SHAKESPEARE'S ENGLAND
Scale of Miles
0 20 40 60 80 100
ST. GEORGE'S CHANNEL
BRISTOL CHANNEL
ENGLISH CHANNEL
Strait of Dover
WALES (Cambria)
Barkloughly Castle (Harlech)
PEMBROKE
Milford Haven
Ha'rford-west
Breck-nock
Monmouth
MON-MOUTH
Abergavenny
R. Wye
HEREFORD
Mortimer's Cross
Ludlow
Bridgnorth
SHROPSHIRE
R. Severn
WORCESTER
Worcester
Tewkesbury
Tamworth
Sutton Co'fi'l'
Bosworth
Leicester
Coventry
WAR-WICK
Warwick
Kenilworth
Daventry
Stratford
NORTHAMPTON
Northampton
Kim-bolton
HUNTING-DON
CAMBRIDGE
Cambridge
Ely
Bury St. Edmunds
SUFFOLK
Ipswich
Plashy
ESSEX
BEDFORD
Bedford
Stony Stratford
BUCKINGHAM
Banbury
OXFORD
Oxford
GLOUCESTER
Gloucester
Cotswold Hills
Berkeley Castle
Cicester
R. Thames
BERK-SHIRE
WILT-SHIRE
Bristol
SOMERSET
Sarum Plain
Salisbury
HAMP-SHIRE
Winchester
Southampton
ISLE OF WIGHT
DORSET
DEVON
Exeter
CORNWALL
HERTFORD
St. Albans
Langley
MIDDLESEX
Westminster
London
Windsor
Eton
Staines
Chertsey
Guildford
SURREY
Eltham
Dartford
Rochester
Gadshill
Chatham
Canterbury
KENT
Weald
Ashford
Dover
SUSSEX
Hastings
Calais
FLANDERS
Ghent
Agincourt
Longavil
Harfleur
NORMANDY
CHANNEL ISLANDS
FRANCE
BRITTANY
MAINE
Alençon
Angiers
ANJOU
TOURAINE

SELECTED PLAYS OF SHAKESPEARE

Selected Plays of Shakespeare

Volume I

KING RICHARD II

KING HENRY IV, PART I

MUCH ADO ABOUT NOTHING

JULIUS CÆSAR

HAMLET

THE WINTER'S TALE

Volume II

THE COMEDY OF ERRORS

ROMEO AND JULIET

A MIDSUMMER NIGHT'S DREAM

KING HENRY V

KING LEAR

ANTONY AND CLEOPATRA

THE TEMPEST

Volume III

KING RICHARD III

AS YOU LIKE IT

TWELFTH NIGHT

OTHELLO

MACBETH

CYMBELINE

SELECTED PLAYS OF SHAKESPEARE

Edited with Introductions and Notes by

KARL J. HOLZKNECHT
New York University

AND

NORMAN E. McCLURE
Ursinus College

VOLUME TWO

AMERICAN BOOK COMPANY
New York Cincinnati Chicago Boston Atlanta Dallas San Francisco

Shakespeare, II
W. P. I.

Made in U. S. A.

PREFACE

The present edition of Shakespeare, designed for the student and the general reader, provides the plays that are usually read in undergraduate college courses. Each volume includes plays that represent not only the several types of drama that Shakespeare wrote, but also the successive stages of his development as a dramatist. Discussion of textual problems and controversial matters has been reduced to a minimum, and the editorial apparatus has been limited to consideration of the plays as drama, to questions of interpretation, and to the elucidation of Elizabethan language. Notes and glossary appear together at the foot of each page, in order that the reader may not need to turn elsewhere in the book for the interpretation of difficult passages, and in order that he may recognize and understand the many words that since Shakespeare's day have changed their meaning but not their form.

The text of the present edition is based upon an independent examination of the more important Quartos and Folios. Universally accepted emendations are, as a rule, admitted without comment, and the punctuation, which in the early editions is of uncertain value, has been modernized. The *dramatis personæ* lists, which have no Shakespearean authority, and which in most modern editions have been merely reprinted from Rowe's edition of 1709, have been rearranged. Further, since nothing but tradition justifies the retention of the spare, formal stage directions found in the early texts or supplied by Rowe, the editors have felt free to amplify the stage directions wherever the reader might have difficulty in following the action. Finally, for the sake of convenience in reference, the standard Globe line-numbering has been adopted, although the prose passages here occupy somewhat less space than in the Globe edition.

The maps of Shakespeare's England and Shakespeare's London mark all of the places mentioned in the plays. Visscher's *View of London and Westminster*, dating from the year of Shakespeare's death, and the other illustrations bring before the reader scenes which Shakespeare knew, or which are closely associated with his plays.

CONTENTS

ILLUSTRATIONS

The Comedy of Errors

Introduction

Dramatic Type

The Comedy of Errors is a Shakespearean example of a type of drama which enjoyed considerable popularity on the Elizabethan stage—the comedy from classical sources. One of the results of Renaissance interest in the classics was a revival of interest in classical drama. The tragedies of Seneca and the comedies of Plautus and Terence (particularly of Plautus) were read and acted in the schools of Tudor England, and imitations of them were occasionally produced as academic exercises. As a consequence, early English comedies, in the words of Stephen Gosson, "smelt of Plautus." *Ralph Roister Doister* (1534–41), often spoken of as the earliest English comedy, was composed about a stock Plautine character-type, the braggart soldier, and *Gammer Gurton's Needle* (1552–3), though thoroughly English, was plainly written upon a Plautine model. In the main, English comedies modeled upon Plautus are school or college plays, but directly or indirectly in the creation of characters which tend to be stock types and often bear tag-names, in the use of patterned themes, in the emphasis upon ludicrous situations, intrigue, amusing mix-ups, and comic wrangles, as well as in general technique, Elizabethan drama owed a great deal to this early writer, who merely reinforced the native English tendencies toward broad humor and riotous farce. *The Comedy of Errors* is but a direct transfer of classical comedy from the academic to the popular stage.

Source

The principal source of *The Comedy of Errors* is the *Menaechmi* of Plautus, which Shakespeare may have read in the original or in a translation by W. W., who is usually identified as William Warner. This translation was not published until 1595, but the printer states that its author had made it "for the use and delight of his friends," and the assumption is that Shakespeare may have seen it in manuscript. Evidence of Shakespeare's obligation to the work, however, is so slight that it is usually assumed that the "small Latin" he must have acquired wherever he went to school would have been sufficient to enable him to work from the original. Other works which evidently suggested modifications of his materials will be alluded to at the proper time below.

In Plautus's story of the two Menaechmi all of the antecedent action is explained in a prologue, and the farce itself is confined to the events of the day when Menaechmus the Traveler at length arrives in Epidamnum, where his lost brother is living. Menaechmus the Citizen has two afflictions—a brazen parasite, Peniculus, and a shrewish wife of whom he has grown tired. The farcical complications arise both from the confusion of the twins and from the Citizen's intrigues with Erotium, a courtesan, about whom the parasite tattles to the neglected wife.

Modification of the Material

Shakespeare's comedy is not a mere imitation of his Latin original, but rather an adaptation of foreign material to Elizabethan conditions.

(1) All of the characters are thoroughly Elizabethanized, and the comic possibilities of each are utilized to the full. Peniculus the parasite, who has no counterpart in Elizabethan society, is transformed into another saucy servant, the twin of Dromio of Syracuse. Another Plautine play, *Amphitruo*, may have suggested this expedient to Shakespeare and certainly furnished the episode in which the husband and his servant are barred out of the house by their doubles (III, i). This incident creates the husband's counter suspicion of his wife to parallel the wife's

baseless jealousy of her husband, and the simple duplication of the twins literally triples the opportunities for mistaken meetings. Likewise the father, to whom the wife complains in the *Menaechmi*, is replaced by Luciana, the sister, who serves as an effective patient-Griselda foil for Adriana and also adds a complicating love interest for the unmarried Antipholus of Syracuse. In the same way, Medicus, the ridiculous physician in Plautus's play who is sent to attend the "madman," is replaced by another "quack," more familiar to the Elizabethan audience, in Pinch, a hungry, lean-faced schoolmaster whose function it is to drive out evil spirits by conjurations and exorcisms in Latin.

(2) In addition, the complications of the farce make possible the creation of characters not to be found in Plautus—Balthasar, who dissuades his friend from rash violence in the streets; Angelo, the goldsmith who delivers a chain to one brother and has the other arrested for non-payment; the merchant to whom Angelo is in debt, and who therefore motivates the goldsmith's action against the Ephesean; and even Luce, "Dowsabel," the mountain of flesh who is only a disembodied voice on the stage, but whose claims to Dromio of Syracuse provide a parody to the amusing situation which has developed above stairs (III, ii).

(3) The material is further adapted to the demands of the popular stage by being shaped on the familiar romantic pattern according to which "all losses are restored and sorrows end." Unlike Plautus, Shakespeare keeps the parents of the Antipholuses alive, increases the element of initial distress by introducing the arrest of Ægeon, and utilizes the story of the family's misfortunes as a contrasting enveloping action to the light farce. The account of Ægeon's woes is put dramatically into the old man's plea before the Duke, instead of into a prologue, and the farcical confusions are disentangled at the close by being brought into contact with the serious action as Ægeon is being led to his execution. Some scholars believe that this framework may have been suggested to Shakespeare by the old story of *Apollonius of*

Tyre, which was known to him through John Gower's *Confessio Amantis*, and which was later to serve as the foundation for *Pericles*. But *Apollonius of Tyre* is only the prototype of the tale of distressful adventure found frequently in medieval and Renaissance literature.

(4) Even the love stories, incidental as they are to the main farce, develop as variations of the same dramatic formula. As the play opens, Antipholus of Ephesus and his wife are out of patience with one another, and the happenings of this eventful day only serve to drive them further apart. On the other hand, Antipholus of Syracuse, who is not at all inclined to the woman who calls him husband, finds a seemingly impassable barrier between him and the fair sister with whom he is enchanted. At sundown when the difficulties are all cleared away, husband and wife are reconciled; the nagging, suspicious Adriana, convicted out of her own mouth, vows to reform; the Syracusian brother has the leisure to make good the declaration of his love from which Luciana had fled before; and the loves of the parents, interrupted by misfortune years before, are renewed in their restoration to one another.

(5) Moreover, by invoking the harsh Ephesean law against Syracusian merchants and placing both father and son in jeopardy, Shakespeare indirectly gave plausibility to the confusions by supplying the spectator with a point of view from which to observe them. The whole action is seen through the jaundiced eye of Antipholus of Syracuse, who walks the streets in danger and at last can find no explanation for these amazing occurrences but witchcraft or trickery (cf. I, ii, 95 ff.; III, ii, 161 ff.; IV, iii, 10 ff.; 48 ff.; and IV, iv, 151 ff.).

(6) Thus a variety of emotional appeal, so essential to dramatic effectiveness, is created; unity is given to what might otherwise have been a series of mildly amusing incidents; the play is lifted into realms of greater dignity by the contrast of pathos and comedy; and the element of surprise is added in the

DRAMATIS PERSONÆ

d merchant of Syracuse.
ɔess of Ephesus, later discovered to be the lost wife

of Ephesus } twin sons of Ægeon and Æmilia.
of Syracuse }

ɛphesus } twin servants of the Antipholuses.
ʖyracuse }

ife of Antipholus of Ephesus.
r unmarried sister.
N.
ıke of Ephesus.
ıoolmaster-exorcist.
oldsmith.
a merchant friend of Antipholus of Ephesus.
friend of Antipholus of Syracuse.
:chant, to whom Angelo the goldsmith is indebted.
ing woman of Adriana's and wife of Dromio of

fficers, and Attendants upon the Duke.

Scene of the Action: Ephesus.

introduction of Æmilia to increase the happiness of the close. Even if it is not a great play, *The Comedy of Errors* reveals the hand of the master.

(7) In addition to these dramatic modifications, Shakespeare gave his Plautine material a thorough moral disinfection. Menaechmus the Traveler is a clever cozener and a thievish rogue. His brother, the Citizen, is habitually immoral; and his wife, though a "brabbling fool" and a "mad-brain scold," has good reason to be resentful. Shakespeare's twins are honest, respected gentlemen; Adriana's jealousy is baseless; and only when he is barred out of his own house does Antipholus of Ephesus seek entertainment elsewhere. Consequently, the role of the Courtesan, an important one in Plautus, is minimized by Shakespeare.

Relation to Other Shakespearean Plays

The Comedy of Errors, written at the beginning of his career, and *The Tempest*, written at its close, are the two of Shakespeare's comedies which conform to the pseudo-classical unities of time, place, and action. Some scholars are inclined to believe that in *The Tempest* Shakespeare's attention to the unities was deliberate, and that the play was almost a demonstration to the confirmed classicists, like Ben Jonson, who had criticized the unrestraint of *The Winter's Tale* and *Pericles*, that a practical dramatist could play the pedantic game of rules if he chose. Whatever may be true, for the unity of *The Comedy of Errors* there was no such motive. The classical orderliness in which he found his materials may, to a certain extent, account for his practice. But it is also apparent that the young playwright feels no restraint; he casts his story in a romantic mold, complicates it infinitely, and works out for himself a unity of action without in the least sacrificing freshness, elasticity, or variety. The dramatic art of *The Comedy of Errors* is sure and apparently effortless.

Yet the play is never thought of as one of Shakespeare's great comedies. Its very lightness has been against it; the characterization is admittedly slight; there are few memorable lines in it, and very little poetry; and the humor is mere horseplay and quibbling. But these very shortcomings, it is often forgotten, are inherent in the farce form, and any super-refinement in these directions would but have spoiled the play utterly. The life of a farce consists in ludicrous situations rather than in fine shades of character. In *The Comedy of Errors* the characterization is always adequate, and it is no mere subtlety which perceives essential differences between the two Antipholuses and the two Dromios. But it is a play to be enjoyed at the moment and not pondered over.

The Comedy of Errors has most frequently been dismissed from serious consideration on the grounds of improbability and artificiality because it turns upon mistaken identity. This expedient, however, was a theatrical convention which the Elizabethans inherited from the Roman drama, and which Shakespeare employed frequently in plays which have larger claims to greatness—notably in *Twelfth Night*, where the "identity" is artificially produced by the disguise of a girl as a boy. But identical twins do exist in real life, and the possibility of ludicrous stage confusions taxes the credulity of no one who has ever seen a pair. Moreover, a willingness to make believe is little enough for any writer of light comedy to demand of his audience. The audience is never confused; it enjoys the complete confidence of the author, and the moment one puts aside his superior airs and surrenders to the comedy the adventures of the twins are irresistible.

The Comedy of Errors is the shortest of Shakespeare's plays—a light entertainment suitable for a night of revels, or as an abridgment of the evening between supper and bedtime.

The Comedy of Errors

ACT I

SCENE I. *A Court of Justice in Ephesus.*

Court is in session; SOLINUS, *Duke of Ephesus, is seated on the judgment seat;* ÆGEON, *in charge of a* Gaoler *and other* Officers, *stands before him. Various Attendants and Spectators are present.*

Æge. Proceed, Solinus, to procure my fall
And by the doom of death end woes and all.
Duke. Merchant of Syracusa, plead no more;
I am not partial to infringe our laws.
The enmity and discord which of late
Sprung from the rancorous outrage of your duke
To merchants, our well-dealing countrymen,
Who, wanting guilders to redeem their lives,
Have seal'd his rigorous statutes with their bloods,
Excludes all pity from our threatening looks. 10
For, since the mortal and intestine jars
'Twixt thy seditious countrymen and us,
It hath in solemn synods been decreed,
Both by the Syracusians and ourselves,

[I. i] 2. *doom:* judgment, sentence. 4. *partial:* inclined. 5. *The enmity and discord.* It is possible that Shakespeare here is thinking in only slightly exaggerated terms of the conflicts of local commercial interests and the trade regulations in the England of his own day. Professor Unwin writes: "The Stratford council employed men armed with cudgels to keep out the traders of Coventry. The Leicester glovers strove with might and main to prevent the glovers of Ashby and Loughborough from buying skins in their market. Between many neighbouring towns there raged an animosity almost as fierce as the feud between Ephesus and Syracuse" (*Shakespeare's England*, I, 315). 11. *mortal:* deadly. *intestine jars:* local or civil discords. *Intestine* also emphasizes *mortal*. 12. *seditious:* i.e., who care nothing for law or justice.

To admit no traffic to our adverse towns.
Nay, more,
If any born at Ephesus be seen
At any Syracusian marts and fairs—
Again, if any Syracusian born
Come to the bay of Ephesus—he dies, 20
His goods confiscate to the duke's dispose,
Unless a thousand marks be levied
To quit the penalty and to ransom him.
Thy substance, valued at the highest rate,
Cannot amount unto a hundred marks;
Therefore by law thou art condemn'd to die.

Æge. Yet this my comfort, when your words are done,
My woes end likewise with the evening sun.

Duke. Well, Syracusian, say in brief the cause
Why thou departed'st from thy native home 30
And for what cause thou camest to Ephesus.

Æge. A heavier task could not have been imposed
Than I to speak my griefs unspeakable.
Yet, that the world may witness that my end
Was wrought by nature, not by vile offense,
I'll utter what my sorrow gives me leave.
In Syracusa was I born, and wed
Unto a woman, happy but for me,
And by me, had not our hap been bad.
With her I lived in joy; our wealth increased 40
By prosperous voyages I often made
To Epidamnum, till my factor's death
And the great care of goods at random left
Drew me from kind embracements of my spouse,
From whom my absence was not six months old
Before herself, almost at fainting under
The pleasing punishment that women bear,

15. *traffic:* commerce. 18. *marts:* markets. 21. *confiscate:* confiscated. *dispose:* disposal. 23. *quit:* pay off. 24. *substance:* goods, possessions. 32. *heavier:* sadder. 35. *nature:* natural affection. 39. *hap:* fortune. 42. *factor's:* commercial agent's.

Had made provision for her following me
And soon and safe arrived where I was.
There had she not been long but she became 50
A joyful mother of two goodly sons;
And, which was strange, the one so like the other
As could not be distinguish'd but by names.
That very hour, and in the self-same inn,
A meaner woman was delivered
Of such a burden, male twins, both alike;
Those, for their parents were exceeding poor,
I bought and brought up to attend my sons.
My wife, not meanly proud of two such boys,
Made daily motions for our home return. 60
Unwilling I agreed; alas, too soon
We came aboard.
A league from Epidamnum had we sail'd,
Before the always wind-obeying deep
Gave any tragic instance of our harm.
But longer did we not retain much hope;
For what obscured light the heavens did grant
Did but convey unto our fearful minds
A doubtful warrant of immediate death,
Which though myself would gladly have embraced, 70
Yet the incessant weepings of my wife,
Weeping before for what she saw must come,
And piteous plainings of the pretty babes,
That mourn'd for fashion, ignorant what to fear,

48. *provision:* preparation. 53. *distinguish'd but by names.* In Plautus's *Menaechmi* one brother is called Sosicles and takes the name of his twin, Menaechmus, after the latter is stolen. In Shakespeare's play, however, no distinction of names is made, and this allusion to different names, therefore, forms an interesting link with the original. 55. *meaner:* of lower rank. 59. *not meanly:* in no slight degree. 60. *motions:* proposals. 65. *instance:* indication. 68. *fearful:* full of fear. 69. *doubtful:* full of apprehensions and misgivings. *warrant:* assurance. 70. *embraced:* submitted to with resignation. 73. *plainings:* complainings, crying. 74. *for fashion:* i.e., because others were weeping.

Forced me to seek delays for them and me.
And this it was, for other means was none:
The sailors sought for safety by our boat,
And left the ship, then sinking-ripe, to us.
My wife, more careful for the latter-born,
Had fasten'd him unto a small spare mast, 80
Such as seafaring men provide for storms;
To him one of the other twins was bound,
Whilst I had been like heedful of the other.
The children thus disposed, my wife and I,
Fixing our eyes on whom our care was fix'd,
Fasten'd ourselves at either end the mast,
And floating straight, obedient to the stream,
Was carried towards Corinth, as we thought.
At length the sun, gazing upon the earth,
Dispersed those vapours that offended us; 90
And, by the benefit of his wished light,
The seas wax'd calm, and we discovered
Two ships from far making amain to us,
Of Corinth that, of Epidaurus this.
But ere they came—O, let me say no more!
Gather the sequel by that went before.

Duke. Nay, forward, old man; do not break off so;
For we may pity, though not pardon thee.

Æge. O, had the gods done so, I had not now
Worthily term'd them merciless to us! 100
For, ere the ships could meet by twice five leagues,
We were encounter'd by a mighty rock;
Which being violently borne upon,
Our helpful ship was splitted in the midst;
So that, in this unjust divorce of us,
Fortune had left to both of us alike

79. *latter-born.* Some editors, following Rowe, emend this line to read *elder-born* to produce consistency with line 125. 90. *vapours:* clouds. 92. *wax'd:* grew. 93. *amain:* with full speed. 96. *that:* that which. 100. *Worthily:* justifiably. 105. *divorce:* separation.

What to delight in, what to sorrow for.
Her part, poor soul, seeming as burdened
With lesser weight, but not with lesser woe,
Was carried with more speed before the wind; 110
And in our sight they three were taken up
By fishermen of Corinth, as we thought.
At length, another ship had seized on us;
And, knowing whom it was their hap to save,
Gave healthful welcome to their shipwreck'd guests;
And would have reft the fishers of their prey,
Had not their bark been very slow of sail;
And therefore homeward did they bend their course.
Thus have you heard me sever'd from my bliss,
That by misfortunes was my life prolong'd, 120
To tell sad stories of my own mishaps.

Duke. And, for the sake of them thou sorrowest for,
Do me the favour to dilate at full
What hath befall'n of them and thee till now.

Æge. My youngest boy, and yet my eldest care,
At eighteen years became inquisitive
After his brother, and importuned me
That his attendant—so his case was like,
Reft of his brother, but retain'd his name—
Might bear him company in the quest of him, 130
Whom whilst I labour'd of a love to see,
I hazarded the loss of whom I loved.
Five summers have I spent in furthest Greece,
Roaming clean through the bounds of Asia,
And, coasting homeward, came to Ephesus;
Hopeless to find, yet loath to leave unsought
Or that or any place that harbours men.
But here must end the story of my life;

108. *seeming as:* apparently, as if. 114. *hap:* fortune. 115. *healthful:* hearty, with a suggestion of "health-restoring." 116. *reft:* robbed, bereft. 123. *dilate at full:* relate at length. 131. *labour'd:* suffered the pains of childbirth (figuratively). 132. *hazarded:* risked. 134. *clean:* completely. 137. *Or . . . or:* either . . . or.

And happy were I in my timely death,
Could all my travels warrant me they live. 140

Duke. Hapless Ægeon, whom the Fates have mark'd
To bear the extremity of dire mishap,
Now, trust me, were it not against our laws,
Against my crown, my oath, my dignity,
Which princes, would they, may not disannul,
My soul should sue as advocate for thee.
But, though thou art adjudged to the death,
And passed sentence may not be recall'd
But to our honour's great disparagement,
Yet I will favour thee in what I can. 150
Therefore, merchant, I'll limit thee this day
To seek thy life by beneficial help.
Try all the friends thou hast in Ephesus;
Beg thou, or borrow, to make up the sum,
And live; if no, then thou art doom'd to die.
Gaoler, take him to thy custody.

Gaol. I will, my lord.

Æge. Hopeless and helpless doth Ægeon wend,
But to procrastinate his lifeless end. [*Exeunt.*

Scene ii. *The Mart of Ephesus, later the same morning.*

Enter Antipholus of Syracuse, *in conversation with a* Merchant, *and attended by* Dromio of Syracuse.

Mer. Therefore give out you are of Epidamnum,
Lest that your goods too soon be confiscate.
This very day a Syracusian merchant
Is apprehended for arrival here,
And not being able to buy out his life

140. *travels:* also *travails;* the two words were not distinguished in Elizabethan English. *warrant:* assure. 145. *would they:* if they wanted to. *disannul:* annul. 151. *limit:* allot. 152. *life.* F_1 reads *help;* the emendation is Rowe's.

[ii] 1. *give out:* say. 3. *Syracusian merchant:* i.e., Ægeon. 4. *apprehended:* arrested. *arrival.* F_1 reads *a rivall.*

According to the statute of the town
Dies ere the weary sun set in the west.
There is your money that I had to keep. [*Giving him a purse.*
Ant. S. Go bear it to the Centaur, where we host,
And stay there, Dromio, till I come to thee. 10
Within this hour it will be dinner-time.
Till that, I'll view the manners of the town,
Peruse the traders, gaze upon the buildings,
And then return and sleep within mine inn,
For with long travel I am stiff and weary.
Get thee away.
Dro. S. Many a man would take you at your word,
And go indeed, having so good a mean. [*Exit.*
Ant. S. A trusty villain, sir, that very oft,
When I am dull with care and melancholy, 20
Lightens my humour with his merry jests.
What, will you walk with me about the town,
And then go to my inn and dine with me?
Mer. I am invited, sir, to certain merchants,
Of whom I hope to make much benefit;
I crave your pardon. Soon at five o'clock,
Please you, I'll meet with you upon the mart,
And afterward consort you till bed-time.
My present business calls me from you now.
Ant. S. Farewell till then; I will go lose myself 30
And wander up and down to view the city.
Mer. Sir, I commend you to your own content. [*Exit.*
Ant. S. He that commends me to mine own content
Commends me to the thing I cannot get.

9. *host:* lodge. 13. *Peruse:* observe, inspect. 18. *mean:* (a) means, opportunity, (b) sum of money. 19. *villain:* used playfully here, but with some of its original meaning of "bondman." 21. *humour:* mood. *Melancholy* (line 20) suggests an allusion to the early physiological belief that the relative proportions of the four fluids of the human body—blood, phlegm, choler, and melancholy or black bile—determined a person's physical and mental qualities. 26. *Soon at:* about. 27. *mart:* market place. 28. *consort you:* keep you company.

I to the world am like a drop of water
That in the ocean seeks another drop,
Who, falling there to find his fellow forth,
Unseen, inquisitive, confounds himself.
So I, to find a mother and a brother,
In quest of them, unhappy, lose myself. 40

Enter DROMIO of Ephesus.

Here comes the almanac of my true date.
What now? How chance thou art return'd so soon?
Dro. E. Return'd so soon? Rather approach'd too late.
The capon burns, the pig falls from the spit,
The clock hath strucken twelve upon the bell—
My mistress made it one upon my cheek—
She is so hot because the meat is cold;
The meat is cold because you come not home;
You come not home because you have no stomach;
You have no stomach having broke your fast; 50
But we, that know what 'tis to fast and pray,
Are penitent for your default today.
Ant. S. Stop in your wind, sir. Tell me this, I pray—
Where have you left the money that I gave you?
Dro. E. O—sixpence, that I had o' Wednesday last
To pay the saddler for my mistress' crupper?
The saddler had it, sir; I kept it not.
Ant. S. I am not in a sportive humour now;
Tell me, and dally not, where is the money?
We being strangers here, how darest thou trust 60
So great a charge from thine own custody?
Dro. E. I pray you, jest, sir, as you sit at dinner.
I from my mistress come to you in post;
If I return, I shall be post indeed,

35. *to the world:* i.e., compared to the world. 41. *almanac . . . date:* i.e., because born on the same day. 44. *spit:* rod on which meat is roasted. 47. *hot:* angry. 49. *stomach:* appetite. 52. *penitent:* doing penance, i.e., fasting. 61. *charge:* trust. 63, 64. *post:* (a) in haste, (b) the doorpost at a tavern on which the reckonings were scored.

For she will score your fault upon my pate.
Methinks your maw, like mine, should be your clock
And strike you home without a messenger.
Ant. S. Come, Dromio, come, these jests are out of season;
Reserve them till a merrier hour than this.
Where is the gold I gave in charge to thee? 70
Dro. E. To me, sir? Why, you gave no gold to me.
Ant. S. Come on, sir knave, have done your foolishness
And tell me how thou hast disposed thy charge.
Dro. E. My charge was but to fetch you from the mart
Home to your house, the Phœnix, sir, to dinner;
My mistress and her sister stays for you.
Ant. S. Now, as I am a Christian, answer me
In what safe place you have bestow'd my money,
Or I shall break that merry sconce of yours,
That stands on tricks when I am undisposed. 80
Where is the thousand marks thou hadst of me?
Dro. E. I have some marks of yours upon my pate,
Some of my mistress' marks upon my shoulders,
But not a thousand marks between you both.
If I should pay your worship those again,
Perchance you will not bear them patiently.
Ant. S. Thy mistress' marks? What mistress, slave, hast thou?
Dro. E. Your worship's wife, my mistress at the Phœnix;
She that doth fast till you come home to dinner,
And prays that you will hie you home to dinner. 90
Ant. S. What, wilt thou flout me thus unto my face,
Being forbid? There, take you that, sir knave. [*Beating him.*
Dro. E. What mean you, sir? For God's sake, hold your hands!
Nay, an you will not, sir, I'll take my heels. [*Exit.*
Ant. S. Upon my life, by some device or other,

65. *score:* keep a reckoning. *pate:* head. 66. *maw:* stomach. *clock.* F1 reads *cooke.* 75. *Phœnix:* the distinguishing sign of Antipholus's house. 79. *sconce:* head. 91. *flout:* mock.

The villain is o'er-raught of all my money.
They say this town is full of cozenage,
As, nimble jugglers that deceive the eye,
Dark-working sorcerers that change the mind,
Soul-killing witches that deform the body, 100
Disguised cheaters, prating mountebanks,
And many such-like liberties of sin.
If it prove so, I will be gone the sooner.
I'll to the Centaur, to go seek this slave;
I greatly fear my money is not safe. [*Exit.*

ACT II

Scene i. *The house of* Antipholus of Ephesus.

Adriana, *his wife, and* Luciana, *her sister, are delaying dinner for the tardy husband.*

Adr. Neither my husband nor the slave return'd,
That in such haste I sent to seek his master?
Sure, Luciana, it is two o'clock.
Luc. Perhaps some merchant hath invited him
And from the mart he's somewhere gone to dinner.
Good sister, let us dine and never fret;
A man is master of his liberty.
Time is their master, and when they see time
They'll go or come; if so, be patient, sister.
Adr. Why should their liberty than ours be more? 10
Luc. Because their business still lies out o' door.
Adr. Look, when I serve him so, he takes it ill.
Luc. O, know he is the bridle of your will.
Adr. There's none but asses will be bridled so.
Luc. Why, headstrong Liberty is lash'd with woe.

96. *o'er-raught:* overreached, cheated. 97. *cozenage:* cheating, trickery. 97 ff. See Introduction for an account of Antipholus's point of view. 99. *change the mind:* i.e., cause madness. 101. *prating:* talking, "barking." 102. *liberties of sin:* sinful or improper freedoms.

[II. i] 15. *lash'd:* scourged; or, perhaps, "leashed," coupled.

There's nothing situate under heaven's eye
But hath his bound, in earth, in sea, in sky.
The beasts, the fishes, and the winged fowls
Are their males' subjects and at their controls;
Men, more divine, the masters of all these, 20
Lords of the wide world and wild watery seas,
Indued with intellectual sense and souls,
Of more pre-eminence than fish and fowls,
Are masters to their females, and their lords.
Then let your will attend on their accords.

Adr. This servitude makes you to keep unwed.

Luc. Not this, but troubles of the marriage-bed.

Adr. But, were you wedded, you would bear some sway.

Luc. Ere I learn love, I'll practice to obey.

Adr. How if your husband start some other where? 30

Luc. Till he come home again, I would forbear.

Adr. Patience unmoved! No marvel though she pause;
They can be meek that have no other cause.
A wretched soul, bruised with adversity,
We bid be quiet when we hear it cry;
But were we burden'd with like weight of pain,
As much, or more, we should ourselves complain.
So thou, that hast no unkind mate to grieve thee,
With urging helpless patience wouldst relieve me;
But, if thou live to see like right bereft, 40
This fool-begg'd patience in thee will be left.

Luc. Well, I will marry one day, but to try.
Here comes your man; now is your husband nigh.

Enter DROMIO of Ephesus.

Adr. Say, is your tardy master now at hand?

Dro. E. Nay, he's at two hands with me, and that my two ears can witness.

16. *situate:* situated. 17. *bound:* boundary, limit. 28. *bear some sway:* have some authority. 30. *start:* go by impulse. *some other where:* somewhere else, after some other woman. 31. *forbear:* i.e., let him alone. 40. *if . . . bereft:* if you live to be similarly ill-treated. 41. *fool-begg'd:* idiotic, foolish.

Adr. Say, didst thou speak with him? Know'st thou his mind?

Dro. E. Ay, ay, he told his mind upon mine ear;
Beshrew his hand, I scarce could understand it.

Luc. Spake he so doubtfully thou couldst not feel his meaning? 51

Dro. E. Nay, he struck so plainly I could too well feel his blows; and withal so doubtfully that I could scarce understand them.

Adr. But say, I prithee, is he coming home?
It seems he hath great care to please his wife.

Dro. E. Why, mistress, sure my master is horn-mad.

Adr. Horn-mad, thou villain?

Dro. E. I mean not cuckold-mad;
But, sure, he is stark mad.
When I desired him to come home to dinner, 60
He ask'd me for a thousand marks in gold.
"'Tis dinner-time," quoth I; "My gold!" quoth he.
"Your meat doth burn," quoth I; "My gold!" quoth he.
"Will you come home?" quoth I; "My gold!" quoth he,
"Where is the thousand marks I gave thee, villain?"
"The pig," quoth I, "is burn'd;" "My gold!" quoth he.
"My mistress, sir—" quoth I; "Hang up thy mistress!
I know not thy mistress; out on thy mistress!"

Luc. Quoth who?

Dro. E. Quoth my master. 70
"I know," quoth he, "no house, no wife, no mistress."
So that my errand, due unto my tongue,
I thank him, I bare home upon my shoulders;
For, in conclusion, he did beat me there.

Adr. Go back again, thou slave, and fetch him home.

Dro. E. Go back again, and be new beaten home?
For God's sake, send some other messenger.

Adr. Back, slave, or I will break thy pate across.

49. *Beshrew:* curse. 50, 53. *doubtfully:* (a) dubiously, (b) dreadfully. 57. *horn-mad:* mad as (a) a bull or (b) a cuckold. 59. *stark:* very, completely. 61. *thousand.* F_1 reads *hundred.*

Dro. E. And he will bless that cross with other beating;
Between you I shall have a holy head. 80
Adr. Hence, prating peasant; fetch thy master home.
Dro. E. Am I so round with you as you with me
That like a football you do spurn me thus?
You spurn me hence, and he will spurn me hither;
If I last in this service, you must case me in leather. [*Exit.*
Luc. Fie, how impatience loureth in your face!
Adr. His company must do his minions grace,
Whilst I at home starve for a merry look.
Hath homely age the alluring beauty took
From my poor cheek? Then he hath wasted it. 90
Are my discourses dull? Barren my wit?
If voluble and sharp discourse be marr'd,
Unkindness blunts it more than marble hard.
Do their gay vestments his affections bait?
That's not my fault; he's master of my state.
What ruins are in me that can be found,
By him not ruin'd? Then is he the ground
Of my defeatures. My decayed fair
A sunny look of his would soon repair.
But, too unruly deer, he breaks the pale 100
And feeds from home; poor I am but his stale.
Luc. Self-harming jealousy! Fie, beat it hence!
Adr. Unfeeling fools can with such wrongs dispense.
I know his eye doth homage otherwhere;
Or else what lets it but he would be here?
Sister, you know he promised me a chain;
Would that alone, alone he would detain,
So he would keep fair quarter with his bed!

79. *bless:* (a) consecrate, (b) beat. 80. *holy:* with a quibble on *holey.* 82. *round:* (a) familiar, (b) spherical. 87. *minions:* hussies, darlings. 89. *homely:* plain, uncomely. 95. *state:* condition. 98. *defeatures:* disfigurement. *fair:* beauty. 100. *deer:* with a quibble on *dear*, i.e., to Adriana. *pale:* fence, paling of the deer park. 101. *stale:* (a) laughingstock, (b) mistress he has grown tired of, (c) harlot. 105. *lets:* prevents, hinders. 107. *alone, alone.* F_1 reads *alone, a loue.*

I see the jewel best enamelled
Will lose his beauty; yet the gold bides still 110
That others touch, and often touching will
Wear gold; and no man that hath a name,
By falsehood and corruption doth it shame.
Since that my beauty cannot please his eye,
I'll weep what's left away, and weeping die. [*She weeps.*

Luc. How many fond fools serve mad Jealousy? [*Exeunt.*

SCENE II. *A public square near the Phœnix, the house of* ANTIPHOLUS of Ephesus.

Enter ANTIPHOLUS of Syracuse.

Ant. S. The gold I gave to Dromio is laid up
Safe at the Centaur, and the heedful slave
Is wander'd forth in care to seek me out.
By computation and mine host's report
I could not speak with Dromio since at first
I sent him from the mart. See, here he comes.

Enter DROMIO of Syracuse.

How now, sir, is your merry humour alter'd?
As you love strokes, so jest with me again.
You know no Centaur? You received no gold?
Your mistress sent to have me home to dinner? 10
My house was at the Phœnix? Wast thou mad,
That thus so madly thou didst answer me?

Dro. S. What answer, sir? When spake I such a word?

Ant. S. Even now, even here, not half an hour since.

Dro. S. I did not see you since you sent me hence,
Home to the Centaur, with the gold you gave me.

Ant. S. Villain, thou didst deny the gold's receipt

109–13. *I see . . . shame:* the most beautiful jewel (the best of men) may lose its beauty (its virtues); though gold will endure a great deal of handling, frequent handling (temptation) will wear gold, and no man who has a reputation that he values will ruin it by falsehood and corruption. 112. *Wear.* F_1 reads *Where.* 116. *fond:* silly.

[ii] 2. *heedful:* mindful.

And told'st me of a mistress and a dinner,
For which, I hope, thou felt'st I was displeased.

Dro. S. I am glad to see you in this merry vein. 20
What means this jest; I pray you, master, tell me?

Ant. S. Yea, dost thou jeer and flout me in the teeth?
Think'st thou I jest? Hold, take thou that, and that. [*Beating him.*

Dro. S. Hold, sir, for God's sake! Now your jest is earnest.
Upon what bargain do you give it me?

Ant. S. Because that I familiarly sometimes
Do use you for my fool and chat with you,
Your sauciness will jest upon my love
And make a common of my serious hours.
When the sun shines let foolish gnats make sport, 30
But creep in crannies when he hides his beams.
If you will jest with me, know my aspect
And fashion your demeanour to my looks,
Or I will beat this method in your sconce.

Dro. S. Sconce call you it? So you would leave battering, I had rather have it a head; an you use these blows long, I must get a sconce for my head and insconce it too, or else I shall seek my wit in my shoulders. But, I pray, sir, why am I beaten? 40

Ant. S. Dost thou not know?

Dro. S. Nothing, sir, but that I am beaten.

Ant. S. Shall I tell you why?

Dro. S. Ay, sir, and wherefore; for they say every "why" hath a "wherefore."

Ant. S. Why, "first," for flouting me; and then, "wherefore,"
For urging it the second time to me.

24. *earnest:* with a quibble on "earnest money," an installment paid to close a bargain. 28. *love:* kindness, good nature. 29. *common . . . hours:* i.e., intrude on my leisure when you please; the allusion is to "common lands," those that belonged to the community as a whole and not to individuals. 32. *aspect:* (a) look, (b) in astrology, the favorable or unfavorable influence of a planet. 34. *sconce:* (a) jocular term for head, (b) helmet, (c) a small fort or earthwork. All are punned upon in the succeeding lines. 38. *insconce:* conceal, entrench. 39. *wit:* intelligence. *in my shoulders:* by showing my back (running away).

Dro. S. Was there ever any man thus beaten out of season,
When in the why and the wherefore is neither rhyme nor
reason?
Well, sir, I thank you. 50

Ant. S. Thank me, sir? For what?

Dro. S. Marry, sir, for this something that you gave me for nothing.

Ant. S. I'll make you amends next, to give you nothing for something. But say, sir, is it dinner-time?

Dro. S. No, sir, I think the meat wants that I have.

Ant. S. In good time, sir; what's that?

Dro. S. Basting.

Ant. S. Well, sir, then 'twill be dry. 60

Dro. S. If it be, sir, I pray you, eat none of it.

Ant. S. Your reason?

Dro. S. Lest it make you choleric and purchase me another dry basting.

Ant. S. Well, sir, learn to jest in good time; there's a time for all things.

Dro. S. I durst have denied that, before you were so choleric.

Ant. S. By what rule, sir?

Dro. S. Marry, sir, by a rule as plain as the plain bald pate of Father Time himself. 71

Ant. S. Let's hear it.

Dro. S. There's no time for a man to recover his hair that grows bald by nature.

Ant. S. May he not do it by fine and recovery?

Dro. S. Yes, to pay a fine for a periwig and recover the lost hair of another man.

48. *out of season:* without reason. 57. *wants:* lacks something. 58. *In good time:* an interjection with several shades of meaning, here a scornful "indeed." 63. *choleric:* irascible. Dry, unbasted meat is frequently alluded to by Shakespeare as likely to induce anger. 64. *dry basting:* severe beating, but one that did not draw blood. 75. *fine and recovery:* a legal phrase meaning an agreement by which an individual gained possession of some property or right by leave or judgment of court (with a quibble on "re-covery").

Ant. S. Why is Time such a niggard of hair, being, as it is, so plentiful an excrement? 79

Dro. S. Because it is a blessing that he bestows on beasts; and what he hath scanted men in hair he hath given them in wit.

Ant. S. Why, but there's many a man hath more hair than wit.

Dro. S. Not a man of those but he hath the wit to lose his hair.

Ant. S. Why, thou didst conclude hairy men plain dealers without wit.

Dro. S. The plainer dealer, the sooner lost; yet he loseth it in a kind of jollity. 90

Ant. S. For what reason?

Dro. S. For two; and sound ones too.

Ant. S. Nay, not sound, I pray you.

Dro. S. Sure ones then.

Ant. S. Nay, not sure, in a thing falsing.

Dro. S. Certain ones then.

Ant. S. Name them.

Dro. S. The one—to save the money that he spends in tiring; the other—that at dinner they should not drop in his porridge. 100

Ant. S. You would all this time have proved there is no time for all things.

Dro. S. Marry, and did, sir; namely, no time to recover hair lost by nature.

Ant. S. But your reason was not substantial why there is no time to recover.

79. *excrement:* outgrowth. 81. *men.* F_1 reads *them.* 82. *wit:* intelligence. 85–6. *Not . . . hair.* "Those who have more hair than wit are easily entrapped by loose women and suffer the consequences of lewdness, one of which, in the first appearance of the disease in Europe, was the loss of hair" (Dr. Johnson). 88. *plain dealers:* virtuous men, free from deceit. Dromio, however, in the next line quibbles on another meaning of *deal*, "divide," "sever." 95. *falsing:* deceptive. 99. *tiring:* hairdressing. 105. *not substantial why:* does not prove why.

Dro. S. Thus I mend it: Time himself is bald, and therefore to the world's end will have bald followers.

Ant. S. I knew 'twould be a bald conclusion. 110

Adriana *and* Luciana *come from the Phœnix and beckon to* Antipholus of Syracuse.

But, soft, who wafts us yonder?

Adr. Ay, ay, Antipholus, look strange and frown;
Some other mistress hath thy sweet aspects;
I am not Adriana nor thy wife.
The time was once when thou unurged wouldst vow
That never words were music to thine ear,
That never object pleasing in thine eye,
That never touch well welcome to thy hand,
That never meat sweet-savour'd in thy taste,
Unless I spake, or look'd, or touch'd, or carved to thee. 120
How comes it now, my husband—O, how comes it—
That thou art then estranged from thyself?
Thy self I call it, being strange to me—
That, undividable, incorporate,
Am better than thy dear self's better part.
Ah, do not tear away thyself from me;
For know, my love, as easy mayst thou fall
A drop of water in the breaking gulf
And take unmingled thence that drop again,
Without addition or diminishing, 130
As take from me thyself and not me too.
How dearly would it touch thee to the quick,
Shouldst thou but hear I were licentious,
And that this body, consecrate to thee,
By ruffian lust should be contaminate!
Wouldst thou not spit at me, and spurn at me,
And hurl the name of husband in my face,
And tear the stain'd skin off my harlot-brow,

108, 109, 110. *bald:* (a) without hair, (b) bareheaded, (c) senseless, trivial. 111. *wafts us:* waves or beckons to us. 113. *aspects:* looks. 127. *fall:* let fall. 128. *breaking gulf:* sea. 132. *dearly:* grievously.

And from my false hand cut the wedding-ring,
And break it with a deep-divorcing vow? 140
I know thou canst, and therefore see thou do it.
I am possess'd with an adulterate blot;
My blood is mingled with the crime of lust;
For if we two be one and thou play false,
I do digest the poison of thy flesh,
Being strumpeted by thy contagion.
Keep then fair league and truce with thy true bed;
I live unstain'd, thou undishonoured.

Ant. S. Plead you to me, fair dame? I know you not.
In Ephesus I am but two hours old, 150
As strange unto your town as to your talk;
Who, every word by all my wit being scann'd,
Wants wit in all one word to understand.

Luc. Fie, brother, how the world is changed with you!
When were you wont to use my sister thus?
She sent for you by Dromio home to dinner.

Ant. S. By Dromio?

Dro. S. By me?

Adr. By thee; and this thou didst return from him,
That he did buffet thee, and in his blows 160
Denied my house for his, me for his wife.

Ant. S. Did you converse, sir, with this gentlewoman?
What is the course and drift of your compact?

Dro. S. I, sir? I never saw her till this time.

Ant. S. Villain, thou liest; for even her very words
Didst thou deliver to me on the mart.

Dro. S. I never spake with her in all my life.

Ant. S. How can she thus then call us by our names,
Unless it be by inspiration?

Adr. How ill agrees it with your gravity 170

147. *league:* alliance. 148. *unstain'd.* F_1 reads *distain'd,* defiled, sullied. 152, 153. *wit:* mind, intelligence. 155. *wont:* accustomed. 159. *return:* bring back by way of answer. 163. *compact:* agreement, conspiracy. 169. *inspiration:* supernatural influence. 170. *gravity:* dignity.

To counterfeit thus grossly with your slave,
Abetting him to thwart me in my mood!
Be it my wrong you are from me exempt,
But wrong not that wrong with a more contempt.
Come, I will fasten on this sleeve of thine;
[*She takes him by the arm.*
Thou art an elm, my husband, I a vine,
Whose weakness married to thy stronger state
Makes me with thy strength to communicate.
If aught possess thee from me, it is dross,
Usurping ivy, brier, or idle moss; 180
Who, all for want of pruning, with intrusion
Infect thy sap and live on thy confusion.

Ant S. [*To the audience*] To me she speaks; she moves me for her theme;
What, was I married to her in my dream?
Or sleep I now and think I hear all this?
What error drives our eyes and ears amiss?
Until I know this sure uncertainty,
I'll entertain the offer'd fallacy.

Luc. Dromio, go bid the servants spread for dinner.

Dro. S. O, for my beads! [*He crosses himself.*] I cross me for a sinner. 190
This is the fairy land, O spite of spites!
We talk with goblins, owls, and sprites;
If we obey them not, this will ensue—
They'll suck our breath or pinch us black and blue.

Luc. Why prat'st thou to thyself and answer'st not?
Dromio, thou drone, thou snail, thou slug, thou sot!

Dro. S. I am transformed, master, am I not?

171. *counterfeit:* dissemble. 173. *exempt:* cut off, separated. 179. *possess:* seize, take. 183. *moves:* addresses, appeals to. 186. *error:* confusion. 187. *know:* unravel. *sure uncertainty:* undeniable mystery. 188. *entertain:* keep up, accept. *offer'd.* F_1 reads *free'd.* 190. *beads:* rosary. 192. *owls:* birds traditionally associated with witchcraft. *sprites:* spirits. 194. *suck our breath.* This bit of folklore may have originated in the old belief that the breath of man was his soul. 197. *transformed:* changed by witchcraft.

Ant. S. I think thou art in mind, and so am I.
Dro. S. Nay, master, both in mind and in my shape.
Ant. S. Thou hast thine own form.
Dro. S. No, I am an ape. 200
Luc. If thou art changed to aught, 'tis to an ass.
Dro. S. 'Tis true; she rides me, and I long for grass.
'Tis so, I am an ass; else it could never be
But I should know her as well as she knows me.
Adr. Come, come, no longer will I be a fool,
To put the finger in the eye and weep,
Whilst man and master laugh my woes to scorn.
Come, sir, to dinner. Dromio, keep the gate.
Husband, I'll dine above with you today
And shrive you of a thousand idle pranks. 210
Sirrah, if any ask you for your master,
Say he dines forth and let no creature enter.
Come, sister. Dromio, play the porter well.
Ant. S. Am I in earth, in heaven, or in hell?
Sleeping or waking? Mad or well-advised?
Known unto these, and to myself disguised!
I'll say as they say, and persevere so,
And in this mist at all adventures go.
Dro. S. Master, shall I be porter at the gate?
Adr. Ay; and let none enter, lest I break your pate. 220
Luc. Come, come, Antipholus, we dine too late.
[*They all go into the Phœnix.*

202. *grass:* freedom, restful pasturage. 209. *above.* Perhaps on the upper stage of the Elizabethan theatre. The amusement of the next scene is conceivably heightened by the possibility that the diners, oblivious of the turmoil at the gate, could be clearly seen by the audience, who thus watched two scenes at the same time. 210. *shrive . . . pranks:* i.e., forgive you for all your defections. 215. *well-advised:* in his right mind. 217. *persevere:* pronounced *persever*, and so spelled in F_1.

ACT III

SCENE I. *In front of the Phœnix, the house of* ANTIPHOLUS of Ephesus.

Enter ANTIPHOLUS of Ephesus, DROMIO *his man*, ANGELO *the Goldsmith*, *and* BALTHASAR *the Merchant*.

Ant. E. Good Signior Angelo, you must excuse us all;
My wife is shrewish when I keep not hours.
Say that I linger'd with you at your shop
To see the making of her carcanet,
And that tomorrow you will bring it home.
[*Turning upon Dromio.*] But here's a villain that would face me down
He met me on the mart, and that I beat him
And charged him with a thousand marks in gold,
And that I did deny my wife and house.
Thou drunkard, thou, what didst thou mean by this? 10
Dro. E. Say what you will, sir, but I know what I know;
That you beat me at the mart, I have your hand to show.
If the skin were parchment, and the blows you gave were ink,
Your own handwriting would tell you what I think.
Ant. E. I think thou art an ass.
Dro. E. Marry, so it doth appear
By the wrongs I suffer and the blows I bear.
I should kick, being kick'd; and, being at that pass,
You would keep from my heels and beware of an ass.
Ant. E. You're sad, Signior Balthasar; pray God our cheer
May answer my good will and your good welcome here. 20
Bal. I hold your dainties cheap, sir, and your welcome dear.
Ant. E. O, Signior Balthasar, either at flesh or fish,
A table full of welcome makes scarce one dainty dish.

[III. i] 4. *carcanet:* an ornamental collar or necklace usually of gold or set with jewels. 8. *charged him with:* i.e., with having received and lost. 11–83. The doggerel verse of these lines recalls the mid-sixteenth-century academic comedies, *Ralph Roister Doister* and *Gammer Gurton's Needle*. 19. *sad:* grave, serious.

Bal. Good meat, sir, is common; that every churl affords.

Ant. E. And welcome more common; for that's nothing but words.

Bal. Small cheer and great welcome makes a merry feast.

Ant. E. Ay, to a niggardly host and more sparing guest.
But though my cates be mean, take them in good part;
Better cheer may you have, but not with better heart.
[*He tries the door.*
But, soft, my door is lock'd. [*To Dromio.*] Go bid them let us in.

Dro. E. [*Knocking*] Maud, Bridget, Marian, Cicely, Gillian, Ginn! 31

Dro. S. [*Inside the gate*] Mome, malt-horse, capon, coxcomb, idiot, patch!
Either get thee from the door or sit down at the hatch.
Dost thou conjure for wenches, that thou call'st for such store,
When one is one too many? Go get thee from the door.

Dro. E. What patch is made our porter? My master stays in the street.

Dro. S. Let him walk from whence he came, lest he catch cold on 's feet.

Ant. E. Who talks within there? Ho, open the door!

Dro. S. Right, sir; I'll tell you when, an you'll tell me wherefore.

Ant. E. Wherefore? For my dinner. I have not dined today. 40

Dro. S. Nor today here you must not; come again when you may.

Ant. E. What art thou that keepest me out from the house I owe?

Dro. S. The porter for this time, sir, and my name is Dromio.

24. *meat:* food. *churl:* peasant, rustic. 26. *cheer:* that which is provided for entertainment, food. 28. *cates:* provisions. 32. *Mome:* blockhead. *malt-horse:* brewer's horse, a clumsy beast; hence, a stupid person. *patch:* fool, in reference to the motley costume. 33. *sit . . . hatch:* i.e., keep quiet, in allusion to the proverb: "It is good to set a hatch before the door." A *hatch* is a Dutch door, a half door, or wicket. 42. *owe:* own.

Dro. E. O villain! Thou hast stolen both mine office and my name.
The one ne'er got me credit, the other mickle blame.
If thou hadst been Dromio today in my place,
Thou wouldst have changed thy face for a name or thy name for an ass.

Luce. [*Calling from inside the house*] What a coil is there, Dromio? Who are those at the gate?

Dro. E. Let my master in, Luce.

Luce. Faith, no; he comes too late;
And so tell your master.

Dro. E. O Lord, I must laugh! 50
Have at you with a proverb—Shall I set in my staff?

Luce. Have at you with another; that's—When? Can you tell?

Dro. S. If thy name be call'd Luce—Luce, thou hast answer'd him well.

Ant. E. Do you hear, you minion? You'll let us in, I hope?

Luce. I thought to have ask'd you.

Dro. S. And you said no.

Dro. E. So, come, help; well struck! There was blow for blow.

Ant. E. Thou baggage, let me in.

Luce. Can you tell for whose sake?

Dro. E. Master, knock the door hard.

Luce. Let him knock till it ache.

Ant. E. You'll cry for this, minion, if I beat the door down.

Luce. What needs all that, and a pair of stocks in the town? 60

Adr. [*Calling from the dining room*] Who is that at the door that keeps all this noise?

Dro. S. By my troth, your town is troubled with unruly boys.

45. *mickle:* much. 48. *Luce.* Here F_1 has a stage direction: *Enter Luce,* but the context makes it certain that the character speaks off-stage. *coil:* disturbance. 51. *set . . . staff:* make myself at home. 54. *minion:* hussy, saucy wench. 61. *Adr.* F_1 has a stage direction: *Enter Adriana;* see note on II, ii, 209.

Ant. E. Are you there, wife? You might have come before.
Adr. Your wife, sir knave? Go get you from the door.
Dro. E. If you went in pain, master, this "knave" would go sore.
Ang. Here is neither cheer, sir, nor welcome; we would fain have either.
Bal. In debating which was best, we shall part with neither.
Dro. E. They stand at the door, master; bid them welcome hither.
Ant. E. There is something in the wind, that we cannot get in.
Dro. E. You would say so, master, if your garments were thin. 70
Your cake there is warm within; you stand here in the cold.
It would make a man mad as a buck, to be so bought and sold.
Ant. E. Go fetch me something; I'll break ope the gate.
Dro. S. Break any breaking here, and I'll break your knave's pate.
Dro. E. A man may break a word with you, sir, and words are but wind,
Ay, and break it in your face, so he break it not behind.
Dro. S. It seems thou want'st breaking; out upon thee, hind!
Dro. E. Here's too much "out upon thee!" I pray thee, let me in.
Dro. S. Ay, when fowls have no feathers, and fish have no fin.
Ant. E. Well, I'll break in; go borrow me a crow. 80
Dro. E. A crow without feather? Master, mean you so?
For a fish without a fin, there's a fowl without a feather.
If a crow help us in, sirrah, we'll pluck a crow together.
Ant. E. Go get thee gone; fetch me an iron crow.
Bal. Have patience, sir; O, let it not be so!

66. *cheer:* hospitable entertainment. 67. *part with:* depart with; i.e., get. 72. *bought and sold:* imposed upon. 80. *crow:* crowbar. 83. *pluck a crow:* a proverbial expression meaning "settle accounts," "quarrel."

Herein you war against your reputation,
And draw within the compass of suspect
The unviolated honour of your wife.
Once this— Your long experience of her wisdom,
Her sober virtue, years, and modesty, 90
Plead on her part some cause to you unknown;
And doubt not, sir, but she will well excuse
Why at this time the doors are made against you.
Be ruled by me; depart in patience,
And let us to the Tiger all to dinner,
And about evening come yourself alone
To know the reason of this strange restraint.
If by strong hand you offer to break in
Now in the stirring passage of the day,
A vulgar comment will be made of it, 100
And that supposed by the common rout
Against your yet ungalled estimation
That may with foul intrusion enter in
And dwell upon your grave when you are dead;
For Slander lives upon succession,
For ever housed where it gets possession.

Ant. E. You have prevail'd; I will depart in quiet,
And, in despite of mirth, mean to be merry.
I know a wench of excellent discourse,
Pretty and witty, wild and yet, too, gentle; 110
There will we dine. This woman that I mean,
My wife—but, I protest, without desert—
Hath oftentimes upbraided me withal;
To her will we to dinner. [*To Angelo.*] Get you home

87. *suspect:* suspicion. 89. *Once this:* in short. 93. *made:* i.e., fastened. 99. *stirring passage:* busy passing to and fro of people. 100. *vulgar:* public. 101. *supposed:* suspected. *common rout:* common herd, rabble. 102. *ungalled:* unblemished. 105. *upon succession:* i.e., by begetting heirs (other exaggerated slanders) to succeed it. Slander, by being repeated, is constantly renewed. 108. *in despite of mirth:* a dubious passage, meaning, probably, "in spite of the mirth which others may have at my expense." 112. *desert:* i.e., my deserving it. 113. *withal:* with it.

And fetch the chain; by this I know 'tis made.
Bring it, I pray you, to the Porpentine;
For there's the house. That chain will I bestow—
Be it for nothing but to spite my wife—
Upon mine hostess there. Good sir, make haste.
Since mine own doors refuse to entertain me, 120
I'll knock elsewhere, to see if they'll disdain me.

Ang. I'll meet you at that place some hour hence.

Ant. E. Do so. This jest shall cost me some expense.

[*Exeunt.*

SCENE II. *The same, some time later.*

Enter LUCIANA *and* ANTIPHOLUS of Syracuse *from the house.*

Luc. And may it be that you have quite forgot
A husband's office? Shall, Antipholus,
Even in the spring of love, thy love-springs rot?
Shall love, in building, grow so ruinous?
If you did wed my sister for her wealth,
Then for her wealth's sake use her with more kindness.
Or if you like elsewhere, do it by stealth;
Muffle your false love with some show of blindness;
Let not my sister read it in your eye;
Be not thy tongue thy own shame's orator; 10
Look sweet, speak fair, become disloyalty;
Apparel Vice like Virtue's harbinger;
Bear a fair presence, though your heart be tainted;
Teach Sin the carriage of a holy saint;
Be secret-false—what need she be acquainted?
What simple thief brags of his own attaint?
'Tis double wrong, to truant with your bed
And let her read it in thy looks at board.

116. *Porpentine:* at the sign of the Porcupine.

[ii] 3. *love-springs. Springs* are the first tender shoots of a plant. 4. *ruinous.* F_1 reads *ruinate.* 11. *become:* make becoming. The next line develops the idea. 12. *harbinger:* attendant; literally, a court officer sent before to prepare lodgings for a royal court. 14. *carriage:* bearing, behavior. 16. *attaint:* disgrace, crime.

Shame hath a bastard fame, well managed;
  Ill deeds are doubled with an evil word. 20
Alas, poor women, make us but believe,
  Being compact of credit, that you love us;
Though others have the arm, show us the sleeve;
  We in your motion turn and you may move us.
Then, gentle brother, get you in again;
  Comfort my sister, cheer her, call her wife.
'Tis holy sport to be a little vain,
  When the sweet breath of flattery conquers strife.

Ant. S. Sweet mistress—what your name is else, I know not,
  Nor by what wonder you do hit of mine— 30
Less in your knowledge and your grace you show not
  Than our earth's wonder, more than earth divine.
Teach me, dear creature, how to think and speak;
  Lay open to my earthly-gross conceit,
Smother'd in errors, feeble, shallow, weak,
  The folded meaning of your words' deceit.
Against my soul's pure truth why labour you
  To make it wander in an unknown field?
Are you a god? Would you create me new?
  Transform me then, and to your power I'll yield. 40
But if that I am I, then well I know
  Your weeping sister is no wife of mine,
Nor to her bed no homage do I owe;
  Far more, far more to you do I decline.
O, train me not, sweet mermaid, with thy note,
  To drown me in thy sister's flood of tears.
Sing, siren, for thyself, and I will dote;
  Spread o'er the silver waves thy golden hairs,

19. *bastard:* spurious. 21. *but.* F_1 reads *not.* 22. *compact:* composed, made up. *credit:* credulity. 24. *in your motion:* at your prompting. 27. *vain:* false. 32. *our earth's wonder.* It has been suggested that this is a compliment to Queen Elizabeth. 34. *conceit:* understanding. 36. *folded:* hidden. 40. *Transform:* change by witchcraft. 44. *decline:* incline. 45. *train:* lure. *mermaid:* siren.

And as a bed I'll take them and there lie,
  And in that glorious supposition think 50
He gains by death that hath such means to die.
  Let Love, being light, be drowned if she sink!
  Luc. What, are you mad, that you do reason so?
  Ant. S. Not mad, but mated; how, I do not know.
  Luc. It is a fault that springeth from your eye.
  Ant. S. For gazing on your beams, fair sun, being by.
  Luc. Gaze where you should, and that will clear your sight.
  Ant. S. As good to wink, sweet love, as look on night.
  Luc. Why call you me "love"? Call my sister so.
  Ant. S. Thy sister's sister.
  Luc. That's my sister.
  Ant. S. No; 60
It is thyself, mine own self's better part,
Mine eye's clear eye, my dear heart's dearer heart,
My food, my fortune, and my sweet hope's aim,
My sole earth's heaven, and my heaven's claim.
  Luc. All this my sister is, or else should be.
  Ant. S. Call thyself sister, sweet, for I am thee.
Thee will I love and with thee lead my life;
Thou hast no husband yet, nor I no wife.
Give me thy hand.
  Luc. O, soft, sir, hold you still; 69
I'll fetch my sister, to get her good will. [*She goes inside.*

DROMIO of Syracuse *comes running out of the house.*

Ant. S. Why, how now, Dromio, where runn'st thou so fast?

Dro. S. Do you know me, sir? Am I Dromio? Am I your man? Am I myself?

49. *bed.* F_1 reads *bud.* 52. *Let . . . sink:* if Love can't take care of herself, let her drown. There is probably a quibble upon *light,* "wanton." 54. *mated:* (a) stupefied, confounded, (b) supplied with a mate. 58. *wink:* close the eyes. 64. *My . . . claim:* my only heaven on earth and my claim of heaven hereafter. 66. *for I am thee:* i.e., you and I are one. Some editors read *aim,* mean to have. 69. *soft:* stay, stop.

Ant. S. Thou art Dromio; thou art my man; thou art thyself.

Dro. S. I am an ass; I am a woman's man, and besides myself.

Ant. S. What woman's man? And how besides thyself? 80

Dro. S. Marry, sir, besides myself, I am due to a woman; one that claims me, one that haunts me, one that will have me.

Ant. S. What claim lays she to thee?

Dro. S. Marry, sir, such claim as you would lay to your horse; and she would have me as a beast; not that, I being a beast, she would have me; but that she, being a very beastly creature, lays claim to me.

Ant. S. What is she? 90

Dro. S. A very reverent body; ay, such a one as a man may not speak of without he say "Sir-reverence." I have but lean luck in the match, and yet is she a wondrous fat marriage.

Ant. S. How dost thou mean a fat marriage?

Dro. S. Marry, sir, she's the kitchen wench and all grease; and I know not what use to put her to, but to make a lamp of her and run from her by her own light. I warrant her rags and the tallow in them will burn a Poland winter. If she lives till Doomsday, she'll burn a week longer than the whole world.

Ant. S. What complexion is she of? 103

Dro. S. Swart, like my shoe, but her face nothing like so clean kept. For why? She sweats; a man may go over shoes in the grime of it.

Ant. S. That's a fault that water will mend.

Dro. S. No, sir, 'tis in grain; Noah's flood could not do it.

Ant. S. What's her name? 110

Dro. S. Nell, sir; but her name and three quarters, that's an ell and three quarters, will not measure her from hip to hip.

Ant. S. Then she bears some breadth?

86. *a beast:* with a quibble on *abased.* 93. "*Sir-reverence*": an apologetic phrase for mentioning an unpleasant fact or an impropriety; a corruption of "save your reverence." 97. *all grease:* a quibble at the expense of this graceless creature. *Grease* and *grace* were pronounced alike in Shakespeare's day. 100. *Poland winter:* i.e., a long winter. 104. *Swart:* swarthy, black. 108. *in grain:* indelible. 112. *ell:* one and a quarter yards.

Dro. S. No longer from head to foot than from hip to hip; she is spherical, like a globe; I could find out countries in her.

Ant. S. In what part of her body stands Ireland?

Dro. S. Marry, sir, in her buttocks; I found it out by the bogs. 121

Ant. S. Where Scotland?

Dro. S. I found it by the barrenness; hard in the palm of the hand.

Ant. S. Where France?

Dro. S. In her forehead, armed and reverted, making war against her heir.

Ant. S. Where England?

Dro. S. I looked for the chalky cliffs, but I could find no whiteness in them; but I guess it stood in her chin, by the salt rheum that ran between France and it. 132

Ant. S. Where Spain?

Dro. S. Faith, I saw it not; but I felt it hot in her breath.

Ant. S. Where America, the Indies?

Dro. S. Oh, sir, upon her nose, all o'er embellished with rubies, carbuncles, sapphires, declining their rich aspect to the hot breath of Spain; who sent whole armadoes of caracks to be ballast at her nose. 141

Ant. S. Where stood Belgia, the Netherlands?

Dro. S. Oh, sir, I did not look so low. To conclude, this drudge, or diviner, laid claim to me; called me Dromio; swore I was assured to her; told me what privy marks I had about me, as, the mark of my shoulder, the mole in my neck, the great wart on my left arm, that I amazed ran from her as a witch.

123. *hard:* exactly. 126–7. *armed . . . heir:* an allusion to the civil wars in France (1589–93), in which the "heir," Henry of Navarre (later Henry IV), fought the "reverted" (i.e., revolted) League for the crown of France. "Mistress Nell's brazen forehead seems to push back her rough and rebellious hair, as France resisted the claims of the Protestant heir to the throne" (Cowden-Clarke). 129. *chalky cliffs:* i.e., her teeth. 136–41. *Where . . . nose:* an early allusion to the supposed fabulous wealth of the New World. 139. *declining:* inclining, bending. *aspect:* glance, look. 140. *caracks:* galleons. 145. *assured:* promised in marriage. 146. *privy:* secret.

And, I think, if my breast had not been made of faith, and my
heart of steel, 150
She had transform'd me to a curtal-dog and made me turn i'
the wheel.

Ant. S. Go hie thee presently, post to the road,
An if the wind blow any way from shore,
I will not harbour in this town tonight.
If any bark put forth, come to the mart,
Where I will walk till thou return to me.
If every one knows us, and we know none,
'Tis time, I think, to trudge, pack, and be gone.

Dro. S. As from a bear a man would run for life,
So fly I from her that would be my wife. [*Exit.*

Ant. S. There's none but witches do inhabit here; 161
And therefore 'tis high time that I were hence.
She that doth call me husband, even my soul
Doth for a wife abhor. But her fair sister,
Possess'd with such a gentle sovereign grace,
Of such enchanting presence and discourse,
Hath almost made me traitor to myself.
But, lest myself be guilty to self-wrong,
I'll stop mine ears against the mermaid's song.

Enter ANGELO *with the chain.*

Ang. Master Antipholus—

Ant. S. Ay, that's my name. 170

Ang. I know it well, sir; lo, here is the chain.
I thought to have ta'en you at the Porpentine;
The chain unfinish'd made me stay thus long.

Ant. S. What is your will that I shall do with this?

151. *curtal-dog:* dog with a docked tail, sometimes confined in a kind of squirrel cage to turn spit in the kitchens. There is probably an allusion to the proverb: "He toils like a dog in a wheel who roasts meat for other people's eating." 152. *presently:* immediately. *post:* in haste. *road:* roadstead, a protected anchorage for ships. 154. *harbour:* lodge. 161. *witches.* In Elizabethan English this word applied to persons of either sex. 172. *ta'en:* found, met. *Porpentine:* at the sign of the Porcupine.

Ang. What please yourself, sir; I have made it for you.
Ant. S. Made it for me, sir? I bespoke it not.
Ang. Not once, nor twice, but twenty times you have.
Go home with it and please your wife withal;
And soon at supper-time I'll visit you
And then receive my money for the chain. 180
Ant. S. I pray you, sir, receive the money now,
For fear you ne'er see chain nor money more.
Ang. You are a merry man, sir; fare you well. [*Exit.*
Ant. S. What I should think of this, I cannot tell;
But this I think, there's no man is so vain
That would refuse so fair an offer'd chain.
I see a man here needs not live by shifts,
When in the streets he meets such golden gifts.
I'll to the mart and there for Dromio stay; 189
If any ship put out, then straight away. [*Exit.*

ACT IV

SCENE I. *A public place near the Porpentine, immediately after.*

Enter a Merchant, ANGELO, *and an* Officer.

Mer. You know since Pentecost the sum is due,
And since I have not much importuned you;
Nor now I had not, but that I am bound
To Persia and want guilders for my voyage.
Therefore make present satisfaction,
Or I'll attach you by this officer.
Ang. Even just the sum that I do owe to you
Is growing to me by Antipholus,

176. *bespoke:* ordered. 178. *withal:* with it. 179. *soon at:* about. 185. *vain:* empty-headed, foolish. 186. *so fair . . . chain:* a chain offered so courteously.

[IV. i] 1. *Pentecost:* Whitsunday. 2. *importuned:* troubled, pressed. 5. *present:* immediate. 6. *attach:* arrest. 8. *growing:* accruing.

And in the instant that I met with you
He had of me a chain. At five o'clock 10
I shall receive the money for the same.
Pleaseth you walk with me down to his house,
I will discharge my bond and thank you too.

Enter ANTIPHOLUS of Ephesus *and* DROMIO of Ephesus *from the Courtesan's.*

Off. That labour may you save; see where he comes.
Ant. E. While I go to the goldsmith's house, go thou
And buy a rope's end; that will I bestow
Among my wife and her confederates,
For locking me out of my doors by day.
But, soft, I see the goldsmith. Get thee gone;
Buy thou a rope and bring it home to me. 20
Dro. E. I buy a thousand pound a year; I buy a rope. [*Exit.*
Ant. E. A man is well holp up that trusts to you;
I promised your presence and the chain,
But neither chain nor goldsmith came to me.
Belike you thought our love would last too long,
If it were chain'd together, and therefore came not.
Ang. Saving your merry humour, here's the note
How much your chain weighs to the utmost carat,
The fineness of the gold and chargeful fashion,
Which doth amount to three odd ducats more 30
Than I stand debted to this gentleman.
I pray you, see him presently discharged,
For he is bound to sea and stays but for it.
Ant. E. I am not furnish'd with the present money;
Besides, I have some business in the town.
Good signior, take the stranger to my house,
And with you take the chain, and bid my wife
Disburse the sum on the receipt thereof;
Perchance I will be there as soon as you.

16. *rope's end:* piece of rope. 21. *pound:* i.e., blows. Cf. *marks* above at I, ii, 81 ff. 22. *holp:* helped. 27. *note:* bill, memorandum. 29. *chargeful:* expensive. *fashion:* workmanship. 33. *stays:* waits.

Ang. Then you will bring the chain to her yourself? 40
Ant. E. No, bear it with you, lest I come not time enough.
Ang. Well, sir, I will. Have you the chain about you?
Ant. E. An if I have not, sir, I hope you have;
Or else you may return without your money.
Ang. Nay, come, I pray you, sir, give me the chain.
Both wind and tide stays for this gentleman,
And I, to blame, have held him here too long.
Ant. E. Good Lord, you use this dalliance to excuse
Your breach of promise to the Porpentine.
I should have chid you for not bringing it, 50
But, like a shrew, you first begin to brawl.
Mer. The hour steals on; I pray you, sir, dispatch.
Ang. You hear how he importunes me—the chain!
Ant. E. Why, give it to my wife and fetch your money.
Ang. Come, come, you know I gave it you even now.
Either send the chain or send me by some token.
Ant. E. Fie, now you run this humour out of breath.
Come, where's the chain? I pray you, let me see it.
Mer. My business cannot brook this dalliance.
Good sir, say whether you'll answer me or no; 60
If not, I'll leave him to the officer.
Ant. E. I answer you? What should I answer you?
Ang. The money that you owe me for the chain.
Ant. E. I owe you none till I receive the chain.
Ang. You know I gave it you half an hour since.
Ant. E. You gave me none; you wrong me much to say so.
Ang. You wrong me more, sir, in denying it.
Consider how it stands upon my credit.
Mer. Well, officer, arrest him at my suit.
Off. I do; and charge you in the duke's name to obey me. 70
Ang. This touches me in reputation.

48. *dalliance:* idle delay, trifling. 51. *shrew:* scolding woman. 52. *dispatch:* make haste. 56. *token:* i.e., send by me some means of identification so that Adriana may know I come on an honest errand. 57. *humour:* whim. 59. *brook:* endure, tolerate. 60. *answer:* pay. 68. *credit:* reputation. 71. *touches:* injures, taints.

Either consent to pay this sum for me,
Or I attach you by this officer.
Ant. E. Consent to pay thee that I never had!
Arrest me, foolish fellow, if thou darest.
Ang. [*Engaging the Officer*] Here is thy fee; arrest him, officer.
I would not spare my brother in this case,
If he should scorn me so apparently.
Off. I do arrest you, sir; you hear the suit.
Ant. E. I do obey thee till I give thee bail. 80
But, sirrah, you shall buy this sport as dear
As all the metal in your shop will answer.
Ang. Sir, sir, I shall have law in Ephesus,
To your notorious shame; I doubt it not.

Enter Dromio of Syracuse, *from the bay.*

Dro. S. Master, there is a bark of Epidamnum
That stays but till her owner comes aboard
And then, sir, she bears away. Our fraughtage, sir,
I have convey'd aboard and I have bought
The oil, the balsamum, and aqua-vitæ.
The ship is in her trim; the merry wind 90
Blows fair from land; they stay for nought at all
But for their owner, master, and yourself.
Ant. E. How now? A madman? Why, thou peevish sheep,
What ship of Epidamnum stays for me?
Dro. S. A ship you sent me to, to hire waftage.
Ant. E. Thou drunken slave, I sent thee for a rope,
And told thee to what purpose and what end.
Dro. S. You sent me for a rope's end as soon;
You sent me to the bay, sir, for a bark.
Ant. E. I will debate this matter at more leisure 100

78. *apparently:* openly. 87. *fraughtage:* cargo, goods. 89. *balsamum:* balm. *aqua-vitæ:* liquor. 90. *in her trim:* i.e., ready to sail. 93. *peevish:* perverse, obstinate. 93–4. *sheep . . . ship:* pronounced alike in Shakespeare's day and frequently quibbled upon. 95. *waftage:* passage. 98. *rope's end:* (a) piece of rope, (b) hangman's halter.

And teach your ears to list me with more heed.
To Adriana, villain, hie thee straight;
Give her this key, and tell her, in the desk
That's cover'd o'er with Turkish tapestry
There is a purse of ducats; let her send it.
Tell her I am arrested in the street
And that shall bail me; hie thee, slave, be gone!
On, officer, to prison till it come.
[*Exeunt Merchant, Angelo, Officer, and Antipholus E.*
Dro. S. To Adriana! That is where we dined,
Where Dowsabel did claim me for her husband. 110
She is too big, I hope, for me to compass.
Thither I must, although against my will,
For servants must their masters' minds fulfil. [*Exit.*

SCENE II. *The house of* ANTIPHOLUS of Ephesus *immediately after.*

Enter ADRIANA *and* LUCIANA.

Adr. Ah, Luciana, did he tempt thee so?
Mightst thou perceive austerely in his eye
That he did plead in earnest? Yea or no?
Look'd he or red or pale, or sad or merrily?
What observation madest thou in this case
Of his heart's meteors tilting in his face?
Luc. First he denied you had in him no right.
Adr. He meant he did me none; the more my spite.
Luc. Then swore he that he was a stranger here.
Adr. And true he swore, though yet forsworn he were. 10
Luc. Then pleaded I for you.

104. *Turkish tapestry:* i.e., Turkey work, a kind of embroidery, or Turkish carpet. 110. *Dowsabel.* This generic name for sweetheart implies both sweetness and beauty, qualities to which the kitchen-vestal could not lay claim. 111. *to compass:* to get under control.

[ii] 1. *tempt:* entice, endeavor to persuade. 2. *austerely:* i.e., by treating him sternly. 4. *or . . . or:* either . . . or. 8. *spite:* vexation, mortification.

Adr. And what said he?
Luc. That love I begg'd for you he begg'd of me.
Adr. With what persuasion did he tempt thy love?
Luc. With words that in an honest suit might move.
First he did praise my beauty, then my speech.
Adr. Didst speak him fair?
Luc. Have patience, I beseech.
Adr. I cannot, nor I will not, hold me still;
My tongue, though not my heart, shall have his will.
He is deformed, crooked, old, and sere,
Ill-faced, worse bodied, shapeless everywhere; 20
Vicious, ungentle, foolish, blunt, unkind,
Stigmatical in making, worse in mind.
Luc. Who would be jealous then of such a one?
No evil lost is wail'd when it is gone.
Adr. Ah, but I think him better than I say,
And yet would herein others' eyes were worse.
Far from her nest the lapwing cries away;
My heart prays for him, though my tongue do curse.

Enter DROMIO of Syracuse *in haste.*

Dro. S. Here, go; the desk, the purse! Sweat now, make haste.
Luc. How hast thou lost thy breath?
Dro. S. By running fast. 30
Adr. Where is thy master, Dromio? Is he well?
Dro. S. No, he's in Tartar limbo, worse than hell.
A devil in an everlasting garment hath him;
One whose hard heart is button'd up with steel;

16. *speak him fair:* i.e., give him any encouragement. 19. *sere:* wrinkled, withered. 22. *Stigmatical:* marked, deformed. 27. *lapwing:* the peewit, which draws an intruder away from its nest in the manner described. 29. *Sweat now:* exert yourselves (Wilson). F_1 reads *sweet;* the two words were pronounced alike in Shakespeare's day. 32. *Tartar limbo.* Both words refer to hell, but a pun is also intended. *Tartar* probably referred to rogues, and *limbo* to prison. 33. *everlasting garment:* i.e., of buff, a stout oxhide garment worn by bailiffs, soldiers, and devils in the old miracle and morality plays.

A fiend, a fairy, pitiless and rough;
A wolf—nay, worse—a fellow all in buff;
A back-friend, a shoulder-clapper, one that countermands
The passages of alleys, creeks, and narrow lands;
A hound that runs counter, and yet draws dry-foot well;
One that, before the Judgment, carries poor souls to hell. 40

Adr. Why, man, what is the matter?

Dro. S. I do not know the matter; he is 'rested on the case.

Adr. What, is he arrested? Tell me at whose suit.

Dro. S. I know not at whose suit he is arrested well;
But he's in a suit of buff which 'rested him, that can I tell.
Will you send him, Mistress Redemption, the money in his desk?

Adr. Go fetch it, sister. [*Exit Luciana.*] This I wonder at,
That he, unknown to me, should be in debt.
Tell me, was he arrested on a band?

Dro. S. Not on a band, but on a stronger thing; 50
A chain, a chain! Do you not hear it ring? [*The clock strikes.*

Adr. What? The chain?

Dro. S. No, no, the bell; 'tis time that I were gone;
It was two ere I left him, and now the clock strikes one.

Adr. The hours come back? That did I never hear.

35. *fairy.* The fairies of folklore were frequently malevolent, malicious beings. (See the Introduction to *A Midsummer Night's Dream.*) Some editors emend the text here to read *fury.* 37. *back-friend:* (a) backslapper, (b) false or pretended friend, (c) sergeant who claps his prisoner on the back. *countermands:* forbids entry to. 38. *creeks:* out-of-the-way corners, winding passages. *narrow lands:* narrow landings on the river (?). The exact meaning is in doubt. 39. *runs counter:* (a) a hunting term, meaning following a scent in the direction opposite to that taken by the game, with a quibble on (b) Counter, a debtors' prison. *draws dry-foot:* tracks game by scent. 40. *before the Judgment:* (a) Day of Judgment, (b) arrest and imprisonment by mesne process (i.e., on some side issue). *hell:* debtors' prison. 46. *Mistress Redemption.* So F_4; F_1 has *Mistris redemption* (uncapitalized). Most modern editors read *mistress, redemption.* If the F_4 emendation is accepted, the allusion is to the old morality plays; and this seems probable, for Dromio's mind runs upon them in this scene and the next. 49. *band:* (a) bond, warrant, (b) leash to tie a dog.

Dro. S. O, yes; if any hour meet a sergeant, a' turns back for very fear.

Adr. As if Time were in debt! How fondly dost thou reason!

Dro. S. Time is a very bankrupt and owes more than he's worth to season.

Nay, he's a thief too. Have you not heard men say
That Time comes stealing on by night and day? 60
If Time be in debt and theft, and a sergeant in the way,
Hath he not reason to turn back an hour in a day?

Re-enter Luciana *with a purse.*

Adr. Go, Dromio; there's the money, bear it straight,
And bring thy master home immediately. [*Dromio goes.*
Come, sister, I am press'd down with conceit—
Conceit, my comfort and my injury. [*Exeunt.*

Scene iii. *A public place near the Porpentine.*

Enter Antipholus of Syracuse, *the chain about his neck.*

Ant. S. There's not a man I meet but doth salute me
As if I were their well-acquainted friend;
And every one doth call me by my name.
Some tender money to me; some invite me;
Some other give me thanks for kindnesses;
Some offer me commodities to buy.
Even now a tailor call'd me in his shop
And show'd me silks that he had bought for me
And therewithal took measure of my body.
Sure, these are but imaginary wiles, 10
And Lapland sorcerers inhabit here.

57. *fondly:* foolishly. 58. *very:* veritable, complete. *season:* a favorable opportunity. 63. *straight:* straightway, without delay. 65. *conceit:* i.e., imaginings.

[iii] 4. *tender:* offer. 10. *imaginary:* existing only in the imagination, not real. 11. *Lapland sorcerers.* A passage on the Lapps in Hakluyt's *Voyages* reads: "For practice of witchcraft and sorcery they pass all nations in the world."

Enter DROMIO of Syracuse.

Dro. S. Master, here's the gold you sent me for. What, have you got the picture of old Adam new-apparelled?

Ant. S. What gold is this? What Adam dost thou mean?

Dro. S. Not that Adam that kept the Paradise, but that Adam that keeps the prison—he that goes in the calf's skin that was killed for the Prodigal—he that came behind you, sir, like an evil angel, and bid you forsake your liberty. 20

Ant. S. I understand thee not.

Dro. S. No? Why, 'tis a plain case—he that went, like a bass-viol, in a case of leather; the man, sir, that, when gentlemen are tired, gives them a sob and 'rests them; he, sir, that takes pity on decayed men and gives them suits of durance; he that sets up his rest to do more exploits with his mace than a morris-pike.

Ant. S. What? Thou meanest an officer? 29

Dro. S. Ay, sir, the sergeant of the band; he that brings any man to answer it that breaks his band; one that thinks a man always going to bed and says, "God give you good rest!"

Ant. S. Well, sir, there rest in your foolery. Is there any ship puts forth tonight? May we be gone?

13–14. *got . . . new-apparelled:* i.e., got the bailiff, who was clad in buff, a new *suit;* hence, got rid of him. The Biblical allusion is to Genesis 3:21—"Unto Adam also and to his wife did the Lord God make coats of skins, and clothed them." Theobald's emendation, *got rid of*, is often adopted by modern editors. 20. *evil angel:* another allusion to the morality plays. *forsake your liberty:* i.e., sell your soul to the Devil. 25. *sob:* an opportunity allowed a horse for recovering its wind after exertion, a rest or respite (*N. E. D.*). Some editors emend to *bob*, tap on the shoulder. *'rests:* arrests. 26. *decayed:* ruined, down-at-the-heel. *suits of durance:* (a) terms of imprisonment, (b) stout garments of buff. 27. *sets . . . rest:* a phrase derived from primero, a popular card game from which poker developed. The *rest* was the stakes, and the phrase originally meant "risk everything"; hence, "be determined." 28. *mace:* the symbol of the constable's office. *morris-pike:* a watchman's weapon, supposed to have been of Moorish origin. 32. *band:* bond. 33. "*God give you good rest*": the call of the night watchman on his rounds.

Dro. S. Why, sir, I brought you word an hour since that the bark *Expedition* put forth tonight; and then were you hindered by the sergeant, to tarry for the hoy *Delay*. Here are the angels that you sent for to deliver you. 41

Ant. S. The fellow is distract, and so am I;
And here we wander in illusions.
Some blessed power deliver us from hence!

The Courtesan *comes from her house.*

Cour. Well met, well met, Master Antipholus.
I see, sir, you have found the goldsmith now.
Is that the chain you promised me today?

Ant. S. Satan, avoid! I charge thee, tempt me not.

Dro. S. Master, is this Mistress Satan?

Ant. S. It is the Devil. 50

Dro. S. Nay, she is worse; she is the Devil's dam; and here she comes in the habit of a light wench; and thereof comes that the wenches say, "God damn me"; that's as much to say, "God make me a light wench." It is written they appear to men like angels of light; light is an effect of fire, and fire will burn; *ergo*, light wenches will burn. Come not near her.

Cour. Your man and you are marvellous merry, sir.
Will you go with me? We'll mend our dinner here? 60

Dro. S. Master, if you do, expect spoon-meat; or bespeak a long spoon.

Ant. S. Why, Dromio?

40. *hoy:* a small coast vessel. 41. *angels:* i.e., the good angels (gold Elizabethan coins stamped with the figure of the Archangel Michael) sent by Mistress Redemption. 42. *distract:* crazy, mad. 49. *Mistress Satan:* another character in Dromio's little morality play. 52. *habit:* garb. *light:* wanton. 55. *It is written.* "Satan himself is transformed into an angel of light" (II Corinthians 11:14). 57. *ergo:* therefore. 60. *mend:* supplement. 61. *spoon-meat:* literally, "food that must be eaten with a spoon"; hence, a delicacy. The modern slang sense of *spoon*, which would be appropriate in this passage, was not known in Elizabethan English. 62. *long spoon:* an allusion to the proverb, "He who feasts with the Devil must get a long spoon" (see line 64).

Dro. S. Marry, he must have a long spoon that must eat with the Devil.

Ant. S. Avoid then, fiend! What tell'st thou me of supping? Thou art, as you are all, a sorceress;
I conjure thee to leave me and be gone.

Cour. Give me the ring of mine you had at dinner,
Or, for my diamond, the chain you promised, 70
And I'll be gone, sir, and not trouble you.

Dro. S. Some devils ask but the parings of one's nail,
A rush, a hair, a drop of blood, a pin,
A nut, a cherry-stone;
But she, more covetous, would have a chain.
Master, be wise; an if you give it her,
The Devil will shake her chain and fright us with it.

Cour. I pray you, sir, my ring, or else the chain;
I hope you do not mean to cheat me so.

Ant. S. Avaunt, thou witch! Come, Dromio, let us go. 80

Dro. S. "Fly pride," says the peacock; mistress, that you know. [*Exeunt Antipholus S. and Dromio S.*

Cour. Now, out of doubt, Antipholus is mad,
Else would he never so demean himself.
A ring he hath of mine worth forty ducats,
And for the same he promised me a chain.
Both one and other he denies me now.
The reason that I gather he is mad,
Besides this present instance of his rage,
Is a mad tale he told today at dinner,
Of his own doors being shut against his entrance. 90
Belike his wife, acquainted with his fits,

72 ff. *Some . . . chain.* To gain power over an intended victim witches were believed to make use of something which had been closely associated with the person of that individual. For an interesting account of this practice by a wizard named Dr. Fian, see *News from Scotland* (1591), reprinted in The Bodley Head Quartos, Volume IX. 76. *an if:* even if. 81. *Fly. . . peacock:* i.e., since you are a cheat, your accusation of my master is worth about as much as a proud peacock's invective against pride. There is also a quibble on *pride* meaning "sexual desire." 83. *demean:* behave, conduct.

On purpose shut the doors against his way.
My way is now to hie home to his house,
And tell his wife that, being lunatic,
He rush'd into my house and took perforce
My ring away. This course I fittest choose,
For forty ducats is too much to lose. [*Exit.*

SCENE IV. *The same.*

Enter ANTIPHOLUS of Ephesus *and the* Officer.

Ant. E. Fear me not, man; I will not break away;
I'll give thee, ere I leave thee, so much money,
To warrant thee, as I am 'rested for.
My wife is in a wayward mood today,
And will not lightly trust the messenger.
That I should be attach'd in Ephesus,
I tell you, 'twill sound harshly in her ears.

Enter DROMIO of Ephesus *with a rope's-end.*

Here comes my man; I think he brings the money.
How now, sir? Have you that I sent you for?
Dro. E. Here's that, I warrant you, will pay them all. 10
Ant. E. But where's the money?
Dro. E. Why, sir, I gave the money for the rope.
Ant. E. Five hundred ducats, villain, for a rope?
Dro. E. I'll serve you, sir, five hundred at the rate.
Ant. E. To what end did I bid thee hie thee home?
Dro. E. To a rope's-end, sir; and to that end am I returned.
Ant. E. And to that end, sir, I will welcome you.
[*Beating him.*
Off. Good sir, be patient.
Dro. E. Nay, 'tis for me to be patient; I am in adversity. 21
Off. Good now, hold thy tongue.
Dro. E. Nay, rather persuade him to hold his hands.

95. *perforce:* forcibly.

[iv] 3. *warrant:* assure. 6. *attach'd:* arrested. 14. *I'll . . . rate.* The Cambridge editors suggest that this speech should be assigned to the Officer.

Ant. E. Thou whoreson, senseless villain!

Dro. E. I would I were senseless, sir, that I might not feel your blows.

Ant. E. Thou art sensible in nothing but blows, and so is an ass. 29

Dro. E. I am an ass, indeed; you may prove it by my long ears. I have served him from the hour of my nativity to this instant, and have nothing at his hands for my service but blows. When I am cold, he heats me with beating; when I am warm, he cools me with beating. I am waked with it when I sleep, raised with it when I sit, driven out of doors with it when I go from home, welcomed home with it when I return; nay, I bear it on my shoulders, as a beggar wont her brat; and, I think, when he hath lamed me, I shall beg with it from door to door. 42

Enter ADRIANA, LUCIANA, *the* Courtesan, *and a Schoolmaster, called* PINCH.

Ant. E. Come, go along; my wife is coming yonder.

Dro. E. Mistress, *respice finem,* respect your end; or rather, to prophesy like the parrot, "beware the rope's-end."

Ant. E. Wilt thou still talk? [*Beating him.*

25. *whoreson:* an epithet of contempt. 28. *sensible:* (a) rational, (b) capable of feeling. 31. *ears:* with a quibble upon *years* (of Dromio's service). 40. *wont:* is wont, or accustomed, to. 44. *respice finem:* look to the end; perhaps, with a pun upon *respice funem*, beware the gallows. 45. *to prophesy . . . parrot:* i.e., to speak by rote, to remark what even a parrot knows (?). Warburton observes on this puzzling passage: "This alludes to people's teaching that bird unlucky words, with which, when any passenger was offended, it was the standing joke of the wise owner to say, 'Take heed, Sir, my parrot prophesies.'" He then quotes a passage from Butler's *Hudibras* (I, i) in which Ralph's skill in augury is described. He

> Could tell what subtlest parrots mean,
> That speak, and think contrary clean;
> What member 'tis of whom they talk,
> When they cry *rope*, and *walk, knave, walk*.

F1 reads *the prophesie.* 46. *rope's end:* (a) piece of rope, (b) hangman's rope.

Cour. How say you now? Is not your husband mad?
Adr. His incivility confirms no less.
Good Doctor Pinch, you are a conjurer; 50
Establish him in his true sense again,
And I will please you what you will demand.
Luc. Alas, how fiery and how sharp he looks!
Cour. Mark how he trembles in his ecstasy!
Pinch. Give me your hand, and let me feel your pulse.
Ant. E. There is my hand, and let it feel your ear.
[*Striking him.*
Pinch. I charge thee, Satan, housed within this man,
To yield possession to my holy prayers,
And to thy state of darkness hie thee straight.
I conjure thee by all the saints in heaven! 60
Ant. E. Peace, doting wizard, peace! I am not mad.
Adr. O, that thou wert not, poor distressed soul!
Ant. E. You minion, you, are these your customers?
Did this companion with the saffron face
Revel and feast it at my house today,
Whilst upon me the guilty doors were shut
And I denied to enter in my house?
Adr. O husband, God doth know you dined at home;
Where would you had remain'd until this time,
Free from these slanders and this open shame! 70
Ant. E. Dined at home! Thou villain, what sayest thou?

50. *Doctor Pinch.* Madness to the Elizabethans (among them, the translators of the Bible) was thought of as possession by an evil spirit which could be cast out if addressed with the proper formula. Latin was popularly thought of as the language spirits were most likely to understand (cf. *Hamlet,* I, i, 42). Pinch, who is described in the stage directions as a "schoolmaster," is more of an exorcist than a physician, and was probably the one person in Ephesus whose Latinity and whose temperament would be equal to the emergency presented by Antipholus. See the Introduction. 52. *please:* give. 54. *ecstasy:* frenzy, madness. 63. *minion:* hussy. *customers:* common familiars, companions. 64. *companion:* fellow, a term of contempt. *saffron:* yellow, sallow. 71 ff. Dromio's answers are a parody of the formal replies that a pedant might exact in a classroom. Does he wish to annoy Pinch still further?

Dro. E. Sir, sooth to say, you did not dine at home.
Ant. E. Were not my doors lock'd up, and I shut out?
Dro. E. Perdie, your doors were lock'd and you shut out.
Ant. E. And did not she herself revile me there?
Dro. E. Sans fable, she herself reviled you there.
Ant. E. Did not her kitchen-maid rail, taunt, and scorn me?
Dro. E. Certes, she did; the kitchen-vestal scorn'd you.
Ant. E. And did not I in rage depart from thence?
Dro. E. In verity you did; my bones bear witness, 80
That since have felt the vigour of his rage.
Adr. Is 't good to soothe him in these contraries?
Pinch. It is no shame; the fellow finds his vein
And yielding to him humours well his frenzy.
Ant. E. Thou hast suborn'd the goldsmith to arrest me.
Adr. Alas, I sent you money to redeem you,
By Dromio here, who came in haste for it.
Dro. E. Money by me! Heart and good-will you might;
But surely, master, not a rag of money.
Ant. E. Went'st not thou to her for a purse of ducats? 90
Adr. He came to me, and I deliver'd it.
Luc. And I am witness with her that she did.
Dro. E. God and the rope-maker bear me witness
That I was sent for nothing but a rope!
Pinch. Mistress, both man and master is possess'd;
I know it by their pale and deadly looks.
They must be bound and laid in some dark room.
Ant. E. Say, wherefore didst thou lock me forth today?
And why dost thou deny the bag of gold?
Adr. I did not, gentle husband, lock thee forth. 100

74. *Perdie: par Dieu*, by God; in Shakespeare's day a mild and innocuous oath. 78. *kitchen-vestal:* Luce, whose name implies that she, like the vestal virgins of old, kept the fire burning. 82. *soothe:* humor. 83. *vein:* disposition, humor. 95. *possess'd:* i.e., of devils, mad. 97. *dark room:* an allusion to the usual treatment for lunacy in Shakespeare's day. Cf. the treatment of Malvolio, *Twelfth Night*, III, iv, 148, and IV, ii.

Dro. E. And, gentle master, I received no gold;
But I confess, sir, that we were lock'd out.

Adr. Dissembling villain, thou speak'st false in both.

Ant. E. Dissembling harlot, thou art false in all,
And art confederate with a damned pack
To make a loathsome abject scorn of me.
But with these nails I'll pluck out these false eyes
That would behold in me this shameful sport.

[*He goes toward her.*

Adr. O, bind him, bind him! Let him not come near me.

Enter three or four, and offer to bind him. He strives.

Pinch. More company! The fiend is strong within him. 110

Luc. Ay me, poor man, how pale and wan he looks!

Ant. E. What, will you murder me? Thou gaoler, thou,
I am thy prisoner; wilt thou suffer them
To make a rescue?

Off. Masters, let him go;
He is my prisoner, and you shall not have him.

Pinch. Go bind this man, for he is frantic too.

[*They offer to bind Dromio E.*

Adr. What wilt thou do, thou peevish officer?
Hast thou delight to see a wretched man
Do outrage and displeasure to himself?

Off. He is my prisoner; if I let him go, 120
The debt he owes will be required of me.

Adr. I will discharge thee ere I go from thee;
Bear me forthwith unto his creditor
And, knowing how the debt grows, I will pay it.
Good master doctor, see him safe convey'd
Home to my house. O most unhappy day!

Ant. E. O most unhappy strumpet!

Dro. E. Master, I am here enter'd in bond for you.

Ant. E. Out on thee, villain! Wherefore dost thou mad me?

105. *pack:* gang of rascals. 110. *company:* assistance. 113. *suffer:* permit. 117. *peevish:* senseless. 123. *Bear:* take. 124. *grows:* becomes due. 129. *mad:* make mad.

Dro. E. Will you be bound for nothing? Be mad, good master; cry, "The Devil!" 131

Luc. God help, poor souls, how idly do they talk!

Adr. Go bear him hence. Sister, go you with me.

[*Pinch and his crew carry off Antipholus E. and Dromio E.*

Say now, whose suit is he arrested at?

Off. One Angelo, a goldsmith; do you know him?

Adr. I know the man. What is the sum he owes?

Off. Two hundred ducats.

Adr. Say, how grows it due?

Off. Due for a chain your husband had of him.

Adr. He did bespeak a chain for me, but had it not.

Cour. When as your husband all in rage today 140
Came to my house and took away my ring—
The ring I saw upon his finger now—
Straight after did I meet him with a chain.

Adr. It may be so, but I did never see it.
Come, gaoler, bring me where the goldsmith is;
I long to know the truth hereof at large.

Enter Antipholus of Syracuse *with his rapier drawn, and* Dromio of Syracuse.

Luc. God, for thy mercy! They are loose again.

Adr. And come with naked swords.
Let's call more help to have them bound again.

Off. Away, they'll kill us. 150

[*They "run all out, as fast as may be, frighted."*

Ant. S. I see these witches are afraid of swords.

Dro. S. She that would be your wife now ran from you.

139. *bespeak:* order. 143. *Straight:* immediately. 150. S. D. After line 149, F1 prints as a stage direction: *Runne all out,* and after line 150: *Exeunt omnes, as fast as may be, frighted.* Some students, explaining this duplication, consider *Exeunt omnes* the original direction, and the more informal phrases a note, or notes, made in the margin of the original manuscript while it served as prompt-copy in the theatre. Others believe the duplication is a result of revision. Neither direction, however, is strictly correct, for Antipholus and Dromio of Syracuse remain on the stage.

Ant. S. Come to the Centaur; fetch our stuff from thence;
I long that we were safe and sound aboard.

Dro. S. Faith, stay here this night; they will surely do us no harm. You saw they speak us fair, give us gold; methinks they are such a gentle nation that, but for the mountain of mad flesh that claims marriage of me, I could find in my heart to stay here still and turn witch. 160

Ant. S. I will not stay tonight for all the town;
Therefore away, to get our stuff aboard. [*Exeunt.*

ACT V

SCENE I. *A street before a Priory.*

Enter ANGELO *and the* Merchant.

Ang. I am sorry, sir, that I have hinder'd you;
But I protest he had the chain of me,
Though most dishonestly he doth deny it.

Mer. How is the man esteem'd here in the city?

Ang. Of very reverend reputation, sir,
Of credit infinite, highly beloved,
Second to none that lives here in the city;
His word might bear my wealth at any time.

Mer. Speak softly; yonder, as I think, he walks.

Enter ANTIPHOLUS of Syracuse *and* DROMIO of Syracuse.

Ang. 'Tis so; and that self chain about his neck 10
Which he forswore most monstrously to have.
Good sir, draw near to me; I'll speak to him.
Signior Antipholus, I wonder much
That you would put me to this shame and trouble;
And, not without some scandal to yourself,
With circumstance and oaths so to deny
This chain which now you wear so openly.
Beside the charge, the shame, imprisonment,

156. *speak us fair:* treat us courteously. 160. *still:* always.
[V. i] 10. *self:* very. 11. *forswore:* denied. 16. *circumstance:* details, particulars.

You have done wrong to this my honest friend,
Who, but for staying on our controversy, 20
Had hoisted sail and put to sea today.
This chain you had of me; can you deny it?

Ant. S. I think I had; I never did deny it.

Mer. Yes, that you did, sir, and forswore it too.

Ant. S. Who heard me to deny it or forswear it?

Mer. These ears of mine, thou know'st, did hear thee.
Fie on thee, wretch! 'Tis pity that thou livest
To walk where any honest men resort.

Ant. S. Thou art a villain to impeach me thus;
I'll prove mine honour and mine honesty 30
Against thee presently, if thou darest stand.

Mer. I dare, and do defy thee for a villain. [*They draw.*

Enter ADRIANA, LUCIANA, *the* Courtesan, *and others.*

Adr. Hold, hurt him not, for God's sake! He is mad.
Some get within him; take his sword away;
Bind Dromio too, and bear them to my house.

Dro. S. Run, master, run; for God's sake, take a house!
This is some priory. In, or we are spoil'd!

They take refuge in the Priory, but when the others try to pursue them, the Lady Abbess *bars the way.*

Abb. Be quiet, people. Wherefore throng you hither?

Adr. To fetch my poor distracted husband hence.
Let us come in that we may bind him fast, 40
And bear him home for his recovery.

Ang. I knew he was not in his perfect wits.

Mer. I am sorry now that I did draw on him.

Abb. How long hath this possession held the man?

Adr. This week he hath been heavy, sour, sad,
And much different from the man he was;

20. *staying:* waiting. 29. *villain:* a man of base birth. *impeach:* discredit. 31. *presently:* immediately. 34. *within him:* within his guard, at close quarters with him. 36. *take:* take refuge in. 37. *spoil'd:* ruined, destroyed. 39. *distracted:* mad. 44. *possession:* madness.

But till this afternoon this passion
Ne'er brake into extremity of rage.
Abb. Hath he not lost much wealth by wreck of sea?
Buried some dear friend? Hath not else his eye 50
Stray'd his affection in unlawful love?
A sin prevailing much in youthful men,
Who give their eyes the liberty of gazing.
Which of these sorrows is he subject to?
Adr. To none of these, except it be the last;
Namely, some love that drew him oft from home.
Abb. You should for that have reprehended him.
Adr. Why, so I did.
Abb. Ay, but not rough enough.
Adr. As roughly as my modesty would let me.
Abb. Haply, in private.
Adr. And in assemblies too. 60
Abb. Ay, but not enough.
Adr. It was the copy of our conference.
In bed he slept not for my urging it;
At board he fed not for my urging it;
Alone, it was the subject of my theme;
In company I often glanced it;
Still did I tell him it was vile and bad.
Abb. And thereof came it that the man was mad.
The venom clamours of a jealous woman
Poisons more deadly than a mad dog's tooth. 70
It seems his sleeps were hinder'd by thy railing,
And thereof comes it that his head is light.
Thou say'st his meat was sauced with thy upbraidings.
Unquiet meals make ill digestions;
Thereof the raging fire of fever bred;
And what's a fever but a fit of madness?
Thou say'st his sports were hinder'd by thy brawls.
Sweet Recreation barr'd, what doth ensue
But moody and dull Melancholy,

51. *Stray'd:* led astray. 62. *copy:* theme, subject set us.
66. *glanced:* alluded to. 67. *Still:* ever, continually.

Kinsman to grim and comfortless Despair, 80
And at her heels a huge infectious troop
Of pale distemperatures and foes to life?
In food, in sport, and life-preserving rest
To be disturb'd, would mad or man or beast.
The consequence is, then, thy jealous fits
Have scared thy husband from the use of wits.
Luc. She never reprehended him but mildly,
When he demean'd himself rough, rude, and wildly.
Why bear you these rebukes and answer not?
Adr. She did betray me to my own reproof. 90
Good people, enter and lay hold on him.
Abb. No, not a creature enters in my house.
Adr. Then let your servants bring my husband forth.
Abb. Neither; he took this place for sanctuary,
And it shall privilege him from your hands
Till I have brought him to his wits again,
Or lose my labour in assaying it.
Adr. I will attend my husband, be his nurse,
Diet his sickness, for it is my office,
And will have no attorney but myself; 100
And therefore let me have him home with me.
Abb. Be patient; for I will not let him stir
Till I have used the approved means I have,
With wholesome syrups, drugs, and holy prayers,
To make of him a formal man again.
It is a branch and parcel of mine oath,
A charitable duty of my order.
Therefore depart and leave him here with me.
Adr. I will not hence and leave my husband here,
And ill it doth beseem your holiness 110
To separate the husband and the wife.

82. *distemperatures:* disorders, ailments. 84. *mad:* make mad. 88. *demean'd:* behaved, conducted. 95. *privilege:* protect, afford the right of sanctuary. 97. *assaying:* trying, attempting. 100. *attorney:* agent, deputy. 103. *approved:* tested. 105. *formal:* normal. 106. *parcel:* part.

Abb. Be quiet and depart; thou shalt not have him.
[*She goes in and closes the gate.*

Luc. Complain unto the duke of this indignity.

Adr. Come, go; I will fall prostrate at his feet
And never rise until my tears and prayers
Have won his Grace to come in person hither
And take perforce my husband from the abbess.

Mer. By this, I think, the dial points at five.
Anon, I'm sure, the duke himself in person
Comes this way to the melancholy vale, 120
The place of death and sorry execution,
Behind the ditches of the abbey here.

Ang. Upon what cause?

Mer. To see a reverend Syracusian merchant,
Who put unluckily into this bay
Against the laws and statutes of this town,
Beheaded publicly for his offense.

Ang. See where they come; we will behold his death.

Luc. Kneel to the duke before he pass the abbey.

Enter in procession Duke, *with his Attendants;* Ægeon, *bareheaded; with the* Headsman *and other* Officers.

Duke. Yet once again proclaim it publicly, 130
If any friend will pay the sum for him,
He shall not die; so much we tender him.

Adr. Justice, most sacred duke, against the abbess!

Duke. She is a virtuous and a reverend lady;
It cannot be that she hath done thee wrong.

Adr. May it please your Grace, Antipholus my husband,
Whom I made lord of me and all I had,
At your important letters—this ill day
A most outrageous fit of madness took him,
That desperately he hurried through the street— 140
With him his bondman, all as mad as he—

117. *perforce:* by force of his authority. 121. *sorry:* sad.
124. *reverend:* old, worthy of reverence. 132. *tender:* regard.
138. *important:* importunate. 141. *all:* quite.

Doing displeasure to the citizens
By rushing in their houses, bearing thence
Rings, jewels, anything his rage did like.
Once did I get him bound and sent him home,
Whilst to take order for the wrongs I went
That here and there his fury had committed.
Anon, I wot not by what strong escape,
He broke from those that had the guard of him;
And with his mad attendant and himself, 150
Each one with ireful passion, with drawn swords,
Met us again and madly bent on us
Chased us away, till raising of more aid
We came again to bind them. Then they fled
Into this abbey, whither we pursued them;
And here the abbess shuts the gates on us
And will not suffer us to fetch him out,
Nor send him forth that we may bear him hence.
Therefore, most gracious duke, with thy command
Let him be brought forth and borne hence for help. 160

Duke. Long since thy husband served me in my wars,
And I to thee engaged a prince's word,
When thou didst make him master of thy bed,
To do him all the grace and good I could.
Go, some of you, knock at the abbey-gate
And bid the lady abbess come to me.
I will determine this before I stir.

Enter a Servant.

Serv. O mistress, mistress, shift and save yourself!
My master and his man are both broke loose,
Beaten the maids a-row and bound the doctor, 170
Whose beard they have singed off with brands of fire;
And ever, as it blazed, they threw on him
Great pails of puddled mire to quench the hair.

146. *take order for:* take measures against. 148. *wot:* know. 157. *suffer:* permit. 161. *Long since:* long ago. 167. *determine:* decide, put an end to. 170. *a-row:* one after another.

My master preaches patience to him and the while
His man with scissors nicks him like a fool,
And sure, unless you send some present help,
Between them they will kill the conjurer.

Adr. Peace, fool! Thy master and his man are here,
And that is false thou dost report to us.

Serv. Mistress, upon my life, I tell you true; 180
I have not breathed almost since I did see it.
He cries for you and vows, if he can take you,
To scorch your face and to disfigure you. [*Cries are heard.*
Hark, hark! I hear him, mistress; fly, be gone!

Duke. Come, stand by me; fear nothing. Guard with halberds!

Enter ANTIPHOLUS of Ephesus *and* DROMIO of Ephesus.

Adr. Ay me, it is my husband! Witness you
That he is borne about invisible.
Even now we housed him in the abbey here;
And now he's there, past thought of human reason.

Ant. E. Justice, most gracious duke, O, grant me justice! 190
Even for the service that long since I did thee,
When I bestrid thee in the wars and took
Deep scars to save thy life; even for the blood
That then I lost for thee, now grant me justice.

Æge. Unless the fear of death doth make me dote,
I see my son Antipholus and Dromio.

Ant. E. Justice, sweet prince, against that woman there!
She whom thou gavest to me to be my wife,
That hath abused and dishonour'd me
Even in the strength and height of injury! 200
Beyond imagination is the wrong
That she this day hath shameless thrown on me.

175. *nicks . . . fool:* gives him a notched or eccentric haircut like a fool's. 176. *present:* immediate, instant. 185. *halberds:* long-handled weapons used by guards. 187. *borne . . . invisible:* i.e., by witches. 192. *bestrid:* i.e., stood over him to defend him. 195. *dote:* act or talk foolishly. 199. *abused:* deceived.

Duke. Discover how, and thou shalt find me just.
Ant. E. This day, great duke, she shut the doors upon me,
While she with harlots feasted in my house.
Duke. A grievous fault! Say, woman, didst thou so?
Adr. No, my good lord; myself, he, and my sister
Today did dine together. So befall my soul
As this is false he burdens me withal!
Luc. Ne'er may I look on day, nor sleep on night, 210
But she tells to your Highness simple truth.
Ang. O perjured woman! They are both forsworn;
In this the madman justly chargeth them.
Ant. E. My liege, I am advised what I say,
Neither disturbed with the effect of wine,
Nor heady-rash, provoked with raging ire,
Albeit my wrongs might make one wiser mad.
This woman lock'd me out this day from dinner;
That goldsmith there, were he not pack'd with her,
Could witness it, for he was with me then; 220
Who parted with me to go fetch a chain,
Promising to bring it to the Porpentine,
Where Balthasar and I did dine together.
Our dinner done, and he not coming thither,
I went to seek him. In the street I met him,
And in his company that gentleman.
There did this perjured goldsmith swear me down
That I this day of him received the chain,
Which, God he knows, I saw not. For the which
He did arrest me with an officer. 230
I did obey, and sent my peasant home
For certain ducats. He with none return'd.
Then fairly I bespoke the officer
To go in person with me to my house.
By the way we met

203. *Discover:* reveal. 205. *harlots:* rascals of either sex. 209. *burdens:* charges. 212. *forsworn:* perjured. 214. *I am advised:* I know very well. 216. *heady-rash:* hot-headed. 219. *pack'd:* in league. 233. *bespoke:* requested, engaged.

My wife, her sister, and a rabble more
Of vile confederates. Along with them
They brought one Pinch, a hungry lean-faced villain,
A mere anatomy, a mountebank,
A threadbare juggler, and a fortune-teller, 240
A needy, hollow-eyed, sharp-looking wretch,
A living-dead man. This pernicious slave,
Forsooth, took on him as a conjurer,
And, gazing in mine eyes, feeling my pulse,
And with no face, as 'twere, outfacing me,
Cries out I was possess'd. Then all together
They fell upon me, bound me, bore me thence,
And in a dark and dankish vault at home
There left me and my man, both bound together;
Till, gnawing with my teeth my bonds in sunder, 250
I gain'd my freedom and immediately
Ran hither to your Grace, whom I beseech
To give me ample satisfaction
For these deep shames and great indignities.

Ang. My lord, in truth, thus far I witness with him—
That he dined not at home, but was lock'd out.

Duke. But had he such a chain of thee or no?

Ang. He had, my lord; and when he ran in here,
These people saw the chain about his neck.

Mer. Besides, I will be sworn these ears of mine 260
Heard you confess you had the chain of him
After you first forswore it on the mart;
And thereupon I drew my sword on you;
And then you fled into this abbey here,
From whence, I think, you are come by miracle.

Ant. E. I never came within these abbey-walls,
Nor ever didst thou draw thy sword on me;
I never saw the chain, so help me Heaven!
And this is false you burden me withal.

239. *anatomy:* skeleton. 243. *took . . . conjurer:* assumed the role of conjurer. 245. *outfacing me:* putting me out of countenance. 246. *possess'd:* mad. 262. *forswore:* denied. 269. *burden:* charge.

Duke. Why, what an intricate impeach is this! 270
I think you all have drunk of Circe's cup.
If here you housed him, here he would have been;
If he were mad, he would not plead so coldly.
You say he dined at home; the goldsmith here
Denies that saying. Sirrah, what say you?
Dro. E. Sir, he dined with her there, at the Porpentine.
Cour. He did, and from my finger snatch'd that ring.
Ant. E. 'Tis true, my liege; this ring I had of her.
Duke. Saw'st thou him enter at the abbey here?
Cour. As sure, my liege, as I do see your Grace. 280
Duke. Why, this is strange. Go call the abbess hither.
I think you are all mated or stark mad.
[*An Attendant goes into the Priory.*
Æge. Most mighty duke, vouchsafe me speak a word;
Haply I see a friend will save my life
And pay the sum that may deliver me.
Duke. Speak freely, Syracusian, what thou wilt.
Æge. Is not your name, sir, call'd Antipholus?
And is not that your bondman, Dromio?
Dro. E. Within this hour I was his bondman, sir,
But he, I thank him, gnaw'd in two my cords; 290
Now am I Dromio and his man unbound.
Æge. I am sure you both of you remember me.
Dro. E. Ourselves we do remember, sir, by you;
For lately we were bound, as you are now.
You are not Pinch's patient, are you, sir?
Æge. Why look you strange on me? You know me well.
Ant. E. I never saw you in my life till now.
Æge. O, grief hath changed me since you saw me last,
And careful hours with Time's deformed hand
Have written strange defeatures in my face. 300
But tell me yet, dost thou not know my voice?

270. *impeach:* accusation. 271. *Circe's cup:* the cup which Circe gave her guests to turn them into beasts. 282. *mated:* amazed. 283. *vouchsafe:* permit. 284. *Haply:* by chance. 299. *careful:* full of care. *deformed:* deforming. 300. *defeatures:* disfigurements.

Ant. E. Neither.

Æge. Dromio, nor thou?

Dro. E. No, trust me, sir, nor I.

Æge. I am sure thou dost.

Dro. E. Ay, sir, but I am sure I do not; and whatsoever a man denies, you are now bound to believe him.

Æge. Not know my voice! O time's extremity,
Hast thou so crack'd and splitted my poor tongue,
In seven short years, that here my only son 310
Knows not my feeble key of untuned cares?
Though now this grained face of mine be hid
In sap-consuming winter's drizzled snow
And all the conduits of my blood froze up,
Yet hath my night of life some memory,
My wasting lamps some fading glimmer left,
My dull deaf ears a little use to hear.
All these old witnesses—I cannot err—
Tell me thou art my son Antipholus.

Ant. E. I never saw my father in my life. 320

Æge. But seven years since, in Syracusa, boy,
Thou know'st we parted. But perhaps, my son,
Thou shamest to acknowledge me in misery.

Ant. E. The duke and all that know me in the city
Can witness with me that it is not so;
I ne'er saw Syracusa in my life.

Duke. I tell thee, Syracusian, twenty years
Have I been patron to Antipholus,
During which time he ne'er saw Syracusa.
I see thy age and dangers make thee dote. 330

The Abbess, Antipholus of Syracuse, *and* Dromio of Syracuse *come from the Priory.*

Abb. Most mighty duke, behold a man much wrong'd.
[*All gather to see them.*

Adr. I see two husbands, or mine eyes deceive me.

308. *extremity:* extreme rigor. 311. *my feeble . . . cares:* the weak tone of my voice, which is altered by sorrow (Onions). 312. *grained:* furrowed, lined like wood.

Photograph by Will F. Taylor, London

GRAY'S INN HALL, LONDON

(See page 9)

Duke. One of these men is Genius to the other;
And so of these, which is the natural man,
And which the spirit? Who deciphers them?
Dro. S. I, sir, am Dromio; command him away.
Dro. E. I, sir, am Dromio; pray, let me stay.
Ant. S. Ægeon art thou not? Or else his ghost?
Dro. S. O, my old master! Who hath bound him here?
Abb. Whoever bound him, I will loose his bonds 340
And gain a husband by his liberty.
Speak, old Ægeon, if thou be'st the man
That hadst a wife once call'd Æmilia
That bore thee at a burden two fair sons;
O, if thou be'st the same Ægeon, speak,
And speak unto the same Æmilia!
Æge. If I dream not, thou art Æmilia.
If thou art she, tell me where is that son
That floated with thee on the fatal raft?
Abb. By men of Epidamnum he and I 350
And the twin Dromio all were taken up;
But by and by rude fishermen of Corinth
By force took Dromio and my son from them
And me they left with those of Epidamnum.
What then became of them I cannot tell—
I to this fortune that you see me in.
Duke. Why, here begins his morning story right;
These two Antipholuses, these two so like,
And these two Dromios, one in semblance—
Besides her urging of her wreck at sea— 360
These are the parents to these children,
Which accidentally are met together.
Antipholus, thou camest from Corinth first?

333. *Genius:* a tutelary god or attendant spirit which classical pagan belief allotted to every man at his birth. 335. *deciphers:* distinguishes, detects. 344. *burden:* birth. 347 ff. In F_1 Ægeon's and the Abbess' speeches follow the duke's (lines 357 ff.). The transposition is an obvious error. 359. *semblance:* appearance. 360. *urging:* emphatic mention. 363. *Antipholus . . . first.* The duke has mixed up the twins again.

Ant. S. No, sir, not I; I came from Syracuse.
Duke. Stay, stand apart; I know not which is which.
Ant. E. I came from Corinth, my most gracious lord—
Dro. E. And I with him.
Ant. E. Brought to this town by that most famous warrior,
Duke Menaphon, your most renowned uncle.
Adr. Which of you two did dine with me today? 370
Ant. S. I, gentle mistress.
Adr. And are not you my husband?
Ant. E. No; I say nay to that.
Ant. S. And so do I; yet did she call me so.
And this fair gentlewoman, her sister here,
Did call me brother. [*To Luciana.*] What I told you then,
I hope I shall have leisure to make good;
If this be not a dream I see and hear.
Ang. That is the chain, sir, which you had of me.
Ant. S. I think it be, sir; I deny it not.
Ant. E. And you, sir, for this chain arrested me. 380
Ang. I think I did, sir; I deny it not.
Adr. I sent you money, sir, to be your bail,
By Dromio; but I think he brought it not.
Dro. E. No, none by me.
Ant. S. This purse of ducats I received from you,
And Dromio my man did bring them me.
I see we still did meet each other's man,
And I was ta'en for him, and he for me,
And thereupon these errors are arose.
Ant. E. These ducats pawn I for my father here. 390
Duke. It shall not need; thy father hath his life.
Cour. Sir, I must have that diamond from you.
Ant. E. There, take it; and much thanks for my good cheer.
Abb. Renowned duke, vouchsafe to take the pains
To go with us into the abbey here
And hear at large discoursed all our fortunes;

387. *still:* always. 389. *errors:* confusions, mistakes. 393. *cheer:* hospitable entertainment. 396. *at large:* at length, in full.

And all that are assembled in this place,
That by this sympathized one day's error
Have suffer'd wrong, go keep us company,
And we shall make full satisfaction. 400
Thirty-three years have I but gone in travail
Of you, my sons; and till this present hour
My heavy burden ne'er delivered.
The duke, my husband, and my children both,
And you the calendars of their nativity,
Go to a gossips' feast, and go with me;
After so long grief, such nativity!

Duke. With all my heart, I'll gossip at this feast.

[*All go into the Priory, but the twin masters and their twin servants.*

Dro. S. Master, shall I fetch your stuff from shipboard?

Ant. E. Dromio, what stuff of mine hast thou embark'd? 410

Dro. S. Your goods that lay at host, sir, in the Centaur.

Ant. S. He speaks to me. I am your master, Dromio.
Come, go with us; we'll look to that anon.
Embrace thy brother there; rejoice with him.

[*The Antipholuses go in.*

Dro. S. There is a fat friend at your master's house,
That kitchen'd me for you today at dinner.
She now shall be my sister, not my wife.

Dro. E. Methinks you are my glass, and not my brother.
I see by you I am a sweet-faced youth.
Will you walk in to see their gossiping? 420

Dro. S. Not I, sir; you are my elder.

Dro. E. That's a question; how shall we try it?

398. *this . . . error:* i.e., this day's confusion in which everyone has been involved. 406. *gossips' feast:* a feast of sponsors at a baptism or christening. 407. *nativity.* Most modern editors follow Dr. Johnson's emendation and read *festivity*. But the allusion to *thirty-three years' travail* (line 401) makes the F_1 meaning perfectly clear. 411. *lay at host:* were stored. 416. *kitchen'd me:* entertained me in the kitchen. 419. *sweet-faced:* handsome. 420. *gossiping:* merrymaking.

Dro. S. We'll draw cuts for the senior; till then lead thou first.

Dro. E. Nay, then, thus.
We came into the world like brother and brother;
And now let's go hand in hand, not one before another.

[*They go in.*

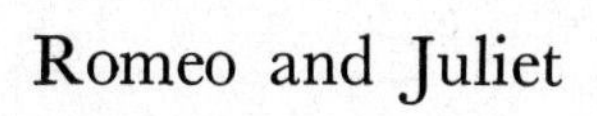

Romeo and Juliet

Introduction

Source

The story of Romeo and Juliet, in its main outlines a very old one, came to England from Italy through France. It was told with various modifications by several other Italian writers before Bandello included it in his *Novelle* (1554). Bandello's version was translated into French by Boisteau or Boaisteau and Belleforest in *Histoires tragiques* (1559), and the French version was in turn translated into English in William Painter's *Palace of Pleasure* (1565–1567). Shakespeare's immediate source, however, was Arthur Brooke's poem *The Tragical History of Romeus and Juliet* (1562), which is based on Boisteau.

Although in the main Shakespeare follows Brooke very closely, he makes several changes. He gains interest and intensity by reducing the duration of the action from several months to five days. His motivation and characterization are more skillful than Brooke's. He added Tybalt's recognition of Romeo at the Capulets' ball, with its train of consequences: the rebuke by old Capulet, Mercutio's death, Tybalt's death, Romeo's banishment. Moreover, by heightening several contrasts Shakespeare added effectiveness to his telling of Brooke's story. He contrasts Romeo's early fancy for Rosaline and his real love for Juliet. With the slow, good-natured Benvolio, the hot-tempered Tybalt, the witty, high-spirited Mercutio, he contrasts Romeo—first the sighing, self-conscious amorist, later the passionate idealist. And as foils to set off the idealist's conception of love he emphasized several contrasted conceptions: to Mercutio love is an amusing folly, a theme for jest and mockery; to Paris, as to Romeo at the opening of the play, a sentimental exercise; to Juliet's parents, in the words of

Sir Edmund Chambers, "part of the customary business of a well-ordered and honourable family life; to the nurse, a gross affair of the physical senses."

Shakespeare's most important change is his complete transformation of the tone of the story. Brooke's poem is a tale of "dishonest love." He represents the love of Romeo and Juliet as an evil power that debases and wrecks life; in Shakespeare their love is beautiful and ennobling. Brooke's Romeo lacks the sentiment and grace of Shakespeare's hero, and his Juliet is a "wily wench" who delights in the deceit she practices on her mother in secretly marrying Romeo, and who sets herself to win the love of Paris so that she may regain her parents' favor. Shakespeare's idealization of youthful love is his principal contribution to the story.

Relation to Other Shakespearean Plays

One striking characteristic of *Romeo and Juliet* is its lyricism. To the influence of Elizabethan lyric poetry, rather than to the influence of earlier Elizabethan drama, the play owes not only its general tone and atmosphere, but the quality of its verse also. The play belongs to that period of Shakespeare's development in which he was experimenting with lyrical verse as a dramatic medium—the period of the lyrical comedy *A Midsummer Night's Dream* and the lyrical history *Richard II.* In *Romeo and Juliet* several well-known lyrical forms are incorporated as parts of the actual dialogue: the sonnet at the first meeting of the lovers (I, v, 95–108), a form which gives Shakespeare, as Mr. Harley Granville-Barker points out, "the very touch of shy formality that he needs"; the epithalamium in Juliet's soliloquy as she awaits her husband's visit (III, i, 1–31); the *aubade* or dawn-song, when Romeo leaves her at daybreak (III, v, 1-36); and the elegy embodied in Romeo's last speech in the tomb (V, iii, 91–120). These lyric poems and many other lyric passages give to the play that "honey-tongued" sweetness which distinguishes it from any other of Shakespeare's tragedies.

A second notable characteristic of this play is its style—the style of Shakespeare's poems and early plays, marked by abundant rhyme, by puns, by fanciful similes and metaphors, and in general by the conventional imagery of Petrarchan amatory verse. At times Shakespeare abandons these conventions and writes with greater freedom and naturalness, as in the "balcony scene," in which the dialogue begins with the use of conventional imagery and ends with the simplest, most natural dramatic speech. Successful as much of the verse is, there are passages in which the effect is marred either by excessive ingenuity or by florid extravagance. It may have been his failure to write effective and appropriate dramatic dialogue throughout the play as a whole that led Shakespeare to abandon tragedy for the easier task of writing comedy and chronicle-history. When, several years later, he returned to tragedy in *Julius Cæsar* and *Hamlet*, he displayed an easy mastery of marvelously revealing dramatic dialogue.

A third difference between *Romeo and Juliet* and the later tragedies is in the causes that bring about the catastrophe and in the very nature of the catastrophe itself. The later tragedies reveal human nature in its more horrible aspects, but in this play evil, active and destructive as it is, is less powerful, less appalling, than in *Othello*, *King Lear*, and *Macbeth*. "Here's much to do with hate, but more with love." Again, the hero in the later tragedies is in conflict with the evil in his own soul, with the baser side of his nature. In *Romeo and Juliet* the evil is entirely external; there is in neither hero nor heroine a tragic weakness that develops to destroy their goodness. The catastrophe, when it overtakes the lovers, is merely external; they are at the end nobler and stronger than at the opening of the play. Futhermore, in the later tragedies, the hero is to some extent "the author of his proper woe"; not only does he in part deserve the catastrophe that overwhelms him, but he also in part brings it upon himself. But although Romeo's precipitancy and his blindness to all considerations but marrying Juliet contribute to the tragedy, the young lovers are victims of the ancient feud between their families: they neither cause nor deserve the suffering and death that come to them. An irresistible power brings them, by a series of accidents, to a foreordained catastrophe. In a very complete sense, *Romeo and Juliet* is a tragedy of fate, not a tragedy of character.

This irresistible power is felt throughout the play. Although the lovers have premonitions of coming disaster, they do not hesitate, and their love strengthens and ennobles them. Romeo the dreamer grows into manhood. The girlish Juliet takes on full womanhood, lovely in fidelity and resolution. But such love cannot live in a world of bitterness and hatred. The young lovers go as sacrifices to the enmity of their elders, a hatred that passes in the "glooming peace" that their love has won. The world of *Romeo and Juliet*, a world in which evil is destined to perish even though its destruction entails the loss of priceless good, is not unlike the world of Shakespeare's later tragedies, and our contemplation of such a world leaves with us for a time a sense of painful mystery. The final impression that *Romeo and Juliet* leaves with us is the recognition of the beauty of youthful love and its tragic brevity—its brief and lovely flowering and its certain passing from our sight. And the spectacle of its passing awakens not pity and fear, but pity and sorrow for beauty and sweetness gone too soon. No other of Shakespeare's plays produces a similar effect.

Finally, *Romeo and Juliet* stands apart from Shakespeare's other plays for further reasons. Juliet is the first and most appealing of his tragic heroines. The nurse—a gross, vulgar, outrageous old woman—is his first complete success in realistic portraiture of low life. Mercutio's famous description of Queen Mab is perhaps the earliest of Shakespeare's "fairy" passages

—passages that transformed English fairies into what they have ever since remained. No other of his plays gives us the same kind of enchanting poetry, the same glow of color and light. If it lacks the power and intensity of the later tragedies, it remains the most beautiful English drama dealing with youthful love.

Date and Text

Modern critics are in substantial agreement that the play was written about 1595. Its style is that of *Richard II* and *A Midsummer Night's Dream.* "I should put it," writes Sir Edmund Chambers, "in 1595, preferably before *Midsummer Night's Dream*, as its theme seems to be parodied in that of Pyramus and Thisbe, and its wall (II, ii, iii) in Snout's wall."

Romeo and Juliet was first printed in 1597 (Q_1). The copy was apparently taken down at the theatre by a reporter, probably in shorthand, or possibly supplied from memory by an actor, and carelessly printed by a piratical publisher. It is possible, though some students think it improbable, that this text is based on an early and incomplete version of the play. Q_1, however, preserves some readings that are preferable to those of Q_2. In 1599 appeared Q_2, printed by a reputable publisher, and presenting a much longer text. The full stage directions, with such notes as "Whistle, Boy" and "Play, Music," indicate that the manuscript had been used in the theatre as a promptbook. Q_3 (1609) was printed from Q_2; Q_4 (undated) and F_1 (1623) were printed from Q_3. The First Folio text is the basis of the present edition.

DRAMATIS PERSONÆ

Capulet } heads of two families in Verona who are at variance
Montague } with each other.

Lady Capulet } their wives.
Lady Montague }

Romeo, heir of the Montagues.
Juliet, daughter of the Capulets.
Escalus, Prince of Verona.
Mercutio, kinsman of the Prince.
Benvolio, nephew of Montague and friend of Romeo.
Tybalt, nephew of Capulet.
Paris, a young nobleman, kinsman of the Prince.
Friar Laurence, a Franciscan, confidant of Romeo.
Nurse, confidante of Juliet.
Peter, attendant of Juliet's nurse.
Friar John, messenger for Friar Laurence.
An Apothecary.
Balthasar, servant of Romeo.
Sampson, servant of Capulet.
Gregory, servant of Capulet.
Abraham, servant of Montague.
Musicians, Maskers, Pages, Watchmen, Officers, Citizens, Attendants.

Scene of the Action: Verona and Mantua.

Romeo and Juliet

PROLOGUE

Enter Chorus.

Two households, both alike in dignity,
  In fair Verona, where we lay our scene,
From ancient grudge break to new mutiny,
  Where civil blood makes civil hands unclean.
From forth the fatal loins of these two foes
  A pair of star-cross'd lovers take their life;
Whose misadventured piteous overthrows
  Do with their death bury their parents' strife.
The fearful passage of their death-mark'd love,
  And the continuance of their parents' rage, 10
Which, but their children's end, nought could remove,
  Is now the two hours' traffic of our stage;
The which if you with patient ears attend,
What here shall miss, our toil shall strive to mend. [*Exit.*

ACT I

Scene i. *Verona. A public place.*

Enter Sampson *and* Gregory, *of the house of Capulet, armed with swords and bucklers.*

Sam. Gregory, o' my word, we'll not carry coals.
Gre. No, for then we should be colliers.

[Prologue] In form, this prologue is a Shakespearean sonnet. 3. *mutiny:* contention. 4. *civil:* of citizens. 6. *star-cross'd:* thwarted by malevolent stars. 9. *passage:* course. 12. *traffic:* business. 14. *miss:* be wanting.

[I. i] 1. *carry coals:* endure insults. In Elizabethan households the lowest servants carried wood and coal.

Sam. I mean, an we be in choler, we'll draw.

Gre. Ay, while you live, draw your neck out o' the collar.

Sam. I strike quickly, being moved.

Gre. But thou art not quickly moved to strike.

Sam. A dog of the house of Montague moves me. 10

Gre. To move is to stir, and to be valiant is to stand; therefore, if thou art moved, thou runn'st away.

Sam. A dog of that house shall move me to stand. I will take the wall of any man or maid of Montague's.

Gre. That shows thee a weak slave, for the weakest goes to the wall. 18

Sam. True; and therefore women, being the weaker vessels, are ever thrust to the wall; therefore I will push Montague's men from the wall, and thrust his maids to the wall.

Gre. The quarrel is between our masters and us their men.

Sam. 'Tis all one; I will show myself a tyrant. When I have fought with the men, I will be cruel with the maids, and cut off their heads.

Gre. The heads of the maids? 29

Sam. Ay, the heads of the maids, or their maidenheads. Take it in what sense thou wilt.

Gre. They must take it in sense that feel it.

Sam. Me they shall feel while I am able to stand; and 'tis known I am a pretty piece of flesh.

Gre. 'Tis well thou art not fish; if thou hadst, thou hadst been poor John. Draw thy tool! Here comes two of the house of the Montagues.

Sam. My naked weapon is out. Quarrel! I will back thee. 40

4. *an . . . draw:* if we be in anger, we'll draw our swords. 7. *moved:* angered. 15. *take the wall.* In Elizabethan London the projecting upper stories of the houses, and the filthy gutter in the middle of the narrow street, made the space nearest the house wall the safest and cleanest place for walking. "To take the wall" was to assert one's superiority. The word-play that follows refers to proverbial expressions: "the weakest goes to the wall" (said of dishes), and "lie next to the wall" (said of married women). 20. *weaker vessels.* See I Peter 3:7. 31. *maidenheads:* maidenhoods. 37. *poor John:* dried fish (alluding, of course, to Sampson's leanness). *tool:* weapon.

Gre. How? Turn thy back and run?

Sam. Fear me not.

Gre. No, marry; I fear thee!

Sam. Let us take the law of our sides; let them begin.

Gre. I will frown as I pass by, and let them take it as they list.

Sam. Nay, as they dare. I will bite my thumb at them, which is a disgrace to them, if they bear it. 50

Enter Abraham *and* Balthasar.

Abr. Do you bite your thumb at us, sir?

Sam. I do bite my thumb, sir.

Abr. Do you bite your thumb at us, sir?

Sam. [*Aside to Gregory*] Is the law of our side, if I say "ay"?

Gre. No.

Sam. No, sir, I do not bite my thumb at you, sir, but I bite my thumb, sir.

Gre. Do you quarrel, sir?

Abr. Quarrel, sir? No, sir. 60

Sam. If you do, sir, I am for you. I serve as good a man as you.

Abr. No better.

Sam. Well, sir.

Gre. [*Aside to Sampson*] Say "better." Here comes one of my master's kinsmen.

Sam. Yes, better, sir.

Abr. You lie.

Sam. Draw, if you be men. Gregory, remember thy swashing blow. [*They fight.*

Enter Benvolio.

Ben. Part, fools! 71
Put up your swords. You know not what you do.
[*Beats down their swords.*

44. *Let . . . sides:* let us have the law on our side. 47. *list:* please. 48. *bite my thumb:* an insulting gesture. 66. *one . . . kinsmen:* i.e., Tybalt, whom he sees in the distance. 70. *swashing:* swinging.

Enter TYBALT.

Tyb. What, art thou drawn among these heartless hinds?
Turn thee, Benvolio! Look upon thy death!

Ben. I do but keep the peace. Put up thy sword,
Or manage it to part these men with me.

Tyb. What, drawn, and talk of peace? I hate the word,
As I hate hell, all Montagues, and thee.
Have at thee, coward! [*They fight.*

Enter several of both houses, who join the fray; then enter Citizens, *with clubs.*

First Cit. Clubs, bills, and partisans! Strike! Beat them down! 80
Down with the Capulets! Down with the Montagues!

Enter CAPULET *in his gown, and* LADY CAPULET.

Cap. What noise is this? Give me my long sword, ho!

La. Cap. A crutch, a crutch! Why call you for a sword?

Cap. My sword, I say! Old Montague is come,
And flourishes his blade in spite of me.

Enter MONTAGUE *and* LADY MONTAGUE.

Mon. Thou villain Capulet!—Hold me not; let me go.

La. Mon. Thou shalt not stir a foot to seek a foe.

Enter PRINCE ESCALUS, *with* Attendants.

Prin. Rebellious subjects, enemies to peace,
Profaners of this neighbour-stained steel—
Will they not hear? What, ho! You men, you beasts, 90
That quench the fire of your pernicious rage
With purple fountains issuing from your veins,
On pain of torture, from those bloody hands

73. *drawn:* with drawn sword. *heartless hinds:* (a) cowardly menials, (b) leaderless (hartless) herd. 80. *Clubs:* the rallying cry of London apprentices, who were expected to help preserve the peace. *bills, partisans:* long-handled spears. S. D. *gown:* dressing gown. 85. *spite:* contempt. 92. *purple:* i.e., the color of venous blood.

Throw your mistemper'd weapons to the ground,
And hear the sentence of your moved prince.
Three civil brawls, bred of an airy word,
By thee, old Capulet, and Montague,
Have thrice disturb'd the quiet of our streets,
And made Verona's ancient citizens
Cast by their grave beseeming ornaments, 100
To wield old partisans, in hands as old,
Canker'd with peace, to part your canker'd hate.
If ever you disturb our streets again,
Your lives shall pay the forfeit of the peace.
For this time, all the rest depart away.
You, Capulet, shall go along with me;
And, Montague, come you this afternoon,
To know our further pleasure in this case,
To old Free-town, our common judgment-place.
Once more, on pain of death, all men depart. 110

[*Exeunt all but Montague, Lady Montague, and Benvolio.*

Mon. Who set this ancient quarrel new abroach?
Speak, nephew; were you by when it began?

Ben. Here were the servants of your adversary,
And yours, close fighting ere I did approach.
I drew to part them. In the instant came
The fiery Tybalt, with his sword prepared,
Which, as he breathed defiance to my ears,
He swung about his head and cut the winds,
Who, nothing hurt withal, hiss'd him in scorn.
While we were interchanging thrusts and blows, 120
Came more and more and fought on part and part,
Till the prince came, who parted either part.

La. Mon. O, where is Romeo? Saw you him today?
Right glad I am he was not at this fray.

94. *mistemper'd:* (a) angry, (b) tempered for an evil purpose. 95. *moved:* angry. 96. *airy:* light, trivial. 100. *grave beseeming:* dignified and suitable. 102. *Canker'd . . . canker'd:* rusted . . . malignant. 104. *forfeit:* penalty for breach. 109. *Free-town:* Brooke's translation of *Villa Franca* in his Italian source. 111. *abroach:* open, running out (as wine from a cask). 121. *part:* side.

Ben. Madam, an hour before the worshipp'd sun
Peer'd forth the golden window of the east,
A troubled mind drave me to walk abroad;
Where, underneath the grove of sycamore
That westward rooteth from the city's side,
So early walking did I see your son. 130
Towards him I made, but he was ware of me
And stole into the covert of the wood.
I, measuring his affections by my own,
That most are busied when they're most alone,
Pursued my humour not pursuing his,
And gladly shunn'd who gladly fled from me.

Mon. Many a morning hath he there been seen,
With tears augmenting the fresh morning's dew,
Adding to clouds more clouds with his deep sighs;
But all so soon as the all-cheering sun 140
Should in the furthest east begin to draw
The shady curtains from Aurora's bed,
Away from light steals home my heavy son,
And private in his chamber pens himself,
Shuts up his windows, locks fair daylight out,
And makes himself an artificial night.
Black and portentous must this humour prove
Unless good counsel may the cause remove.

Ben. My noble uncle, do you know the cause?

Mon. I neither know it nor can learn of him. 150

Ben. Have you importuned him by any means?

Mon. Both by myself and many other friends;
But he, his own affections' counsellor,
Is to himself—I will not say how true—

125 ff. Like other conventional Elizabethan amorists, Romeo before he meets Juliet suffers from conventional love-melancholy. With his symptoms compare those of Valentine (*Two Gentlemen of Verona*, II, i, 18 ff.) and those of Rosalind's ideal lover (*As You Like It*, III, ii, 397). 131. *ware:* aware. 133. *affections:* inclinations. 134. *That . . . alone.* So Q_1; Q_2 and F_1 read *Which then most sought, where most might not be found: Being one too many by my weary self.* 135. *humour:* mood. 143. *heavy:* sad.

But to himself so secret and so close,
So far from sounding and discovery,
As is the bud bit with an envious worm,
Ere he can spread his sweet leaves to the air,
Or dedicate his beauty to the sun.
Could we but learn from whence his sorrows grow, 160
We would as willingly give cure as know.

Enter ROMEO.

Ben. See, where he comes! So please you step aside;
I'll know his grievance, or be much denied.
Mon. I would thou wert so happy by thy stay
To hear true shrift. Come, madam, let's away.
[*Exeunt Montague and Lady.*
Ben. Good morrow, cousin.
Rom. Is the day so young?
Ben. But new struck nine.
Rom. Ay me! Sad hours seem long.
Was that my father that went hence so fast?
Ben. It was. What sadness lengthens Romeo's hours?
Rom. Not having that, which, having, makes them short. 170
Ben. In love?
Rom. Out—
Ben. Of love?
Rom. Out of her favour where I am in love.
Ben. Alas, that Love, so gentle in his view,
Should be so tyrannous and rough in proof!
Rom. Alas, that Love, whose view is muffled still,
Should, without eyes, see pathways to his will!
Where shall we dine? O me! What fray was here?
Yet tell me not, for I have heard it all. 180

156. *sounding:* fathoming. *discovery:* disclosure. 157. *envious:* spiteful. 165. *To . . . shrift:* as to hear honest confession. 166. *Good morrow:* good morning. 175. *his view:* its appearance. 176. *proof:* experience. 177. *view:* sight. *still:* always. 177–8. *Love . . . will:* Cupid, though blind, can shoot his arrows where he will.

Here's much to do with hate, but more with love.
Why, then, O brawling love! O loving hate!
O anything, of nothing first create!
O heavy lightness! Serious vanity!
Mis-shapen chaos of well-seeming forms!
Feather of lead, bright smoke, cold fire, sick health!
Still-waking sleep, that is not what it is!
This love feel I, that feel no love in this.
Dost thou not laugh?

Ben. No, coz, I rather weep.

Rom. Good heart, at what?

Ben. At thy good heart's oppression.

Rom. Why, such is love's transgression. 191
Griefs of mine own lie heavy in my breast,
Which thou wilt propagate, to have it prest
With more of thine. This love that thou hast shown
Doth add more grief to too much of mine own.
Love is a smoke raised with the fume of sighs;
Being purged, a fire sparkling in lovers' eyes;
Being vex'd, a sea nourish'd with lovers' tears.
What is it else? A madness most discreet,
A choking gall, and a preserving sweet. 200
Farewell, my coz.

Ben. Soft! I will go along;
An if you leave me so, you do me wrong.

Rom. Tut, I have lost myself; I am not here.
This is not Romeo; he's some other where.

Ben. Tell me in sadness, who is that you love.

Rom. What, shall I groan and tell thee?

Ben. Groan? Why, no;
But sadly tell me who.

181. *Here's . . . love.* The feud between the families interferes with Romeo's love for Rosaline, who is a Capulet. (See I, ii, 73.) 182–8. *O brawling . . . this.* Paradoxes of this kind are frequent in Elizabethan love sonnets. 193. *propagate:* increase. *to have:* by having. 197. *purged:* purified (from smoke). 205. *sadness:* seriousness.

Rom. Bid a sick man in sadness make his will—
Ah, word ill urged to one that is so ill!
In sadness, cousin, I do love a woman. 210

Ben. I aim'd so near when I supposed you loved.

Rom. A right good mark-man! And she's fair I love.

Ben. A right fair mark, fair coz, is soonest hit.

Rom. Well, in that hit you miss. She'll not be hit
With Cupid's arrow. She hath Dian's wit;
And, in strong proof of chastity well arm'd,
From Love's weak childish bow she lives unharm'd.
She will not stay the siege of loving terms,
Nor bide the encounter of assailing eyes,
Nor ope her lap to saint-seducing gold. 220
O, she is rich in beauty, only poor
That, when she dies, with beauty dies her store.

Ben. Then she hath sworn that she will still live chaste?

Rom. She hath, and in that sparing makes huge waste,
For beauty, starved with her severity,
Cuts beauty off from all posterity.
She is too fair, too wise, wisely too fair,
To merit bliss by making me despair.
She hath forsworn to love, and in that vow
Do I live dead that live to tell it now. 230

Ben. Be ruled by me; forget to think of her.

Rom. O, teach me how I should forget to think.

Ben. By giving liberty unto thine eyes;
Examine other beauties.

Rom. 'Tis the way
To call hers, exquisite, in question more.
These happy masks that kiss fair ladies' brows
Being black put us in mind they hide the fair;

214–22. This resembles the conventional compliments that poets addressed to Queen Elizabeth. 215. *Dian's wit:* the goddess Diana's wisdom to remain single. 216. *proof:* impenetrable armor. 218. *stay:* wait for, abide. 222. *That . . . store:* in that when she dies (childless) her wealth of beauty perishes. (See *Sonnets*, i-xvii.) 229. *forsworn to love:* sworn not to love. 235. *in question more:* into greater consideration.

He that is strucken blind cannot forget
The precious treasure of his eyesight lost.
Show me a mistress that is passing fair, 240
What doth her beauty serve but as a note
Where I may read who pass'd that passing fair?
Farewell! Thou canst not teach me to forget.
Ben. I'll pay that doctrine, or else die in debt. [*Exeunt.*

SCENE II. *A street.*

Enter CAPULET, COUNTY PARIS, *and* Servant.

Cap. But Montague is bound as well as I,
In penalty alike; and 'tis not hard, I think,
For men so old as we to keep the peace.
Par. Of honourable reckoning are you both,
And pity 'tis you lived at odds so long.
But now, my lord, what say you to my suit?
Cap. But saying o'er what I have said before.
My child is yet a stranger in the world;
She hath not seen the change of fourteen years.
Let two more summers wither in their pride 10
Ere we may think her ripe to be a bride.
Par. Younger than she are happy mothers made.
Cap. And too soon marr'd are those so early made.
The earth hath swallow'd all my hopes but she;
She is the hopeful lady of my earth.
But woo her, gentle Paris; get her heart;
My will to her consent is but a part.
An she agree, within her scope of choice
Lies my consent and fair according voice.
This night I hold an old accustom'd feast, 20
Whereto I have invited many a guest,

240. *passing fair:* surpassingly fair. 244. *pay that doctrine:* give that instruction (despite cost or difficulty).

[ii] 4. *reckoning:* reputation. 15. *lady of my earth:* probably a translation of the French phrase for "heiress," *fille de terre*, or, possibly, "she is the one in whom my hopes are centered."

Such as I love; and you, among the store,
One more, most welcome, makes my number more.
At my poor house look to behold this night
Earth-treading stars that make dark heaven light.
Such comfort as do lusty young men feel
When well-apparell'd April on the heel
Of limping winter treads, even such delight
Among fresh female buds shall you this night
Inherit at my house; hear all, all see, 30
And like her most whose merit most shall be;
Which, on more view of many, mine—being one—
May stand in number, though in reckoning none.
Come, go with me. [*To Servant, giving him a paper.*] Go, sirrah,
trudge about
Through fair Verona; find those persons out
Whose names are written there, and to them say
My house and welcome on their pleasure stay. 37
[*Exeunt Capulet and Paris.*

Serv. Find them out whose names are written here! It is written that the shoemaker should meddle with his yard, and the tailor with his last, the fisher with his pencil, and the painter with his nets; but I am sent to find those persons whose names are here writ, and can never find what names the writing person hath here writ. I must to the learned. In good time!

Enter BENVOLIO *and* ROMEO.

Ben. Tut, man, one fire burns out another's burning;
One pain is lessen'd by another's anguish;
Turn giddy, and be holp by backward turning;

30. *Inherit:* receive. 32–3. *Which . . . none.* The meaning is not clear. Perhaps Capulet means, "When you see the many beautiful girls, you may include my daughter among the number, though you consider her nothing in comparison with them." 45. *In good time.* Benvolio and Romeo appear at the opportune moment. 46–51. These lines, like lines 93–8, are the concluding six lines of a Shakespearean sonnet. (See also V, iii, 12–17, 305–10.) The prologue, the chorus before Act II, and I, v, 95–108 are complete sonnets. Shakespeare was at this time experimenting with metrical forms. 48. *holp:* helped.

One desperate grief cures with another's languish.
Take thou some new infection to thy eye, 50
And the rank poison of the old will die.

Rom. Your plaintain-leaf is excellent for that.

Ben. For what, I pray thee?

Rom. For your broken shin.

Ben. Why, Romeo, art thou mad?

Rom. Not mad, but bound more than a madman is;
Shut up in prison, kept without my food,
Whipp'd and tormented and—God-den, good fellow.

Serv. God gi' god-den. I pray, sir, can you read?

Rom. Ay, mine own fortune in my misery. 60

Serv. Perhaps you have learned it without book. But, I pray, can you read anything you see?

Rom. Ay, if I know the letters and the language.

Serv. Ye say honestly. Rest you merry!

Rom. Stay, fellow; I can read. [*Reads the paper.*

"Signior Martino and his wife and daughters; County Anselme and his beauteous sisters; the lady widow of Vitruvio; Signior Placentio and his lovely nieces; Mercutio and his brother Valentine; mine uncle Capulet, his wife, and daughters; my fair niece Rosaline; Livia; Signior Valentio and his cousin Tybalt; Lucio and the lively Helena." 74
A fair assembly. Whither should they come?

Serv. Up.

Rom. Whither?

Serv. To supper; to our house.

Rom. Whose house?

Serv. My master's. 80

Rom. Indeed, I should have asked you that before.

Serv. Now I'll tell you without asking. My master is the great rich Capulet; and if you be not of the house of Montagues, I pray, come and crush a cup of wine. Rest you merry! [*Exit.*

49. *cures with:* is healed by. 59. *God gi' god-den:* God give you good evening. 65. *Rest you merry:* God keep you merry (a parting salutation). 68. *County:* count (Italian *conte*). 86. *crush:* drink.

Ben. At this same ancient feast of Capulet's
Sups the fair Rosaline whom thou so lovest,
With all the admired beauties of Verona.
Go thither, and with unattainted eye 90
Compare her face with some that I shall show,
And I will make thee think thy swan a crow.
Rom. When the devout religion of mine eye
Maintains such falsehood, then turn tears to fires;
And these, who, often drown'd, could never die,
Transparent heretics, be burnt for liars!
One fairer than my love? The all-seeing sun
Ne'er saw her match since first the world begun.
Ben. Tut, you saw her fair, none else being by,
Herself poised with herself in either eye; 100
But in that crystal scales let there be weigh'd
Your lady's love against some other maid
That I will show you shining at this feast,
And she shall scant show well that now shows best.
Rom. I'll go along no such sight to be shown,
But to rejoice in splendour of mine own. [*Exeunt.*

SCENE III. *A room in* CAPULET'S *house.*

Enter LADY CAPULET *and* NURSE.

La. Cap. Nurse, where's my daughter? Call her forth to me.
Nurse. Now, by my maidenhead at twelve year old,
I bade her come. What, lamb! What, ladybird!
God forbid! Where's this girl? What, Juliet!

Enter JULIET.

Jul. How now? Who calls?
Nurse. Your mother.
Jul. Madam, I am here.
What is your will?
La. Cap. This is the matter. Nurse, give leave awhile;

87. *ancient:* customary. 90. *unattainted:* impartial. 95. *these:* these eyes. 100. *poised:* weighed. 104. *scant:* scarcely.
[iii] 7. *give leave:* leave us.

We must talk in secret. Nurse, come back again;
I have remember'd me, thou 's hear our counsel.
Thou know'st my daughter's of a pretty age. 10

Nurse. Faith, I can tell her age unto an hour.

La. Cap. She's not fourteen.

Nurse. I'll lay fourteen of my teeth—
And yet, to my teen be it spoken, I have but four—
She is not fourteen. How long is it now
To Lammastide?

La. Cap. A fortnight and odd days.

Nurse. Even or odd, of all days in the year,
Come Lammas Eve at night shall she be fourteen.
Susan and she—God rest all Christian souls!—
Were of an age. Well, Susan is with God;
She was too good for me. But, as I said, 20
On Lammas Eve at night shall she be fourteen;
That shall she, marry; I remember it well.
'Tis since the earthquake now eleven years;
And she was wean'd—I never shall forget it—
Of all the days of the year, upon that day;
For I had then laid wormwood to my dug,
Sitting in the sun under the dove-house wall.
My lord and you were then at Mantua—
Nay, I do bear a brain—but, as I said,
When it did taste the wormwood on the nipple 30
Of my dug and felt it bitter, pretty fool,
To see it tetchy and fall out with the dug!
"Shake," quoth the dove-house! 'Twas no need, I trow,
To bid me trudge.
And since that time it is eleven years,
For then she could stand alone; nay, by the rood,
She could have run and waddled all about;
For even the day before, she broke her brow.

9. *thou 's:* thou shalt. 12. *lay:* wager. 13. *teen:* sorrow. 15. *Lammastide:* August 1. 29. *bear a brain:* have a memory. 32. *tetchy:* fretful. 33–4. *Shake . . . trudge.* This refers to the earthquake. 33. *trow:* dare say. 36. *rood:* cross.

And then my husband—God be with his soul!
A' was a merry man—took up the child. 40
"Yea," quoth he, "dost thou fall upon thy face?
Thou wilt fall backward when thou hast more wit;
Wilt thou not, Jule?" and, by my holidame,
The pretty wretch left crying and said, "Ay."
To see now how a jest shall come about!
I warrant, an I should live a thousand years,
I never should forget it. "Wilt thou not, Jule?" quoth he;
And, pretty fool, it stinted and said, "Ay."

La. Cap. Enough of this; I pray thee hold thy peace.

Nurse. Yes, madam; yet I cannot choose but laugh, 50
To think it should leave crying and say, "Ay."
And yet, I warrant, it had upon its brow
A bump as big as a young cockerel's stone;
A parlous knock; and it cried bitterly.
"Yea," quoth my husband, "fall'st upon thy face?
Thou wilt fall backward when thou comest to age;
Wilt thou not, Jule?" It stinted and said, "Ay."

Jul. And stint thou too, I pray thee, nurse, say I.

Nurse. Peace, I have done. God mark thee to His grace!
Thou wast the prettiest babe that e'er I nursed. 60
An I might live to see thee married once,
I have my wish.

La. Cap. Marry, that "marry" is the very theme
I came to talk of. Tell me, daughter Juliet,
How stands your disposition to be married?

Jul. It is an honour that I dream not of.

Nurse. An honour! Were not I thine only nurse,
I would say thou hadst suck'd wisdom from thy teat.

La. Cap. Well, think of marriage now. Younger than you,
Here in Verona, ladies of esteem, 70
Are made already mothers. By my count,
I was your mother much upon these years

40. *A':* he. 42. *wit:* sense, intelligence. 43. *holidame:* a mild oath. 46. *an:* if. 48. *stinted:* stopped. 59. *mark:* set apart. 65. *disposition:* inclination, humor.

That you are now a maid. Thus then in brief:
The valiant Paris seeks you for his love.
Nurse. A man, young lady! Lady, such a man
As all the world—why, he's a man of wax.
La. Cap. Verona's summer hath not such a flower.
Nurse. Nay, he's a flower; in faith, a very flower.
La. Cap. What say you? Can you love the gentleman?
This night you shall behold him at our feast. 80
Read o'er the volume of young Paris' face
And find delight writ there with beauty's pen;
Examine every married lineament
And see how one another lends content,
And what obscured in this fair volume lies
Find written in the margent of his eyes.
This precious book of love, this unbound lover,
To beautify him only lacks a cover.
The fish lives in the sea, and 'tis much pride
For fair without the fair within to hide. 90
That book in many's eyes doth share the glory,
That in gold clasps locks in the golden story;
So shall you share all that he doth possess,
By having him, making yourself no less.
Nurse. No less? Nay, bigger! Women grow by men.
La. Cap. Speak briefly; can you like of Paris' love?
Jul. I'll look to like, if looking liking move;
But no more deep will I endart mine eye
Than your consent gives strength to make it fly. 99

76. *man of wax:* perfect as a wax figure. 81–94. With this fantastic passage, in which the young poet is obviously more interested in his imagery than in his idea, compare another description of a lover in *Antony and Cleopatra* (V, ii, 76–94), written in Shakespeare's maturity, which is more dramatic, and in which there is more nearly a balance of thought and expression. 83. *married:* harmonious. 86. *margent:* margin, where commentary was printed. 89–90. *The fish . . . hide.* The meaning has puzzled the commentators. Since fishskin was sometimes used for binding books, the meaning may be that the girl who is to be the binding of this book is still uncaught.

Enter a Servant.

Serv. Madam, the guests are come, supper served up, you called, my young lady asked for, the nurse cursed in the pantry, and everything in extremity. I must hence to wait; I beseech you follow straight.

La. Cap. We follow thee. [*Exit Servant.*] Juliet, the county stays.

Nurse. Go, girl; seek happy nights to happy days. 106

[*Exeunt.*

SCENE IV. *A street.*

Enter ROMEO, MERCUTIO, BENVOLIO, *with five or six* Maskers, Torchbearers, *and others.*

Rom. What, shall this speech be spoke for our excuse?
Or shall we on without apology?
Ben. The date is out of such prolixity.
We'll have no Cupid hoodwink'd with a scarf,
Bearing a Tartar's painted bow of lath,
Scaring the ladies like a crow-keeper;
Nor no without-book prologue, faintly spoke
After the prompter, for our entrance;
But, let them measure us by what they will,
We'll measure them a measure, and be gone. 10
Rom. Give me a torch. I am not for this ambling;
Being but heavy, I will bear the light.
Mer. Nay, gentle Romeo, we must have you dance.
Rom. Not I, believe me. You have dancing shoes
With nimble soles; I have a soul of lead
So stakes me to the ground I cannot move.

104. *straight:* at once. 105. *stays:* waits.

[iv] 1. *speech.* It was customary for maskers to announce their arrival by a messenger, sometimes dressed as Cupid, who made a formal, complimentary speech. Benvolio considers such tiresome formality out of date. 4. *hoodwink'd:* blindfolded. 6. *like a crow-keeper:* dressed like a scarecrow. 7–8. *Nor . . . entrance.* Omitted in Q_2 and subsequent editions. 10. *measure:* stately dance. 11. *torch.* A torchbearer, of course, did not dance. 12. *heavy:* sad. 16. *So stakes:* which so fastens.

Mer. You are a lover; borrow Cupid's wings,
And soar with them above a common bound.
Rom. I am too sore enpierced with his shaft
To soar with his light feathers; and, so bound, 20
I cannot bound a pitch above dull woe.
Under love's heavy burden do I sink.
Mer. And, to sink in it, should you burden love—
Too great oppression for a tender thing.
Rom. Is love a tender thing? It is too rough,
Too rude, too boisterous, and it pricks like thorn.
Mer. If love be rough with you, be rough with love;
Prick love for pricking, and you beat love down.
Give me a case to put my visage in. [*Puts on a mask.*
A visor for a visor! What care I 30
What curious eye doth quote deformities?
Here are the beetle brows shall blush for me.
Ben. Come; knock and enter; and no sooner in,
But every man betake him to his legs.
Rom. A torch for me. Let wantons light of heart
Tickle the senseless rushes with their heels,
For I am proverb'd with a grandsire phrase;
I'll be a candle-holder, and look on.
The game was ne'er so fair, and I am done.
Mer. Tut, dun's the mouse, the constable's own word! 40
If thou art dun, we'll draw thee from the mire
Of this sir-reverence love, wherein thou stick'st
Up to the ears. Come, we burn daylight, ho!

21. *pitch:* highest point in the falcon's flight. 30. *A . . . visor:* a mask for my ugly face! 31. *quote:* observe. 32. *beetle brows:* prominent eyebrows, i.e., the mask. 35. *wantons:* triflers. 36. *rushes:* used as a floor-covering. 37. *grandsire phrase:* old saying, viz., a good candleholder (spectator) proves a good gamester. 40. *dun's the mouse:* be still as a mouse (a phrase of uncertain origin). 41. *If . . . mire.* He alludes to a Christmas game, "Dun (a log representing a dun horse) in the mire." *dun:* done (with this silly love). 42. *sir-reverence:* a contraction of "saving your reverence." This phrase, used as an apology for a liberty or an impropriety, is here a euphemism for "dung." 43. *burn daylight:* burn candles by day.

Rom. Nay, that's not so.
Mer. I mean, sir, in delay
We waste our lights in vain, like lamps by day.
Take our good meaning, for our judgment sits
Five times in that ere once in our five wits.
Rom. And we mean well in going to this mask;
But 'tis no wit to go.
Mer. Why, may one ask?
Rom. I dream'd a dream tonight.
Mer. And so did I. 50
Rom. Well, what was yours?
Mer. That dreamers often lie.
Rom. In bed asleep, while they do dream things true.
Mer. O, then, I see Queen Mab hath been with you.
She is the fairies' midwife, and she comes
In shape no bigger than an agate-stone
On the fore-finger of an alderman,
Drawn with a team of little atomies
Athwart men's noses as they lie asleep;
Her waggon-spokes made of long spinners' legs,
Her cover of the wings of grasshoppers, 60
Her traces of the smallest spider's web,
Her collars of the moonshine's watery beams,
Her whip of cricket's bone, the lash of film,
Her waggoner a small grey-coated gnat,
Not half so big as a round little worm

45. *lights:* intellectual ability. 47. *five wits:* common wit, imagination, fantasy, judgment, memory. Mercutio says, "Consider our real meaning, for sound sense is there more often than in the fanciful speech that our *five wits* suggest." 49. *wit:* good sense. 53–95. A comparison between this description of Queen Mab, in which Mercutio's—and Shakespeare's—imagination runs riot, and the description of another supernatural being, Ariel (*Tempest*, I, ii, 195 ff.), will reveal the difference between Shakespeare's youthful and his more mature style. 54. *fairies' midwife:* i.e., the fairy who brings dreams to birth, *the children of an idle brain* (97). 55. *agate-stone:* tiny figures cut in the agate set in a ring. 57. *atomies:* tiny creatures. 58. *Athwart:* across. 59. *spinners':* spiders'. 63. *film:* gossamer thread. 64. *waggoner:* coachman.

Prick'd from the lazy finger of a maid.
Her chariot is an empty hazel-nut
Made by the joiner squirrel or old grub,
Time out o' mind the fairies' coachmakers.
And in this state she gallops night by night 70
Through lovers' brains, and then they dream of love;
O'er courtiers' knees, that dream on curtsies straight;
O'er lawyers' fingers, who straight dream on fees;
O'er ladies' lips, who straight on kisses dream,
Which oft the angry Mab with blisters plagues,
Because their breaths with sweetmeats tainted are.
Sometime she gallops o'er a courtier's nose,
And then dreams he of smelling out a suit;
And sometime comes she with a tithe-pig's tail
Tickling a parson's nose as a' lies asleep; 80
Then dreams he of another benefice.
Sometime she driveth o'er a soldier's neck,
And then dreams he of cutting foreign throats,
Of breaches, ambuscadoes, Spanish blades,
Of healths five-fathom deep; and then anon
Drums in his ear, at which he starts and wakes,
And being thus frighted swears a prayer or two
And sleeps again. This is that very Mab
That plats the manes of horses in the night,
And bakes the elf-locks in foul sluttish hairs, 90
Which, once untangled, much misfortune bodes.
This is the hag, when maids lie on their backs,
That presses them and learns them first to bear,
Making them women of good carriage.
This is she—

Rom. Peace, peace, Mercutio, peace!
Thou talk'st of nothing.

Mer. True, I talk of dreams,

66. *lazy finger.* An allusion to the belief that worms grew in the fingers of lazy girls. 70. *state:* chair of state. 78. *suit:* petition at court. 79. *tithe-pig's tail:* tail of a pig paid to the church as tithe. 90. *bakes the elf-locks:* makes a cake or mass of tangles.

Which are the children of an idle brain,
Begot of nothing but vain fantasy,
Which is as thin of substance as the air
And more inconstant than the wind, who woos 100
Even now the frozen bosom of the north,
And, being anger'd, puffs away from thence,
Turning his face to the dew-dropping south.

Ben. This wind you talk of blows us from ourselves.
Supper is done, and we shall come too late.

Rom. I fear, too early; for my mind misgives
Some consequence yet hanging in the stars
Shall bitterly begin his fearful date
With this night's revels, and expire the term
Of a despised life closed in my breast 110
By some vile forfeit of untimely death.
But He that hath the steerage of my course
Direct my sail! On, lusty gentlemen!

Ben. Strike, drum. [*Exeunt.*

SCENE V. *A hall in* CAPULET'S *house.*

Musicians *waiting. Enter* Servingmen, *with napkins.*

First Serv. Where's Potpan, that he helps not to take away? He shift a trencher! He scrape a trencher!

Sec. Serv. When good manners shall lie all in one or two men's hands, and they unwashed too, 'tis a foul thing.

First Serv. Away with the joint-stools, remove the court-cupboard, look to the plate. Good thou, save me a piece of

98. *vain:* empty. 103. *dew-dropping:* misty. 108. *date:* time. 109. *expire the term:* end the duration.

[v] On Shakespeare's stage no break in the action occurred here, and none is indicated in the early editions. In Scene iv the action took place on the platform, and as the drum was beaten and the maskers passed through the door of Capulet's house, the curtains of the inner stage were drawn open, and the platform, which a moment before had been a street, now became part of a hall, in the rear of which servingmen were setting out a banquet. 2. *trencher:* wooden plate. 7. *joint-stools:* stools made by a joiner. 8. *court-cupboard:* movable sideboard used to display plate.

marchpane; and, as thou lovest me, let the porter let in Susan Grindstone and Nell. Antony and Potpan! 11

Sec. Serv. Ay, boy, ready.

First Serv. You are looked for and called for, asked for and sought for, in the great chamber.

Sec. Serv. We cannot be here and there too. Cheerly, boys! Be brisk awhile, and the longer liver take all.

Enter Capulet, *with* Juliet *and others of his house, meeting the* Guests *and* Maskers.

Cap. Welcome, gentlemen! Ladies that have their toes
Unplagued with corns will have a bout with you.
Ah ha, my mistresses, which of you all 20
Will now deny to dance? She that makes dainty,
She, I'll swear, hath corns. Am I come near ye now?
Welcome, gentlemen! I have seen the day
That I have worn a visor and could tell
A whispering tale in a fair lady's ear,
Such as would please. 'Tis gone, 'tis gone, 'tis gone!
You are welcome, gentlemen! Come, musicians, play.
A hall, a hall! Give room! And foot it, girls.
[*Music plays, and they dance.*
More light, you knaves; and turn the tables up,
And quench the fire, the room is grown too hot. 30
Ah, sirrah, this unlook'd-for sport comes well.
Nay, sit, nay, sit, good cousin Capulet,
For you and I are past our dancing days.
How long is 't now since last yourself and I
Were in a mask?

Sec. Cap. By 'r lady, thirty years.

Cap. What, man! 'Tis not so much; 'tis not so much!
'Tis since the nuptial of Lucentio,

9. *marchpane:* marzipan, confectionery made of pounded almonds, sugar, flour, etc. 19. *bout:* turn. 21. *deny:* refuse. *makes dainty:* affects reluctance. 22. *Am I come near ye:* do my words fit you? 24. *visor:* mask. 28. *A hall:* make room! 29. *turn the tables up.* Tables were made of hinged leaves placed on trestles.

Come Pentecost as quickly as it will,
Some five and twenty years; and then we mask'd.
Sec. Cap. 'Tis more; 'tis more. His son is elder, sir; 40
His son is thirty.
Cap. Will you tell me that?
His son was but a ward two years ago.
Rom. [*To a Servingman*] What lady's that which doth enrich the hand
Of yonder knight?
Serv. I know not, sir.
Rom. O, she doth teach the torches to burn bright!
It seems she hangs upon the cheek of night
Like a rich jewel in an Ethiope's ear—
Beauty too rich for use, for earth too dear!
So shows a snowy dove trooping with crows, 50
As yonder lady o'er her fellows shows.
The measure done, I'll watch her place of stand,
And, touching hers, make blessed my rude hand.
Did my heart love till now? Forswear it, sight!
For I ne'er saw true beauty till this night.
Tyb. This, by his voice, should be a Montague.
Fetch me my rapier, boy. What dares the slave
Come hither, cover'd with an antic face,
To fleer and scorn at our solemnity?
Now, by the stock and honour of my kin, 60
To strike him dead I hold it not a sin.
Cap. Why, how now, kinsman! Wherefore storm you so?
Tyb. Uncle, this is a Montague, our foe,
A villain that is hither come in spite
To scorn at our solemnity this night.
Cap. Young Romeo is it?
Tyb. 'Tis he, that villain Romeo.
Cap. Content thee, gentle coz; let him alone;
He bears him like a portly gentleman;

51. *shows:* appears. 57. *What dares:* how dares. 58. *antic face:* fantastic mask. 59. *fleer:* sneer. *solemnity:* festivity. 68. *portly:* dignified, well-bred.

And, to say truth, Verona brags of him
To be a virtuous and well govern'd youth. 70
I would not for the wealth of all the town
Here in my house do him disparagement.
Therefore be patient; take no note of him.
It is my will, the which if thou respect,
Show a fair presence and put off these frowns,
An ill-beseeming semblance for a feast.

Tyb. It fits, when such a villain is a guest.
I'll not endure him.

Cap. He shall be endured.
What, goodman boy! I say, he shall. Go to!
Am I the master here, or you? Go to! 80
You'll not endure him! God shall mend my soul!
You'll make a mutiny among my guests!
You will set cock-a-hoop! You'll be the man!

Tyb. Why, uncle, 'tis a shame.

Cap. Go to, go to!
You are a saucy boy. Is 't so, indeed?
This trick may chance to scathe you; I know what.
You must contrary me! Marry, 'tis time—
Well said, my hearts!—You are a princox; go!
Be quiet, or—More light, more light!—For shame!
I'll make you quiet.—What, cheerly, my hearts! 90

Tyb. Patience perforce with wilful choler meeting
Makes my flesh tremble in their different greeting.
I will withdraw, but this intrusion shall,
Now seeming sweet, convert to bitter gall. [*Exit.*

Rom. [*To Juliet*] If I profane with my unworthiest hand
This holy shrine, the gentle fine is this:
My lips, two blushing pilgrims, ready stand
To smooth that rough touch with a tender kiss.

79. *What, goodman boy:* see here, young man! 81. *mend:* amend, save. 82. *mutiny:* disturbance. 83. *set cock-a-hoop:* start disorder. 86. *scathe:* injure. 88. *princox:* saucy boy. 91. *Patience perforce:* enforced patience. 94. *convert:* change. 96. *gentle fine:* pleasant penalty.

Jul. Good pilgrim, you do wrong your hand too much,
Which mannerly devotion shows in this; 100
For saints have hands that pilgrims' hands do touch,
And palm to palm is holy palmers' kiss.
Rom. Have not saints lips, and holy palmers too?
Jul. Ay, pilgrim, lips that they must use in prayer.
Rom. O, then, dear saint, let lips do what hands do!
They pray; grant thou, lest faith turn to despair.
Jul. Saints do not move, though grant for prayers' sake.
Rom. Then move not, while my prayer's effect I take.
Thus from my lips, by thine, my sin is purged. [*He kisses her.*
Jul. Then have my lips the sin that they have took. 110
Rom. Sin from my lips? O trespass sweetly urged!
Give me my sin again. [*He kisses her again.*
Jul. You kiss by the book.
Nurse. Madam, your mother craves a word with you.
[*Juliet withdraws.*
Rom. What is her mother?
Nurse. Marry, bachelor,
Her mother is the lady of the house,
And a good lady, and a wise and virtuous.
I nursed her daughter, that you talk'd withal.
I tell you he that can lay hold of her
Shall have the chinks.
Rom. Is she a Capulet?
O dear account! My life is my foe's debt. 120
Ben. Away, be gone; the sport is at the best.
Rom. Ay, so I fear; the more is my unrest.
Cap. Nay, gentlemen, prepare not to be gone;
We have a trifling foolish banquet towards.
Is it e'en so? Why, then, I thank you all;

99. *pilgrim.* Romeo wore the costume of a pilgrim or palmer, a conventional disguise often assumed by the lover worshipping at the shrine of his "saint." 107. *move:* propose, urge. 112. *by the book:* according to rule. 119. *chinks:* money. 120. *My life . . . debt:* i.e., since he cannot live without Juliet, his life is in his foe's power. 124. *foolish banquet towards:* insignificant dessert in preparation. 125. *Is it e'en so?* Here, according to Q_1, "they wisper in his eare."

I thank you, honest gentlemen; good night.
More torches here! Come on then, let's to bed.
Ah, sirrah, by my fay, it waxes late;
I'll to my rest. [*All but Juliet and Nurse begin to leave.*

Jul. Come hither, nurse. What is yond gentleman? 130

Nurse. The son and heir of old Tiberio.

Jul. What's he that now is going out of door?

Nurse. Marry, that, I think, be young Petrucio.

Jul. What's he that follows there, that would not dance?

Nurse. I know not.

Jul. Go, ask his name.—If he be married,
My grave is like to be my wedding bed.

Nurse. His name is Romeo, and a Montague;
The only son of your great enemy.

Jul. My only love sprung from my only hate! 140
Too early seen unknown, and known too late!
Prodigious birth of love it is to me
That I must love a loathed enemy.

Nurse. What's this? What's this?

Jul. A rhyme I learn'd even now
Of one I danced withal. [*One calls within*, "Juliet."

Nurse. Anon, anon!
Come, let's away; the strangers all are gone. [*Exeunt.*

ACT II

PROLOGUE

Enter Chorus.

Chor. Now old Desire doth in his death-bed lie,
And young Affection gapes to be his heir;
That fair for which love groan'd for and would die,
With tender Juliet match'd, is now not fair.

128. *fay:* faith. *waxes:* grows. 142. *Prodigious:* (a) monstrous, (b) ominous.

[II. Prologue] 3. *That fair:* that fair one (Rosaline). 4. *match'd:* compared.

Now Romeo is beloved and loves again,
  Alike bewitched by the charm of looks,
But to his foe supposed he must complain,
  And she steal love's sweet bait from fearful hooks.
Being held a foe, he may not have access
  To breathe such vows as lovers use to swear, 10
And she as much in love, her means much less
  To meet her new-beloved anywhere.
But passion lends them power, time means, to meet.
Tempering extremities with extreme sweet. [*Exit.*

SCENE I. *A lane by the wall of* CAPULET'S *orchard.*

Enter ROMEO.

Rom. Can I go forward when my heart is here?
Turn back, dull earth, and find thy centre out.
[*He climbs the wall, and leaps down within it.*

Enter BENVOLIO *and* MERCUTIO.

Ben. Romeo! My cousin Romeo!
Mer. He is wise;
And, on my life, hath stol'n him home to bed.
Ben. He ran this way, and leap'd this orchard wall.
Call, good Mercutio.
Mer. Nay, I'll conjure too.
Romeo! Humours! Madman! Passion! Lover!
Appear thou in the likeness of a sigh;
Speak but one rhyme, and I am satisfied;
Cry but "Ay me!" Pronounce but "love" and "dove"; 10
Speak to my gossip Venus one fair word,
One nick-name for her purblind son and heir,

6. *Alike:* i.e., both he and she. 10. *use to:* are accustomed to. 14. *extremities:* extreme difficulties or dangers.

[i] 2. *dull earth:* i.e., my body. *centre:* heart or soul, i.e., Juliet. 6. *conjure:* summon by incantation. 7. *Humours:* whims. 11. *gossip:* friend.

Young Adam Cupid, he that shot so trim
When King Cophetua loved the beggar-maid!
He heareth not, he stirreth not, he moveth not;
The ape is dead, and I must conjure him.
I conjure thee by Rosaline's bright eyes,
By her high forehead and her scarlet lip,
By her fine foot, straight leg, and quivering thigh,
And the demesnes that there adjacent lie, 20
That in thy likeness thou appear to us!

Ben. An if he hear thee, thou wilt anger him.

Mer. This cannot anger him; 'twould anger him
To raise a spirit in his mistress' circle
Of some strange nature, letting it there stand
Till she had laid it and conjured it down.
That were some spite; my invocation
Is fair and honest; and in his mistress' name
I conjure only but to raise up him.

Ben. Come, he hath hid himself among these trees 30
To be consorted with the humorous night.
Blind is his love and best befits the dark.

Mer. If Love be blind, Love cannot hit the mark.
Now will he sit under a medlar tree,
And wish his mistress were that kind of fruit
As maids call medlars, when they laugh alone.
O, Romeo, that she were, O, that she were
An open *et cetera*, thou a poperin pear!

13. *Adam.* Qq and F_1 read *Abraham*, which may mean *abram* or *auburn*, "light-haired," or it may mean that Cupid is still young, though actually as old as Father Abraham; or some allusion now lost may be hidden in the name. Upton proposed the emendation *Adam*, as referring to Adam Bell, the famous archer of the old ballads. *trim:* neatly. This is a reference to a stanza from the ballad *King Cophetua and the Beggar-Maid*. 15–16. *He heareth . . . him:* a reference to the showman with the performing ape. 20. *demesnes:* regions. 24. *circle:* the ring drawn by a magician. 27. *spite:* injury. 31. *consorted:* associated. *humorous:* (a) moist, (b) full of whims. 34. *medlar:* the tree *Mespilus germanica*. The fruit resembles a small, brown-skinned apple. 38. *poperin:* a variety of pear from Poperinghe, a town in Flanders.

Romeo, good night! I'll to my truckle-bed;
This field-bed is too cold for me to sleep. 40
Come, shall we go?

Ben. Go, then; for 'tis in vain
To seek him here that means not to be found. [*Exeunt.*

SCENE II. CAPULET'S *orchard.*

Enter ROMEO.

Rom. He jests at scars that never felt a wound.
[*Juliet appears above at a window.*
But, soft! What light through yonder window breaks?
It is the east, and Juliet is the sun!
Arise, fair sun, and kill the envious moon,
Who is already sick and pale with grief
That thou, her maid, art far more fair than she.
Be not her maid, since she is envious.
Her vestal livery is but sick and green,
And none but fools do wear it. Cast it off.
It is my lady; O, it is my love! 10
O that she knew she were!
She speaks, yet she says nothing. What of that?
Her eye discourses; I will answer it.
I am too bold; 'tis not to me she speaks.
Two of the fairest stars in all the heaven,
Having some business, do entreat her eyes
To twinkle in their spheres till they return.

39. *truckle-bed:* trundle-bed.
[ii] There is no necessity for a scene-division here. The dialogue is continuous: line 1 rhymes with line 42 of scene i. Modern stage versions place the lane on the right of the stage, the orchard center, and the balcony left. As Benvolio and Mercutio leave, Romeo emerges from the shadows of the orchard. 1. *He:* Mercutio. 2. *window.* Not until much later did this famous scene become a "balcony scene." 4. *envious:* malicious, spiteful. 6. *her maid:* a follower of Diana, virgin goddess of the moon. 8. *vestal:* virgin. 17. *spheres:* orbits.

What if her eyes were there, they in her head?
The brightness of her cheek would shame those stars
As daylight doth a lamp; her eyes in heaven 20
Would through the airy region stream so bright
That birds would sing and think it were not night.
See, how she leans her cheek upon her hand!
O, that I were a glove upon that hand,
That I might touch that cheek!

Jul. Ay me!

Rom. She speaks!
O, speak again, bright angel, for thou art
As glorious to this night, being o'er my head,
As is a winged messenger of heaven
Unto the white-upturned wondering eyes
Of mortals that fall back to gaze on him 30
When he bestrides the lazy-pacing clouds
And sails upon the bosom of the air.

Jul. O Romeo, Romeo! Wherefore art thou Romeo?
Deny thy father and refuse thy name!
Or, if thou wilt not, be but sworn my love,
And I'll no longer be a Capulet.

Rom. [*Aside*] Shall I hear more, or shall I speak at this?

Jul. 'Tis but thy name that is my enemy;
Thou art thyself, though not a Montague.
What's Montague? It is nor hand, nor foot, 40
Nor arm, nor face, nor any other part
Belonging to a man. O, be some other name!
What's in a name? That which we call a rose
By any other name would smell as sweet.
So Romeo would, were he not Romeo call'd,
Retain that dear perfection which he owes
Without that title. Romeo, doff thy name,
And for that name, which is no part of thee,
Take all myself.

Rom. I take thee at thy word.

39. *Thou . . . Montague:* thou wouldst be thyself even though thou wert not a Montague. 46. *owes:* owns.

Call me but love, and I'll be new baptized; 50
Henceforth I never will be Romeo.

Jul. What man art thou that thus bescreen'd in night
So stumblest on my counsel?

Rom. By a name
I know not how to tell thee who I am.
My name, dear saint, is hateful to myself,
Because it is an enemy to thee;
Had I it written, I would tear the word.

Jul. My ears have not yet drunk a hundred words
Of that tongue's utterance, yet I know the sound.
Art thou not Romeo and a Montague? 60

Rom. Neither, fair saint, if either thee dislike.

Jul. How camest thou hither, tell me, and wherefore?
The orchard walls are high and hard to climb,
And the place death, considering who thou art,
If any of my kinsmen find thee here.

Rom. With Love's light wings did I o'erperch these walls;
For stony limits cannot hold love out,
And what love can do, that dares love attempt;
Therefore thy kinsmen are no let to me.

Jul. If they do see thee, they will murder thee. 70

Rom. Alack, there lies more peril in thine eye
Than twenty of their swords! Look thou but sweet,
And I am proof against their enmity.

Jul. I would not for the world they saw thee here.

Rom. I have night's cloak to hide me from their sight;
And but thou love me, let them find me here.
My life were better ended by their hate,
Than death prorogued, wanting of thy love.

Jul. By whose direction found'st thou out this place?

Rom. By Love, who first did prompt me to inquire; 80

53. *counsel:* secrets. 55. *dear saint.* Romeo in the dark identifies himself by alluding to the conversation with Juliet (I, v, 105) which no one else had heard. 61. *dislike:* displease. 66. *o'erperch:* fly over. 69. *let:* obstacle. 76. *but:* unless. 78. *prorogued:* postponed. *wanting of:* lacking. 79. *direction:* guidance.

He lent me counsel and I lent him eyes.
I am no pilot; yet, wert thou as far
As that vast shore wash'd with the farthest sea,
I would adventure for such merchandise.

Jul. Thou know'st the mask of night is on my face,
Else would a maiden blush bepaint my cheek
For that which thou hast heard me speak tonight.
Fain would I dwell on form—fain, fain deny
What I have spoke—but farewell compliment!
Dost thou love me? I know thou wilt say "Ay," 90
And I will take thy word; yet, if thou swear'st,
Thou mayst prove false. At lovers' perjuries,
They say Jove laughs. O gentle Romeo,
If thou dost love, pronounce it faithfully;
Or if thou think'st I am too quickly won,
I'll frown and be perverse and say thee nay,
So thou wilt woo; but else, not for the world.
In truth, fair Montague, I am too fond,
And therefore thou mayst think my haviour light.
But trust me, gentleman, I'll prove more true 100
Than those that have more cunning to be strange.
I should have been more strange, I must confess,
But that thou overheard'st, ere I was ware,
My true love's passion. Therefore pardon me,
And not impute this yielding to light love,
Which the dark night hath so discovered.

Rom. Lady, by yonder blessed moon I swear,
That tips with silver all these fruit-tree tops—

Jul. O, swear not by the moon, the inconstant moon,
That monthly changes in her circled orb, 110
Lest that thy love prove likewise variable.

Rom. What shall I swear by?

Jul. Do not swear at all;
Or, if thou wilt, swear by thy gracious self,

89. *compliment:* conventional speech. 97. *So:* provided that. 101. *cunning:* skill. *strange:* reserved. 106. *discovered:* revealed. 110. *circled orb:* circular orbit.

Which is the god of my idolatry,
And I'll believe thee.

Rom. If my heart's dear love—

Jul. Well, do not swear. Although I joy in thee,
I have no joy of this contract tonight;
It is too rash, too unadvised, too sudden,
Too like the lightning, which doth cease to be
Ere one can say it lightens. Sweet, good night! 120
This bud of love, by summer's ripening breath,
May prove a beauteous flower when next we meet.
Good night, good night! As sweet repose and rest
Come to thy heart as that within my breast!

Rom. O, wilt thou leave me so unsatisfied?

Jul. What satisfaction canst thou have tonight?

Rom. The exchange of thy love's faithful vow for mine.

Jul. I gave thee mine before thou didst request it,
And yet I would it were to give again.

Rom. Wouldst thou withdraw it? For what purpose, love?

Jul. But to be frank, and give it thee again. 131
And yet I wish but for the thing I have.
My bounty is as boundless as the sea,
My love as deep; the more I give to thee,
The more I have, for both are infinite.
I hear some noise within. Dear love, adieu! [*Nurse calls within.*
Anon, good nurse! Sweet Montague, be true.
Stay but a little; I will come again. [*Exit, above.*

Rom. O blessed, blessed night! I am afeard,
Being in night, all this is but a dream, 140
Too flattering-sweet to be substantial.

Re-enter JULIET, *above.*

Jul. Three words, dear Romeo, and good night indeed.
If that thy bent of love be honourable,
Thy purpose marriage, send me word tomorrow,
By one that I'll procure to come to thee,
Where and what time thou wilt perform the rite;

131. *frank:* generous. 141. *substantial:* real. 143. *bent:* inclination. 145. *procure:* cause.

And all my fortunes at thy foot I'll lay
And follow thee my lord throughout the world.
Nurse. [*Within*] Madam!
Jul. I come, anon.—But if thou mean'st not well, 150
I do beseech thee—
Nurse. [*Within*] Madam!
Jul. By and by, I come.—
To cease thy suit, and leave me to my grief.
Tomorrow will I send.
Rom. So thrive my soul—
Jul. A thousand times good night! [*Exit, above.*
Rom. A thousand times the worse, to want thy light!
Love goes toward love, as schoolboys from their books,
But love from love, toward school with heavy looks.
[*Retiring.*

Re-enter Juliet, *above.*

Jul. Hist! Romeo, hist! O, for a falconer's voice
To lure this tassel-gentle back again! 160
Bondage is hoarse and may not speak aloud;
Else would I tear the cave where Echo lies,
And make her airy tongue more hoarse than mine,
With repetition of my Romeo's name.
Rom. It is my soul that calls upon my name.
How silver-sweet sound lovers' tongues by night,
Like softest music to attending ears!
Jul. Romeo!
Rom. My dear?
Jul. At what o'clock tomorrow
Shall I send to thee?
Rom. At the hour of nine.
Jul. I will not fail; 'tis twenty years till then. 170
I have forgot why I did call thee back.
Rom. Let me stand here till thou remember it.
Jul. I shall forget, to have thee still stand there,
Remembering how I love thy company.

151. *By and by:* at once. 156. *want:* lack. 160. *tassel-gentle:* tercel-gentle, male falcon. 167. *attending:* listening.

Rom. And I'll still stay, to have thee still forget,
Forgetting any other home but this.
Jul. 'Tis almost morning. I would have thee gone—
And yet no further than a wanton's bird,
Who lets it hop a little from her hand,
Like a poor prisoner in his twisted gyves, 180
And with a silk thread plucks it back again,
So loving-jealous of his liberty.
Rom. I would I were thy bird.
Jul. Sweet, so would I;
Yet I should kill thee with much cherishing.
Good night, good night! Parting is such sweet sorrow
That I shall say good night till it be morrow. [*Exit above.*
Rom. Sleep dwell upon thine eyes, peace in thy breast!
Would I were sleep and peace, so sweet to rest!
Hence will I to my ghostly father's cell, 189
His help to crave and my dear hap to tell. [*Exit.*

SCENE III. FRIAR LAURENCE'S *cell.*

Enter FRIAR LAURENCE, *with a basket.*

Fri. L. The grey-eyed morn smiles on the frowning night,
Chequering the eastern clouds with streaks of light,
And flecked darkness like a drunkard reels
From forth day's path and Titan's fiery wheels.
Now, ere the sun advance his burning eye
The day to cheer and night's dank dew to dry,
I must up-fill this osier cage of ours
With baleful weeds and precious-juiced flowers.
The earth that's nature's mother is her tomb;
What is her burying grave that is her womb, 10
And from her womb children of divers kind
We sucking on her natural bosom find,

178. *wanton's:* pampered child's. 180. *gyves:* fetters. 189. *ghostly:* spiritual. 190. *dear hap:* good fortune.

[iii] 3. *flecked:* dappled. 4. *Titan's:* the sun-god's. 7. *osier cage:* willow basket.

Many for many virtues excellent,
None but for some, and yet all different.
O, mickle is the powerful grace that lies
In herbs, plants, stones, and their true qualities;
For nought so vile that on the earth doth live
But to the earth some special good doth give,
Nor aught so good but, strain'd from that fair use,
Revolts from true birth, stumbling on abuse. 20
Virtue itself turns vice, being misapplied;
And vice sometime 's by action dignified.
Within the infant rind of this small flower
Poison hath residence and medicine power;
For this, being smelt, with that part cheers each part;
Being tasted, slays all senses with the heart.
Two such opposed kings encamp them still
In man as well as herbs—grace and rude will;
And where the worser is predominant,
Full soon the canker death eats up that plant. 30

Enter ROMEO.

Rom. Good morrow, father.
Fri. L. Benedicite!
What early tongue so sweet saluteth me?
Young son, it argues a distemper'd head
So soon to bid good morrow to thy bed.
Care keeps his watch in every old man's eye,
And where care lodges, sleep will never lie;
But where unbruised youth with unstuff'd brain
Doth couch his limbs, there golden sleep doth reign.
Therefore thy earliness doth me assure
Thou art up-roused by some distemperature; 40

15. *mickle:* much. *grace:* efficacy. 19. *strain'd:* forced. 25. *that part:* the odor. 27. *encamp them still:* are always encamped. 28. *grace . . . will:* divine grace and undisciplined desire. 30. *canker:* cankerworm. 31. *Benedicite:* God bless you. 33. *distemper'd:* disordered. 34. *morrow:* morning. 37. *unbruised:* undamaged. *unstuff'd:* not overloaded.

Or if not so, then here I hit it right—
Our Romeo hath not been in bed tonight.
Rom. That last is true; the sweeter rest was mine.
Fri. L. God pardon sin! Wast thou with Rosaline?
Rom. With Rosaline, my ghostly father? No!
I have forgot that name, and that name's woe.
Fri. L. That's my good son. But where hast thou been then?
Rom. I'll tell thee ere thou ask it me again.
I have been feasting with mine enemy,
Where on a sudden one hath wounded me 50
That's by me wounded. Both our remedies
Within thy help and holy physic lies.
I bear no hatred, blessed man, for, lo,
My intercession likewise steads my foe.
Fri. L. Be plain, good son, and homely in thy drift;
Riddling confession finds but riddling shrift.
Rom. Then plainly know my heart's dear love is set
On the fair daughter of rich Capulet.
As mine on hers, so hers is set on mine;
And all combined, save what thou must combine 60
By holy marriage. When and where and how
We met, we woo'd, and made exchange of vow,
I'll tell thee as we pass; but this I pray,
That thou consent to marry us today.
Fri. L. Holy Saint Francis, what a change is here!
Is Rosaline, whom thou didst love so dear,
So soon forsaken? Young men's love then lies
Not truly in their hearts, but in their eyes.
Jesu Maria, what a deal of brine
Hath wash'd thy sallow cheeks for Rosaline! 70
How much salt water thrown away in waste,
To season love, that of it doth not taste!
The sun not yet thy sighs from heaven clears,
Thy old groans ring yet in my ancient ears.

51. *Both our remedies:* a remedy for both of us. 52. *physic:* healing art. 54. *intercession:* prayer. *steads:* helps. 55. *homely in thy drift:* simple in thy speech. 56. *shrift:* absolution. 60. *combined:* bound.

Lo, here upon thy cheek the stain doth sit
Of an old tear that is not wash'd off yet.
If e'er thou wast thyself and these woes thine,
Thou and these woes were all for Rosaline.
And art thou changed? Pronounce this sentence then:
Women may fall when there's no strength in men. 80
Rom. Thou chid'st me oft for loving Rosaline.
Fri. L. For doting, not for loving, pupil mine.
Rom. And bad'st me bury love.
Fri. L. Not in a grave
To lay one in, another out to have.
Rom. I pray thee, chide not. She whom I love now
Doth grace for grace and love for love allow;
The other did not so.
Fri. L. O, she knew well
Thy love did read by rote and could not spell.
But come, young waverer, come, go with me,
In one respect I'll thy assistant be; 90
For this alliance may so happy prove,
To turn your households' rancour to pure love.
Rom. O, let us hence! I stand on sudden haste.
Fri. L. Wisely and slow. They stumble that run fast.
[*Exeunt.*

SCENE IV. *A street.*

Enter BENVOLIO *and* MERCUTIO.

Mer. Where the devil should this Romeo be?
Came he not home tonight?
Ben. Not to his father's; I spoke with his man.
Mer. Ah, that same pale hard-hearted wench, that Rosaline,
Torments him so, that he will sure run mad.
Ben. Tybalt, the kinsman of old Capulet,
Hath sent a letter to his father's house.

79. *sentence:* pithy saying. 86. *grace:* favor. 88. *rote:* memory. 90. *In one respect:* for one reason. 92. *To turn:* as to turn. 93. *stand on:* insist on.
[iv] 2. *tonight:* last night.

Mer. A challenge, on my life.

Ben. Romeo will answer it.

Mer. Any man that can write may answer a letter. 10

Ben. Nay, he will answer the letter's master, how he dares, being dared.

Mer. Alas, poor Romeo! He is already dead, stabbed with a white wench's black eye, shot thorough the ear with a love-song, the very pin of his heart cleft with the blind bow-boy's butt-shaft; and is he a man to encounter Tybalt?

Ben. Why, what is Tybalt? 18

Mer. More than Prince of Cats, I can tell you. O, he is the courageous captain of compliments. He fights as you sing prick-song; keeps time, distance, and proportion; rests me his minim rest, one, two, and the third in your bosom! The very butcher of a silk button, a duellist, a duellist! A gentleman of the very first house, of the first and second cause. Ah, the immortal *passado!* The *punto reverso!* The *hai!*

Ben. The what? 28

Mer. The pox of such antic, lisping, affecting fantasticoes! These new tuners of accents! "By Jesu, a very good blade! A very tall man! A very good whore!" Why, is not this a lamentable thing, grandsire, that we should be thus afflicted with these strange flies, these fashion-mongers, these *perdona-mi's*, who stand so much on the new form that they cannot sit at ease on the old bench? O, their bones, their bones!

12. *dared:* challenged. 15. *pin:* peg in the center of a target. 16. *butt-shaft:* blunt arrow for target-shooting. 19. *Prince of Cats.* Tibalt or Tibert is the cat in the old story of *Reynard the Fox.* 20. *captain of compliments:* observer of formalities. 21. *prick-song:* music "pricked" or written out. 22. *proportion:* rhythm. 23. *minim rest:* short rest. 25. *first house:* the best school of fence (?). 26. *first and second cause:* recognized reasons for quarrel. See *As You Like It*, V, iv, 69–108. 27. *passado, hai:* technical terms for maneuvers in fencing. 29. *The pox of:* plague take. *antic:* ludicrous. *affecting:* affected. 30. *fantasticoes:* absurd persons. This is the Q_1 reading; Q_2 and F_1 read *phantacies. accents:* language. 31. *tall:* valiant. 33. *grandsire:* old man. 34. *flies:* affected persons. 35. *perdona-mi's:* persons who affect foreign manners and phrases. 36. *form:* (a) fashion, (b) bench. 37. *bones:* pun on French *bon* or Italian *buon*, "good."

Enter ROMEO.

Ben. Here comes Romeo! Here comes Romeo! 38

Mer. Without his roe, like a dried herring. O flesh, flesh, how art thou fishified! Now is he for the numbers that Petrarch flowed in. Laura, to his lady, was but a kitchen-wench; marry, she had a better love to be-rhyme her; Dido a dowdy; Cleopatra a gipsy; Helen and Hero hildings and harlots; Thisbe a grey eye or so, but not to the purpose. Signior Romeo, *bon jour!* There's a French salutation to your French slop. You gave us the counterfeit fairly last night.

Rom. Good morrow to you both. What counterfeit did I give you? 50

Mer. The slip, sir, the slip. Can you not conceive?

Rom. Pardon, good Mercutio. My business was great, and in such a case as mine a man may strain courtesy.

Mer. That's as much as to say, such a case as yours constrains a man to bow in the hams.

Rom. Meaning, to curtsy.

Mer. Thou hast most kindly hit it.

Rom. A most courteous exposition. 60

Mer. Nay, I am the very pink of courtesy.

Rom. Pink for flower.

Mer. Right.

Rom. Why, then is my pump well flowered.

Mer. Well said! Follow me this jest now till thou hast worn out thy pump, that, when the single sole of it is worn, the jest may remain, after the wearing, sole singular. 68

Rom. O single-soled jest, solely singular for the singleness!

Mer. Come between us, good Benvolio! My wits faint.

39. *Without his roe:* Romeo = *roe* (fish roe) and *me O* (a sigh). Only the sigh remains. 41. *Petrarch:* the Italian poet whose sonnets to Laura were the models of the Elizabethans. 45. *hildings:* worthless persons. 47. *slop:* loose breeches. 48. *counterfeit.* Counterfeit coins were often called "slips." 51. *conceive:* understand. 56–106. These lines are often cut in a modern performance. The wit displayed is typically Elizabethan. The puns that crowd this passage scarcely deserve explanation.

Rom. Switch and spurs, switch and spurs, or I'll cry a match.

Mer. Nay, if thy wits run the wild-goose chase, I have done; for thou hast more of the wild-goose in one of thy wits than, I am sure, I have in my whole five. Was I with you there for the goose?

Rom. Thou wast never with me for anything when thou wast not there for the goose. 80

Mer. I will bite thee by the ear for that jest.

Rom. Nay, good goose, bite not!

Mer. Thy wit is a very bitter sweeting; it is a most sharp sauce.

Rom. And is it not well served in to a sweet goose?

Mer. O, here's a wit of cheveril, that stretches from an inch narrow to an ell broad!

Rom. I stretch it out for that word "broad," which, added to the goose, proves thee far and wide a broad goose. 91

Mer. Why, is not this better now than groaning for love? Now art thou sociable; now art thou Romeo; now art thou what thou art, by art as well as by nature; for this drivelling love is like a great natural that runs lolling up and down to hide his bauble in a hole.

Ben. Stop there, stop there.

Mer. Thou desirest me to stop in my tale against the hair. 100

Ben. Thou wouldst else have made thy tale large.

Mer. O, thou art deceived. I would have made it short, for I was come to the whole depth of my tale, and meant indeed to occupy the argument no longer.

Rom. Here's goodly gear!

Enter NURSE *and* PETER.

Mer. A sail, a sail!

Ben. Two, two; a shirt and a smock.

87. *cheveril:* kid leather, very flexible. 96. *natural:* idiot, fool (hence the allusion to *bauble,* line 97). 100. *against the hair:* against the grain. 105. *occupy:* have to do with carnally, but "an excellent good word before it was ill-sorted" (*2 Henry IV*, II, iv, 160). 107. *gear:* business.

Nurse. Peter! 110

Peter. Anon!

Nurse. My fan, Peter.

Mer. Good Peter, to hide her face; for her fan's the fairer face of the two.

Nurse. God ye good morrow, gentlemen.

Mer. God ye good den, fair gentlewoman.

Nurse. Is it good den?

Mer. 'Tis no less, I tell you, for the bawdy hand of the dial is now upon the prick of noon.

Nurse. Out upon you! What a man are you! 120

Rom. One, gentlewoman, that God hath made for himself to mar.

Nurse. By my troth, it is well said; "for himself to mar," quoth a'? Gentlemen, can any of you tell me where I may find the young Romeo?

Rom. I can tell you; but young Romeo will be older when you have found him than he was when you sought him. I am the youngest of that name, for fault of a worse.

Nurse. You say well. 130

Mer. Yea, is the worst well? Very well took, i' faith; wisely, wisely.

Nurse. If you be he, sir, I desire some confidence with you.

Ben. She will indite him to some supper.

Mer. A bawd, a bawd, a bawd! So ho!

Rom. What hast thou found?

Mer. No hare, sir; unless a hare, sir, in a lenten pie, that is something stale and hoar ere it be spent.

[*Sings*] An old hare hoar, 141
And an old hare hoar,
Is very good meat in Lent;

115. *God ye good morrow:* God give you a good morning. 116. *God ye good den:* God give you a good evening. 119. *prick:* point. 123. *By my troth:* upon my word. 124. *quoth a':* said he. 129. *fault:* lack. 134. *confidence:* blunder for "conference." 135. *indite:* intentional blunder for "invite." 136. *So ho:* the huntsman's cry when he sights a hare. 138. *hare:* courtesan (slang). 139. *hoar:* mouldy.

But a hare that is hoar
Is too much for a score,
When it hoars ere it be spent.
Romeo, will you come to your father's? We'll to dinner thither.

Rom. I will follow you. 149

Mer. Farewell, ancient lady; farewell, [*Singing.*] "lady, lady, lady." [*Exeunt Mercutio and Benvolio.*

Nurse. Marry, farewell! I pray you, sir, what saucy merchant was this that was so full of his ropery?

Rom. A gentleman, nurse, that loves to hear himself talk and will speak more in a minute than he will stand to in a month.

Nurse. An a' speak anything against me, I'll take him down, an a' were lustier than he is, and twenty such Jacks; and if I cannot, I'll find those that shall. Scurvy knave! I am none of his flirt-gills; I am none of his skains-mates. [*To Peter.*] And thou must stand by too, and suffer every knave to use me at his pleasure! 164

Peter. I saw no man use you at his pleasure. If I had, my weapon should quickly have been out, I warrant you. I dare draw as soon as another man, if I see occasion in a good quarrel, and the law on my side. 169

Nurse. Now, afore God, I am so vexed that every part about me quivers. Scurvy knave! Pray you, sir, a word; and, as I told you, my young lady bade me inquire you out. What she bade me say, I will keep to myself. But first let me tell ye, if ye should lead her into a fool's paradise, as they say, it were a very gross kind of behaviour, as they say; for the gentlewoman is young, and, therefore, if you should deal double with her, truly it were an ill thing to be offered to any gentlewoman, and very weak dealing. 181

Rom. Nurse, commend me to thy lady and mistress. I protest unto thee—

151. "*lady, lady, lady*": refrain from the ballad *Chaste Susanna.* 153. *merchant:* rude fellow. 154. *ropery:* blunder for "roguery." 160. *Jacks:* saucy fellows. 162. *flirt-gills:* flirting women. *skains-mates:* ruffians (?). 183. *protest:* vow.

Nurse. Good heart, and, i' faith, I will tell her as much. Lord, Lord! She will be a joyful woman.

Rom. What wilt thou tell her, nurse? Thou dost not mark me.

Nurse. I will tell her, sir, that you do protest; which, as I take it, is a gentlemanlike offer. 190

Rom. Bid her devise
Some means to come to shrift this afternoon;
And there she shall at Friar Laurence' cell
Be shrived and married. Here is for thy pains.

Nurse. No, truly, sir; not a penny.

Rom. Go to! I say you shall.

Nurse. This afternoon, sir? Well, she shall be there.

Rom. And stay, good nurse; behind the abbey wall
Within this hour my man shall be with thee, 200
And bring thee cords made like a tackled stair,
Which to the high top-gallant of my joy
Must be my convoy in the secret night.
Farewell. Be trusty, and I'll quit thy pains.
Farewell. Commend me to thy mistress.

Nurse. Now God in heaven bless thee! Hark you, sir.

Rom. What say'st thou, my dear nurse?

Nurse. Is your man secret? Did you ne'er hear say
Two may keep counsel, putting one away?

Rom. I warrant thee my man's as true as steel. 210

Nurse. Well, sir; my mistress is the sweetest lady—Lord, Lord! When 'twas a little prating thing—O, there is a nobleman in town, one Paris, that would fain lay knife aboard; but she, good soul, had as lief see a toad, a very toad, as see him. I anger her sometimes and tell her that Paris is the properer man; but, I'll warrant you, when I say so, she looks as pale as any clout in the versal world. Doth not rosemary and Romeo begin both with a letter? 220

188. *mark:* heed. 192. *shrift:* confession. 201. *tackled stair:* rope ladder, such as sailors might use. 202. *top-gallant:* summit (highest mast on a ship). 203. *convoy:* conveyance. 204. *quit:* requite. 208. *secret:* trustworthy. 217. *properer:* more handsome. 219. *clout:* rag. *versal:* universal. 220. *a letter:* the same letter.

Rom. Ay, nurse; what of that? Both with an R.

Nurse. Ah, mocker! That's the dog's name. R is for the— No; I know it begins with some other letter—and she hath the prettiest sententious of it, of you and rosemary, that it would do you good to hear it.

Rom. Commend me to thy lady.

Nurse. Ay, a thousand times. [*Exit Romeo.*] Peter! 230

Peter. Anon!

Nurse. Peter, take my fan, and go before, and apace.

[*Exeunt.*

SCENE V. CAPULET'S *orchard.*

Enter JULIET.

Jul. The clock struck nine when I did send the nurse;
In half an hour she promised to return.
Perchance she cannot meet him. That's not so.
O, she is lame! Love's heralds should be thoughts,
Which ten times faster glide than the sun's beams
Driving back shadows over louring hills.
Therefore do nimble-pinion'd doves draw Love,
And therefore hath the wind-swift Cupid wings.
Now is the sun upon the highmost hill
Of this day's journey, and from nine till twelve 10
Is three long hours; yet she is not come.
Had she affections and warm youthful blood,
She would be as swift in motion as a ball;
My words would bandy her to my sweet love,
And his to me.
But old folks, marry, feign as they were dead—
Unwieldy, slow, heavy and pale as lead.

Enter Nurse *and* PETER.

O God, she comes! O honey nurse, what news?
Hast thou met with him? Send thy man away.

223. *dog's name.* R was called the dog's letter because the sound is like a growl. 226. *sententious:* blunder for "sentences," pithy sayings.
[v] 4. *heralds:* messengers. 6. *louring:* frowning. 7. *Love:* Venus. 14. *bandy:* toss to and fro.

Nurse. Peter, stay at the gate. [*Exit Peter.*

Jul. Now, good sweet nurse—O Lord, why look'st thou sad? 21
Though news be sad, yet tell them merrily;
If good, thou shamest the music of sweet news
By playing it to me with so sour a face.

Nurse. I am aweary; give me leave awhile.
Fie, how my bones ache! What a jaunt have I had!

Jul. I would thou hadst my bones, and I thy news.
Nay, come, I pray thee, speak; good, good nurse, speak.

Nurse. Jesu, what haste! Can you not stay awhile?
Do you not see that I am out of breath? 30

Jul. How art thou out of breath when thou hast breath
To say to me that thou art out of breath?
The excuse that thou dost make in this delay
Is longer than the tale thou dost excuse.
Is thy news good or bad? Answer to that.
Say either, and I'll stay the circumstance.
Let me be satisfied; is 't good or bad? 37

Nurse. Well, you have made a simple choice; you know not how to choose a man. Romeo! No, not he; though his face be better than any man's, yet his leg excels all men's; and for a hand and a foot and a body, though they be not to be talked on, yet they are past compare. He is not the flower of courtesy, but, I'll warrant him, as gentle as a lamb. Go thy ways, wench; serve God. What, have you dined at home?

Jul. No, no! But all this did I know before.
What says he of our marriage? What of that?

Nurse. Lord, how my head aches! What a head have I!
It beats as it would fall in twenty pieces. 50
My back o' t' other side—O, my back, my back!
Beshrew your heart for sending me about,
To catch my death with jaunting up and down!

22. *them:* i.e., *news*, which was in Shakespeare's day either singular or plural. 25. *give me leave:* i.e., to go or rest. 29. *stay:* wait. 36. *stay the circumstance:* wait for the details. 52. *Beshrew:* ill luck to.

Jul. I' faith, I am sorry that thou art not well.
Sweet, sweet, sweet nurse, tell me, what says my love?

Nurse. Your love says, like an honest gentleman, and a courteous, and a kind, and a handsome, and, I warrant, a virtuous— Where is your mother?

Jul. Where is my mother! Why, she is within; 60
Where should she be? How oddly thou repliest!
"Your love says, like an honest gentleman,
Where is your mother?"

Nurse. O God's lady dear!
Are you so hot? Marry, come up, I trow;
Is this the poultice for my aching bones?
Henceforward do your messages yourself.

Jul. Here's such a coil! Come, what says Romeo?

Nurse. Have you got leave to go to shrift today?

Jul. I have.

Nurse. Then hie you hence to Friar Laurence' cell; 70
There stays a husband to make you a wife.
Now comes the wanton blood up in your cheeks;
They'll be in scarlet straight at any news.
Hie you to church; I must another way,
To fetch a ladder, by the which your love
Must climb a bird's nest soon when it is dark.
I am the drudge and toil in your delight,
But you shall bear the burden soon at night.
Go; I'll to dinner; hie you to the cell. 79

Jul. Hie to high fortune! Honest nurse, farewell. [*Exeunt.*

SCENE VI. FRIAR LAURENCE'S *cell.*

Enter FRIAR LAURENCE *and* ROMEO.

Fri. L. So smile the heavens upon this holy act
That after hours with sorrow chide us not!

Rom. Amen, amen! But come what sorrow can,

63. *God's lady dear:* the Virgin Mary. 64. *hot:* (a) impatient, (b) ardent. 67. *coil:* fuss. 70. *hie:* hasten. 78. *soon at night:* towards evening.

It cannot countervail the exchange of joy
That one short minute gives me in her sight.
Do thou but close our hands with holy words,
Then love-devouring Death do what he dare;
It is enough I may but call her mine.
Fri. L. These violent delights have violent ends,
And in their triumph die, like fire and powder, 10
Which, as they kiss, consume. The sweetest honey
Is loathsome in his own deliciousness
And in the taste confounds the appetite.
Therefore love moderately; long love doth so;
Too swift arrives as tardy as too slow.

Enter JULIET.

Here comes the lady. O, so light a foot
Will ne'er wear out the everlasting flint.
A lover may bestride the gossamer
That idles in the wanton summer air,
And yet not fall; so light is vanity. 20
Jul. Good even to my ghostly confessor.
Fri. L. Romeo shall thank thee, daughter, for us both.
Jul. As much to him, else is his thanks too much.
Rom. Ah, Juliet, if the measure of thy joy
Be heap'd like mine, and that thy skill be more
To blazon it, then sweeten with thy breath
This neighbour air, and let rich music's tongue
Unfold the imagined happiness that both
Receive in either by this dear encounter.
Jul. Conceit, more rich in matter than in words, 30
Brags of his substance, not of ornament.
They are but beggars that can count their worth;
But my true love is grown to such excess
I cannot sum up sum of half my wealth.

[vi] 4. *countervail:* equal. 12. *his:* its. 13. *confounds:* destroys. 18. *gossamer:* spider's thread. 20. *vanity:* earthly joys. 26. *blazon:* describe fitly. 30. *Conceit:* imagination.

Fri. L. Come, come with me, and we will make short work;
For, by your leaves, you shall not stay alone
Till Holy Church incorporate two in one. [*Exeunt.*

ACT III

SCENE I. *A public place.*

Enter MERCUTIO, BENVOLIO, Page, *and* Servants.

Ben. I pray thee, good Mercutio, let's retire.
The day is hot, the Capulets abroad,
And, if we meet, we shall not scape a brawl,
For now, these hot days, is the mad blood stirring.

Mer. Thou art like one of those fellows that when he enters the confines of a tavern claps me his sword upon the table and says, "God send me no need of thee!" and by the operation of the second cup draws it on the drawer, when indeed there is no need. 10

Ben. Am I like such a fellow?

Mer. Come, come, thou art as hot a Jack in thy mood as any in Italy, and as soon moved to be moody, and as soon moody to be moved.

Ben. And what to? 15

Mer. Nay, an there were two such, we should have none shortly, for one would kill the other. Thou! Why, thou wilt quarrel with a man that hath a hair more, or a hair less, in his beard than thou hast. Thou wilt quarrel with a man for cracking nuts, having no other reason but because thou hast hazel eyes. What eye but such an eye would spy out such a quarrel? Thy head is as full of quarrels as an egg is full of meat, and yet thy head hath been beaten as addle as an egg for quarrelling. Thou hast quarrelled with a man for coughing in the street, because he hath wakened thy dog that hath lain asleep in the sun. Didst thou not fall out with a tailor for wearing his new doublet before Easter? With another, for tying his new shoes with old riband? And yet thou wilt tutor me from quarrelling! 33

[III. i] 8. *operation:* effect. 9. *drawer:* waiter. 13. *mood:* anger. 16. *an:* if.

Ben. An I were so apt to quarrel as thou art, any man should buy the fee-simple of my life for an hour and a quarter.

Mer. The fee-simple! O simple!

Enter TYBALT *and others.*

Ben. By my head, here come the Capulets.

Mer. By my heel, I care not.

Tyb. Follow me close, for I will speak to them. 40
Gentlemen, good den; a word with one of you.

Mer. And but one word with one of us? Couple it with something; make it a word and a blow.

Tyb. You shall find me apt enough to that, sir, an you will give me occasion.

Mer. Could you not take some occasion without giving?

Tyb. Mercutio, thou consort'st with Romeo— 48

Mer. Consort! What, dost thou make us minstrels? An thou make minstrels of us, look to hear nothing but discords. Here's my fiddlestick; here's that shall make you dance. 'Zounds, consort!

Ben. We talk here in the public haunt of men.
Either withdraw unto some private place,
And reason coldly of your grievances,
Or else depart. Here all eyes gaze on us.

Mer. Men's eyes were made to look, and let them gaze.
I will not budge for no man's pleasure, I.

Enter ROMEO.

Tyb. Well, peace be with you, sir. Here comes my man.

Mer. But I'll be hang'd, sir, if he wear your livery. 60
Marry, go before to field; he'll be your follower.
Your worship in that sense may call him "man."

Tyb. Romeo, the love I bear thee can afford
No better term than this—thou art a villain.

35. *fee-simple:* absolute possession. 49. *Consort:* (a) associate with, (b) company of minstrels. 55. *coldly:* calmly. 61. *field:* battle.

Rom. Tybalt, the reason that I have to love thee
Doth much excuse the appertaining rage
To such a greeting. Villain am I none;
Therefore farewell; I see thou know'st me not.
Tyb. Boy, this shall not excuse the injuries
That thou hast done me; therefore turn and draw. 70
Rom. I do protest I never injured thee,
But love thee better than thou canst devise
Till thou shalt know the reason of my love.
And so, good Capulet—which name I tender
As dearly as my own—be satisfied.
Mer. O calm, dishonourable, vile submission!
Alla stoccata carries it away. [*Draws.*
Tybalt, you rat-catcher, will you walk?
Tyb. What wouldst thou have with me? 79
Mer. Good King of Cats, nothing but one of your nine lives; that I mean to make bold withal, and, as you shall use me hereafter, dry-beat the rest of the eight. Will you pluck your sword out of his pilcher by the ears? Make haste, lest mine be about your ears ere it be out.
Tyb. I am for you. [*Drawing.*
Rom. Gentle Mercutio, put thy rapier up.
Mer. Come, sir, your *passado.* [*They fight.*
Rom. Draw, Benvolio; beat down their weapons.
Gentlemen, for shame, forbear this outrage! 90
Tybalt, Mercutio, the prince expressly hath
Forbidden bandying in Verona streets.
Hold, Tybalt! Good Mercutio!
[*Tybalt under Romeo's arm stabs Mercutio, and flies with his followers.*
Mer. I am hurt.

66. *appertaining rage:* rage appertaining to. 69. *Boy.* Used contemptuously. *injuries:* insults. 72. *devise:* think. 74. *tender:* hold. 77. *Alla stoccata:* literally, "with a rapier thrust," i.e., the blusterer, Tybalt. 78. *rat-catcher.* See II, iv, 19. 82. *dry-beat:* beat severely without drawing blood. 84. *his pilcher:* its scabbard. 88. *passado:* forward thrust with the rapier. 92. *bandying:* fighting.

A plague o' both your houses! I am sped.
Is he gone and hath nothing?

Ben. What, art thou hurt?

Mer. Ay, ay, a scratch, a scratch; marry, 'tis enough.
Where is my page? Go, villain, fetch a surgeon. [*Exit Page.*

Rom. Courage, man; the hurt cannot be much. 98

Mer. No, 'tis not so deep as a well, nor so wide as a church-door; but 'tis enough; 'twill serve. Ask for me tomorrow, and you shall find me a grave man. I am peppered, I warrant, for this world. A plague o' both your houses! 'Zounds, a dog, a rat, a mouse, a cat, to scratch a man to death! A braggart, a rogue, a villain, that fights by the book of arithmetic! Why the devil came you between us? I was hurt under your arm.

Rom. I thought all for the best.

Mer. Help me into some house, Benvolio, 110
Or I shall faint. A plague o' both your houses!
They have made worms' meat of me. I have it,
And soundly too. Your houses—

[*Exit, led by Benvolio and servants.*

Rom. This gentleman, the prince's near ally,
My very friend, hath got his mortal hurt
In my behalf—my reputation stain'd
With Tybalt's slander—Tybalt, that an hour
Hath been my kinsman! O sweet Juliet,
Thy beauty hath made me effeminate
And in my temper soften'd valour's steel! 120

Re-enter BENVOLIO.

Ben. O Romeo, Romeo, brave Mercutio's dead!
That gallant spirit hath aspired the clouds,
Which too untimely here did scorn the earth.

Rom. This day's black fate on more days doth depend;
This but begins the woe others must end.

94. *sped:* killed. 106. *book of arithmetic.* See II, iv, 21–3. 114. *ally:* relative. 115. *very:* true. 120. *temper:* temperament (with pun on the "tempering" of steel). 122. *aspired:* reached. 124. *on . . . depend:* hangs over future days.

Re-enter TYBALT.

Ben. Here comes the furious Tybalt back again.
Rom. Alive, in triumph, and Mercutio slain!
Away to heaven, respective lenity,
And fire-eyed fury be my conduct now!
Now, Tybalt, take the "villain" back again 130
That late thou gavest me; for Mercutio's soul
Is but a little way above our heads,
Staying for thine to keep him company.
Either thou or I, or both, must go with him.
Tyb. Thou, wretched boy, that didst consort him here,
Shalt with him hence.
Rom. This shall determine that.
[*They fight; Tybalt falls.*
Ben. Romeo, away, be gone!
The citizens are up, and Tybalt slain.
Stand not amazed; the prince will doom thee death,
If thou art taken. Hence, be gone, away! 140
Rom. O, I am Fortune's fool!
Ben. Why dost thou stay?
[*Exit Romeo.*

Enter Citizens.

First Cit. Which way ran he that kill'd Mercutio?
Tybalt, that murderer, which way ran he?
Ben. There lies that Tybalt.
First Cit. Up, sir, go with me.
I charge thee, in the prince's name, obey.

Enter PRINCE. *attended;* MONTAGUE, CAPULET, *their* Wives, *and others.*

Prin. Where are the vile beginners of this fray?
Ben. O noble prince, I can discover all
The unlucky manage of this fatal brawl.

128. *respective lenity:* considerate gentleness. 129. *conduct:* guide. 133. *Staying:* waiting. 139. *amazed:* bewildered. *doom:* condemn to. 141. *fool:* dupe, victim. 147. *discover:* reveal. 148. *manage:* course.

There lies the man, slain by young Romeo,
That slew thy kinsman, brave Mercutio. 150
La. Cap. Tybalt, my cousin! O my brother's child!
O prince! O husband! O, the blood is spilt
Of my dear kinsman! Prince, as thou art true,
For blood of ours shed blood of Montague.
O cousin, cousin!
Prin. Benvolio, who began this bloody fray?
Ben. Tybalt, here slain, whom Romeo's hand did slay.
Romeo, that spoke him fair, bade him bethink
How nice the quarrel was, and urged withal
Your high displeasure, all this—uttered 160
With gentle breath, calm look, knees humbly bow'd—
Could not take truce with the unruly spleen
Of Tybalt, deaf to peace, but that he tilts
With piercing steel at bold Mercutio's breast,
Who, all as hot, turns deadly point to point,
And, with a martial scorn, with one hand beats
Cold death aside, and with the other sends
It back to Tybalt, whose dexterity
Retorts it. Romeo he cries aloud,
"Hold, friends! Friends, part!" and, swifter than his tongue,
His agile arm beats down their fatal points, 171
And 'twixt them rushes; underneath whose arm
An envious thrust from Tybalt hit the life
Of stout Mercutio, and then Tybalt fled,
But by and by comes back to Romeo,
Who had but newly entertain'd revenge,
And to 't they go like lightning, for, ere I
Could draw to part them, was stout Tybalt slain,
And, as he fell, did Romeo turn and fly.
This is the truth, or let Benvolio die. 180

158. *spoke him fair:* addressed him courteously. 159. *nice:* trivial. *urged:* stressed. 162. *take truce:* make peace. *unruly spleen:* uncontrolled rage. 163. *tilts:* thrusts. 169. *Retorts:* throws back. 171. *agile.* So Q_1; Q_2 and F_1 read *aged.* 173. *envious:* malicious. 176. *entertain'd:* taken into mind.

La. Cap. He is a kinsman to the Montague;
Affection makes him false; he speaks not true.
Some twenty of them fought in this black strife,
And all those twenty could but kill one life.
I beg for justice, which thou, prince, must give.
Romeo slew Tybalt; Romeo must not live.
Prin. Romeo slew him; he slew Mercutio.
Who now the price of his dear blood doth owe?
Mon. Not Romeo, prince; he was Mercutio's friend;
His fault concludes but what the law should end, 190
The life of Tybalt.
Prin. And for that offense
Immediately we do exile him hence.
I have an interest in your hate's proceeding;
My blood for your rude brawls doth lie ableeding.
But I'll amerce you with so strong a fine
That you shall all repent the loss of mine.
I will be deaf to pleading and excuses;
Nor tears nor prayers shall purchase out abuses.
Therefore use none. Let Romeo hence in haste,
Else, when he's found, that hour is his last. 200
Bear hence this body, and attend our will.
Mercy but murders, pardoning those that kill. [*Exeunt.*

SCENE II. CAPULET'S *orchard.*

Enter JULIET.

Jul. Gallop apace, you fiery-footed steeds,
Towards Phœbus' lodging! Such a waggoner
As Phaëthon would whip you to the west,
And bring in cloudy night immediately.
Spread thy close curtain, love-performing night,

195. *amerce:* punish. 198. *purchase out abuses:* obtain remission of punishment for offenses. 201. *attend:* await.

[ii] 3. *Phaëthon:* son of Helios, the sun god. Allowed for one day to drive the chariot of the sun, he could not restrain the steeds and would have destroyed the world, had not Zeus struck him down with a thunderbolt.

That runaways' eyes may wink, and Romeo
Leap to these arms, untalk'd of and unseen.
Lovers can see to do their amorous rites
By their own beauties; or, if love be blind,
It best agrees with night. Come, civil night, 10
Thou sober-suited matron, all in black,
And learn me how to lose a winning match,
Play'd for a pair of stainless maidenhoods.
Hood my unmann'd blood, bating in my cheeks,
With thy black mantle till strange love grow bold,
Think true love acted simple modesty.
Come, night; come, Romeo; come, thou day in night;
For thou wilt lie upon the wings of night
Whiter than new snow on a raven's back.
Come, gentle night; come, loving, black-brow'd night; 20
Give me my Romeo; and, when he shall die,
Take him and cut him out in little stars,
And he will make the face of heaven so fine
That all the world will be in love with night
And pay no worship to the garish sun.
O, I have bought the mansion of a love,
But not possess'd it, and, though I am sold,
Not yet enjoy'd. So tedious is this day
As is the night before some festival
To an impatient child that hath new robes 30
And may not wear them. O, here comes my nurse,

6. *That . . . wink.* These words have never been satisfactorily explained, although many emendations and interpretations have been suggested. (See Furness, *Variorum*, pp. 367–95.) *Wink* means "close." Q_2 reads *runnawayes*, F_1 *run-awayes*, both either singular or plural. If singular, the *runaway* may be the sun, the day, the night; if plural, the *runaways* may be the lovers themselves, or else vagabonds, whose eyes, Juliet hopes, will not be able to see Romeo. 10. *civil:* orderly. 12. *learn:* teach. 14. *Hood* (cover), *unmann'd* (untamed), *bating* (fluttering) are terms of falconry. 15. *strange:* shy.

Enter Nurse, *with cords.*

And she brings news; and every tongue that speaks
But Romeo's name speaks heavenly eloquence.
Now, nurse, what news? What hast thou there? The cords
That Romeo bid thee fetch?

Nurse. Ay, ay, the cords.

[*Throws them down.*

Jul. Ay me! What news? Why dost thou wring thy hands?

Nurse. Ah, well-a-day! He's dead, he's dead, he's dead!
We are undone, lady, we are undone!
Alack the day! He's gone, he's kill'd, he's dead!

Jul. Can heaven be so envious?

Nurse. Romeo can, 40
Though heaven cannot. O Romeo, Romeo!
Who ever would have thought it? Romeo!

Jul. What devil art thou that dost torment me thus?
This torture should be roar'd in dismal hell.
Hath Romeo slain himself? Say thou but "ay,"
And that bare vowel "I" shall poison more
Than the death-darting eye of cockatrice.
I am not I, if there be such an ay;
Or those eyes shut, that make thee answer "ay."
If he be slain, say "ay"; or if not, "no." 50
Brief sounds determine of my weal or woe.

Nurse. I saw the wound; I saw it with mine eyes—
God save the mark!—here on his manly breast.
A piteous corse, a bloody piteous corse!
Pale, pale as ashes, all bedaub'd in blood,
All in gore-blood. I swounded at the sight.

Jul. O, break, my heart! Poor bankrupt, break at once!
To prison, eyes; ne'er look on liberty!
Vile earth, to earth resign; end motion here;
And thou and Romeo press one heavy bier! 60

Nurse. O Tybalt, Tybalt, the best friend I had!

40. *envious:* malicious. 47. *cockatrice:* fabulous serpent with deadly glance. 56. *gore-blood:* clotted blood. *swounded:* swooned. 59. *Vile earth:* body. *resign:* yield.

O courteous Tybalt! Honest gentleman!
That ever I should live to see thee dead!
Jul. What storm is this that blows so contrary?
Is Romeo slaughter'd, and is Tybalt dead?
My dear-loved cousin, and my dearer lord?
Then, dreadful trumpet, sound the general doom!
For who is living, if those two are gone?
Nurse. Tybalt is gone, and Romeo banished;
Romeo that kill'd him, he is banished. 70
Jul. O God! Did Romeo's hand shed Tybalt's blood?
Nurse. It did, it did; alas the day, it did!
Jul. O serpent heart, hid with a flowering face!
Did ever dragon keep so fair a cave?
Beautiful tyrant! Fiend angelical!
Dove-feather'd raven! Wolvish-ravening lamb!
Despised substance of divinest show!
Just opposite to what thou justly seem'st,
A damned saint, an honourable villain!
O Nature, what hadst thou to do in hell, 80
When thou didst bower the spirit of a fiend
In mortal paradise of such sweet flesh?
Was ever book containing such vile matter
So fairly bound? O, that deceit should dwell
In such a gorgeous palace!
Nurse. There's no trust,
No faith, no honesty in men; all perjured,
All forsworn, all naught, all dissemblers.
Ah, where's my man? Give me some *aqua vitæ;*
These griefs, these woes, these sorrows make me old.
Shame come to Romeo!
Jul. Blister'd be thy tongue 90
For such a wish! He was not born to shame.
Upon his brow shame is ashamed to sit,
For 'tis a throne where honour may be crown'd
Sole monarch of the universal earth.
O, what a beast was I to chide at him!

77. *show:* appearance. 81. *bower:* enclose. 87. *naught:* wicked.

Nurse. Will you speak well of him that kill'd your cousin?
Jul. Shall I speak ill of him that is my husband?
Ah, poor my lord, what tongue shall smooth thy name,
When I, thy three-hours wife, have mangled it?
But wherefore, villain, didst thou kill my cousin? 100
That villain cousin would have kill'd my husband.
Back, foolish tears, back to your native spring!
Your tributary drops belong to woe,
Which you, mistaking, offer up to joy.
My husband lives, that Tybalt would have slain;
And Tybalt's dead, that would have slain my husband.
All this is comfort; wherefore weep I then?
Some word there was, worser than Tybalt's death,
That murder'd me. I would forget it fain;
But, O, it presses to my memory, 110
Like damned guilty deeds to sinners' minds!
"Tybalt is dead, and Romeo—banished."
That "banished," that one word "banished,"
Hath slain ten thousand Tybalts. Tybalt's death
Was woe enough, if it had ended there;
Or, if sour woe delights in fellowship
And needly will be rank'd with other griefs,
Why follow'd not, when she said, "Tybalt's dead,"
Thy father, or thy mother, nay, or both,
Which modern lamentation might have moved? 120
But with a rearward following Tybalt's death,
"Romeo is banished"—to speak that word,
Is father, mother, Tybalt, Romeo, Juliet,
All slain, all dead. "Romeo is banished"—
There is no end, no limit, measure, bound,
In that word's death; no words can that woe sound.
Where is my father and my mother, nurse?
Nurse. Weeping and wailing over Tybalt's corse.
Will you go to them? I will bring you thither.

98. *smooth:* flatter, praise. 114. *Hath . . . Tybalts:* i.e., is worse than the loss of ten thousand Tybalts. 117. *needly:* of necessity. 120. *modern:* ordinary. 121. *rearward:* (a) rearguard, (b) final word.

Jul. Wash they his wounds with tears. Mine shall be spent,
When theirs are dry, for Romeo's banishment. 131
Take up those cords. Poor ropes, you are beguiled,
Both you and I, for Romeo is exiled.
He made you for a highway to my bed,
But I, a maid, die maiden-widowed.
Come, cords; come, nurse; I'll to my wedding-bed;
And death, not Romeo, take my maidenhead!

Nurse. Hie to your chamber. I'll find Romeo
To comfort you. I wot well where he is.
Hark ye, your Romeo will be here at night. 140
I'll to him; he is hid at Laurence' cell.

Jul. O, find him! Give this ring to my true knight,
And bid him come to take his last farewell. [*Exeunt.*

SCENE III. FRIAR LAURENCE'S *cell.*

Enter FRIAR LAURENCE.

Fri. L. Romeo, come forth; come forth, thou fearful man.
Affliction is enamour'd of thy parts,
And thou art wedded to calamity.

Enter ROMEO.

Rom. Father, what news? What is the prince's doom?
What sorrow craves acquaintance at my hand
That I yet know not?

Fri. L. Too familiar
Is my dear son with such sour company.
I bring thee tidings of the prince's doom.

Rom. What less than doomsday is the prince's doom?

Fri. L. A gentler judgment vanish'd from his lips— 10
Not body's death, but body's banishment.

139. *wot:* know.
[iii] 1. *fearful:* full of fear. 10. *vanish'd:* issued (a very odd use of the word). Dowden suggests that *banishment* in the next line misled the printer, and that Shakespeare may have written *A gentler judgment—"banish'd"—from his lips.*

Rom. Ha, banishment! Be merciful; say "death,"
For exile hath more terror in his look,
Much more than death. Do not say "banishment."
Fri. L. Hence from Verona art thou banished.
Be patient, for the world is broad and wide.
Rom. There is no world without Verona walls
But purgatory, torture, hell itself.
Hence-banished is banish'd from the world,
And world's exile is death. Then "banished" 20
Is death mis-term'd. Calling death "banishment,"
Thou cutt'st my head off with a golden axe,
And smilest upon the stroke that murders me.
Fri. L. O deadly sin! O rude unthankfulness!
Thy fault our law calls death; but the kind prince,
Taking thy part, hath rush'd aside the law,
And turn'd that black word death to banishment.
This is dear mercy, and thou seest it not.
Rom. 'Tis torture, and not mercy. Heaven is here,
Where Juliet lives; and every cat and dog 30
And little mouse, every unworthy thing,
Live here in heaven and may look on her;
But Romeo may not. More validity,
More honourable state, more courtship lives
In carrion-flies than Romeo. They may seize
On the white wonder of dear Juliet's hand
And steal immortal blessing from her lips,
Who, even in pure and vestal modesty,
Still blush, as thinking their own kisses sin;
But Romeo may not; he is banished. 40
This may flies do, but I from this must fly.
They are free men, but I am banished,
And say'st thou yet that exile is not death?
Hadst thou no poison mix'd, no sharp-ground knife,
No sudden mean of death, though ne'er so mean,

26. *rush'd:* brushed. 28. *dear:* unusual, loving. 33. *validity:* value. 34. *courtship:* (a) courtliness, (b) wooing. 45. *mean:* instrument, means.

But "banished" to kill me—"banished"?
O friar, the damned use that word in hell;
Howlings attend it. How hast thou the heart,
Being a divine, a ghostly confessor,
A sin-absolver, and my friend profess'd, 50
To mangle me with that word "banished"?

Fri. L. Thou fond mad man, hear me but speak a word.

Rom. O, thou wilt speak again of banishment.

Fri. L. I'll give thee armour to keep off that word;
Adversity's sweet milk, philosophy,
To comfort thee, though thou art banished.

Rom. Yet "banished"? Hang up philosophy!
Unless philosophy can make a Juliet,
Displant a town, reverse a prince's doom,
It helps not, it prevails not. Talk no more. 60

Fri. L. O, then I see that madmen have no ears.

Rom. How should they, when that wise men have no eyes?

Fri. L. Let me dispute with thee of thy estate.

Rom. Thou canst not speak of that thou dost not feel.
Wert thou as young as I, Juliet thy love,
An hour but married, Tybalt murdered,
Doting like me, and like me banished,
Then mightst thou speak, then mightst thou tear thy hair,
And fall upon the ground, as I do now, 69
Taking the measure of an unmade grave. [*Knocking within.*

Fri. L. Arise; one knocks. Good Romeo, hide thyself.

Rom. Not I; unless the breath of heart-sick groans,
Mist-like, infold me from the search of eyes. [*Knocking.*

Fri. L. Hark, how they knock! Who's there? Romeo, arise;
Thou wilt be taken.—Stay awhile!—Stand up; [*Knocking.*
Run to my study.—By and by!—God's will,
What simpleness is this!—I come, I come! [*Knocking.*
Who knocks so hard? Whence come you? What's your will?

49. *ghostly:* spiritual. 52. *fond:* foolish. 59. *Displant:* uproot, transplant. 60. *prevails:* avails. 63. *dispute:* discuss. *estate:* condition of affairs. 77. *simpleness:* folly.

Nurse. [*Within*] Let me come in, and you shall know my errand.
I come from Lady Juliet.

Fri. L. Welcome, then. 80

Enter Nurse.

Nurse. O holy friar, O, tell me, holy friar,
Where is my lady's lord, where's Romeo?

Fri. L. There on the ground, with his own tears made drunk.

Nurse. O, he is even in my mistress' case,
Just in her case! O woeful sympathy!
Piteous predicament! Even so lies she,
Blubbering and weeping, weeping and blubbering.
Stand up, stand up. Stand, an you be a man.
For Juliet's sake, for her sake, rise and stand!
Why should you fall into so deep an O? 90

Rom. Nurse! [*He rises.*

Nurse. Ah sir! Ah sir! Well, death's the end of all.

Rom. Spakest thou of Juliet? How is it with her?
Doth she not think me an old murderer,
Now I have stain'd the childhood of our joy
With blood removed but little from her own?
Where is she? And how doth she? And what says
My conceal'd lady to our cancell'd love?

Nurse. O, she says nothing, sir, but weeps and weeps,
And now falls on her bed, and then starts up, 100
And Tybalt calls, and then on Romeo cries,
And then down falls again.

Rom. As if that name,
Shot from the deadly level of a gun,
Did murder her, as that name's cursed hand
Murder'd her kinsman. O, tell me, friar, tell me,
In what vile part of this anatomy

87. *Blubbering:* weeping hard. The word had no ridiculous connotation in Shakespeare's day. 88. *an:* if. 90. *an O:* a lament. 94. *old:* practiced, confirmed. 98. *conceal'd lady:* i.e., the fact that she is Romeo's lady is concealed. 103. *level:* aim.

Doth my name lodge? Tell me, that I may sack
The hateful mansion. [*Drawing his dagger.*

Fri. L. Hold thy desperate hand!
Art thou a man? Thy form cries out thou art;
Thy tears are womanish; thy wild acts denote 110
The unreasonable fury of a beast.
Unseemly woman in a seeming man!
Or ill-beseeming beast in seeming both!
Thou hast amazed me! By my holy order,
I thought thy disposition better temper'd.
Hast thou slain Tybalt? Wilt thou slay thyself,
And slay thy lady too that lives in thee,
By doing damned hate upon thyself?
Why rail'st thou on thy birth, the heaven, and earth?
Since birth and heaven and earth, all three do meet 120
In thee at once, which thou at once wouldst lose.
Fie, fie, thou shamest thy shape, thy love, thy wit,
Which, like a usurer, abound'st in all,
And usest none in that true use indeed
Which should bedeck thy shape, thy love, thy wit.
Thy noble shape is but a form of wax,
Digressing from the valour of a man;
Thy dear love sworn but hollow perjury,
Killing that love which thou hast vow'd to cherish;
Thy wit, that ornament to shape and love, 130
Mis-shapen in the conduct of them both,
Like powder in a skilless soldier's flask,
Is set a-fire by thine own ignorance,
And thou dismember'd with thine own defense.
What, rouse thee, man! Thy Juliet is alive,
For whose dear sake thou wast but lately dead;
There art thou happy. Tybalt would kill thee,
But thou slew'st Tybalt; there art thou happy too.
The law that threaten'd death becomes thy friend

107. *sack:* destroy. 113. *ill-beseeming:* ill-appearing. 123. *Which:* who. 125. *shape:* form, appearance. 127. *Digressing:* deviating. 130. *wit:* intelligence. *shape:* physical body. 134. *defense:* weapons.

And turns it to exile; there art thou happy. 140
A pack of blessings lights upon thy back;
Happiness courts thee in her best array;
But, like a misbehaved and sullen wench,
Thou pout'st upon thy fortune and thy love.
Take heed, take heed, for such die miserable.
Go get thee to thy love, as was decreed;
Ascend her chamber; hence and comfort her.
But look thou stay not till the watch be set,
For then thou canst not pass to Mantua,
Where thou shalt live till we can find a time 150
To blaze your marriage, reconcile your friends,
Beg pardon of the prince, and call thee back
With twenty hundred thousand times more joy
Than thou went'st forth in lamentation.
Go before, nurse. Commend me to thy lady,
And bid her hasten all the house to bed,
Which heavy sorrow makes them apt unto.
Romeo is coming.

Nurse. O Lord, I could have stay'd here all the night
To hear good counsel. O, what learning is! 160
My lord, I'll tell my lady you will come.

Rom. Do so, and bid my sweet prepare to chide.

Nurse. Here, sir, a ring she bid me give you, sir.
Hie you, make haste, for it grows very late. [*Exit.*

Rom. How well my comfort is revived by this!

Fri. L. Go hence; good night; and here stands all your state:
Either be gone before the watch be set,
Or by the break of day disguised from hence.
Sojourn in Mantua. I'll find out your man,
And he shall signify from time to time 170
Every good hap to you that chances here.
Give me thy hand. 'Tis late. Farewell; good night.

148. *watch:* guard. 151. *blaze:* announce. 157. *apt unto:* ready for. 162. S. D. in Q_1 read *Nurse offers to go and turns again.* 166. *here . . . state:* here is the state of your affairs. 171. *hap:* chance occurrence. *chances:* happens.

Rom. But that a joy past joy calls out on me,
It were a grief so brief to part with thee.
Farewell. [*Exeunt.*

SCENE IV. *A room in* CAPULET'S *house.*

Enter CAPULET, LADY CAPULET, *and* PARIS.

Cap. Things have fall'n out, sir, so unluckily
That we have had no time to move our daughter.
Look you, she loved her kinsman Tybalt dearly,
And so did I. Well, we were born to die.
'Tis very late; she'll not come down tonight;
I promise you, but for your company,
I would have been abed an hour ago.
Par. These times of woe afford no time to woo.
Madam, good night. Commend me to your daughter.
La. Cap. I will, and know her mind early tomorrow; 10
Tonight she is mew'd up to her heaviness.
Cap. Sir Paris, I will make a desperate tender
Of my child's love. I think she will be ruled
In all respects by me; nay, more, I doubt it not.
Wife, go you to her ere you go to bed;
Acquaint her here of my son Paris' love,
And bid her—mark you me—on Wednesday next—
But, soft! What day is this?
Par. Monday, my lord.
Cap. Monday! Ha, ha! Well, Wednesday is too soon;
O' Thursday let it be—o' Thursday, tell her, 20
She shall be married to this noble earl.
Will you be ready? Do you like this haste?
We'll keep no great ado—a friend or two;
For, hark you, Tybalt being slain so late,
It may be thought we held him carelessly,
Being our kinsman, if we revel much.
Therefore we'll have some half a dozen friends,
And there an end. But what say you to Thursday?

[iv] 2. *move:* urge. 11. *mew'd:* shut. *heaviness:* grief. 12. *desperate tender:* bold offer. 23. *keep:* make.

Par. My lord, I would that Thursday were tomorrow.
Cap. Well, get you gone; o' Thursday be it, then. 30
Go you to Juliet ere you go to bed;
Prepare her, wife, against this wedding-day.
Farewell, my lord.—Light to my chamber, ho!
Afore me, it is so very, very late
That we may call it early by and by.
Good night. [*Exeunt.*

SCENE V. CAPULET'S *orchard.*

Enter ROMEO *and* JULIET *above, at the window.*

Jul. Wilt thou be gone? It is not yet near day.
It was the nightingale, and not the lark,
That pierced the fearful hollow of thine ear.
Nightly she sings on yond pomegranate-tree.
Believe me, love, it was the nightingale.
Rom. It was the lark, the herald of the morn,
No nightingale. Look, love, what envious streaks
Do lace the severing clouds in yonder east.
Night's candles are burnt out, and jocund day
Stands tiptoe on the misty mountain tops. 10
I must be gone and live, or stay and die.
Jul. Yond light is not daylight, I know it, I;
It is some meteor that the sun exhales
To be to thee this night a torchbearer
And light thee on thy way to Mantua.
Therefore stay yet; thou need'st not to be gone.
Rom. Let me be ta'en; let me be put to death;
I am content, so thou wilt have it so.
I'll say yon grey is not the morning's eye,
'Tis but the pale reflex of Cynthia's brow; 20

32. *against:* before, in expectation of. 34. *Afore me:* God before me. [v] S. D. *Capulet's orchard.* In the modern theatre this scene is often played in Juliet's bedroom. 1–35. A conventional *aubade*, or dawn-song. 8. *lace:* streak. 13. *exhales:* draws forth, i.e., the sun draws up vapors and thereby produces meteors. 20. *reflex:* reflected light. *Cynthia's:* the moon's.

Nor that is not the lark, whose notes do beat
The vaulty heaven so high above our heads.
I have more care to stay than will to go.
Come, death, and welcome! Juliet wills it so.
How is't, my soul? Let's talk; it is not day.
Jul. It is; it is! Hie hence, be gone, away!
It is the lark that sings so out of tune,
Straining harsh discords and unpleasing sharps.
Some say the lark makes sweet division;
This doth not so, for she divideth us. 30
Some say the lark and loathed toad changed eyes;
O, now I would they had changed voices too,
Since arm from arm that voice doth us affray,
Hunting thee hence with hunt's-up to the day!
O, now be gone! More light and light it grows.
Rom. More light and light—more dark and dark our woes!

Enter Nurse.

Nurse. Madam!
Jul. Nurse?
Nurse. Your lady mother is coming to your chamber.
The day is broke; be wary; look about. [*Exit.*
Jul. Then, window, let day in, and let life out. 41
Rom. Farewell, farewell! One kiss, and I'll descend.
[*He goes down.*
Jul. Art thou gone so? Love, lord, ay, husband, friend!
I must hear from thee every day in the hour,
For in a minute there are many days.
O, by this count I shall be much in years
Ere I again behold my Romeo!
Rom. Farewell!
I will omit no opportunity
That may convey my greetings, love, to thee. 50
Jul. O, think'st thou we shall ever meet again?

23. *care:* desire. 28. *Straining:* forcing out. *sharps:* shrill high notes. 29. *division:* rapid melodic passage. 33. *affray:* frighten. 34. *hunt's-up:* morning song to awaken huntsmen.

Rom. I doubt it not; and all these woes shall serve
For sweet discourses in our time to come.
Jul. O God, I have an ill-divining soul!
Methinks I see thee, now thou art below,
As one dead in the bottom of a tomb.
Either my eyesight fails, or thou look'st pale.
Rom. And trust me, love, in my eye so do you.
Dry sorrow drinks our blood. Adieu, adieu! [*Exit.*
Jul. O Fortune, Fortune! All men call thee fickle. 60
If thou art fickle, what dost thou with him
That is renown'd for faith? Be fickle, Fortune;
For then I hope thou wilt not keep him long,
But send him back.
La. Cap. [*Within*] Ho, daughter! Are you up?
Jul. Who is 't that calls? Is it my lady mother?
Is she not down so late, or up so early?
What unaccustom'd cause procures her hither?

Enter LADY CAPULET.

La. Cap. Why, how now, Juliet?
Jul. Madam, I am not well.
La. Cap. Evermore weeping for your cousin's death? 70
What, wilt thou wash him from his grave with tears?
An if thou couldst, thou couldst not make him live;
Therefore, have done. Some grief shows much of love,
But much of grief shows still some want of wit.
Jul. Yet let me weep for such a feeling loss.
La. Cap. So shall you feel the loss, but not the friend
Which you weep for.
Jul. Feeling so the loss,
I cannot choose but ever weep the friend.
La. Cap. Well, girl, thou weep'st not so much for his death
As that the villain lives which slaughter'd him. 80
Jul. What villain, madam?

54. *ill-divining:* foreboding evil. 59. *Dry:* thirsty. Sorrow was thought to dry up the blood and make lovers pale. 68. *procures:* brings. 75. *feeling:* heartfelt.

La. Cap. That same villain, Romeo.
Jul. [*Aside*] Villain and he be many miles asunder.—
God pardon him! I do, with all my heart;
And yet no man like he doth grieve my heart.
La. Cap. That is because the traitor murderer lives.
Jul. Ay, madam, from the reach of these my hands.
Would none but I might venge my cousin's death!
La. Cap. We will have vengeance for it, fear thou not.
Then weep no more. I'll send to one in Mantua,
Where that same banish'd runagate doth live, 90
Shall give him such an unaccustom'd dram
That he shall soon keep Tybalt company;
And then, I hope, thou wilt be satisfied.
Jul. Indeed, I never shall be satisfied
With Romeo, till I behold him—dead—
Is my poor heart so for a kinsman vex'd.
Madam, if you could find out but a man
To bear a poison, I would temper it,
That Romeo should, upon receipt thereof,
Soon sleep in quiet. O, how my heart abhors 100
To hear him named, and cannot come to him
To wreak the love I bore my cousin
Upon his body that hath slaughter'd him!
La. Cap. Find thou the means, and I'll find such a man.
But now I'll tell thee joyful tidings, girl.
Jul. And joy comes well in such a needy time.
What are they, I beseech your ladyship?
La. Cap. Well, well, thou hast a careful father, child;
One who, to put thee from thy heaviness,
Hath sorted out a sudden day of joy 110
That thou expect'st not nor I look'd not for.
Jul. Madam, in happy time, what day is that?

84. *like:* so much as. 90. *runagate:* vagabond. 91. *dram:* dose of poison. 95. *dead.* Juliet, of course, intends her mother to understand this word as part of the preceding clause. Note the careful ambiguity of her statements. 98. *temper:* (a) mix, (b) mollify. 109. *heaviness:* grief. 110. *sorted out:* selected. 112. *in happy time:* opportunely.

La. Cap. Marry, my child, early next Thursday morn,
The gallant, young, and noble gentleman,
The county Paris, at Saint Peter's Church,
Shall happily make thee there a joyful bride.

Jul. Now, by Saint Peter's Church and Peter too,
He shall not make me there a joyful bride!
I wonder at this haste, that I must wed
Ere he that should be husband comes to woo. 120
I pray you tell my lord and father, madam,
I will not marry yet; and, when I do, I swear
It shall be Romeo, whom you know I hate,
Rather than Paris. These are news indeed!

La. Cap. Here comes your father; tell him so yourself,
And see how he will take it at your hands.

Enter CAPULET *and* Nurse.

Cap. When the sun sets, the air doth drizzle dew,
But for the sunset of my brother's son
It rains downright.
How now? A conduit, girl? What, still in tears? 130
Evermore showering? In one little body
Thou counterfeit'st a bark, a sea, a wind;
For still thy eyes, which I may call the sea,
Do ebb and flow with tears; the bark thy body is,
Sailing in this salt flood; the winds, thy sighs,
Who, raging with thy tears, and they with them,
Without a sudden calm, will overset
Thy tempest-tossed body. How now, wife?
Have you deliver'd to her our decree? 139

La. Cap. Ay, sir; but she will none; she gives you thanks.
I would the fool were married to her grave!

Cap. Soft! Take me with you, take me with you, wife.

130. *conduit:* fountain, often in the form of a human figure. 132. *Thou counterfeit'st:* you represent, imitate. 137. *Without . . . calm:* unless a calm comes. *overset:* upset, overwhelm. 140. *will none:* i.e., rejects it. 142. *Take me with you:* let me understand you.

How? Will she none? Doth she not give us thanks?
Is she not proud? Doth she not count her blest,
Unworthy as she is, that we have wrought
So worthy a gentleman to be her bridegroom?
Jul. Not proud you have, but thankful that you have.
Proud can I never be of what I hate.
But thankful even for hate that is meant love.
Cap. How now, how now, chop-logic? What is this? 150
"Proud," and "I thank you," and "I thank you not";
And yet "not proud." Mistress minion, you,
Thank me no thankings, nor proud me no prouds,
But fettle your fine joints 'gainst Thursday next,
To go with Paris to Saint Peter's Church,
Or I will drag thee on a hurdle thither.
Out, you green-sickness carrion! Out, you baggage!
You tallow-face!
La. Cap. Fie, fie! What, are you mad?
Jul. Good father, I beseech you on my knees, [*Kneels.*
Hear me with patience but to speak a word. 160
Cap. Hang thee, young baggage! Disobedient wretch!
I tell thee what—get thee to church o' Thursday,
Or never after look me in the face.
Speak not, reply not, do not answer me!
My fingers itch. Wife, we scarce thought us blest
That God had lent us but this only child;
But now I see this one is one too much,
And that we have a curse in having her.
Out on her, hilding!
Nurse. God in heaven bless her!
You are to blame, my lord, to rate her so. 170
Cap. And why, my Lady Wisdom? Hold your tongue,
Good Prudence. Smatter with your gossips, go.

145. *wrought:* arranged for. 150. *chop-logic:* sophistical arguer. 152. *minion:* saucy girl. 154. *fettle:* prepare. 156. *hurdle:* rude sledge for carrying criminals. 157. *green-sickness:* a kind of anemia. 169. *hilding:* good-for-nothing. 170. *rate:* berate, scold. 172. *Smatter:* chatter.

Nurse. I speak no treason.
Cap. O, God ye god-den.
Nurse. May not one speak?
Cap. Peace, you mumbling fool!
Utter your gravity o'er a gossip's bowl,
For here we need it not.
La. Cap. You are too hot.
Cap. God's bread! It makes me mad.
Day, night, hour, tide, time, work, play,
Alone, in company, still my care hath been
To have her match'd; and having now provided 180
A gentleman of noble parentage,
Of fair demesnes, youthful, and nobly train'd,
Stuff'd, as they say, with honourable parts,
Proportion'd as one's thought would wish a man—
And then to have a wretched puling fool,
A whining mammet, in her fortune's tender,
To answer, "I'll not wed; I cannot love;
I am too young; I pray you, pardon me."
But, an you will not wed, I'll pardon you!
Graze where you will, you shall not house with me. 190
Look to 't; think on 't; I do not use to jest.
Thursday is near; lay hand on heart; advise.
An you be mine, I'll give you to my friend;
An you be not, hang, beg, starve, die in the streets,
For, by my soul, I'll ne'er acknowledge thee,
Nor what is mine shall never do thee good.
Trust to 't. Bethink you. I'll not be forsworn. [*Exit.*
Jul. Is there no pity sitting in the clouds
That sees into the bottom of my grief?
O sweet my mother, cast me not away! 200

173. *God ye god-den:* God give you a good evening. 175. *gravity:* wise words. *gossip's bowl:* a christening cup of wine or ale. Gossips were originally sponsors or invited guests at a baptism. 182. *demesnes:* estates. 186. *mammet:* doll. *in . . . tender:* when good fortune offers itself. 189. *an:* if. 191. *do not use:* am not accustomed. 192. *advise:* consider. 197. *I'll . . . forsworn:* I'll not break my word.

Delay this marriage for a month, a week;
Or, if you do not, make the bridal bed
In that dim monument where Tybalt lies.

La. Cap. Talk not to me, for I'll not speak a word.
Do as thou wilt, for I have done with thee. [*Exit.*

Jul. O God!—O nurse, how shall this be prevented?
My husband is on earth, my faith in heaven;
How shall that faith return again to earth,
Unless that husband send it me from heaven
By leaving earth? Comfort me, counsel me. 210
Alack, alack, that heaven should practice stratagems
Upon so soft a subject as myself!
What say'st thou? Hast thou not a word of joy?
Some comfort, nurse.

Nurse. Faith, here it is.
Romeo is banish'd; and all the world to nothing
That he dares ne'er come back to challenge you;
Or, if he do, it needs must be by stealth.
Then, since the case so stands as now it doth,
I think it best you married with the county.
O, he's a lovely gentleman! 220
Romeo's a dishclout to him. An eagle, madam,
Hath not so green, so quick, so fair an eye
As Paris hath. Beshrew my very heart,
I think you are happy in this second match,
For it excels your first; or, if it did not,
Your first is dead; or 'twere as good he were,
As living here and you no use of him.

Jul. Speakest thou from thy heart?

Nurse. And from my soul too;
Or else beshrew them both.

Jul. Amen!

Nurse. What?

Jul. Well, thou hast comforted me marvellous much. 230
Go in and tell my lady I am gone,

207. *faith:* pledged word. 211. *practice stratagems:* plot deeds of violence. 216. *challenge:* accuse, claim. 223. *Beshrew:* curse.

Having displeased my father, to Laurence' cell,
To make confession and to be absolved.

Nurse. Marry, I will; and this is wisely done. [*Exit.*

Jul. Ancient damnation! O most wicked fiend!

[*She looks after Nurse.*

Is it more sin to wish me thus forsworn,
Or to dispraise my lord with that same tongue
Which she hath praised him with above compare
So many thousand times? Go, counsellor!
Thou and my bosom henceforth shall be twain. 240
I'll to the friar to know his remedy;
If all else fail, myself have power to die. [*Exit.*

ACT IV

SCENE I. FRIAR LAURENCE'S *cell.*

Enter FRIAR LAURENCE *and* PARIS.

Fri. L. On Thursday, sir? The time is very short.

Par. My father Capulet will have it so;
And I am nothing slow to slack his haste.

Fri. L. You say you do not know the lady's mind.
Uneven is the course; I like it not.

Par. Immoderately she weeps for Tybalt's death,
And therefore have I little talk'd of love,
For Venus smiles not in a house of tears.
Now, sir, her father counts it dangerous
That she doth give her sorrow so much sway, 10
And in his wisdom hastes our marriage
To stop the inundation of her tears,
Which, too much minded by herself alone,
May be put from her by society.
Now do you know the reason of this haste.

[IV. i] 3. *I . . . haste:* "his haste shall not be abated by my slowness" (Johnson). 5. *Uneven:* not straightforward. *course:* method of procedure. 14. *society:* companionship.

Fri. L. [*Aside*] I would I knew not why it should be slow'd—
Look, sir, here comes the lady towards my cell.

Enter JULIET.

Par. Happily met, my lady and my wife!
Jul. That may be, sir, when I may be a wife.
Par. That may be must be, love, on Thursday next. 20
Jul. What must be shall be.
Fri. L. That's a certain text.
Par. Come you to make confession to this father?
Jul. To answer that, I should confess to you.
Par. Do not deny to him that you love me.
Jul. I will confess to you that I love him.
Par. So will ye, I am sure, that you love me.
Jul. If I do so, it will be of more price
Being spoke behind your back than to your face.
Par. Poor soul, thy face is much abused with tears.
Jul. The tears have got small victory by that, 30
For it was bad enough before their spite.
Par. Thou wrong'st it, more than tears, with that report.
Jul. That is no slander, sir, which is a truth;
And what I spake, I spake it to my face.
Par. Thy face is mine, and thou hast slander'd it.
Jul. It may be so, for it is not mine own.
Are you at leisure, holy father, now,
Or shall I come to you at evening mass?
Fri. L. My leisure serves me, pensive daughter, now.
My lord, we must entreat the time alone. 40
Par. God shield I should disturb devotion!
Juliet, on Thursday early will I rouse ye;
Till then, adieu; and keep this holy kiss. [*Exit.*
Jul. O, shut the door! And when thou hast done so,
Come weep with me—past hope, past cure, past help!
Fri. L. Ah, Juliet, I already know thy grief;
It strains me past the compass of my wits.

27. *price:* worth, estimation. 29. *abused:* disfigured. 41. *shield:* forbid. 47. *compass:* limits, reach.

I hear thou must, and nothing may prorogue it,
On Thursday next be married to this county.
Jul. Tell me not, friar, that thou hear'st of this, 50
Unless thou tell me how I may prevent it.
If, in thy wisdom, thou canst give no help,
Do thou but call my resolution wise,
And with this knife I'll help it presently.
God join'd my heart and Romeo's, thou our hands;
And ere this hand, by thee to Romeo seal'd,
Shall be the label to another deed,
Or my true heart with treacherous revolt
Turn to another, this shall slay them both.
Therefore, out of thy long-experienced time, 60
Give me some present counsel, or, behold,
'Twixt my extremes and me this bloody knife
Shall play the umpire, arbitrating that
Which the commission of thy years and art
Could to no issue of true honour bring.
Be not so long to speak; I long to die,
If what thou speak'st speak not of remedy.
Fri. L. Hold, daughter! I do spy a kind of hope,
Which craves as desperate an execution
As that is desperate which we would prevent. 70
If, rather than to marry county Paris,
Thou hast the strength of will to slay thyself,
Then is it likely thou wilt undertake
A thing like death to chide away this shame,
That copest with Death himself to scape from it;
And, if thou darest, I'll give thee remedy.
Jul. O, bid me leap, rather than marry Paris,
From off the battlements of yonder tower,
Or walk in thievish ways, or bid me lurk

48. *prorogue:* postpone. 54. *presently:* at once. 57. *label:* strip of parchment for appending the seal to a deed. 62. *extremes:* extreme suffering. 64. *commission:* warrant. 65. *issue:* point at which decision becomes possible (legal term). 74. *chide:* drive. 75. *copest:* meets. 79. *thievish ways:* roads frequented by robbers.

Where serpents are; chain me with roaring bears; 80
Or shut me nightly in a charnel-house,
O'er-cover'd quite with dead men's rattling bones,
With reeky shanks and yellow chapless skulls;
Or bid me go into a new-made grave
And hide me with a dead man in his shroud—
Things that, to hear them told, have made me tremble—
And I will do it without fear or doubt,
To live an unstain'd wife to my sweet love.

Fri. L. Hold, then. Go home, be merry, give consent
To marry Paris. Wednesday is tomorrow. 90
Tomorrow night look that thou lie alone;
Let not thy nurse lie with thee in thy chamber.
Take thou this vial, being then in bed,
And this distilled liquor drink thou off;
When presently through all thy veins shall run
A cold and drowsy humour, for no pulse
Shall keep his native progress, but surcease;
No warmth, no breath, shall testify thou livest;
The roses in thy lips and cheeks shall fade
To paly ashes, thy eyes' windows fall, 100
Like death, when he shuts up the day of life;
Each part, deprived of supple government,
Shall, stiff and stark and cold, appear like death;
And in this borrow'd likeness of shrunk death
Thou shalt continue two and forty hours,
And then awake as from a pleasant sleep.
Now, when the bridegroom in the morning comes
To rouse thee from thy bed, there art thou dead.
Then, as the manner of our country is,
In thy best robes uncover'd on the bier 110
Thou shalt be borne to that same ancient vault
Where all the kindred of the Capulets lie.

81. *charnel-house:* vault in which dead bodies or bones are kept. 83. *reeky:* ill-smelling. *chapless:* lacking the lower jaw. 96. *drowsy humour:* sleep-inducing fluid. 97. *native progress:* natural motion. *surcease:* cease.

In the mean time, against thou shalt awake,
Shall Romeo by my letters know our drift,
And hither shall he come; and he and I
Will watch thy waking, and that very night
Shall Romeo bear thee hence to Mantua.
And this shall free thee from this present shame,
If no inconstant toy nor womanish fear
Abate thy valour in the acting it. 120

Jul. Give me, give me! O, tell not me of fear!

Fri. L. Hold! Get you gone! Be strong and prosperous
In this resolve. I'll send a friar with speed
To Mantua, with my letters to thy lord.

Jul. Love give me strength! And strength shall help afford.
Farewell, dear father! [*Exeunt.*

SCENE II. *Hall in* CAPULET'S *house.*

Enter CAPULET, LADY CAPULET, Nurse, *and* Servingmen.

Cap. So many guests invite as here are writ.
[*Exit First Servant.*
Sirrah, go hire me twenty cunning cooks.

Sec. Serv. You shall have none ill, sir; for I'll try if they can lick their fingers.

Cap. How canst thou try them so?

Sec. Serv. Marry, sir, 'tis an ill cook that cannot lick his own fingers. Therefore he that cannot lick his fingers goes not with me.

Cap. Go, be gone. [*Exit Second Servant.*
We shall be much unfurnish'd for this time. 10
What, is my daughter gone to Friar Laurence?

Nurse. Ay, forsooth.

Cap. Well, he may chance to do some good on her.
A peevish self-will'd harlotry it is.

Nurse. See where she comes from shrift with merry look.

113. *against:* before. 114. *drift:* plot. 119. *toy:* whim. 122. *Hold:* here, take it!

[ii] 2. *cunning:* skillful. 10. *unfurnish'd:* unprepared. 14. *peevish:* silly, perverse. *harlotry:* silly girl.

Enter JULIET.

Cap. How now, my headstrong? Where have you been gadding?
Jul. Where I have learn'd me to repent the sin
Of disobedient opposition
To you and your behests, and am enjoin'd
By holy Laurence to fall prostrate here, [*Kneels.*
And beg your pardon. Pardon, I beseech you! 21
Henceforward I am ever ruled by you.
Cap. Send for the county; go tell him of this.
I'll have this knot knit up tomorrow morning.
Jul. I met the youthful lord at Laurence' cell
And gave him what becomed love I might,
Not stepping o'er the bounds of modesty.
Cap. Why, I am glad on 't. This is well; stand up.
[*Juliet rises.*
This is as 't should be. Let me see the county;
Ay, marry, go, I say, and fetch him hither. 30
Now, afore God, this reverend holy friar,
All our whole city is much bound to him.
Jul. Nurse, will you go with me into my closet,
To help me sort such needful ornaments
As you think fit to furnish me tomorrow?
La. Cap. No, not till Thursday. There is time enough.
Cap. Go, nurse, go with her. We'll to church tomorrow.
[*Exeunt Juliet and Nurse.*
La. Cap. We shall be short in our provision.
'Tis now near night.
Cap. Tush, I will stir about,
And all things shall be well, I warrant thee, wife. 40
Go thou to Juliet; help to deck up her.
I'll not to bed tonight; let me alone;
I'll play the housewife for this once. What, ho!
They are all forth. Well, I will walk myself

26. *becomed:* becoming, befitting. 32. *bound:* indebted. 33. *closet:* private room. 34. *sort:* select. 35. *furnish:* adorn.

To county Paris, to prepare him up
Against tomorrow. My heart is wondrous light
Since this same wayward girl is so reclaim'd. [*Exeunt.*

Scene iii. Juliet's *bedroom.*

Enter Juliet *and* Nurse.

Jul. Ay, those attires are best; but, gentle nurse,
I pray thee leave me to myself tonight,
For I have need of many orisons
To move the heavens to smile upon my state,
Which, well thou know'st, is cross and full of sin.

Enter Lady Capulet.

La. Cap. What, are you busy, ho? Need you my help?
Jul. No, madam; we have cull'd such necessaries
As are behoveful for our state tomorrow.
So please you, let me now be left alone,
And let the nurse this night sit up with you, 10
For I am sure you have your hands full all
In this so sudden business.
La. Cap. Good night.
Get thee to bed, and rest; for thou hast need.
[*Exeunt Lady Capulet and Nurse.*
Jul. Farewell! God knows when we shall meet again.
I have a faint cold fear thrills through my veins
That almost freezes up the heat of life.
I'll call them back again to comfort me.
Nurse!—What should she do here?
My dismal scene I needs must act alone.
Come, vial. 20
What if this mixture do not work at all?
Shall I be married then tomorrow morning?
No, no! This shall forbid it. Lie thou there.
[*Laying down her dagger.*

[iii] 3. *orisons:* prayers. 5. *cross:* perverse. 8. *behoveful:* necessary. *state:* dignity.

What if it be a poison which the friar
Subtly hath minister'd to have me dead,
Lest in this marriage he should be dishonour'd,
Because he married me before to Romeo?
I fear it is; and yet, methinks, it should not,
For he hath still been tried a holy man.
I will not entertain so bad a thought. 30
How if, when I am laid into the tomb,
I wake before the time that Romeo
Come to redeem me? There's a fearful point!
Shall I not then be stifled in the vault,
To whose foul mouth no healthsome air breathes in,
And there die strangled ere my Romeo comes?
Or, if I live, is it not very like
The horrible conceit of death and night,
Together with the terror of the place—
As in a vault, an ancient receptacle, 40
Where, for these many hundred years, the bones
Of all my buried ancestors are pack'd;
Where bloody Tybalt, yet but green in earth,
Lies festering in his shroud; where, as they say,
At some hours in the night spirits resort—
Alack, alack, is it not like that I,
So early waking—what with loathsome smells,
And shrieks like mandrakes' torn out of the earth,
That living mortals, hearing them, run mad—
O, if I wake, shall I not be distraught, 50
Environed with all these hideous fears,
And madly play with my forefathers' joints,
And pluck the mangled Tybalt from his shroud,
And, in this rage, with some great kinsman's bone

25. *minister'd:* administered. 29. *still:* always. *tried:* proved. 33. *redeem:* save, recover. 38. *conceit:* imagination. 40. *As:* namely. 43. *green in earth:* recently buried. 48. *mandrakes'*. The mandragora or mandrake is a plant that was thought to grow on criminals' graves. Its forked root was believed to resemble the human figure, and when pulled from the ground to utter shrieks that killed or drove mad anyone who heard them. 50. *distraught:* insane.

As with a club dash out my desperate brains?
O, look! Methinks I see my cousin's ghost
Seeking out Romeo, that did spit his body
Upon a rapier's point. Stay, Tybalt, stay!
Romeo, I come! This do I drink to thee.

[*She falls upon her bed, within the curtains.*

SCENE IV. *Hall in* CAPULET'S *house.*

Enter LADY CAPULET *and* Nurse.

La. Cap. Hold, take these keys, and fetch more spices, nurse.

Nurse. They call for dates and quinces in the pastry.

Enter CAPULET.

Cap. Come, stir, stir, stir! The second cock hath crow'd;
The curfew-bell hath rung; 'tis three o'clock.
Look to the baked meats, good Angelica;
Spare not for cost.

Nurse. Go, you cot-quean, go,
Get you to bed! Faith, you'll be sick tomorrow
For this night's watching.

Cap. No, not a whit. What, I have watch'd ere now
All night for lesser cause, and ne'er been sick. 10

La. Cap. Ay, you have been a mouse-hunt in your time;
But I will watch you from such watching now.

[*Exeunt Lady Capulet and Nurse.*

Cap. A jealous-hood, a jealous-hood!

Enter three or four Servingmen, *with spits, logs, and baskets.*

Now, fellow,
What's there?

First Serv. Things for the cook, sir; but I know not what.

57. *spit:* impale, as on a spit.
[iv] 2. *pastry:* place where pastry is made. 5. *baked meats:* meat pies, pastry. 6. *cot-quean:* housewife. 8. *watching:* waking. 11. *mouse-hunt:* woman-hunter. 13. *jealous-hood:* jealousy, or, perhaps, "jealous hooded spy."

Cap. Make haste, make haste. [*Exit First Servingman.*]
Sirrah, fetch drier logs;
Call Peter; he will show thee where they are.

Sec. Serv. I have a head, sir, that will find out logs,
And never trouble Peter for the matter. [*Exit.*

Cap. Mass, and well said; a merry whoreson, ha!
Thou shalt be logger-head. Good faith, 'tis day. 20
The county will be here with music straight,
For so he said he would. I hear him near. [*Music within.*
Nurse! Wife! What, ho! What, nurse, I say!

Re-enter Nurse.

Go waken Juliet; go and trim her up;
I'll go and chat with Paris. Hie, make haste,
Make haste! The bridegroom he is come already.
Make haste, I say. [*Exeunt.*

Scene v. Juliet's *bedroom.*

Enter Nurse.

Nurse. Mistress! What, mistress! Juliet! Fast, I warrant her,
she—
Why, lamb! Why, lady! Fie, you slug-a-bed!
Why, love, I say! Madam! Sweetheart! Why, bride!
What, not a word? You take your pennyworths now!
Sleep for a week; for the next night, I warrant,
The county Paris hath set up his rest
That you shall rest but little. God forgive me!
Marry, and amen, how sound is she asleep!
I must needs wake her. Madam, madam, madam!
Ay, let the county take you in your bed; 10
He'll fright you up, i' faith. Will it not be? [*Opens the curtains.*
What, dress'd, and in your clothes, and down again!

19. *Mass:* by the Mass. *whoreson:* rascal. 20. *logger-head:* blockhead. 21. *straight:* straightway.

[v] 1. *Fast:* fast asleep. 4. *pennyworths:* money's worth. 6. *set up his rest:* resolved, determined (a phrase from the game of primero).

I must needs wake you. Lady, lady, lady!
Alas, alas! Help, help! My lady's dead!
O well-a-day that ever I was born!
Some *aqua vitæ*, ho! My lord! My lady!

Enter LADY CAPULET.

La. Cap. What noise is here?
Nurse. O lamentable day!
La. Cap. What is the matter?
Nurse. Look, look! O heavy day!
La. Cap. O me, O me! My child, my only life,
Revive, look up, or I will die with thee! 20
Help, help! Call help.

Enter CAPULET.

Cap. For shame, bring Juliet forth; her lord is come.
Nurse. She's dead, deceased; she's dead; alack the day!
La. Cap. Alack the day, she's dead, she's dead, she's dead!
Cap. Ha! Let me see her. Out, alas! She's cold;
Her blood is settled, and her joints are stiff;
Life and these lips have long been separated.
Death lies on her like an untimely frost
Upon the sweetest flower of all the field.
Nurse. O lamentable day!
La. Cap. O woeful time! 30
Cap. Death, that hath ta'en her hence to make me wail,
Ties up my tongue and will not let me speak.

Enter FRIAR LAURENCE *and* PARIS, *with* Musicians.

Fri. L. Come, is the bride ready to go to church?
Cap. Ready to go, but never to return.
O son, the night before thy wedding-day
Hath Death lain with thy wife. See, there she lies,
Flower as she was, deflowered by him.
Death is my son-in-law, Death is my heir;
My daughter he hath wedded. I will die
And leave him all. Life, living, all is Death's. 40

26. *settled:* congealed, stagnant. 40. *living:* possessions.

Par. Have I thought long to see this morning's face,
And doth it give me such a sight as this?

La. Cap. Accursed, unhappy, wretched, hateful day!
Most miserable hour that e'er time saw
In lasting labour of his pilgrimage!
But one, poor one, one poor and loving child,
But one thing to rejoice and solace in,
And cruel Death hath catch'd it from my sight!

Nurse. O woe! O woeful, woeful, woeful day!
Most lamentable day, most woeful day 50
That ever, ever, I did yet behold!
O day! O day! O day! O hateful day!
Never was seen so black a day as this.
O woeful day! O woeful day!

Par. Beguiled, divorced, wronged, spited, slain!
Most detestable Death, by thee beguiled,
By cruel, cruel thee quite overthrown!
O love! O life! Not life, but love in death!

Cap. Despised, distressed, hated, martyr'd, kill'd!
Uncomfortable time, why camest thou now 60
To murder, murder our solemnity?
O child! O child! My soul, and not my child!
Dead art thou! Alack! My child is dead,
And with my child my joys are buried.

Fri. L. Peace, ho, for shame! Confusion's cure lives not
In these confusions. Heaven and yourself
Had part in this fair maid; now heaven hath all,
And all the better is it for the maid.
Your part in her you could not keep from death,
But heaven keeps his part in eternal life. 70
The most you sought was her promotion,
For 'twas your heaven she should be advanced;
And weep ye now, seeing she is advanced
Above the clouds, as high as heaven itself?

41. *thought long:* longed. 60. *Uncomfortable:* joyless. 61. *solemnity:* festivity. 65. *Confusion's:* ruin's. 66. *confusions:* disorders. 73. *advanced:* raised.

O, in this love, you love your child so ill
That you run mad, seeing that she is well.
She's not well married that lives married long,
But she's best married that dies married young.
Dry up your tears, and stick your rosemary
On this fair corse; and, as the custom is, 80
In all her best array bear her to church;
For though fond nature bids us all lament,
Yet nature's tears are reason's merriment.

Cap. All things that we ordained festival,
Turn from their office to black funeral—
Our instruments to melancholy bells,
Our wedding cheer to a sad burial feast,
Our solemn hymns to sullen dirges change,
Our bridal flowers serve for a buried corse,
And all things change them to the contrary. 90

Fri. L. Sir, go you in; and, madam, go with him;
And go, Sir Paris; everyone prepare
To follow this fair corse unto her grave.
The heavens do lour upon you for some ill;
Move them no more by crossing their high will.

[*Exeunt Capulet, Lady Capulet, Paris, and Friar.*

First Mus. Faith, we may put up our pipes and be gone.

Nurse. Honest good fellows, ah, put up, put up,
For well you know this is a pitiful case. [*Exit.*

First Mus. Ay, by my troth, the case may be amended. 101

Enter PETER.

Peter. Musicians, O, musicians, *Heart's ease, Heart's ease!* O, an you will have me live, play *Heart's ease.*

First Mus. Why *Heart's ease?*

79. *rosemary:* emblem of immortality and enduring love. 83. *nature's . . . merriment:* natural grief, if excessive, is unreasonable. 85. *office:* function. 100. *case:* situation. 101. *case.* He refers to the cover for his instrument. *amended:* bettered. S. D. *Enter Peter.* Q1-2 read *Enter Will Kemp.* He was the most famous clown and dancer of his day. 102, 107. Peter mentions two popular songs.

Peter. O, musicians, because my heart itself plays *My heart is full of woe.* O, play me some merry dump to comfort me.

First Mus. Not a dump we. 'Tis no time to play now. 110

Peter. You will not, then?

First Mus. No.

Peter. I will then give it you soundly.

First Mus. What will you give us?

Peter. No money, on my faith, but the gleek. I will give you the minstrel.

First Mus. Then will I give you the serving-creature.

Peter. Then will I lay the serving-creature's dagger on your pate. I will carry no crotchets; I'll *re* you, I'll *fa* you. Do you note me? 121

First Mus. An you *re* us and *fa* us, you note us.

Sec. Mus. Pray you, put up your dagger, and put out your wit.

Peter. Then have at you with my wit! I will dry-beat you with an iron wit, and put up my iron dagger. Answer me like men.

"When griping grief the heart doth wound,
And doleful dumps the mind oppress,
Then music with her silver sound"— 130

Why "silver sound"? Why "music with her silver sound"? What say you, Simon Catling?

First Mus. Marry, sir, because silver hath a sweet sound.

Peter. Pretty! What say you, Hugh Rebeck?

Sec. Mus. I say "silver sound," because musicians sound for silver.

Peter. Pretty too! What say you, James Soundpost?

Third Mus. Faith, I know not what to say. 140

108. *dump:* melody or song (usually mournful). 115. *gleek:* scoff. 115–16. *the gleek . . . minstrel:* I shall call you minstrel, i.e., a gleeman or gleekman. The word *minstrel* had apparently a contemptuous connotation. 120. *carry:* endure. *crotchets:* (a) whims, (b) eighth-notes. 121. *note:* observe. 124. *put out:* (a) extinguish, (b) exercise. 128–30. Lines from a song in *The Paradise of Dainty Devices* (1576). 132. *Catling:* small lute-string of catgut. 135. *Rebeck:* three-stringed fiddle. 139. *Soundpost:* peg supporting the body of a stringed instrument.

Peter. O, I cry you mercy; you are the singer. I will say for you. It is "music with her silver sound" because musicians have no gold for sounding.

"Then music with her silver sound
With speedy help doth lend redress." [*Exit.*

First Mus. What a pestilent knave is this same!

Sec. Mus. Hang him, Jack! Come, we'll in here, tarry for the mourners, and stay dinner. [*Exeunt.*

ACT V

SCENE I. *Mantua. A street.*

Enter ROMEO.

Rom. If I may trust the flattering truth of sleep,
My dreams presage some joyful news at hand.
My bosom's lord sits lightly in his throne;
And all this day an unaccustom'd spirit
Lifts me above the ground with cheerful thoughts.
I dreamt my lady came and found me dead—
Strange dream, that gives a dead man leave to think!—
And breathed such life with kisses in my lips
That I revived, and was an emperor.
Ah me! How sweet is love itself possess'd, 10
When but love's shadows are so rich in joy!

Enter BALTHASAR, *booted.*

News from Verona!—How now, Balthasar?
Dost thou not bring me letters from the friar?
How doth my lady? Is my father well?
How fares my Juliet? That I ask again,
For nothing can be ill if she be well.

Bal. Then she is well, and nothing can be ill.
Her body sleeps in Capels' monument,

141. *cry you mercy:* beg your pardon. 143. *sounding:* making music. 149. *Jack:* lowbred or ill-mannered fellow.

[V. i] 1. *flattering:* illusive. 3. *bosom's lord:* heart. 11. *shadows:* phantoms.

And her immortal part with angels lives.
I saw her laid low in her kindred's vault 20
And presently took post to tell it you.
O, pardon me for bringing these ill news,
Since you did leave it for my office, sir.

Rom. Is it even so? Then I defy you, stars!
Thou know'st my lodging. Get me ink and paper,
And hire post-horses. I will hence tonight.

Bal. I do beseech you, sir, have patience.
Your looks are pale and wild, and do import
Some misadventure.

Rom. Tush, thou art deceived.
Leave me, and do the thing I bid thee do. 30
Hast thou no letters to me from the friar?

Bal. No, my good lord.

Rom. No matter; get thee gone,
And hire those horses. I'll be with thee straight.

[*Exit Balthasar.*

Well, Juliet, I will lie with thee tonight.
Let's see for means. O mischief, thou art swift
To enter in the thoughts of desperate men!
I do remember an apothecary—
And hereabouts he dwells—which late I noted
In tatter'd weeds, with overwhelming brows,
Culling of simples. Meagre were his looks; 40
Sharp misery had worn him to the bones.
And in his needy shop a tortoise hung,
An alligator stuff'd, and other skins
Of ill-shaped fishes; and about his shelves
A beggarly account of empty boxes,
Green earthen pots, bladders and musty seeds,
Remnants of packthread and old cakes of roses,

21. *presently:* at once. *took post:* started with post-horses. 23. *office:* duty. 28. *import:* indicate. 39. *weeds:* clothes. *overwhelming:* overhanging. 40. *simples:* medicinal herbs. 45. *beggarly account:* poor array. 47. *cakes of roses:* cakes of perfume made from rose petals.

Were thinly scatter'd, to make up a show.
Noting this penury, to myself I said,
"An if a man did need a poison now, 50
Whose sale is present death in Mantua,
Here lives a caitiff wretch would sell it him."
O, this same thought did but forerun my need,
And this same needy man must sell it me.
As I remember, this should be the house.
Being holiday, the beggar's shop is shut.
What, ho, apothecary!

Enter Apothecary.

Ap. Who calls so loud?
Rom. Come hither, man. I see that thou art poor.
Hold, there is forty ducats. Let me have
A dram of poison, such soon-speeding gear 60
As will disperse itself through all the veins
That the life-weary taker may fall dead,
And that the trunk may be discharged of breath
As violently as hasty powder fired
Doth hurry from the fatal cannon's womb.
Ap. Such mortal drugs I have, but Mantua's law
Is death to any he that utters them.
Rom. Art thou so bare and full of wretchedness,
And fear'st to die? Famine is in thy cheeks,
Need and oppression starveth in thine eyes, 70
Contempt and beggary hangs upon thy back;
The world is not thy friend nor the world's law;
The world affords no law to make thee rich;
Then be not poor, but break it, and take this.
[*Offers him money.*
Ap. My poverty, but not my will, consents.
Rom. I pay thy poverty, and not thy will.
[*Apothecary enters shop and returns with drug.*
Ap. Put this in any liquid thing you will,

52. *caitiff:* miserable. 60. *gear:* stuff. 63. *trunk:* body. 67. *he:* man. *utters:* offers for sale.

And drink it off; and, if you had the strength
Of twenty men, it would dispatch you straight.

Rom. There is thy gold, worse poison to men's souls, 80
Doing more murders in this loathsome world,
Than these poor compounds that thou mayst not sell.
I sell thee poison; thou hast sold me none.
Farewell. Buy food, and get thyself in flesh.
Come, cordial and not poison, go with me
To Juliet's grave, for there must I use thee. [*Exeunt.*

SCENE II. *Verona.* FRIAR LAURENCE'S *cell.*

Enter FRIAR JOHN.

Fri. J. Holy Franciscan friar! Brother, ho!

Enter FRIAR LAURENCE.

Fri. L. This same should be the voice of Friar John.
Welcome from Mantua. What says Romeo?
Or, if his mind be writ, give me his letter.

Fri. J. Going to find a bare-foot brother out,
One of our order, to associate me
Here in this city visiting the sick,
And finding him, the searchers of the town,
Suspecting that we both were in a house
Where the infectious pestilence did reign, 10
Seal'd up the doors, and would not let us forth,
So that my speed to Mantua there was stay'd.

Fri. L. Who bare my letter, then, to Romeo?

Fri. J. I could not send it—here it is again—
Nor get a messenger to bring it thee,
So fearful were they of infection.

Fri. L. Unhappy fortune! By my brotherhood,
The letter was not nice but full of charge
Of dear import, and the neglecting it

79. *dispatch:* kill.
[ii] 6. *associate:* accompany. 8. *searchers:* i.e., health officers. 12. *stay'd:* stopped. 18. *nice:* trivial. *charge:* weight. 19. *Of dear import:* of great importance.

May do much danger. Friar John, go hence; 20
Get me an iron crow, and bring it straight
Unto my cell.

Fri. J. Brother, I'll go and bring it thee. [*Exit.*

Fri. L. Now must I to the monument alone.
Within this three hours will fair Juliet wake.
She will beshrew me much that Romeo
Hath had no notice of these accidents;
But I will write again to Mantua,
And keep her at my cell till Romeo come— 29
Poor living corse, closed in a dead man's tomb! [*Exit.*

SCENE III. *Verona. A churchyard; in it a tomb belonging to the Capulets.*

Enter PARIS *and his* Page *with flowers and a torch.*

Par. Give me thy torch, boy. Hence, and stand aloof.
Yet put it out, for I would not be seen.
Under yond yew-trees lay thee all along,
Holding thine ear close to the hollow ground;
So shall no foot upon the churchyard tread,
Being loose, unfirm, with digging up of graves,
But thou shalt hear it. Whistle then to me,
As signal that thou hear'st something approach.
Give me those flowers. Do as I bid thee, go.

Page. [*Aside*] I am almost afraid to stand alone 10
Here in the churchyard; yet I will adventure. [*Retires.*

Par. Sweet flower, with flowers thy bridal bed I strew—
O woe! Thy canopy is dust and stones—
Which with sweet water nightly I will dew,
Or, wanting that, with tears distill'd by moans.
The obsequies that I for thee will keep
Nightly shall be to strew thy grave and weep.
[*The Page whistles.*

The boy gives warning something doth approach

21. *iron crow:* crowbar. 26. *beshrew:* blame.
[iii] 3. *all along:* flat. 15. *wanting:* lacking.

What cursed foot wanders this way tonight
To cross my obsequies and true love's rite? 20
What, with a torch? Muffle me, night, awhile. [*Retires.*

Enter ROMEO *and* BALTHASAR, *with a torch, a mattock, and a crow of iron.*

Rom. Give me that mattock and the wrenching iron.
Hold, take this letter; early in the morning
See thou deliver it to my lord and father.
Give me the light. Upon thy life, I charge thee,
Whate'er thou hear'st or seest, stand all aloof,
And do not interrupt me in my course.
Why I descend into this bed of death,
Is partly to behold my lady's face,
But chiefly to take thence from her dead finger 30
A precious ring, a ring that I must use
In dear employment. Therefore hence, be gone.
But if thou, jealous, dost return to pry
In what I further shall intend to do,
By heaven, I will tear thee joint by joint
And strew this hungry churchyard with thy limbs.
The time and my intents are savage-wild,
More fierce and more inexorable far
Than empty tigers or the roaring sea.

Bal. I will be gone, sir, and not trouble you. 40

Rom. So shalt thou show me friendship. Take thou that. [*Gives him a purse.*
Live, and be prosperous; and farewell, good fellow.

Bal. [*Aside*] For all this same, I'll hide me hereabout.
His looks I fear, and his intents I doubt. [*Retires.*

Rom. Thou detestable maw, thou womb of death,
Gorged with the dearest morsel of the earth,
Thus I enforce thy rotten jaws to open,
And, in despite, I'll cram thee with more food! [*Opens the tomb.*

20. *cross:* thwart. 21. *Muffle:* hide. 32. *dear:* important.
33. *jealous:* suspicious. 44. *doubt:* suspect. 48. *despite:* defiance.

Par. This is that banish'd haughty Montague
That murder'd my love's cousin—with which grief, 50
It is supposed, the fair creature died—
And here is come to do some villainous shame
To the dead bodies. I will apprehend him. [*Comes forward.*
Stop thy unhallow'd toil, vile Montague!
Can vengeance be pursued further than death?
Condemned villain, I do apprehend thee.
Obey, and go with me; for thou must die.

Rom. I must indeed; and therefore came I hither.
Good gentle youth, tempt not a desperate man.
Fly hence, and leave me. Think upon these gone; 60
Let them affright thee. I beseech thee, youth,
Put not another sin upon my head
By urging me to fury. O, be gone!
By heaven, I love thee better than myself,
For I come hither arm'd against myself.
Stay not; be gone. Live, and hereafter say
A madman's mercy bade thee run away.

Par. I do defy thy conjurations
And apprehend thee for a felon here.

Rom. Wilt thou provoke me? Then have at thee, boy! 70
[*They fight.*

Page. O Lord, they fight! I will go call the watch. [*Exit.*

Par. O, I am slain! [*Falls.*] If thou be merciful,
Open the tomb; lay me with Juliet. [*Dies.*

Rom. In faith, I will. Let me peruse this face.
Mercutio's kinsman, noble county Paris!
What said my man when my betossed soul
Did not attend him as we rode? I think
He told me Paris should have married Juliet.
Said he not so? Or did I dream it so?
Or am I mad, hearing him talk of Juliet, 80
To think it was so? O, give me thy hand,
One writ with me in sour misfortune's book!

53. *apprehend:* arrest. 68. *conjurations:* earnest entreaties. 74. *peruse:* scrutinize. 76. *betossed:* troubled.

I'll bury thee in a triumphant grave.
A grave? O, no, a lantern, slaughter'd youth,
For here lies Juliet, and her beauty makes
This vault a feasting presence full of light.
Death, lie thou there, by a dead man interr'd.
[*Lays Paris in the tomb.*
How oft when men are at the point of death
Have they been merry—which their keepers call
A lightning before death. O, how may I 90
Call this a lightning? O my love! My wife!
Death, that hath suck'd the honey of thy breath,
Hath had no power yet upon thy beauty.
Thou art not conquer'd; Beauty's ensign yet
Is crimson in thy lips and in thy cheeks,
And Death's pale flag is not advanced there.
Tybalt, liest thou there in thy bloody sheet?
O, what more favour can I do to thee
Than with that hand that cut thy youth in twain
To sunder his that was thine enemy? 100
Forgive me, cousin! Ah, dear Juliet,
Why art thou yet so fair? Shall I believe
That unsubstantial Death is amorous,
And that the lean abhorred monster keeps
Thee here in dark to be his paramour?
For fear of that, I still will stay with thee,
And never from this palace of dim night
Depart again. Here, here will I remain
With worms that are thy chamber-maids. O, here
Will I set up my everlasting rest, 110
And shake the yoke of inauspicious stars
From this world-wearied flesh. Eyes, look your last!
Arms, take your last embrace! And, lips, O you
The doors of breath, seal with a righteous kiss

84. *lantern:* windowed turret. 86. *presence:* presence-chamber, great room of state. 89. *keepers:* nurses. 96. *advanced:* raised. 106. *still:* always. 110. *set . . . rest:* take my stand, with pun on *rest,* repose. (See IV, v, 6.)

A dateless bargain to engrossing Death!
Come, bitter conduct! Come, unsavoury guide!
Thou desperate pilot, now at once run on
The dashing rocks thy sea-sick weary bark!
Here's to my love! [*Drinks.*] O true apothecary!
Thy drugs are quick. Thus with a kiss I die. [*Dies.*

Enter, at the other end of the churchyard, FRIAR LAURENCE, *with lantern, crow, and spade.*

Fri. L. Saint Francis be my speed! How oft tonight 121
Have my old feet stumbled at graves! Who's there?
Bal. Here's one, a friend, and one that knows you well.
Fri. L. Bliss be upon you! Tell me, good my friend,
What torch is yond that vainly lends his light
To grubs and eyeless skulls? As I discern,
It burneth in the Capels' monument.
Bal. It doth so, holy sir; and there's my master,
One that you love.
Fri. L. Who is it?
Bal. Romeo.
Fri. L. How long hath he been there?
Bal. Full half an hour.
Fri. L. Go with me to the vault.
Bal. I dare not, sir. 131
My master knows not but I am gone hence,
And fearfully did menace me with death
If I did stay to look on his intents.
Fri. L. Stay, then; I'll go alone. Fear comes upon me;
O, much I fear some ill unlucky thing.
Bal. As I did sleep under this yew-tree here,
I dreamt my master and another fought,
And that my master slew him.
Fri. L. Romeo! [*Advances.*
Alack, alack, what blood is this which stains 140
The stony entrance of this sepulchre?
What mean these masterless and gory swords

115. *dateless:* endless. *engrossing:* all-consuming. 121. *speed:* help.

To lie discolour'd by this place of peace? [*Enters the tomb.*
Romeo! O, pale! Who else? What, Paris too?
And steep'd in blood? Ah, what an unkind hour
Is guilty of this lamentable chance!
The lady stirs. [*Juliet wakes.*

Jul. O comfortable friar! Where is my lord?
I do remember well where I should be, 149
And there I am. Where is my Romeo? [*Noise within.*

Fri. L. I hear some noise. Lady, come from that nest
Of death, contagion, and unnatural sleep.
A greater power than we can contradict
Hath thwarted our intents. Come, come away.
Thy husband in thy bosom there lies dead;
And Paris too. Come, I'll dispose of thee
Among a sisterhood of holy nuns.
Stay not to question, for the watch is coming.
Come, go, good Juliet. [*Noise again.*] I dare no longer stay.

Jul. Go, get thee hence, for I will not away. 160
[*Exit Friar Laurence.*
What's here? A cup, closed in my true love's hand?
Poison, I see, hath been his timeless end.
O churl! Drunk all, and left no friendly drop
To help me after? I will kiss thy lips;
Haply some poison yet doth hang on them
To make me die with a restorative. [*Kisses him.*
Thy lips are warm.

First Watch. [*Within*] Lead, boy. Which way?

Jul. Yea, noise? Then I'll be brief. O happy dagger! 169
[*Takes Romeo's dagger.*
This is thy sheath [*Stabs herself.*]; there rest, and let me die.
[*Falls on Romeo's body, and dies.*

Enter Watch, *with the* Page *of* PARIS.

Page. This is the place—there, where the torch doth burn.

First Watch. The ground is bloody; search about the churchyard.

148. *comfortable:* comforting. 162. *timeless:* untimely. 165. *Haply:* perhaps.

Go, some of you, whoe'er you find attach.
[*Exeunt some of the Watch.*
Pitiful sight! Here lies the county slain,
And Juliet bleeding, warm, and newly dead,
Who here hath lain these two days buried.
Go, tell the prince; run to the Capulets;
Raise up the Montagues; some others search.
We see the ground whereon these woes do lie;
But the true ground of all these piteous woes 180
We cannot without circumstance descry.

Re-enter some of the Watch, *with* BALTHASAR.

Sec. Watch. Here's Romeo's man; we found him in the churchyard.

First Watch. Hold him in safety till the prince come hither.

Re-enter others of the Watch, *with* FRIAR LAURENCE.

Third Watch. Here is a friar that trembles, sighs, and weeps.
We took this mattock and this spade from him
As he was coming from this churchyard side.

First Watch. A great suspicion! Stay the friar too.

Enter the PRINCE *and* Attendants.

Prince. What misadventure is so early up,
That calls our person from our morning's rest?

Enter CAPULET, LADY CAPULET, *and others.*

Cap. What should it be, that they so shriek abroad? 190

La. Cap. The people in the street cry "Romeo,"
Some "Juliet," and some "Paris"; and all run,
With open outcry, toward our monument.

Prince. What fear is this which startles in our ears?

First Watch. Sovereign, here lies the county Paris slain;
And Romeo dead; and Juliet, dead before,
Warm and new kill'd.

173. *attach:* arrest. 180. *ground:* cause. 181. *circumstance:* further details. 187. *Stay:* stop, arrest.

Prince. Search, seek, and know how this foul murder comes.
First Watch. Here is a friar, and slaughter'd Romeo's man,
With instruments upon them fit to open 200
These dead men's tombs.
Cap. O heavens! O wife, look how our daughter bleeds!
This dagger hath mista'en—for, lo, his house
Is empty on the back of Montague,
And is mis-sheathed in my daughter's bosom!
La. Cap. O me! This sight of death is as a bell
That warns my old age to a sepulchre.

Enter Montague *and others.*

Prince. Come, Montague; for thou art early up
To see thy son and heir more early down.
Mon. Alas, my liege, my wife is dead tonight. 210
Grief of my son's exile hath stopp'd her breath.
What further woe conspires against mine age?
Prince. Look, and thou shalt see.
Mon. O thou untaught! What manners is in this,
To press before thy father to a grave?
Prince. Seal up the mouth of outrage for a while,
Till we can clear these ambiguities
And know their spring, their head, their true descent;
And then will I be general of your woes
And lead you even to death. Meantime forbear, 220
And let mischance be slave to patience.
Bring forth the parties of suspicion.
Fri. L. I am the greatest, able to do least,
Yet most suspected, as the time and place
Doth make against me, of this direful murder;
And here I stand, both to impeach and purge
Myself condemned and myself excused.
Prince. Then say at once what thou dost know in this.
Fri. L. I will be brief, for my short date of breath

203. *his house:* its sheath. 207. *warns:* summons. 214. *untaught:* unmannerly. 216. *outrage:* violent language, fury. 222. *of:* under. 226. *impeach:* accuse, discredit. *purge:* free from suspicion.

Is not so long as is a tedious tale. 230
Romeo, there dead, was husband to that Juliet;
And she, there dead, that Romeo's faithful wife.
I married them; and their stol'n marriage-day
Was Tybalt's doomsday, whose untimely death
Banish'd the new-made bridegroom from this city,
For whom, and not for Tybalt, Juliet pined.
You, to remove that siege of grief from her,
Betroth'd and would have married her perforce
To county Paris. Then comes she to me,
And with wild looks bid me devise some mean 240
To rid her from this second marriage,
Or in my cell there would she kill herself.
Then gave I her, so tutor'd by my art,
A sleeping potion, which so took effect
As I intended, for it wrought on her
The form of death. Meantime I writ to Romeo
That he should hither come as this dire night
To help to take her from her borrow'd grave,
Being the time the potion's force should cease.
But he which bore my letter, Friar John, 250
Was stay'd by accident, and yesternight
Return'd my letter back. Then all alone
At the prefixed hour of her waking,
Came I to take her from her kindred's vault,
Meaning to keep her closely at my cell
Till I conveniently could send to Romeo.
But when I came, some minute ere the time
Of her awaking, here untimely lay
The noble Paris and true Romeo dead.
She wakes; and I entreated her come forth, 260
And bear this work of heaven with patience.
But then a noise did scare me from the tomb;
And she, too desperate, would not go with me,
But, as it seems, did violence on herself.

247. *as this:* on this. 253. *prefixed:* previously fixed. 255. *closely:* secretly.

All this I know; and to the marriage
Her nurse is privy; and, if aught in this
Miscarried by my fault, let my old life
Be sacrificed, some hour before his time,
Unto the rigour of severest law.

Prince. We still have known thee for a holy man. 270
Where's Romeo's man? What can he say in this?

Bal. I brought my master news of Juliet's death;
And then in post he came from Mantua
To this same place, to this same monument.
This letter he early bid me give his father,
And threaten'd me with death, going in the vault,
If I departed not and left him there.

Prince. Give me the letter; I will look on it.
Where is the county's page that raised the watch?
Sirrah, what made your master in this place? 280

Page. He came with flowers to strew his lady's grave;
And bid me stand aloof, and so I did.
Anon comes one with light to ope the tomb,
And by and by my master drew on him;
And then I ran away to call the watch.

Prince. This letter doth make good the friar's words,
Their course of love, the tidings of her death.
And here he writes that he did buy a poison
Of a poor 'pothecary, and therewithal
Came to this vault to die, and lie with Juliet. 290
Where be these enemies? Capulet! Montague!
See what a scourge is laid upon your hate,
That heaven finds means to kill your joys with love.
And I, for winking at your discords too,
Have lost a brace of kinsmen. All are punish'd.

Cap. O brother Montague, give me thy hand.
This is my daughter's jointure, for no more
Can I demand.

266. *privy:* secretly cognizant. 270. *still:* always. 273. *post:* haste. 280. *made:* was doing. 295. *brace of kinsmen:* i.e., Mercutio and Paris. 297. *jointure:* marriage portion.

Mon. But I can give thee more,
For I will raise her statue in pure gold,
That while Verona by that name is known, 300
There shall no figure at such rate be set
As that of true and faithful Juliet.
Cap. As rich shall Romeo's by his lady's lie,
Poor sacrifices of our enmity!
Prince. A glooming peace this morning with it brings;
The sun, for sorrow, will not show his head.
Go hence, to have more talk of these sad things;
Some shall be pardon'd, and some punished;
For never was a story of more woe 309
Than this of Juliet and her Romeo. [*Exeunt.*

301. *rate:* value. 305. *glooming:* dark.

A Midsummer Night's Dream

Introduction

Relation to Other Shakespearean Plays

Among the thirty-seven dramas in the Shakespeare canon, only three—*Love's Labor's Lost*, *A Midsummer Night's Dream*, and *The Tempest*—bear the marks of having been written originally, not for the public theatre, but for the more limited audience of the court. Two of these are youthful works, inspired, perhaps, by the court dramas of John Lyly; the third is a mature play, akin in mood and theme to the dramatic romances which Shakespeare produced toward the end of his career. Taken together, however, all three may be described as lyrical and poetic rather than strictly dramatic. In each a delicate theme of courtly romance is unraveled in a more or less mock-serious vein which would be suitable for a courtly revel. Two of them, *A Midsummer Night's Dream* and *The Tempest*, are definitely marriage plays and end in happy unions and epithalamia, while *Love's Labor's Lost*, composed of a series of courtly flirtations, has the unusual and amusing result of a series of deferred betrothals. No one of the three dramas can be referred to any recognizable source, and each has been suspected—not without reason—of some allegorical reference to contemporary events. Masquelike scenes appear in all three, and their bipartite structure of contrast between differing social groups and of minor plot burlesquing main plot, suggests the conventional pattern of the court entertainment in which the delicate masque was balanced by the grotesque antimasque. Moreover, the two early plays culminate in the same device—amateur theatricals produced before a highly critical court audience by a troupe of village yokels—while the more mature drama introduces a formal marriage-masque acted by spirits for the delectation of a betrothed pair. Finally, two of this trio of plays, *A Midsummer Night's Dream* and *The Tempest*, stand together as Shakespeare's only excursions for comic purposes into the realm of the supernatural.

For the student of Shakespeare's varying moods, *A Midsummer Night's Dream*, as the most lyrical of the comedies, bears an interesting relation to *Romeo and Juliet*, the most lyrical of the tragedies. The two plays are contrasting treatments of similar themes and present tragic and comic views of the same central idea. *Romeo and Juliet* is the young dramatist's serious, sympathetic treatment of the tragic tale of star-crossed lovers whose lives are wrecked and at the same time ennobled by their love. Its whole temper is summed up by Lysander's words in *A Midsummer Night's Dream:* "The course of true love never did run smooth," and his lament for Love, "Brief as the lightning in the collied night," (I, i, 145 ff.) is an echo of Juliet's,

> I have no joy of this contract tonight;
> It is too rash, too unadvised, too sudden,
> Too like the lightning, which doth cease to be
> Ere one can say it lightens. (II, ii, 117 ff.)

A Midsummer Night's Dream, on the other hand, interprets the theme from something like the point of view of Mercutio, to whom love is not an integral part of life, but an amusing disturbance and a kind of lunacy in the brain. In both plays, lovers are beings of strange caprices, at odds with the established order of things, rebellious against parental control, disregardful of the claims of friendship, and inconstant even to their own vows. But, whereas in the tragedy "violent delights have violent ends," in the comedy love is at once lawless and laughable, and the best commentary upon its perplexities is the Puck's,

> Lord, what fools these mortals be!

Source

Like the other court dramas, *A Midsummer Night's Dream* appears to have had no single origin, but to be instead a fantasy composed of divers elements drawn from widely separated sources. The play, however, is woven of four readily distinguishable strands, and for each of these analogues have been found: (1) the core plot of Theseus and Hippolyta; (2) the romantic perplexities of the inconstant lovers, Lysander and Demetrius, and their constant ladies, Hermia and Helena; (3) the grotesque comic plot on a lower social level of Bottom and the amateur actors; and (4) on a supernatural plane, the fairy plot of Oberon and Titania. For (1) Shakespeare seems to have drawn from both Plutarch's *Life of Theseus* and Chaucer's *Knight's Tale*. The account in the latter of the rivalry of Palamon and Arcite for the love of Emily may also have suggested (2), which is constructed, however, upon a familiar Elizabethan pattern. For the characters in (3) Shakespeare probably went no further than his own Warwickshire or London, but their play is a *reductio ad absurdum* of a popular classical story from Ovid's *Metamorphoses*, which had been retold in Chaucer's *Legend of Good Women* and elsewhere. But for (4), though numerous analogues exist, Shakespeare, without doubt, drew not only upon written literature, but also upon the folk tales and nursery legends he had learned at his mother's knee in Warwickshire. The interweaving of these various threads—classical and medieval legend, contemporary life, and Gothic folklore—is a peculiarly Shakespearean feat.

Unification of the Material

To keep to the fore the central theme of the amusing perplexities of love, the dramatist has constructed his play around a series of variations on the romantic theme of the course of true love with contrasting varieties of affection. The unstable, intense romance of the pairs of lovers is contrasted with the mature conjugal devotion of Theseus and his Amazonian princess, which has reached its stable conclusion only after injury and wooing by the sword. The irresponsible, childlike bickering and making up of the tiny fairy king and queen furnishes an amusing parallel to the romantic theme, while the ups and downs of the "rude mechanicals" and the play they present is but a mock-heroic parody of the situation which in *Romeo and Juliet* had asked tears in the performing of it. The hub around which all the action revolves is the marriage of Theseus and Hippolyta. Like an Elizabethan, if not a classical ruler, Theseus bids his Master of the Revels "stir up the Athenian youth to merriments," and prepares to celebrate his wedding "with pomp, with triumph, and with revelling." Accordingly, to grace this occasion, "hard-handed men of Athens," who "never labour'd in their minds till now," make ready their "tragical mirth." On their nuptial day, by the Duke's decree, Hermia must announce her decision to wed with Demetrius, enter a nunnery, or die as the harsh Athenian law provides for disobedient daughters. To bless the marriage of their sometime protégés, both Oberon and Titania with their trains have made the journey "from the farthest steppe of India" and in the forest around Athens, which becomes their enchanted abode, all of the amazing adventures take place.

The active instrument for interweaving these plots is Oberon's tricksy sprite, the elvish Puck, to whom things are most pleasant "that befall preposterously." It is he who fetches the little western flower—called significantly "love-in-idleness," and an emblem of capricious fancy. With it, at Oberon's behest, he anoints the eyes of Titania and those of a sleeping youth whom he identifies as the quarreling lover merely by the Athenian garments he has on. It is he, also, who seeks a suitable monster with whom Titania may be enamored and finds him all but ready made in the asinine Bottom. Yet never is he seen by any of those whom he affects, nor does his magic flower bring about anything which love-in-idleness in the human heart might not have brought about as readily.

In addition, as another unifying element, there are the recurring variations on the dream motif: the perplexities of the lovers, when they awake, seem "but as the fierce vexation of a dream"; Titania's dotage likewise appears to her as a terrible nightmare; and Bottom's adventures are to him so rare a vision that he will get Peter Quince to write a ballad about it and sing it at the latter end of the play before the Duke. And Shakespeare himself, through his Epilogue, the Puck, invites us to consider

> That you have but slumber'd here
> While these visions did appear.
> And this weak and idle theme,
> No more yielding but a dream.

Herein lies the significance of the title—the events of this May-Day Eve are but a vision of life as one might see it on Midsummer Night, when anything may happen.

The Fairies

Shakespeare was not the first to introduce fairies to the English stage. Lyly had enlivened his *Endymion* (*c.* 1588) with fairy dances and songs, and a dramatization of the romance of *Huon of Bordeaux* had presented Oberon as early at least as 1593–4, as had Greene's *Scottish History of James IV* (*c.* 1591). But it was Shakespeare who took from romance the hints which made his fairy king the friend of young lovers, and transformed the mischievous, malevolent creatures of folklore into the delightful beings they have been ever since. It was Shakespeare who diminished their size and made them, not smallish men and women, but dainty elemental beings capable of lighting torches at the glow-worm's eyes, warring with rere-mice for their leathern wings, or creeping into acorn-cups. Charles

Lamb was right when he spoke of Shakespeare as having "invented the Fairies." "There were no real fairies before Shakespeare's. What were called 'fairies' have existed ever since stories were told to wide-eyed listeners round a winter's fire. But these are not the fairies of Shakespeare, nor the fairies of today. They are the fairies of Grimm's *Mythology*. Our fairies are spirits of another sort, but unless they wear Shakespeare's livery they are counterfeit. The fairies of Folk Lore were rough and repulsive, taking their style from the hempen homespuns who invented them; they were gnomes, cobbolds, lubberlouts, and, descendants though they may have been of the Greek Nereids, they had lost every vestige of charm along their Northern route" (Furness).

Not all of Shakespeare's little beings are alike, however. There is that "merry wanderer of the night" and tricksy house-spirit, the Celtic puck or poukie, who frights the slatterns of the villagery and performs domestic labors for cleanly housemaids. But there are also orders of elves and dainty, dancing beings who attend the fairy queen.

Date and Text

All that is certainly known concerning the date of *A Midsummer Night's Dream* is that it was written some time before 1598, when it was mentioned in a list of Shakespeare's plays in Francis Meres's *Palladis Tamia*. Over the significance of possible topical allusions in the text, speculation has run riot. The hymeneal character of the drama makes it almost certain that it was written for some court wedding, and Oberon's compliment to the "fair vestal throned by the west" makes it probable that it was a wedding at which Queen Elizabeth was present. No less than six occasions have been suggested, but the wedding of William Stanley, Earl of Derby (brother of Lord Strange, for whose players Shakespeare had written), and Elizabeth de Vere in January, 1595; or that of Thomas Berkeley and Elizabeth Carey, the granddaughter of the company's patron, Lord Hunsdon, in February, 1596, seem most likely. Titania's description of the effects upon the weather of her quarrel with Oberon (II, i, 81 ff.) has been taken by some to be an allusion to the unusually bad weather referred to by the chroniclers in 1594, and the date, on that account, is put earlier still. For these and other reasons, scholars generally date the play somewhat uncertainly 1594–8, with the majority leaning to an early date. Whether it preceded or followed *Romeo and Juliet* is not known, though the parallels between the plays suggest that it came after.

A Midsummer Night's Dream was first printed in 1600, two editions bearing the date of this year. Of these, that printed for Thomas Fisher has been accepted as genuine (Q_1); the other, "printed by Iames Roberts, 1600" (Q_2), has now been proved to bear both a false imprint and a false date. It is a reprint of Q_1 known to have been the work of Thomas Pavier, who in 1619 attempted, but abandoned, a collected edition of Shakespearean quartos in which this printing of *A Midsummer Night's Dream* was to have been included. (For details consult A. W. Pollard, *Shakespeare's Fight with the Pirates*, 2d ed., 1920; or E. K. Chambers, *William Shakespeare, a Study of Facts and Problems*, 1930.) The First Folio (F_1) text in 1623 was apparently set up not from Q_1, but from a copy of Q_2 that had seen service in the playhouse as prompt-copy. The present text is based upon Q_1.

DRAMATIS PERSONÆ

THESEUS, Duke of Athens.
HIPPOLYTA, Queen of the Amazons and the betrothed of Theseus.
LYSANDER, DEMETRIUS — young men of Athens, both in love with Hermia.
HERMIA, daughter of Egeus, in love with Lysander.
HELENA, her friend, in love with Demetrius.
EGEUS, father of Hermia.
PHILOSTRATE, Master of the Revels at Theseus' court.
PETER QUINCE, a carpenter and an amateur director of theatricals.
NICK BOTTOM, a weaver, the "leading man."
FRANCIS FLUTE, a bellows-mender.
TOM SNOUT, a tinker.
ROBIN STARVELING, a tailor.
SNUG, a joiner.
OBERON, King of the Fairies.
TITANIA, Queen of the Fairies.
ROBIN GOODFELLOW, a Puck, attendant on Oberon.
PEASEBLOSSOM, COBWEB, MOTH, MUSTARDSEED — fairy attendants on Queen Titania.
Attendants upon Theseus and Hippolyta; Fairy Attendants upon Oberon and Titania.

Scene of the Action: Athens and the palace wood near it.

A Midsummer Night's Dream

ACT I

Scene i. *Athens. A hall in the palace of* Theseus.

Enter Theseus *and* Hippolyta *in conversation, attended by* Philostrate *and others.*

The. Now, fair Hippolyta, our nuptial hour
Draws on apace. Four happy days bring in
Another moon; but, O, methinks, how slow
This old moon wanes! She lingers my desires,
Like to a step-dame, or a dowager,
Long withering out a young man's revenue.
Hip. Four days will quickly steep themselves in night;
Four nights will quickly dream away the time;
And then the moon, like to a silver bow
New-bent in heaven, shall behold the night 10
Of our solemnities.
The. Go, Philostrate,
Stir up the Athenian youth to merriments,
Awake the pert and nimble spirit of mirth,
Turn Melancholy forth to funerals;
The pale companion is not for our pomp. [*Exit Philostrate.*
Hippolyta, I woo'd thee with my sword,
And won thy love, doing thee injuries;
But I will wed thee in another key,
With pomp, with triumph, and with revelling.

[I. i] 4. *lingers:* delays. 5–6. *step-dame . . . revenue:* a widow whose "dowage" or jointure is a burden upon an estate. 10. *New-bent.* Qq and Ff read *Now-bent;* the emendation is Rowe's. 11. *solemnities:* i.e., the solemnization of the wedding. 13. *pert:* lively. 15. *companion:* fellow, a term of contempt. 19. *pomp . . . triumph . . . revelling:* i.e., processions, bonfires, shows, and all sorts of public merrymaking.

Enter Egeus, *with his daughter* Hermia, *followed by* Lysander *and* Demetrius.

Ege. Happy be Theseus, our renownèd duke! 20
The. Thanks, good Egeus. What's the news with thee?
Ege. Full of vexation come I, with complaint
Against my child, my daughter Hermia.
Stand forth, Demetrius. My noble lord,
This man hath my consent to marry her.
Stand forth, Lysander. And, my gracious duke,
This man hath bewitch'd the bosom of my child.
Thou, thou, Lysander, thou hast given her rhymes
And interchanged love-tokens with my child;
Thou hast by moonlight at her window sung, 30
With faining voice, verses of faining love,
And stolen the impression of her fantasy
With bracelets of thy hair, rings, gawds, conceits,
Knacks, trifles, nosegays, sweetmeats—messengers
Of strong prevailment in unharden'd youth.
With cunning hast thou filch'd my daughter's heart,
Turn'd her obedience—which is due to me—
To stubborn harshness. And, my gracious duke,
Be it so she will not here before your Grace
Consent to marry with Demetrius, 40
I beg the ancient privilege of Athens,
As she is mine, I may dispose of her,
Which shall be either to this gentleman
Or to her death, according to our law
Immediately provided in that case.

20. *duke.* This modern title Shakespeare found in Chaucer's *Knight's Tale.* 24, 26. *Stand forth, Demetrius, Lysander.* Qq and Ff print these phrases in italics as stage directions. It is likely that the compositor found them set apart as separate half lines in the original manuscript and was led astray. 31. *faining:* probably "lovesick," "yearning"; some editors emend to *feigning.* 32. *And . . . fantasy:* and imprinted thyself by stealth upon her fancy (Chambers). 33. *gawds:* playthings. *conceits:* remembrances. 34. *Knacks:* knick-knacks. 45. *Immediately:* expressly, precisely.

The. What say you, Hermia? Be advised, fair maid,
To you your father should be as a god,
One that composed your beauties, yea, and one
To whom you are but as a form in wax,
By him imprinted, and within his power 50
To leave the figure or disfigure it.
Demetrius is a worthy gentleman.

Her. So is Lysander.

The. In himself he is;
But in this kind, wanting your father's voice,
The other must be held the worthier.

Her. I would my father look'd but with my eyes.

The. Rather your eyes must with his judgment look.

Her. I do entreat your Grace to pardon me.
I know not by what power I am made bold,
Nor how it may concern my modesty, 60
In such a presence here to plead my thoughts;
But I beseech your Grace that I may know
The worst that may befall me in this case,
If I refuse to wed Demetrius.

The. Either to die the death, or to abjure
Forever the society of men.
Therefore, fair Hermia, question your desires,
Know of your youth, examine well your blood,
Whether, if you yield not to your father's choice,
You can endure the livery of a nun, 70
For aye to be in shady cloister mew'd,
To live a barren sister all your life,
Chanting faint hymns to the cold fruitless moon.
Thrice-blessed they that master so their blood,

46. *Be advised:* consider. 54. *in this kind:* i.e., as a suitor. *wanting:* lacking. *voice:* approval. 60. *concern my modesty:* affect my reputation for modesty. 67. *question:* inquire into. 68. *Know:* ascertain. *blood:* disposition, temperament (i.e., the emotions as opposed to the reason). 70. *livery:* distinctive dress. *nun:* an anachronism, but not Shakespeare's. "A Nun of the Temple" is the description of a Delphic priestess in North's Plutarch (*Life of Theseus*). 71. *aye:* ever. *mew'd:* caged in.

To undergo such maiden pilgrimage;
But earthlier happy is the rose distill'd
Than that which withering on the virgin thorn
Grows, lives, and dies in single blessedness.
Her. So will I grow, so live, so die, my lord,
Ere I will yield my virgin patent up 80
Unto his lordship, whose unwished yoke
My soul consents not to give sovereignty.
The. Take time to pause; and, by the next new moon—
The sealing-day betwixt my love and me,
For everlasting bond of fellowship—
Upon that day either prepare to die
For disobedience to your father's will,
Or else to wed Demetrius, as he would,
Or on Diana's altar to protest
For aye austerity and single life. 90
Dem. Relent, sweet Hermia; and, Lysander, yield
Thy crazed title to my certain right.
Lys. You have her father's love, Demetrius;
Let me have Hermia's. Do you marry him.
Ege. Scornful Lysander! True, he hath my love,
And what is mine my love shall render him,
And she is mine, and all my right of her
I do estate unto Demetrius.
Lys. I am, my lord, as well derived as he,
As well possess'd; my love is more than his; 100
My fortunes every way as fairly rank'd,
If not with vantage, as Demetrius';
And, which is more than all these boasts can be,

76. *earthlier happy:* more happy on this earth. 78. *single blessedness:* divine blessing accorded a life of celibacy. In modern parlance this phrase has an altered meaning. 80. *virgin patent:* privilege of remaining unmarried, or, the liberty of my unmarried state. 81. *his lordship, whose:* the sovereignty or control of him to whose. 88. *would:* wishes. 92. *crazed:* cracked, unsound. 98. *estate:* settle or bestow. In legal phraseology the word ordinarily is used with *upon.* 99. *derived:* descended. 100. *well possess'd:* wealthy. 102. *vantage:* superiority.

I am beloved of beauteous Hermia.
Why should not I then prosecute my right?
Demetrius, I'll avouch it to his head,
Made love to Nedar's daughter, Helena,
And won her soul; and she, sweet lady, dotes,
Devoutly dotes, dotes in idolatry,
Upon this spotted and inconstant man. 110

The. I must confess that I have heard so much,
And with Demetrius thought to have spoke thereof;
But, being over-full of self-affairs,
My mind did lose it. But, Demetrius, come;
And come, Egeus; you shall go with me.
I have some private schooling for you both.
For you, fair Hermia, look you arm yourself
To fit your fancies to your father's will;
Or else the law of Athens yields you up—
Which by no means we may extenuate— 120
To death, or to a vow of single life.
Come, my Hippolyta, what cheer, my love?
Demetrius and Egeus, go along;
I must employ you in some business
Against our nuptial and confer with you
Of something nearly that concerns yourselves.

Ege. With duty and desire we follow you.

[*Exeunt all but Hermia and Lysander.*

Lys. How now, my love? Why is your cheek so pale?
How chance the roses there do fade so fast?

106. *to his head:* i.e., to his face, openly. 110. *spotted:* wicked (the opposite of *spotless*). 113. *over-full of self-affairs:* too much absorbed in my own affairs. 114 ff. Is this "a strange oversight on the part of Egeus to leave his daughter with Lysander" (Wright), "only the playwright's rather crude device to clear the stage for Lysander and Hermia" (Chambers), or a deliberate opportunity provided for the lovers by the understanding duke, himself a lover, and hence a sympathizer with lovers? 114. *lose:* let slip. 116. *schooling:* information, reprimand (Onions). 120. *extenuate:* mitigate, make light. 125. *Against:* in anticipation of, for. 126. *nearly . . . yourselves:* i.e., that concerns you closely.

Her. Belike for want of rain, which I could well 130
Beteem them from the tempest of my eyes.

Lys. Ay me, for aught that I could ever read,
Could ever hear by tale or history,
The course of true love never did run smooth;
But, either it was different in blood—

Her. O cross! Too high to be enthrall'd to low.

Lys. Or else misgraffed in respect of years—

Her. O spite! Too old to be engaged to young.

Lys. Or else it stood upon the choice of friends—

Her. O hell! To choose love by another's eyes. 140

Lys. Or, if there were a sympathy in choice,
War, death, or sickness did lay siege to it,
Making it momentary as a sound,
Swift as a shadow, short as any dream;
Brief as the lightning in the collied night,
That, in a spleen, unfolds both heaven and earth,
And ere a man hath power to say "Behold!"
The jaws of darkness do devour it up.
So quick bright things come to confusion.

Her. If then true lovers have been ever cross'd, 150
It stands as an edict in destiny;
Then let us teach our trial patience,
Because it is a customary cross,
As due to love as thoughts, and dreams, and sighs,
Wishes, and tears, poor Fancy's followers.

Lys. A good persuasion; therefore, hear me, Hermia.
I have a widow aunt, a dowager
Of great revenue, and she hath no child.

131. *Beteem:* grant, perhaps with a secondary reference to *teem*, "pour" (Onions). 133. *history:* story, narrative. 136. *low.* Qq and Ff read *love;* the emendation is Theobald's. This is one of the sorrows which Venus, seeing Adonis dead, prophesied should attend on love (*Venus and Adonis*, lines 1135 ff.). 137. *misgraffed:* ill-matched. 145–8. *Brief . . . up.* Cf. *Romeo and Juliet*, II, ii, 119 ff. 145. *collied:* dark, blackened as by coal. 146. *spleen:* sudden outburst. 153. *customary:* ordained by custom, usual. 155. *Fancy's:* Love's. 158. *revenue:* wealth, income.

From Athens is her house remote seven leagues;
And she respects me as her only son. 160
There, gentle Hermia, may I marry thee;
And to that place the sharp Athenian law
Cannot pursue us. If thou lovest me, then
Steal forth thy father's house tomorrow night;
And in the wood, a league without the town
(Where I did meet thee once with Helena,
To do observance to a morn of May),
There will I stay for thee.

Her. My good Lysander!
I swear to thee, by Cupid's strongest bow,
By his best arrow with the golden head, 170
By the simplicity of Venus' doves,
By that which knitteth souls and prospers loves,
And by that fire which burn'd the Carthage queen,
When the false Trojan under sail was seen,
By all the vows that ever men have broke
(In number more than ever women spoke),
In that same place thou hast appointed me,
Tomorrow truly will I meet with thee.

Lys. Keep promise, love. Look, here comes Helena.

160. *respects:* looks upon. 162. *the sharp Athenian law.* Shakespeare is probably thinking of his own London, outside the walls of which the civic authority of the Lord Mayor and the Aldermen did not extend. 165. *without:* outside. 167. *To . . . May.* Observing May Day is an English, not an Athenian, rite. The anachronism, however, is not Shakespeare's; Chaucer had introduced it in *The Knight's Tale.* 168. *stay:* wait. 170. *best arrow:* an allusion to Cupid's two arrows, one of which produced love, the other dispelled it:

> That causeth love is all of gold with point full sharp and bright,
> That chaseth love is blunt, whose steel with leaden head is dight.
> (Ovid's *Metamorphoses*, tr. Golding.)

171. *simplicity:* harmlessness, innocence. *doves.* Venus's car was drawn by a team of doves. 172. *prospers loves:* i.e., causes love to prosper. 173. *Carthage queen:* Dido, in Virgil's *Aeneid.* She killed herself for grief when deserted by the "false Trojan," Aeneas. The allusion, of course, is an anachronism.

Enter Helena.

Her. God speed fair Helena! Whither away? 180
Hel. Call you me fair? That fair again unsay.
Demetrius loves your fair, O happy fair!
Your eyes are lode-stars, and your tongue's sweet air
More tuneable than lark to shepherd's ear,
When wheat is green, when hawthorn buds appear.
Sickness is catching; O, were favour so,
Yours would I catch, fair Hermia, ere I go.
My ears should catch your voice, my eye your eye,
My tongue should catch your tongue's sweet melody.
Were the world mine, Demetrius being bated, 190
The rest I 'ld give to be to you translated.
O, teach me how you look, and with what art
You sway the motion of Demetrius' heart.
Her. I frown upon him, yet he loves me still.
Hel. O that your frowns would teach my smiles such skill!
Her. I give him curses, yet he gives me love.
Hel. O that my prayers could such affection move!
Her. The more I hate, the more he follows me.
Hel. The more I love, the more he hateth me.
Her. His folly, Helena, is no fault of mine. 200
Hel. None; but your beauty—would that fault were mine!
Her. Take comfort. He no more shall see my face;
Lysander and myself will fly this place.
Before the time I did Lysander see,
Seem'd Athens as a paradise to me.
O, then, what graces in my love do dwell,
That he hath turn'd a heaven unto a hell!
Lys. Helen, to you our minds we will unfold.
Tomorrow night, when Phœbe doth behold

182. *fair:* beauty. 183. *lode-stars:* leading or guiding stars. The sense here, however, seems to be crossed with *lodestone*, magnet, leading-stone. 186. *favour:* charm, beauty. 190. *bated:* deducted, excepted. 191. *translated:* transformed. 192. *art:* i.e., magic art. 209. *Phœbe:* Diana, the moon.

Her silver visage in the watery glass, 210
Decking with liquid pearl the bladed grass
(A time that lovers' flights doth still conceal),
Through Athens' gates have we devised to steal.

Her. And in the wood, where often you and I
Upon faint primrose-beds were wont to lie,
Emptying our bosoms of their counsel sweet,
There my Lysander and myself shall meet,
And thence from Athens turn away our eyes,
To seek new friends and stranger companies.
Farewell, sweet playfellow, pray thou for us; 220
And good luck grant thee thy Demetrius!
Keep word, Lysander; we must starve our sight
From lovers' food till morrow deep midnight.

Lys. I will, my Hermia. [*Exit Hermia*.
Helena, adieu;
As you on him, Demetrius dote on you! [*Exit*.

Hel. How happy some o'er other some can be!
Through Athens I am thought as fair as she.
But what of that? Demetrius thinks not so.
He will not know what all but he do know;
And as he errs, doting on Hermia's eyes, 230
So I, admiring of his qualities.
Things base and vile, holding no quantity,
Love can transpose to form and dignity.
Love looks not with the eyes, but with the mind;
And therefore is wing'd Cupid painted blind.
Nor hath Love's mind of any judgment taste;
Wings and no eyes figure unheedy haste.
And therefore is Love said to be a child,
Because in choice he is so oft beguiled.

212. *still:* always, ever. 215. *faint:* pale. 216. *counsel:* inmost thoughts. 219. *stranger companies:* i.e., companies of strangers. Qq and Ff read *strange companions;* the emendation is Theobald's. 226. *How . . . be:* how much more happy some can be than others. 229. *will not know:* doesn't want to know. 232. *quantity:* proportion. 237. *figure:* symbolize.

As waggish boys in game themselves forswear, 240
So the boy Love is perjured everywhere.
For ere Demetrius look'd on Hermia's eyne,
He hail'd down oaths that he was only mine;
And when this hail some heat from Hermia felt,
So he dissolved, and showers of oaths did melt.
I will go tell him of fair Hermia's flight;
Then to the wood will he tomorrow night
Pursue her; and for this intelligence
If I have thanks, it is a dear expense.
But herein mean I to enrich my pain, 250
To have his sight thither and back again. [*Exit.*

SCENE II. *Athens.* PETER QUINCE'S *carpenter shop.*

QUINCE, BOTTOM, SNUG, FLUTE, SNOUT, *and* STARVELING *are assembled.*

Quin. Is all our company here?

Bot. You were best to call them generally, man by man, according to the scrip.

Quin. Here is the scroll of every man's name which is thought fit, through all Athens, to play in our interlude before the duke and the duchess, on his wedding-day at night.

242. *eyne:* an archaic plural of *eye.* 245. *dissolved:* (a) broke faith, (b) melted. 248. *intelligence:* information. 249. *dear expense:* a bitter bargain, i.e., thanks dearly bought.

[ii] S. D. The surnames of the "mechanicals" are tags indicative of their callings. Bottom the Weaver takes his name from the *bottom* or bobbin upon which a skein of weaver's yarn is wound; Quince the Carpenter has his from *quoins* or *quines*, the wedge-like blocks used in building; Snug's is an appropriate name for a joiner or cabinetmaker; Flute's is suggestive of the wheezy sounds emitted by the bellows he mended, and Snout's of the tinker's trade of repairing pots and kettles, while that of Starveling the Tailor is an allusion to the proverbial undernourished, unpaid condition of members of his trade. Cf. Francis Feeble, the woman's tailor, in *2 Henry IV*, III, ii, 160 ff.

2. *generally.* To explain every Bottomism is unnecessary. Usually, Bottom and his brethren mean the opposite of what they say and have merely confused words which have antithetical meanings but which sound alike. Here, of course, he means *severally*.

Bot. First, good Peter Quince, say what the play treats on, then read the names of the actors, and so grow to a point. 10

Quin. Marry, our play is *The Most Lamentable Comedy, and Most Cruel Death of Pyramus and Thisby.*

Bot. A very good piece of work, I assure you, and a merry. Now, good Peter Quince, call forth your actors by the scroll. Masters, spread yourselves.

Quin. Answer as I call you. Nick Bottom, the weaver.

Bot. Ready. Name what part I am for, and proceed. 21

Quin. You, Nick Bottom, are set down for Pyramus.

Bot. What is Pyramus? A lover, or a tyrant?

Quin. A lover that kills himself most gallant for love.

Bot. That will ask some tears in the true performing of it. If I do it, let the audience look to their eyes. I will move storms; I will condole in some measure. To the rest—yet my chief humour is for a tyrant. I could play Ercles rarely, or a part to tear a cat in, to make all split. 32

The raging rocks
And shivering shocks
Shall break the locks
Of prison gates,

10. *grow:* come. 11. *Marry:* indeed, to be sure; originally the name of the Virgin Mary used as an oath or an invocation. 11–13. *The Most . . . Thisby:* a parody of the fantastic names given to Elizabethan plays upon title pages, and probably also upon the playbills announcing performances. 14. *piece of work.* This is probably an instance of lost humor. Ben Jonson, publishing a collected edition of his dramas in Shakespeare's death-year, 1616, was the first seriously to call a "play" a "work," and merriment at Jonson's expense lasted nearly a generation. These amateurs are taking everything too seriously. 30. *To the rest:* i.e., go on and name the other players. 31. *humour:* disposition, liking. *Ercles:* Hercules, a ranter on the early stage; like Termagant and Herod, "robustious, periwig-pated fellows" who tore "a passion to tatters, to very rags." 33 ff. These lines have been thought a rough parody of a passage from Jasper Heywood's translation of Seneca's *Hercules Furens* (1581). At least Bottom's fustian lines are intended to suggest a comparison with some old theatrical piece; they are not his own composition.

And Phibbus' car
Shall shine from far
And make and mar
The foolish Fates. 40

This was lofty! [*To Quince.*] Now name the rest of the players. [*To the rest.*] This is Ercles' vein, a tyrant's vein; a lover is more condoling. [*He is interrupted.*

Quin. Francis Flute, the bellows-mender.

Flu. Here, Peter Quince.

Quin. Flute, you must take Thisby on you.

Flu. What is Thisby? A wandering knight?

Quin. It is the lady that Pyramus must love.

Flu. Nay, faith, let not me play a woman; I have a beard coming. 50

Quin. That's all one. You shall play it in a mask, and you may speak as small as you will.

Bot. An I may hide my face, let me play Thisby too. I'll speak in a monstrous little voice, thisne, thisne: "Ah Pyramus, my lover dear! Thy Thisby dear, and lady dear!"

Quin. No, no; you must play Pyramus; and, Flute, you Thisby.

Bot. Well, proceed.

Quin. Robin Starveling, the tailor. 60

Star. Here, Peter Quince.

Quin. Robin Starveling, you must play Thisby's mother. Tom Snout, the tinker.

37. *Phibbus:* Phoebus, god of the sun. 46. *take . . . on you:* undertake. 47. *wandering knight.* Young Flute's yearning for the role of knight-errant, like that of Ralph the grocer's apprentice in Beaumont's *Knight of the Burning Pestle*, has probably come from reading too many chivalric romances like *Palmerin d'Oliva* and *Amadis of Gaul*. 49–52. *Nay . . . will.* In Shakespeare's day women's roles in the theatre were played by boys, some of whom, like Flute, were not altogether suitable for their parts and obliged sometimes to wear masks. 52. *small:* i.e., high-pitched, feminine. 55. *thisne, thisne:* printed in italics and with capital letters in the old texts, and hence usually taken for a proper name and (somewhat illogically here) an affected variation of *Thisby*. *Thisne*, however, is Midland dialect for "in this manner." 62–6. *Thisby's mother . . . Pyramus' father . . . Thisby's father*. These characters do not appear in the play.

Snout. Here, Peter Quince.

Quin. You, Pyramus' father; myself, Thisby's father. Snug, the joiner—you, the lion's part; and, I hope, here is a play fitted.

Snug. Have you the lion's part written? Pray you, if it be, give it me, for I am slow of study.

Quin. You may do it extempore, for it is nothing but roaring. 71

Bot. Let me play the lion too. I will roar that I will do any man's heart good to hear me. I will roar that I will make the duke say, "Let him roar again; let him roar again."

Quin. An you should do it too terribly, you would fright the duchess and the ladies that they would shriek; and that were enough to hang us all.

All. That would hang us, every mother's son. 80

Bot. I grant you, friends, if you should fright the ladies out of their wits, they would have no more discretion but to hang us. But I will aggravate my voice so that I will roar you as gently as any sucking dove; I will roar you an 'twere any nightingale.

Quin. You can play no part but Pyramus; for Pyramus is a sweet-faced man, a proper man as one shall see in a summer's day, a most lovely gentleman-like man—therefore you must needs play Pyramus. 91

Bot. Well, I will undertake it. What beard were I best to play it in?

Quin. Why, what you will.

Bot. I will discharge it in either your straw-colour beard, your orange-tawny beard, your purple-in-grain beard, or your French-crown-colour beard—your perfect yellow. 98

Quin. Some of your French crowns have no hair at all, and

84. *you:* the redundant ethical dative, "for you." 85. *sucking dove.* Is Bottom thinking of the way in which doves and pigeons feed their young? 86. *an 'twere:* as if it were. 88. *sweet-faced:* handsome. *proper:* elegant, good-looking. 97. *purple-in-grain:* fast-dyed red. *French-crown:* (a) the écu, a gold coin, (b) baldness produced by the "French disease."

then you will play barefaced. But, masters, here are your parts; and I am to entreat you, request you, and desire you, to con them by tomorrow night; and meet me in the palace wood, a mile without the town, by moonlight. There will we rehearse, for if we meet in the city, we shall be dogged with company, and our devices known. In the meantime, I will draw a bill of properties, such as our play wants. I pray you, fail me not.

Bot. We will meet; and there we may rehearse most obscenely and courageously. Take pains; be perfect. Adieu. 112

Quin. At the Duke's Oak we meet.

Bot. Enough; hold, or cut bow-strings. [*Exeunt.*

ACT II

SCENE I. *The palace wood, a short distance outside of Athens, the next night.*

Enter, from opposite directions, PUCK *and a* Fairy.

Puck. How now, spirit? Whither wander you?

Fai. Over hill, over dale,
Thorough bush, thorough brier,
Over park, over pale,
Thorough flood, thorough fire—

102. *entreat, request, desire.* It is characteristic that Quince should use these words in an anticlimactic order. *con:* learn by heart. 108. *bill:* list. 111. *obscenely.* Bottom, like Costard the Clown (*Love's Labor's Lost,* IV, i, 142), apparently thinks that this word has some connection with *seemly* and means "fittingly" or "smoothly." 114. *hold, or cut bow-strings:* a doubtful phrase; probably, keep this engagement, or quit.

[II. i] S. D. In the early editions this stage direction reads: *Enter a Fairy at one door, and Robin Goodfellow at another.* The practical playwright is clearly thinking of the entrances to the platform stage. 2 ff. Although these lines are not specifically called a song in any of the early texts, they have frequently been set to music and sung in performance. Observe that they are the Fairy's conversation, a reply to the Puck's question, and that throughout this play all of the fairies' lines are in lyrical, rhymed verse. 3. *Thorough:* through. 4. *pale:* the fence enclosing a deer park.

I do wander everywhere,
Swifter than the moon's sphere;
And I serve the fairy queen,
To dew her orbs upon the green.
The cowslips tall her pensioners be; 10
In their gold coats spots you see;
Those be rubies, fairy favours;
In those freckles live their savours.
I must go seek some dewdrops here
And hang a pearl in every cowslip's ear.
Farewell, thou lob of spirits; I'll be gone.
Our queen and all her elves come here anon.

Puck. The king doth keep his revels here tonight.
Take heed the queen come not within his sight,
For Oberon is passing fell and wrath, 20
Because that she as her attendant hath
A lovely boy, stolen from an Indian king.
She never had so sweet a changeling,
And jealous Oberon would have the child
Knight of his train, to trace the forests wild.
But she perforce withholds the loved boy,
Crowns him with flowers, and makes him all her joy.
And now they never meet in grove or green,
By fountain clear, or spangled starlight sheen,
But they do square, that all their elves for fear 30
Creep into acorn-cups and hide them there.

7. *moon's sphere.* According to the Ptolemaic astronomy, the moon and all of the planets and stars were supposed to be fixed in hollow, concentric, crystalline spheres or globes, which, revolving rapidly, produced the "music of the spheres." (Cf. Marlowe's *Dr. Faustus*, lines 649 ff.) 9. *dew:* spread with dew. *orbs:* fairy rings, circles formed by certain mushroom fungi, but popularly thought to be fairy dancing places. 10. *pensioners:* bodyguards, retainers. 13. *savours:* perfume. 16. *lob:* lubber, country bumpkin. 20. *fell:* angry. 23. *She . . . changeling:* she never had a changeling (i.e., a child stolen by the fairies from its cradle) who was so sweet. *Changeling* is usually applied to the infant, often stupid and ugly, which the fairies left for the one they stole. 25. *trace:* walk over, traverse. 26. *perforce:* forcibly. 30. *square:* quarrel noisily.

Fai. Either I mistake your shape and making quite,
Or else you are that shrewd and knavish sprite
Call'd Robin Goodfellow. Are not you he
That frights the maidens of the villagery,
Skim milk, and sometimes labour in the quern,
And bootless make the breathless housewife churn;
And sometime make the drink to bear no barm,
Mislead night-wanderers, laughing at their harm?
Those that Hobgoblin call you and sweet Puck, 40
You do their work, and they shall have good luck.
Are not you he?
Puck. Thou speak'st aright;
I am that merry wanderer of the night.
I jest to Oberon and make him smile
When I a fat and bean-fed horse beguile,
Neighing in likeness of a filly foal;
And sometime lurk I in a gossip's bowl,
In very likeness of a roasted crab,
And when she drinks, against her lips I bob
And on her wither'd dewlap pour the ale. 50
The wisest aunt, telling the saddest tale,
Sometime for three-foot stool mistaketh me;
Then slip I from her bum, down topples she,
And "tailor" cries, and falls into a cough;

33. *shrewd:* mischievous. 34. *Robin Goodfellow. Puck,* strictly speaking, is a generic name for a class of mischievous sprite like the brownie or leprechaun, a "lob of spirits"; *Robin Goodfellow* is the name of an individual, Oberon's court jester, the "Sir Dagonet of Fairyland." Titania's midsummer fairy does not consider the Puck one of her own race. 35. *villagery:* village folk. 36. *quern:* a hand mill for grinding corn. 37. *bootless:* in vain. 38. *barm:* yeast formed on brewing liquors. 47. *gossip's bowl:* a spiced cup at any merrymaking. *Gossips* were originally sponsors or invited guests at a baptism. 48. *very:* exact. *crab:* crab apple. 50. *dewlap:* the fold of loose skin hanging from the necks of some animals. 51. *wisest aunt:* most sedate old dame. *saddest:* most serious. 54. "*tailor.*" Unexplained. Furness suggests substituting *e* for *o;* "as boys in swimming take a *header*, the wisest aunt was suggested to take the opposite." Or, perhaps in falling she sat down tailor-fashion.

And then the whole quire hold their hips and laugh,
And waxen in their mirth, and neeze, and swear
A merrier hour was never wasted there.
But, room, fairy! Here comes Oberon.
Fai. And here my mistress. Would that he were gone!

Enter, from opposite directions, OBERON *with his train and* TITANIA *with hers. The King and Queen face each other.*

Obe. Ill met by moonlight, proud Titania. 60
Tita. What, jealous Oberon! Fairies, skip hence;
I have forsworn his bed and company.
Obe. Tarry, rash wanton; am not I thy lord?
Tita. Then I must be thy lady. But I know
When thou hast stolen away from fairy land,
And in the shape of Corin sat all day,
Playing on pipes of corn and versing love
To amorous Phillida. Why art thou here,
Come from the farthest steppe of India?
But that, forsooth, the bouncing Amazon, 70
Your buskin'd mistress and your warrior love,
To Theseus must be wedded; and you come
To give their bed joy and prosperity.
Obe. How canst thou thus for shame, Titania,

55. *quire:* choir, company. 56. *waxen:* increase. *neeze:* an archaic form of *sneeze.* S. D. *from . . . directions.* Qq and Ff read *at one door, at another.* Cf. II, i, S. D. and note. 66–8. *Corin . . . Phillida:* conventional names of swain and nymph in pastoral literature. 67. *pipes of corn:* the "oaten pipes" frequently referred to as the musical instruments of shepherds. *versing:* telling in verse. 68. *Why art thou here?* "One of the strokes of humour in this whole scene, between atomies who can creep into acorn-cups, and for whom the waxen thigh of a bee affords an ample torch, lies in the assumption by them of human powers and of super-human importance. Not only is Titania jealous of the bouncing Amazon, but this their quarrel influences the moon in the sky, changes the seasons, and affects disastrously the whole human race. There is a touch of the same humour, but deeply coarsened, in the scandal which Gulliver's conduct started when he was at the court of Laputa" (Furness). 70. *bouncing:* buxom, stout. 71. *buskin'd:* booted.

Glance at my credit with Hippolyta,
Knowing I know thy love to Theseus?
Didst thou not lead him through the glimmering night
From Perigenia, whom he ravished?
And make him with fair Ægle break his faith,
With Ariadne and Antiopa? 80

Tita. These are the forgeries of jealousy;
And never, since the middle summer's spring,
Met we on hill, in dale, forest, or mead,
By paved fountain, or by rushy brook,
Or in the beached margent of the sea,
To dance our ringlets to the whistling wind,
But with thy brawls thou hast disturb'd our sport.
Therefore the winds, piping to us in vain,
As in revenge, have suck'd up from the sea
Contagious fogs; which falling in the land 90
Have every pelting river made so proud
That they have overborne their continents.
The ox hath therefore stretch'd his yoke in vain,
The ploughman lost his sweat, and the green corn
Hath rotted ere his youth attain'd a beard;
The fold stands empty in the drowned field,
And crows are fatted with the murrion flock;
The nine men's morris is fill'd up with mud,
And the quaint mazes in the wanton green
For lack of tread are undistinguishable. 100
The human mortals want their winter here;
No night is now with hymn or carol blest.
Therefore the moon, the governess of floods,

75. *Glance at:* hit at, indirectly attack. *credit:* reputation. 78–80. *Perigenia, Ægle, Ariadne, Antiopa.* All of these affairs of this early Don Juan are mentioned in Plutarch's *Life of Theseus.* 81. *forgeries:* fictions, inventions. 82. *middle summer's spring:* i.e., the beginning of midsummer. 91. *pelting.* F_1 reads *petty. proud:* swollen. 92. *continents:* banks. 94. *corn:* grain, wheat. 97. *murrion:* diseased. 98. *nine men's morris:* a game for two or more players, played on a square with pegs or stones. 99. *quaint:* intricate. *wanton:* luxuriant. 101. *want:* lack.

Pale in her anger, washes all the air,
That rheumatic diseases do abound.
And thorough this distemperature we see
The seasons alter—hoary-headed frosts
Fall in the fresh lap of the crimson rose,
And on old Hiems' chin and icy crown
An odorous chaplet of sweet summer buds 110
Is, as in mockery, set. The spring, the summer,
The childing autumn, angry winter, change
Their wonted liveries, and the mazed world,
By their increase, now knows not which is which.
And this same progeny of evils comes
From our debate, from our dissension;
We are their parents and original.

Obe. Do you amend it, then; it lies in you.
Why should Titania cross her Oberon?
I do but beg a little changeling boy, 120
To be my henchman.

Tita. Set your heart at rest.
The fairy land buys not the child of me.
His mother was a votress of my order;
And, in the spiced Indian air, by night,
Full often hath she gossip'd by my side,
And sat with me on Neptune's yellow sands,
Marking the embarked traders on the flood,
When we have laugh'd to see the sails conceive
And grow big-bellied with the wanton wind;
Which she, with pretty and with swimming gait 130
Following—her womb then rich with my young squire—
Would imitate, and sail upon the land,
To fetch me trifles, and return again,
As from a voyage, rich with merchandise.
But she, being mortal, of that boy did die;

105. *rheumatic diseases:* head colds. 109. *Hiems':* Winter's. 112. *childing:* fruitful. 113. *mazed:* bewildered. 117. *original:* origin. 123. *votress:* woman who has made a vow; here, a member. 127. *Marking:* watching. 129. *wanton:* (a) sportive, (b) lascivious.

And for her sake do I rear up her boy,
And for her sake I will not part with him.
Obe. How long within this wood intend you stay?
Tita. Perchance till after Theseus' wedding-day.
If you will patiently dance in our round 140
And see our moonlight revels, go with us;
If not, shun me, and I will spare your haunts.
Obe. Give me that boy, and I will go with thee.
Tita. Not for thy fairy kingdom. Fairies, away!
We shall chide downright, if I longer stay.
[*Exit Titania with her train.*
Obe. Well, go thy way; thou shalt not from this grove
Till I torment thee for this injury.
My gentle Puck, come hither. Thou rememberest
Since once I sat upon a promontory
And heard a mermaid on a dolphin's back 150
Uttering such dulcet and harmonious breath
That the rude sea grew civil at her song
And certain stars shot madly from their spheres
To hear the sea-maid's music.
Puck. I remember.
Obe. That very time I saw, but thou couldst not,
Flying between the cold moon and the earth,
Cupid all arm'd. A certain aim he took
At a fair vestal throned by the west,
And loosed his love-shaft smartly from his bow,

140. *round:* circular dance. 142. *spare:* avoid. 147. *injury:* insult. 149. *Since:* when. 150. *a mermaid on a dolphin's back.* The imagery of this description and the obvious flattery of Queen Elizabeth as the "fair vestal throned by the west" has inclined most scholars to regard this passage as a reminiscence of an episode in the "princely pleasures" invariably arranged by her loving subjects when the Queen went on "progress" through her kingdom. But there is no agreement as to the occasion referred to. At both Kenilworth (1575) and Elvetham (1591) there were water-shows, but no mermaid on a dolphin's back. Many of these entertainments, however, were much alike, and the allusion may be a general one. 151. *dulcet:* sweet, melodious. 153. *certain:* fixed. *spheres.* See above, II, i, 7 note 157. *certain:* sure.

As it should pierce a hundred thousand hearts. 160
But I might see young Cupid's fiery shaft
Quench'd in the chaste beams of the watery moon,
And the imperial votress passed on,
In maiden meditation, fancy-free.
Yet mark'd I where the bolt of Cupid fell.
It fell upon a little western flower,
Before milk-white, now purple with love's wound,
And maidens call it love-in-idleness.
Fetch me that flower—the herb I shew'd thee once.
The juice of it on sleeping eye-lids laid 170
Will make or man or woman madly dote
Upon the next live creature that it sees.
Fetch me this herb, and be thou here again
Ere the leviathan can swim a league.

Puck. I'll put a girdle round about the earth
In forty minutes. [*Exit.*

Obe. Having once this juice,
I'll watch Titania when she is asleep,
And drop the liquor of it in her eyes.
The next thing then she, waking, looks upon
(Be it on lion, bear, or wolf, or bull, 180
On meddling monkey, or on busy ape),
She shall pursue it with the soul of love.
And ere I take this charm from off her sight
(As I can take it with another herb),
I'll make her render up her page to me.
But who comes here? I am invisible;
And I will overhear their conference.

166. *little western flower.* Numerous attempts have been made to identify the "little western flower" as the girl wounded by the arrow intended for the queen. 167. *purple:* crimson. 168. *love-in-idleness:* (a) heartsease or pansy, (b) love without seriousness. 174. *leviathan:* sea monster of Biblical literature, probably the whale. 186. *I am invisible.* On the Elizabethan stage Oberon probably wore some special garment which to the audience symbolized his invisibility. Among the accounts kept by Philip Henslowe, owner of several of the Bankside theatres, there is mention of "a robe for to go invisible."

Enter Demetrius, Helena *following him.*

Dem. I love thee not; therefore pursue me not.
Where is Lysander and fair Hermia?
The one I'll stay; the other stayeth me. 190
Thou told'st me they were stolen unto this wood;
And here am I, and wode within this wood,
Because I cannot meet my Hermia.
Hence; get thee gone, and follow me no more.
Hel. You draw me, you hard-hearted adamant;
But yet you draw not iron, for my heart
Is true as steel. Leave you your power to draw,
And I shall have no power to follow you.
Dem. Do I entice you? Do I speak you fair?
Or, rather, do I not in plainest truth 200
Tell you, I do not, nor I cannot love you?
Hel. And even for that do I love you the more.
I am your spaniel; and, Demetrius,
The more you beat me, I will fawn on you.
Use me but as your spaniel, spurn me, strike me,
Neglect me, lose me; only give me leave,
Unworthy as I am, to follow you.
What worser place can I beg in your love—
And yet a place of high respect with me—
Than to be used as you use your dog? 210
Dem. Tempt not too much the hatred of my spirit,
For I am sick when I do look on thee.
Hel. And I am sick when I look not on you.
Dem. You do impeach your modesty too much,
To leave the city and commit yourself
Into the hands of one that loves you not,
To trust the opportunity of night

190. *stay:* check, stop. Some editors emend to *slay* and *slayeth.* 192. *wode:* mad; *wode* and *wood* were pronounced alike. 195. *adamant:* a stone of excessive hardness identified with the lodestone or magnet. 199. *Do I speak you fair:* do I give you any encouragement? 209. *respect:* estimation. 211. *Tempt:* try. 214. *impeach:* discredit.

And the ill counsel of a desert place
With the rich worth of your virginity.
Hel. Your virtue is my privilege, for that 220
It is not night when I do see your face.
Therefore I think I am not in the night,
Nor doth this wood lack worlds of company,
For you in my respect are all the world.
Then how can it be said I am alone,
When all the world is here to look on me?
Dem. I'll run from thee and hide me in the brakes,
And leave thee to the mercy of wild beasts.
Hel. The wildest hath not such a heart as you.
Run when you will, the story shall be changed— 230
Apollo flies, and Daphne holds the chase.
The dove pursues the griffin; the mild hind
Makes speed to catch the tiger—bootless speed,
When cowardice pursues and valour flies.
Dem. I will not stay thy questions; let me go.
Or, if thou follow me, do not believe
But I shall do thee mischief in the wood.
[*He breaks away from her, and exit.*
Hel. Ay, in the temple, in the town, the field,
You do me mischief. Fie, Demetrius!
Your wrongs do set a scandal on my sex. 240
We cannot fight for love, as men may do;
We should be woo'd and were not made to woo.
I'll follow thee and make a heaven of hell,
To die upon the hand I love so well. [*She follows him.*
Obe. Fare thee well, nymph; ere he do leave this grove,
Thou shalt fly him and he shall seek thy love.

224. *respect:* estimation. 227. *brakes:* thickets. 231. *Apollo, Daphne.* Daphne, a nymph of whom the god Apollo became enamored, fled from his importunities and, appealing to the gods for assistance, was transformed into a laurel. 232. *griffin:* a fabulous beast, half eagle, half lion. *hind:* female of the red deer. 233. *bootless:* useless, vain. 235. *stay:* wait for. *questions:* arguments. 244. *To die:* in dying.

Re-enter Puck.

Hast thou the flower there? Welcome, wanderer.
Puck. Ay, there it is.
Obe. I pray thee, give it me.
I know a bank where the wild thyme blows,
Where oxlips and the nodding violet grows, 250
Quite over-canopied with luscious woodbine,
With sweet musk-roses and with eglantine.
There sleeps Titania sometime of the night,
Lull'd in these flowers with dances and delight;
And there the snake throws her enamell'd skin,
Weed wide enough to wrap a fairy in.
And with the juice of this I'll streak her eyes,
And make her full of hateful fantasies.
Take thou some of it, and seek through this grove;
A sweet Athenian lady is in love 260
With a disdainful youth. Anoint his eyes,
But do it when the next thing he espies
May be the lady. Thou shalt know the man
By the Athenian garments he hath on.
Effect it with some care that he may prove
More fond on her than she upon her love.
And look thou meet me ere the first cock crow.
Puck. Fear not, my lord, your servant shall do so. [*Exeunt.*

Scene ii. *The palace wood, near the Duke's Oak.*

Enter Titania, *with her train.*

Tita. Come, now a roundel and a fairy song;
Then, for the third part of a minute, hence;
Some to kill cankers in the musk-rose buds,
Some war with rere-mice for their leathern wings,

251. *woodbine:* honeysuckle. 252. *eglantine:* sweetbriar. 256. *Weed:* garment. 258. *fantasies:* imaginings.
[ii] 1. *roundel:* round dance. 3. *cankers:* worms. 4. *rere-mice:* bats.

To make my small elves coats, and some keep back
The clamorous owl that nightly hoots and wonders
At our quaint spirits. [*She lies down.*] Sing me now asleep;
Then to your offices and let me rest.

The Fairies *sing.*

First Fairy. You spotted snakes with double tongue,
Thorny hedgehogs, be not seen; 10
Newts and blind-worms, do no wrong;
Come not near our fairy queen.

All. Philomel, with melody
Sing in our sweet lullaby;
Lulla, lulla, lullaby, lulla, lulla, lullaby.
Never harm,
Nor spell nor charm,
Come our lovely lady nigh;
So, good night, with lullaby.

Sec. Fairy. Weaving spiders, come not here; 20
Hence, you long-legg'd spinners, hence!
Beetles black, approach not near;
Worm nor snail, do no offense.

All. Philomel, with melody, &c.

[*Titania sleeps.*

First Fairy. Hence, away! Now all is well;
One aloof stand sentinel. [*Exeunt Fairies.*

Enter OBERON, *and squeezes the flower on* TITANIA'S *eyelids.*

Obe. What thou seest when thou dost wake,
Do it for thy true-love take,

7. *quaint:* dainty. 8. *offices:* duties. 9 ff. *The Fairies sing.* How easily and naturally this song accomplishes its dramatic purpose! A fairy atmosphere is created, Oberon's plot is facilitated (he is not included in the charm), and this dainty lullaby is very different from the cacophonous braying with which Bottom awakens the little queen. 9. *double:* forked. 11. *Newts:* small lizards. 13. *Philomel:* the nightingale. 23. *Worm:* applied to all small creeping things, including snakes. *offense:* harm, injury.

Love and languish for his sake.
Be it ounce, or cat, or bear, 30
Pard, or boar with bristled hair,
In thy eye that shall appear
When thou wakest, it is thy dear.
Wake when some vile thing is near. [*Exit.*

Enter LYSANDER *and* HERMIA.

Lys. Fair love, you faint with wandering in the wood;
And, to speak troth, I have forgot our way.
We'll rest us, Hermia, if you think it good,
And tarry for the comfort of the day.
Her. Be it so, Lysander; find you out a bed,
For I upon this bank will rest my head. 40
Lys. One turf shall serve as pillow for us both;
One heart, one bed, two bosoms, and one troth.
Her. Nay, good Lysander; for my sake, my dear,
Lie further off yet; do not lie so near.
Lys. O, take the sense, sweet, of my innocence!
Love takes the meaning in love's conference.
I mean that my heart unto yours is knit
So that but one heart we can make of it;
Two bosoms interchained with an oath;
So then two bosoms and a single troth. 50
Then by your side no bed-room me deny;
For lying so, Hermia, I do not lie.
Her. Lysander riddles very prettily.
Now much beshrew my manners and my pride,
If Hermia meant to say Lysander lied.
But, gentle friend, for love and courtesy
Lie further off; in human modesty,
Such separation as may well be said

30. *ounce:* lynx. 31. *Pard:* leopard. 32. *that:* what. 45. *O . . . innocence:* i.e., I mean no harm (with a quibble upon *sense* and *innocence*). 46. *Love . . . conference:* Love enables lovers to understand each other's true meaning (Chambers). 54. *beshrew:* curse (a mild imprecation). 57. *human:* humane, seemly.

Becomes a virtuous bachelor and a maid,
So far be distant; and, good night, sweet friend. 60
Thy love ne'er alter till thy sweet life end!

Lys. Amen, amen, to that fair prayer, say I;
And then end life when I end loyalty!
Here is my bed; sleep give thee all his rest!

Her. With half that wish the wisher's eyes be press'd!

[*They sleep.*

Enter PUCK.

Puck. Through the forest have I gone,
But Athenian found I none
On whose eyes I might approve
This flower's force in stirring love.
Night and silence—[*He spies the sleepers.*] Who is here? 70
Weeds of Athens he doth wear.
This is he, my master said,
Despised the Athenian maid;
And here the maiden, sleeping sound,
On the dank and dirty ground.
Pretty soul! She durst not lie
Near this lack-love, this kill-courtesy.
Churl, upon thy eyes I throw
All the power this charm doth owe.

[*He anoints the eyelids of Lysander.*

When thou wakest, let love forbid 80
Sleep his seat on thy eyelid.
So awake when I am gone,
For I must now to Oberon. [*Exit.*

Enter DEMETRIUS *and* HELENA, *running.*

Hel. Stay, though thou kill me, sweet Demetrius.

Dem. I charge thee, hence, and do not haunt me thus.

Hel. O, wilt thou darkling leave me? Do not so.

68. *approve:* test. 71. *Weeds:* garments. 75. *dank:* damp.
79. *owe:* own, possess. 86. *darkling:* in the dark. F_4 reads *darling*.

Dem. Stay, on thy peril; I alone will go.
[*Exit into the wood.*

Hel. O, I am out of breath in this fond chase!
The more my prayer, the lesser is my grace.
Happy is Hermia, wheresoe'er she lies; 90
For she hath blessed and attractive eyes.
How came her eyes so bright? Not with salt tears.
If so, my eyes are oftener wash'd than hers.
No, no, I am as ugly as a bear;
For beasts that meet me run away for fear.
Therefore no marvel though Demetrius
Do, as a monster, fly my presence thus.
What wicked and dissembling glass of mine
Made me compare with Hermia's sphery eyne?
But who is here? Lysander! On the ground? 100
Dead? Or asleep? I see no blood, no wound.
Lysander, if you live, good sir, awake!

Lys. [*Awaking*] And run through fire I will for thy sweet sake.
Transparent Helena! Nature shows art,
That through thy bosom makes me see thy heart.
Where is Demetrius? O, how fit a word
Is that vile name to perish on my sword!

Hel. Do not say so, Lysander; say not so.
What though he love your Hermia? Lord, what though?
Yet Hermia still loves you. Then be content. 110

Lys. Content with Hermia? No; I do repent
The tedious minutes I with her have spent.
Not Hermia but Helena I love.
Who will not change a raven for a dove?
The will of man is by his reason sway'd;
And reason says you are the worthier maid.

88. *fond:* foolish. 98. *glass:* mirror. 99. *sphery:* starlike. *eyne:* an archaic plural of *eye.* 104. *Transparent:* (a) frank, ingenuous, (b) diaphanous, pellucid. 110. *still:* ever. 111. *repent:* regret. 114. *raven:* an allusion to Hermia's dark hair. Cf. note on III, ii, 257-305.

Things growing are not ripe until their season;
So I, being young, till now ripe not to reason.
And touching now the point of human skill,
Reason becomes the marshal to my will 120
And leads me to your eyes, where I o'erlook
Love's stories written in love's richest book.

Hel. Wherefore was I to this keen mockery born?
When at your hands did I deserve this scorn?
Is 't not enough, is 't not enough, young man,
That I did never—no, nor never can—
Deserve a sweet look from Demetrius' eye,
But you must flout my insufficiency?
Good troth, you do me wrong—good sooth, you do,
In such disdainful manner me to woo. 130
But fare you well; perforce I must confess
I thought you lord of more true gentleness.
O, that a lady, of one man refused,
Should of another therefore be abused! [*Exit into the wood.*

Lys. She sees not Hermia. Hermia, sleep thou there;
And never mayst thou come Lysander near!
For as a surfeit of the sweetest things
The deepest loathing to the stomach brings,
Or as the heresies that men do leave
Are hated most of those they did deceive; 140
So thou, my surfeit and my heresy,
Of all be hated, but the most of me!
And, all my powers, address your love and might
To honour Helen and to be her knight! [*He follows her.*

Her. [*Awaking*] Help me, Lysander, help me! Do thy best
To pluck this crawling serpent from my breast!
Ay me, for pity! What a dream was here!
Lysander, look how I do quake with fear.
Methought a serpent eat my heart away,
And you sat smiling at his cruel prey. 150

119. *And . . . skill:* i.e., having now become maturely sensible or discerning. 128. *flout:* scoff at. 131. *perforce:* an intensive. 140. *of:* by. 150. *prey:* preying.

Lysander! What, removed? Lysander! Lord!
What, out of hearing? Gone? No sound, no word?
Alack, where are you? Speak, an if you hear;
Speak, of all loves! I swoon almost with fear.
No? Then I well perceive you are not nigh.
Either death or you I'll find immediately.

[*Exit into the wood.*

ACT III

SCENE I. *The palace wood, near the Duke's Oak;*
TITANIA *still lying asleep.*

Enter QUINCE, BOTTOM, SNUG, FLUTE, SNOUT, *and* STARVELING.

Bot. Are we all met?

Quin. Pat, pat; and here's a marvellous convenient place for our rehearsal. This green plot shall be our stage, this hawthorn brake our tiring-house; and we will do it in action as we will do it before the duke.

Bot. Peter Quince?

Quin. What sayest thou, bully Bottom? 8

Bot. There are things in this comedy of Pyramus and Thisby that will never please. First, Pyramus must draw a sword to kill himself, which the ladies cannot abide. How answer you that?

Snout. By 'r lakin, a parlous fear.

Star. I believe we must leave the killing out, when all is done. 16

Bot. Not a whit. I have a device to make all well. Write me a prologue, and let the prologue seem to say we will do no harm with our swords and that Pyramus is not killed indeed; and, for the more better assurance, tell them that I Pyramus am not Pyramus, but Bottom the weaver. This will put them out of fear.

153. *an if:* if. 154. *of all loves:* by all loves.
[III. i] 5. *tiring-house:* attiring-house, dressing room. 8. *bully:* a term of familiarity. 14. *By 'r lakin:* by our Ladykin, i.e., the Virgin Mary. *parlous:* perilous (used as an intensive).

Quin. Well, we will have such a prologue; and it shall be written in eight and six.

Bot. No, make it two more; let it be written in eight and eight.

Snout. Will not the ladies be afeard of the lion?

Star. I fear it, I promise you. 29

Bot. Masters, you ought to consider with yourselves. To bring in—God shield us!—a lion among ladies, is a most dreadful thing; for there is not a more fearful wild-fowl than your lion living; and we ought to look to 't.

Snout. Therefore, another prologue must tell he is not a lion. 36

Bot. Nay, you must name his name, and half his face must be seen through the lion's neck, and he himself must speak through, saying thus, or to the same defect: "Ladies"—or "Fair ladies—I would wish you"—or "I would request you"—or "I would entreat you—not to fear, not to tremble; my life for yours. If you think I come hither as a lion, it were pity of my life. No, I am no such thing; I am a man as other men are." And there indeed let him name his name, and tell them plainly he is Snug the joiner. 47

25. *eight and six:* the fourteen-syllabic line, with a marked caesura, which was usual in early sixteenth-century drama. 32. *a lion among ladies.* Perhaps a sly glance at the baptismal festivities for Prince Henry of Scotland on August 30, 1594. A triumphal chariot, wherein stood Fecundity, Faith, Liberality, and other Virtues, was to have been brought in, drawn by a lion (the heraldic device of timorous King James). In practice, however, it was thought best to substitute a blackamoor for the tame lion, "because his presence might have brought some fear to the nearest." A pamphlet, entitled *A True Reportary of the . . . Baptism of . . . Prince Frederick Henry* (1594), gave an account of the ceremonies and seems to have produced some merriment in London. 46. *name his name.* This also seems to be an allusion to an actual happening. Once when water-pageants were being presented before the Queen, Arion upon the Dolphin's back, finding himself hoarse, "tears off his Disguise, and swears he was none of Arion, not he, but e'en honest Har. Goldingham; which blunt discovery pleased the Queen better, than if he had gone through in the right way" (*Merry Passages and Jests*, cited by Malone). Readers of Scott's *Kenilworth* will recall his use of this episode (Ch. XXX).

Quin. Well, it shall be so. But there is two hard things: that is, to bring the moonlight into a chamber; for, you know, Pyramus and Thisby meet by moonlight.

Snout. Doth the moon shine that night we play our play?

Bot. A calendar, a calendar! Look in the almanac; find out moonshine, find out moonshine.

[*Quince produces an almanac and turns through it.*

Quin. Yes, it doth shine that night.

Bot. Why, then may you leave a casement of the great chamber window, where we play, open, and the moon may shine in at the casement. 59

Quin. Ay; or else one must come in with a bush of thorns and a lanthorn, and say he comes to disfigure, or to present, the person of Moonshine. Then, there is another thing: we must have a wall in the great chamber; for Pyramus and Thisby, says the story, did talk through the chink of a wall.

Snout. You can never bring in a wall. What say you, Bottom? 68

Bot. Some man or other must present Wall. And let him have some plaster, or some loam, or some rough-cast about him, to signify wall; and let him hold his fingers thus, and through that cranny shall Pyramus and Thisby whisper.

Quin. If that may be, then all is well. [*He takes up his prompt-book.*] Come, sit down, every mother's son, and rehearse your parts. Pyramus, you begin. When you have spoken your speech, enter into that brake, and so every one according to his cue.

Enter Puck *behind.*

Puck. What hempen home-spuns have we swaggering here,
So near the cradle of the fairy queen? 80
What, a play toward? I'll be an auditor,
An actor too perhaps, if I see cause.

Quin. Speak, Pyramus. Thisby, stand forth.

Bot. Thisby, the flowers of odious savours sweet—

Quin. Odours, odours.

69. *present:* represent. 81. *toward:* in preparation, about to take place.

Bot. —odours savours sweet.
So hath thy breath, my dearest Thisby dear.
But hark, a voice! Stay thou but here awhile,
And by and by I will to thee appear.
[*Exit into the hawthorn brake.*

Puck. A stranger Pyramus than e'er played here. [*He follows.*

Flu. Must I speak now? 91

Quin. Ay, marry, must you; for you must understand he goes but to see a noise that he heard, and is to come again.

Flu. Most radiant Pyramus, most lily-white of hue,
Of colour like the red rose on triumphant brier,
Most brisky juvenal and eke most lovely Jew,
As true as truest horse that yet would never tire,
I'll meet thee, Pyramus, at Ninny's tomb. 99

Quin. "Ninus' tomb," man. Why, you must not speak that yet; that you answer to Pyramus. You speak all your part at once, cues and all. Pyramus enter. Your cue is past; it is "never tire."

Flu. O—As true as truest horse that yet would never tire.

Re-enter BOTTOM *with an ass's head*, PUCK *following him.*

Bot. If I were fair, Thisby, I were only thine.

Quin. O monstrous! O strange! We are haunted. Pray, masters! Fly, masters! Help!
[*Exeunt Bottom's companions into the bushes.*

Puck. I'll follow you, I'll lead you about, around,
Through bog, through bush, through brake, through brier.
Sometime a horse I'll be, sometime a hound, 111
A hog, a headless bear, sometime a fire;
And neigh, and bark, and grunt, and roar, and burn,
Like horse, hound, hog, bear, fire, at every turn.
[*Pursuing them.*

97. *juvenal:* i.e., youth. *eke:* also. 102. *cues and all.* An Elizabethan actor's part consisted of the player's lines and the cues furnished by the other speakers. Flute, the inexperienced player, memorized everything he found in his script and spoke it all at once.

Bot. Why do they run away? This is a knavery of them to make me afeard.

Re-enter SNOUT.

Snout. O Bottom, thou art changed! What do I see on thee? [*He flies.*

Bot. What do you see? You see an ass-head of your own, do you?

Re-enter QUINCE.

Quin. Bless thee, Bottom! Bless thee! Thou art translated. [*He flies.*

Bot. I see their knavery. This is to make an ass of me; to fright me, if they could. But I will not stir from this place, do what they can. I will walk up and down here, and I will sing, that they shall hear I am not afraid. [*He brays out a song.*

The woosell cock so black of hue,
With orange-tawny bill,
The throstle with his note so true, 130
The wren with little quill—

Tita. [*Awaking*] What angel wakes me from my flowery bed?

Bot. [*Sings*] The finch, the sparrow, and the lark,
The plain-song cuckoo gray,
Whose note full many a man doth mark,
And dares not answer nay—

for, indeed, who would set his wit to so foolish a bird? Who would give a bird the lie, though he cry "cuckoo" never so?

Tita. I pray thee, gentle mortal, sing again. 140
Mine ear is much enamour'd of thy note;
So is mine eye enthralled to thy shape;

116. *afeard:* afraid. 122. *translated:* transformed. 128 ff. This song which wakes the fairy queen is almost a parody of the delicate little lullaby which put her to sleep. (Cf. II, ii, 9 ff.) 128. *woosell:* blackbird. 131. *quill:* pipe, note. 134. *plain-song:* simple-air (used as an adjective). 135–6. *Whose . . . nay.* The cuckoo supposedly mocked married men with their wives' infidelity. Bottom appears to be somewhat fatalistic about it.

And thy fair virtue's force perforce doth move me
On the first view to say—to swear—I love thee.

Bot. Methinks, mistress, you should have little reason for that. And yet, to say the truth, reason and love keep little company together now-a-days. The more the pity that some honest neighbours will not make them friends. Nay, I can gleek upon occasion. 150

Tita. Thou art as wise as thou art beautiful.

Bot. Not so, neither; but if I had wit enough to get out of this wood, I have enough to serve mine own turn.

Tita. Out of this wood do not desire to go.
Thou shalt remain here, whether thou wilt or no.
I am a spirit of no common rate.
The summer still doth tend upon my state,
And I do love thee. Therefore, go with me;
I'll give thee fairies to attend on thee, 160
And they shall fetch thee jewels from the deep,
And sing while thou on pressed flowers dost sleep;
And I will purge thy mortal grossness so
That thou shalt like an airy spirit go.
Peaseblossom! Cobweb! Moth! and Mustardseed!

Enter PEASEBLOSSOM, COBWEB, MOTH, *and* MUSTARDSEED.

Peas. Ready.

Cob. And I.

Moth. And I.

Mus. And I.

All. Where shall we go?

Tita. Be kind and courteous to this gentleman;
Hop in his walks and gambol in his eyes;
Feed him with apricocks and dewberries,
With purple grapes, green figs, and mulberries; 170
The honey-bags steal from the humble-bees,
And for night-tapers crop their waxen thighs
And light them at the fiery glow-worm's eyes,

143. *perforce:* forcibly. 150. *gleek:* jest. 153–4. *serve . . . turn:* be sufficient, "do." 157. *rate:* worth. 158. *still:* always. *state:* majesty, power. 169. *apricocks:* apricots. 172. *crop:* cut off.

To have my love to bed and to arise;
And pluck the wings from painted butterflies
To fan the moonbeams from his sleeping eyes.
Nod to him, elves, and do him courtesies. [*They curtsy.*

Peas. Hail, mortal!

Cob. Hail!

Moth. Hail! 180

Mus. Hail!

Bot. I cry your worships mercy, heartily; I beseech your worship's name.

Cob. Cobweb.

Bot. I shall desire you of more acquaintance, good Master Cobweb; if I cut my finger, I shall make bold with you. Your name, honest gentleman?

Peas. Peaseblossom. 189

Bot. I pray you, commend me to Mistress Squash, your mother, and to Master Peascod, your father. Good Master Peaseblossom, I shall desire you of more acquaintance too. Your name, I beseech you, sir?

Mus. Mustardseed.

Bot. Good Master Mustardseed, I know your patience well. That same cowardly, giant-like ox-beef hath devoured many a gentleman of your house. I promise you your kindred hath made my eyes water ere now. I desire your more acquaintance, good Master Mustardseed. 201

Tita. Come, wait upon him; lead him to my bower.
The moon methinks looks with a watery eye;
And when she weeps, weeps every little flower,
Lamenting some enforced chastity.
Tie up my love's tongue; bring him silently. [*Exeunt.*

185. *you . . . acquaintance:* i.e., more acquaintance of you. 186. *if . . . finger:* i.e., to stop the blood. 191. *Squash:* an unripe pea-pod, not the American squash. *Peascod:* pea-pod. 205. *enforced:* i.e., violated. 206. *Tie . . . silently.* "Is it insinuated that however deeply Titania may be enamoured with Bottom's fair large ears, and her eye enthralled to his shape, she can find no corresponding charm in his talk? There is a limit even to the powers of the magic love-juice" (Furness).

SCENE II. *Another part of the wood.*

OBERON *is waiting.*

Obe. I wonder if Titania be awaked;
Then, what it was that next came in her eye,
Which she must dote on in extremity.

Enter PUCK.

Here comes my messenger. How now, mad spirit?
What night-rule now about this haunted grave?
Puck. My mistress with a monster is in love.
Near to her close and consecrated bower,
While she was in her dull and sleeping hour,
A crew of patches, rude mechanicals,
That work for bread upon Athenian stalls, 10
Were met together to rehearse a play
Intended for great Theseus' nuptial-day.
The shallowest thick-skin of that barren sort,
Who Pyramus presented, in their sport
Forsook his scene and enter'd in a brake.
When I did him at this advantage take,
An ass's nole I fixed on his head.
Anon his Thisbe must be answered,
And forth my mimic comes. When they him spy,
As wild geese that the creeping fowler eye, 20
Or russet-pated choughs, many in sort,
Rising and cawing at the gun's report,
Sever themselves and madly sweep the sky,
So, at his sight, away his fellows fly;
And, at our stamp, here o'er and o'er one falls;
He murder cries and help from Athens calls.
Their sense thus weak, lost with their fears thus strong,

[ii] 3. *in extremity:* in the highest degree. 5. *night-rule:* diversion for the night. 9. *patches:* fools, louts. *mechanicals:* mechanics. 13. *The shallowest . . . sort:* the shallowest blockhead of that empty-headed company. 16. *advantage:* opportunity. 17. *nole:* head. 21. *choughs:* jackdaws. 25. *stamp:* noisy blow with the foot.

Made senseless things begin to do them wrong;
For briers and thorns at their apparel snatch;
Some sleeves, some hats, from yielders all things catch. 30
I led them on in this distracted fear,
And left sweet Pyramus translated there;
When in that moment, so it came to pass,
Titania waked and straightway loved an ass.

Obe. This falls out better than I could devise.
But hast thou yet latch'd the Athenian's eyes
With the love-juice, as I did bid thee do?

Puck. I took him sleeping—that is finish'd too—
And the Athenian woman by his side;
That, when he waked, of force she must be eyed. 40

Enter Hermia *and* Demetrius.

Obe. Stand close; this is the same Athenian.

Puck. This is the woman, but not this the man.

Dem. O, why rebuke you him that loves you so?
Lay breath so bitter on your bitter foe.

Her. Now I but chide; but I should use thee worse,
For thou, I fear, hast given me cause to curse.
If thou hast slain Lysander in his sleep,
Being o'er shoes in blood, plunge in the deep,
And kill me too.
The sun was not so true unto the day 50
As he to me. Would he have stolen away
From sleeping Hermia? I'll believe as soon
This whole earth may be bored and that the moon
May through the centre creep and so displace
Her brother's noontide with th' Antipodes.
It cannot be but thou hast murder'd him.
So should a murderer look, so dead, so grim.

30. *yielders:* persons who give something up. 32. *translated:* transformed. 36. *latch'd:* moistened. 37. *love-juice:* juice causing love. 41. *Stand close:* hide, get out of sight. 43, 46. *you . . . thou.* Demetrius uses the respectful *you,* while Hermia, in her contempt, uses the more familiar *thou.* 54. *displace.* Qq and Ff read *displease.* 57. *dead:* deadly pale.

Dem. So should the murder'd look, and so should I,
Pierced through the heart with your stern cruelty.
Yet you, the murderer, look as bright, as clear, 60
As yonder Venus in her glimmering sphere.
Her. What's this to my Lysander? Where is he?
Ah, good Demetrius, wilt thou give him me?
Dem. I had rather give his carcass to my hounds.
Her. Out, dog! Out, cur! Thou drivest me past the bounds
Of maiden's patience. Hast thou slain him, then?
Henceforth be never number'd among men!
O, once tell true, tell true, even for my sake!
Durst thou have look'd upon him being awake?
And hast thou kill'd him sleeping? O brave touch! 70
Could not a worm, an adder, do so much?
An adder did it, for with doubler tongue
Than thine, thou serpent, never adder stung.
Dem. You spend your passion on a misprised mood.
I am not guilty of Lysander's blood;
Nor is he dead, for aught that I can tell.
Her. I pray thee, tell me then that he is well.
Dem. An if I could, what should I get therefore?
Her. A privilege never to see me more.
And from thy hated presence part I so; 80
See me no more, whether he be dead or no. [*Exit.*
Dem. There is no following her in this fierce vein.
Here therefore for a while I will remain.
So sorrow's heaviness doth heavier grow
For debt that bankrupt sleep doth sorrow owe;
Which now in some slight measure it will pay,
If for his tender here I make some stay. [*Lies down and sleeps.*
Obe. What hast thou done? Thou hast mistaken quite
And laid the love-juice on some true-love's sight.
Of thy misprision must perforce ensue 90
Some true love turn'd and not a false turn'd true.

71. *worm:* serpent. 72. *doubler:* more forked. 74. *passion:* emotion, anger. *misprised:* mistaken. 84. *heaviness:* sadness. 87. *tender:* offer. 90. *misprision:* mistake. *perforce:* of necessity.

Puck. Then fate o'er-rules, that, one man holding troth,
A million fail, confounding oath on oath.

Obe. About the wood go swifter than the wind,
And Helena of Athens look thou find.
All fancy-sick she is and pale of cheer,
With sighs of love that costs the fresh blood dear.
By some illusion see thou bring her here;
I'll charm his eyes against she do appear.

Puck. I go, I go; look how I go, 100
Swifter than arrow from the Tartar's bow. [*Exit.*

[*Oberon anoints the eyes of the sleeper.*

Obe. Flower of this purple dye,
Hit with Cupid's archery,
Sink in apple of his eye.
When his love he doth espy,
Let her shine as gloriously
As the Venus of the sky.
When thou wakest, if she be by,
Beg of her for remedy.

Re-enter PUCK.

Puck. Captain of our fairy band, 110
Helena is here at hand;
And the youth, mistook by me,
Pleading for a lover's fee.
Shall we their fond pageant see?
Lord, what fools these mortals be!

Obe. Stand aside. The noise they make
Will cause Demetrius to awake.

Puck. Then will two at once woo one;
That must needs be sport alone;

92. *o'er-rules:* annuls, sets aside as by a higher authority. 93. *confounding:* breaking. 96. *fancy-sick:* lovesick. *cheer:* face. 97. *With . . . dear:* an allusion to the old belief that each sigh cost the heart a drop of blood. 99. *against:* before. 102. *purple:* crimson. 104. *apple of his eye:* pupil, which was thought to be a solid globular body. 114. *their fond pageant:* the foolish spectacle they present. 119. *alone:* in itself.

And those things do best please me 120
That befall preposterously.

Enter HELENA *followed by* LYSANDER.

Lys. Why should you think that I should woo in scorn?
Scorn and derision never come in tears.
Look, when I vow, I weep; and vows so born,
In their nativity all truth appears.
How can these things in me seem scorn to you,
Bearing the badge of faith to prove them true?
Hel. You do advance your cunning more and more.
When truth kills truth, O devilish-holy fray!
These vows are Hermia's. Will you give her o'er? 130
Weigh oath with oath, and you will nothing weigh.
Your vows to her and me, put in two scales,
Will even weigh, and both as light as tales.
Lys. I had no judgment when to her I swore.
Hel. Nor none, in my mind, now you give her o'er.
Lys. Demetrius loves her, and he loves not you.
Dem. [*Awaking*] O Helen, goddess, nymph, perfect, divine!
To what, my love, shall I compare thine eyne?
Crystal is muddy. O, how ripe in show
Thy lips, those kissing cherries, tempting grow! 140
That pure congealed white, high Taurus' snow,
Fann'd with the eastern wind, turns to a crow
When thou hold'st up thy hand. O, let me kiss
This princess of pure white, this seal of bliss!
Hel. O spite! O hell! I see you all are bent
To set against me for your merriment.
If you were civil and knew courtesy,
You would not do me thus much injury.
Can you not hate me, as I know you do,

121. *preposterously:* topsy-turvily. 127. *badge:* a device or emblem which identified a knight and distinguished his followers. 130. *give her o'er:* give her up, desert her. 139. *show:* appearance. 141. *Taurus':* a lofty mountain range in Asia Minor. 147. *civil:* well-mannered, polite.

But you must join in souls to mock me too? 150
If you were men, as men you are in show,
You would not use a gentle lady so—
To vow, and swear, and superpraise my parts,
When I am sure you hate me with your hearts.
You both are rivals, and love Hermia;
And now both rivals, to mock Helena.
A trim exploit, a manly enterprise,
To conjure tears up in a poor maid's eyes
With your derision! None of noble sort
Would so offend a virgin and extort 160
A poor soul's patience, all to make you sport.

Lys. You are unkind, Demetrius; be not so,
For you love Hermia; this you know I know.
And here, with all good will, with all my heart,
In Hermia's love I yield you up my part;
And yours of Helena to me bequeath,
Whom I do love and will do till my death.

Hel. Never did mockers waste more idle breath.

Dem. Lysander, keep thy Hermia; I will none.
If e'er I loved her, all that love is gone. 170
My heart to her but as guest-wise sojourn'd,
And now to Helen is it home return'd,
There to remain.

Lys. Helen, it is not so.

Dem. Disparage not the faith thou dost not know,
Lest, to thy peril, thou aby it dear.

Re-enter Hermia.

Look, where thy love comes; yonder is thy dear.

Her. [*Running to Lysander*] Dark night, that from the eye his function takes,
The ear more quick of apprehension makes;

150. *in souls:* in the same mind. 151. *show:* appearance. 153. *superpraise:* overpraise. *parts:* qualities. 159. *sort:* rank. 175. *aby:* atone for. 178. *quick:* lively. *apprehension:* perception, understanding.

Wherein it doth impair the seeing sense,
It pays the hearing double recompense. 180
Thou art not by mine eye, Lysander, found;
Mine ear, I thank it, brought me to thy sound.
But why unkindly didst thou leave me so?

Lys. [*Repulsing her*] Why should he stay, whom love doth press to go?

Her. What love could press Lysander from my side?

Lys. Lysander's love (that would not let him bide)
For Helena, who more engilds the night
Than all yon fiery O's and eyes of light.
Why seek'st thou me? Could not this make thee know,
The hate I bear thee made me leave thee so? 190

Her. You speak not as you think; it cannot be.

Hel. Lo, she is one of this confederacy!
Now I perceive they have conjoin'd all three
To fashion this false sport, in spite of me.
Injurious Hermia! Most ungrateful maid!
Have you conspired, have you with these contrived
To bait me with this foul derision?
Is all the counsel that we two have shared,
The sisters' vows, the hours that we have spent,
When we have chid the hasty-footed time 200
For parting us—O, is it all forgot?
All school-days' friendship, childhood innocence?
We, Hermia, like two artificial gods,
Have with our needles created both one flower,
Both on one sampler, sitting on one cushion,
Both warbling of one song, both in one key,
As if our hands, our sides, voices, and minds,
Had been incorporate. So we grew together,
Like to a double cherry, seeming parted,
But yet an union in partition; 210

187. *For.* Qq and Ff read *Fair.* 195. *Injurious:* insulting. 197. *bait:* torment. 198. *counsel:* secret or inmost thought. 203. *artificial:* skillful. 204. *needles:* a monosyllable, pronounced "neels." 208. *incorporate:* made into one body.

Two lovely berries moulded on one stem;
So, with two seeming bodies, but one heart;
Two of the first, like coats in heraldry,
Due but to one and crowned with one crest.
And will you rent our ancient love asunder,
To join with men in scorning your poor friend?
It is not friendly, 'tis not maidenly.
Our sex, as well as I, may chide you for it,
Though I alone do feel the injury.

Her. I am amazed at your passionate words. 220
I scorn you not. It seems that you scorn me.

Hel. Have you not set Lysander, as in scorn,
To follow me and praise my eyes and face?
And made your other love, Demetrius,
Who even but now did spurn me with his foot,
To call me goddess, nymph, divine, and rare,
Precious, celestial? Wherefore speaks he this
To her he hates? And wherefore doth Lysander
Deny your love, so rich within his soul,
And tender me, forsooth, affection, 230
But by your setting on, by your consent?
What though I be not so in grace as you,
So hung upon with love, so fortunate,
But miserable most, to love unloved?
This you should pity rather than despise.

Her. I understand not what you mean by this.

Hel. Ay, do, persevere, counterfeit sad looks,
Make mouths upon me when I turn my back;
Wink each at other; hold the sweet jest up.

213. *Two of the first:* i.e., bodies. The allusion is to the double coats of arms which belong to husband and wife and are crowned with one crest. The phrase *of the first* in heraldry refers, however, not to quartering or impaling, but to the color first mentioned in blazoning. Helena's figure of speech may be technically incorrect, but her meaning is perfectly clear. 215. *rent:* rend. 220. *passionate:* angry. 230. *tender:* offer. 237. *persevere:* pronounced *persêver*, and so spelled in Qq and Ff. *counterfeit:* pretend. *sad:* serious. 239. *hold . . . up:* keep . . . going.

This sport, well carried, shall be chronicled. 240
If you have any pity, grace, or manners,
You would not make me such an argument.
But fare ye well; 'tis partly my own fault;
Which death or absence soon shall remedy.

Lys. Stay, gentle Helena; hear my excuse,
My love, my life, my soul, fair Helena!

Hel. O excellent!

Her. Sweet, do not scorn her so.

Dem. If she cannot entreat, I can compel.

Lys. Thou canst compel no more than she entreat.
Thy threats have no more strength than her weak prayers. 250
Helen, I love thee; by my life, I do.
I swear by that which I will lose for thee,
To prove him false that says I love thee not.

Dem. I say I love thee more than he can do.

Lys. If thou say so, withdraw, and prove it too.

Dem. Quick, come!

Her. [*Clinging to him*] Lysander, whereto tends all this?

Lys. Away, you Ethiope!

Dem. No, no, sir;
Seem to break loose; take on as you would follow,
But yet come not. You are a tame man, go!

Lys. Hang off, thou cat, thou burr! Vile thing, let loose, 260
Or I will shake thee from me like a serpent.

Her. Why are you grown so rude? What change is this?
Sweet love—

Lys. Thy love! Out, tawny Tartar, out!
Out, loathed medicine! Hated potion, hence!

Her. Do you not jest?

Hel. Yes, sooth; and so do you.

Lys. Demetrius, I will keep my word with thee.

240. *chronicled:* written up in history. 242. *argument:* subject of merriment. 257. *sir.* So F_1; Q_1 reads *heele*, and most editors consider the line corrupt. 257–305. The epithets used in this squabble make it evident that Hermia is short, high-spirited, and dark, and that Helena is tall, timid, and blonde. Helena's pink and white complexion suggests the comparison with "a painted maypole."

Dem. I would I had your bond, for I perceive
A weak bond holds you. I'll not trust your word.
Lys. What, should I hurt her, strike her, kill her dead?
Although I hate her, I'll not harm her so. 270
Her. What, can you do me greater harm than hate?
Hate me? Wherefore? O me! What news, my love?
Am not I Hermia? Are not you Lysander?
I am as fair now as I was erewhile.
Since night you loved me; yet since night you left me.
Why, then you left me—O, the gods forbid!—
In earnest, shall I say?
Lys. Ay, by my life;
And never did desire to see thee more.
Therefore be out of hope, of question, of doubt;
Be certain, nothing truer; 'tis no jest 280
That I do hate thee and love Helena.
Her. [*Turning upon Helena*] O me! You juggler! You canker-blossom!
You thief of love! What, have you come by night
And stolen my love's heart from him?
Hel. Fine, i' faith!
Have you no modesty, no maiden shame,
No touch of bashfulness? What, will you tear
Impatient answers from my gentle tongue?
Fie, fie! You counterfeit, you puppet, you!
Her. Puppet? Why so? Ay, that way goes the game.
Now I perceive that she hath made compare 290
Between our statures; she hath urged her height;
And with her personage, her tall personage,
Her height, forsooth, she hath prevail'd with him.
And are you grown so high in his esteem,
Because I am so dwarfish and so low?
How low am I, thou painted May-pole? Speak!
How low am I? I am not yet so low

268. *A weak bond:* i.e., Hermia's arms. 282. *canker-blossom:* worm that destroys blossoms. 288. *counterfeit:* imitation in miniature. 290. *compare:* comparison.

But that my nails can reach unto thine eyes.
[*She flies at her; Helena takes refuge behind Demetrius, and Lysander restrains Hermia.*

Hel. I pray you, though you mock me, gentlemen,
Let her not hurt me. I was never curst; 300
I have no gift at all in shrewishness;
I am a right maid for my cowardice;
Let her not strike me. You perhaps may think,
Because she is something lower than myself,
That I can match her.

Her. Lower? Hark, again.

Hel. Good Hermia, do not be so bitter with me.
I evermore did love you, Hermia,
Did ever keep your counsels, never wrong'd you;
Save that, in love unto Demetrius,
I told him of your stealth unto this wood. 310
He follow'd you; for love I follow'd him;
But he hath chid me hence and threaten'd me
To strike me, spurn me, nay, to kill me too.
And now, so you will let me quiet go,
To Athens will I bear my folly back
And follow you no further. Let me go.
You see how simple and how fond I am.

Her. Why, get you gone. Who is 't that hinders you?

Hel. A foolish heart, that I leave here behind.

Her. What, with Lysander?

Hel. With Demetrius. 320

Lys. Be not afraid; she shall not harm thee, Helena.

Dem. No, sir, she shall not, though you take her part.

Hel. O, when she's angry, she is keen and shrewd!
She was a vixen when she went to school;
And though she be but little, she is fierce.

Her. "Little" again? Nothing but "low" and "little"?

300. *curst:* shrewish, savage. 301. *shrewishness:* sharpness of tongue. 302. *right:* real, downright. 308. *counsels:* confidences, secrets. 317. *fond:* foolish. 323. *keen:* sharp. *shrewd:* sharp-tongued.

Why will you suffer her to flout me thus?
Let me come to her. [*She tries to fly at Helena again.*
Lys. Get you gone, you dwarf;
You minimus, of hindering knot-grass made;
You bead, you acorn. [*He pushes Hermia aside.*
Dem. [*With a protecting arm about Helena*] You are too officious 330
In her behalf that scorns your services.
Let her alone; speak not of Helena;
Take not her part; for, if thou dost intend
Never so little show of love to her,
Thou shalt aby it.
Lys. Now she holds me not;
Now follow, if thou darest, to try whose right,
Or thine or mine, is most in Helena.
Dem. Follow? Nay, I'll go with thee, cheek by jowl.
[*Lysander and Demetrius go into the wood.*
Her. [*Turning upon Helena, who retreats*] You, mistress, all this coil is 'long of you.
Nay, go not back.
Hel. I will not trust you, I, 340
Nor longer stay in your curst company.
Your hands than mine are quicker for a fray,
My legs are longer though, to run away. [*Exit.*
Her. I am amazed, and know not what to say. [*She follows.*
Obe. This is thy negligence; still thou mistak'st,
Or else committ'st thy knaveries wilfully.
Puck. Believe me, king of shadows, I mistook.
Did not you tell me I should know the man
By the Athenian garments he had on?

327. *suffer:* permit. *flout:* mock. 329. *minimus:* diminutive creature. *knot-grass:* a common weed, an infusion of which was supposed to stunt the growth. 330. *officious:* zealous in duty. 333. *intend:* give a sign of. 335. *aby:* answer for. 337. *Or.* Theobald's emendation; Qq and Ff read *Of.* 338. *cheek by jowl:* i.e., side by side. 339. *coil:* disturbance. *'long of:* because of. 341. *curst:* shrewish, savage. 344. *Her. . . . say.* Omitted in F_1. 345. *still:* always.

And so far blameless proves my enterprise, 350
That I have 'nointed an Athenian's eyes;
And so far am I glad it so did sort
As this their jangling I esteem a sport.

Obe. Thou see'st these lovers seek a place to fight;
Hie therefore, Robin, overcast the night,
The starry welkin cover thou anon
With drooping fog as black as Acheron,
And lead these testy rivals so astray
As one come not within another's way.
Like to Lysander sometime frame thy tongue; 360
Then stir Demetrius up with bitter wrong;
And sometime rail thou like Demetrius;
And from each other look thou lead them thus,
Till o'er their brows death-counterfeiting sleep
With leaden legs and batty wings doth creep.
Then crush this herb into Lysander's eye;
Whose liquor hath this virtuous property,
To take from thence all error with his might,
And make his eyeballs roll with wonted sight.
When they next wake, all this derision 370
Shall seem a dream and fruitless vision,
And back to Athens shall the lovers wend,
With league whose date till death shall never end.
Whiles I in this affair do thee employ,
I'll to my queen and beg her Indian boy;
And then I will her charmed eye release
From monster's view, and all things shall be peace.

Puck. My fairy lord, this must be done with haste,
For night's swift dragons cut the clouds full fast,
And yonder shines Aurora's harbinger; 380
At whose approach, ghosts, wandering here and there,

352. *sort:* fall out. 356. *welkin:* sky. 357. *Acheron:* a river of Hades. 358. *testy:* angry. 364. *death-counterfeiting:* death-imitating. 367. *liquor:* juice. *virtuous:* powerful. 373. *league:* alliance, friendship. *date:* term of existence. 380. *Aurora's harbinger:* the morning star.

Troop home to churchyards. Damned spirits all
That in crossways and floods have burial
Already to their wormy beds are gone;
For fear lest day should look their shames upon,
They wilfully themselves exile from light
And must for aye consort with black-brow'd night.

Obe. But we are spirits of another sort.
I with the morning's love have oft made sport,
And, like a forester, the groves may tread, 390
Even till the eastern gate, all fiery-red,
Opening on Neptune with fair blessed beams,
Turns into yellow gold his salt, green streams.
But, notwithstanding, haste; make no delay.
We may effect this business yet ere day. [*Exit.*

Puck. Up and down, up and down,
I will lead them up and down.
I am fear'd in field and town.
Goblin, lead them up and down.
Here comes one. 400

Re-enter LYSANDER.

Lys. Where art thou, proud Demetrius? Speak thou now.

Puck. [*Imitating Demetrius' voice*] Here, villain; drawn and ready. Where art thou?

Lys. I will be with thee straight.

Puck. [*Far off*] Follow me, then,
To plainer ground. [*Exit Lysander, following the voice.*

Re-enter DEMETRIUS.

Dem. Lysander! Speak again.
Thou runaway, thou coward, art thou fled?
Speak! In some bush? Where dost thou hide thy head?

Puck. [*Imitating Lysander's voice*] Thou coward, art thou bragging to the stars,

382–3. *Damned . . . burial:* suicides, who were buried in unhallowed ground at the crossroads, and the drowned, over whom funeral rites had not been performed. 387. *consort:* keep company. 402. *drawn:* with sword drawn. 403. *straight:* straightway. 404. *plainer:* more level.

Telling the bushes that thou look'st for wars,
And wilt not come? Come, recreant; come, thou child,
I'll whip thee with a rod. He is defiled 410
That draws a sword on thee.

Dem. Yea, art thou there?

Puck. [*Far off*] Follow my voice; we'll try no manhood here. [*Exeunt.*

Re-enter LYSANDER.

Lys. He goes before me and still dares me on;
When I come where he calls, then he is gone.
The villain is much lighter-heel'd than I;
I follow'd fast, but faster he did fly;
That fallen am I in dark uneven way,
And here will rest me. [*Lies down.*] Come, thou gentle day!
For if but once thou show me thy grey light, 419
I'll find Demetrius and revenge this spite. [*Sleeps.*

Re-enter PUCK *and* DEMETRIUS.

Puck. [*Imitating Lysander's voice*] Ho, ho, ho! Coward, why comest thou not?

Dem. Abide me, if thou darest; for well I wot
Thou runn'st before me, shifting every place,
And darest not stand, nor look me in the face.
Where art thou now?

Puck. [*Far off*] Come hither; I am here.

Dem. Nay, then, thou mock'st me. Thou shalt buy this dear,
If ever I thy face by daylight see.
Now, go thy way. Faintness constraineth me
To measure out my length on this cold bed. 429
By day's approach look to be visited. [*Lies down and sleeps.*

Re-enter HELENA.

Hel. O weary night, O long and tedious night,
Abate thy hours! Shine comforts from the east
That I may back to Athens by daylight,

409. *recreant:* coward. 410. *rod:* stick, switch. 412. *try:* test. 420. *spite:* outrage. 422. *Abide:* wait for. *wot:* know. 426. *buy this dear:* pay dearly for this. 432. *Abate:* lessen, shorten.

From these that my poor company detest;
And Sleep, that sometimes shuts up Sorrow's eye,
Steal me awhile from mine own company.
[*Lies down and sleeps.*

Puck. Yet but three? Come one more;
Two of both kinds makes up four.
Here she comes, curst and sad.
Cupid is a knavish lad, 440
Thus to make poor females mad.

Re-enter HERMIA.

Her. Never so weary, never so in woe,
Bedabbled with the dew and torn with briers,
I can no further crawl, no further go;
My legs can keep no pace with my desires.
Here will I rest me till the break of day.
Heavens shield Lysander, if they mean a fray!
[*Lies down and sleeps.*

Puck. On the ground
Sleep sound.
I'll apply 450
To your eye,
Gentle lover, remedy.
[*Squeezing the juice on Lysander's eyes.*
When thou wakest,
Thou takest
True delight
In the sight
Of thy former lady's eye.
And the country proverb known,
That every man should take his own,
In your waking shall be shown. 460
Jack shall have Jill;
Nought shall go ill;
The man shall have his mare again, and all shall be well. [*Exit.*

439. *curst:* angry.

ACT IV

SCENE I. *The same.*

LYSANDER, DEMETRIUS, HELENA, *and* HERMIA
are still lying asleep.

Enter TITANIA *and* BOTTOM, *his ass's head decked with flowers;* PEASEBLOSSOM, COBWEB, MOTH, MUSTARDSEED, *and other Fairies attending;* OBERON *behind unseen.*

Tita. Come, sit thee down upon this flowery bed,
While I thy amiable cheeks do coy,
And stick musk-roses in thy sleek smooth head,
And kiss thy fair large ears, my gentle joy. [*They sit.*

Bot. Where's Peaseblossom?

Peas. Ready.

Bot. Scratch my head, Peaseblossom. Where's Mounsieur Cobweb?

Cob. Ready. 9

Bot. Mounsieur Cobweb, good Mounsieur, get you your weapons in your hand, and kill me a red-hipped humble-bee on the top of a thistle; and, good Mounsieur, bring me the honey-bag. Do not fret yourself too much in the action, Mounsieur; and, good Mounsieur, have a care the honey-bag break not; I would be loath to have you overflown with a honey-bag, Signior. Where's Mounsieur Mustardseed?

Mus. Ready. 19

Bot. Give me your neaf, Mounsieur Mustardseed. [*He extends a hairy hand, which Mustardseed takes with a courtly bow.*] Pray you, leave your courtesy, good Mounsieur.

Mus. What's your will?

Bot. Nothing, good Mounsieur, but to help Cavalery Cobweb to scratch. I must to the barber's, Mounsieur; for methinks

[IV. i] 2. *amiable:* lovable. *coy:* fondle. 14. *fret:* exert, trouble. 20. *neaf:* fist (Midland dialect). 21. *leave your courtesy:* i.e., omit your formality. 24. *Cavalery:* Cavalier. Bottom has forgotten that Peaseblossom, and not Cobweb, was scratching.

I am marvellous hairy about the face; and I am such a tender ass, if my hair do but tickle me, I must scratch.

Tita. What, wilt thou hear some music, my sweet love? 30

Bot. I have a reasonable good ear in music. Let's have the tongs and the bones. [*"Rural music" is played.*

Tita. Or say, sweet love, what thou desirest to eat.

Bot. Truly, a peck of provender. I could munch your good dry oats. Methinks I have a great desire to a bottle of hay; good hay, sweet hay, hath no fellow.

Tita. I have a venturous fairy that shall seek
The squirrel's hoard, and fetch thee new nuts. 40

Bot. I had rather have a handful or two of dried peas. But, I pray you, let none of your people stir me; I have an exposition of sleep come upon me.

Tita. Sleep thou, and I will wind thee in my arms.
Fairies, be gone, and be all ways away. [*Exeunt Fairies.*
So doth the woodbine the sweet honeysuckle
Gentle entwist; the female ivy so
Enrings the barky fingers of the elm. 49
O, how I love thee! How I dote on thee! [*They sleep.*

Enter Puck.

Obe. [*Advancing*] Welcome, good Robin. See'st thou this sweet sight?
Her dotage now I do begin to pity;
For, meeting her of late behind the wood,
Seeking sweet favours for this hateful fool,
I did upbraid her and fall out with her;
For she his hairy temples then had rounded
With coronet of fresh and fragrant flowers;
And that same dew, which sometime on the buds
Was wont to swell like round and orient pearls,
Stood now within the pretty flowerets' eyes 60

32. *tongs and the bones:* some rude musical instruments. 37. *bottle:* truss, bundle. 38. *fellow:* equal, match. 42. *stir:* disturb. 45. *all ways:* in all directions. 56. *rounded:* surrounded. 59. *orient:* Eastern, of superior quality and size.

Like tears that did their own disgrace bewail.
When I had at my pleasure taunted her
And she in mild terms begg'd my patience,
I then did ask of her her changeling child,
Which straight she gave me, and her fairy sent
To bear him to my bower in fairy land.
And now I have the boy, I will undo
This hateful imperfection of her eyes.
And, gentle Puck, take this transformed scalp
From off the head of this Athenian swain, 70
That, he awaking when the other do,
May all to Athens back again repair
And think no more of this night's accidents
But as the fierce vexation of a dream.
But first I will release the fairy queen. [*He anoints her eyes.*
Be as thou wast wont to be;
See as thou wast wont to see.
Dian's bud o'er Cupid's flower
Hath such force and blessed power.
Now, my Titania; wake you, my sweet queen. 80

Tita. My Oberon! What visions have I seen!
Methought I was enamour'd of an ass.

Obe. There lies your love.

Tita. How came these things to pass?
O, how mine eyes do loathe his visage now!

Obe. Silence awhile. Robin, take off this head.
Titania, music call; and strike more dead
Than common sleep of all these five the sense.

Tita. Music, ho! Music, such as charmeth sleep!
[*Soft music is played.*

Puck. Now, when thou wakest, with thine own fool's eyes peep. [*He removes the ass's head.*

Obe. Sound, music! Come, my queen, take hands with me,
And rock the ground whereon these sleepers be. [*They dance.*
Now thou and I are new in amity 92

65. *straight:* straightway. 72. *repair:* return. 76. *wont:* accustomed.

And will tomorrow midnight solemnly
Dance in Duke Theseus' house triumphantly
And bless it to all fair prosperity.
There shall the pairs of faithful lovers be
Wedded, with Theseus, all in jollity.

Puck. Fairy king, attend, and mark;
I do hear the morning lark.

Obe. Then, my queen, in silence sad, 100
Trip we after night's shade.
We the globe can compass soon,
Swifter than the wandering moon.

Tita. Come, my lord, and in our flight
Tell me how it came this night
That I sleeping here was found
With these mortals on the ground. [*Exeunt.*

Horns sound in the distance; enter THESEUS, HIPPOLYTA, EGEUS, *and train, dressed for the hunt.*

The. Go, one of you, find out the forester;
For now our observation is perform'd.
And since we have the vaward of the day, 110
My love shall hear the music of my hounds.
Uncouple in the western valley; let them go.
Dispatch, I say, and find the forester. [*Exit an Attendant.*
We will, fair queen, up to the mountain's top
And mark the musical confusion
Of hounds and echo in conjunction.

Hip. I was with Hercules and Cadmus once,
When in a wood of Crete they bay'd the bear
With hounds of Sparta. Never did I hear
Such gallant chiding; for, besides the groves, 120
The skies, the fountains, every region near
Seem'd all one mutual cry. I never heard
So musical a discord, such sweet thunder.

93. *solemnly:* formally, ceremoniously. 100. *sad:* solemn. 109. *observation:* "the rite of May" mentioned in line 138. 110. *vaward:* vanguard. 112. *Uncouple:* loose the hounds. 113. *Dispatch:* make haste. 120. *chiding:* noise. 122. *cry:* pack of hounds.

The. My hounds are bred out of the Spartan kind,
So flew'd, so sanded, and their heads are hung
With ears that sweep away the morning dew;
Crook-knee'd, and dew-lapp'd like Thessalian bulls;
Slow in pursuit, but match'd in mouth like bells,
Each under each. A cry more tuneable
Was never holla'd to, nor cheer'd with horn, 130
In Crete, in Sparta, nor in Thessaly.
Judge when you hear. But, soft! What nymphs are these?
Ege. My lord, this is my daughter here asleep;
And this, Lysander; this Demetrius is;
This Helena, old Nedar's Helena.
I wonder of their being here together.
The. No doubt they rose up early to observe
The rite of May, and, hearing our intent,
Came here in grace of our solemnity.
But speak, Egeus; is not this the day 140
That Hermia should give answer of her choice?
Ege. It is, my lord.
The. Go, bid the huntsmen wake them with their horns.
[*Horns and a shout. The lovers wake and start up.*

125. *flew'd:* having large chaps. *sanded:* of a sandy color. 127. *dew-lapp'd:* having a "dewlap" or fold of loose skin hanging from the throat. 128–9. *Slow . . . each.* Theseus's hounds are selected, not for excellence in hunting, but for their musical voices. Henry II is said to have made sure that his hounds were not only fleet, but "well-tongued and consonous," and in Shakespeare's day Gervase Markham gave this advice: "If you would have your kennel for sweetness of cry, then you must compound it of some large dogs that have deep solemn mouths and are swift in spending, which must, as it were, bear the bass in the consort; then a double number of roaring and loud ringing mouths, which must bear the counter-tenor; then some hollow, plain, sweet mouths, which must bear the mean or middle part; and so with these three parts of music you shall make your cry perfect" (*Country Contentments*, 1611). Can one take this seriously? Cf. *The Spectator*, No. 116, where Sir Roger de Coverly returns the gift of a fine hound because he was a bass and not a counter-tenor. 129. *tuneable:* tuneful. 139. *grace:* honor. *solemnity:* festivity. 140–1. *is . . . choice.* Cf. I, i, 83 ff.

Good morrow, friends. Saint Valentine is past.
Begin these wood-birds but to couple now?

Lys. Pardon, my lord.

The. I pray you all, stand up.
I know you two are rival enemies.
How comes this gentle concord in the world
That hatred is so far from jealousy
To sleep by hate and fear no enmity? 150

Lys. My lord, I shall reply amazedly,
Half sleep, half waking. But as yet, I swear,
I cannot truly say how I came here;
But, as I think—for truly would I speak,
And now I do bethink me, so it is—
I came with Hermia hither. Our intent
Was to be gone from Athens, where we might,
Without the peril of the Athenian law—

Ege. Enough, enough, my lord; you have enough.
I beg the law, the law, upon his head. 160
They would have stolen away; they would, Demetrius,
Thereby to have defeated you and me—
You of your wife and me of my consent,
Of my consent that she should be your wife.

Dem. My lord, fair Helen told me of their stealth,
Of this their purpose hither to this wood;
And I in fury hither follow'd them,
Fair Helena in fancy following me.
But, my good lord, I wot not by what power—
But by some power it is—my love to Hermia, 170
Melted as the snow, seems to me now
As the remembrance of an idle gawd
Which in my childhood I did dote upon;
And all the faith, the virtue of my heart,
The object and the pleasure of mine eye,

144. *Saint Valentine.* Birds were supposed to select their mates on St. Valentine's Day. Cf. Chaucer's *Parlement of Foules.* 145. *couple:* mate. 149. *jealousy:* suspicion. 158. *Without the peril:* outside the jurisdiction. 168. *fancy:* love. 169. *wot:* know. 172. *gawd:* toy, trifle.

Is only Helena. To her, my lord,
Was I betroth'd ere I saw Hermia;
But, like in sickness, did I loathe this food.
But, as in health, come to my natural taste,
Now I do wish it, love it, long for it, 180
And will for evermore be true to it.

The. Fair lovers, you are fortunately met;
Of this discourse we more will hear anon.
Egeus, I will overbear your will;
For in the temple, by and by, with us
These couples shall eternally be knit.
And, for the morning now is something worn,
Our purposed hunting shall be set aside.
Away with us to Athens; three and three,
We'll hold a feast in great solemnity. 190
Come, Hippolyta. [*Exeunt Theseus, Hippolyta, Egeus, and train.*

Dem. These things seem small and undistinguishable,
Like far-off mountains turned into clouds.

Her. Methinks I see these things with parted eye,
When everything seems double.

Hel. So methinks;
And I have found Demetrius like a jewel,
Mine own, and not mine own.

Dem. Are you sure
That we are awake? It seems to me
That yet we sleep, we dream. Do not you think
The duke was here, and bid us follow him? 200

Her. Yea, and my father.

Hel. And Hippolyta.

Lys. And he did bid us follow to the temple.

Dem. Why, then, we are awake. Let's follow him,
And by the way let us recount our dreams. [*They follow.*

Bot. [*Awaking*] When my cue comes, call me, and I will

184. *overbear:* overrule. 185. *by and by.* This phrase usually means "immediately"; here, however, it has its modern meaning. 192–9. *These . . . dream.* Demetrius, it should be remembered, is still enchanted. 194. *Methinks:* it seems to me. 204. *recount:* relate.

answer. My next is, "Most fair Pyramus." Heigh-ho! [*Yawning.*] Peter Quince! Flute, the bellows-mender! Snout, the tinker! Starveling! God's my life, stolen hence, and left me asleep! I have had a most rare vision. I have had a dream, past the wit of man to say what dream it was. Man is but an ass, if he go about to expound this dream. Methought I was—there is no man can tell what. Methought I was—and methought I had—but man is but a patched fool, if he will offer to say what methought I had. The eye of man hath not heard, the ear of man hath not seen, man's hand is not able to taste, his tongue to conceive, nor his heart to report, what my dream was. I will get Peter Quince to write a ballad of this dream; it shall be called *Bottom's Dream*, because it hath no bottom; and I will sing it in the latter end of a play, before the duke. Peradventure, to make it the more gracious, I shall sing it at her death. [*Exit.* 225

SCENE II. *Athens.* QUINCE'S *carpenter shop, some time later.*

QUINCE, FLUTE, SNOUT, *and* STARVELING *are assembled.*

Quin. Have you sent to Bottom's house? Is he come home yet?

Star. He cannot be heard of. Out of doubt he is transported.

Flu. If he come not, then the play is marred. It goes not forward, doth it?

Quin. It is not possible. You have not a man in all Athens able to discharge Pyramus but he.

Flu. No, he hath simply the best wit of any handicraft man in Athens. 10

Quin. Yea, and the best person too; and he is a very paramour for a sweet voice.

Flu. You must say "paragon." A paramour is, God bless us, a thing of naught.

211. *wit:* intelligence. 216. *patched fool:* a professional jester dressed in motley. 225. *her death:* Thisby's (?).

[ii] 4. *transported:* carried away. 8. *discharge:* perform. 11. *person:* bodily figure.

Enter SNUG.

Snug. Masters, the duke is coming from the temple, and there is two or three lords and ladies more married. If our sport had gone forward, we had all been made men. 18

Flu. O sweet bully Bottom! Thus hath he lost sixpence a day during his life; he could not have 'scaped sixpence a day. An the duke had not given him sixpence a day for playing Pyramus, I'll be hanged; he would have deserved it—sixpence a day in Pyramus, or nothing.

Enter BOTTOM.

Bot. Where are these lads? Where are these hearts?

Quin. Bottom! O most courageous day! O most happy hour! 28

Bot. Masters, I am to discourse wonders. But ask me not what; for if I tell you, I am no true Athenian. I will tell you everything, right as it fell out.

Quin. Let us hear, sweet Bottom. 33

Bot. Not a word of me. All that I will tell you is that the duke hath dined. Get your apparel together, good strings to your beards, new ribbons to your pumps; meet presently at the palace; every man look o'er his part; for the short and the long is our play is preferred. In any case, let Thisby have clean linen; and let not him that plays the lion pare his nails, for they shall hang out for the lion's claws. And, most dear actors, eat no onions nor garlic, for we are to utter sweet breath; and I do not doubt but to hear them say it is a sweet comedy. No more words. Away! Go, away! [*Exeunt.* 46

18. *made men:* i.e., generously rewarded. 20. *sixpence a day:* i.e., as a pension. 37. *presently:* at once.

ACT V

SCENE I. *Athens. A hall in the palace of* THESEUS *at night.*

Enter THESEUS, HIPPOLYTA, PHILOSTRATE, Lords, *and* Attendants.

Hip. 'Tis strange, my Theseus, that these lovers speak of.
The. More strange than true. I never may believe
These antic fables, nor these fairy toys.
Lovers and madmen have such seething brains,
Such shaping fantasies, that apprehend
More than cool reason ever comprehends.
The lunatic, the lover, and the poet
Are of imagination all compact.
One sees more devils than vast hell can hold—
That is the madman. The lover, all as frantic, 10
Sees Helen's beauty in a brow of Egypt.
The poet's eye, in a fine frenzy rolling,
Doth glance from heaven to earth, from earth to heaven;
And as imagination bodies forth
The forms of things unknown, the poet's pen
Turns them to shapes and gives to airy nothing
A local habitation and a name.
Such tricks hath strong imagination,
That, if it would but apprehend some joy,
It comprehends some bringer of that joy; 20
Or in the night, imagining some fear,
How easy is a bush supposed a bear!
Hip. But all the story of the night told over,
And all their minds transfigured so together,

[V. i] 1. *that:* i.e., that which. 3. *antic:* fantastic; most editions follow the spelling of Q1, *antique.* 5. *fantasies:* imaginations. *apprehend:* imagine, conceive. 8. *all compact:* entirely composed or made up. 11. *Helen's:* Helen of Troy's. *brow of Egypt:* gypsy's brow; i.e., dark. The Elizabethans considered light hair and eyes especially beautiful. The Queen herself had reddish-golden hair. 19. *apprehend:* imagine. 24. *transfigured:* changed, altered.

More witnesseth than fancy's images
And grows to something of great constancy,
But, howsoever, strange and admirable.
The. Here comes the lovers, full of joy and mirth.

Enter LYSANDER, DEMETRIUS, HERMIA, *and* HELENA.

Joy, gentle friends! Joy and fresh days of love
Accompany your hearts!
Lys. More than to us 30
Wait in your royal walks, your board, your bed!
The. Come now; what masques, what dances shall we have,
To wear away this long age of three hours
Between our after-supper and bed-time?
Where is our usual manager of mirth?
What revels are in hand? Is there no play
To ease the anguish of a torturing hour?
Call Philostrate.
Phil. Here, mighty Theseus.
The. Say, what abridgment have you for this evening?
What masque? What music? How shall we beguile 40
The lazy time, if not with some delight?
Phil. There is a brief how many sports are ripe;
Make choice of which your Highness will see first.
[*Giving a paper.*
The. [*Reads*] "The battle with the Centaurs, to be sung
By an Athenian eunuch to the harp."
We'll none of that; that have I told my love,
In glory of my kinsman Hercules.
[*Reads*] "The riot of the tipsy Bacchanals,
Tearing the Thracian singer in their rage."
That is an old device; and it was play'd 50

25. *fancy's:* imagination's. 27. *admirable:* wonderful. 32. *masques:* costume-dances and elaborate allegorical shows popular as court entertainments in the sixteenth century. 34. *after-supper:* dessert. 39. *abridgment:* pastime. 42. *brief:* short list. 49. *Thracian singer:* Orpheus; his story is found in Ovid's *Metamorphoses.*

When I from Thebes came last a conqueror.
[*Reads*] "The thrice three Muses mourning for the death
Of Learning, late deceased in beggary."
That is some satire, keen and critical,
Not sorting with a nuptial ceremony.
[*Reads*] "A tedious brief scene of young Pyramus
And his love Thisbe—very tragical mirth."
Merry and tragical? Tedious and brief?
That is, hot ice and wondrous strange snow.
How shall we find the concord of this discord? 60

Phil. A play there is, my lord, some ten words long,
Which is as brief as I have known a play;
But by ten words, my lord, it is too long,
Which makes it tedious; for in all the play
There is not one word apt, one player fitted.
And tragical, my noble lord, it is;
For Pyramus therein doth kill himself,
Which, when I saw rehearsed, I must confess,
Made mine eyes water; but more merry tears
The passion of loud laughter never shed. 70

The. What are they that do play it?

Phil. Hard-handed men that work in Athens here,
Which never labour'd in their minds till now,
And now have toil'd their unbreathed memories
With this same play, against your nuptial.

The. And we will hear it.

Phil. No, my noble lord;
It is not for you. I have heard it over,
And it is nothing, nothing in the world,
Unless you can find sport in their intents,
Extremely stretch'd and conn'd with cruel pain, 80
To do you service.

54. *satire:* i.e., directed against a nobility that neglected its duty of patronage of the arts. 55. *sorting with:* suitable to. 65. *fitted:* suited to his role. 70. *passion:* emotion. 74. *unbreathed:* unexercised, unpracticed. 75. *against:* in preparation for. 79. *intents:* intentions. 80. *conn'd:* committed to memory.

The. I will hear that play,
For never anything can be amiss,
When simpleness and duty tender it.
Go, bring them in; and take your places, ladies.
[*Exit Philostrate; space is cleared for the play.*

Hip. I love not to see wretchedness o'ercharged
And duty in his service perishing.

The. Why, gentle sweet, you shall see no such thing.

Hip. He says they can do nothing in this kind.

The. The kinder we, to give them thanks for nothing.
Our sport shall be to take what they mistake; 90
And what poor duty cannot do, noble respect
Takes it in might, not merit.
Where I have come, great clerks have purposed
To greet me with premeditated welcomes;
Where I have seen them shiver and look pale,
Make periods in the midst of sentences,
Throttle their practiced accent in their fears,
And in conclusion dumbly have broke off,
Not paying me a welcome. Trust me, sweet,
Out of this silence yet I pick'd a welcome; 100
And in the modesty of fearful duty,
I read as much as from the rattling tongue
Of saucy and audacious eloquence.
Love, therefore, and tongue-tied simplicity
In least speak most, to my capacity.

Re-enter PHILOSTRATE.

Phil. So please your Grace, the Prologue is address'd.

The. Let him approach. [*Flourish of trumpets.*

83. *tender:* offer. 85. *o'ercharged:* overladen, too great demands made upon. 88. *kind:* sort of thing. 92. *Takes . . . merit:* accepts the good intention for the accomplishment. 93. *clerks:* men of learning. 101. *And . . . duty:* in the moderate welcome of a respect which was full of fear. 104. *tongue-tied simplicity:* silent artlessness, unaffected humility. 105. *to my capacity:* to my way of thinking. 106. *address'd:* ready.

Enter QUINCE *for the* Prologue.

Pro. If we offend, it is with our good will.
That you should think, we come not to offend,
But with good will. To show our simple skill, 110
That is the true beginning of our end.
Consider then we come but in despite.
We do not come as minding to content you,
Our true intent is. All for your delight
We are not here. That you should here repent you,
The actors are at hand and by their show
You shall know all that you are like to know.

The. This fellow doth not stand upon points. 118

Lys. He hath rid his prologue like a rough colt; he knows not the stop. A good moral, my lord; it is not enough to speak, but to speak true.

Hip. Indeed he hath played on his prologue like a child on a recorder; a sound, but not in government.

The. His speech was like a tangled chain; nothing impaired, but all disordered. Who is next?

Enter PYRAMUS *and* THISBE, WALL, MOONSHINE, *and* LION, *preceded by a Trumpeter.*

Pro. Gentles, perchance you wonder at this show;
But wonder on, till truth make all things plain.
This man is Pyramus, if you would know; 130
This beauteous lady Thisby is certain.
This man, with lime and rough-cast, doth present

118. *stand upon points:* (a) bother about trifles, (b) pay attention to punctuation marks. The distortion of this Prologue by Quince's ill-timed pauses is indicated by the punctuation. It can be made to have some meaning, if not much sense, by repunctuation. Cf. Ralph's letter to Dame Custance in *Ralph Roister Doister*, III, ii. 120. *stop:* a term in horsemanship, here punned upon. 123. *recorder:* a kind of flute. 124. *government:* control. 126. *impaired:* broken. S. D. Ff reads *Tawyer with a Trumpet before them.* William Tawyer is known to have been a member of the Shakespearean company, and the note probably originated in the playhouse.

Wall, that vile Wall which did these lovers sunder;
And through Wall's chink, poor souls, they are content
To whisper. At the which let no man wonder.
This man, with lanthorn, dog, and bush of thorn,
Presenteth Moonshine; for, if you will know,
By moonshine did these lovers think no scorn
To meet at Ninus' tomb, there, there to woo.
This grisly beast, which Lion hight by name, 140
The trusty Thisby, coming first by night,
Did scare away, or rather did affright;
And, as she fled, her mantle she did fall,
Which Lion vile with bloody mouth did stain.
Anon comes Pyramus, sweet youth and tall,
And finds his trusty Thisby's mantle slain;
Whereat, with blade, with bloody blameful blade,
He bravely broach'd his boiling bloody breast;
And Thisby, tarrying in mulberry shade,
His dagger drew, and died. For all the rest, 150
Let Lion, Moonshine, Wall, and lovers twain
At large discourse, while here they do remain.
[*Exeunt Prologue, Pyramus, Thisbe, Lion, and Moonshine.*

The. I wonder if the lion be to speak.

Dem. No wonder, my lord; one lion may, when many asses do.

Wall. In this same interlude it doth befall
That I, one Snout by name, present a wall;
And such a wall, as I would have you think,
That had in it a crannied hole or chink,
Through which the lovers, Pyramus and Thisby, 160
Did whisper often very secretly.
This loam, this rough-cast, and this stone doth show
That I am that same wall; the truth is so.
And this the cranny is, right and sinister, [*Holds up his fingers.*
Through which the fearful lovers are to whisper.

The. Would you desire lime and hair to speak better?

138. *think no scorn:* did not disdain. 140. *hight:* is called. 143. *fall:* let fall. 156. *interlude:* play. 157. *present:* represent.

Dem. It is the wittiest partition that ever I heard discourse, my lord.

Re-enter PYRAMUS.

The. Pyramus draws near the wall. Silence! 170

Pyr. O grim-look'd night! O night with hue so black!
O night, which ever art when day is not!
O night, O night! Alack, alack, alack,
I fear my Thisby's promise is forgot!
And thou, O wall, O sweet, O lovely wall,
That stand'st between her father's ground and mine!
Thou wall, O wall, O sweet and lovely wall,
Show me thy chink, to blink through with mine eyne!

[*Wall holds up his fingers.*

Thanks, courteous wall. Jove shield thee well for this!
But what see I? No Thisby do I see. 180
O wicked wall, through whom I see no bliss!
Cursed be thy stones for thus deceiving me!

The. The wall, methinks, being sensible, should curse again.

Pyr. No, in truth, sir, he should not. "Deceiving me" is Thisby's cue; she is to enter now, and I am to spy her through the wall. You shall see; it will fall pat as I told you. Yonder she comes.

Re-enter THISBE.

This. O wall, full often hast thou heard my moans, 190
For parting my fair Pyramus and me!
My cherry lips have often kiss'd thy stones,
Thy stones with lime and hair knit up in thee.

Pyr. I see a voice; now will I to the chink,
To spy an I can hear my Thisby's face.
Thisby!

This. My love thou art, my love I think.

Pyr. Think what thou wilt, I am thy lover's grace;
And, like Limander, am I trusty still.

This. And I like Helen, till the Fates me kill.

183. *sensible:* capable of feeling. 198. *Limander:* Leander (?). 199. *Helen.* Hardly a model of constancy and fidelity.

Pyr. Not Shafalus to Procrus was so true. 200

This. As Shafalus to Procrus, I to you.

Pyr. O, kiss me through the hole of this vile wall!

This. I kiss the wall's hole, not your lips at all.

Pyr. Wilt thou at Ninny's tomb meet me straightway?

This. 'Tide life, 'tide death, I come without delay.

[*Exeunt Pyramus and Thisbe.*

Wall. Thus have I, Wall, my part discharged so;
And, being done, thus Wall away doth go. [*Exit.*

The. Now is the moon used between the two neighbours.

Dem. No remedy, my lord, when walls are so wilful to hear without warning. 211

Hip. This is the silliest stuff that ever I heard.

The. The best in this kind are but shadows; and the worst are no worse, if imagination amend them.

Hip. It must be your imagination then, and not theirs.

The. If we imagine no worse of them than they of themselves, they may pass for excellent men. Here come two noble beasts in, a man and a lion. 221

Re-enter LION *and* MOONSHINE.

Lion. You, ladies, you, whose gentle hearts do fear
The smallest monstrous mouse that creeps on floor,
May now perchance both quake and tremble here,
When lion rough in wildest rage doth roar.
Then know that I, one Snug the joiner, am
A lion fell, nor else no lion's dam;
For, if I should as lion come in strife
Into this place, 'twere pity on my life.

The. A very gentle beast, and of a good conscience. 231

200. *Shafalus:* Cephalus. *Procrus:* Procris. 208. *moon used.* So Qq; Ff read *moral down*, which also makes sense after a fashion. Most editors adopt Pope's conjectural emendation to Ff, *mural down.* 213. *The best in this kind:* i.e., the best actors. *shadows:* with a possible allusion to shadow puppets. 220. *man.* Theobald emends to *moon.* 227. *lion fell:* (a) fierce lion, (b) lion's skin. *nor else . . . dam:* (a) and not a lioness, (b) and in no other way a lion (save by this lion-fell).

Dem. The very best at a beast, my lord, that e'er I saw.

Lys. This lion is a very fox for his valour.

The. True; and a goose for his discretion.

Dem. Not so, my lord; for his valour cannot carry his discretion, and the fox carries the goose.

The. His discretion, I am sure, cannot carry his valour; for the goose carries not the fox. It is well; leave it to his discretion, and let us listen to the moon. 242

Moon. This lanthorn doth the horned moon present—

Dem. He should have worn the horns on his head.

The. He is no crescent, and his horns are invisible within the circumference.

Moon. This lanthorn doth the horned moon present;
Myself the man i' the moon do seem to be. 249

The. This is the greatest error of all the rest; the man should be put into the lanthorn. How is it else the man i' the moon?

Dem. He dares not come there for the candle; for, you see, it is already in snuff.

Hip. I am aweary of this moon; would he would change!

The. It appears, by his small light of discretion, that he is in the wane; but yet, in courtesy, in all reason, we must stay the time.

Lys. Proceed, Moon. 260

Moon. All that I have to say, is, to tell you that the lanthorn is the moon; I, the man in the moon; this thorn-bush, my thorn-bush; and this dog, my dog.

Dem. Why, all these should be in the lanthorn; for all these are in the moon. But silence! Here comes Thisbe.

Re-enter THISBE.

This. This is old Ninny's tomb. Where is my love?

Lion. [*Roaring*] Oh——[*Thisbe runs off, dropping her mantle.*

232. *best . . . beast.* In Shakespeare's day these words were pronounced more nearly alike than they are today. 243. *lanthorn.* Perhaps a pun on *horn* is intended. 246. *crescent:* i.e., the crescent or increasing moon; this moon is visibly on the wane. 254. *in snuff:* (a) on the wane, (b) in a huff, flustered. 259. *stay:* await.

Dem. Well roared, Lion. 270

The. Well run, Thisbe.

Hip. Well shone, Moon. Truly, the moon shines with a good grace. [*The Lion shakes Thisbe's mantle, and exit.*

The. Well moused, Lion.

Re-enter PYRAMUS.

Dem. And then came Pyramus.

Lys. And so the lion vanished.

Pyr. Sweet Moon, I thank thee for thy sunny beams;
I thank thee, Moon, for shining now so bright;
For, by thy gracious, golden, glittering gleams,
I trust to take of truest Thisby sight. 280
But stay, O spite!
But mark, poor knight,
What dreadful dole is here!
Eyes, do you see?
How can it be?
O dainty duck! O dear!
Thy mantle good,
What, stain'd with blood!
Approach, ye Furies fell!
O Fates, come, come, 290
Cut thread and thrum;
Quail, crush, conclude, and quell!

The. This passion—and the death of a dear friend—would go near to make a man look sad.

Hip. Beshrew my heart, but I pity the man.

Pyr. O wherefore, Nature, didst thou lions frame?
Since lion vile hath here deflower'd my dear,
Which is—no, no—which was the fairest dame
That lived, that loved, that liked, that look'd with cheer.

274. *moused:* i.e., caught and shaken as a cat does a mouse. 279. *gleams.* Qq and Ff read *beams;* the emendation is Knight's. 291. *thrum:* the tuft beyond the tie at the end of the warp in weaving; hence, tie (verb). Bottom as Pyramus has not altered his vocabulary. 292. *Quail:* destroy. *quell:* kill. 299. *cheer:* face, countenance.

Come, tears, confound; 300
Out, sword, and wound
The pap of Pyramus;
Ay, that left pap,
Where heart doth hop. [*Stabs himself repeatedly.*
Thus die I, thus, thus, thus.
Now am I dead,
Now am I fled;
My soul is in the sky.
Tongue, lose thy light; 309
Moon, take thy flight; [*Exit Moonshine.*
Now die, die, die, die, die. [*Dies.*

Dem. No die, but an ace, for him; for he is but one.

Lys. Less than an ace, man; for he is dead; he is nothing.

The. With the help of a surgeon he might yet recover, and prove an ass.

Hip. How chance Moonshine is gone before Thisbe comes back and finds her lover?

The. She will find him by starlight. Here she comes; and her passion ends the play. 321

Re-enter THISBE.

Hip. Methinks she should not use a long one for such a Pyramus. I hope she will be brief.

Dem. A mote will turn the balance, which Pyramus, which Thisbe, is the better; he for a man, God warrant us; she for a woman, God bless us.

Lys. She hath spied him already with those sweet eyes.

Dem. And thus she moans, videlicet— 330

This. Asleep, my love?
What, dead, my dove?

312–13. *die:* singular of *dice.* 314. *ace:* pronounced like *ass;* hence the pun. *but one:* with a possible suggestion of "unique." 321. *passion:* sorrow. 324. *mote.* Qq and Ff read *Moth;* the two words were pronounced alike in Shakespeare's day. 330. *moans.* Qq and Ff read *meanes;* the emendation is Theobald's. Onions, glossing *mean* as "lament," adds: "This form had become restricted to the north by Shakespeare's time."

O Pyramus, arise!
Speak, speak. Quite dumb?
Dead, dead? A tomb
Must cover thy sweet eyes.
These lily lips,
This cherry nose,
These yellow cowslip cheeks,
Are gone, are gone. 340
Lovers, make moan.
His eyes were green as leeks.
O Sisters Three,
Come, come to me,
With hands as pale as milk;
Lay them in gore,
Since you have shore
With shears his thread of silk.
Tongue, not a word;
Come, trusty sword; 350
Come, blade, my breast imbrue—

[*After vainly groping for the dagger, she stabs herself with its sheath.*

And, farewell, friends;
Thus Thisby ends;
Adieu, adieu, adieu. [*Dies.*

The. Moonshine and Lion are left to bury the dead.

Dem. Ay, and Wall too.

Bot. [*Starting up*] No, I assure you; the wall is down that parted their fathers. Will it please you to see the epilogue, or to hear a Bergomask dance between two of our company? 361

343. *Sisters Three:* the Fates. 347. *shore:* shorn, cut. 348. *thread of silk:* i.e., life. 351. *imbrue:* stain. S. D. Edward Sharpham's play *The Fleir* (1607) alludes to contemporary stage business in this scene: "Faith, like Thisbe in the play, a' has almost killed himself with the scabbard." 360. *Bergomask:* a rustic dance named from Bergamo, a suburb of Venice. This Bergomask and the dance of the Fairies, of which the Puck is the presenter, provides here precisely that combination of grotesquerie and daintiness of which the Elizabethan court masque consisted.

The. No epilogue, I pray you; for your play needs no excuse. Never excuse; for when the players are all dead, there need none to be blamed. Marry, if he that writ it had played Pyramus and hanged himself in Thisbe's garter, it would have been a fine tragedy; and so it is, truly; and very notably discharged. But, come, your Bergomask; let your epilogue alone. [*The players dance and depart.*
The iron tongue of midnight hath told twelve. 370
Lovers, to bed; 'tis almost fairy time.
I fear we shall out-sleep the coming morn
As much as we this night have overwatch'd.
This palpable-gross play hath well beguiled
The heavy gait of night. Sweet friends, to bed.
A fortnight hold we this solemnity,
In nightly revels and new jollity. [*Exeunt.*

Enter PUCK *with a broom.*

Puck. Now the hungry lion roars,
And the wolf behowls the moon;
Whilst the heavy ploughman snores, 380
All with weary task fordone.
Now the wasted brands do glow,
Whilst the screech-owl, screeching loud,
Puts the wretch that lies in woe
In remembrance of a shroud.
Now it is the time of night
That the graves all gaping wide,
Every one lets forth his sprite
In the church-way paths to glide.
And we fairies, that do run 390
By the triple Hecate's team,

368. *discharged:* performed. 370. *told:* (a) counted, (b) tolled. 371. *fairy time:* midnight to dawn. 373. *overwatch'd:* stayed awake longer than usual. 374. *palpable-gross:* obviously stupid. 375. *heavy:* slow. 376. *solemnity:* nuptial celebration. 379. *behowls.* Qq and Ff read *beholds;* the emendation is Warburton's. 381. *fordone:* worn out. 382. *wasted:* consumed. 388. *sprite:* spirit. 391. *triple Hecate:* Diana, who was Cynthia or Phoebe in heaven, Diana on earth, and Proserpina or Hecate in hell.

From the presence of the sun,
Following darkness like a dream,
Now are frolic. Not a mouse
Shall disturb this hallow'd house.
I am sent with broom before,
To sweep the dust behind the door.

Enter OBERON *and* TITANIA *with their train.*

Obe. Through the house give glimmering light,
By the dead and drowsy fire.
Every elf and fairy sprite 400
Hop as light as bird from brier;
And this ditty, after me,
Sing, and dance it trippingly.
Tita. First, rehearse your song by rote,
To each word a warbling note.
Hand in hand, with fairy grace,
Will we sing, and bless this place. [*Song and dance.*
Obe. Now, until the break of day,
Through this house each fairy stray.
Fairies. To the best bride-bed will we, 410
Which by us shall blessed be;
And the issue there create
Ever shall be fortunate.
So shall all the couples three
Ever true in loving be;
And the blots of Nature's hand
Shall not in their issue stand;
Never mole, hare lip, nor scar,
Nor mark prodigious, such as are
Despised in nativity, 420
Shall upon their children be.
Obe. Through this palace, with sweet peace,
Every fairy take his gait,

422 ff. These lines seem confused in the early texts; the re-arrangement here adopted is that of Richmond Noble (*Shakespeare's Use of Song*, pp. 58–9).

And each several chamber bless,
  With this field-dew consecrate,
And the owner of it blest
Ever shall in safety rest.
Trip away; make no stay;
Meet me all by break of day.
[*Exeunt Oberon, Titania, and train.*

EPILOGUE

Spoken by Puck

If we shadows have offended, 430
Think but this, and all is mended:
That you have but slumber'd here
While these visions did appear.
And this weak and idle theme,
No more yielding but a dream,
Gentles, do not reprehend;
If you pardon, we will mend.
And, as I am an honest Puck,
If we have unearned luck
Now to 'scape the serpent's tongue, 440
We will make amends ere long;
Else the Puck a liar call.
So, good night unto you all.
Give me your hands, if we be friends,
And Robin shall restore amends. [*Exit.*

425. *field-dew consecrate:* consecrated dew, the fairies' equivalent of holy water. 430. *shadows:* (a) fairies (IV, i, 347), (b) players (V, i, 253). 439. *unearned:* undeserved. 440. *serpent's tongue:* i.e., the hiss of disapproval. 444. *your hands:* i.e., your applause.

The Life of King Henry V

Introduction

Relation to Other Shakespearean Plays

Henry V is the last of a tetralogy of plays dealing with the rise of the House of Lancaster (*Richard II*, the two parts of *Henry IV*, *Henry V*), and this series is introductory to another tetralogy (the three parts of *Henry VI*, *Richard III*), written earlier in Shakespeare's career, and dealing with the civil wars of Lancaster and York. The Lancastrian tetralogy, which covers English history from 1398 to 1420, opens with the downfall of Richard II, follows the course of Henry IV's disturbed and unhappy reign, and concludes with the triumphant exploits of the soldier-king, Henry V.

Henry V differs in several respects from the other plays in the series. Although *Henry V* lacks the poetic delicacy and lyricism of *Richard II* and the vigorous and witty prose of Falstaff in *Henry IV*, the play is notable for King Henry's eloquent blank verse and his clear and simple prose. In his public utterances the soldier and the hero speaks. "Once more unto the breach, dear friends" (III, i, 1), "We few, we happy few, we band of brothers" (IV, iii, 60), and many another passage of stirring blank verse mark Henry as the most eloquent of Shakespeare's English kings. Richer and more moving than any of his martial speeches is the soliloquy on "ceremony" (IV, i, 247–301). And in the grave and beautiful prose of his conversation with the soldiers, as Francis Thompson, the poet, has observed, it is perhaps not fanciful to imagine that we hear something not unlike Shakespeare's own talk.

The king is but a man, as I am. The violet smells to him as it doth to me; the element shows to him as it doth to me; all his senses have but human conditions. His ceremonies laid by, in his nakedness he appears but a man; and though his affections are higher mounted than ours, yet, when they stoop, they stoop with the like wing. (IV, i, 104–11.)

Every subject's duty is the king's, but every subject's soul is his own. Therefore should every soldier in the wars do as every sick man in his bed—wash every mote out of his conscience; and dying so, death is to him advantage; or not dying, the time was blessedly lost wherein such preparation was gained; and in him that escapes, it were not sin to think that, making God so free an offer, He let him outlive that day to see His greatness and to teach others how they should prepare. (IV, iii, 188–96.)

There is no prose like this in the earlier histories.

A second marked difference is in its plan and general structure. *Richard II* is essentially a tragedy. Weaknesses in Richard's character combine with external causes to bring about his deposition and death. Moreover, this play includes no comedy and no humorous characters. The two parts of *Henry IV* are chronicle-histories of an older type, in which the serious plot is balanced by an underplot of low comedy. *Henry V*, though admitting comic relief, is of still another type—a dramatic epic, glorifying the deeds of the hero-king, a series of pageant-like episodes bound together by choric prologues.

A third difference between *Henry V* and the other plays in the series is no less apparent. Instead of the revealing study of two sharply contrasted characters in *Richard II*, instead of the equally striking contrasts presented by the king, Prince Hal, and Hotspur in *Henry IV*, and the unforgettable pictures of low life that are so conspicuous a feature of that play, *Henry V* presents a single character and a single theme—England's soldier-king leading a united people to victory. Never, as in the two parts of *Henry IV*, is the serious action overshadowed by the comic byplay.

The four plays of the Lancastrian tetralogy are bound together not merely by their theme—the rise of the House of Lancaster—and by their continuous account of English history from 1398 to 1420, but by the character of Henry V. From the first mention of him in *Richard II* (V, ii), through the years of his youthful wildness and growing seriousness in the two parts of *Henry IV*, to his emergence as "the mirror of all Christian kings" in *Henry V*, he serves to give to the tetralogy as a whole a kind of structural unity. As king, he serves also as a norm for Shakespeare's study of kingship, and as a striking foil to his father, Henry IV, the usurper, crafty, suspicious, trembling on his throne, and to Richard II, the weak and ineffectual dreamer.

Character of Henry V

Whatever modern critics may think of Shakespeare's hero-king—and many, from Hazlitt to A. C. Bradley, W. B. Yeats, and John Masefield, have admired him neither as king nor as man—it is clear that in his own day he was considered the perfect monarch, and that the chronicles and popular tradition preserved the legend of the madcap prince who became the ideal king, the very incarnation of the spirit of England. He was, wrote Holinshed, "a king, of life without spot; a prince whom all men loved, and of none disdained; a captain against whom Fortune never frowned, nor mischance once spurned; whose people him, so severe a justicer, both loved and obeyed, and so humane withal that he left no offense unpunished nor friendship unrewarded. . . . A majesty was he that both lived and died a pattern in princehood, a loadstar in honor, and mirror of magnificence." Holinshed's estimate of Henry V is that of Shakespeare and his contemporaries. Wise, courageous, modest, genial, understanding the common man, confident of God's support, proud of England's past, merciless to her enemies, keeping foremost in his thoughts the welfare of his subjects, he reveals himself to Shakespeare's audience—if not to us—as the ideal leader at a time of national crisis.

Sources

As in his other plays dealing with English history, Shakespeare's principal source is Holinshed's *Chronicles of England, Scotland, and Ireland* (second edition, 1587). In the main, Shakespeare follows Holinshed very closely, at times even borrowing his phrases, as in the Archbishop of Canterbury's statement of Henry's claim to the French crown. In adapting the chronicler's account to the requirements of drama, he makes several changes. He omits all mention of the insurrections early in Henry's reign, and shows instead a united nation. He omits also, for the sake of brevity and increased interest, the campaigns and negotiations that occurred after the victory at Agincourt (1415) and before the betrothal of King Henry and the Princess Katharine (1420). Other modifications of Holinshed's account are the addition of the contrast between the two armies before the battle, King Henry's easy comradeship with the common soldiers, his eloquent speeches before Harfleur and on St. Crispin's day, his moralizing upon "ceremony," his soliloquy and prayer before the battle, and the emphasis upon his piety in general. From *The Famous Victories of Henry the Fifth*, a crude chronicle-history that Shakespeare had utilized in the two parts of *Henry IV*, he borrowed suggestions for the episode of the tennis balls, for the scene between Pistol and his captive, and for Henry's wooing of Katharine.

The epilogue to the second part of *Henry IV* makes clear that Shakespeare thought of carrying over into *Henry V* that most fascinating comic character in all his plays—Falstaff. But the fat knight had served his purpose; Prince Hal's tavern companion would have been out of place in King Henry's heroic little army at Agincourt, and all that we have of him is the humorous-pathetic account of his death.

Pistol and his friends are original with Shakespeare, as are the other comic characters. In each of them a single peculiarity is emphasized, and they are clearly imitations and at times travesties of the "humorous" character recently made popular by Ben Jonson in his *Every Man in His Humour*, a play in which Shakespeare himself had been one of the actors.

Date and Text

The first edition (Q_1) appeared in 1600. It was reprinted in 1602 (Q_2) and again in 1619 (Q_3), the latter edition bearing the date 1608. (For details see A. W. Pollard, *Shakespeare's Fight with the Pirates*, second edition, 1920; or E. K. Chambers, *William Shakespeare, a Study of Facts and Problems*, 1930.) This text, which is less than half the length of the version included in the First Folio of 1623, is based on a text reported by shorthand or by an actor. The omissions—which include the prologue, the other four choruses, the epilogue, three complete scenes (I, i; II, i; IV, ii), and parts of other scenes—point to a performance for which the Folio text had been "cut." All modern editions are based on the Folio text.

All evidence points to the spring or summer of 1599 as the date of composition and production. The play is not included in Francis Meres's list in *Palladis Tamia* (1598). It is certainly later than the second part of *Henry IV*. In the last chorus the reference to the Earl of Essex's expedition against the Irish rebels places the date of that chorus between March, 1599, and August, 1599, and there is no sufficient reason for assuming that the play as a whole was written at another time.

Indeed, it is not unreasonable to suppose that *Henry V* was written for the opening of the new Globe Theatre in 1599. In *Henry V* Shakespeare seems to have planned to please a London audience rather than a court audience for whom such plays as *Love's Labor's Lost*, *A Midsummer Night's Dream*, and *The Tempest* were certainly written. Henry is bourgeois rather than aristocratic; he lacks all courtly accomplishments; he despises all Frenchmen; he is bluff, hearty, fond of practical jokes, perfectly at home with all his subjects, a "king of good fellows." Shakespeare introduces, moreover, an unusual number of characters of various rank and type, including a great many plain people with "humorous" peculiarities. Again, he employs the unusual device of a chorus, not merely to bridge the gaps between the acts but to explain the action so completely that the unsophisticated and inexperienced playgoer may easily understand. Finally, he includes in the prologue to the last act a tribute to the Earl of Essex, who was at the moment the especial favorite of Londoners. To an unusual extent, *Henry V* is a "popular" play.

Judged as a "popular" play that deals easily with conventional patriotism, with conventional ideals, with accepted idols, with externalities, *Henry V* is wholly successful. To look in it for enchanting poetry or for profound meditations on human life and destiny is to look for what Shakespeare obviously did not intend to include. Shakespeare seems here to be writing in a complaisant and uncritical mood for complaisant and uncritical Londoners, and his play is a masterpiece of its kind.

Political Significance

The political philosophy that underlies all of Shakespeare's plays dealing with English history stresses the importance of order and national unity, of loyalty to the monarch as God's vicegerent. They all support throughout the thesis stated in *3 Henry VI* (IV, i, 40), "England is safe, if true within itself," and repeated in the closing lines of *King John:*

> This England never did, nor never shall,
> Lie at the proud foot of a conqueror,
> But when it first did help to wound itself.

Henry V, in particular, emphasizes the importance of national unity. Shakespeare here glorifies not Henry only but the whole nation—Saxon, Scot, Welshman, Irishman, king, nobles, yeomen, peasants—united in a common cause and displaying the dauntless spirit of Englishmen.

The play reflects very completely the patriotic enthusiasm which was so marked during the years immediately following the defeat of the Spanish Armada, an enthusiasm which waned somewhat during the next decade, but which was again fanned into flame by the departure of Essex and his army for Ireland in March, 1599. But the play is more than praise of England's greatness. To the Englishmen of Shakespeare's day it had a further meaning. Fear of what might follow the death of the aging Queen Elizabeth was in the mind of everyone—the possibility of civil war and of foreign invasion. *Henry V* and his loyal band of brothers, united by their unselfish devotion to England, must have suggested to the Englishmen of 1599 their own duty at a time of national peril.

DRAMATIS PERSONÆ

KING HENRY V.
THE DUKE OF GLOUCESTER } the King's brothers.
THE DUKE OF BEDFORD }
THE DUKE OF EXETER, the King's uncle.
THE DUKE OF YORK, the King's cousin.
THE ARCHBISHOP OF CANTERBURY.
THE BISHOP OF ELY.
THE EARL OF SALISBURY } leaders of the English forces in France.
THE EARL OF WARWICK }
THE EARL OF WESTMORELAND }
SIR THOMAS ERPINGHAM } English officers in the King's army.
GOWER }
FLUELLEN, a Welsh captain in the English army.
JAMY, a Scots captain in the English army.
MACMORRIS, an Irish captain in the English army.
BATES, COURT, WILLIAMS, soldiers in the King's army in France.
THE EARL OF CAMBRIDGE, LORD SCROOP, SIR THOMAS GREY, English traitors.
PISTOL, NYM, BARDOLPH, rogues of the Boar's Head Tavern group.
A Boy attending the three rogues in France.
An English Herald.
Hostess of the Boar's Head Tavern, formerly Nell Quickly but now the wife of Pistol.
CHARLES VI, King of France.
ISABEL, his Queen.
LEWIS, the Dauphin.
KATHARINE, daughter of King Charles and Queen Isabel.
ALICE, a lady attending Princess Katherine.
THE DUKE OF BURGUNDY.
THE CONSTABLE OF FRANCE.
THE DUKE OF ORLEANS.
THE DUKE OF BOURBON.
RAMBURES, GRANDPRÉ, French noblemen.
THE GOVERNOR OF HARFLEUR.
MONTJOY, a French Herald.
Ambassadors from the Dauphin to Henry V.
Lords, Ladies, Officers, Citizens, Messengers, Attendants.

Scene of the Action: England and France.

Time: Spring, 1414, to May, 1420.

The Life of King Henry V

PROLOGUE

Enter Chorus.

Chor. O for a Muse of fire, that would ascend
The brightest heaven of invention,
A kingdom for a stage, princes to act,
And monarchs to behold the swelling scene!
Then should the warlike Harry, like himself,
Assume the port of Mars; and at his heels,
Leash'd in like hounds, should famine, sword, and fire
Crouch for employment. But pardon, gentles all,
The flat unraised spirits that have dared
On this unworthy scaffold to bring forth 10
So great an object. Can this cockpit hold
The vasty fields of France? Or may we cram
Within this wooden O the very casques
That did affright the air at Agincourt?
O, pardon! since a crooked figure may
Attest in little place a million;
And let us, ciphers to this great accompt,
On your imaginary forces work.
Suppose within the girdle of these walls

[Prologue] S. D. *Chorus.* The usual function of the classical chorus was to explain the significance of the action. Shakespeare, however, uses it here to bridge the gaps in time between the acts and to give the audience necessary information of what has occurred during the intervals. 2. *invention:* inventiveness, imagination. 6. *port:* bearing. 9. *unraised:* i.e., unlike the mounting spirit of the *Muse of fire.* 10. *scaffold:* stage. 11. *cockpit:* a small pit for cock-fighting; here used contemptuously for the theatre. 13. *this wooden O:* this circular theatre, probably the Globe Theatre, built in 1599. 15. *crooked figure:* probably the numeral "1." 16. *Attest:* stand for, represent. 18. *imaginary forces:* powers of imagination.

Are now confined two mighty monarchies, 20
Whose high-upreared and abutting fronts
The perilous narrow ocean parts asunder;
Piece out our imperfections with your thoughts;
Into a thousand parts divide one man,
And make imaginary puissance;
Think, when we talk of horses, that you see them
Printing their proud hoofs i' the receiving earth.
For 'tis your thoughts that now must deck our kings,
Carry them here and there, jumping o'er times,
Turning the accomplishment of many years 30
Into an hour-glass; for the which supply,
Admit me Chorus to this history,
Who prologue-like your humble patience pray,
Gently to hear, kindly to judge, our play. [*Exit.*

ACT I

SCENE I. *London. An ante-chamber in the* KING'S *palace.*

Enter the ARCHBISHOP OF CANTERBURY *and the* BISHOP OF ELY.

Cant. My lord, I'll tell you: that self bill is urged
Which in the eleventh year of the last king's reign
Was like, and had indeed against us pass'd,
But that the scambling and unquiet time
Did push it out of farther question.
Ely. But how, my lord, shall we resist it now?
Cant. It must be thought on. If it pass against us,
We lose the better half of our possession;
For all the temporal lands which men devout
By testament have given to the Church 10
Would they strip from us; being valued thus:

21. *abutting:* adjacent. 22. *narrow ocean:* English Channel. 25. *puissance:* armed forces. 29. *jumping o'er times.* The action of the play covers the period from 1414 to 1420. 31. *for . . . supply:* for the supply of which.

[I. i] 1. *self:* same. 3. *like:* likely (to pass). 4. *scambling:* disturbed. 5. *question:* consideration.

As much as would maintain, to the king's honour,
Full fifteen earls and fifteen hundred knights,
Six thousand and two hundred good esquires;
And, to relief of lazars and weak age,
Of indigent faint souls past corporal toil,
A hundred almshouses right well supplied;
And to the coffers of the king beside,
A thousand pounds by the year. Thus runs the bill. 19

Ely. This would drink deep.

Cant. 'Twould drink the cup and all.

Ely. But what prevention?

Cant. The king is full of grace and fair regard.

Ely. And a true lover of the holy church.

Cant. The courses of his youth promised it not.
The breath no sooner left his father's body
But that his wildness, mortified in him,
Seem'd to die too; yea, at that very moment
Consideration, like an angel, came
And whipp'd the offending Adam out of him,
Leaving his body as a paradise 30
To envelop and contain celestial spirits.
Never was such a sudden scholar made;
Never came reformation in a flood
With such a heady currance, scouring faults;
Nor never Hydra-headed wilfulness
So soon did lose his seat, and all at once,
As in this king.

Ely. We are blessed in the change.

Cant. Hear him but reason in divinity,
And, all-admiring, with an inward wish
You would desire the king were made a prelate; 40
Hear him debate of commonwealth affairs,

15. *lazars:* poor and diseased persons like Lazarus. 26. *mortified:* destroyed, dead. 28. *Consideration:* thoughtfulness. 28–30. *like . . . paradise.* The reference is to the expulsion of Adam from Eden. See Genesis 3 : 23–4. 34. *heady currance:* headlong current. 35. *Hydra-headed:* many-headed. 36. *his:* its. *all at once:* all the rest (of his faults).

You would say it hath been all in all his study;
List his discourse of war, and you shall hear
A fearful battle render'd you in music;
Turn him to any cause of policy,
The Gordian knot of it he will unloose,
Familiar as his garter; that, when he speaks,
The air, a charter'd libertine, is still,
And the mute wonder lurketh in men's ears
To steal his sweet and honey'd sentences; 50
So that the art and practic part of life
Must be the mistress to this theoric;
Which is a wonder how his Grace should glean it,
Since his addiction was to courses vain,
His companies unletter'd, rude, and shallow,
His hours fill'd up with riots, banquets, sports,
And never noted in him any study,
Any retirement, any sequestration
From open haunts and popularity.

Ely. The strawberry grows underneath the nettle, 60
And wholesome berries thrive and ripen best
Neighbour'd by fruit of baser quality;
And so the prince obscured his contemplation
Under the veil of wildness, which, no doubt,
Grew like the summer grass, fastest by night,
Unseen, yet crescive in his faculty.

Cant. It must be so, for miracles are ceased,
And therefore we must needs admit the means
How things are perfected.

45. *cause of policy:* problem of government. 46. *The Gordian knot:* the intricate knot tied by Gordius and cut by Alexander the Great. 48. *charter'd:* privileged. 51. *art:* practical application of knowledge. *practic:* practical. 52. *theoric:* theory. 54. *addiction:* inclination. 55. *companies:* companions. 57. *never noted:* never denoted, or, there was never noted. 58. *sequestration:* seclusion, withdrawal. 59. *popularity:* association with the common people. 63. *contemplation:* thoughtfulness, thoughtful nature. 64. *which.* The antecedent is *contemplation.* 66. *crescive . . . faculty:* growing by its own powers.

Ely. But, my good lord,
How now for mitigation of this bill 70
Urged by the commons? Doth his Majesty
Incline to it, or no?
Cant. He seems indifferent,
Or rather swaying more upon our part
Than cherishing the exhibiters against us;
For I have made an offer to his Majesty—
Upon our spiritual convocation
And in regard of causes now in hand,
Which I have open'd to his Grace at large,
As touching France—to give a greater sum
Than ever at one time the clergy yet 80
Did to his predecessors part withal.
Ely. How did this offer seem received, my lord?
Cant. With good acceptance of his Majesty;
Save that there was not time enough to hear,
As I perceived his Grace would fain have done,
The severals and unhidden passages
Of his true titles to some certain dukedoms
And generally to the crown and seat of France,
Derived from Edward, his great-grandfather.
Ely. What was the impediment that broke this off? 90
Cant. The French ambassador upon that instant
Craved audience; and the hour, I think, is come
To give him hearing. Is it four o'clock?
Ely. It is.
Cant. Then go we in to know his embassy,

73. *upon our part:* to our side. 74. *exhibiters:* presenters of the bill in Parliament. 76. *Upon . . . convocation:* in consequence of, or on behalf of, the assembly of bishops and clergy. 86. *severals:* details. *unhidden passages:* plain facts or, perhaps, lines of succession. 89. *Edward.* Henry's great-grandfather, Edward III, was the son of Isabelle, daughter of Philip IV of France. Her three brothers having died without male heirs, she claimed the French throne for her son. The claim was rejected on the ground that, since custom barred a woman from succeeding to the French throne, it barred also succession through her. This principle was later known as the Salic Law.

Which I could with a ready guess declare
Before the Frenchman speak a word of it.
Ely. I'll wait upon you, and I long to hear it. [*Exeunt.*

Scene ii. *The same. The presence chamber.*

Enter King Henry, Gloucester, Bedford, Exeter, Warwick, Westmoreland, *and* Attendants.

K. Hen. Where is my gracious Lord of Canterbury?
Exe. Not here in presence.
K. Hen. Send for him, good uncle.
West. Shall we call in the ambassador, my liege?
K. Hen. Not yet, my cousin. We would be resolved,
Before we hear him, of some things of weight
That task our thoughts, concerning us and France.

Enter the Archbishop of Canterbury *and the* Bishop of Ely.

Cant. God and his angels guard your sacred throne
And make you long become it!
K. Hen. Sure, we thank you.
My learned lord, we pray you to proceed
And justly and religiously unfold 10
Why the Law Salique, that they have in France,
Or should, or should not, bar us in our claim;
And God forbid, my dear and faithful lord,
That you should fashion, wrest, or bow your reading,
Or nicely charge your understanding soul
With opening titles miscreate, whose right

[ii] On Shakespeare's stage the action of Scenes i and ii was continuous. The setting of Scene i was the platform; the moment the two churchmen left, the curtains of the inner stage were drawn open, revealing King Henry on his throne and surrounded by his nobles. 4. *cousin:* title of courtesy used by the sovereign in addressing a nobleman. 4–5. *resolved . . . of:* satisfied about. 10. *justly:* precisely. 11. *Law Salique.* See I, i, 89, note. 14. *wrest . . . reading:* twist or pervert your interpretation. 15. *nicely:* subtly. *charge:* burden. 16. *opening:* revealing. *miscreate:* spurious.

Suits not in native colours with the truth;
For God doth know how many now in health
Shall drop their blood in approbation
Of what your Reverence shall incite us to. 20
Therefore take heed how you impawn our person,
How you awake our sleeping sword of war.
We charge you, in the name of God, take heed;
For never two such kingdoms did contend
Without much fall of blood, whose guiltless drops
Are every one a woe, a sore complaint
'Gainst him whose wrongs give edge unto the swords
That make such waste in brief mortality.
Under this conjuration speak, my lord;
For we will hear, note, and believe in heart 30
That what you speak is in your conscience wash'd
As pure as sin with baptism.

Cant. Then hear me, gracious sovereign, and you peers,
That owe yourselves, your lives, and services
To this imperial throne. There is no bar
To make against your Highness' claim to France
But this which they produce from Pharamond,
"*In terram Salicam mulieres ne succedant*":
"No woman shall succeed in Salique land";
Which Salique land the French unjustly glose 40
To be the realm of France, and Pharamond
The founder of this law and female bar.
Yet their own authors faithfully affirm
That the land Salique is in Germany,
Between the floods of Sala and of Elbe;
Where Charles the Great, having subdued the Saxons,
There left behind and settled certain French;
Who, holding in disdain the German women
For some dishonest manners of their life,

19. *approbation:* proving. 21. *impawn:* pledge. 27. *wrongs:* wrongdoings. 28. *mortality:* human life. 29. *conjuration:* solemn appeal. 37. *Pharamond:* legendary Frankish king. 40. *glose:* interpret. 45. *floods:* rivers. 49. *dishonest:* unchaste.

Establish'd then this law: to wit, no female 50
Should be inheritrix in Salique land;
Which Salique, as I said, 'twixt Elbe and Sala,
Is at this day in Germany call'd Meisen.
Then doth it well appear the Salique Law
Was not devised for the realm of France;
Nor did the French possess the Salique land
Until four hundred one and twenty years
After defunction of King Pharamond,
Idly supposed the founder of this law,
Who died within the year of our redemption 60
Four hundred twenty-six; and Charles the Great
Subdued the Saxons, and did seat the French
Beyond the river Sala, in the year
Eight hundred five. Besides, their writers say,
King Pepin, which deposed Childeric,
Did, as heir general, being descended
Of Blithild, which was daughter to King Clothair,
Make claim and title to the crown of France.
Hugh Capet also—who usurp'd the crown
Of Charles the Duke of Lorraine, sole heir male 70
Of the true line and stock of Charles the Great—
To find his title with some shows of truth,
Though, in pure truth, it was corrupt and naught,
Convey'd himself as heir to the Lady Lingare,
Daughter to Charlemain, who was the son
To Lewis the emperor, and Lewis the son
Of Charles the Great. Also King Lewis the Tenth,
Who was sole heir to the usurper Capet,
Could not keep quiet in his conscience,
Wearing the crown of France, till satisfied 80
That fair Queen Isabel, his grandmother,

57. This error in arithmetic is in Holinshed. 58. *defunction:* death. 61. *Charles the Great:* Charlemagne. 66. *heir general:* heir to the whole kingdom. 72. *find:* furnish. *shows:* appearances. 74. *Convey'd:* represented. 75. *Charlemain:* not Charlemagne (lines 61, 77), but Charles the Bald. 77. *Lewis the Tenth:* Louis IX (St. Louis). The error is in Holinshed.

Was lineal of the Lady Ermengare,
Daughter to Charles the foresaid Duke of Lorraine;
By the which marriage the line of Charles the Great
Was reunited to the crown of France.
So that, as clear as is the summer's sun,
King Pepin's title and Hugh Capet's claim,
King Lewis his satisfaction, all appear
To hold in right and title of the female.
So do the kings of France unto this day, 90
Howbeit they would hold up this Salique Law
To bar your Highness claiming from the female,
And rather choose to hide them in a net
Than amply to imbar their crooked titles
Usurp'd from you and your progenitors.

K. Hen. May I with right and conscience make this claim?

Cant. The sin upon my head, dread sovereign!
For in the book of Numbers is it writ,
When the man dies, let the inheritance
Descend unto the daughter. Gracious lord, 100
Stand for your own! Unwind your bloody flag!
Look back into your mighty ancestors!
Go, my dread lord, to your great-grandsire's tomb,
From whom you claim; invoke his warlike spirit,
And your great-uncle's, Edward the Black Prince,
Who on the French ground play'd a tragedy,
Making defeat on the full power of France,
Whiles his most mighty father on a hill
Stood smiling to behold his lion's whelp
Forage in blood of French nobility. 110
O noble English, that could entertain
With half their forces the full pride of France
And let another half stand laughing by,
All out of work and cold for action!

82. *lineal of:* descended from. 88. *Lewis his:* Lewis's. 93. *net:* tangle (of contradictions). 94. *imbar:* defend. 98. *Numbers.* See Numbers 27 : 8. 106. *tragedy:* Battle of Crécy (1346). 114. *for:* for want of.

Ely. Awake remembrance of these valiant dead
And with your puissant arm renew their feats.
You are their heir; you sit upon their throne;
The blood and courage that renowned them
Runs in your veins; and my thrice-puissant liege
Is in the very May-morn of his youth, 120
Ripe for exploits and mighty enterprises.

Exe. Your brother kings and monarchs of the earth
Do all expect that you should rouse yourself,
As did the former lions of your blood.

West. They know your Grace hath cause and means and might;
So hath your Highness. Never king of England
Had nobles richer and more loyal subjects,
Whose hearts have left their bodies here in England
And lie pavilion'd in the fields of France.

Cant. O, let their bodies follow, my dear liege, 130
With blood and sword and fire, to win your right;
In aid whereof we of the spiritualty
Will raise your Highness such a mighty sum
As never did the clergy at one time
Bring in to any of your ancestors.

K. Hen. We must not only arm to invade the French,
But lay down our proportions to defend
Against the Scot, who will make road upon us
With all advantages.

Cant. They of those marches, gracious sovereign, 140
Shall be a wall sufficient to defend
Our inland from the pilfering borderers.

K. Hen. We do not mean the coursing snatchers only,
But fear the main intendment of the Scot,

118. *renowned them:* brought them renown. 120. *May-morn . . . youth.* He was twenty-six years old. 126. *So . . . Highness:* and indeed your Highness hath *cause and means and might.* 132. *spiritualty:* clergy. 137. *lay . . . proportions:* estimate the necessary number of troops. 138. *road:* raid. 139. *With all advantages:* whenever advantageous. 140. *marches:* borders. 143. *coursing snatchers:* marauding raiders. 144. *intendment:* plan.

Who hath been still a giddy neighbour to us;
For you shall read that my great-grandfather
Never went with his forces into France
But that the Scot on his unfurnish'd kingdom
Came pouring, like the tide into a breach,
With ample and brim fulness of his force, 150
Galling the gleaned land with hot assays,
Girding with grievous siege castles and towns,
That England, being empty of defense,
Hath shook and trembled at the ill neighbourhood.

Cant. She hath been then more fear'd than harm'd, my liege;
For hear her but exampled by herself:
When all her chivalry hath been in France
And she a mourning widow of her nobles,
She hath herself not only well defended
But taken and impounded as a stray 160
The King of Scots, whom she did send to France,
To fill King Edward's fame with prisoner kings
And make her chronicle as rich with praise
As is the ooze and bottom of the sea
With sunken wreck and sumless treasuries.

West. But there's a saying very old and true,
"If that you will France win,
Then with Scotland first begin."
For once the eagle England being in prey,
To her unguarded nest the weasel Scot 170
Comes sneaking and so sucks her princely eggs,
Playing the mouse in absence of the cat,
To tear and havoc more than she can eat.

Exe. It follows then the cat must stay at home;
Yet that is but a crush'd necessity,

145. *still:* always. *giddy:* unstable. 148. *unfurnish'd:* undefended. 151. *gleaned:* stripped (of defenders). *assays:* attacks. 155. *fear'd:* frightened. 160–1. *taken . . . Scots.* David Bruce was captured and imprisoned in 1346, while Edward III was in France. 160. *impounded as a stray:* i.e., as stray cattle are shut up in a pound. 169. *in prey:* in search of prey. 173. *havoc:* the signal for pillaging; here, destroy. 175. *crush'd:* forced.

Since we have locks to safeguard necessaries,
And pretty traps to catch the petty thieves.
While that the armed hand doth fight abroad,
The advised head defends itself at home;
For government, though high and low and lower, 180
Put into parts, doth keep in one consent,
Congreeing in a full and natural close,
Like music.

Cant. Therefore doth heaven divide
The state of man in divers functions,
Setting endeavour in continual motion,
To which is fixed, as an aim or butt,
Obedience. For so work the honey-bees,
Creatures that by a rule in nature teach
The act of order to a peopled kingdom.
They have a king and officers of sorts, 190
Where some, like magistrates, correct at home,
Others, like merchants, venture trade abroad,
Others, like soldiers, armed in their stings,
Make boot upon the summer's velvet buds,
Which pillage they with merry march bring home
To the tent-royal of their emperor,
Who, busied in his majesty, surveys
The singing masons building roofs of gold,
The civil citizens kneading up the honey,
The poor mechanic porters crowding in 200
Their heavy burdens at his narrow gate,
The sad-eyed justice, with his surly hum,
Delivering o'er to executors pale
The lazy yawning drone. I this infer,
That many things, having full reference
To one consent, may work contrariously.

179. *advised:* cautious. 181. *parts:* i.e., as in music. *consent:* harmony. 182. *Congreeing:* agreeing. *close:* cadence. 190. *sorts:* different ranks. 194. *Make boot upon:* plunder. 199. *civil:* orderly. 202. *sad-eyed:* grave-eyed. 203. *executors:* executioners.

As many arrows loosed several ways
Come to one mark; as many ways meet in one town;
As many fresh streams meet in one salt sea;
As many lines close in the dial's centre; 210
So may a thousand actions, once afoot,
End in one purpose, and be all well borne
Without defeat. Therefore to France, my liege!
Divide your happy England into four,
Whereof take you one quarter into France,
And you withal shall make all Gallia shake.
If we, with thrice such powers left at home,
Cannot defend our own doors from the dog,
Let us be worried and our nation lose
The name of hardiness and policy. 220

K. Hen. Call in the messengers sent from the Dauphin.
[*Exeunt some Attendants.*

Now are we well resolved, and by God's help
And yours, the noble sinews of our power,
France being ours, we'll bend it to our awe,
Or break it all to pieces. Or there we'll sit,
Ruling in large and ample empery
O'er France and all her almost kingly dukedoms,
Or lay these bones in an unworthy urn,
Tombless, with no remembrance over them.
Either our history shall with full mouth 230
Speak freely of our acts, or else our grave,
Like Turkish mute, shall have a tongueless mouth,
Not worshipp'd with a waxen epitaph.

Enter Ambassadors *of France.*

Now are we well prepared to know the pleasure
Of our fair cousin Dauphin, for we hear
Your greeting is from him, not from the king.

207. *several ways:* from several directions. 212. *borne:* managed. 216. *Gallia:* France. 219. *worried:* harassed as dogs harass a bear. 220. *hardiness and policy:* bravery and shrewdness. 224. *our awe:* awe of us. 226. *empery:* absolute dominion. 233. *worshipp'd:* honored. *waxen:* perishable.

First Amb. May 't please your Majesty to give us leave
Freely to render what we have in charge,
Or shall we sparingly show you far off
The Dauphin's meaning and our embassy? 240
K. Hen. We are no tyrant, but a Christian king,
Unto whose grace our passion is as subject
As are our wretches fetter'd in our prisons.
Therefore with frank and with uncurbed plainness
Tell us the Dauphin's mind.
First Amb. Thus, then, in few.
Your Highness, lately sending into France,
Did claim some certain dukedoms, in the right
Of your great predecessor, King Edward the Third.
In answer of which claim, the prince our master
Says that you savour too much of your youth, 250
And bids you be advised. There's nought in France
That can be with a nimble galliard won.
You cannot revel into dukedoms there.
He therefore sends you, meeter for your spirit,
This tun of treasure; and, in lieu of this,
Desires you let the dukedoms that you claim
Hear no more of you. This the Dauphin speaks.
K. Hen. What treasure, uncle?
Exe. Tennis-balls, my liege.
K. Hen. We are glad the Dauphin is so pleasant with us.
His present and your pains we thank you for. 260
When we have match'd our rackets to these balls,
We will, in France, by God's grace, play a set
Shall strike his father's crown into the hazard.
Tell him he hath made a match with such a wrangler
That all the courts of France will be disturb'd
With chaces. And we understand him well,

242. *grace:* sense of duty. 245. *in few:* in few words. 251. *advised:* discreet. 252. *galliard:* a lively dance. 254. *meeter:* more suitable. 255. *tun:* cask. *in lieu of:* in return for. 263–6. *hazard* (a winning opening in the court), *wrangler* (opponent), *chaces* (strokes) are terms used in the old game of court tennis. *Hazard, courts,* and *chaces* are puns.

How he comes o'er us with our wilder days,
Not measuring what use we made of them.
We never valued this poor seat of England;
And therefore, living hence, did give ourself 270
To barbarous license; as 'tis ever common
That men are merriest when they are from home.
But tell the Dauphin I will keep my state,
Be like a king, and show my sail of greatness,
When I do rouse me in my throne of France.
For that I have laid by my majesty
And plodded like a man for working-days,
But I will rise there with so full a glory
That I will dazzle all the eyes of France,
Yea, strike the Dauphin blind to look on us. 280
And tell the pleasant prince this mock of his
Hath turn'd his balls to gun-stones, and his soul
Shall stand sore charged for the wasteful vengeance
That shall fly with them; for many a thousand widows
Shall this his mock mock out of their dear husbands,
Mock mothers from their sons, mock castles down;
And some are yet ungotten and unborn
That shall have cause to curse the Dauphin's scorn.
But this lies all within the will of God,
To whom I do appeal, and in whose name 290
Tell you the Dauphin I am coming on
To venge me as I may and to put forth
My rightful hand in a well-hallow'd cause.
So get you hence in peace; and tell the Dauphin
His jest will savour but of shallow wit
When thousands weep more than did laugh at it.
Convey them with safe conduct. Fare you well.

[*Exeunt Ambassadors.*

Exe. This was a merry message.

267. *comes o'er:* taunts. 269–72. *We . . . home.* This is spoken ironically. 269. *seat:* throne. 270. *hence:* away from court. 273. *state:* royal pomp and power. 282. *gun-stones:* cannon balls. 287. *ungotten:* unbegotten.

K. Hen. We hope to make the sender blush at it.
Therefore, my lords, omit no happy hour 300
That may give furtherance to our expedition;
For we have now no thought in us but France,
Save those to God, that run before our business.
Therefore let our proportions for these wars
Be soon collected and all things thought upon
That may with reasonable swiftness add
More feathers to our wings; for, God before,
We'll chide this Dauphin at his father's door.
Therefore let every man now task his thought
That this fair action may on foot be brought. 310
[*Exeunt. Flourish.*

ACT II

PROLOGUE

Flourish. Enter Chorus.

Chor. Now all the youth of England are on fire,
And silken dalliance in the wardrobe lies.
Now thrive the armourers, and honour's thought
Reigns solely in the breast of every man.
They sell the pasture now to buy the horse,
Following the mirror of all Christian kings,
With winged heels, as English Mercuries.
For now sits Expectation in the air
And hides a sword from hilts unto the point
With crowns imperial, crowns, and coronets, 10
Promised to Harry and his followers.
The French, advised by good intelligence
Of this most dreadful preparation,

300. *omit . . . hour:* neglect no opportunity. 304. *proportions.* forces. 307. *God before:* with God's help.

[II. Prologue] 2. *silken . . . lies:* i.e., silken dress and courtly pleasures are forgotten. 12. *advised . . . intelligence:* reliably informed.

Shake in their fear and with pale policy
Seek to divert the English purposes.
O England, model to thy inward greatness,
Like little body with a mighty heart,
What mightst thou do that honour would thee do,
Were all thy children kind and natural!
But see thy fault! France hath in thee found out 20
A nest of hollow bosoms, which he fills
With treacherous crowns; and three corrupted men—
One, Richard Earl of Cambridge, and the second,
Henry Lord Scroop of Masham, and the third,
Sir Thomas Grey, knight, of Northumberland—
Have, for the gilt of France—O guilt indeed!—
Confirm'd conspiracy with fearful France;
And by their hands this grace of kings must die,
If hell and treason hold their promises,
Ere he take ship for France, and in Southampton. 30
Linger your patience on, and we'll digest
The abuse of distance, force a play.
The sum is paid, the traitors are agreed,
The king is set from London, and the scene
Is now transported, gentles, to Southampton.
There is the playhouse now, there must you sit,
And thence to France shall we convey you safe,
And bring you back, charming the narrow seas
To give you gentle pass; for, if we may,
We'll not offend one stomach with our play. 40
But, till the king come forth, and not till then,
Unto Southampton do we shift our scene. [*Exit.*

14. *pale policy:* cowardly intrigue. 16–19. *O England . . . natural!* Shakespeare here states an idea that is central in his plays based on English history. 18. *would:* would have. 19. *kind:* natural, true to their kinship. 20. *France:* the king of France. 22. *crowns:* crown-pieces, bribes. 26. *gilt:* gold. 28. *grace of kings:* ornament of all kings, best of kings. 31–2. *Linger . . . play:* prolong your patience, and we'll dispose of the difficulties of distance and in spite of them make a play. 39. *pass:* passage. 41. *till the king:* when the king.

SCENE I. *London. A street.*

Enter Corporal NYM *and* Lieutenant BARDOLPH.

Bard. Well met, Corporal Nym.

Nym. Good morrow, Lieutenant Bardolph.

Bard. What, are Ancient Pistol and you friends yet?

Nym. For my part, I care not. I say little; but when time shall serve, there shall be smiles—but that shall be as it may. I dare not fight, but I will wink and hold out mine iron. It is a simple one, but what though? It will toast cheese, and it will endure cold as another man's sword will—and there's an end. 11

Bard. I will bestow a breakfast to make you friends, and we'll be all three sworn brothers to France. Let it be so, good Corporal Nym.

Nym. Faith, I will live so long as I may, that's the certain of it; and when I cannot live any longer, I will do as I may. That is my rest; that is the rendezvous of it.

Bard. It is certain, corporal, that he is married to Nell Quickly; and certainly she did you wrong, for you were troth-plight to her. 21

Nym. I cannot tell. Things must be as they may. Men may sleep, and they may have their throats about them at that time, and some say knives have edges. It must be as it may. Though Patience be a tired mare, yet she will plod. There must be conclusions. Well, I cannot tell.

Enter PISTOL *and* Hostess.

Bard. Here comes Ancient Pistol and his wife. Good corporal, be patient here. How now, mine host Pistol? 30

Pist. Base tike, call'st thou me host?

[i] 3. *Ancient:* ensign. 5–7. *I say . . . may.* Nym's peculiarities are his fondness for dark hints and meaningless formulas, and his misuse of words. 8. *wink:* shut the eyes. *iron:* sword. 14. *to France:* as we go to France. 17. *rest:* determination. 21. *troth-plight:* betrothed. 31. *tike:* cur. Pistol's "humor" is to use extravagant epithets, phrases borrowed from plays, and scraps of foreign languages.

Now, by this hand, I swear, I scorn the term;
Nor shall my Nell keep lodgers!

Host. No, by my troth, not long; for we cannot lodge and board a dozen or fourteen gentlewomen that live honestly by the prick of their needles but it will be thought we keep a bawdy-house straight. [*Nym and Pistol draw.*] O well-a-day, Lady, if he be not drawn now! We shall see wilful adultery and murder committed. 40

Bard. Good lieutenant! Good corporal! Offer nothing here!

Nym. Pish!

Pist. Pish for thee, Iceland dog! Thou prick-ear'd cur of Iceland!

Host. Good Corporal Nym, show thy valour, and put up your sword.

Nym. Will you shog off? I would have you solus.

Pist. "Solus," egregious dog? O viper vile!
The "solus" in thy most mervailous face; 50
The "solus" in thy teeth, and in thy throat,
And in thy hateful lungs, yea, in thy maw, perdy,
And, which is worse, within thy nasty mouth!
I do retort the "solus" in thy bowels;
For I can take, and Pistol's cock is up,
And flashing fire will follow.

Nym. I am not Barbason; you cannot conjure me. I have an humour to knock you indifferently well. If you grow foul with me, Pistol, I will scour you with my rapier, as I may, in fair terms. If you would walk off, I would prick your guts a little, in good terms, as I may, and that's the humour of it. 63

Pist. O braggart vile and damned furious wight!
The grave doth gape, and doting Death is near.
Therefore exhale!

39. *Lady:* by our Lady, an oath. *be not drawn:* has not drawn his sword. 47. *shog:* jog; slang for *move.* 52. *maw:* stomach. *perdy: par Dieu.* 55. *take:* (a) catch fire, (b) bewitch. *Pistol's . . . up:* the pistol is cocked. 57. *Barbason:* a fiend. 58. *humour:* inclination. 59–60. *I will . . . rapier:* I will run you through as one would *scour* a pistol-barrel that has grown *foul* from shooting. 66. *exhale:* draw (your sword).

C. J. Visscher's *View of London and Westminster* (1616).

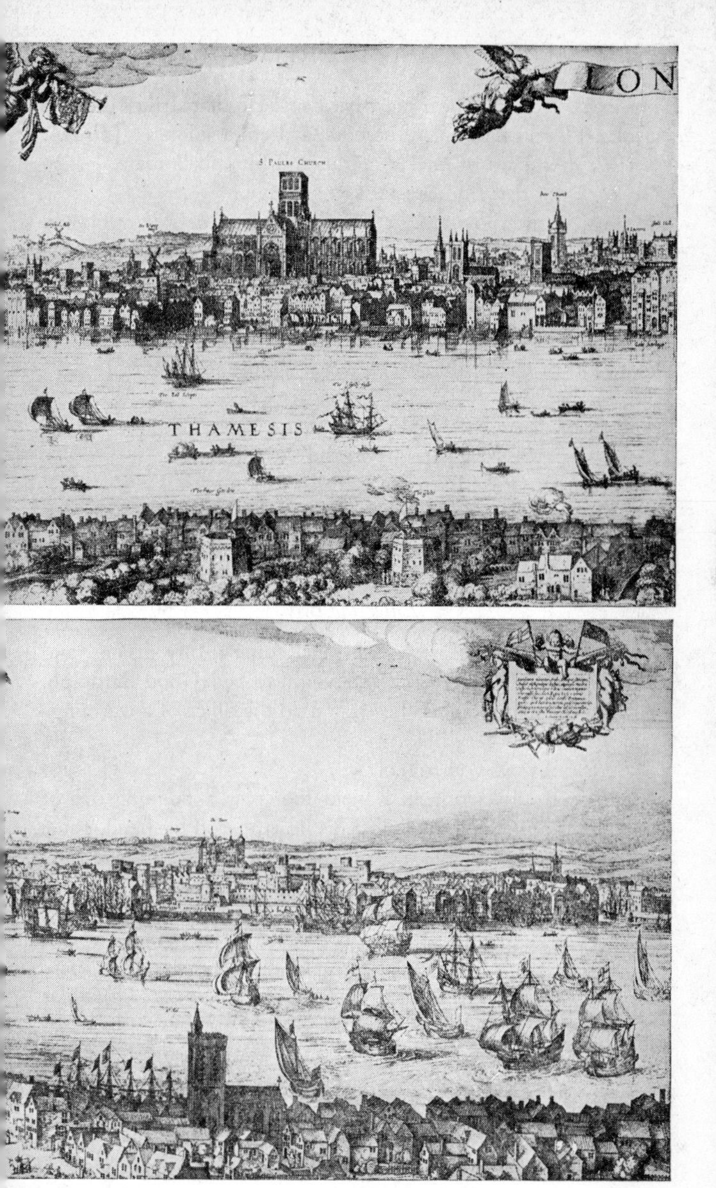

(Read from left to right across both pages.)

Bard. Hear me, hear me what I say! He that strikes the first stroke, I'll run him up to the hilts, as I am a soldier. [*Draws.*

Pist. An oath of mickle might, and fury shall abate. 70
Give me thy fist, thy fore-foot to me give.
Thy spirits are most tall. [*They sheathe their swords.*

Nym. I will cut thy throat, one time or other, in fair terms. That is the humour of it.

Pist. *Couple a gorge!*
That is the word. I thee defy again.
O hound of Crete, think'st thou my spouse to get?
No; to the spital go,
And from the powdering-tub of infamy
Fetch forth the lazar kite of Cressid's kind, 80
Doll Tearsheet she by name, and her espouse.
I have, and I will hold, the quondam Quickly
For the only she; and—*pauca*, there's enough.
Go to!

Enter the Boy.

Boy. Mine host Pistol, you must come to my master, and you, hostess. He is very sick and would to bed. Good Bardolph, put thy face between his sheets, and do the office of a warming-pan. Faith, he's very ill.

Bard. Away, you rogue! 90

Host. By my troth, he'll yield the crow a pudding one of these days. The king has killed his heart. Good husband, come home presently. [*Exeunt Hostess and Boy.*

70. *mickle:* great. 72. *tall:* brave. 75. *Couple a gorge: coupez la gorge,* cut the throat. 78. *spital:* hospital. 79. *powdering-tub:* tub used for salting meat; here alluding to a method of curing a disease. 80. *lazar:* leprous. *kite:* an indefinite term of reproach. Perhaps, as Onions suggests, the reading should be *kit* (i.e., kitten), as in F_4. *Cressid's kind.* Cressida was the type of inconstancy. In Henryson's fifteenth-century *Testament of Cresseid*, Chaucer's inconstant girl becomes a beggar and leper. 82. *quondam:* former. 83. *she:* woman. *pauca* (*verba*): few words. 88. *face.* His face was permanently red from drinking. 91–2. *yield . . . pudding:* come to the gallows (referring to the Boy). 93. *his:* Falstaff's. See *2 Henry IV*, V, v, 93. *presently:* at once.

Bard. Come, shall I make you two friends? We must to France together. Why the devil should we keep knives to cut one another's throats?

Pist. Let floods o'erswell, and fiends for food howl on!

Nym. You'll pay me the eight shillings I won of you at betting?

Pist. Base is the slave that pays. 100

Nym. That now I will have; that's the humour of it.

Pist. As manhood shall compound. Push home.

[*They draw.*

Bard. By this sword, he that makes the first thrust, I'll kill him! By this sword, I will. [*Draws.*

Pist. "Sword" is an oath, and oaths must have their course.

Bard. Corporal Nym, an thou wilt be friends, be friends; an thou wilt not, why then be enemies with me too. Prithee, put up. 109

Nym. I shall have my eight shillings I won of you at betting?

Pist. A noble shalt thou have, and present pay;
And liquor likewise will I give to thee,
And friendship shall combine, and brotherhood.
I'll live by Nym, and Nym shall live by me.
Is not this just? For I shall sutler be
Unto the camp, and profits will accrue.
Give me thy hand. [*They sheathe their swords.*

Nym. I shall have my noble?

Pist. In cash most justly paid. 120

Nym. Well, then, that's the humour of 't.

Re-enter Hostess.

Host. As ever you came of women, come in quickly to Sir John. Ah, poor heart! He is so shaked of a burning quotidian tertian that it is most lamentable to behold. Sweet men, come to him.

103. *compound:* settle (a quarrel). 107. *an:* if. 112. *noble:* a gold coin. 116. *sutler:* one who sells provisions to the soldiers. 120. *justly:* exactly. 124. *quotidian:* a fever recurring daily. *tertian:* a fever recurring every third day.

Nym. The king hath run bad humours on the knight; that's the even of it.

Pist. Nym, thou hast spoke the right.
His heart is fracted and corroborate. 130

Nym. The king is a good king, but it must be as it may. He passes some humours and careers.

Pist. Let us condole the knight; for, lambkins, we will live.
[*Exeunt.*

SCENE II. *Southampton. A council chamber.*

Enter EXETER, BEDFORD, *and* WESTMORELAND.

Bed. 'Fore God, his Grace is bold, to trust these traitors.

Exe. They shall be apprehended by and by.

West. How smooth and even they do bear themselves,
As if allegiance in their bosoms sat,
Crowned with faith and constant loyalty!

Bed. The king hath note of all that they intend,
By interception which they dream not of.

Exe. Nay, but the man that was his bedfellow,
Whom he hath dull'd and cloy'd with gracious favours—
That he should, for a foreign purse, so sell 10
His sovereign's life to death and treachery!

Trumpets sound. Enter KING HENRY, SCROOP, CAMBRIDGE, GREY, *and* Attendants.

K. Hen. Now sits the wind fair, and we will aboard.
My Lord of Cambridge, and my kind Lord of Masham,
And you, my gentle knight, give me your thoughts.
Think you not that the powers we bear with us
Will cut their passage through the force of France,
Doing the execution and the act
For which we have in head assembled them?

Scroop. No doubt, my liege, if each man do his best.

K. Hen. I doubt not that, since we are well persuaded 20

128. *even:* plain truth. 130. *fracted:* broken. *corroborate:* strengthened. 132. *He . . . careers:* he has his whims and caprices.
[ii] 15. *powers:* forces. 18. *head:* armed force.

We carry not a heart with us from hence
That grows not in a fair consent with ours,
Nor leave not one behind that doth not wish
Success and conquest to attend on us.
Cam. Never was monarch better fear'd and loved
Than is your Majesty. There's not, I think, a subject
That sits in heart-grief and uneasiness
Under the sweet shade of your government.
Grey. True! Those that were your father's enemies
Have steep'd their galls in honey and do serve you 30
With hearts create of duty and of zeal.
K. Hen. We therefore have great cause of thankfulness,
And shall forget the office of our hand
Sooner than quittance of desert and merit
According to the weight and worthiness.
Scroop. So service shall with steeled sinews toil,
And labour shall refresh itself with hope,
To do your Grace incessant services.
K. Hen. We judge no less. Uncle of Exeter,
Enlarge the man committed yesterday 40
That rail'd against our person. We consider
It was excess of wine that set him on,
And on his more advice we pardon him.
Scroop. That's mercy, but too much security.
Let him be punish'd, sovereign, lest example
Breed, by his sufferance, more of such a kind.
K. Hen. O, let us yet be merciful!
Cam. So may your Highness, and yet punish too.
Grey. Sir,
You show great mercy if you give him life 50
After the taste of much correction.
K. Hen. Alas, your too much love and care of me
Are heavy orisons 'gainst this poor wretch!

22. *consent:* agreement. 33. *office:* use. 34. *quittance:* reward. 40. *Enlarge:* release. *committed:* imprisoned. 43. *advice:* thought. 44. *security:* overconfidence. 46. *by his sufferance:* by permitting him to go unpunished. 53. *orisons:* prayers.

If little faults, proceeding on distemper,
Shall not be wink'd at, how shall we stretch our eye
When capital crimes, chew'd, swallow'd, and digested,
Appear before us? We'll yet enlarge that man,
Though Cambridge, Scroop, and Grey, in their dear care
And tender preservation of our person,
Would have him punish'd. And now to our French causes. 60
Who are the late commissioners?

Cam. I one, my lord.
Your Highness bade me ask for it today.

Scroop. So did you me, my liege.

Grey. And I, my royal sovereign.

K. Hen. Then, Richard Earl of Cambridge, there is yours;
There yours, Lord Scroop of Masham; and, sir knight,
Grey of Northumberland, this same is yours.
Read them, and know I know your worthiness.
My Lord of Westmoreland and uncle Exeter, 70
We will aboard tonight.—Why, how now, gentlemen?
What see you in those papers that you lose
So much complexion?—Look ye, how they change!
Their cheeks are paper.—Why, what read you there
That hath so cowarded and chased your blood
Out of appearance?

Cam. I do confess my fault,
And do submit me to your Highness' mercy.

Grey.
Scroop. } To which we all appeal.

K. Hen. The mercy that was quick in us but late,
By your own counsel is suppress'd and kill'd. 80
You must not dare, for shame, to talk of mercy,
For your own reasons turn into your bosoms,
As dogs upon their masters, worrying you.
See you, my princes and my noble peers,
These English monsters! My Lord of Cambridge here—

54. *on distemper:* from physical disorder. 55. *stretch:* open wide. 61. *late:* lately appointed. 63. *it:* i.e., the commission. 79. *quick:* alive.

You know how apt our love was to accord
To furnish him with all appertinents
Belonging to his honour; and this man
Hath, for a few light crowns, lightly conspired
And sworn unto the practices of France	90
To kill us here in Hampton; to the which
This knight, no less for bounty bound to us
Than Cambridge is, hath likewise sworn. But, O,
What shall I say to thee, Lord Scroop? Thou cruel,
Ingrateful, savage, and inhuman creature!
Thou that didst bear the key of all my counsels,
That knew'st the very bottom of my soul,
That almost mightst have coin'd me into gold,
Wouldst thou have practiced on me for thy use?
May it be possible that foreign hire	100
Could out of thee extract one spark of evil
That might annoy my finger? 'Tis so strange
That, though the truth of it stands off as gross
As black and white, my eye will scarcely see it.
Treason and murder ever kept together,
As two yoke-devils sworn to either's purpose,
Working so grossly in a natural cause
That admiration did not whoop at them;
But thou, 'gainst all proportion, didst bring in
Wonder to wait on treason and on murder;	110
And whatsoever cunning fiend it was
That wrought upon thee so preposterously
Hath got the voice in hell for excellence.
All other devils that suggest by treasons
Do botch and bungle up damnation
With patches, colours, and with forms being fetch'd
From glistering semblances of piety.

86. *apt:* ready. *accord:* consent. 87. *appertinents:* things pertaining to him. 90. *practices:* plots. 99. *practiced on:* conspired against. 103. *gross:* plain. 108. *admiration:* wonder. 109. *'gainst all proportion:* contrary to all reason. 113. *voice:* reputation. 114. *suggest:* tempt. 115. *botch:* patch unskillfully. 116. *colours:* pretenses. 117. *glistering:* shining.

But he that temper'd thee bade thee stand up,
Gave thee no instance why thou shouldst do treason,
Unless to dub thee with the name of traitor. 120
If that same demon that hath gull'd thee thus
Should with his lion gait walk the whole world,
He might return to vasty Tartar back,
And tell the legions, "I can never win
A soul so easy as that Englishman's."
O, how hast thou with jealousy infected
The sweetness of affiance! Show men dutiful?
Why, so didst thou. Seem they grave and learned?
Why, so didst thou. Come they of noble family?
Why, so didst thou. Seem they religious? 130
Why, so didst thou. Or are they spare in diet,
Free from gross passion or of mirth or anger,
Constant in spirit, not swerving with the blood,
Garnish'd and deck'd in modest complement,
Not working with the eye without the ear,
And but in purged judgment trusting neither?
Such and so finely bolted didst thou seem.
And thus thy fall hath left a kind of blot
To mark the full-fraught man and best indued
With some suspicion. I will weep for thee, 140
For this revolt of thine, methinks, is like
Another fall of man.—Their faults are open.
Arrest them to the answer of the law;
And God acquit them of their practices!

Exe. I arrest thee of high treason, by the name of Richard Earl of Cambridge.

118. *temper'd:* worked upon. 119. *instance:* motive. 121. *gull'd:* deceived. 122. *lion gait.* See I Peter 5 : 8—"Your adversary the devil, as a roaring lion, walketh about, seeking whom he may devour." 123. *Tartar:* Tartarus, the hell of classical mythology. 124. *legions:* i.e., of devils. (Mark 5 : 9.) 126. *jealousy:* mistrust. 127. *affiance:* confidence. *Show:* seem. 133. *swerving with the blood:* swayed by passion. 134. *complement:* demeanor. 137. *bolted:* sifted and cleansed. 139. *full-fraught:* full-stored (with virtues). *indued:* endowed.

I arrest thee of high treason, by the name of Henry Lord Scroop of Masham.

I arrest thee of high treason, by the name of Thomas Grey, knight, of Northumberland. 150

Scroop. Our purposes God justly hath discover'd,
And I repent my fault more than my death,
Which I beseech your Highness to forgive,
Although my body pay the price of it.

Cam. For me, the gold of France did not seduce,
Although I did admit it as a motive
The sooner to effect what I intended.
But God be thanked for prevention,
Which I in sufferance heartily will rejoice,
Beseeching God and you to pardon me. 160

Grey. Never did faithful subject more rejoice
At the discovery of most dangerous treason
Than I do at this hour joy o'er myself,
Prevented from a damned enterprise.
My fault, but not my body, pardon, sovereign.

K. Hen. God quit you in his mercy! Hear your sentence.
You have conspired against our royal person,
Join'd with an enemy proclaim'd, and from his coffers
Received the golden earnest of our death;
Wherein you would have sold your king to slaughter, 170
His princes and his peers to servitude,
His subjects to oppression and contempt,
And his whole kingdom into desolation.
Touching our person seek we no revenge;
But we our kingdom's safety must so tender,
Whose ruin you have sought, that to her laws
We do deliver you. Get you therefore hence,
Poor miserable wretches, to your death,

151. *discover'd:* revealed. 155–7. *For . . . intended.* According to Holinshed, his motive was to bring to the throne his brother-in-law, the Earl of March, whose heirs were Cambridge's children. 159. *in sufferance:* in suffering the penalty. 166. *quit:* acquit. 169. *earnest:* pledge money. 175. *tender:* hold dear.

The taste whereof God of his mercy give
You patience to endure and true repentance 180
Of all your dear offenses! Bear them hence.
[*Exeunt Cambridge, Scroop, and Grey, guarded.*
Now, lords, for France; the enterprise whereof
Shall be to you, as us, like glorious.
We doubt not of a fair and lucky war,
Since God so graciously hath brought to light
This dangerous treason lurking in our way
To hinder our beginnings. We doubt not now
But every rub is smoothed on our way.
Then forth, dear countrymen! Let us deliver
Our puissance into the hand of God, 190
Putting it straight in expedition.
Cheerly to sea! The signs of war advance!
No king of England, if not king of France! [*Exeunt.*

SCENE III. *London. Before a tavern.*

Enter PISTOL, Hostess, NYM, BARDOLPH, *and* BOY.

Host. Prithee, honey-sweet husband, let me bring thee to Staines.

Pist. No; for my manly heart doth yearn.
Bardolph, be blithe; Nym, rouse thy vaunting veins;
Boy, bristle thy courage up; for Falstaff he is dead,
And we must yearn therefore.

Bard. Would I were with him, wheresome'er he is, either in heaven or in hell!

Host. Nay, sure, he's not in hell. He's in Arthur's bosom, if ever man went to Arthur's bosom. A' made a finer end and

181. *dear:* grievous. 188. *rub:* obstacle; a term from bowls. 190. *puissance:* power. 191. *expedition:* motion. 192. *The . . . advance:* lift up the banners.

[iii] 1. *bring:* accompany. 2. *Staines:* a village on the road to Southampton. 3. *yearn:* mourn. 10. *Arthur's bosom.* She probably means Abraham's bosom. See Luke 16 : 22. 11. *A':* he. *an:* as if.

went away an it had been any christom child. A' parted even just between twelve and one, even at the turning o' the tide, for after I saw him fumble with the sheets and play with flowers and smile upon his fingers' ends, I knew there was but one way, for his nose was as sharp as a pen, and a' babbled of green fields. "How now, Sir John?" quoth I. "What, man? Be o' good cheer." So a' cried out, "God, God, God!" three or four times. Now I, to comfort him, bid him a' should not think of God; I hoped there was no need to trouble himself with any such thoughts yet. So a' bade me lay more clothes on his feet. I put my hand into the bed and felt them, and they were as cold as any stone. Then I felt to his knees, and they were as cold as any stone, and so upward and upward, and all was as cold as any stone.

Nym. They say he cried out of sack.

Host. Ay, that a' did. 30

Bard. And of women.

Host. Nay, that a' did not.

Boy. Yes, that a' did; and said they were devils incarnate.

Host. A' could never abide carnation; 'twas a colour he never liked.

Boy. A' said once, the Devil would have him about women.

Host. A' did in some sort, indeed, handle women; but then he was rheumatic, and talked of the whore of Babylon. 41

Boy. Do you not remember, a' saw a flea stick upon Bardolph's nose, and a' said it was a black soul burning in hell-fire?

Bard. Well, the fuel is gone that maintained that fire. That's all the riches I got in his service.

Nym. Shall we shog? The king will be gone from Southampton.

Pist. Come, let's away. My love, give me thy lips.
Look to my chattels and my movables. 50
Let senses rule; the word is "Pitch and Pay."

12. *christom child:* child in its chrisom-cloth or christening-robe. 17–18. *a' babbled of green fields*. Theobald's famous emendation of the Folio reading: *a Table of greene fields*. 29. *of:* against. *sack:* a white wine. 39. *handle:* discuss. 40. *rheumatic:* error for lunatic (?). 51. *senses:* common sense (?). "*Pitch and Pay*": pay cash (?).

Trust none;
For oaths are straws, men's faiths are wafer-cakes,
And Hold-fast is the only dog, my duck.
Therefore Caveto be thy counsellor.
Go, clear thy crystals. Yoke-fellows in arms,
Let us to France; like horse-leeches, my boys,
To suck, to suck, the very blood to suck!

Boy. And that's but unwholesome food, they say. 60

Pist. Touch her soft mouth, and march.

Bard. Farewell, hostess. [*Kissing her.*

Nym. I cannot kiss—that is the humour of it; but adieu!

Pist. Let housewifery appear. Keep close, I thee command.

Host. Farewell! Adieu! [*Exeunt.*

SCENE IV. *France. The* KING'S *palace.*

Flourish. Enter the FRENCH KING, *the* DAUPHIN, *the* DUKE OF BURGUNDY, *the* CONSTABLE, *and others.*

Fr. King. Thus comes the English with full power upon us,
And more than carefully it us concerns
To answer royally in our defenses.
Therefore the Dukes of Berri and of Bretagne,
Of Brabant and of Orleans, shall make forth,
And you, Prince Dauphin, with all swift dispatch,
To line and new repair our towns of war
With men of courage and with means defendant;
For England his approaches makes as fierce
As waters to the sucking of a gulf. 10
It fits us then to be as provident
As fear may teach us out of late examples
Left by the fatal and neglected English
Upon our fields.

53. *faiths are wafer-cakes:* oaths are easily broken. 54. *Hold-fast.* Cf. the proverb, "Brag is a good dog, but Hold-fast is a better." 55. *Caveto:* be cautious. 56. *clear thy crystals:* dry your eyes. 65. *housewifery:* (good) housekeeping. *keep close:* stay at home.

[iv] 5. *make:* go. 7. *line:* strengthen. 8. *defendant:* of defense. 9. *England:* the king of England. 10. *gulf:* whirlpool. 13. *fatal and neglected:* ominous and underrated.

Dau. My most redoubted father,
It is most meet we arm us 'gainst the foe;
For peace itself should not so dull a kingdom,
Though war nor no known quarrel were in question,
But that defenses, musters, preparations,
Should be maintain'd, assembled, and collected,
As were a war in expectation. 20
Therefore I say 'tis meet we all go forth
To view the sick and feeble parts of France.
And let us do it with no show of fear—
No, with no more than if we heard that England
Were busied with a Whitsun morris-dance;
For, my good liege, she is so idly king'd,
Her sceptre so fantastically borne
By a vain, giddy, shallow, humorous youth,
That fear attends her not.
Con. O peace, Prince Dauphin!
You are too much mistaken in this king. 30
Question your Grace the late ambassadors,
With what great state he heard their embassy,
How well supplied with noble counsellors,
How modest in exception, and withal
How terrible in constant resolution,
And you shall find his vanities forespent
Were but the outside of the Roman Brutus,
Covering discretion with a coat of folly,
As gardeners do with ordure hide those roots
That shall first spring and be most delicate. 40
Dau. Well, 'tis not so, my lord high constable!
But though we think it so, it is no matter.
In cases of defense 'tis best to weigh
The enemy more mighty than he seems.

25. *Whitsun morris-dance:* grotesque dance in fantastic costumes, performed at Whitsuntide and other festivals. 26. *idly:* foolishly. 28. *humorous:* capricious. 34. *modest in exception:* moderate in expressing disapproval. 36. *vanities forespent:* past follies. 37. *Brutus.* The elder Brutus feigned insanity in order to conquer the Tarquins.

So the proportions of defense are fill'd;
Which of a weak and niggardly projection
Doth, like a miser, spoil his coat with scanting
A little cloth.

Fr. King. Think we King Harry strong;
And, princes, look you strongly arm to meet him.
The kindred of him hath been flesh'd upon us; 50
And he is bred out of that bloody strain
That haunted us in our familiar paths.
Witness our too much memorable shame
When Crécy battle fatally was struck,
And all our princes captived by the hand
Of that black name, Edward, Black Prince of Wales;
Whiles that his mountain sire, on mountain standing,
Up in the air, crown'd with the golden sun,
Saw his heroical seed, and smiled to see him,
Mangle the work of nature and deface 60
The patterns that by God and by French fathers
Had twenty years been made. This is a stem
Of that victorious stock, and let us fear
The native mightiness and fate of him.

Enter a Messenger.

Mess. Ambassadors from Harry King of England
Do crave admittance to your Majesty.

Fr. King. We'll give them present audience. Go and bring
them. [*Exeunt Messenger and certain Lords.*
You see this chase is hotly follow'd, friends.

Dau. Turn head, and stop pursuit; for coward dogs
Most spend their mouths when what they seem to threaten 70
Runs far before them. Good my sovereign,
Take up the English short, and let them know

46–8. *Which . . . cloth:* i.e., a niggardly plan of defense is worthless. 50. *flesh'd:* made eager (as a hawk or hound) by feeding it the flesh of the game killed; hence, inflamed by a foretaste of success. 51. *strain:* stock, race. 57. *mountain sire:* great father. 64. *fate:* what he is destined to do. 67. *present:* instant. 70. *spend their mouths:* bay.

Of what a monarchy you are the head.
Self-love, my liege, is not so vile a sin
As self-neglecting.

Re-enter Lords, *with* EXETER *and train.*

Fr. King. From our brother England?
Exe. From him, and thus he greets your Majesty:
He wills you, in the name of God Almighty,
That you divest yourself, and lay apart
The borrow'd glories that by gift of heaven,
By law of nature and of nations, 'long 80
To him and to his heirs, namely, the crown
And all wide-stretched honours that pertain
By custom and the ordinance of times
Unto the crown of France. That you may know
'Tis no sinister nor no awkward claim,
Pick'd from the worm-holes of long-vanish'd days,
Nor from the dust of old oblivion raked,
He sends you this most memorable line, [*Gives him a paper.*
In every branch truly demonstrative;
Willing you overlook this pedigree; 90
And when you find him evenly derived
From his most famed of famous ancestors,
Edward the Third, he bids you then resign
Your crown and kingdom, indirectly held
From him, the native and true challenger.
Fr. King. Or else what follows?
Exe. Bloody constraint; for if you hide the crown
Even in your hearts, there will he rake for it.
Therefore in fierce tempest is he coming,
In thunder and in earthquake, like a Jove, 100
That, if requiring fail, he will compel;

80. *'long:* belong. 85. *sinister:* left-handed, indirect. *awkward:* perverse. 88. *line:* pedigree. 89. *demonstrative:* proving. 90. *Willing:* desiring you to. *overlook:* peruse. 91. *evenly:* directly. 94. *indirectly:* unjustly. 95. *native:* rightful. *challenger:* claimant. 101. *requiring:* asking.

And bids you, in the bowels of the Lord,
Deliver up the crown, and to take mercy
On the poor souls for whom this hungry war
Opens his vasty jaws; and on your head
Turning the widows' tears, the orphans' cries,
The dead men's blood, the pining maidens' groans,
For husbands, fathers, and betrothed lovers
That shall be swallow'd in this controversy.
This is his claim, his threatening, and my message; 110
Unless the Dauphin be in presence here,
To whom expressly I bring greeting too.

Fr. King. For us, we will consider of this further.
Tomorrow shall you bear our full intent
Back to our brother England.

Dau. For the Dauphin,
I stand here for him. What to him from England?

Exe. Scorn and defiance, slight regard, contempt,
And anything that may not misbecome
The mighty sender, doth he prize you at.
Thus says my king. An if your father's Highness 120
Do not, in grant of all demands at large,
Sweeten the bitter mock you sent his Majesty,
He'll call you to so hot an answer of it
That caves and womby vaultages of France
Shall chide your trespass and return your mock
In second accent of his ordinance.

Dau. Say, if my father render fair return,
It is against my will, for I desire
Nothing but odds with England. To that end,
As matching to his youth and vanity, 130
I did present him with the Paris balls.

Exe. He'll make your Paris Louvre shake for it,
Were it the mistress-court of mighty Europe;

102. *bowels:* mercy. See Philippians 1 : 8. 124. *womby vaultages:* hollow caverns. 126. *second accent:* echo. 129. *odds:* discord. 131. *Paris balls:* tennis balls. 132. *Louvre:* the royal palace. 133. *mistress-court:* the principal court, whether for tennis or of a king.

And be assured you'll find a difference,
As we his subjects have in wonder found,
Between the promise of his greener days
And these he masters now. Now he weighs time
Even to the utmost grain. That you shall read
In your own losses, if he stay in France.

Fr. King. Tomorrow shall you know our mind at full. 140

Exe. Dispatch us with all speed, lest that our king
Come here himself to question our delay,
For he is footed in this land already.

Fr. King. You shall be soon dispatch'd with fair conditions.
A night is but small breath and little pause
To answer matters of this consequence. [*Flourish. Exeunt.*

ACT III

PROLOGUE

Enter Chorus.

Chor. Thus with imagined wing our swift scene flies
In motion of no less celerity
Than that of thought. Suppose that you have seen
The well-appointed king at Hampton pier
Embark his royalty, and his brave fleet
With silken streamers the young Phœbus fanning.
Play with your fancies, and in them behold
Upon the hempen tackle ship-boys climbing;
Hear the shrill whistle which doth order give
To sounds confused; behold the threaden sails, 10
Borne with the invisible and creeping wind,
Draw the huge bottoms through the furrow'd sea,
Breasting the lofty surge. O, do but think
You stand upon the rivage and behold

136. *greener:* younger. 143. *footed:* established. 145. *breath:* breathing-space.

[III. Prologue] 1. *imagined wing:* wings of imagination. 4. *well-appointed:* well-equipped. 5. *brave:* fine. 12. *bottoms:* ships. 14. *rivage:* shore.

A city on the inconstant billows dancing;
For so appears this fleet majestical,
Holding due course to Harfleur. Follow, follow!
Grapple your minds to sternage of this navy,
And leave your England, as dead midnight still,
Guarded with grandsires, babies, and old women, 20
Either past or not arrived to pith and puissance;
For who is he whose chin is but enrich'd
With one appearing hair that will not follow
These cull'd and choice-drawn cavaliers to France?
Work, work your thoughts, and therein see a siege;
Behold the ordnance on their carriages,
With fatal mouths gaping on girded Harfleur.
Suppose the ambassador from the French comes back,
Tells Harry that the king doth offer him
Katharine his daughter, and with her, to dowry, 30
Some petty and unprofitable dukedoms.
The offer likes not; and the nimble gunner
With linstock now the devilish cannon touches,
[*Alarum, and chambers go off, within.*
And down goes all before them. Still be kind,
And eke out our performance with your mind. [*Exit.*

SCENE I. *France. Before Harfleur.*

Alarum. Enter KING HENRY, EXETER, BEDFORD, GLOUCESTER, *and* Soldiers, *with scaling-ladders.*

K. Hen. Once more unto the breach, dear friends, once more;
Or close the wall up with our English dead!
In peace there's nothing so becomes a man
As modest stillness and humility;
But when the blast of war blows in our ears,

18. *to sternage:* astern. 27. *girded:* besieged. 30. *to dowry:* as a dowry. 31. *unprofitable:* worthless. 32. *likes:* pleases. 33. *linstock:* staff holding a gunner's match. S. D. *Alarum:* call to arms. *chambers:* small cannon.

Then imitate the action of the tiger;
Stiffen the sinews, summon up the blood,
Disguise fair nature with hard-favour'd rage;
Then lend the eye a terrible aspect;
Let it pry through the portage of the head 10
Like the brass cannon; let the brow o'erwhelm it
As fearfully as doth a galled rock
O'erhang and jutty his confounded base,
Swill'd with the wild and wasteful ocean.
Now set the teeth and stretch the nostril wide;
Hold hard the breath and bend up every spirit
To his full height. On, on, you noblest English,
Whose blood is fet from fathers of war-proof!
Fathers that, like so many Alexanders,
Have in these parts from morn till even fought, 20
And sheathed their swords for lack of argument.
Dishonour not your mothers; now attest
That those whom you call'd fathers did beget you!
Be copy now to men of grosser blood,
And teach them how to war! And you, good yeomen,
Whose limbs were made in England, show us here
The mettle of your pasture; let us swear
That you are worth your breeding; which I doubt not;
For there is none of you so mean and base
That hath not noble lustre in your eyes. 30
I see you stand like greyhounds in the slips,
Straining upon the start. The game's afoot!
Follow your spirit, and upon this charge
Cry, "God for Harry, England, and Saint George!"
[*Exeunt. Alarum, and chambers go off, within.*

[i] 8. *hard-favour'd:* ugly. 10. *portage:* porthole. 11. *o'erwhelm:* project over. 12. *galled:* worn. 13. *jutty his confounded base:* overhang its wasted base. 14. *Swill'd with:* gulped down by. 18. *fet:* fetched. *war-proof:* valor tested in war. 21. *argument:* subject of contention. 24. *copy:* example. 27. *mettle . . . pasture:* quality of your breeding (literally, feeding). 31. *in the slips:* in leash.

Scene II. *France. Before Harfleur.*

Enter Nym, Bardolph, Pistol, *and* Boy.

Bard. On, on, on, on, on! To the breach, to the breach!

Nym. Pray thee, corporal, stay. The knocks are too hot; and, for mine own part, I have not a case of lives. The humour of it is too hot; that is the very plain-song of it.

Pist. The plain-song is most just, for humours do abound.
Knocks go and come; God's vassals drop and die;

And sword and shield,
In bloody field, 10
Doth win immortal fame.

Boy. Would I were in an alehouse in London! I would give all my fame for a pot of ale and safety.

Pist. And I!

If wishes would prevail with me,
My purpose should not fail with me,
But thither would I hie.

Boy. As duly, but not as truly,
As bird doth sing on bough. 20

Enter Fluellen.

Flu. Up to the breach, you dogs! Avaunt, you cullions! [*Driving them forward.*

Pist. Be merciful, great duke, to men of mould!
Abate thy rage, abate thy manly rage,
Abate thy rage, great duke!
Good bawcock, bate thy rage! Use lenity, sweet chuck!

Nym. These be good humours! Your honour wins bad humours. [*Exeunt all but Boy.*

Boy. As young as I am, I have observed these three swashers. I am boy to them all three; but all they three, though they would serve me, could not be man to me; for indeed three

[ii] 5. *case:* set. 6. *plain-song:* simple melody. 22. *cullions:* rascals. 23. *men of mould:* men of earth, mere mortals. 26. *bawcock:* fine fellow (French *beau coq*). *chuck:* a term of endearment. 30. *swashers:* blusterers.

such antics do not amount to a man. For Bardolph, he is white-livered and red-faced; by the means whereof a' faces it out, but fights not. For Pistol, he hath a killing tongue and a quiet sword; by the means whereof a' breaks words, and keeps whole weapons. For Nym, he hath heard that men of few words are the best men; and therefore he scorns to say his prayers, lest a' should be thought a coward. But his few bad words are matched with as few good deeds, for a' never broke any man's head but his own, and that was against a post when he was drunk. They will steal anything, and call it purchase. Bardolph stole a lute-case, bore it twelve leagues, and sold it for three half-pence. Nym and Bardolph are sworn brothers in filching, and in Calais they stole a fire-shovel. I knew by that piece of service the men would carry coals. They would have me as familiar with men's pockets as their gloves or their handkerchers; which makes much against my manhood, if I should take from another's pocket to put into mine; for it is plain pocketing up of wrongs. I must leave them and seek some better service. Their villainy goes against my weak stomach, and therefore I must cast it up. [*Exit.*

Re-enter FLUELLEN, GOWER *following.*

Gow. Captain Fluellen, you must come presently to the mines. The Duke of Gloucester would speak with you. 60

Flu. To the mines? Tell you the duke it is not so good to come to the mines; for, look you, the mines is not according to the disciplines of the war. The concavities of it is not sufficient; for, look you, th' athversary, you may discuss unto the duke, look you, is digt himself four yard under the countermines. By Cheshu, I think a' will plow up all, if there is not better directions.

Gow. The Duke of Gloucester, to whom the order of the siege is given, is altogether directed by an Irishman, a very valiant gentleman, i' faith. 71

32. *antics:* buffoons. 34. *white-livered:* cowardly. 45. *purchase:* thieves' cant for *booty.* 50. *carry coals:* do dirty work; hence, submit to insults. 55. *pocketing up of:* submitting to. 65. *discuss:* explain.

Flu. It is Captain Macmorris, is it not?

Gow. I think it be.

Flu. By Cheshu, he is an ass, as in the world! I will verify as much in his beard. He has no more directions in the true disciplines of the wars, look you, of the Roman disciplines, than is a puppy-dog.

Enter Macmorris *and* Captain Jamy.

Gow. Here a' comes, and the Scots captain, Captain Jamy, with him. 80

Flu. Captain Jamy is a marvellous falorous gentleman, that is certain, and of great expedition and knowledge in th' aunchient wars, upon my particular knowledge of his directions. By Cheshu, he will maintain his argument as well as any military man in the world in the disciplines of the pristine wars of the Romans.

Jamy. I say gud-day, Captain Fluellen.

Flu. God-den to your worship, good Captain James. 90

Gow. How now, Captain Macmorris! Have you quit the mines? Have the pioners given o'er?

Mac. By Chrish, la, tish ill done! The work ish give over; the trompet sound the retreat. By my hand, I swear, and my father's soul, the work ish ill done! It ish give over. I would have blowed up the town, so Chrish save me, la, in an hour. O, tish ill done, tish ill done! By my hand, tish ill done! 99

Flu. Captain Macmorris, I beseech you now, will you voutsafe me, look you, a few disputations with you, as partly touching or concerning the disciplines of the war, the Roman wars? In the way of argument, look you, and friendly communication; partly to satisfy my opinion, and partly for the satisfaction, look you, of my mind, as touching the direction of the military discipline; that is the point. 108

Jamy. It sall be vary gud, gud feith, gud captains bath; and I sall quit you with gud leve, as I may pick occasion. That sall I, marry.

74. *as:* as great as any. 89. *God-den:* good evening. 92. *pioners:* pioneers, sappers, miners. 110. *quit:* requite.

Mac. It is no time to discourse, so Chrish save me! The day is hot, and the weather, and the wars, and the king, and the dukes. It is no time to discourse. The town is beseeched, and the trumpet call us to the breach, and we talk, and, be Chrish, do nothing. 'Tis shame for us all. So God sa' me, 'tis shame to stand still; it is shame, by my hand; and there is throats to be cut, and works to be done; and there ish nothing done, so Chrish sa' me, la! 121

Jamy. By the mess, ere theise eyes of mine take themselves to slomber, ay'll de gud service, or ay'll lig i' the grund for it! Ay, or go to death! And ay'll pay 't as valorously as I may, that sall I suerly do, that is the breff and the long. Marry, I wad full fain hear some question 'tween you tway.

Flu. Captain Macmorris, I think, look you, under your correction, there is not many of your nation— 131

Mac. Of my nation? What ish my nation? Ish a villain, and a bastard, and a knave, and a rascal—What ish my nation? Who talks of my nation?

Flu. Look you, if you take the matter otherwise than is meant, Captain Macmorris, peradventure I shall think you do not use me with that affability as in discretion you ought to use me, look you, being as good a man as yourself, both in the disciplines of war, and in the derivation of my birth, and in other particularities. 142

Mac. I do not know you so good a man as myself. So Chrish save me, I will cut off your head!

Gow. Gentlemen both, you will mistake each other.

Jamy. Ah, that's a foul fault! [*A parley sounded.*

Gow. The town sounds a parley. 149

Flu. Captain Macmorris, when there is more better opportunity to be required, look you, I will be so bold as to tell you I know the disciplines of war; and there is an end. [*Exeunt.*

118. *sa':* save. 122. *mess:* Mass. 124. *lig:* lie. 126. *breff:* brief. 128. *tway:* two. 132–5. *What . . . nation:* Macmorris is ready to fight at the mere mention of his country.

Scene iii. *Before the gates of Harfleur.*

The Governor *and some* Citizens *on the walls; the English forces below. Enter* King Henry *and his train.*

K. Hen. How yet resolves the governor of the town?
This is the latest parle we will admit.
Therefore to our best mercy give yourselves,
Or like to men proud of destruction
Defy us to our worst; for, as I am a soldier,
A name that in my thoughts becomes me best,
If I begin the battery once again,
I will not leave the half-achieved Harfleur
Till in her ashes she lie buried.
The gates of mercy shall be all shut up, 10
And the flesh'd soldier, rough and hard of heart,
In liberty of bloody hand shall range
With conscience wide as hell, mowing like grass
Your fresh-fair virgins and your flowering infants.
What is it then to me, if impious War,
Array'd in flames like to the prince of fiends,
Do, with his smirch'd complexion, all fell feats
Enlink'd to waste and desolation?
What is 't to me, when you yourselves are cause,
If your pure maidens fall into the hand 20
Of hot and forcing violation?
What rein can hold licentious Wickedness
When down the hill he holds his fierce career?
We may as bootless spend our vain command
Upon the enraged soldiers in their spoil
As send precepts to the leviathan
To come ashore. Therefore, you men of Harfleur,
Take pity of your town and of your people
Whiles yet my soldiers are in my command,
Whiles yet the cool and temperate wind of grace 30

[iii] 2. *latest:* last. *parle:* parley. 11. *flesh'd.* See II, iv, 50, note. 17. *fell feats:* savage practices. 18. *Enlink'd to:* associated with. 26. *precepts:* commands. *leviathan:* whale.

O'erblows the filthy and contagious clouds
Of heady murder, spoil, and villainy.
If not, why, in a moment look to see
The blind and bloody soldier with foul hand
Defile the locks of your shrill-shrieking daughters;
Your fathers taken by the silver beards,
And their most reverend heads dash'd to the walls;
Your naked infants spitted upon pikes,
Whiles the mad mothers with their howls confused
Do break the clouds, as did the wives of Jewry 40
At Herod's bloody-hunting slaughtermen.
What say you? Will you yield, and this avoid,
Or, guilty in defense, be thus destroy'd?

Gov. Our expectation hath this day an end.
The Dauphin, whom of succours we entreated,
Returns us that his powers are yet not ready
To raise so great a siege. Therefore, great king,
We yield our town and lives to thy soft mercy.
Enter our gates; dispose of us and ours;
For we no longer are defensible. 50

K. Hen. Open your gates. Come, uncle Exeter,
Go you and enter Harfleur; there remain,
And fortify it strongly 'gainst the French.
Use mercy to them all. For us, dear uncle,
The winter coming on and sickness growing
Upon our soldiers, we will retire to Calais.
Tonight in Harfleur will we be your guest;
Tomorrow for the march are we addrest.

[*Flourish. The King and his train enter the town.*

31. *O'erblows:* blows away. *contagious:* pestilential. 32. *heady:* headlong. 40. *Jewry:* Judea. See Matthew 2 : 16–18. 46. *Returns:* answers. 50. *defensible:* capable of defense. 54. *Use . . . all.* According to Holinshed, Henry V sacked Harfleur and drove out the citizens. 58. *addrest:* prepared.

SCENE IV. *The* FRENCH KING'S *palace.*

Enter KATHARINE *and* ALICE.

Kath. *Alice, tu as été en Angleterre, et tu parles bien le langage.*

Alice. *Un peu, madame.*

Kath. *Je te prie, m'enseignez; il faut que j'apprenne à parler. Comment appelez-vous la main en Anglois?*

Alice. *La main? Elle est appelée* de hand.

Kath. De hand. *Et les doigts?*

Alice. *Les doigts? Ma foi, j'oublie les doigts; mais je me souviendrai. Les doigts? Je pense qu'ils sont appelés* de fingres; *oui*, de fingres. 11

Kath. *La main*, de hand; *les doigts*, de fingres. *Je pense que je suis le bon écolier; j'ai gagné deux mots d'Anglois vîtement. Comment appelez-vous les ongles?*

Alice. *Les ongles? Nous les appelons* de nails.

Kath. De nails. *Écoutez; dites-moi, si je parle bien:* de hand, de fingres, *et* de nails.

Alice. *C'est bien dit, madame; il est fort bon Anglois.* 20

Kath. *Dites-moi l'Anglois pour le bras.*

[iv] Translation:
Kath. Alice, you have been in England, and you speak the language well.
Alice. A little, madame.
Kath. I pray you, teach me; I must learn to speak. What do you call *la main* in English?
Alice. *La main?* It is called de hand.
Kath. De hand. And *les doigts?*
Alice. *Les doigts?* My faith, I forget *les doigts;* but I shall remember. *Les doigts?* I think that they are called de fingres; yes, de fingres.
Kath. *La main*, de hand; *les doigts*, de fingres. I think that I am a good scholar; I have learned two English words quickly. What do you call *les ongles?*
Alice. *Les ongles?* We call them de nails.
Kath. De nails. Listen; tell me if I speak well: de hand, de fingres, and de nails.
Alice. That is well said, madame; it is very good English.
Kath. Tell me the English for *le bras.*

Alice. De arm, *madame.*

Kath. *Et le coude?*

Alice. De elbow.

Kath. De elbow. *Je m'en fais la répétition de tous les mots que vous m'avez appris dès à présent.*

Alice. *Il est trop difficile, madame, comme je pense.*

Kath. *Excusez-moi, Alice; écoutez:* de hand, de fingres, de nails, de arma, de bilbow. 31

Alice. De elbow, *madame.*

Kath. *O Seigneur Dieu, je m'en oublie!* De elbow. *Comment appelez-vous le col?*

Alice. De neck, *madame.*

Kath. De nick. *Et le menton?*

Alice. De chin.

Kath. De sin. *Le col*, de nick; *le menton*, de sin. 39

Alice. *Oui. Sauf votre honneur, en vérité, vous prononcez les mots aussi droit que les natifs d'Angleterre.*

Kath. *Je ne doute point d'apprendre, par la grace de Dieu, et en peu de temps.*

Alice. *N'avez vous pas déjà oublié ce que je vous ai enseigné?*

Alice. De arm, madame.

Kath. And *le coude?*

Alice. De elbow.

Kath. De elbow. I will repeat all the words that you have taught me so far.

Alice. It is too difficult, madame, I think.

Kath. Excuse me, Alice; listen: de hand, de fingres, de nails, de arma, de bilbow.

Alice. De elbow, madame.

Kath. O Lord, I forget! De elbow. What do you call *le col?*

Alice. De neck, madame.

Kath. De nick. And *le menton?*

Alice. De chin.

Kath. De sin. *Le col*, de nick; *le menton*, de sin.

Alice. Yes. By your leave, truly you pronounce the words as correctly as the natives of England.

Kath. I do not doubt that I shall learn, by God's grace, and in a short time.

Alice. Have you not already forgotten what I have taught you?

Kath. *Non, je réciterai à vous promptement:* de hand, de fingres, de mails—

Alice. De nails, *madame.*

Kath. De nails, de arm, de ilbow. 50

Alice. *Sauf votre honneur*, de elbow.

Kath. *Ainsi dis-je;* de elbow, de nick, *et* de sin. *Comment appelez-vous le pied et la robe?*

Alice. De foot, *madame; et* de coun.

Kath. De foot *et* de coun! *O Seigneur Dieu! Ce sont mots de son mauvais, corruptible, gros, et impudique, et non pour les dames d'honneur d'user. Je ne voudrais prononcer ces mots devant les seigneurs de France pour tout le monde. Foh! Le* foot *et le* coun! *Néanmoins, je réciterai une autre fois ma leçon ensemble:* de hand, de fingres, de nails, de arm, de elbow, de nick, de sin, de foot, de coun. 63

Alice. *Excellent, madame!*

Kath. *C'est assez pour une fois. Allons-nous à dîner.*

[*Exeunt.*

Kath. No, I will recite to you promptly: de hand, de fingres, de mails—

Alice. De nails, madame.

Kath. De nails, de arm, de ilbow.

Alice. By your leave, de elbow.

Kath. So I said; de elbow, de nick, and de sin. What do you call *le pied* and *la robe?*

Alice. De foot, madame; and de coun.

Kath. De foot and de coun! O Lord! These are words of bad, corrupt, coarse, and immodest sound, and not for honorable ladies to use. I would not say these words before French gentlemen for all the world. Foh! Le foot and le coun! Nevertheless, I will recite once more my whole lesson: de hand, de fingres, de nails, de arm, de elbow, de nick, de sin, de foot, de coun.

Alice. Excellent, madame.

Kath. That is enough for one time. Let us go to dinner.

SCENE V. *The same.*

Enter the KING OF FRANCE, *the* DAUPHIN, *the* DUKE OF BOURBON, *the* CONSTABLE OF FRANCE, *and others.*

Fr. King. 'Tis certain he hath pass'd the river Somme.
Con. And if he be not fought withal, my lord,
Let us not live in France; let us quit all
And give our vineyards to a barbarous people.
Dau. *O Dieu vivant!* Shall a few sprays of us,
The emptying of our fathers' luxury,
Our scions, put in wild and savage stock,
Spirt up so suddenly into the clouds,
And overlook their grafters? 9
Bour. Normans, but bastard Normans, Norman bastards!
Mort de ma vie! If they march along
Unfought withal, but I will sell my dukedom,
To buy a slobbery and a dirty farm
In that nook-shotten isle of Albion.
Con. *Dieu de batailles!* Where have they this mettle?
Is not their climate foggy, raw, and dull,
On whom, as in despite, the sun looks pale,
Killing their fruit with frowns? Can sodden water,
A drench for sur-rein'd jades, their barley-broth,
Decoct their cold blood to such valiant heat? 20
And shall our quick blood, spirited with wine,
Seem frosty? O, for honour of our land,
Let us not hang like roping icicles

[v] 5. *O Dieu vivant:* O living God! *sprays:* branches. 6. *emptying:* issue. *luxury:* lust. 7. *scions:* twigs cut from one tree and grafted upon another (*stock*). The allusion is to William the Conqueror, an illegitimate son, and to the Norman ancestry of the English. 8. *Spirt:* sprout. 9. *overlook:* overtop. 11. *Mort de ma vie:* death of my life! 13. *slobbery:* sloppy. 14. *nook-shotten:* full of inlets; full of capes; thrust into a corner. *Albion:* England (in allusion to the white cliffs seen from the Channel). 15. *Dieu de batailles:* God of battles. 18. *sodden water:* boiled water, i.e., beer. 19. *drench:* drink. *sur-rein'd jades:* overridden horses. *barley-broth:* ale. 20. *Decoct:* warm. 21. *quick:* lively. 23. *roping:* hanging down like a rope.

Upon our houses' thatch, whiles a more frosty people
Sweat drops of gallant youth in our rich fields!
"Poor" we may call them in their native lords!

Dau. By faith and honour,
Our madams mock at us and plainly say
Our mettle is bred out, and they will give
Their bodies to the lust of English youth 30
To new-store France with bastard warriors.

Bour. They bid us to the English dancing-schools
And teach lavoltas high and swift corantos,
Saying our grace is only in our heels,
And that we are most lofty runaways.

Fr. King. Where is Montjoy the herald? Speed him hence.
Let him greet England with our sharp defiance.
Up, princes, and, with spirit of honour edged
More sharper than your swords, hie to the field!
Charles Delabreth, high constable of France; 40
You Dukes of Orleans, Bourbon, and of Berri,
Alençon, Brabant, Bar, and Burgundy;
Jaques Chatillon, Rambures, Vaudemont,
Beaumont, Grandpré, Roussi, and Fauconberg,
Foix, Lestrale, Bouciqualt, and Charolois;
High dukes, great princes, barons, lords, and knights,
For your great seats now quit you of great shames.
Bar Harry England, that sweeps through our land
With pennons painted in the blood of Harfleur.
Rush on his host as doth the melted snow 50
Upon the valleys whose low vassal seat
The Alps doth spit and void his rheum upon.
Go down upon him—you have power enough—
And in a captive chariot into Rouen
Bring him our prisoner.

26. *them:* the rich fields of France. 33. *lavoltas, corantos:* lively dances. 36. *Montjoy:* title of the chief herald of France. 37. *England:* i.e., the king of England. 47. *For . . . shames:* for the sake of your great rank free yourselves from great shame. 52. *rheum:* moisture, saliva.

Con. This becomes the great.
Sorry am I his numbers are so few,
His soldiers sick and famish'd in their march,
For I am sure, when he shall see our army,
He'll drop his heart into the sink of fear
And for achievement offer us his ransom. 60

Fr. King. Therefore, lord constable, haste on Montjoy,
And let him say to England that we send
To know what willing ransom he will give.
Prince Dauphin, you shall stay with us in Rouen.

Dau. Not so, I do beseech your Majesty.

Fr. King. Be patient, for you shall remain with us.
Now forth, lord constable and princes all,
And quickly bring us word of England's fall. [*Exeunt.*

SCENE VI. *The English camp in Picardy.*

Enter GOWER *and* FLUELLEN, *meeting.*

Gow. How now, Captain Fluellen? Come you from the bridge?

Flu. I assure you there is very excellent services committed at the bridge.

Gow. Is the Duke of Exeter safe?

Flu. The Duke of Exeter is as magnanimous as Agamemnon, and a man that I love and honour with my soul, and my heart, and my duty, and my life, and my living, and my uttermost power. He is not—God be praised and plessed!—any hurt in the world, but keeps the bridge most valiantly, with excellent discipline. There is an aunchient lieutenant there at the pridge; I think in my very conscience he is as valiant a man as Mark Antony, and he is a man of no estimation in the world, but I did see him do as gallant service.

Gow. What do you call him?

60. *for:* instead of.

[vi] 13. *aunchient lieutenant.* Fluellen, in his enthusiasm, gives Pistol two titles. 16. *estimation:* reputation.

Flu. He is called Aunchient Pistol.

Gow. I know him not. 20

Enter PISTOL.

Flu. Here is the man.

Pist. Captain, I thee beseech to do me favours.
The Duke of Exeter doth love thee well.

Flu. Ay, I praise God; and I have merited some love at his hands.

Pist. Bardolph, a soldier firm and sound of heart,
And of buxom valour, hath by cruel fate
And giddy Fortune's furious fickle wheel,
That goddess blind,
That stands upon the rolling restless stone— 30

Flu. By your patience, Aunchient Pistol. Fortune is painted plind, with a muffler afore her eyes, to signify to you that Fortune is plind; and she is painted also with a wheel, to signify to you, which is the moral of it, that she is turning, and inconstant, and mutability, and variation; and her foot, look you, is fixed upon a spherical stone, which rolls, and rolls, and rolls. In good truth, the poet makes a most excellent description of it. Fortune is an excellent moral. 40

Pist. Fortune is Bardolph's foe, and frowns on him;
For he hath stolen a pax, and hanged must a' be—
A damned death!
Let gallows gape for dog; let man go free,
And let not hemp his wind-pipe suffocate.
But Exeter hath given the doom of death
For pax of little price.
Therefore, go speak; the duke will hear thy voice;
And let not Bardolph's vital thread be cut
With edge of penny cord and vile reproach. 50
Speak, captain, for his life, and I will thee requite.

27. *buxom:* lively. 42. *pax:* tablet bearing a representation of the Crucifixion or other sacred subject, used in the Mass. Holinshed describes the object stolen as a *pyx*, the casket containing the consecrated wafer.

Flu. Aunchient Pistol, I do partly understand your meaning.

Pist. Why then, rejoice therefore.

Flu. Certainly, aunchient, it is not a thing to rejoice at; for if, look you, he were my brother, I would desire the duke to use his good pleasure, and put him to execution; for discipline ought to be used.

Pist. Die and be damn'd! and *figo* for thy friendship! 60

Flu. It is well.

Pist. The fig of Spain! [*Exit.*

Flu. Very good.

Gow. Why, this is an arrant counterfeit rascal. I remember him now—a bawd, a cutpurse.

Flu. I'll assure you, a' uttered as prave words at the pridge as you shall see in a summer's day. But it is very well; what he has spoke to me, that is well, I warrant you, when time is serve. 69

Gow. Why, 'tis a gull, a fool, a rogue, that now and then goes to the wars, to grace himself at his return into London under the form of a soldier. And such fellows are perfect in the great commanders' names, and they will learn you by rote where services were done, at such and such a sconce, at such a breach, at such a convoy; who came off bravely, who was shot, who disgraced, what terms the enemy stood on; and this they con perfectly in the phrase of war, which they trick up with new-tuned oaths; and what a beard of the general's cut and a horrid suit of the camp will do among foaming bottles and ale-washed wits, is wonderful to be thought on. But you must learn to know such slanders of the age, or else you may be marvellously mistook. 85

Flu. I tell you what, Captain Gower; I do perceive he is not the man that he would gladly make show to the world he is. If I find a hole in his coat, I will tell him my mind. [*Drum*

60. *figo:* Spanish for "fig." The *fig of Spain* was a contemptuous gesture. 70. *gull:* dupe. 74. *learn:* teach, tell. 76. *sconce:* fort. 78. *stood on:* insisted on. 79. *con:* learn by heart. 84. *slanders of the age:* persons who disgrace the age.

within.] Hark you, the king is coming, and I must speak with him from the pridge. 91

Drum and colours. Enter KING HENRY, GLOUCESTER, *and* Soldiers.

God pless your Majesty!

K. Hen. How now, Fluellen? Camest thou from the bridge?

Flu. Ay, so please your Majesty. The Duke of Exeter has very gallantly maintained the pridge. The French is gone off, look you; and there is gallant and most prave passages. Marry, th' athversary was have possession of the pridge; but he is enforced to retire, and the Duke of Exeter is master of the pridge. I can tell your Majesty, the duke is a prave man. 101

K. Hen. What men have you lost, Fluellen?

Flu. The perdition of th' athversary hath been very great, reasonable great. Marry, for my part, I think the duke hath lost never a man but one that is like to be executed for robbing a church, one Bardolph, if your Majesty know the man. His face is all bubukles, and whelks, and knobs, and flames o' fire; and his lips blows at his nose, and it is like a coal of fire, sometimes plue and sometimes red; but his nose is executed, and his fire's out. 112

K. Hen. We would have all such offenders so cut off; and we give express charge that in our marches through the country there be nothing compelled from the villages, nothing taken but paid for, none of the French upbraided or abused in disdainful language; for when lenity and cruelty play for a kingdom, the gentler gamester is the soonest winner. 120

Tucket. Enter MONTJOY.

Mont. You know me by my habit.

K. Hen. Well, then, I know thee. What shall I know of thee?

Mont. My master's mind.

K. Hen. Unfold it.

91. *from:* of news from. 97. *passages:* deeds. 103. *perdition:* losses. 108. *bubukles.* He confuses *bubo* and *carbuncle. whelks:* boils. S. D. *Tucket:* trumpet signal. 121. *habit:* dress. 122. *of:* from.

Mont. Thus says my king: Say thou to Harry of England: Though we seemed dead, we did but sleep. Advantage is a better soldier than rashness. Tell him we could have rebuked him at Harfleur, but that we thought not good to bruise an injury till it were full ripe. Now we speak upon our cue, and our voice is imperial. England shall repent his folly, see his weakness, and admire our sufferance. Bid him therefore consider of his ransom, which must proportion the losses we have borne, the subjects we have lost, the disgrace we have digested; which in weight to re-answer, his pettiness would bow under. For our losses, his exchequer is too poor; for the effusion of our blood, the muster of his kingdom too faint a number; and for our disgrace, his own person kneeling at our feet but a weak and worthless satisfaction. To this add defiance; and tell him, for conclusion, he hath betrayed his followers, whose condemnation is pronounced. So far my king and master; so much my office.

K. Hen. What is thy name? I know thy quality.

Mont. Montjoy.

K. Hen. Thou dost thy office fairly. Turn thee back,
And tell thy king I do not seek him now,
But could be willing to march on to Calais 150
Without impeachment; for, to say the sooth,
Though 'tis no wisdom to confess so much
Unto an enemy of craft and vantage,
My people are with sickness much enfeebled,
My numbers lessen'd, and those few I have
Almost no better than so many French;
Who when they were in health, I tell thee, herald,
I thought upon one pair of English legs
Did march three Frenchmen. Yet forgive me, God,
That I do brag thus! This your air of France 160

127. *Advantage:* waiting for favorable opportunity. 130. *upon our cue:* i.e., at the proper time. 132. *admire our sufferance:* wonder at our forbearance. 136. *re-answer:* compensate. *pettiness:* insignificance. 146. *quality:* rank, office. 151. *impeachment:* hindrance. 153. *vantage:* superior position.

Hath blown that vice in me. I must repent.
Go therefore; tell thy master here I am,
My ransom is this frail and worthless trunk,
My army but a weak and sickly guard;
Yet, God before, tell him we will come on,
Though France himself and such another neighbour
Stand in our way. There's for thy labour, Montjoy.
[*Gives a purse.*
Go, bid thy master well advise himself.
If we may pass, we will; if we be hinder'd,
We shall your tawny ground with your red blood 170
Discolour; and so, Montjoy, fare you well.
The sum of all our answer is but this:
We would not seek a battle, as we are;
Nor, as we are, we say we will not shun it.
So tell your master.

Mont. I shall deliver so. Thanks to your Highness. [*Exit.*

Glou. I hope they will not come upon us now.

K. Hen. We are in God's hand, brother, not in theirs.
March to the bridge. It now draws toward night.
Beyond the river we'll encamp ourselves, 180
And on tomorrow bid them march away. [*Exeunt.*

SCENE VII. *The French camp, near Agincourt.*

Enter the CONSTABLE OF FRANCE, *the* LORD RAMBURES, ORLEANS, DAUPHIN, *with others.*

Con. Tut! I have the best armour of the world. Would it were day!

Orl. You have an excellent armour, but let my horse have his due.

Con. It is the best horse of Europe.

Orl. Will it never be morning?

161. *blown:* made blossom. 168. *advise himself:* consider. 176. *deliver:* report.

[vii] S. D. The Dauphin was not present at Agincourt.

Dau. My lord of Orleans, and my lord high constable, you talk of horse and armour?

Orl. You are as well provided of both as any prince in the world. 10

Dau. What a long night is this! I will not change my horse with any that treads but on four pasterns. *Ça, ha!* He bounds from the earth, as if his entrails were hairs; *le cheval volant*, the Pegasus, *chez les narines de feu!* When I bestride him, I soar, I am a hawk; he trots the air; the earth sings when he touches it; the basest horn of his hoof is more musical than the pipe of Hermes.

Orl. He's of the colour of the nutmeg. 20

Dau. And of the heat of the ginger. It is a beast for Perseus. He is pure air and fire, and the dull elements of earth and water never appear in him, but only in patient stillness while his rider mounts him. He is indeed a horse, and all other jades you may call beasts.

Con. Indeed, my lord, it is a most absolute and excellent horse.

Dau. It is the prince of palfreys. His neigh is like the bidding of a monarch, and his countenance enforces homage. 31

Orl. No more, cousin.

Dau. Nay, the man hath no wit that cannot, from the rising of the lark to the lodging of the lamb, vary deserved praise on my palfrey. It is a theme as fluent as the sea. Turn the sands into eloquent tongues, and my horse is argument for them all. 'Tis a subject for a sovereign to reason on, and for a sovereign's sovereign to ride on; and for the world, familiar to us and unknown, to lay apart their particular functions and wonder at him. I once writ a sonnet in his praise and began thus: "Wonder of nature—" 43

Orl. I have heard a sonnet begin so to one's mistress.

Dau. Then did they imitate that which I composed to my courser, for my horse is my mistress.

14. *hairs.* Tennis balls were stuffed with hair. 14–15. *le cheval . . . feu:* the flying horse, Pegasus, with nostrils of fire. 27. *absolute:* perfect. 34. *lodging:* lying down. 37. *argument:* subject.

Orl. Your mistress bears well.

Dau. Me well, which is the prescript praise and perfection of a good and particular mistress. 50

Con. Nay, for methought yesterday your mistress shrewdly shook your back.

Dau. So perhaps did yours.

Con. Mine was not bridled.

Dau. O, then belike she was old and gentle; and you rode, like a kern of Ireland, your French hose off, and in your strait strossers.

Con. You have good judgment in horsemanship. 59

Dau. Be warned by me then. They that ride so, and ride not warily, fall into foul bogs. I had rather have my horse to my mistress.

Con. I had as lief have my mistress a jade.

Dau. I tell thee, constable, my mistress wears his own hair.

Con. I could make as true a boast as that, if I had a sow to my mistress.

Dau. "*Le chien est retourné à son propre vomissement, et la truie lavée au bourbier.*" Thou makest use of anything. 70

Con. Yet do I not use my horse for my mistress, or any such proverb so little kin to the purpose.

Ram. My lord constable, the armour that I saw in your tent tonight—are those stars or suns upon it?

Con. Stars, my lord.

Dau. Some of them will fall tomorrow, I hope.

Con. And yet my sky shall not want.

Dau. That may be, for you bear a many superfluously, and 'twere more honour some were away. 81

Con. Even as your horse bears your praises, who would trot as well, were some of your brags dismounted.

Dau. Would I were able to load him with his desert! Will

49. *prescript:* prescribed. 50. *particular:* private, personal. 52. *shrewdly:* viciously. 56. *kern:* light-armed Irish foot soldier. 57. *French hose:* wide breeches. *strait strossers:* narrow trousers. 62. *to:* as. 68–9. *Le chien . . . bourbier.* See II Peter 2 : 22—"The dog is turned to his own vomit again, and the sow that was washed to her wallowing in the mire."

it never be day? I will trot tomorrow a mile, and my way shall be paved with English faces.

Con. I will not say so, for fear I should be faced out of my way. But I would it were morning, for I would fain be about the ears of the English. 92

Ram. Who will go to hazard with me for twenty prisoners?

Con. You must first go yourself to hazard ere you have them.

Dau. 'Tis midnight; I'll go arm myself. [*Exit.*

Orl. The Dauphin longs for morning.

Ram. He longs to eat the English.

Con. I think he will eat all he kills. 100

Orl. By the white hand of my lady, he's a gallant prince.

Con. Swear by her foot, that she may tread out the oath.

Orl. He is simply the most active gentleman of France.

Con. Doing is activity, and he will still be doing.

Orl. He never did harm, that I heard of.

Con. Nor will do none tomorrow. He will keep that good name still. 111

Orl. I know him to be valiant.

Con. I was told that by one that knows him better than you.

Orl. What's he?

Con. Marry, he told me so himself, and he said he cared not who knew it.

Orl. He needs not; it is no hidden virtue in him. 119

Con. By my faith, sir, but it is! Never anybody saw it but his lackey. 'Tis a hooded valour; and when it appears, it will bate.

Orl. Ill will never said well.

Con. I will cap that proverb with "There is flattery in friendship."

Orl. And I will take up that with "Give the Devil his due."

90. *faced . . . way:* forced out of my way, outfaced. 93. *go to hazard:* risk a wager. 107. *still:* always. 121–2. *hooded . . . bate.* In hawking, the hawk was kept hooded until it was allowed to fly at its game. When the hood was removed, the hawk *baited* (flapped its wings). When action begins, the Dauphin's courage will prepare for flight, and will *bate* (abate, decrease).

Con. Well placed! There stands your friend for the Devil. Have at the very eye of that proverb with "A pox of the Devil."

Orl. You are the better at proverbs, by how much "a fool's bolt is soon shot." 132

Con. You have shot over.

Orl. 'Tis not the first time you were overshot.

Enter a Messenger.

Mess. My lord high constable, the English lie within fifteen hundred paces of your tents.

Con. Who hath measured the ground?

Mess. The Lord Grandpré.

Con. A valiant and most expert gentleman. Would it were day! Alas, poor Harry of England! He longs not for the dawning as we do. 141

Orl. What a wretched and peevish fellow is this king of England, to mope with his fat-brained followers so far out of his knowledge!

Con. If the English had any apprehension, they would run away.

Orl. That they lack; for if their heads had any intellectual armour, they could never wear such heavy head-pieces. 149

Ram. That island of England breeds very valiant creatures. Their mastiffs are of unmatchable courage.

Orl. Foolish curs, that run winking into the mouth of a Russian bear and have their heads crushed like rotten apples! You may as well say that's a valiant flea that dare eat his breakfast on the lip of a lion. 157

Con. Just, just! And the men do sympathize with the mastiffs in robustious and rough coming on, leaving their wits with their wives; and then give them great meals of beef and iron and steel, they will eat like wolves and fight like devils.

134. *overshot:* (a) defeated at shooting, (b) wide of the mark, (c) intoxicated. 142. *peevish:* foolish. 143. *mope:* act without thought. 144. *out of his knowledge:* without reflection. 145. *apprehension:* (a) sense, (b) fear. 153. *winking:* with eyes shut. 158. *sympathize with:* resemble.

Orl. Ay, but these English are shrewdly out of beef.

Con. Then shall we find tomorrow they have only stomachs to eat and none to fight. Now is it time to arm. Come, shall we about it?

Orl. It is now two o'clock; but, let me see, by ten 168
We shall have each a hundred Englishmen. [*Exeunt.*

ACT IV

PROLOGUE

Enter Chorus.

Chor. Now entertain conjecture of a time
When creeping murmur and the poring dark
Fills the wide vessel of the universe.
From camp to camp through the foul womb of night
The hum of either army stilly sounds,
That the fix'd sentinels almost receive
The secret whispers of each other's watch.
Fire answers fire, and through their paly flames
Each battle sees the other's umber'd face;
Steed threatens steed, in high and boastful neighs 10
Piercing the night's dull ear; and from the tents
The armourers, accomplishing the knights,
With busy hammers closing rivets up,
Give dreadful note of preparation.
The country cocks do crow, the clocks do toll,
And the third hour of drowsy morning name.
Proud of their numbers and secure in soul,
The confident and over-lusty French
Do the low-rated English play at dice;
And chide the cripple tardy-gaited Night 20
Who, like a foul and ugly witch, doth limp

163. *shrewdly:* very much, sorely. 166. *stomachs:* (a) appetite, (b) courage.

[IV. Prologue] 1. *entertain . . . of:* imagine. 2. *poring:* peering. 5. *stilly:* softly. 9. *battle:* army. *umber'd:* shadowed. 12. *accomplishing:* equipping. 17. *secure:* confident. 18. *over-lusty:* too lively.

So tediously away. The poor condemned English,
Like sacrifices, by their watchful fires
Sit patiently and inly ruminate
The morning's danger; and their gesture sad,
Investing lank-lean cheeks and war-worn coats,
Presenteth them unto the gazing moon
So many horrid ghosts. O, now, who will behold
The royal captain of this ruin'd band
Walking from watch to watch, from tent to tent, 30
Let him cry, "Praise and glory on his head!"
For forth he goes and visits all his host,
Bids them good morrow with a modest smile,
And calls them brothers, friends, and countrymen.
Upon his royal face there is no note
How dread an army hath enrounded him;
Nor doth he dedicate one jot of colour
Unto the weary and all-watched night,
But freshly looks and overbears attaint
With cheerful semblance and sweet majesty; 40
That every wretch, pining and pale before,
Beholding him, plucks comfort from his looks.
A largess universal, like the sun,
His liberal eye doth give to everyone,
Thawing cold fear, that mean and gentle all
Behold, as may unworthiness define,
A little touch of Harry in the night.
And so our scene must to the battle fly,
Where—O for pity!—we shall much disgrace
With four or five most vile and ragged foils, 50
Right ill-disposed in brawl ridiculous,
The name of Agincourt. Yet sit and see,
Minding true things by what their mockeries be. [*Exit.*

25. *gesture sad:* grave bearing. 26. *Investing:* accompanying. 39. *overbears attaint:* overcomes depressing influences. 45. *mean and gentle:* those of low and of high birth. 46. *as . . . define:* so far as their inferiority can appreciate. 47. *touch:* dash, trace. 51. *ill-disposed:* ill-managed. 53. *Minding:* imagining.

SCENE I. *The English camp at Agincourt.*

Enter KING HENRY, BEDFORD, *and* GLOUCESTER.

K. Hen. Gloucester, 'tis true that we are in great danger;
The greater therefore should our courage be.
Good morrow, brother Bedford. God Almighty!
There is some soul of goodness in things evil,
Would men observingly distil it out,
For our bad neighbour makes us early stirrers,
Which is both healthful and good husbandry.
Besides, they are our outward consciences
And preachers to us all, admonishing
That we should dress us fairly for our end. 10
Thus may we gather honey from the weed
And make a moral of the Devil himself.

Enter ERPINGHAM.

Good morrow, old Sir Thomas Erpingham.
A good soft pillow for that good white head
Were better than a churlish turf of France.
Erp. Not so, my liege. This lodging likes me better,
Since I may say, "Now lie I like a king."
K. Hen. 'Tis good for men to love their present pains
Upon example; so the spirit is eased;
And when the mind is quicken'd, out of doubt 20
The organs, though defunct and dead before,
Break up their drowsy grave and newly move,
With casted slough and fresh legerity.
Lend me thy cloak, Sir Thomas. Brothers both,
Commend me to the princes in our camp;
Do my good morrow to them, and anon
Desire them all to my pavilion.
Glou. We shall, my liege.

[i] 8. *they:* things evil, or, perhaps, the French. 10. *dress:* prepare. 16. *likes:* pleases. 19. *Upon example:* in consequence of the example of others, or, perhaps, as an example to others. 20. *out of doubt:* certainly. 23. *With . . . legerity:* freed of the old skin (as a snake) and with fresh nimbleness. 27. *Desire:* summon.

Erp. Shall I attend your Grace?

K. Hen. No, my good knight;
Go with my brothers to my lords of England. 30
I and my bosom must debate a while,
And then I would no other company.

Erp. The Lord in heaven bless thee, noble Harry!

[*Exeunt all but King.*

K. Hen. God-a-mercy, old heart! Thou speak'st cheerfully.

Enter PISTOL.

Pist. *Qui va là?*

K. Hen. A friend.

Pist. Discuss unto me; art thou officer?
Or art thou base, common, and popular?

K. Hen. I am a gentleman of a company.

Pist. Trail'st thou the puissant pike? 40

K. Hen. Even so. What are you?

Pist. As good a gentleman as the emperor.

K. Hen. Then you are a better than the king.

Pist. The king's a bawcock, and a heart of gold,
A lad of life, an imp of fame,
Of parents good, of fist most valiant.
I kiss his dirty shoe, and from heart-string
I love the lovely bully. What is thy name?

K. Hen. Harry le Roy.

Pist. Le Roy? A Cornish name. Art thou of Cornish crew?

K. Hen. No, I am a Welshman. 51

Pist. Know'st thou Fluellen?

K. Hen. Yes.

Pist. Tell him I'll knock his leek about his pate
Upon Saint Davy's day.

34. *God-a-mercy:* God have mercy. 35. *Qui va là:* who goes there? 38. *popular:* of the people. 44. *bawcock.* See III, ii, 26, note. 45. *imp:* child. 48. *bully:* fine fellow. 49. *le Roy:* the king. 51. *Welshman.* He was born at Monmouth, on the Welsh border. 54–5. *leek . . . Saint Davy's day.* When the Welsh defeated the Saxons in 540, Saint David, according to the legend, told the Welsh to take leeks from the garden where they fought and wear them in their caps. Thereafter, they wore leeks on Saint David's Day, March 1.

K. Hen. Do not you wear your dagger in your cap that day, lest he knock that about yours.

Pist. Art thou his friend?

K. Hen. And his kinsman too.

Pist. The *figo* for thee, then! 60

K. Hen. I thank you. God be with you!

Pist. My name is Pistol call'd. [*Exit.*

K. Hen. It sorts well with your fierceness.

Enter FLUELLEN *and* GOWER, *meeting.*

Gow. Captain Fluellen!

Flu. So! In the name of Jesu Christ, speak lower. It is the greatest admiration in the universal world, when the true and aunchient prerogatifes and laws of the wars is not kept. If you would take the pains but to examine the wars of Pompey the Great, you shall find, I warrant you, that there is no tiddle taddle nor pibble pabble in Pompey's camp. I warrant you, you shall find the ceremonies of the wars, and the cares of it, and the forms of it, and the sobriety of it, and the modesty of it, to be otherwise. 75

Gow. Why, the enemy is loud; you hear him all night.

Flu. If the enemy is an ass and a fool and a prating coxcomb, is it meet, think you, that we should also, look you, be an ass and a fool and a prating coxcomb? In your own conscience, now? 81

Gow. I will speak lower.

Flu. I pray you and beseech you that you will.

[*Exeunt Gower and Fluellen.*

K. Hen. Though it appear a little out of fashion,
There is much care and valour in this Welshman.

Enter three soldiers, JOHN BATES, ALEXANDER COURT, *and* MICHAEL WILLIAMS.

Court. Brother John Bates, is not that the morning which breaks yonder?

60. *figo.* See III, vi, 60, note. 63. *sorts:* agrees. 66. *admiration:* wonder.

Bates. I think it be; but we have no great cause to desire the approach of day. 90

Will. We see yonder the beginning of the day, but I think we shall never see the end of it. Who goes there?

K. Hen. A friend.

Will. Under what captain serve you?

K. Hen. Under Sir Thomas Erpingham.

Will. A good old commander and a most kind gentleman. I pray you, what thinks he of our estate?

K. Hen. Even as men wrecked upon a sand, that look to be washed off the next tide. 101

Bates. He hath not told his thought to the king?

K. Hen. No; nor it is not meet he should. For, though I speak it to you, I think the king is but a man, as I am. The violet smells to him as it doth to me; the element shows to him as it doth to me; all his senses have but human conditions. His ceremonies laid by, in his nakedness he appears but a man; and though his affections are higher mounted than ours, yet, when they stoop, they stoop with the like wing. Therefore when he sees reason of fears, as we do, his fears, out of doubt, be of the same relish as ours are; yet, in reason, no man should possess him with any appearance of fear, lest he, by showing it, should dishearten his army. 117

Bates. He may show what outward courage he will; but I believe, as cold a night as 'tis, he could wish himself in Thames up to the neck; and so I would he were, and I by him, at all adventures, so we were quit here.

K. Hen. By my troth, I will speak my conscience of the king. I think he would not wish himself anywhere but where he is.

99. *estate:* condition, position. 104. *meet:* proper. 107. *element shows:* sky appears. 108. *conditions:* characteristics. 109. *ceremonies:* symbols of office. 111. *his affections are higher mounted:* his feelings rise higher. 112. *stoop:* swoop down. *Mount* and *stoop* are terms of falconry. 114. *out of doubt:* certainly. *relish:* kind, quality. 115. *possess him with:* put himself in possession of, i.e., no man should show fear. *possess:* infect. 121–2. *at all adventures:* at all hazards, whatever the consequences. 124. *conscience:* inmost thought.

Bates. Then I would he were here alone; so should he be sure to be ransomed, and a many poor men's lives saved. 128

K. Hen. I dare say you love him not so ill to wish him here alone, howsoever you speak this to feel other men's minds. Methinks I could not die anywhere so contented as in the king's company, his cause being just and his quarrel honourable.

Will. That's more than we know. 135

Bates. Ay, or more than we should seek after; for we know enough, if we know we are the king's subjects. If his cause be wrong, our obedience to the king wipes the crime of it out of us.

Will. But if the cause be not good, the king himself hath a heavy reckoning to make, when all those legs and arms and heads, chopped off in a battle, shall join together at the latter day and cry all, "We died at such a place"; some swearing, some crying for a surgeon, some upon their wives left poor behind them, some upon the debts they owe, some upon their children rawly left. I am afeard there are few die well that die in a battle, for how can they charitably dispose of anything when blood is their argument? Now, if these men do not die well, it will be a black matter for the king that led them to it, whom to disobey were against all proportion of subjection. 153

K. Hen. So, if a son that is by his father sent about merchandise do sinfully miscarry upon the sea, the imputation of his wickedness, by your rule, should be imposed upon his father that sent him. Or if a servant, under his master's command transporting a sum of money, be assailed by robbers and die in many irreconciled iniquities, you may call the business of the master the author of the servant's damnation. But this is not so. The king is not bound to answer the particular endings of his soldiers, the father of his son, nor the master of his servant; for they purpose not their death when they purpose their services. Besides, there is no king, be his cause never so spotless, if it come to the arbitrement of swords, can try it out with all

147. *rawly:* without proper provision. 150. *argument:* theme, business. 153. *proportion of subjection:* proper relation of subject to king. 155. *sinfully miscarry:* perish in his sin. 160. *irreconciled:* unatoned for. 168. *arbitrement:* decision.

unspotted soldiers. Some peradventure have on them the guilt of premeditated and contrived murder; some, of beguiling virgins with the broken seals of perjury; some, making the wars their bulwark, that have before gored the gentle bosom of Peace with pillage and robbery. Now, if these men have defeated the law and outrun native punishment, though they can outstrip men, they have no wings to fly from God. War is His beadle, war is His vengeance; so that here men are punished for before-breach of the king's laws in now the king's quarrel. Where they feared the death, they have borne life away; and where they would be safe, they perish. Then if they die unprovided, no more is the king guilty of their damnation than he was before guilty of those impieties for the which they are now visited. Every subject's duty is the king's, but every subject's soul is his own. Therefore should every soldier in the wars do as every sick man in his bed—wash every mote out of his conscience; and dying so, death is to him advantage; or not dying, the time was blessedly lost wherein such preparation was gained; and in him that escapes, it were not sin to think that, making God so free an offer, He let him outlive that day to see His greatness and to teach others how they should prepare. 196

Will. 'Tis certain, every man that dies ill, the ill upon his own head—the king is not to answer it. 199

Bates. I do not desire he should answer for me; and yet I determine to fight lustily for him.

K. Hen. I myself heard the king say he would not be ransomed.

Will. Ay, he said so, to make us fight cheerfully; but when our throats are cut, he may be ransomed, and we ne'er the wiser.

K. Hen. If I live to see it, I will never trust his word after.

Will. You pay him then! That's a perilous shot out of an

171. *contrived:* plotted. 173. *bulwark:* refuge. 176. *native:* at home. 178. *beadle:* inferior police officer. 181. *the death:* death as legal punishment for crime. 183. *unprovided:* without spiritual preparation. 185. *visited:* punished. 209. *pay:* repay, punish.

elder-gun that a poor and a private displeasure can do against a monarch! You may as well go about to turn the sun to ice with fanning in his face with a peacock's feather. You'll never trust his word after! Come, 'tis a foolish saying.

K. Hen. Your reproof is something too round. I should be angry with you if the time were convenient.

Will. Let it be a quarrel between us, if you live. 220

K. Hen. I embrace it.

Will. How shall I know thee again?

K. Hen. Give me any gage of thine, and I will wear it in my bonnet. Then, if ever thou darest acknowledge it, I will make it my quarrel.

Will. Here's my glove; give me another of thine.

K. Hen. There.

Will. This will I also wear in my cap. If ever thou come to me and say, after tomorrow, "This is my glove," by this hand, I will take thee a box on the ear. 232

K. Hen. If ever I live to see it, I will challenge it.

Will. Thou darest as well be hanged.

K. Hen. Well, I will do it, though I take thee in the king's company.

Will. Keep thy word. Fare thee well.

Bates. Be friends, you English fools, be friends! We have French quarrels enow, if you could tell how to reckon. 241

K. Hen. Indeed, the French may lay twenty French crowns to one they will beat us, for they bear them on their shoulders; but it is no English treason to cut French crowns, and tomorrow the king himself will be a clipper. [*Exeunt Soldiers.*

Upon the king! Let us our lives, our souls,
Our debts, our careful wives,
Our children, and our sins lay on the king!
We must bear all. O hard condition, 250

210. *elder-gun:* popgun made of a hollowed shoot of elder. 212. *go about:* attempt. 216. *round:* brusque, plain-spoken. 223. *gage:* pledge. 231. *take:* give. 245. *crowns:* (a) coins, (b) heads. 246. *clipper:* one who mutilates coins by fraudulently paring the edges. 248. *careful:* anxious.

Twin-born with greatness, subject to the breath
Of every fool, whose sense no more can feel
But his own wringing! What infinite heart's-ease
Must kings neglect that private men enjoy!
And what have kings that privates have not too,
Save ceremony, save general ceremony?
And what art thou, thou idol Ceremony?
What kind of god art thou, that suffer'st more
Of mortal griefs than do thy worshippers?
What are thy rents? What are thy comings in? 260
O Ceremony, show me but thy worth!
What is thy soul of adoration?
Art thou aught else but place, degree, and form,
Creating awe and fear in other men?
Wherein thou art less happy being fear'd
Than they in fearing.
What drink'st thou oft, instead of homage sweet,
But poison'd flattery? O, be sick, great greatness,
And bid thy Ceremony give thee cure!
Think'st thou the fiery fever will go out 270
With titles blown from adulation?
Will it give place to flexure and low bending?
Canst thou, when thou command'st the beggar's knee,
Command the health of it? No, thou proud dream,
That play'st so subtly with a king's repose;
I am a king that find thee, and I know
'Tis not the balm, the sceptre, and the ball,
The sword, the mace, the crown imperial,
The intertissued robe of gold and pearl,
The farced title running 'fore the king, 280
The throne he sits on, nor the tide of pomp
That beats upon the high shore of this world—

253. *wringing:* pain. 262. *What . . . adoration:* what is the real reason men adore thee? 271. *blown from adulation:* breathed or puffed up by flatterers. 272. *flexure:* bending the knee. 276. *find:* find out. 277. *balm:* consecrated oil used at coronation. *ball:* carried as a symbol of sovereignty. 279. *intertissued:* interwoven. 280. *farced:* "stuffed out with pompous phrases" (Onions).

No, not all these, thrice-gorgeous Ceremony,
Not all these, laid in bed majestical,
Can sleep so soundly as the wretched slave,
Who with a body fill'd and vacant mind
Gets him to rest, cramm'd with distressful bread;
Never sees horrid night, the child of hell,
But, like a lackey, from the rise to set
Sweats in the eye of Phœbus and all night 290
Sleeps in Elysium; next day after dawn,
Doth rise and help Hyperion to his horse,
And follows so the ever-running year,
With profitable labour, to his grave;
And, but for Ceremony, such a wretch,
Winding up days with toil and nights with sleep,
Had the forehand and vantage of a king.
The slave, a member of the country's peace,
Enjoys it, but in gross brain little wots
What watch the king keeps to maintain the peace, 300
Whose hours the peasant best advantages.

Re-enter ERPINGHAM.

Erp. My lord, your nobles, jealous of your absence,
Seek through your camp to find you.
K. Hen. Good old knight,
Collect them all together at my tent.
I'll be before thee.
Erp. I shall do 't, my lord. [*Exit.*
K. Hen. O God of battles, steel my soldiers' hearts!
Possess them not with fear! Take from them now
The sense of reckoning, if the opposed numbers
Pluck their hearts from them. Not today, O Lord,

287. *distressful:* gained by hard toil. 291. *Elysium:* the abode of the blessed. 292. *Hyperion:* the sun-god. The peasant rises before the sun. 297. *Had the forehand:* would have the upper hand. 298. *member:* sharer. 299. *wots:* knows. 301. *Whose . . . advantages:* whose hours most benefit the peasant. 302. *jealous:* watchful. 309. *hearts:* courage.

O, not today, think not upon the fault 310
My father made in compassing the crown!
I Richard's body have interred new,
And on it have bestow'd more contrite tears
Than from it issued forced drops of blood.
Five hundred poor I have in yearly pay,
Who twice a day their wither'd hands hold up
Toward heaven, to pardon blood; and I have built
Two chantries, where the sad and solemn priests
Sing still for Richard's soul. More will I do,
Though all that I can do is nothing worth, 320
Since that my penitence comes after all,
Imploring pardon.

Re-enter GLOUCESTER.

Glou. My liege!

K. Hen. My brother Gloucester's voice? Ay;
I know thy errand, I will go with thee.
The day, my friends, and all things stay for me. [*Exeunt.*

SCENE II. *The French camp.*

Enter the DAUPHIN, ORLEANS, RAMBURES, *and others.*

Orl. The sun doth gild our armour. Up, my lords!

Dau. *Montez à cheval!* My horse! Varlet! *Laquais!* Ha!

Orl. O brave spirit!

Dau. *Via! Les eaux et la terre*—

Orl. *Rien puis? L'air et le feu.*

Dau. *Ciel*, cousin Orleans!

310–11. *the fault . . . crown:* the deposition and murder of Richard II. 311. *compassing:* obtaining. 318. *chantries:* chapels endowed for the maintenance of priests to sing masses for departed souls.

[ii] 2. *Montez à cheval:* to horse. *Laquais:* lackey. 4–6. *Via . . . Ciel.* The Dauphin says, "Away! Water and earth. (Such dull elements are not in my horse)." Orleans adds, "Nothing (in him) but air and fire." The Dauphin replies, "(There is also) heaven." See III, vii, 22 ff.

Enter CONSTABLE.

Now, my lord constable?
Con. Hark how our steeds for present service neigh!
Dau. Mount them and make incision in their hides
That their hot blood may spin in English eyes, 10
And dout them with superfluous courage, ha!
Ram. What, will you have them weep our horses' blood?
How shall we, then, behold their natural tears?

Enter Messenger.

Mess. The English are embattled, you French peers.
Con. To horse, you gallant princes! Straight to horse!
Do but behold yon poor and starved band,
And your fair show shall suck away their souls,
Leaving them but the shales and husks of men.
There is not work enough for all our hands,
Scarce blood enough in all their sickly veins 20
To give each naked curtle-axe a stain
That our French gallants shall today draw out
And sheathe for lack of sport. Let us but blow on them,
The vapour of our valour will o'erturn them.
'Tis positive 'gainst all exceptions, lords,
That our superfluous lackeys and our peasants,
Who in unnecessary action swarm
About our squares of battle, were enow
To purge this field of such a hilding foe,
Though we upon this mountain's basis by 30
Took stand for idle speculation,
But that our honours must not. What's to say?
A very little little let us do,
And all is done. Then let the trumpets sound
The tucket sonance and the note to mount,

9. *incision:* i.e., with spurs. 11. *dout:* put out. 18. *shales:* shells. 21. *curtle-axe:* cutlass (a corruption of French *coutelas*). 25. *exceptions:* objections. 29. *hilding:* worthless, contemptible. 31. *speculation:* looking on. 35. *tucket sonance:* preliminary trumpet call.

For our approach shall so much dare the field
That England shall couch down in fear and yield.

Enter GRANDPRÉ.

Grand. Why do you stay so long, my lords of France?
Yon island carrions, desperate of their bones,
Ill-favouredly become the morning field. 40
Their ragged curtains poorly are let loose,
And our air shakes them passing scornfully.
Big Mars seems bankrupt in their beggar'd host
And faintly through a rusty beaver peeps.
The horsemen sit like fixed candlesticks,
With torch-staves in their hand; and their poor jades
Lob down their heads, dropping the hides and hips,
The gum down-roping from their pale-dead eyes,
And in their pale dull mouths the gimmal bit
Lies foul with chew'd grass, still and motionless; 50
And their executors, the knavish crows,
Fly o'er them, all impatient for their hour.
Description cannot suit itself in words
To demonstrate the life of such a battle
In life so lifeless as it shows itself.

Con. They have said their prayers, and they stay for death.

Dau. Shall we go send them dinners and fresh suits
And give their fasting horses provender,
And after fight with them?

Con. I stay but for my guidon. To the field! 60
I will the banner from a trumpet take
And use it for my haste. Come, come, away!
The sun is high, and we outwear the day. [*Exeunt.*

36. *dare the field:* terrify the enemy. 37. *couch:* lie, crouch. *Dare* and *couch* are terms of falconry. 39. *desperate:* reckless. 41. *curtains:* banners. 42. *passing:* surpassing. 44. *beaver:* face-guard of helmet. 46. *torch-staves:* staves to hold torches. *jades:* ill-conditioned horses. 47. *Lob:* droop. 48. *down-roping:* flowing down. 49. *gimmal:* jointed, hinged. 61. *trumpet:* trumpeter. 63. *outwear:* waste, spend.

SCENE III. *The English camp.*

Enter GLOUCESTER, BEDFORD, EXETER, ERPINGHAM, *with all his host,* SALISBURY *and* WESTMORELAND.

Glou. Where is the king?
Bed. The king himself is rode to view their battle.
West. Of fighting men they have full three score thousand.
Exe. There's five to one; besides, they all are fresh.
Sal. God's arm strike with us! 'Tis a fearful odds.
God be wi' you, princes all; I'll to my charge.
If we no more meet till we meet in heaven,
Then, joyfully, my noble Lord of Bedford,
My dear Lord Gloucester, and my good Lord Exeter,
And my kind kinsman, warriors all, adieu! 10
Bed. Farewell, good Salisbury, and good luck go with thee!
Exe. Farewell, kind lord; fight valiantly today!
And yet I do thee wrong to mind thee of it,
For thou art framed of the firm truth of valour. [*Exit Salisbury.*
Bed. He is full of valour as of kindness,
Princely in both.

Enter the KING.

West. O that we now had here
But one ten thousand of those men in England
That do no work today!
K. Hen. What's he that wishes so?
My cousin Westmoreland? No, my fair cousin.
If we are mark'd to die, we are enow 20
To do our country loss; and if to live,
The fewer men, the greater share of honour.
God's will! I pray thee, wish not one man more.
By Jove, I am not covetous for gold,
Nor care I who doth feed upon my cost;
It yearns me not if men my garments wear;
Such outward things dwell not in my desires.
But if it be a sin to covet honour,

[iii] 2. *battle:* battle lines. 13. *mind:* remind. 26. *yearns:* grieves.

I am the most offending soul alive.
No, faith, my coz, wish not a man from England. 30
God's peace! I would not lose so great an honour
As one man more, methinks, would share from me
For the best hope I have. O, do not wish one more!
Rather proclaim it, Westmoreland, through my host,
That he which hath no stomach to this fight,
Let him depart; his passport shall be made
And crowns for convoy put into his purse.
We would not die in that man's company
That fears his fellowship to die with us.
This day is call'd the feast of Crispian. 40
He that outlives this day, and comes safe home,
Will stand a-tiptoe when this day is named
And rouse him at the name of Crispian.
He that shall live this day, and see old age,
Will yearly on the vigil feast his neighbours,
And say, "Tomorrow is Saint Crispian."
Then will he strip his sleeve and show his scars,
And say, "These wounds I had on Crispin's day."
Old men forget; yet all shall be forgot,
But he'll remember with advantages 50
What feats he did that day. Then shall our names,
Familiar in his mouth as household words,
Harry the king, Bedford and Exeter,
Warwick and Talbot, Salisbury and Gloucester,
Be in their flowing cups freshly remember'd.
This story shall the good man teach his son;
And Crispin Crispian shall ne'er go by,
From this day to the ending of the world,
But we in it shall be remembered,
We few, we happy few, we band of brothers; 60

30. *coz:* cousin. 37. *crowns for convoy:* money for transportation. 39. *That . . . us:* that fears his sharing death with us. 40. *Crispian.* Crispinus and Crispianus were martyred at Soissons in the fourth century. St. Crispian's Day is October 25. 45. *vigil:* eve of a festival. 50. *advantages:* additions.

For he today that sheds his blood with me
Shall be my brother; be he ne'er so vile,
This day shall gentle his condition.
And gentlemen in England now a-bed
Shall think themselves accursed they were not here,
And hold their manhoods cheap whiles any speaks
That fought with us upon Saint Crispin's day.

Re-enter SALISBURY.

Sal. My sovereign lord, bestow yourself with speed.
The French are bravely in their battles set
And will with all expedience charge on us. 70

K. Hen. All things are ready, if our minds be so.

West. Perish the man whose mind is backward now!

K. Hen. Thou dost not wish more help from England, coz?

West. God's will! My liege, would you and I alone,
Without more help, could fight this royal battle!

K. Hen. Why, now thou hast unwish'd five thousand men,
Which likes me better than to wish us one.
You know your places. God be with you all!

Tucket. Enter MONTJOY.

Mont. Once more I come to know of thee, King Harry,
If for thy ransom thou wilt now compound, 80
Before thy most assured overthrow;
For certainly thou art so near the gulf
Thou needs must be englutted. Besides, in mercy,
The constable desires thee thou wilt mind
Thy followers of repentance, that their souls
May make a peaceful and a sweet retire
From off these fields, where, wretches, their poor bodies
Must lie and fester.

K. Hen. Who hath sent thee now?

Mont. The constable of France.

62. *vile:* low-born. 63. *gentle his condition:* raise him to the rank of gentleman. 68. *bestow yourself:* take your place. 70. *expedience:* speed. 77. *likes:* pleases. 80. *compound:* make terms. 83. *englutted:* swallowed up. 84. *mind:* remind.

K. Hen. I pray thee, bear my former answer back: 90
Bid them achieve me and then sell my bones.
Good God! Why should they mock poor fellows thus?
The man that once did sell the lion's skin
While the beast lived, was killed with hunting him.
A many of our bodies shall no doubt
Find native graves, upon the which, I trust,
Shall witness live in brass of this day's work;
And those that leave their valiant bones in France,
Dying like men, though buried in your dunghills,
They shall be famed; for there the sun shall greet them 100
And draw their honours reeking up to heaven,
Leaving their earthly parts to choke your clime,
The smell whereof shall breed a plague in France.
Mark then abounding valour in our English,
That, being dead, like to the bullet's grazing,
Break out into a second course of mischief,
Killing in relapse of mortality.
Let me speak proudly. Tell the constable
We are but warriors for the working-day.
Our gayness and our gilt are all besmirch'd 110
With rainy marching in the painful field.
There's not a piece of feather in our host—
Good argument, I hope, we will not fly—
And time hath worn us into slovenry.
But, by the mass, our hearts are in the trim;
And my poor soldiers tell me, yet ere night
They'll be in fresher robes, or they will pluck
The gay new coats o'er the French soldiers' heads
And turn them out of service. If they do this—
As, if God please, they shall—my ransom then 120
Will soon be levied. Herald, save thou thy labour.
Come thou no more for ransom, gentle herald.

91. *achieve:* kill. 96. *native:* in their own land. 105. *grazing:* glancing off. 107. *in . . . mortality:* as they die, or "with renewed deadliness," or "with a deadly rebound" (Onions). 114. *slovenry:* slovenliness. 117. *in fresher robes:* i.e., dead.

They shall have none, I swear, but these my joints,
Which if they have as I will leave 'em them,
Shall yield them little, tell the constable.

Mont. I shall, King Harry. And so fare thee well.
Thou never shalt hear herald any more. [*Exit.*

K. Hen. I fear thou 'lt once more come again for ransom.

Enter YORK.

York. My lord, most humbly on my knee I beg
The leading of the vaward. 130

K. Hen. Take it, brave York. Now, soldiers, march away;
And how thou pleasest, God, dispose the day! [*Exeunt.*

SCENE IV. *The field of battle.*

Alarum. Excursions. Enter PISTOL, French Soldier, *and* Boy.

Pist. Yield, cur!

Fr. Sol. *Je pense que vous êtes gentilhomme de bonne qualité.*

Pist. *Qualtitie calmie custure me!* Art thou a gentleman?
What is thy name? Discuss.

Fr. Sol. *O Seigneur Dieu!*

Pist. O, Signieur Dew should be a gentleman.
Perpend my words, O Signieur Dew, and mark.
O Signieur Dew, thou diest on point of fox,
Except, O signieur, thou do give to me 10
Egregious ransom.

Fr. Sol. *O, prenez miséricorde! Ayez pitié de moi!*

Pist. Moy shall not serve; I will have forty moys,
Or I will fetch thy rim out at thy throat
In drops of crimson blood.

130. *vaward:* vanguard.
[iv] S. D. *Excursions.* Small groups of armed men hurry across the stage. 2–3. *Je . . . qualité:* I think that you are a gentleman of high rank. 4. *Qualtitie . . . me!* Pistol repeats the French soldier's last word and adds meaningless jargon probably suggested by the refrain of a popular song. 6. *O Seigneur Dieu:* O Lord God! 8. *Perpend:* consider. 9. *fox:* sword. 12–13. *O . . . moi:* O have mercy! Have pity on me! 14. *Moy . . . moys.* Pistol supposes ransom is spoken of. 15. *rim:* diaphragm.

Fr. Sol. *Est-il impossible d'échapper la force de ton bras?*

Pist. Brass, cur!
Thou damned and luxurious mountain goat, 20
Offer'st me brass?

Fr. Sol. *O, pardonnez moi!*

Pist. Say'st thou me so? Is that a ton of moys?
Come hither, boy; ask me this slave in French
What is his name.

Boy. *Écoutez: comment êtes-vous appelé?*

Fr. Sol. *Monsieur le Fer.*

Boy. He says his name is Master Fer.

Pist. Master Fer? I'll fer him, and firk him, and ferret him.
Discuss the same in French unto him. 31

Boy. I do not know the French for "fer," and "ferret," and "firk."

Pist. Bid him prepare, for I will cut his throat.

Fr. Sol. *Que dit-il, monsieur?*

Boy. *Il me commande de vous dire que vous faites vous prêt, car ce soldat ici est disposé tout à cette heure de couper votre gorge.*

Pist. *Owy, cuppele gorge, permafoy,*
Peasant, unless thou give me crowns, brave crowns; 40
Or mangled shalt thou be by this my sword.

Fr. Sol. *O, je vous supplie, pour l'amour de Dieu, me pardonner! Je suis gentilhomme de bonne maison; gardez ma vie, et je vous donnerai deux cents écus.*

Pist. What are his words?

Boy. He prays you to save his life. He is a gentleman of a good house; and for his ransom he will give you two hundred crowns.

17–18. *Est-il . . . bras:* is it impossible to escape the strength of your arm? 20. *luxurious:* lustful. 22. *O . . . moi:* Oh, pardon me! 26. *Écoutez . . . appelé:* listen: what is your name? 29. *firk:* beat. 30. *ferret:* worry (as a ferret does its prey). 35–8. *Que . . . gorge.* What does he say, sir? *Boy.* He bids me tell you to make yourself ready, for this soldier intends to cut your throat at once. 42–5. *O . . . écus.* O, I beg you, for the love of God, pardon me! I am a gentleman of a good house; preserve my life, and I will give you two hundred crowns.

Pist. Tell him my fury shall abate, and I　　50
The crowns will take.

Fr. Sol. *Petit monsieur, que dit-il?*

Boy. *Encore qu'il est contre son jurement de pardonner aucun prisonnier, néanmoins, pour les écus que vous l'avez promis, il est content de vous donner la liberté, le franchisement.*

Fr. Sol. *Sur mes genoux je vous donne mille remercîmens; et je m'estime heureux que je suis tombé entre les mains d'un chevalier, je pense, le plus brave, vaillant, et très distingué seigneur d'Angleterre.*　　61

Pist. Expound unto me, boy.

Boy. He gives you, upon his knees, a thousand thanks; and he esteems himself happy that he hath fallen into the hands of one, as he thinks, the most brave, valorous, and thrice-worthy signieur of England.

Pist. As I suck blood, I will some mercy show.
Follow me!　　69

Boy. *Suivez-vous le grand capitaine.* [*Exeunt Pistol and French Soldier.*] I did never know so full a voice issue from so empty a heart; but the saying is true, "The empty vessel makes the greatest sound." Bardolph and Nym had ten times more valour than this roaring devil i' the old play that everyone may pare his nails with a wooden dagger; and they are both hanged; and so would this be, if he durst steal anything adventurously. I must stay with the lackeys, with the luggage of our camp. The French might have a good prey of us, if he knew of it; for there is none to guard it but boys.　　[*Exit.* 82

52–61. *Petit . . . d'Angleterre.* Little sir, what does he say? *Boy.* Again, that it is contrary to his oath to pardon any prisoner; nevertheless, for the crowns that you have promised him, he is willing to give you liberty, freedom. *Fr. Sol.* On my knees I give you a thousand thanks; and I consider myself fortunate that I have fallen into the hands of a knight, I think, the bravest, most valiant, and distinguished gentleman of England.　70. *Suivez-vous . . . capitaine:* follow the great captain.　75. *devil.* In some of the moralities and interludes the Devil, a coward and braggart, supplies the boisterous humor. The Vice was often armed with a wooden dagger.

Scene v. *Another part of the field.*

Enter Constable, Orleans, Bourbon, Dauphin, *and* Rambures.

Con. *O diable!*
Orl. *O Seigneur! Le jour est perdu, tout est perdu!*
Dau. *Mort de ma vie!* All is confounded, all!
Reproach and everlasting shame
Sits mocking in our plumes. *O méchante fortune!*
Do not run away. [*A short alarum.*
Con. Why, all our ranks are broke.
Dau. O perdurable shame! Let's stab ourselves.
Be these the wretches that we play'd at dice for?
Orl. Is this the king we sent to for his ransom?
Bour. Shame and eternal shame! Nothing but shame! 10
Let us die in honour! Once more back again!
And he that will not follow Bourbon now,
Let him go hence, and with his cap in hand,
Like a base pandar, hold the chamber-door
Whilst by a slave, no gentler than my dog,
His fairest daughter is contaminated.
Con. Disorder, that hath spoil'd us, friend us now!
Let us on heaps go offer up our lives.
Orl. We are enow yet living in the field
To smother up the English in our throngs, 20
If any order might be thought upon.
Bour. The devil take order now! I'll to the throng.
Let life be short; else shame will be too long. [*Exeunt.*

Scene vi. *Another part of the field.*

Alarums. Enter King Henry *and forces*, Exeter, *and others.*

K. Hen. Well have we done, thrice valiant countrymen.
But all's not done; yet keep the French the field.

[v] 1. *O diable:* O the Devil! 2. *O . . . perdu:* O Lord, the day is lost, all is lost! 3. *Mort . . . vie:* death of my life! 5. *méchante:* evil. 7. *perdurable:* lasting. 18. *on heaps:* in crowds.

Exe. The Duke of York commends him to your Majesty.
K. Hen. Lives he, good uncle? Thrice within this hour
I saw him down, thrice up again and fighting.
From helmet to the spur all blood he was.
Exe. In which array, brave soldier, doth he lie,
Larding the plain; and by his bloody side,
Yoke-fellow to his honour-owing wounds,
The noble Earl of Suffolk also lies. 10
Suffolk first died, and York, all haggled over,
Comes to him, where in gore he lay insteep'd,
And takes him by the beard, kisses the gashes
That bloodily did yawn upon his face,
And cries aloud, "Tarry, dear cousin Suffolk!
My soul shall thine keep company to heaven.
Tarry, sweet soul, for mine; then fly abreast,
As in this glorious and well-foughten field
We kept together in our chivalry!"
Upon these words I came and cheer'd him up. 20
He smiled me in the face, raught me his hand,
And, with a feeble gripe, says, "Dear my lord,
Commend my service to my sovereign."
So did he turn and over Suffolk's neck
He threw his wounded arm and kiss'd his lips,
And so, espoused to death, with blood he seal'd
A testament of noble-ending love.
The pretty and sweet manner of it forced
Those waters from me which I would have stopp'd;
But I had not so much of man in me, 30
And all my mother came into mine eyes
And gave me up to tears.
K. Hen. I blame you not;
For, hearing this, I must perforce compound
With mistful eyes, or they will issue too. [*Alarum.*

[vi] 8. *Larding:* garnishing; enriching (with his blood). 9. *honour-owing:* honor-owning, honorable. 11. *haggled:* hacked, mangled. 21. *raught:* reached. 31. *mother:* gentle nature, womanish qualities. 33. *compound:* come to terms. 34. *issue:* shed tears.

But, hark! What new alarum is this same?
The French have reinforced their scatter'd men.
Then every soldier kill his prisoners!
Give the word through. [*Exeunt.*

SCENE VII. *Another part of the field.*

Enter FLUELLEN *and* GOWER.

Flu. Kill the poys and the luggage? 'Tis expressly against the law of arms. 'Tis as arrant a piece of knavery, mark you now, as can be offer't. In your conscience, now, is it not?

Gow. 'Tis certain there's not a boy left alive, and the cowardly rascals that ran from the battle ha' done this slaughter. Besides, they have burned and carried away all that was in the king's tent; wherefore the king, most worthily, hath caused every soldier to cut his prisoner's throat. O, 'tis a gallant king!

Flu. Ay, he was porn at Monmouth, Captain Gower. What call you the town's name where Alexander the Pig was born?

Gow. Alexander the Great.

Flu. Why, I pray you, is not "pig" great? The pig, or the great, or the mighty, or the huge, or the magnanimous, are all one reckonings, save the phrase is a little variations. 19

Gow. I think Alexander the Great was born in Macedon. His father was called Philip of Macedon, as I take it.

Flu. I think it is in Macedon where Alexander is porn. I tell you, captain, if you look in the maps of the 'orld, I warrant you sall find, in the comparisons between Macedon and Monmouth, that the situations, look you, is both alike. There is a river in Macedon, and there is also moreover a river at Monmouth. It is called Wye at Monmouth; but it is out of my prains what is the name of the other river. But 'tis all one; 'tis alike as my fingers is to my fingers, and there is salmons in both. If you mark Alexander's life well, Harry of Monmouth's life is come after it indifferent well, for there is figures in all things.

[vii] 34. *is come after:* resembles. 35. *figures:* analogies, comparisons.

Alexander, God knows, and you know, in his rages, and his furies, and his wraths, and his cholers, and his moods, and his displeasures, and his indignations, and also being a little intoxicates in his prains, did, in his ales and his angers, look you, kill his best friend, Cleitus. 41

Gow. Our king is not like him in that. He never killed any of his friends.

Flu. It is not well done, mark you now, to take the tales out of my mouth ere it is made and finished. I speak but in the figures and comparisons of it. As Alexander killed his friend Cleitus, being in his ales and his cups, so also Harry Monmouth, being in his right wits and his good judgments, turned away the fat knight with the great-belly doublet. He was full of jests, and gipes, and knaveries, and mocks. I have forgot his name. 53

Gow. Sir John Falstaff.

Flu. That is he. I'll tell you there is good men porn at Monmouth.

Gow. Here comes his Majesty.

Alarum. Enter KING HENRY, WARWICK, GLOUCESTER, EXETER, *and others.*

K. Hen. I was not angry since I came to France
Until this instant. Take a trumpet, herald;
Ride thou unto the horsemen on yon hill. 60
If they will fight with us, bid them come down,
Or void the field; they do offend our sight.
If they'll do neither, we will come to them
And make them skirr away as swift as stones
Enforced from the old Assyrian slings.
Besides, we'll cut the throats of those we have,
And not a man of them that we shall take
Shall taste our mercy. Go and tell them so.

38. *cholers:* angers. 51. *great-belly doublet:* "no doubt a jocose allusion to his circumference rather than a precise description of his attire" (*Shakespeare's England*, II, 104). 52. *gipes:* gibes. 62. *void:* leave. 64. *skirr:* scurry. 65. *Enforced:* driven, hurled.

Enter MONTJOY.

Exe. Here comes the herald of the French, my liege.
Glo. His eyes are humbler than they used to be. 70
K. Hen. How now? What means this, herald? Know'st thou not
That I have fined these bones of mine for ransom?
Comest thou again for ransom?
Mont. No, great king.
I come to thee for charitable license
That we may wander o'er this bloody field
To book our dead, and then to bury them,
To sort our nobles from our common men,
For many of our princes—woe the while!—
Lie drown'd and soak'd in mercenary blood;
So do our vulgar drench their peasant limbs 80
In blood of princes, and their wounded steeds
Fret fetlock deep in gore, and with wild rage
Yerk out their armed heels at their dead masters,
Killing them twice. O, give us leave, great king,
To view the field in safety and dispose
Of their dead bodies!
K. Hen. I tell thee truly, herald,
I know not if the day be ours or no,
For yet a many of your horsemen peer
And gallop o'er the field.
Mont. The day is yours.
K. Hen. Praised be God, and not our strength, for it! 90
What is this castle call'd that stands hard by?
Mont. They call it Agincourt.
K. Hen. Then call we this the field of Agincourt,
Fought on the day of Crispin Crispianus.
Flu. Your grandfather of famous memory, an 't please your Majesty, and your great-uncle Edward the Plack Prince of

72. *fined:* agreed to pay as a fine. 76. *book:* record. 80. *vulgar:* common soldiers. 83. *Yerk:* kick. 88. *peer:* appear. 95. *grandfather:* i.e., great-grandfather, Edward III, at Crécy.

Wales, as I have read in the chronicles, fought a most prave pattle here in France.

K. Hen. They did, Fluellen. 100

Flu. Your Majesty says very true. If your Majesties is remembered of it, the Welshmen did good service in a garden where leeks did grow, wearing leeks in their Monmouth caps; which your Majesty know to this hour is an honourable badge of the service; and I do believe your Majesty takes no scorn to wear the leek upon Saint Tavy's day.

K. Hen. I wear it for a memorable honour,
For I am Welsh, you know, good countryman. 110

Flu. All the water in Wye cannot wash your Majesty's Welsh plood out of your pody, I can tell you that. God pless it and preserve it, as long as it pleases His grace, and His majesty too!

K. Hen. Thanks, good my countryman.

Flu. By Jeshu, I am your Majesty's countryman; I care not who know it! I will confess it to all the 'orld. I need not to be ashamed of your Majesty, praised be God, so long as your Majesty is an honest man. 120

K. Hen. God keep me so! Our heralds go with him.
Bring me just notice of the numbers dead
On both our parts. Call yonder fellow hither.

[*Points to Williams. Exeunt Heralds with Montjoy.*

Exe. Soldier, you must come to the king.

K. Hen. Soldier, why wearest thou that glove in thy cap?

Will. An 't please your Majesty, 'tis the gage of one that I should fight withal, if he be alive.

K. Hen. An Englishman? 129

Will. An 't please your Majesty, a rascal that swaggered with me last night; who, if alive and ever dare to challenge this glove, I have sworn to take him a box o' th' ear; or if I can see my glove in his cap, which he swore, as he was a soldier, he would wear if alive, I will strike it out soundly.

103. *in a garden.* See IV, i, 54–5, note. 122. *just notice:* exact information.

K. Hen. What think you, Captain Fluellen? Is it fit this soldier keep his oath?

Flu. He is a craven and a villain else, an 't please your Majesty, in my conscience. 140

K. Hen. It may be his enemy is a gentleman of great sort, quite from the answer of his degree.

Flu. Though he be as good a gentleman as the Devil is, as Lucifer and Belzebub himself, it is necessary, look your Grace, that he keep his vow and his oath. If he be perjured, see you now, his reputation is as arrant a villain and a Jacksauce as ever his black shoe trod upon God's ground and his earth, in my conscience, la! 150

K. Hen. Then keep thy vow, sirrah, when thou meetest the fellow.

Will. So I will, my liege, as I live.

K. Hen. Who servest thou under?

Will. Under Captain Gower, my liege.

Flu. Gower is a good captain and is good knowledge and literatured in the wars.

K. Hen. Call him hither to me, soldier.

Will. I will, my liege. [*Exit.*

K. Hen. Here, Fluellen, wear thou this favour for me and stick it in thy cap. When Alençon and myself were down together, I plucked this glove from his helm. If any man challenge this, he is a friend to Alençon, and an enemy to our person. If thou encounter any such, apprehend him, an thou dost me love.

Flu. Your Grace doo's me as great honours as can be desired in the hearts of his subjects. I would fain see the man, that has but two legs, that shall find himself aggriefed at this glove. That is all; but I would fain see it once, an please God of His grace that I might see. 172

K. Hen. Knowest thou Gower?

Flu. He is my dear friend, an please you.

K. Hen. Pray thee go seek him and bring him to my tent.

Flu. I will fetch him. [*Exit.*

142. *sort:* rank. 142–3. *from . . . degree:* above answering the challenge of one of his rank. 148. *Jacksauce:* saucy knave.

K. Hen. My Lord of Warwick, and my brother Gloucester,
Follow Fluellen closely at the heels.
The glove which I have given him for a favour 180
May haply purchase him a box o' th' ear.
It is the soldier's; I by bargain should
Wear it myself. Follow, good cousin Warwick.
If that the soldier strike him, as I judge
By his blunt bearing he will keep his word,
Some sudden mischief may arise of it;
For I do know Fluellen valiant
And, touch'd with choler, hot as gunpowder,
And quickly will return an injury.
Follow and see there be no harm between them. 190
Go you with me, uncle of Exeter. [*Exeunt.*

SCENE VIII. *Before* KING HENRY'S *pavilion.*

Enter GOWER *and* WILLIAMS.

Will. I warrant it is to knight you, captain.

Enter FLUELLEN.

Flu. God's will and his pleasure, captain, I beseech you now, come apace to the king. There is more good toward you peradventure than is in your knowledge to dream of.

Will. Sir, know you this glove?

Flu. Know the glove? I know the glove is a glove.

Will. I know this, and thus I challenge it. [*Strikes him.*

Flu. 'Sblood! An arrant traitor as any is in the universal world, or in France, or in England! 11

Gow. How now, sir? You villain!

Will. Do you think I'll be forsworn?

Flu. Stand away, Captain Gower. I will give treason his payment into plows, I warrant you.

Will. I am no traitor.

188. *choler:* anger.
[viii] 3. *toward:* intended for. 10. *'Sblood:* God's blood.

Flu. That's a lie in thy throat. I charge you in his Majesty's name, apprehend him. He's a friend of the Duke Alençon's.

Enter Warwick *and* Gloucester.

War. How now, how now? What's the matter? 20

Flu. My Lord of Warwick, here is—praised be God for it!—a most contagious treason come to light, look you, as you shall desire in a summer's day. Here is his Majesty.

Enter King Henry *and* Exeter.

K. Hen. How now? What's the matter?

Flu. My liege, here is a villain and a traitor, that, look your Grace, has struck the glove which your Majesty is take out of the helmet of Alençon. 28

Will. My liege, this was my glove; here is the fellow of it; and he that I gave it to in change promised to wear it in his cap. I promised to strike him if he did. I met this man with my glove in his cap, and I have been as good as my word.

Flu. Your Majesty hear now, saving your Majesty's manhood, what an arrant, rascally, beggarly, lousy knave it is! I hope your Majesty is pear me testimony and witness, and will avouchment, that this is the glove of Alençon that your Majesty is give me. In your conscience, now! 40

K. Hen. Give me thy glove, soldier. Look, here is the fellow of it.
'Twas I indeed thou promised'st to strike,
And thou hast given me most bitter terms.

Flu. And please your Majesty, let his neck answer for it, if there is any martial law in the world.

K. Hen. How canst thou make me satisfaction?

Will. All offenses, my lord, come from the heart. Never came any from mine that might offend your Majesty. 51

K. Hen. It was ourself thou didst abuse.

Will. Your Majesty came not like yourself. You appeared

22. *contagious:* blunder for "outrageous." 38. *is pear:* will bear. *avouchment:* acknowledge. 44. *terms:* words.

to me but as a common man; witness the night, your garments, your lowliness. And what your Highness suffered under that shape, I beseech you take it for your own fault and not mine; for had you been as I took you for, I made no offense. Therefore I beseech your Highness pardon me. 60

K. Hen. Here, uncle Exeter, fill this glove with crowns,
And give it to this fellow. Keep it, fellow,
And wear it for an honour in thy cap
Till I do challenge it. Give him the crowns;
And, captain, you must needs be friends with him.

Flu. By this day and this light, the fellow has mettle enough in his belly. Hold, there is twelve pence for you; and I pray you to serve God, and keep you out of prawls, and prabbles, and quarrels, and dissensions, and, I warrant you, it is the better for you. 71

Will. I will none of your money.

Flu. It is with a good will. I can tell you it will serve you to mend your shoes. Come, wherefore should you be so pashful? Your shoes is not so good. 'Tis a good silling, I warrant you, or I will change it.

Enter an English Herald.

K. Hen. Now, herald, are the dead number'd?

Her. Here is the number of the slaughter'd French.
[*Gives a paper.*

K. Hen. What prisoners of good sort are taken, uncle? 80

Exe. Charles Duke of Orleans, nephew to the king;
John Duke of Bourbon, and Lord Bouciqualt;
Of other lords and barons, knights and squires,
Full fifteen hundred, besides common men.

K. Hen. This note doth tell me of ten thousand French
That in the field lie slain. Of princes, in this number,
And nobles bearing banners, there lie dead
One hundred twenty six; added to these,
Of knights, esquires, and gallant gentlemen,

55. *lowliness:* humble bearing. 69. *prabbles:* brabbles, quarrels.
80. *good sort:* rank.

Eight thousand and four hundred; of the which, 90
Five hundred were but yesterday dubb'd knights;
So that, in these ten thousand they have lost,
There are but sixteen hundred mercenaries;
The rest are princes, barons, lords, knights, squires,
And gentlemen of blood and quality.
The names of those their nobles that lie dead:
Charles Delabreth, high constable of France;
Jacques of Chatillon, admiral of France;
The master of the cross-bows, Lord Rambures;
Great Master of France, the brave Sir Guichard Dolphin, 100
John Duke of Alençon; Anthony Duke of Brabant,
The brother to the Duke of Burgundy,
And Edward Duke of Bar; of lusty earls,
Grandpré and Roussi, Fauconberg and Foix,
Beaumont and Marle, Vaudemont and Lestrale.
Here was a royal fellowship of death!
Where is the number of our English dead?

[*Herald presents another paper.*

Edward the Duke of York, the Earl of Suffolk,
Sir Richard Ketly, Davy Gam, esquire;
None else of name; and of all other men 110
But five and twenty. O God, Thy arm was here!
And not to us, but to Thy arm alone,
Ascribe we all! When, without stratagem,
But in plain shock and even play of battle,
Was ever known so great and little loss
On one part and on the other? Take it, God,
For it is none but Thine!

Exe. 'Tis wonderful!

K. Hen. Come, go we in procession to the village,
And be it death proclaimed through our host
To boast of this or take that praise from God 120
Which is His only.

Flu. Is it not lawful, an please your Majesty, to tell how many is killed?

110. *name:* rank, eminence.

K. Hen. Yes, captain, but with this acknowledgment,
That God fought for us.

Flu. Yes, my conscience, he did us great good.

K. Hen. Do we all holy rites.
Let there be sung *Non nobis* and *Te Deum;*
The dead with charity enclosed in clay;
And then to Calais; and to England then, 130
Where ne'er from France arrived more happy men. [*Exeunt.*

ACT V

PROLOGUE

Enter Chorus.

Chor. Vouchsafe to those that have not read the story
That I may prompt them; and of such as have,
I humbly pray them to admit the excuse
Of time, of numbers, and due course of things
Which cannot in their huge and proper life
Be here presented. Now we bear the king
Toward Calais. Grant him there. There seen,
Heave him away upon your winged thoughts
Athwart the sea. Behold, the English beach
Pales in the flood with men, with wives and boys, 10
Whose shouts and claps outvoice the deep-mouth'd sea,
Which like a mighty whiffler 'fore the king
Seems to prepare his way. So let him land,
And solemnly see him set on to London.
So swift a pace hath thought that even now
You may imagine him upon Blackheath,

128. *Non nobis and Te Deum.* According to Holinshed, Psalm 115, beginning *Non nobis, Domine, non nobis, sed nomini tuo da gloriam,* and the great hymn of praise, *Te deum laudamus,* were sung after the battle.

[V. Prologue] Between Acts IV and V there is an interval of five years during which Henry made a second campaign ended by the treaty of Troyes. 10. *Pales:* fences. 12. *whiffler:* officer who clears the way for a procession. 14. *solemnly:* ceremoniously.

Where that his lords desire him to have borne
His bruised helmet and his bended sword
Before him through the city. He forbids it,
Being free from vainness and self-glorious pride; 20
Giving full trophy, signal, and ostent
Quite from himself to God. But now behold,
In the quick forge and working-house of thought,
How London doth pour out her citizens!
The mayor and all his brethren in best sort—
Like to the senators of the antique Rome,
With the plebeians swarming at their heels—
Go forth and fetch their conquering Cæsar in;
As, by a lower but loving likelihood,
Were now the general of our gracious empress, 30
As in good time he may, from Ireland coming,
Bringing rebellion broached on his sword,
How many would the peaceful city quit,
To welcome him! Much more, and much more cause,
Did they this Harry. Now in London place him;
As yet the lamentation of the French
Invites the King of England's stay at home—
The emperor's coming in behalf of France,
To order peace between them—and omit
All the occurrences, whatever chanced, 40
Till Harry's back-return again to France.
There must we bring him; and myself have play'd
The interim, by remembering you 'tis past.
Then brook abridgment, and your eyes advance,
After your thoughts, straight back again to France. [*Exit.*

21. *Giving . . . ostent:* transferring the token and show of triumph. 25. *sort:* array. 30. *the general.* Robert Devereux, second Earl of Essex, left England in March, 1599, to subdue the Irish rebels, and returned in disgrace the following September. 32. *broached:* spitted. 38. *The emperor's coming.* Sigismund, Emperor of Germany, came to England in May, 1416. 39. *order:* arrange. 43. *remembering:* reminding. 44. *brook:* accept, tolerate.

SCENE I. *France. The English camp.*

Enter FLUELLEN *and* GOWER.

Gow. Nay, that's right. But why wear you your leek today? Saint Davy's day is past.

Flu. There is occasions and causes why and wherefore in all things. I will tell you ass my friend, Captain Gower. The rascally, scauld, beggarly, lousy, pragging knave, Pistol, which you and yourself and all the world know to be no petter than a fellow, look you now, of no merits, he is come to me and prings me pread and salt yesterday, look you, and bid me eat my leek. It was in a place where I could not breed no contention with him; but I will be so bold as to wear it in my cap till I see him once again, and then I will tell him a little piece of my desires.

Enter PISTOL.

Gow. Why, here he comes, swelling like a turkey-cock.

Flu. 'Tis no matter for his swellings nor his turkey-cocks. God pless you, Aunchient Pistol! You scurvy, lousy knave, God pless you! 19

Pist. Ha! Art thou bedlam? Dost thou thirst, base Trojan,
To have me fold up Parca's fatal web?
Hence! I am qualmish at the smell of leek.

Flu. I peseech you heartily, scurvy, lousy knave, at my desires, and my requests, and my petitions, to eat, look you, this leek. Because, look you, you do not love it, nor your affections and your appetites and your disgestions doo's not agree with it, I would desire you to eat it.

Pist. Not for Cadwallader and all his goats.

Flu. There is one goat for you. [*Strikes him.*] Will you be so good, scauld knave, as eat it? 31

Pist. Base Trojan, thou shalt die!

Flu. You say very true, scauld knave, when God's will is.

[i] 5. *scauld:* scurvy. 20. *bedlam:* crazy. *Trojan:* cant term for "boon companion." 21. *Parca's:* the Parcae's, the Fates'. 29. *Cadwallader:* last king of the Welsh. Even he, Pistol implies, was a goatherd.

I will desire you to live in the meantime, and eat your victuals. Come, there is sauce for it. [*Strikes him.*] You called me yesterday mountain-squire; but I will make you today a squire of low degree. I pray you fall to. If you can mock a leek, you can eat a leek.

Gow. Enough, captain. You have astonished him. 41

Flu. I say I will make him eat some part of my leek, or I will peat his pate four days. Bite, I pray you; it is good for your green wound and your ploody coxcomb.

Pist. Must I bite?

Flu. Yes, certainly, and out of doubt and out of question too, and ambiguities.

Pist. By this leek, I will most horribly revenge. I eat and eat, I swear— 50

Flu. Eat, I pray you. Will you have some more sauce to your leek? There is not enough leek to swear by.

Pist. Quiet thy cudgel. Thou dost see I eat.

Flu. Much good do you, scauld knave, heartily. Nay, pray you, throw none away. The skin is good for your broken coxcomb. When you take occasions to see leeks hereafter, I pray you, mock at 'em; that is all.

Pist. Good. 60

Flu. Ay, leeks is good. Hold you, there is a groat to heal your pate.

Pist. Me a groat!

Flu. Yes, verily and in truth, you shall take it; or I have another leek in my pocket, which you shall eat.

Pist. I take thy groat in earnest of revenge.

Flu. If I owe you anything, I will pay you in cudgels. You shall be a woodmonger and buy nothing of me but cudgels. God b' wi' you, and keep you, and heal your pate. [*Exit.*

Pist. All hell shall stir for this! 72

Gow. Go, go. You are a counterfeit cowardly knave. Will

37. *mountain-squire.* An allusion to mountainous Wales. 38. *squire of low degree.* This was the title of a popular romance. 40. *astonished:* stunned. 45. *coxcomb:* head. 62. *groat:* fourpence. 67. *in earnest:* as an installment to secure a bargain.

you mock at an ancient tradition, begun upon an honourable respect, and worn as a memorable trophy of predeceased valour, and dare not avouch in your deeds any of your words? I have seen you gleeking and galling at this gentleman twice or thrice. You thought, because he could not speak English in the native garb, he could not therefore handle an English cudgel. You find it otherwise; and henceforth let a Welsh correction teach you a good English condition. Fare ye well. [*Exit.*

Pist. Doth Fortune play the huswife with me now? 85
News have I that my Nell is dead i' the spital
Of malady of France;
And there my rendezvous is quite cut off.
Old I do wax, and from my weary limbs
Honour is cudgelled. Well, bawd I'll turn, 90
And something lean to cutpurse of quick hand.
To England will I steal, and there I'll steal;
And patches will I get unto these cudgell'd scars
And swear I got them in the Gallia wars. [*Exit.*

SCENE II. *France. A royal palace.*

Enter, at one door, KING HENRY, GLOUCESTER, BEDFORD, EXETER, WARWICK, WESTMORELAND, *and other* Lords; *at another, the* FRENCH KING, QUEEN ISABEL, *the* PRINCESS KATHARINE, ALICE, *and other* Ladies; *the* DUKE OF BURGUNDY *and his train.*

K. Hen. Peace to this meeting, wherefore we are met!
Unto our brother France and to our sister,
Health and fair time of day; joy and good wishes
To our most fair and princely cousin Katharine;
And, as a branch and member of this royalty,
By whom this great assembly is contrived,

75. *respect:* consideration. 77. *avouch:* support. 78. *gleeking and galling:* jesting and scoffing. 80. *garb:* manner. 83. *condition:* temper. 85. *huswife:* hussy. 86. *spital:* hospital. 91. *cutpurse:* thief.

[ii] 1. *wherefore:* on account of which (the peace). 3. *fair time of day:* a common greeting.

We do salute you, Duke of Burgundy;
And, princes French, and peers, health to you all!
Fr. King. Right joyous are we to behold your face,
Most worthy brother England. Fairly met! 10
So are you, princes English, every one.
Q. Isa. So happy be the issue, brother England,
Of this good day and of this gracious meeting,
As we are now glad to behold your eyes—
Your eyes, which hitherto have borne in them
Against the French that met them in their bent
The fatal balls of murdering basilisks.
The venom of such looks, we fairly hope,
Have lost their quality, and that this day
Shall change all griefs and quarrels into love. 20
K. Hen. To cry amen to that, thus we appear.
Q. Isa. You English princes all, I do salute you!
Bur. My duty to you both, on equal love,
Great Kings of France and England! That I have labour'd,
With all my wits, my pains, and strong endeavours,
To bring your most imperial Majesties
Unto this bar and royal interview,
Your mightiness on both parts best can witness.
Since, then, my office hath so far prevail'd
That, face to face and royal eye to eye, 30
You have congreeted, let it not disgrace me
If I demand, before this royal view,
What rub or what impediment there is
Why that the naked, poor, and mangled Peace,
Dear nurse of arts, plenties, and joyful births,
Should not in this best garden of the world,
Our fertile France, put up her lovely visage.
Alas, she hath from France too long been chased,
And all her husbandry doth lie on heaps,

16. *bent:* glance. 17. *basilisks:* cannon. The basilisk was a fabulous serpent said to kill by its breath and look. 27. *bar:* court. 31. *congreeted:* exchanged greetings. 33. *rub:* obstacle. 39. *on heaps:* in ruins.

Corrupting in it own fertility. 40
Her vine, the merry cheerer of the heart,
Unpruned dies; her hedges even-pleach'd,
Like prisoners wildly over-grown with hair,
Put forth disorder'd twigs; her fallow leas
The darnel, hemlock, and rank fumitory
Doth root upon, while that the coulter rusts
That should deracinate such savagery.
The even mead, that erst brought sweetly forth
The freckled cowslip, burnet, and green clover,
Wanting the scythe, all uncorrected, rank, 50
Conceives by idleness, and nothing teems
But hateful docks, rough thistles, kecksies, burs,
Losing both beauty and utility.
And as our vineyards, fallows, meads, and hedges,
Defective in their natures, grow to wildness,
Even so our houses and ourselves and children
Have lost, or do not learn for want of time,
The sciences that should become our country;
But grow like savages—as soldiers will
That nothing do but meditate on blood— 60
To swearing and stern looks, defused attire,
And everything that seems unnatural.
Which to reduce into our former favour
You are assembled; and my speech entreats
That I may know the let, why gentle Peace
Should not expel these inconveniences
And bless us with her former qualities.

K. Hen. If, Duke of Burgundy, you would the peace
Whose want gives growth to the imperfections

40. *it:* its. 42. *even-pleach'd:* evenly interwoven. 44. *fallow leas:* uncultivated open land. 45. *darnel:* a grass. *fumitory:* a plant with a bitter taste. 47. *deracinate:* uproot. 48. *erst:* formerly. 51. *nothing teems:* brings forth nothing. 52. *kecksies:* plants with hollow stalks. 54. *fallows:* ground plowed and harrowed but left unplanted. 55. *natures:* natural functions, i.e., to supply food. 61. *defused:* disordered. 63. *reduce:* bring back. *favour:* appearance. 65. *let:* hindrance.

Which you have cited, you must buy that peace 70
With full accord to all our just demands;
Whose tenours and particular effects
You have, enscheduled briefly, in your hands.

Bur. The king hath heard them; to the which as yet
There is no answer made.

K. Hen. Well, then, the peace,
Which you before so urged, lies in his answer.

Fr. King. I have but with a cursorary eye
O'erglanced the articles. Pleaseth your Grace
To appoint some of your council presently
To sit with us once more, with better heed 80
To re-survey them, we will suddenly
Pass our accept and peremptory answer.

K. Hen. Brother, we shall. Go, uncle Exeter,
And brother Clarence, and you, brother Gloucester,
Warwick, and Huntingdon, go with the king;
And take with you free power to ratify,
Augment, or alter, as your wisdoms best
Shall see advantageable for our dignity,
Anything in or out of our demands,
And we'll consign thereto. Will you, fair sister, 90
Go with the princes or stay here with us?

Q. Isa. Our gracious brother, I will go with them.
Haply a woman's voice may do some good
When articles too nicely urged be stood on.

K. Hen. Yet leave our cousin Katharine here with us.
She is our capital demand, comprised
Within the fore-rank of our articles.

Q. Isa. She hath good leave.

[*Exeunt all except King Henry, Katharine, and Alice.*

K. Hen. Fair Katharine, and most fair,

72. *tenours . . . effects:* purport and specific details. 73. *enscheduled:* written. 77. *cursorary:* cursory. 81. *suddenly:* soon. 82. *accept:* accepted (as decisive). *peremptory:* final. 90. *consign:* agree. 94. *nicely:* with attention to detail. *stood on:* insisted on. 96. *capital:* chief.

Will you vouchsafe to teach a soldier terms
Such as will enter at a lady's ear		100
And plead his love-suit to her gentle heart?

Kath. Your Majesty shall mock at me; I cannot speak your England.

K. Hen. O fair Katharine, if you will love me soundly with your French heart, I will be glad to hear you confess it brokenly with your English tongue. Do you like me, Kate?

Kath. *Pardonnez-moi*, I cannot tell vat is "like me."

K. Hen. An angel is like you, Kate, and you are like an angel.		111

Kath. *Que dit-il? Que je suis semblable à les anges?*

Alice. *Oui, vraiment, sauf votre grace, ainsi dit-il.*

K. Hen. I said so, dear Katharine, and I must not blush to affirm it.

Kath. *O bon Dieu! Les langues des hommes sont pleines de tromperies.*

K. Hen. What says she, fair one? That the tongues of men are full of deceits?		121

Alice. *Oui*, dat de tongues of de mans is be full of deceits. Dat is de princess.

K. Hen. The princess is the better Englishwoman. I' faith, Kate, my wooing is fit for thy understanding. I am glad thou canst speak no better English, for, if thou couldst, thou wouldst find me such a plain king that thou wouldst think I had sold my farm to buy my crown. I know no ways to mince it in love, but directly to say, "I love you." Then if you urge me farther than to say, "Do you in faith?" I wear out my suit. Give me your answer; i' faith, do; and so clap hands and a bargain. How say you, lady?		134

Kath. *Sauf votre honneur*, me understand vell.

K. Hen. Marry, if you would put me to verses or to dance for your sake, Kate, why, you undid me. For the one, I have neither words nor measure, and for the other, I have no strength

112–15. *Que . . . dit-il:* what does he say? That I am like the angels? *Alice.* Yes, truly, by your leave, so he says. 133. *clap:* clasp. 138. *undid:* would undo.

in measure, yet a reasonable measure in strength. If I could win a lady at leap-frog, or by vaulting into my saddle with my armour on my back, under the correction of bragging be it spoken, I should quickly leap into a wife. Or if I might buffet for my love, or bound my horse for her favours, I could lay on like a butcher and sit like a jackanapes, never off. But, before God, Kate, I cannot look greenly nor gasp out my eloquence, nor I have no cunning in protestation; only downright oaths, which I never use till urged, nor never break for urging. If thou canst love a fellow of this temper, Kate, whose face is not worth sunburning, that never looks in his glass for love of anything he sees there, let thine eye be thy cook. I speak to thee plain soldier. If thou canst love me for this, take me; if not, to say to thee that I shall die, is true—but for thy love, by the Lord, no; yet I love thee too. And while thou livest, dear Kate, take a fellow of plain and uncoined constancy; for he perforce must do thee right, because he hath not the gift to woo in other places; for these fellows of infinite tongue, that can rhyme themselves into ladies' favours, they do always reason themselves out again. What! A speaker is but a prater; a rhyme is but a ballad. A good leg will fall; a straight back will stoop; a black beard will turn white; a curled pate will grow bald; a fair face will wither; a full eye will wax hollow; but a good heart, Kate, is the sun and the moon, or rather the sun and not the moon, for it shines bright and never changes, but keeps his course truly. If thou would have such a one, take me; and take me, take a soldier; take a soldier, take a king. And what sayest thou then to my love? Speak, my fair, and fairly, I pray thee.

Kath. Is it possible dat I sould love de enemy of France? 179

K. Hen. No, it is not possible you should love the enemy of France, Kate; but, in loving me you should love the friend of France; for I love France so well that I will not part with a

139–41. *measure:* (a) versification, (b) dancing, (c) amount. 146. *buffet:* box. *bound:* make leap. 148. *jackanapes:* monkey. 149. *greenly:* foolishly. 155–6. *let . . . cook:* i.e., let your eye dress me with attractive qualities as a cook garnishes meat. 161. *uncoined:* unalloyed (?). 167. *fall:* shrink.

village of it—I will have it all mine. And, Kate, when France is mine and I am yours, then yours is France and you are mine.

Kath. I cannot tell vat is dat.

K. Hen. No, Kate? I will tell thee in French; which I am sure will hang upon my tongue like a new-married wife about her husband's neck, hardly to be shook off. *Je quand sur le possession de France, et quand vous avez le possession de moi*—let me see, what then? Saint Denis be my speed!—*donc votre est France et vous êtes mienne.* It is as easy for me, Kate, to conquer the kingdom as to speak so much more French. I shall never move thee in French, unless it be to laugh at me.

Kath. Sauf votre honneur, le François que vous parlez, il est meilleur que l'Anglois lequel je parle. 201

K. Hen. No, faith, is't not, Kate; but thy speaking of my tongue, and I thine, most truly-falsely, must needs be granted to be much at one. But, Kate, dost thou understand thus much English: canst thou love me?

Kath. I cannot tell. 207

K. Hen. Can any of your neighbours tell, Kate? I'll ask them. Come, I know thou lovest me; and at night, when you come into your closet, you'll question this gentlewoman about me; and I know, Kate, you will to her dispraise those parts in me that you love with your heart. But, good Kate, mock me mercifully; the rather, gentle princess, because I love thee cruelly. If ever thou beest mine, Kate, as I have a saving faith within me tells me thou shalt, I get thee with scambling, and thou must therefore needs prove a good soldier-breeder. Shall not thou and I, between Saint Denis and Saint George, compound a boy, half French, half English, that shall go to Con-

191–5. *Je quand . . . mienne:* when I have possession of France, and you have possession of me . . . then France is yours and you are mine. 193. *Saint Denis:* the patron saint of France. 194. *speed:* help. 199–201. *Sauf . . . parle:* save your honor, the French that you speak is better than the English that I speak. 204. *truly-falsely:* with truth badly expressed. 205. *at one:* alike. 211. *closet:* private apartment. 218. *scambling:* fighting. 221. *boy.* His son, Henry VI, was one of the weakest and most unfortunate of English kings. See Epilogue.

stantinople and take the Turk by the beard? Shall we not? What sayest thou, my fair flower-de-luce? 224

Kath. I do not know dat.

K. Hen. No; 'tis hereafter to know, but now to promise. Do but now promise, Kate, you will endeavour for your French part of such a boy; and for my English moiety take the word of a king and a bachelor. How answer you, *la plus belle Katharine du monde, mon très cher et devin déesse?* 232

Kath. Your Majestee ave *fausse* French enough to deceive de most *sage demoiselle* dat is *en France*.

K. Hen. Now, fie upon my false French! By mine honour, in true English, I love thee, Kate; by which honour I dare not swear thou lovest me; yet my blood begins to flatter me that thou dost, notwithstanding the poor and untempering effect of my visage. Now beshrew my father's ambition! He was thinking of civil wars when he got me; therefore was I created with a stubborn outside, with an aspect of iron, that, when I come to woo ladies, I fright them. But, in faith, Kate, the elder I wax, the better I shall appear. My comfort is that old age, that ill layer-up of beauty, can do no more spoil upon my face. Thou hast me, if thou hast me, at the worst; and thou shalt wear me, if thou wear me, better and better; and therefore tell me, most fair Katharine, will you have me? Put off your maiden blushes; avouch the thoughts of your heart with the looks of an empress; take me by the hand, and say, "Harry of England, I am thine." Which word thou shalt no sooner bless mine ear withal, but I will tell thee aloud, "England is thine, Ireland is thine, France is thine, and Henry Plantagenet is thine," who, though I speak it before his face, if he be not fellow with the best king, thou shalt find the best king of good fellows. Come, your answer in broken music, for thy voice is music and thy

222. *Turk.* The Turks did not take Constantinople until 1453. 224. *flower-de-luce:* fleur-de-lis, the emblem of France. 229. *moiety:* half. 230–2. *la plus . . . déesse:* the most beautiful Katharine in the world, my very dear and divine goddess. 241. *untempering:* lacking power to soften. 242. *beshrew:* a plague upon. 247. *wax:* grow. 248. *layer-up:* preserver. 261. *fellow with:* the equal of. 263. *broken music:* music "in parts" for different instruments.

English broken. Therefore, queen of all, Katharine, break thy mind to me in broken English. Wilt thou have me? 266

Kath. Dat is as it sall please de *roi mon père.*

K. Hen. Nay, it will please him well, Kate. It shall please him, Kate.

Kath. Den it sall also content me. 270

K. Hen. Upon that I kiss your hand, and I call you my queen.

Kath. *Laissez, mon seigneur, laissez, laissez! Ma foi, je ne veux point que vous abaissiez votre grandeur en baisant la main d'une de votre seigneurie indigne serviteur. Excusez-moi, je vous supplie, mon très-puissant seigneur.*

K. Hen. Then I will kiss your lips, Kate.

Kath. *Les dames et demoiselles pour être baisées devant leur noces, il n'est pas la coutume de France.* 281

K. Hen. Madam my interpreter, what says she?

Alice. Dat it is not be de fashion *pour les* ladies of France— I cannot tell vat is *baiser en* Anglish.

K. Hen. To kiss.

Alice. Your Majesty *entendre* bettre *que moi.*

K. Hen. It is not a fashion for the maids in France to kiss before they are married, would she say? 291

Alice. *Oui, vraiment.*

K. Hen. O Kate, nice customs curtsy to great kings. Dear Kate, you and I cannot be confined within the weak list of a country's fashion. We are the makers of manners, Kate; and the liberty that follows our places stops the mouth of all find-faults, as I will do yours for upholding the nice fashion of your country in denying me a kiss. Therefore, patiently and

265. *break:* reveal. 267. *de . . . père:* the king, my father. 273–7. *Laissez . . . seigneur:* let be, my lord, let be, let be! My faith, I do not at all wish you to lower your greatness by kissing the hand of your lordship's humble servant. Excuse me, I beg you, my most powerful lord. 279–81. *Les dames . . . France:* it is not the custom in France for ladies and young girls to be kissed before their marriage. 288. *entendre . . . moi:* understands better than I. 292. *Oui, vraiment:* yes, truly. 293–9. *nice:* subtle, prudish. 295. *list:* boundary (edge of cloth).

yielding. [*Kisses her.*] You have witchcraft in your lips, Kate. There is more eloquence in a sugar touch of them than in the tongues of the French council, and they should sooner persuade Harry of England than a general petition of monarchs. Here comes your father. 306

Re-enter the FRENCH KING *and his* QUEEN, BURGUNDY, *and other* Lords.

Bur. God save your Majesty! My royal cousin, teach you our princess English?

K. Hen. I would have her learn, my fair cousin, how perfectly I love her, and that is good English. 311

Bur. Is she not apt?

K. Hen. Our tongue is rough, coz, and my condition is not smooth; so that, having neither the voice nor the heart of flattery about me, I cannot so conjure up the spirit of love in her that he will appear in his true likeness. 317

Bur. Pardon the frankness of my mirth if I answer you for that. If you would conjure in her, you must make a circle; if conjure up Love in her in his true likeness, he must appear naked and blind. Can you blame her then, being a maid yet rosed over with the virgin crimson of modesty, if she deny the appearance of a naked blind boy in her naked seeing self? It were, my lord, a hard condition for a maid to consign to.

K. Hen. Yet they do wink and yield, as love is blind and enforces.

Bur. They are then excused, my lord, when they see not what they do. 330

K. Hen. Then, good my lord, teach your cousin to consent winking.

Bur. I will wink on her to consent, my lord, if you will teach her to know my meaning; for maids, well summered and warm kept, are like flies at Bartholomew-tide, blind, though they have their eyes; and then they will endure handling, which before would not abide looking on. 338

314. *condition:* disposition. 320. *circle:* i.e., the conjurer's circle. 326. *consign:* agree. 327. *wink:* shut the eyes. 336. *Bartholomew-tide:* St. Bartholomew's Day, August 24.

K. Hen. This moral ties me over to time and a hot summer; and so I shall catch the fly, your cousin, in the latter end and she must be blind too.

Bur. As love is, my lord, before it loves.

K. Hen. It is so; and you may, some of you, thank love for my blindness, who cannot see many a fair French city for one fair French maid that stands in my way.

Fr. King. Yes, my lord, you see them perspectively—the cities turned into a maid; for they are all girdled with maiden walls that war hath never entered. 350

K. Hen. Shall Kate be my wife?

Fr. King. So please you.

K. Hen. I am content, so the maiden cities you talk of may wait on her. So the maid that stood in the way for my wish shall show me the way to my will.

Fr. King. We have consented to all terms of reason.

K. Hen. Is 't so, my lords of England?

West. The king hath granted every article; 360
His daughter first and in sequel all,
According to their firm proposed natures.

Exe. Only he hath not yet subscribed this:
Where your Majesty demands that the King of France, having any occasion to write for matter of grant, shall name your Highness in this form and with this addition, in French, *Notre très-cher fils Henri, Roi d'Angleterre, Héritier de France;* and thus in Latin, *Præclarissimus filius noster Henricus, Rex Angliæ, et Hæres Franciæ.* 370

Fr. King. Nor this I have not, brother, so denied,
But your request shall make me let it pass.

K. Hen. I pray you then, in love and dear alliance,
Let that one article rank with the rest,
And thereupon give me your daughter.

347. *perspectively:* as through a perspective, i.e., a glass for producing fantastic images. 363. *subscribed:* signed. 367. *addition:* title. 367–9. *Notre . . . France:* our very dear son Henry, King of England, Heir of France. 369. *Præclarissimus:* most renowned. Shakespeare repeats Holinshed's error for *præcarissimus* (most dear).

Fr. King. Take her, fair son, and from her blood raise up
Issue to me, that the contending kingdoms
Of France and England, whose very shores look pale
With envy of each other's happiness,
May cease their hatred, and this dear conjunction 380
Plant neighbourhood and Christian-like accord
In their sweet bosoms, that never war advance
His bleeding sword 'twixt England and fair France.

All. Amen!

K. Hen. Now, welcome, Kate; and bear me witness all
That here I kiss her as my sovereign queen. [*Flourish.*

Q. Isa. God, the best maker of all marriages,
Combine your hearts in one, your realms in one!
As man and wife, being two, are one in love,
So be there 'twixt your kingdoms such a spousal 390
That never may ill office, or fell jealousy,
Which troubles oft the bed of blessed marriage,
Thrust in between the paction of these kingdoms,
To make divorce of their incorporate league;
That English may as French, French Englishmen,
Receive each other! God speak this Amen!

All. Amen!

K. Hen. Prepare we for our marriage; on which day,
My Lord of Burgundy, we'll take your oath,
And all the peers', for surety of our leagues. 400
Then shall I swear to Kate, and you to me;
And may our oaths well kept and prosperous be!

[*Sennet. Exeunt.*

378. *look pale.* An allusion to the white chalk cliffs on both sides of the English Channel. 381. *neighbourhood:* neighborly feeling. 393. *paction:* alliance. S. D. *Sennet:* processional trumpet call.

EPILOGUE

Enter Chorus.

Chor. Thus far, with rough and all-unable pen,
Our bending author hath pursued the story,
In little room confining mighty men,
Mangling by starts the full course of their glory.
Small time, but in that small most greatly lived
This star of England. Fortune made his sword,
By which the world's best garden he achieved,
And of it left his son imperial lord.
Henry the Sixth, in infant bands crown'd King
Of France and England, did this king succeed; 10
Whose state so many had the managing
That they lost France and made his England bleed;
Which oft our stage hath shown; and, for their sake,
In your fair minds let this acceptance take. [*Exit.*

[Epilogue] The Epilogue is a regular Shakespearean sonnet. 2. *bending:* (a) suppliant, (b) bending under the weight of his task. 4. *by starts:* by sudden fits or impulses. 11. *Whose state:* of whose kingdom. 13. *Which . . . shown.* The reference is to the three parts of *Henry VI.* 14. *this:* this play.

The Tragedy of King Lear

Introduction

Source

Of all the stories utilized by Shakespeare for his dramas, the one which had perhaps the longest history and was at the same time most familiar to his audiences was that of King Lear and his three daughters. The king himself has been identified with Lir or Llyr, the sea-god of ancient Gaelic and British mythology, whose city, Leircestre or Leicester, still bears his name. The legend of his division of his kingdom, developed apparently from a folk tale, was first made historical in Geoffrey of Monmouth's *Historia Britonum* in the twelfth century, and from that time to Shakespeare's own day more than fifty redactions of it appeared. All of the important chroniclers from Layamon to Holinshed gave space to it, and, in addition, versions of the story appeared in the *Gesta Romanorum, A Mirror for Magistrates* (1574), Warner's *Albion's England* (1586), Spenser's *Faerie Queene* (1590), and Camden's *Remains* (1605). It had also been adapted to the stage in *The True Chronicle History of King Leir and his Three Daughters*, a drama of unknown authorship, which was acted in 1594 and put into print in 1605. Any or all of these narratives Shakespeare may have seen, but on the whole his version bears a closer resemblance to the play than to any other. A ballad on the subject which appeared in Richard Johnson's *Golden Garland of Princely Pleasures and Delicate Delights* (1620) is thought of generally, not as a source, but as a redaction of Shakespeare's play.

The story of King Lear underwent singularly little change through the centuries, and all of the possible sources for Shakespeare's play, therefore, contain the same essential elements: a trial of love, the disinheritance of the sincere daughter, the subsequent ill-treatment of the father at the hands of the favored sisters, his succour by his wronged child, and a happy ending—the restoration of the kingdom to the aged ruler. But *The True Chronicle History of King Leir* is the only version which fully supplies motives for the various stages of the action. A comparison of the two plays, therefore, reveals not only a tragicomedy transformed into a tragedy, but also some other divergences which are of great interest to a student of Shakespeare's dramatic technique. If the old play was indeed his source, Shakespeare departed from it much more frequently than he usually did from borrowed material.

Relation to the Old Play

(1) At the outset, between the old *King Leir* and Shakespeare's *King Lear* there is a significant difference in the circumstances attending the professions of love upon which both plays turn. In the old play, Leir, having recently lost his queen, knows little of his daughters' real feeling for him because they have been brought up by their mother while he attended to state affairs, and he hungers now for their affection. Moreover, like a dutiful father, he has determined to find husbands for them. The neighboring kings of Cornwall and Cambria are suitors for the hands of the eldest daughters, but the youngest, though solicited by divers peers, taxes her father's patience by vowing to marry only for love. The contest of love, therefore, is proposed by the king, not merely as a basis for distributing dowries to his daughters, but also as a possible means of tricking his youngest daughter into marriage. When she protests that she loves him best and will do anything for him, he plans to ask as proof that she marry the husband he shall choose for her. Of this guileful purpose there is no suggestion in Shakespeare. Furthermore, in the old play the wicked sisters are told everything by Skalliger (Shakespeare's Oswald), the courtier who had originally suggested the expedient to Leir, and when the

time arrives they are unfairly prepared for the king's test. Like Shakespeare's Cordelia, Cordella abhors flattery, and somehow, instinctively, she feels the significance of her father's question. Her simple, honest answer, therefore, not only contrasts strikingly with the fulsome replies of her sisters (as in Shakespeare), but is additionally unfortunate in thwarting the tricky old king and so doubly earning for her his displeasure.

(2) In Shakespeare's play, the removal of any special motive for the love-test throws an additional burden upon the characters. King Lear, therefore, is developed not only as an irascible, headstrong monarch whom no one has ever dared to cross, but as a vain old man as well. Unlike Leir, Shakespeare's king believes he knows his daughters; the division of his realm is already agreed upon; and the love-test is of no importance except as the pageantry of an old man's vanity. Shakespeare's Cordelia, on the other hand, does not have Cordella's justification for her equivocal answer, and however admirable her honesty may be, she reveals as a tragic flaw in her nature the same inability to bend which characterizes her father. Likewise, Kent, whose selfless devotion is second only to Cordelia's, in his blunt, outspoken opposition to the king, reveals a similar lack of compromise and tact, and throughout his disguise does the master he loves more harm than good. Thus, the three—Lear, Kent, and Cordelia—present tragic varieties of the same misapplied strength.

(3) In order that he might concentrate his attention upon Lear's act of wrath and the consequences of this clash of wills, Shakespeare compresses into one tremendous scene material which corresponds to two acts of the old play. As a result, there is no time for the more leisurely romantic wooing of Cordella by the Gallian king, who had heard rumors of the beauty of the British princess, but who, like her, wishes to be loved for himself alone, and who comes in disguise to Britain and meets the outcast daughter on the road.

(4) To reinforce his main plot Shakespeare grafted to it a complementary sub-plot of which there is no suggestion in the old play, but which he found developed in detail in the story of "the Paphlagonian unkind king and his kind son" in Sidney's *Arcadia* (1590). Gloucester, another Lear, casts off his faithful son, and the story of the unfilial daughters is paralleled by the story of the bastard who is also a Machiavellian villain. The two plots are closely interrelated—both Goneril and Regan love Edmund, Gloucester is blinded because of his loyalty to Lear, mad Tom o' Bedlam meets the unsettled king on the heath, and Edgar at last becomes the agent of retributive justice.

(5) To provide a bitter, clear-eyed commentator upon the action and a parallel on a lower social level for Kent's devotion, Shakespeare created the Fool, a masterly drawing of a traditional comic type now employed for tragic purposes. Under cover of his coxcomb, Lear's Fool is almost a personification of his master's conscience. During the early half of the play he serves as a kind of Greek chorus in his commentary upon the happenings, and his wisdom constantly throws into relief the old king's folly.

(6) Doubtless because he conceived of Lear as an oak unable to bend, Shakespeare also made his aged king not merely travel-worn and weary because of his misfortunes, but mad as well. Adversity breaks him, and the scenes (III, iv and vi) which bring together the "natural," the feigned madman, and the old king whose wits are beginning to totter, are among the most artfully intense situations in all of Shakespeare's tragedies. This contact with Edgar and the Fool—the last persons who would wish Lear harm—causes the king's mind to break, and the three varieties of madness intensify and throw one another into relief, and, at the same time, divide the interest and keep it from centering too much upon Lear. The storm on the heath, however, is the only suggestion for this tremendous scene that Shakespeare received from his source.

(7) Shakespeare's drama differs from the old play and from all preceding versions in its tragic ending. In the old *King Leir*, even at the risk of showing a patriotic Elizabethan audience a Gallic army victorious over British forces, the kingdom is restored to Leir, and the king at last is made to understand the depth of his daughter's modest declaration that she loved him as in duty bound. In Shakespeare the good go down with the evil; Gloucester, Cordelia, and Lear are sacrificed, and only Albany, Kent, and Edgar are left to put together the broken bits of what Fate has left of the kingdom. Perhaps the tragic conclusion for his play was suggested to Shakespeare by some versions of the story, notably that in *A Mirror for Magistrates*, which continued the story and told how Cordelia succeeded her father as ruler of Britain, how her nephews (the sons of the wicked sisters) rebelled against her rule and threw her into prison, and how in despair she took her own life. Shakespeare preferred to link together the fates of father and daughter.

(8) Above all, to the Lear story Shakespeare contributed the atmosphere of poetic tragedy, the tremendous energy and poignancy of the drama, the pathos of the "poor, infirm, weak, and despised old man," "more sinned against than sinning," and the bitterness of its fatalistic philosophy:

> As flies to wanton boys are we to the gods;
> They kill us for their sport.

Critical Comment

King Lear is in many respects the most moving of all of Shakespeare's tragedies, a painful story viewed through the eyes of the aged, as *Romeo and Juliet* had been seen through the eyes of the young. Indeed, no greater contrast could be imagined than that between these two plays. The one is a youthful work, a tragic treatment of the old romantic theme of the course of true love, and its catastrophe grows, not inevitably out of the characters themselves, but out of a series of tragic accidents which move pity and not fear. *King Lear*, on the other hand, is a mature play in which a remorseless logic, like the workings of a grim, satiric Force, crushes everything before it.

Yet, as a whole, *King Lear* has been more praised as poetry than as drama. Lamb's remark that "the *Lear* of Shakespeare cannot be acted" is frequently quoted with approval by those who have forgotten that Lamb said the like about almost all of Shakespeare's plays. Keats loved "the bitter-sweet of this Shakespearean fruit"; Shelley considered it "the most perfect specimen of dramatic art in the world," and in our own day John Masefield has written, "No image in the world is so fierce with imaginative energy." Most readers of the play have confirmed the opinion of Dr. Johnson:

> There is perhaps no play which keeps the attention so strongly fixed; which so much agitates our passions and interests our curiosity. The artful involutions of distinct interests, the striking opposition of contrary characters, the sudden changes of fortune, and the quick succession of events, fill the mind with a perpetual tumult of indignation, pity, and hope.

But even Dr. Johnson agreed with the sentiment which led Nahum Tate to produce in 1681 an adaptation of Shakespeare's play which ended happily and permitted Cordelia to retire "with victory and felicity." Addison in the eighteenth century stands alone as approving Shakespeare's ending, and Tate's version in some form held the stage until the time of W. C. MacCready (1838). In recent years the great English critic, A. C. Bradley, has raised the same question. Traditions are against the play as acting drama, and it is most attractive when read for its poetry and its philosophy of life. To the modern reader—more than to the Elizabethan spectator, perhaps—*Lear*, like *Othello*, comes close to everyday life and appeals strongly as a domestic tragedy.

Date and Text

Scholars are agreed that *King Lear* is a play of Shakespeare's maturity, and most believe that it belongs to 1605–6, the years which also produced *Macbeth*. But it is difficult to fix the date with precision. The play was registered for publication on November 26, 1607, and Q_1 bears the date of 1608. For better identification, Q_1 is sometimes called the "Pied Bull" quarto from its imprint: "Printed for Nathaniel Butter, and are to be sold at his shop in Paul's Churchyard at the sign of the Pied Bull near St. Austin's Gate, 1608." Another edition (Q_2)—also said to have been "Printed for Nathaniel Butter, 1608"—is now known to have been produced in 1619 by the stationer Thomas Pavier with both a false date and a false imprint. (For details see E. K. Chambers, *William Shakespeare, a Study of Facts and Problems* [1930], I, 133 ff.)

The text of *King Lear* is one of the most complicated. Q_1 (1608) is an unusually poor text to be an authentic quarto, and some students agree with Sir Edmund Chambers that it may have been taken down by a stenographer in the theatre and pirated. The matter is further complicated by what is certain evidence that the sheets were corrected while the play was in press; most of the sheets of Q_1 are found both in corrected and uncorrected states, variously combined in existing copies of the book. Q_2 (1619) appears to have been set up from a copy of Q_1 containing uncorrected sheets D, G, H. F_1 appears to rest both upon copy from an independent source and upon a first quarto with uncorrected sheets E, H, K. Q_1, however, omits about 100 lines found in F_1, and F_1 omits about 300 lines, including a whole scene (IV, iii), to be found in Q_1. In addition there are numerous verbal and phrasal differences between the two versions. The present text, though based upon Q_1, is a composite containing the missing lines of both Q_1 and F_1 and readings from F_1 when these are obviously preferable.

DRAMATIS PERSONÆ

LEAR, King of Britain.

GONERIL, REGAN, CORDELIA — his daughters.

THE DUKE OF ALBANY, husband of Goneril.

THE DUKE OF CORNWALL, husband of Regan.

THE KING OF FRANCE, THE DUKE OF BURGUNDY — rival suitors for the hand of Cordelia.

THE EARL OF GLOUCESTER.

EDGAR, his elder, legitimate son.

EDMUND, his bastard son.

THE EARL OF KENT.

A FOOL, Lear's jester.

OSWALD, steward of Goneril.

CURAN, a courtier.

An Old Tenant of Gloucester's.

A Doctor.

Knights, Captains, Heralds, Soldiers, Messengers, and Attendants.

Scene of the Action: Britain.

The Tragedy of King Lear

ACT I

SCENE I. *The throne-room in* KING LEAR'S *palace.*

Enter KENT, GLOUCESTER, *and* EDMUND.

Kent. I thought the king had more affected the Duke of Albany than Cornwall.

Glou. It did always seem so to us. But now, in the division of the kingdom, it appears not which of the dukes he values most, for equalities are so weighed that curiosity in neither can make choice of either's moiety.

Kent. Is not this your son, my lord?

Glou. His breeding, sir, hath been at my charge. I have so often blushed to acknowledge him that now I am brazed to it.

Kent. I cannot conceive you. 12

Glou. Sir, this young fellow's mother could, whereupon she grew round-wombed, and had, indeed, sir, a son for her cradle ere she had a husband for her bed. Do you smell a fault?

Kent. I cannot wish the fault undone, the issue of it being so proper. 18

Glou. But I have, sir, a son by order of law, some year elder than this, who yet is no dearer in my account. Though this knave came something saucily into the world before he was sent for, yet was his mother fair; there was good sport at his

[I. i] 1. *affected:* favored, had affection for. 2. *Albany.* The old name for all Great Britain north of the Humber, later used for Scotland, especially that portion north of the Firths of Forth and Clyde. 4. *division of the kingdom.* It is clear, therefore, that Lear has already divided his realm, though he has not as yet announced it publicly. The distribution is in no sense dependent upon the daughters' professions of love; this condition is an afterthought and springs from an old man's vanity. 6. *curiosity:* captiousness. 7. *moiety:* share; literally, a half. 11. *brazed:* hardened. 12. *conceive:* (a) understand, (b) become pregnant. 18. *proper:* handsome.

making, and the whoreson must be acknowledged. Do you know this noble gentleman, Edmund? 25

Edm. No, my lord.

Glou. My lord of Kent. Remember him hereafter as my honourable friend.

Edm. My services to your lordship.

Kent. I must love you, and sue to know you better. 31

Edm. Sir, I shall study deserving.

Glou. He hath been out nine years, and away he shall again. The king is coming.

A Sennet is sounded. Enter a Court Officer *bearing a Coronet, then* KING LEAR, CORNWALL, ALBANY, GONERIL, REGAN, CORDELIA, *and* Attendants. *The* KING *ascends his throne.*

Lear. Attend the lords of France and Burgundy, Gloucester.

Glou. I shall, my liege. [*Exeunt Gloucester and Edmund.*

Lear. Meantime we shall express our darker purpose.
Give me the map there. [*Spreading out a chart.*] Know that we have divided
In three our kingdom; and 'tis our fast intent
To shake all cares and business from our age, 40
Conferring them on younger strengths while we
Unburden'd crawl toward death. Our son of Cornwall,
And you, our no less loving son of Albany,
We have this hour a constant will to publish
Our daughters' several dowers, that future strife
May be prevented now. The princes, France and Burgundy,
Great rivals in our youngest daughter's love,
Long in our court have made their amorous sojourn,
And here are to be answer'd. Tell me, my daughters—
Since now we will divest us, both of rule, 50
Interest of territory, cares of state—

24. *whoreson:* rascal (used playfully). 30. *love:* be friends with. 33. *out:* abroad. S. D. *Coronet.* This is intended for Cordelia; her sisters, as duchesses, already have crowns. 37. *darker:* more secret. 39. *fast:* firm. 40. *from our age.* Q_1 reads *of our state.* 41. *Conferring . . . strengths.* Q_1 reads *Confirming . . . years.* 41–6. *while . . . now.* Omitted in Q_1. 50–1. *Since . . . state.* Omitted in Q_1.

Which of you shall we say doth love us most?
That we our largest bounty may extend
Where nature doth with merit challenge. Goneril,
Our eldest-born, speak first.

Gon. Sir, I love you more than words can wield the matter;
Dearer than eye-sight, space, and liberty;
Beyond what can be valued, rich or rare;
No less than life, with grace, health, beauty, honour;
As much as child e'er loved, or father found; 60
A love that makes breath poor, and speech unable;
Beyond all manner of so much I love you.

Cor. [*Aside*] What shall Cordelia do? Love, and be silent.

Lear. [*Tracing it on the map*] Of all these bounds, even from this line to this,
With shadowy forests and with champaigns rich'd,
With plenteous rivers and wide-skirted meads,
We make thee lady. To thine and Albany's issue
Be this perpetual. What says our second daughter,
Our dearest Regan, wife to Cornwall? Speak.

Reg. Sir, I am made 70
Of the selfsame metal that my sister is,
And prize me at her worth. In my true heart
I find she names my very deed of love;
Only she comes too short, that I profess
Myself an enemy to all other joys
Which the most precious square of sense possesses;

54. *Where . . . challenge:* where there are claims of both relationship and merit. 56. *wield:* express. 61. *unable:* weak, impotent. 65. *champaigns:* plains. 67. *issue:* children. 73. *names . . . love:* states my love exactly. 76. *square of sense.* Bartholomeus Anglicus' *Of the Properties of Things* divides the soul into three parts: (a) the vegetable soul, which consists of the three virtues of self-sustainment, growth, and reproduction, "like to a triangle in Geometry"; (b) the sensible soul, "like to a quadrangle, square and four cornered. For in a quadrangle is a line drawn from one corner to another corner, afore it maketh two triangles; and the soul sensible maketh two triangles of virtues. For wherever the soul sensible is, there is also the soul vegetabilis"; and (c) the rational soul, which is likened to a circle, the most perfect of figures. It is to the sensible soul that Regan alludes.

And find I am alone felicitate
In your dear Highness' love.
Cor. [*Aside*] Then poor Cordelia!
And yet not so; since I am sure my love's
More richer than my tongue. 80
Lear. To thee and thine hereditary ever
Remain this ample third of our fair kingdom,
No less in space, validity, and pleasure,
Than that conferr'd on Goneril. Now, our joy,
Although our last and least—to whose young love
The vines of France and milk of Burgundy
Strive to be interess'd—what can you say to draw
A third more opulent than your sisters? Speak.
Cor. Nothing, my lord.
Lear. Nothing? 90
Cor. Nothing.
Lear. Nothing will come of nothing. Speak again.
Cor. Unhappy that I am, I cannot heave
My heart into my mouth. I love your Majesty
According to my bond, nor more nor less.
Lear. How, how, Cordelia? Mend your speech a little,
Lest it may mar your fortunes.
Cor. Good my lord,
You have begot me, bred me, loved me. I
Return those duties back as are right fit,
Obey you, love you, and most honour you. 100
Why have my sisters husbands, if they say
They love you all? Haply, when I shall wed,
That lord whose hand must take my plight shall carry
Half my love with him, half my care and duty.
Sure I shall never marry like my sisters,
To love my father all.

77. *felicitate:* made happy. 83. *validity:* value, worth. 85. *our last and least.* Q_1 reads *the last, not least in our dear love. least:* smallest, youngest. 86. *milk.* Burgundy was a dairy country. 87. *be interess'd:* have a right or share. 90–1. *Lear . . . Nothing.* Omitted in Q_1. 95. *bond:* bounden duty, obligation. 102. *all:* only. 103. *plight:* pledge, plighting. 106. *To . . . all.* Omitted in F_1.

Lear. But goes thy heart with this?
Cor. Ay, good my lord.
Lear. So young, and so untender?
Cor. So young, my lord, and true.
Lear. Let it be so; thy truth, then, be thy dower! 110
For, by the sacred radiance of the sun,
The mysteries of Hecate and the night;
By all the operation of the orbs
From whom we do exist and cease to be;
Here I disclaim all my paternal care,
Propinquity and property of blood,
And as a stranger to my heart and me
Hold thee from this forever. The barbarous Scythian,
Or he that makes his generation messes
To gorge his appetite, shall to my bosom 120
Be as well neighbour'd, pitied, and relieved,
As thou my sometime daughter.
Kent. Good my liege—
Lear. Peace, Kent!
Come not between the dragon and his wrath.
I loved her most, and thought to set my rest
On her kind nursery. [*To Cordelia.*] Hence, and avoid my sight!
So be my grave my peace, as here I give
Her father's heart from her! [*To the Attendants.*] Call France! Who stirs?
Call Burgundy! Cornwall and Albany,
With my two daughters' dowers digest this third. 130
Let Pride, which she calls Plainness, marry her.
I do invest you jointly with my power,

112. *Hecate:* in Greek mythology, the goddess of the underworld, supposed to preside over witchcraft and magical rites. 113. *operation:* influence. *orbs:* stars. 116. *Propinquity . . . blood:* kinship. 118. *from this:* from this time. 119. *generation:* progeny, offspring. Herodotus states that the Scythians ate their aged and impotent relations. *messes:* dishes of food. 120. *to my bosom.* Omitted in Q_1. 125. *set my rest:* stake all I have (a phrase from primero, a card game, with an allusion to the sense "repose"). 126. *nursery:* nursing. 130. *digest:* divide, dispose of. 131. *marry:* find her a husband.

Pre-eminence, and all the large effects
That troop with majesty. Ourself, by monthly course,
With reservation of an hundred knights,
By you to be sustain'd, shall our abode
Make with you by due turns. Only we still retain
The name, and all th' additions to a king;
The sway, revenue, execution of the rest,
Beloved sons, be yours, which to confirm, 140
This coronet part betwixt you. [*Giving the crown.*

Kent. Royal Lear,
Whom I have ever honour'd as my king,
Loved as my father, as my master follow'd,
As my great patron thought on in my prayers—

Lear. The bow is bent and drawn; make from the shaft.

Kent. Let it fall rather, though the fork invade
The region of my heart! Be Kent unmannerly
When Lear is mad. What wilt thou do, old man?
Think'st thou that duty shall have dread to speak 149
When Power to Flattery bows? To plainness honour's bound
When majesty stoops to folly. Reverse thy doom;
And, in thy best consideration, check
This hideous rashness. Answer my life my judgment,
Thy youngest daughter does not love thee least,
Nor are those empty-hearted whose low sound
Reverbs no hollowness.

Lear. Kent, on thy life, no more!

Kent. My life I never held but as a pawn
To wage against thy enemies; nor fear to lose it,
Thy safety being the motive.

Lear. Out of my sight!

Kent. See better, Lear, and let me still remain 160
The true blank of thine eye.

133. *effects:* outward signs. 138. *additions:* titles. 146. *fork:* barb. 151. *stoops.* F_1 reads *falls*. *Reverse thy doom.* F_1 reads *Reserve thy state.* 153. *Answer my life:* let my life answer for. 156. *Reverbs:* re-echoes (shortened from *reverberates*). 158. *wage:* lay a wager. 161. *blank:* literally, the white center of a target.

Lear. Now, by Apollo—

Kent. Now, by Apollo, king,
Thou swear'st thy gods in vain.

Lear. O, vassal! Miscreant!
[*Laying his hand on his sword.*

Alb.
Corn. } Dear sir, forbear.

Kent. Do!
Kill thy physician, and the fee bestow
Upon thy foul disease. Revoke thy doom;
Or, whilst I can vent clamour from my throat,
I'll tell thee thou dost evil.

Lear. Hear me, recreant!
On thine allegiance, hear me! 170
Since thou hast sought to make us break our vow,
Which we durst never yet, and with strain'd pride
To come between our sentence and our power,
Which nor our nature nor our place can bear,
Our potency made good, take thy reward.
Five days we do allot thee for provision
To shield thee from diseases of the world,
And on the sixth to turn thy hated back
Upon our kingdom. If, on the tenth day following,
Thy banish'd trunk be found in our dominions, 180
The moment is thy death. Away! By Jupiter,
This shall not be revoked!

Kent. Fare thee well, king. Sith thus thou wilt appear,
Freedom lives hence, and banishment is here.
[*To Cordelia.*] The gods to their dear shelter take thee, maid,
That justly think'st, and hast most rightly said!
[*To Regan and Goneril.*] And your large speeches may your deeds
approve,

163. *Miscreant:* villain. 164. *Alb. . . . forbear.* Omitted in Q_1. 167. *doom.* F_1 reads *gift.* 169. *recreant:* traitor. Omitted in Q_1. 172. *strain'd.* Q_1 reads *straied.* 175. *potency:* authority. 176. *Five.* Q_1 reads *Four.* 177. *diseases:* discomforts. 183. *Sith:* since. 184. *Freedom.* Q_1 reads *Friendship.* 187. *large:* pompous. *approve:* confirm.

That good effects may spring from words of love.
Thus Kent, O princes, bids you all adieu;
He'll shape his old course in a country new. [*Exit.*

Flourish. Re-enter Gloucester, *with* France, Burgundy, *and* Attendants.

Glou. Here's France and Burgundy, my noble lord. 191
Lear. My lord of Burgundy,
We first address towards you, who with this king
Hath rivall'd for our daughter. What in the least
Will you require in present dower with her,
Or cease your quest of love?
Bur. Most royal Majesty,
I crave no more than what your Highness offer'd,
Nor will you tender less.
Lear. Right noble Burgundy,
When she was dear to us, we did hold her so;
But now her price is fall'n. Sir, there she stands. 200
If aught within that little seeming substance—
Or all of it—with our displeasure pieced,
And nothing more, may fitly like your Grace,
She's there, and she is yours.
Bur. I know no answer.
Lear. Will you, with those infirmities she owes,
Unfriended, new-adopted to our hate,
Dower'd with our curse, and stranger'd with our oath,
Take her, or leave her?
Bur. Pardon me, royal sir;
Election makes not up on such conditions. 209
Lear. Then leave her, sir; for, by the power that made me,
I tell you all her wealth. [*To France.*] For you, great king,
I would not from your love make such a stray
To match you where I hate. Therefore, beseech you

194. *rivall'd:* competed. 195. *present:* immediate, "ready." 198. *tender:* give. 199. *so:* i.e., dear. 203. *like:* please. 205. *owes:* possesses. 209. *Election . . . conditions:* there is no choice under such conditions. 212. *make such a stray:* stray so far.

To avert your liking a more worthier way
Than on a wretch whom nature is ashamed
Almost to acknowledge hers.

France. This is most strange,
That she, that even but now was your best object,
The argument of your praise, balm of your age,
Most best, most dearest, should in this trice of time
Commit a thing so monstrous to dismantle 220
So many folds of favour. Sure her offense
Must be of such unnatural degree
That monsters it, or your fore-vouch'd affection
Fall'n into taint, which to believe of her,
Must be a faith that reason without miracle
Could never plant in me.

Cor. I yet beseech your Majesty—
If for I want that glib and oily art
To speak and purpose not, since what I well intend,
I'll do 't before I speak—that you make known
It is no vicious blot, murder, or foulness, 230
No unchaste action, or dishonour'd step,
That hath deprived me of your grace and favour;
But even for want of that for which I am richer,
A still-soliciting eye, and such a tongue
As I am glad I have not, though not to have it
Hath lost me in your liking.

Lear. Better thou
Hadst not been born than not to have pleased me better.

France. Is it but this? A tardiness in nature
Which often leaves the history unspoke
That it intends to do? My lord of Burgundy, 240
What say you to the lady? Love's not love
When it is mingled with regards that stands

218. *argument:* subject. 219. *trice:* moment. 223. *monsters it:* makes it monstrous. 224. *taint:* corruption, decay. 225. *faith:* belief. 227. *for:* because. *want:* lack. 228. *purpose:* intend. 234. *still-soliciting:* ever-begging. 239. *history:* narrative. 242. *regards:* considerations.

Aloof from the entire point. Will you have her?
She is herself a dowry.

Bur. Royal Lear,
Give but that portion which yourself proposed,
And here I take Cordelia by the hand,
Duchess of Burgundy.

Lear. Nothing! I have sworn; I am firm.

Bur. [*To Cordelia*] I am sorry, then, you have so lost a father
That you must lose a husband.

Cor. Peace be with Burgundy! 250
Since that respects of fortune are his love,
I shall not be his wife.

France. Fairest Cordelia, that art most rich, being poor;
Most choice, forsaken; and most loved, despised!
Thee and thy virtues here I seize upon,
Be it lawful I take up what's cast away.
Gods, gods! 'Tis strange that from their cold'st neglect
My love should kindle to inflamed respect.
Thy dowerless daughter, king, thrown to my chance,
Is queen of us, of ours, and our fair France. 260
Not all the dukes of waterish Burgundy
Can buy this unprized precious maid of me.
Bid them farewell, Cordelia, though unkind.
Thou losest here, a better where to find.

Lear. Thou hast her, France. Let her be thine, for we
Have no such daughter, nor shall ever see
That face of hers again. Therefore be gone
Without our grace, our love, our benison.
Come, noble Burgundy.

[*Flourish. Exeunt all but France, Goneril, Regan, and Cordelia.*

France. Bid farewell to your sisters. 270

Cor. The jewels of our father, with wash'd eyes

243. *entire:* unmixed, pure (?) (Onions). 251. *respects:* considerations of. 261. *waterish:* well-watered, with a note of contempt. The old dukedom of Burgundy at one time included the Netherlands. 262. *unprized:* i.e., by others, but highly valued by me. 263. *unkind:* unnatural; or perhaps, *unkinn'd*, deprived of kindred.

Cordelia leaves you. I know you what you are,
And like a sister am most loath to call
Your faults as they are named. Use well our father;
To your professed bosoms I commit him.
But yet, alas, stood I within his grace,
I would prefer him to a better place.
So farewell to you both.

Reg. Prescribe not us our duties.

Gon. Let your study
Be to content your lord, who hath received you 280
At Fortune's alms. You have obedience scanted,
And well are worth the want that you have wanted.

Cor. Time shall unfold what pleated cunning hides;
Who cover faults, at last shame them derides.
Well may you prosper!

France. Come, my fair Cordelia.

[*Exeunt France and Cordelia.*

Gon. Sister, it is not a little I have to say of what most nearly appertains to us both. I think our father will hence tonight.

Reg. That's most certain, and with you; next month with us. 290

Gon. You see how full of changes his age is; the observation we have made of it hath not been little. He always loved our sister most, and with what poor judgment he hath now cast her off appears too grossly.

Reg. 'Tis the infirmity of his age. Yet he hath ever but slenderly known himself.

Gon. The best and soundest of his time hath been but rash; then must we look to receive from his age, not alone the im-

274. *Use.* F_1 reads *Love.* 275. *professed bosoms:* i.e., hearts that have professed love for him. 277. *prefer:* recommend. 281. *At:* as. 282. *are worth:* deserve. *want . . . wanted:* lack (i.e., of dowry) that you have lacked. *want.* F_1 reads *worth.* 283. *pleated.* F_1 reads *plighted.* 291 ff. If the sisters did not subsequently prove themselves such fiends, these remarks might be accepted as just and logical. 295. *grossly:* plainly. 298. *The best . . . time:* his best and soundest years. The tragic flaw in Lear's character is not altogether produced by senility.

perfections of long-engraffed condition, but therewithal the unruly waywardness that infirm and choleric years bring with them. 303

Reg. Such unconstant starts are we like to have from him as this of Kent's banishment.

Gon. There is further compliment of leave-taking between France and him. Pray you, let's hit together. If our father carry authority with such dispositions as he bears, this last surrender of his will but offend us. 310

Reg. We shall further think on 't.

Gon. We must do something, and i' the heat. [*Exeunt.*

Scene ii. *The* Earl of Gloucester's *castle.*

Enter Edmund, *with a letter.*

Edm. Thou, Nature, art my goddess; to thy law
My services are bound. Wherefore should I
Stand in the plague of custom, and permit
The curiosity of nations to deprive me,
For that I am some twelve or fourteen moonshines
Lag of a brother? Why bastard? Wherefore base?
When my dimensions are as well compact,
My mind as generous, and my shape as true,
As honest madam's issue? Why brand they us
With base? With baseness? Bastardy? Base, base? 10
Who, in the lusty stealth of nature, take
More composition and fierce quality
Than doth, within a dull, stale, tired bed,
Go to the creating a whole tribe of fops,

301. *long-engraffed:* long-implanted, firmly fixed. 302. *choleric:* irascible, inclined to wrath. 308. *hit:* agree. 310. *offend:* harm. 312. *i' the heat:* at once.

[ii] 1. *Nature:* i.e., because he is a natural son. Edmund's villainy has at least this justification which that of the sisters does not have — he is baseborn. 3. *Stand . . . custom:* suffer the injustice of custom. 4. *curiosity:* strictness. 6. *Lag:* tardy. 7. *dimensions:* bodily frame. *compact:* put together. 8. *generous:* noble. 9. *honest:* chaste. 12. *composition:* fashioning. *quality:* character.

Got 'tween asleep and wake? Well, then,
Legitimate Edgar, I must have your land.
Our father's love is to the bastard Edmund
As to the legitimate. Fine word—"legitimate"!
Well, my legitimate, if this letter speed,
And my invention thrive, Edmund the base 20
Shall top the legitimate. I grow; I prosper.
Now, gods, stand up for bastards!

Enter GLOUCESTER.

Glou. Kent banish'd thus? And France in choler parted?
And the king gone tonight? Subscribed his power?
Confined to exhibition? All this done
Upon the gad? Edmund, how now? What news?

Edm. So please your lordship, none. [*Putting up the letter.*

Glou. Why so earnestly seek you to put up that letter?

Edm. I know no news, my lord.

Glou. What paper were you reading? 30

Edm. Nothing, my lord.

Glou. No? What needed, then, that terrible dispatch of it into your pocket? The quality of nothing hath not such need to hide itself. Let's see. Come, if it be nothing, I shall not need spectacles.

Edm. I beseech you, sir, pardon me. It is a letter from my brother that I have not all o'er-read; and for so much as I have perused, I find it not fit for your o'er-looking. 40

Glou. Give me the letter, sir.

Edm. I shall offend, either to detain or give it. The contents, as in part I understand them, are to blame.

Glou. Let's see, let's see.

Edm. I hope, for my brother's justification, he wrote this but as an essay or taste of my virtue. 47

Glou. [*Reads*] "This policy and reverence of age makes the

18. *Fine . . . "legitimate."* Omitted in Q1. 19. *speed:* succeed. 20. *invention:* plan, scheme. 24. *Subscribed:* surrendered. 25. *exhibition:* an allowance of money. 26. *gad:* spur of the moment. 32. *terrible:* terrified. 33. *dispatch:* haste. 47. *essay:* trial.

world bitter to the best of our times; keeps our fortunes from us till our oldness cannot relish them. I begin to find an idle and fond bondage in the oppression of aged tyranny, who sways, not as it hath power, but as it is suffered. Come to me, that of this I may speak more. If our father would sleep till I waked him, you should enjoy half his revenue for ever, and live the beloved of your brother, EDGAR." 57

Hum—conspiracy? "Sleep till I waked him, you should enjoy half his revenue"—My son Edgar? Had he a hand to write this? A heart and brain to breed it in? When came this to you? Who brought it?

Edm. It was not brought me, my lord; there's the cunning of it. I found it thrown in at the casement of my closet.

Glou. You know the character to be your brother's? 67

Edm. If the matter were good, my lord, I durst swear it were his; but, in respect of that, I would fain think it were not.

Glou. It is his.

Edm. It is his hand, my lord; but I hope his heart is not in the contents.

Glou. Hath he never heretofore sounded you in this business?

Edm. Never, my lord. But I have heard him oft maintain it to be fit that, sons at perfect age, and fathers declining, the father should be as ward to the son, and the son manage his revenue. 79

Glou. O villain, villain! His very opinion in the letter! Abhorred villain! Unnatural, detested, brutish villain! Worse than brutish! Go, sirrah, seek him; I'll apprehend him. Abominable villain! Where is he? 84

Edm. I do not well know, my lord. If it shall please you to suspend your indignation against my brother till you can de-

49. *best of our times:* the best years of our lives. 51. *idle:* weak. 52. *fond:* foolish. *aged tyranny:* tyranny of age. 54. *suffered:* allowed. 65. *closet:* private room. 66. *character:* handwriting. 79. *revenue:* income. 83. *sirrah:* ordinary form of address for inferiors and servants. *apprehend:* arrest, seize. 84. *Abominable:* inhuman. Spelled *abhominable* in Q_1 and F_1.

rive from him better testimony of his intent, you shall run a certain course; where, if you violently proceed against him, mistaking his purpose, it would make a great gap in your own honour, and shake in pieces the heart of his obedience. I dare pawn down my life for him that he hath wrote this to feel my affection to your Honour, and to no further pretense of danger.

Glou. Think you so? 96

Edm. If your Honour judge it meet, I will place you where you shall hear us confer of this and by an auricular assurance have your satisfaction, and that without any further delay than this very evening. 101

Glou. He cannot be such a monster—

Edm. Nor is not, sure.

Glou. To his father, that so tenderly and entirely loves him. Heaven and earth! Edmund, seek him out; wind me into him, I pray you. Frame the business after your own wisdom. I would unstate myself to be in a due resolution.

Edm. I will seek him, sir, presently, convey the business as I shall find means, and acquaint you withal. 111

Glou. These late eclipses in the sun and moon portend no good to us. Though the wisdom of nature can reason it thus and thus, yet nature finds itself scourged by the sequent effects. Love cools, friendship falls off, brothers divide. In cities, mutinies; in countries, discord; in palaces, treason; and the bond cracked 'twixt son and father. This villain of mine comes under the prediction; there's son against father. The king falls from bias of nature; there's father against child. We have seen

89. *where:* whereas. 95. *pretense of danger:* dangerous intention. 97. *meet:* fitting. 99. *auricular:* perceived by the ear. 103–5. *Edm. . . . earth.* Omitted in F_1. 106. *wind me into:* worm your way into his confidence for me. 108. *unstate . . . resolution:* give up my position to know how matters really stand. 109. *presently:* at once. *convey:* manage. 112. *These late eclipses:* thought to be a reference to an eclipse of the sun on October 2, and one of the moon on September 27, 1605. 113. *wisdom of nature:* natural science. 115. *yet . . . effects:* yet the world suffers the consequences. 118–24. *This . . . graves.* Omitted in Q_1. 120. *falls . . . nature:* departs from his natural inclination, behaves unnaturally.

the best of our time. Machinations, hollowness, treachery, and all ruinous disorders, follow us disquietly to our graves. Find out this villain, Edmund; it shall lose thee nothing; do it carefully. And the noble and true-hearted Kent banished! His offense, honesty! 'Tis strange. [*Exit.* 127

Edm. This is the excellent foppery of the world, that, when we are sick in fortune—often the surfeit of our own behaviour—we make guilty of our disasters the sun, the moon, and the stars, as if we were villains by necessity; fools by heavenly compulsion; knaves, thieves, and treachers, by spherical predominance; drunkards, liars, and adulterers, by an enforced obedience of planetary influence; and all that we are evil in, by a divine thrusting on. An admirable evasion of whoremaster man, to lay his goatish disposition to the charge of a star! My father compounded with my mother under the dragon's tail; and my nativity was under Ursa Major; so that it follows, I am rough and lecherous. Fut, I should have been that I am, had the maidenliest star in the firmament twinkled on my bastardizing. Edgar— 145

Enter EDGAR.

and pat he comes like the catastrophe of the old comedy; my cue is villainous melancholy, with a sigh like Tom o' Bedlam. O, these eclipses do portend these divisions! Fa, sol, la, mi.

Edg. How now, brother Edmund? What serious contemplation are you in? 151

Edm. I am thinking, brother, of a prediction I read this other day, what should follow these eclipses.

Edg. Do you busy yourself about that?

128. *foppery:* folly. 133. *treachers:* traitors. 134. *spherical predominance:* influence of the stars. 137. *divine thrusting on:* heavenly, i.e., astrological compulsion. *admirable:* wonderful. 138. *goatish:* lascivious. 139. *compounded:* came to terms. 140. *dragon's tail:* the ascending node of the moon's orbit with the ecliptic (an astronomical term). 143. *that:* that which. 148. *Tom o' Bedlam:* a madman, an inmate of the hospital of St. Mary of Bethlehem in London. 149. *divisions:* (a) dissensions, (b) in music, melodic runs. Edmund illustrates his pun by running the scale.

Edm. I promise you, the effects he writes of succeed unhappily; as of unnaturalness between the child and the parent; death, dearth, dissolutions of ancient amities; divisions in state, menaces and maledictions against king and nobles; needless diffidences, banishment of friends, dissipation of cohorts, nuptial breaches, and I know not what. 163

Edg. How long have you been a sectary astronomical?

Edm. Come, come; when saw you my father last?

Edg. Why, the night gone by.

Edm. Spake you with him?

Edg. Ay, two hours together. 170

Edm. Parted you in good terms? Found you no displeasure in him by word or countenance?

Edg. None at all.

Edm. Bethink yourself wherein you may have offended him, and at my entreaty forbear his presence till some little time hath qualified the heat of his displeasure, which at this instant so rageth in him that with the mischief of your person it would scarcely allay.

Edg. Some villain hath done me wrong. 180

Edm. That's my fear. I pray you, have a continent forbearance till the speed of his rage goes slower; and, as I say, retire with me to my lodging, from whence I will fitly bring you to hear my lord speak. Pray ye, go; [*Giving him a key.*] there's my key. If you do stir abroad, go armed.

Edg. Armed, brother?

Edm. Brother, I advise you to the best; go armed. I am no honest man if there be any good meaning towards you. I have told you what I have seen and heard; but faintly, nothing like the image and horror of it. Pray you, away. 192

Edg. Shall I hear from you anon?

157. *succeed:* come to pass. 157–66. *as . . . come.* Omitted in F_1. 159. *amities:* friendships. 161. *diffidences:* distrusts. 162. *dissipation of cohorts:* disbanding of troops. 164. *sectary astronomical:* student of astrology. 176. *qualified:* moderated. 178–9. *that . . . allay:* that harm to you would hardly satisfy him. 182. *continent:* self-restraining.

Edm. I do serve you in this business. [*Exit Edgar.*
A credulous father, and a brother noble,
Whose nature is so far from doing harms,
That he suspects none; on whose foolish honesty
My practices ride easy! I see the business.
Let me, if not by birth, have lands by wit. 199
All with me's meet that I can fashion fit. [*Exit.*

Scene III. *A room in the* Duke of Albany's *palace some days later.*

Goneril *and* Oswald, *her steward, in conversation.*

Gon. Did my father strike my gentleman for chiding of his fool?
Osw. Yes, madam.
Gon. By day and night he wrongs me; every hour
He flashes into one gross crime or other
That sets us all at odds. I'll not endure it.
His knights grow riotous, and himself upbraids us
On every trifle. When he returns from hunting,
I will not speak with him; say I am sick.
If you come slack of former services,
You shall do well; the fault of it I'll answer. 10
Osw. He's coming, madam; I hear him. [*Horns are heard.*
Gon. Put on what weary negligence you please,
You and your fellows; I'ld have it come to question.
If he dislike it, let him to our sister,
Whose mind and mine, I know, in that are one,
Not to be over-ruled. Idle old man,
That still would manage those authorities
That he hath given away! Now, by my life,
Old fools are babes again, and must be used
With checks as flatteries—when they are seen abused. 20
Remember what I tell you.

198. *practices:* plots. 199. *wit:* strategy, contriving.
[iii] 1. *chiding:* scolding. 10. *answer:* answer for. 13. *to question:* to an issue. 16–20. *Not . . . abused.* Omitted in F_1. 20. *checks as flatteries:* rebukes as well as flatteries. *abused:* to be deceived.

Osw. Well, madam.

Gon. And let his knights have colder looks among you;
What grows of it, no matter; advise your fellows so.
I would breed from hence occasions, and I shall
That I may speak. I'll write straight to my sister
To hold my very course. Prepare for dinner. [*Exeunt.*

SCENE IV. *Another hall in the same.*

Enter KENT, *disguised.*

Kent. If but as well I other accents borrow,
That can my speech defuse, my good intent
May carry through itself to that full issue
For which I razed my likeness. Now, banish'd Kent,
If thou canst serve where thou dost stand condemn'd,
So may it come, thy master, whom thou lovest,
Shall find thee full of labours.

Horns are heard. Enter LEAR, Knights, *and* Attendants, *from hunting.*

Lear. Let me not stay a jot for dinner; go get it ready. [*Exit an Attendant.*] How now? What art thou? 10

Kent. A man, sir.

Lear. What dost thou profess? What wouldst thou with us?

Kent. I do profess to be no less than I seem; to serve him truly that will put me in trust; to love him that is honest; to converse with him that is wise, and says little; to fear judgment; to fight when I cannot choose; and to eat no fish.

Lear. What art thou?

Kent. A very honest-hearted fellow, and as poor as the king. 21

24–5. *I . . . speak.* Omitted in F_1.

[iv] 1–2. *If . . . defuse:* if I can disguise my voice as well as I have disguised my person. 2. *defuse:* render indistinguishable. 4. *razed:* erased. 12. *dost thou profess:* is your profession. Kent's reply plays on the other meaning of the word. 18. *eat no fish.* In Elizabethan parlance "he's an honest man and eats no fish" meant "he is favorable to the government and a Protestant."

Lear. If thou be as poor for a subject as he is for a king, thou art poor enough. What wouldst thou?

Kent. Service.

Lear. Who wouldst thou serve?

Kent. You.

Lear. Dost thou know me, fellow?

Kent. No, sir; but you have that in your countenance which I would fain call master. 30

Lear. What's that?

Kent. Authority.

Lear. What services canst thou do?

Kent. I can keep honest counsel, ride, run, mar a curious tale in telling it, and deliver a plain message bluntly. That which ordinary men are fit for, I am qualified in; and the best of me is diligence.

Lear. How old art thou? 39

Kent. Not so young, sir, to love a woman for singing, nor so old to dote on her for anything. I have years on my back forty-eight.

Lear. Follow me; thou shalt serve me. If I like thee no worse after dinner, I will not part from thee yet. Dinner, ho, dinner! Where's my knave? My fool? Go you, and call my fool hither. [*Exit an Attendant.*

Enter OSWALD.

You, you, sirrah, where's my daughter?

Osw. So please you— [*He turns abruptly and leaves.*

Lear. What says the fellow there? Call the clotpoll back. [*A Knight goes after him.*] Where's my fool, ho? I think the world's asleep. 52

Re-enter Knight.

How now? Where's that mongrel?

Knight. He says, my lord, your daughter is not well.

Lear. Why came not the slave back to me when I called him?

35. *curious:* skillfully wrought. 51. *clotpoll:* clodpoll, blockhead.

Knight. Sir, he answered me in the roundest manner, he would not.

Lear. He would not? 60

Knight. My lord, I know not what the matter is; but, to my judgment, your Highness is not entertained with that ceremonious affection as you were wont. There's a great abatement of kindness appears as well in the general dependants as in the duke himself also and your daughter.

Lear. Ha? Sayest thou so?

Knight. I beseech you, pardon me, my lord, if I be mistaken; for my duty cannot be silent when I think your Highness wronged. 71

Lear. Thou but rememberest me of mine own conception. I have perceived a most faint neglect of late, which I have rather blamed as mine own jealous curiosity than as a very pretense and purpose of unkindness. I will look further into't. But where's my fool? I have not seen him this two days.

Knight. Since my young lady's going into France, sir, the fool hath much pined away. 80

Lear. No more of that; I have noted it well. Go you, and tell my daughter I would speak with her. [*Exit an Attendant.*] Go you, call hither my fool. [*Exit another Attendant.*

Re-enter OSWALD.

O, you sir, you, come you hither, sir. Who am I, sir?

Osw. My lady's father.

Lear. "My lady's father"? My lord's knave. You whoreson dog! You slave! You cur! 89

Osw. I am none of these, my lord; I beseech your pardon.

Lear. Do you bandy looks with me, you rascal?

[*Striking him.*

Osw. I'll not be struck, my lord.

58. *roundest:* bluntest, plainest. 63. *entertained:* treated. 64. *abatement:* diminution. 72. *rememberest:* remindest. 75. *jealous:* suspicious. *curiosity:* fastidiousness. *pretense:* design. 81. *No . . . well.* This is the first indication that Lear regrets his treatment of Cordelia.

Kent. Nor tripped neither, you base football player.

[*Tripping up his heels.*

Lear. [*To Kent*] I thank thee, fellow; thou servest me, and I'll love thee.

Kent. [*To Oswald*] Come, sir, arise, away! I'll teach you differences. Away, away! If you will measure your lubber's length again, tarry. But away! Go to; have you wisdom? So. 102

[*Pushes Oswald out.*

Lear. Now, my friendly knave, I thank thee. There's earnest of thy service. [*Giving Kent money.*

Enter Fool.

Fool. Let me hire him too. Here's my coxcomb.

[*Offering Kent his cap.*

Lear. How now, my pretty knave, how dost thou?

Fool. Sirrah, you were best take my coxcomb.

Kent. Why, fool? 110

Fool. Why, for taking one's part that's out of favour. Nay, an thou canst not smile as the wind sits, thou'lt catch cold shortly. There, take my coxcomb. Why, this fellow has banished two on's daughters, and did the third a blessing against his will; if thou follow him, thou must needs wear my coxcomb. How now, nuncle? Would I had two coxcombs and two daughters!

Lear. Why, my boy? 119

Fool. If I gave them all my living, I'ld keep my coxcombs myself. There's mine; beg another of thy daughters.

Lear. Take heed, sirrah; the whip.

Fool. Truth's a dog must to kennel; he must be whipped out, when Lady Brach may stand by the fire and stink.

Lear. A pestilent gall to me!

Fool. Sirrah, I'll teach thee a speech.

104. *earnest:* handsel, money paid as an installment to secure a bargain. 105. *coxcomb:* cap worn by a professional fool, like a cock's comb in shape and color. 110–11. *Kent . . . Fool.* Omitted in F_1. 114. *on 's:* of his. 117. *nuncle:* a contraction of *mine uncle*, the customary address of the fool to his master. 125. *Lady Brach:* i.e., the dog.

Lear. Do.

Fool. Mark it, nuncle: 130

Have more than thou showest,
Speak less than thou knowest,
Lend less than thou owest,
Ride more than thou goest,
Learn more than thou trowest,
Set less than thou throwest;
Leave thy drink and thy whore,
And keep in-a-door,
And thou shalt have more
Than two tens to a score. 140

Lear. This is nothing, fool.

Fool. Then 'tis like the breath of an unfee'd lawyer; you gave me nothing for 't. Can you make no use of nothing, nuncle?

Lear. Why, no, boy; nothing can be made out of nothing.

Fool. [*To Kent*] Prithee, tell him, so much the rent of his land comes to. He will not believe a fool.

Lear. A bitter fool! 150

Fool. Dost thou know the difference, my boy, between a bitter fool and a sweet fool?

Lear. No, lad; teach me.

Fool. That lord that counsell'd thee
To give away thy land,
Come place him here by me,
Do thou for him stand.
The sweet and bitter fool
Will presently appear;
The one in motley here, 160
The other found out there.

Lear. Dost thou call me fool, boy?

133. *owest:* possessest. 134. *goest:* walkest. 135. *Learn . . . trowest:* don't believe all you hear. 136. *Set:* wager. *throwest:* i.e., at dice. 141. *Lear.* F_1 gives the speech to Kent. 154–69. *Fool . . . snatching.* Omitted in F_1. 154. *lord . . . thee.* In the old *King Leir* the division of the kingdom is made at the suggestion of a courtier named Skalliger. 159. *presently:* at once.

Fool. All thy other titles thou hast given away; that thou wast born with.

Kent. This is not altogether fool, my lord.

Fool. No, faith, lords and great men will not let me; if I had a monopoly out, they would have part on 't. And ladies too, they will not let me have all fool to myself; they'll be snatching. Give me an egg, nuncle, and I'll give thee two crowns. 171

Lear. What two crowns shall they be?

Fool. Why, after I have cut the egg i' the middle, and eat up the meat, the two crowns of the egg. When thou clovest thy crown i' the middle and gavest away both parts, thou borest thy ass on thy back o'er the dirt. Thou hadst little wit in thy bald crown when thou gavest thy golden one away. If I speak like myself in this, let him be whipped that first finds it so. 180

[*Singing*] Fools had ne'er less grace in a year;
For wise men are grown foppish,
They know not how their wits to wear,
Their manners are so apish.

Lear. When were you wont to be so full of songs, sirrah?

Fool. I have used it, nuncle, ever since thou madest thy daughters thy mother. For when thou gavest them the rod, and put'st down thine own breeches, 190

[*Singing*] Then they for sudden joy did weep,
And I for sorrow sung,
That such a king should play bo-peep,
And go the fools among.

Prithee, nuncle, keep a schoolmaster that can teach thy fool to lie. I would fain learn to lie.

Lear. An you lie, sirrah, we'll have you whipped. 198

Fool. I marvel what kin thou and thy daughters are. They'll have me whipped for speaking true, thou'lt have me whipped for lying; and sometimes I am whipped for holding my peace.

177. *ass on thy back:* an allusion to Aesop's fable. 178. *wit:* intelligence. 179. *like myself:* i.e., like a fool. 181 ff. *Singing.* The Fool's snatches of song are merely long enough to emphasize unpleasant truths. 181. *grace:* good luck. Q_1 reads *wit.* 182. *foppish:* foolish.

I had rather be any kind o' thing than a fool. And yet I would not be thee, nuncle; thou hast pared thy wit o' both sides, and left nothing i' the middle. Here comes one o' the parings.

Enter GONERIL, *scowling.*

Lear. How now, daughter? What makes that frontlet on?
Methinks you are too much of late i' the frown. 209

Fool. Thou wast a pretty fellow when thou hadst no need to care for her frowning; now thou art an O without a figure. I am better than thou art now; I am a fool, thou art nothing. [*To Goneril.*] Yes, forsooth, I will hold my tongue; so your face bids me, though you say nothing. Mum, mum,

He that keeps nor crust nor crum,
Weary of all, shall want some.

[*Pointing to Lear.*] That's a shealed peascod.

Gon. Not only, sir, this your all-licensed fool, 220
But other of your insolent retinue
Do hourly carp and quarrel, breaking forth
In rank and not-to-be-endured riots. Sir,
I had thought, by making this well known unto you,
To have found a safe redress; but now grow fearful,
By what yourself too late have spoke and done,
That you protect this course, and put it on
By your allowance; which if you should, the fault
Would not 'scape censure, nor the redresses sleep,
Which, in the tender of a wholesome weal, 230
Might in their working do you that offense,
Which else were shame, that then necessity
Will call discreet proceeding.

Fool. For, you know, nuncle,

The hedge-sparrow fed the cuckoo so long,
That it had it head bit off by it young.

So, out went the candle, and we were left darkling.

208. *frontlet:* a band worn on the forehead, here used figuratively for a frown. 219. *shealed peascod:* empty pea-pod. 220. *all-licensed:* wholly unrestrained. 223. *rank:* gross. 227. *put it on:* promote it. 228. *allowance:* approval. 230. *tender:* care. *wholesome weal:* healthily organized state. 236. *it:* its. 237. *darkling:* in the dark.

Lear. Are you our daughter?

Gon. Come, sir,
I would you would make use of that good wisdom, 240
Whereof I know you are fraught, and put away
These dispositions that of late transform you
From what you rightly are.

Fool. May not an ass know when the cart draws the horse?
Whoop, Jug! I love thee.

Lear. Doth any here know me? This is not Lear.
Doth Lear walk thus? Speak thus? Where are his eyes?
Either his notion weakens, his discernings
Are lethargied—Ha! Waking? 'Tis not so.
Who is it that can tell me who I am? 250

Fool. Lear's shadow.

Lear. I would learn that; for, by the marks of sovereignty, knowledge, and reason, I should be false persuaded I had daughters.

Fool. Which they will make an obedient father.

Lear. Your name, fair gentlewoman?

Gon. This admiration, sir, is much o' the savour
Of other your new pranks. I do beseech you
To understand my purposes aright. 260
As you are old and reverend, you should be wise.
Here do you keep a hundred knights and squires;
Men so disorder'd, so debosh'd and bold,
That this our court, infected with their manners,
Shows like a riotous inn. Epicurism and lust
Make it more like a tavern or a brothel
Than a graced palace. The shame itself doth speak
For instant remedy. Be then desired

241. *fraught:* laden, stored. 245. *Whoop, Jug.* May the Fool, by this snatch of drunken song, be pretending to be tipsy and so trying to avoid the danger he has incurred by his outspoken remarks to Goneril? 248. *notion:* understanding, mind. 251. *Fool.* Q_1 gives his speech to Lear. 252–6. *Lear . . . father.* Omitted in F_1. 258. *admiration:* wonder. 259. *other your:* your other. 261. *reverend:* worthy of respect or reverence. 263. *debosh'd:* debauched. 265. *Shows:* appears. *Epicurism:* luxury.

By her that else will take the thing she begs
A little to disquantity your train, 270
And the remainder that shall still depend
To be such men as may besort your age,
And know themselves and you.

Lear. Darkness and devils!
Saddle my horses; call my train together!
Degenerate bastard! I'll not trouble thee.
Yet have I left a daughter.

Gon. You strike my people, and your disorder'd rabble
Make servants of their betters.

Enter ALBANY.

Lear. Woe, that too late repents—[*To Albany.*] O, sir, are you come?
Is it your will? Speak, sir.—Prepare my horses. 280
Ingratitude, thou marble-hearted fiend,
More hideous when thou show'st thee in a child
Than the sea-monster.

Alb. Pray, sir, be patient.

Lear. [*To Goneril*] Detested kite, thou liest.
My train are men of choice and rarest parts,
That all particulars of duty know,
And in the most exact regard support
The worships of their name. O most small fault,
How ugly didst thou in Cordelia show!
That, like an engine, wrench'd my frame of nature 290
From the fix'd place; drew from my heart all love
And added to the gall. O Lear, Lear, Lear!
Beat at this gate that let thy folly in, [*Striking his head.*
And thy dear judgment out! Go, go, my people.

270. *disquantity:* diminish, reduce. 271. *depend:* be your dependants. 272. *besort:* befit. 283. *Alb. Pray . . . patient.* Omitted in Q_1. 284. *kite:* hawk; hence, rapacious person. 285. *choice and rarest.* The superlative belongs to both adjectives. 288. *worships:* dignities. 290. *engine:* i.e., of torture, the rack. *frame of nature:* natural body. 294. *dear:* precious.

Alb. My lord, I am guiltless, as I am ignorant
Of what hath moved you.

Lear. It may be so, my lord.
Hear, Nature; hear, dear goddess, hear!
Suspend thy purpose, if thou didst intend
To make this creature fruitful!
Into her womb convey sterility! 300
Dry up in her the organs of increase;
And from her derogate body never spring
A babe to honour her! If she must teem,
Create her child of spleen, that it may live,
And be a thwart disnatured torment to her!
Let it stamp wrinkles in her brow of youth,
With cadent tears fret channels in her cheeks;
Turn all her mother's pains and benefits
To laughter and contempt, that she may feel
How sharper than a serpent's tooth it is 310
To have a thankless child! Away, away! [*Exit.*

Alb. Now, gods that we adore, whereof comes this?

Gon. Never afflict yourself to know the cause;
But let his disposition have that scope
That dotage gives it.

Re-enter LEAR.

Lear. What, fifty of my followers at a clap?
Within a fortnight?

Alb. What's the matter, sir?

Lear. I'll tell thee—[*To Goneril.*] Life and death! I am ashamed
That thou hast power to shake my manhood thus;
That these hot tears, which break from me perforce, 320
Should make thee worth them. Blasts and fogs upon thee!

302. *derogate:* debased. 303. *teem:* be fruitful. 304. *spleen:* malice, hatred. 305. *thwart:* perverse. *disnatured:* unnatural. 306. *brow of youth:* youthful brow. 307. *cadent:* falling; Q_1 reads *accent. fret:* wear away. 313. *the cause.* F_1 reads *more of it.* 314. *scope:* license. 316. *What . . . clap.* Cf. line 270; Goneril had already carried out her plan before mentioning it to her father.

The untented woundings of a father's curse
Pierce every sense about thee! Old fond eyes,
Beweep this cause again, I'll pluck ye out,
And cast you, with the waters that you lose,
To temper clay. Yea, is it come to this?
Let it be so. Yet have I left a daughter,
Who I am sure is kind and comfortable.
When she shall hear this of thee, with her nails
She'll flay thy wolvish visage. Thou shalt find 330
That I'll resume the shape which thou dost think
I have cast off for ever. Thou shalt, I warrant thee.

[*Exeunt Lear*, *Kent*, *and Attendants*.

Gon. Do you mark that, my lord?

Alb. I cannot be so partial, Goneril,
To the great love I bear you—

Gon. Pray you, content. What, Oswald, ho!
[*To the Fool.*] You, sir, more knave than fool, after your master.

Fool. Nuncle Lear, nuncle Lear, tarry and take the fool with thee.

A fox, when one has caught her, 340
And such a daughter,
Should sure to the slaughter,
If my cap would buy a halter.
So the fool follows after. [*Exit.*

Gon. This man hath had good counsel—a hundred knights!
'Tis politic and safe to let him keep
At point a hundred knights. Yes, that, on every dream,
Each buzz, each fancy, each complaint, dislike,
He may enguard his dotage with their powers,
And hold our lives in mercy. Oswald, I say! 350

Alb. Well, you may fear too far.

322. *untented:* not cleansed and so liable to fester. 323. *fond:* foolish. 324. *Beweep:* if you beweep. 326. *temper:* mix. 327. *Yet . . . daughter.* F_1 reads *I have another daughter.* 328. *comfortable:* comforting. 332. *Thou . . . thee.* Omitted in F_1. 345–56. *Gon. . . . unfitness.* Omitted in Q_1. 345. *counsel:* advice. 346. *politic:* wise. 347. *At point:* in readiness. 348. *buzz:* whisper.

Gon. Safer than trust too far.
Let me still take away the harms I fear,
Not fear still to be taken. I know his heart.
What he hath utter'd I have writ my sister.
If she sustain him and his hundred knights,
When I have show'd the unfitness—

Re-enter OSWALD.

How now, Oswald?
What, have you writ that letter to my sister?

Osw. Yes, madam.

Gon. Take you some company, and away to horse.
Inform her full of my particular fear; 360
And thereto add such reasons of your own
As may compact it more. Get you gone;
And hasten your return. [*Exit Oswald.*] No, no, my lord,
This milky gentleness and course of yours
Though I condemn not, yet, under pardon,
You are much more attask'd for want of wisdom
Than praised for harmful mildness.

Alb. How far your eyes may pierce I cannot tell;
Striving to better, oft we mar what's well.

Gon. Nay, then— 370

Alb. Well, well; the event. [*Exeunt.*

SCENE V. *Court before the same.*

Enter LEAR, KENT, *and* Fool.

Lear. Go you before to Gloucester with these letters. Acquaint my daughter no further with anything you know than comes from her demand out of the letter. If your diligence be not speedy, I shall be there afore you.

Kent. I will not sleep, my lord, till I have delivered your letter. [*Exit.*

352–3. *still:* ever. 359. *company:* attendants. 360. *particular:* personal. 362. *compact:* strengthen. 364. *milky . . . course:* i.e., the milky gentleness of your course. 365. *under pardon:* i.e., if I may say so. 366. *attask'd:* blamed. 371. *event:* i.e., let's wait and see.

Fool. If a man's brains were in 's heels, were't not in danger of kibes?

Lear. Ay, boy. 10

Fool. Then, I prithee, be merry; thy wit shall ne'er go slip-shod.

Lear. Ha, ha, ha!

Fool. Shalt see thy other daughter will use thee kindly; for though she's as like this as a crab's like an apple, yet I can tell what I can tell.

Lear. Why, what canst thou tell, my boy?

Fool. She will taste as like this as a crab does to a crab. Thou canst tell why one's nose stands i' the middle on's face? 20

Lear. No.

Fool. Why, to keep one's eyes of either side's nose, that what a man cannot smell out, he may spy into.

Lear. I did her wrong—

Fool. Canst tell how an oyster makes his shell?

Lear. No.

Fool. Nor I neither; but I can tell why a snail has a house. 30

Lear. Why?

Fool. Why, to put 's head in; not to give it away to his daughters, and leave his horns without a case.

Lear. I will forget my nature. So kind a father? Be my horses ready?

Fool. Thy asses are gone about 'em. The reason why the seven stars are no more than seven is a pretty reason.

Lear. Because they are not eight? 40

Fool. Yes, indeed. Thou wouldst make a good fool.

Lear. To take't again perforce! Monster ingratitude!

Fool. If thou wert my fool, nuncle, I'ld have thee beaten for being old before thy time.

Lear. How's that?

Fool. Thou shouldst not have been old till thou hadst been wise.

---

[v] 9. *kibes:* chilblains. 12. *go slip-shod:* wear slippers; i.e., you have no brains. 15. *kindly:* (a) with kindness, (b) after her nature. 16. *crab's:* crab-apple's. 38. *seven stars:* the Pleiades.

Lear. O, let me not be mad, not mad, sweet heaven! 50
Keep me in temper; I would not be mad!

Enter a Gentleman.

How now, are the horses ready?

Gent. Ready, my lord.

Lear. Come, boy.

Fool. [*To the Audience*] She that's a maid now, and laughs at my departure,
Shall not be a maid long, unless things be cut shorter. [*Exeunt.*

ACT II

Scene i. *Night, outside the* Earl of Gloucester's *castle.*

Edmund *and* Curan *meeting.*

Edm. Save thee, Curan.

Cur. And you, sir. I have been with your father, and given him notice that the Duke of Cornwall and Regan his duchess will be here with him this night.

Edm. How comes that?

Cur. Nay, I know not. You have heard of the news abroad; I mean the whispered ones, for they are yet but ear-bussing arguments?

Edm. Not I; pray you, what are they? 10

Cur. Have you heard of no likely wars toward, 'twixt the Dukes of Cornwall and Albany?

Edm. Not a word.

Cur. You may do, then, in time. Fare you well, sir. [*Exit.*

Edm. The duke be here tonight? The better best!
This weaves itself perforce into my business.
My father hath set guard to take my brother;
And I have one thing, of a queasy question,

[II. i] 9. *ear-bussing:* ear-kissing, i.e., whispered, with a pun on *buzzing. Buss* is dialectal for *kiss.* F_1 reads *ear-kissing. arguments:* subjects. 11. *toward:* in preparation. One of Lear's objects in dividing his kingdom was that future strife might be prevented. 19. *queasy question:* i.e., that requires delicate handling.

Which I must act; briefness and fortune, work! 20
Brother, a word; descend. [*Calling at a window.*] Brother, I say!

Enter EDGAR.

My father watches. O sir, fly this place;
Intelligence is given where you are hid;
You have now the good advantage of the night.
Have you not spoken 'gainst the Duke of Cornwall?
He's coming hither; now, i' the night, i' the haste,
And Regan with him. Have you nothing said
Upon his party 'gainst the Duke of Albany?
Advise yourself.

Edg. I am sure on 't, not a word.

Edm. I hear my father coming. Pardon me; 30
In cunning I must draw my sword upon you.
Draw; seem to defend yourself; [*They clash swords.*] now quit you well.
[*Loudly.*] Yield! Come before my father! Light, ho, here!—
Fly, brother. [*Loudly.*] Torches, torches!—So, farewell.

[*Exit Edgar.*

Some blood drawn on me would beget opinion

[*Wounds his arm.*

Of my more fierce endeavour. I have seen drunkards
Do more than this in sport. [*Aloud.*] Father, father!
Stop, stop! No help?

Enter GLOUCESTER, *and* Servants *with torches.*

Glou. Now, Edmund, where's the villain?

Edm. Here stood he in the dark, his sharp sword out, 40
Mumbling of wicked charms, conjuring the moon
To stand auspicious mistress—

Glou. But where is he?

Edm. Look, sir, I bleed.

Glou. Where is the villain, Edmund?

20. *briefness:* promptness. 23. *Intelligence:* secret information. 28. *party:* side, i.e., in his favor. 29. *Advise yourself:* consider, recollect yourself. Edmund, of course, wishes to make Edgar afraid of both sides. 32. *quit:* acquit. 41. *conjuring:* imploring.

Edm. [*Pointing the wrong way*] Fled this way, sir. When by no means he could—

Glou. Pursue him, ho! Go after. [*Exeunt some Servants.* By no means what?

Edm. Persuade me to the murder of your lordship;
But that I told him the revengive gods
'Gainst parricides did all their thunders bend;
Spoke with how manifold and strong a bond
The child was bound to the father; sir, in fine, 50
Seeing how loathly opposite I stood
To his unnatural purpose, in fell motion,
With his prepared sword, he charges home
My unprovided body, latch'd mine arm.
But when he saw my best alarum'd spirits,
Bold in the quarrel's right, roused to the encounter,
Or whether gasted by the noise I made,
Full suddenly he fled.

Glou. Let him fly far.
Not in this land shall he remain uncaught;
And found— Dispatch. The noble duke my master, 60
My worthy arch and patron, comes tonight.
By his authority I will proclaim it,
That he which finds him shall deserve our thanks,
Bringing the murderous coward to the stake;
He that conceals him, death.

Edm. When I dissuaded him from his intent
And found him pight to do it, with curst speech
I threaten'd to discover him. He replied,
"Thou unpossessing bastard, dost thou think,

47. *revengive.* F1 reads *revenging.* 48. *bend:* aim. 50. *in fine:* finally. 51. *how . . . stood:* with what loathing I opposed. 52. *fell motion:* fierce movement. 54. *unprovided:* unarmed. *latch'd:* caught. 55. *best . . . spirits:* best spirits alarmed, or, spirits alarmed in the best cause. 57. *gasted:* frightened. 61. *arch:* chief. 67. *pight:* determined. *curst:* savage. 68. *discover:* expose. 69. *unpossessing:* without lands because of bastardy. "Thus the secret poison of Edmund's own heart steals forth; and then observe poor Gloucester's 'Loyal and *natural* boy!' as if praising the crime of Edmund's birth" (Coleridge).

If I would stand against thee, would the reposal 70
Of any trust, virtue, or worth in thee
Make thy words faith'd? No, what I should deny—
As this I would; ay, though thou didst produce
My very character—I 'ld turn it all
To thy suggestion, plot, and damned practice.
And thou must make a dullard of the world,
If they not thought the profits of my death
Were very pregnant and potential spurs
To make thee seek it."

Glou. Strong and fasten'd villain! 79
Would he deny his letter? I never got him. [*A tucket sounds.*
Hark, the duke's trumpets! I know not why he comes.
All ports I'll bar; the villain shall not 'scape;
The duke must grant me that. Besides, his picture
I will send far and near, that all the kingdom
May have due note of him; and of my land,
Loyal and natural boy, I'll work the means
To make thee capable.

Enter CORNWALL, REGAN, *and* Attendants.

Corn. How now, my noble friend? Since I came hither,
Which I can call but now, I have heard strange news.

Reg. If it be true, all vengeance comes too short 90
Which can pursue the offender. How dost, my lord?

Glou. O, madam, my old heart is crack'd, is crack'd!

Reg. What, did my father's godson seek your life?
He whom my father named? Your Edgar?

Glou. O, lady, lady, shame would have it hid!

Reg. Was he not companion with the riotous knights
That tend upon my father?

72. *faith'd:* believed. 74. *character:* handwriting. 75. *suggestion:* prompting to evil, temptation. *practice:* plot, scheme. 78. *pregnant:* cogent, compelling. *potential:* powerful. *spurs.* F_1 reads *spirits.* 79. *Strong.* F_1 reads *O strange. fasten'd:* confirmed. 80. *I . . . him.* F_1 reads *said he? got:* begot. 82. *ports:* gates. 86. *natural.* See note to II, i, 69 above. 87. *capable:* i.e., of inheriting. 93 ff. Observe Regan's venomous innuendo.

Glou. I know not, madam; 'tis too bad, too bad.
Edm. Yes, madam, he was of that consort.
Reg. No marvel, then, though we were ill affected; 100
'Tis they have put him on the old man's death,
To have the expense and waste of his revenues.
I have this present evening from my sister
Been well inform'd of them; and with such cautions,
That if they come to sojourn at my house,
I'll not be there.
Corn. Nor I, assure thee, Regan.
Edmund, I hear that you have shown your father
A child-like office.
Edm. 'Twas my duty, sir.
Glou. He did bewray his practice, and received
This hurt you see, striving to apprehend him. 110
Corn. Is he pursued?
Glou. Ay, my good lord.
Corn. If he be taken, he shall never more
Be fear'd of doing harm; make your own purpose,
How in my strength you please. For you, Edmund,
Whose virtue and obedience doth this instant
So much commend itself, you shall be ours.
Natures of such deep trust we shall much need;
You we first seize on.
Edm. I shall serve you, sir,
Truly, however else.
Glou. For him I thank your Grace.
Corn. You know not why we came to visit you— 120
Reg. Thus out of season, threading dark-eyed night.
Occasions, noble Gloucester, of some poise,
Wherein we must have use of your advice.
Our father he hath writ, so hath our sister,
Of differences, which I least thought it fit

99. *consort:* fellowship, company. 101. *put him on:* incited him to. 102. *expense:* spending. 109. *bewray:* expose. *practice:* scheme, treachery. 110. *apprehend:* arrest. 122. *Occasions:* reasons. *poise:* weight, importance; F_1 reads *prize.*

To answer from our home; the several messengers
From hence attend dispatch. Our good old friend,
Lay comforts to your bosom; and bestow
Your needful counsel to our business,
Which craves the instant use.

Glou. I serve you, madam. 130
Your Graces are right welcome. [*Exeunt.*

SCENE II. *Before* GLOUCESTER'S *castle.*

KENT *and* OSWALD, *meeting.*

Osw. Good dawning to thee, friend. Art of this house?

Kent. Ay.

Osw. Where may we set our horses?

Kent. I' the mire.

Osw. Prithee, if thou lovest me, tell me.

Kent. I love thee not.

Osw. Why, then, I care not for thee.

Kent. If I had thee in Lipsbury pinfold, I would make thee care for me. 10

Osw. Why dost thou use me thus? I know thee not.

Kent. Fellow, I know thee.

Osw. What dost thou know me for?

Kent. A knave; a rascal; an eater of broken meats; a base, proud, shallow, beggarly, three-suited, hundred-pound, filthy, worsted-stocking knave; a lily-livered, action-taking knave, a whoreson, glass-gazing, superserviceable, finical rogue; one-trunk-inheriting slave; one that wouldst be a bawd in way of

127. *attend dispatch:* await dismissal.

[ii] 9. *Lipsbury pinfold.* The reference is unexplained; a *pinfold* is a pound or enclosure. 16–17. *three-suited:* owning but three suits of clothes, the usual allowance to menials. 17. *hundred-pound:* poor. *worsted-stocking:* unable to buy silk stockings. 18. *lily-livered.* The liver was considered the seat of the emotions, and a bloodless or white liver was indicative of cowardice. *action-taking:* taking disputes to law rather than fighting them out. 19. *whoreson:* rascal. *glass-gazing:* wasting time gazing in a mirror. *superserviceable:* one who is over-officious or thinks he is above his work. 20. *one-trunk-inheriting:* either "possessing but one pair of trunk hose" or "owning but one coffer." *Inherit* also had its modern meaning in Shakespeare's day.

good service, and art nothing but the composition of a knave, beggar, coward, pandar, and the son and heir of a mongrel bitch; one whom I will beat into clamorous whining, if thou deniest the least syllable of thy addition.

Osw. Why, what a monstrous fellow art thou, thus to rail on one that is neither known of thee nor knows thee! 29

Kent. What a brazen-faced varlet art thou, to deny thou knowest me! Is it two days ago since I tripped up thy heels and beat thee before the king? Draw, you rogue; for, though it be night, yet the moon shines; I'll make a sop o' the moonshine of you. Draw, you whoreson cullionly barber-monger, draw. [*Drawing his sword.*

Osw. Away! I have nothing to do with thee.

Kent. Draw, you rascal. You come with letters against the king; and take Vanity the puppet's part against the royalty of her father. Draw, you rogue, or I'll so carbonado your shanks. Draw, you rascal; come your ways. 42

Osw. Help, ho! Murder! Help!

Kent. Strike, you slave; stand, rogue, stand; you neat slave, strike. [*Beating him.*

Osw. Help, ho! Murder! Murder!

Enter EDMUND, *with his rapier drawn*, CORNWALL, REGAN, GLOUCESTER, *and* Servants.

Edm. How now? What's the matter? Part!

Kent. With you, goodman boy, an you please. Come, I'll flesh ye. Come on, young master.

Glou. Weapons? Arms? What's the matter here? 51

Corn. Keep peace, upon your lives;
He dies that strikes again. What is the matter?

22. *composition:* combination. 26. *addition:* title. 35. *sop o' the moonshine:* unexplained; perhaps "a mess," with allusion to a 16th–17th-century dish called "eggs in moonshine." 36. *cullionly:* base. *barber-monger:* patron of barbers, fop. 39. *Vanity the puppet's:* an allusion to a common character in the old morality plays. 41. *carbonado:* slash or score for broiling. 42. *come your ways:* come on. 45. *neat:* (a) elegant, (b) ox-like. 47. *Part.* Omitted in Q1. 49. *flesh:* initiate you to bloodshed.

Reg. The messengers from our sister and the king?
Corn. What is your difference? Speak.
Osw. I am scarce in breath, my lord.
Kent. No marvel, you have so bestirred your valour. You cowardly rascal, nature disclaims in thee. A tailor made thee. 60
Corn. Thou art a strange fellow. A tailor make a man?
Kent. Ay, a tailor, sir. A stone-cutter or a painter could not have made him so ill, though he had been but two hours at the trade.
Corn. Speak yet, how grew your quarrel?
Osw. This ancient ruffian, sir, whose life I have spared at suit of his gray beard— 68
Kent. Thou whoreson zed! Thou unnecessary letter! My lord, if you will give me leave, I will tread this unbolted villain into mortar and daub the walls of a jakes with him. Spare my gray beard, you wagtail?
Corn. Peace, sirrah!
You beastly knave, know you no reverence?
Kent. Yes, sir; but anger hath a privilege.
Corn. Why art thou angry?
Kent. That such a slave as this should wear a sword,
Who wears no honesty. Such smiling rogues as these,
Like rats, oft bite the holy cords a-twain 80
Which are too intrinse t' unloose; smooth every passion
That in the natures of their lords rebel;
Bring oil to fire, snow to their colder moods;
Renege, affirm, and turn their halcyon beaks
With every gale and vary of their masters,
Knowing nought, like dogs, but following.
A plague upon your epileptic visage!

59. *disclaims in:* disowns. 65. *hours.* F_1 reads *years.* 69. *zed:* the letter Z. 71. *unbolted:* unsifted, coarse. 72. *jakes:* privy. 73. *wagtail:* a bird which habitually bobs its tail up and down. The allusion is to Oswald's obsequious bowing. 79. *honesty:* honor. 81. *intrinse:* tangled. 84. *halcyon:* the kingfisher. A dried specimen, hung up so as to swing freely, was thought to turn in the direction of the wind. 85. *vary:* variation. 87. *epileptic:* "distorted and pale like that of a man in a fit of epilepsy" (Wright).

Smoyle you my speeches, as I were a fool?
Goose, if I had you upon Sarum Plain,
I'ld drive ye cackling home to Camelot. 90

Corn. What, art thou mad, old fellow?

Glou. How fell you out? Say that.

Kent. No contraries hold more antipathy
Than I and such a knave.

Corn. Why dost thou call him knave? What's his offense?

Kent. His countenance likes me not.

Corn. No more, perchance, does mine, nor his, nor hers.

Kent. Sir, 'tis my occupation to be plain.
I have seen better faces in my time
Than stands on any shoulder that I see 100
Before me at this instant.

Corn. This is some fellow,
Who, having been praised for bluntness, doth affect
A saucy roughness, and constrains the garb
Quite from his nature. He cannot flatter, he,
An honest mind and plain, he must speak truth!
An they will take it, so; if not, he's plain.
These kind of knaves I know, which in this plainness
Harbour more craft, and more corrupter ends,
Than twenty silly ducking observants
That stretch their duties nicely. 110

Kent. Sir, in good sooth, in sincere verity,
Under the allowance of your great aspect,
Whose influence, like the wreath of radiant fire
On flickering Phœbus' front—

Corn. What mean'st by this?

88. *Smoyle:* sneer or mock at. Most modern editions accept the F_4 reading, *smile.* 89. *Sarum:* Salisbury. 90. *Camelot:* an unexplained allusion. Camelot was the legendary capital of King Arthur, usually identified as Winchester. 96. *likes:* pleases. 98. *occupation:* business. 103. *constrains:* assumes, put on by an effort. 109. *ducking:* bowing. *observants:* homagers, obsequious courtiers. 110. *nicely:* with the utmost exactness. 112. *aspect:* an allusion to the relative positions of the heavenly bodies and the influence attributed to them. 114. *front:* forehead, face.

Kent. To go out of my dialect, which you discommend so much. I know, sir, I am no flatterer. He that beguiled you in a plain accent was a plain knave, which, for my part, I will not be, though I should win your displeasure to entreat me to 't. 120

Corn. What was the offense you gave him?

Osw. I never gave him any.
It pleased the king his master very late
To strike at me, upon his misconstruction;
When he, conjunct, and flattering his displeasure,
Tripp'd me behind; being down, insulted, rail'd,
And put upon him such a deal of man,
That worthied him, got praises of the king
For him attempting who was self-subdued;
And, in the fleshment of this dread exploit, 130
Drew on me here again.

Kent. None of these rogues and cowards
But Ajax is their fool.

Corn. Fetch forth the stocks!
You stubborn ancient knave, you reverend braggart,
We'll teach you.

Kent. Sir, I am too old to learn.
Call not your stocks for me. I serve the king,
On whose employment I was sent to you;
You shall do small respect, show too bold malice
Against the grace and person of my master,
Stocking his messenger.

Corn. Fetch forth the stocks! As I have life and honour, 140
There shall he sit till noon.

Reg. Till noon? Till night, my lord; and all night too.

115. *dialect.* Q_1 reads *dialogue.* 119–20. *win . . . to 't:* win you in your displeasure to beg me to be a flatterer. 124. *misconstruction:* misunderstanding. 125. *conjunct.* F_1 reads *compact.* 128. *worthied:* made him worthy. 129. *attempting:* subduing. 130. *fleshment:* excitement resulting from this first success. *dread.* F_1 reads *dead.* 132. *Ajax:* one of the Greek heroes in the Trojan war, described by Shakespeare in *Troilus and Cressida* as a "beef-witted" braggart. Kent's exact meaning here is dependent upon whether he admired Ajax or not.

Kent. Why, madam, if I were your father's dog,
You should not use me so.
Reg. Sir, being his knave, I will.
[*Stocks are brought out.*

Corn. This is a fellow of the selfsame colour
Our sister speaks of. Come, bring away the stocks!
Glou. Let me beseech your Grace not to do so.
His fault is much, and the good king his master
Will check him for 't. Your purposed low correction
Is such as basest and contemned'st wretches 150
For pilferings and most common trespasses
Are punish'd with. The king must take it ill,
That he's so slightly valued in his messenger,
Should have him thus restrain'd.
Corn. I'll answer that.
Reg. My sister may receive it much more worse,
To have her gentleman abused, assaulted,
For following her affairs. Put in his legs.
[*Kent is put in the stocks.*
Come, my good lord, away.
[*Exeunt all but Gloucester and Kent.*
Glou. I am sorry for thee, friend; 'tis the duke's pleasure,
Whose disposition, all the world well knows, 160
Will not be rubb'd nor stopp'd. I'll entreat for thee.
Kent. Pray, do not, sir. I have watched and travell'd hard;
Some time I shall sleep out, the rest I'll whistle.
A good man's fortune may grow out at heels.
Give you good morrow!
Glou. The duke's to blame in this; 'twill be ill taken. [*Exit.*
Kent. Good king, that must approve the common saw,
Thou out of heaven's benediction comest
To the warm sun!
Approach, thou beacon to this under globe, 170

145. *colour:* kind. 148–52. *His . . . with.* Omitted in F_1. 148. *much:* great. 157. *For . . . legs.* Omitted in F_1. 161. *rubb'd:* hindered, obstructed (a term from bowling). 162. *watched:* not slept. 167. *approve:* prove the truth of. *saw:* saying.

That by thy comfortable beams I may
Peruse this letter! Nothing almost sees miracles
But misery. I know 'tis from Cordelia,
Who hath most fortunately been inform'd
Of my obscured course; and shall find time
From this enormous state, seeking to give
Losses their remedies. All weary and o'erwatch'd,
Take vantage, heavy eyes, not to behold
This shameful lodging. 179
Fortune, good night; smile once more; turn thy wheel! [*Sleeps.*

SCENE III. *A wood.*

Enter EDGAR.

Edg. I heard myself proclaim'd,
And by the happy hollow of a tree
Escaped the hunt. No port is free, no place
That guard and most unusual vigilance
Does not attend my taking. Whiles I may 'scape,
I will preserve myself; and am bethought
To take the basest and most poorest shape
That ever penury, in contempt of man,
Brought near to beast. My face I'll grime with filth,
Blanket my loins, elf all my hair in knots, 10
And with presented nakedness out-face
The winds and persecutions of the sky.
The country gives me proof and precedent
Of Bedlam beggars, who, with roaring voices,

171. *comfortable:* comforting. 172. *Nothing:* i.e., nothing so much as misery. 175. *obscured:* (a) lowly, (b) secret. *course:* line of action. 177. *o'erwatch'd:* too long sleepless. 178. *vantage:* opportunity. 180. S. D. *Sleeps.* On the Elizabethan stage, Kent, asleep in the stocks, remained in the background during Scene iii, ignored by player and audience, while the platform took on the locality of the wood in which Edgar was hiding.

[iii] 3. *port:* gate. 5. *attend:* wait for, look for. 6. *am bethought:* intend. 10. *elf:* twist, tangle. 11. *out-face:* defy. 14. *Bedlam beggars.* "The Abraham-man . . . swears he hath been in Bedlam, and will talk franticly of purpose; you see pins stuck in sundry

Strike in their numb'd and mortified bare arms
Pins, wooden pricks, nails, sprigs of rosemary;
And with this horrible object, from low farms,
Poor pelting villages, sheep-cotes, and mills,
Sometime with lunatic bans, sometime with prayers,
Enforce their charity. Poor Turlygod! Poor Tom! 20
That's something yet; Edgar I nothing am. [*Exit.*

SCENE IV. *Before* GLOUCESTER'S *castle.* KENT *in the stocks.*

Enter LEAR, Fool, *and* Gentleman.

Lear. 'Tis strange that they should so depart from home,
And not send back my messenger.

Gent. As I learn'd,
The night before there was no purpose in them
Of this remove.

Kent. Hail to thee, noble master!

Lear. Ha?
Makest thou this shame thy pastime?

Kent. No, my lord.

Fool. Ha, ha! He wears crewell garters. Horses are tied by the heads, dogs and bears by the neck, monkeys by the loins, and men by the legs. When a man's over-lusty at legs, then he wears wooden nether-stocks. 11

---

places of his naked flesh, especially in his arms, which pain he gladly puts himself to (being indeed no torment at all, his skin is either so dead with some foul disease, or so hardened with weather) only to make you believe he is out of his wits. He calls himself by the name of Poor Tom, and coming near any body, cries out, 'Poor Tom is a-cold.' Of these Abraham-men, some be exceeding merry, . . . others are dogged and so sullen both in look and speech, that spying but small company in a house, they boldly and bluntly enter, compelling the servants through fear to give them what they demand." (Dekker's *Bellman of London*, of which three editions appeared in 1608, the year *King Lear* was first printed.) 15. *mortified:* deadened, hardened. 17. *object:* appearance. *low farms.* Q_1 reads *low service.* 18. *pelting:* petty. 19. *bans:* curses. 20. *Turlygod:* apparently another name for a Bedlam beggar.

[iv] 7. *crewell:* (a) embroidered worsted, (b) cruel. 11. *nether-stocks:* stockings.

Lear. What's he that hath so much thy place mistook
To set thee here?
Kent. It is both he and she;
Your son and daughter.
Lear. No.
Kent. Yes.
Lear. No, I say.
Kent. I say, yea.
Lear. No, no, they would not.
Kent. Yes, they have. 20
Lear. By Jupiter, I swear, no.
Kent. By Juno, I swear, ay.
Lear. They durst not do't;
They could not, would not do't; 'tis worse than murder
To do upon respect such violent outrage.
Resolve me, with all modest haste, which way
Thou mightst deserve, or they impose, this usage,
Coming from us.
Kent. My lord, when at their home
I did commend your Highness' letters to them,
Ere I was risen from the place that show'd
My duty kneeling, came there a reeking post, 30
Stew'd in his haste, half breathless, panting forth
From Goneril, his mistress, salutations;
Deliver'd letters, spite of intermission,
Which presently they read. On those contents,
They summon'd up their meiny, straight took horse;
Commanded me to follow, and attend
The leisure of their answer; gave me cold looks,
And meeting here the other messenger,
Whose welcome, I perceived, had poison'd mine—

19–20. *Lear . . . have.* Omitted in F_1. 22. *Kent . . . ay.* Omitted in Q_1. 24. *upon respect:* upon consideration, deliberately; or upon one entitled to respect. 25. *Resolve:* inform. *modest haste:* as much haste as is consistent with telling the truth. 28. *commend:* deliver. 30. *reeking post:* sweating courier. 33. *intermission:* delay. 34. *presently:* immediately. 35. *meiny:* body of retainers. 36. *attend:* await.

Being the very fellow that of late 40
Display'd so saucily against your Highness—
Having more man than wit about me, drew.
He raised the house with loud and coward cries.
Your son and daughter found this trespass worth
The shame which here it suffers.

Fool. Winter's not gone yet, if the wild-geese fly that way.

Fathers that wear rags
Do make their children blind;
But fathers that bear bags 50
Shall see their children kind.
Fortune, that arrant whore,
Ne'er turns the key to the poor.

But, for all this, thou shalt have as many dolours for thy daughters as thou canst tell in a year.

Lear. O, how this mother swells up toward my heart!
Hysterica passio, down, thou climbing sorrow,
Thy element's below! Where is this daughter?

Kent. With the earl, sir, here within.

Lear. Follow me not; 59
Stay here. [*Exit.*

Gent. Made you no more offense but what you speak of?

Kent. None.
How chance the king comes with so small a train?

Fool. An thou hadst been set i' the stocks for that question, thou hadst well deserved it.

Kent. Why, fool? 67

Fool. We'll set thee to school to an ant, to teach thee there's no labouring i' the winter. All that follow their noses are led by their eyes but blind men, and there's not a nose among twenty but can smell him that's stinking. Let go thy hold when a great wheel runs down a hill, lest it break thy neck with following it; but the great one that goes up the hill, let him

46–55. *Fool . . . year.* Omitted in Q_1. 54. *dolours:* (a) sorrows, (b) dollars. 55. *tell:* count. 56. *mother:* a popular name for hysteria, for which the medical name was *hysterica passio*. 68–9. *We'll . . . winter.* See Proverbs 6 : 6–8. 75. *up the hill.* F_1 reads *upward.*

draw thee after. When a wise man gives thee better counsel, give me mine again. I would have none but knaves follow it, since a fool gives it.

That sir which serves and seeks for gain,
  And follows but for form, 80
Will pack when it begins to rain,
  And leave thee in the storm.
But I will tarry; the fool will stay,
  And let the wise man fly.
The knave turns fool that runs away;
  The fool no knave, perdy.

Kent. Where learned you this, fool?

Fool. Not i' the stocks, fool.

Re-enter LEAR, *with* GLOUCESTER.

Lear. Deny to speak with me? They are sick? They are weary?
They have travell'd all the night? Mere fetches, 90
The images of revolt and flying off.
Fetch me a better answer.

Glou. My dear lord,
You know the fiery quality of the duke;
How unremoveable and fix'd he is
In his own course.

Lear. Vengeance! Plague! Death! Confusion!
Fiery? What quality? Why, Gloucester, Gloucester,
I'ld speak with the Duke of Cornwall and his wife.

Glou. Well, my good lord, I have inform'd them so.

Lear. Inform'd them? Dost thou understand me, man? 100

Glou. Ay, my good lord.

Lear. The king would speak with Cornwall; the dear father
Would with his daughter speak, commands her service.
Are they inform'd of this? My breath and blood!

77. *counsel:* advice. 79. *sir:* man. 81. *pack:* take himself off. 86. *perdy:* an Anglicization of *par Dieu*. 89. *Deny:* refuse. 90. *fetches:* pretexts, excuses. 93. *quality:* character. 104. *Are . . . blood*. Omitted in Q1.

Fiery? The fiery duke? Tell the hot duke that—
No, but not yet. May be he is not well.
Infirmity doth still neglect all office
Whereto our health is bound; we are not ourselves
When nature, being oppress'd, commands the mind
To suffer with the body. I'll forbear; 110
And am fall'n out with my more headier will,
To take the indisposed and sickly fit
For the sound man. Death on my state! Wherefore
[*Looking on Kent.*
Should he sit here? This act persuades me
That this remotion of the duke and her
Is practice only. Give me my servant forth.
Go tell the duke and's wife I'ld speak with them—
Now, presently. Bid them come forth and hear me,
Or at their chamber-door I'll beat the drum
Till it cry sleep to death. 120

Glou. I would have all well betwixt you. [*Exit.*

Lear. O me, my heart, my rising heart! But, down!

Fool. Cry to it, nuncle, as the cockney did to the eels when she put 'em i' the paste alive; she knapped 'em o' the coxcombs with a stick and cried, "Down, wantons, down!" 'Twas her brother that, in pure kindness to his horse, buttered his hay.

Enter CORNWALL, REGAN, GLOUCESTER, *and* Servants.

Lear. Good morrow to you both.

Corn. Hail to your Grace!
[*Kent is set at liberty.*

Reg. I am glad to see your Highness. 130

Lear. Regan, I think you are; I know what reason
I have to think so. If thou shouldst not be glad,
I would divorce me from thy mother's tomb,
Sepulchring an adultress. [*To Kent.*] O, are you free?

107. *still:* ever, constantly. *office:* service, duty. 112. *To take:* for taking. 113. *sound:* healthy. 115. *remotion:* removal. 116. *practice:* trickery. 118. *presently:* at once. 120. *cry sleep to death:* put an end to sleep. 123. *cockney:* foolish cook.

Some other time for that. Beloved Regan,
Thy sister's naught. O Regan, she hath tied
Sharp-tooth'd unkindness, like a vulture, here.
[*Points to his heart.*
I can scarce speak to thee; thou'lt not believe
With how depraved a quality—O Regan!
Reg. I pray you, sir, take patience; I have hope 140
You less know how to value her desert
Than she to scant her duty.
Lear. Say, how is that?
Reg. I cannot think my sister in the least
Would fail her obligation. If, sir, perchance
She have restrain'd the riots of your followers,
'Tis on such ground, and to such wholesome end,
As clears her from all blame.
Lear. My curses on her!
Reg. O, sir, you are old;
Nature in you stands on the very verge
Of her confine. You should be ruled, and led 150
By some discretion that discerns your state
Better than you yourself. Therefore, I pray you,
That to our sister you do make return;
Say you have wrong'd her, sir.
Lear. Ask her forgiveness?
Do you but mark how this becomes the house?
"Dear daughter, I confess that I am old; [*Kneeling.*
Age is unnecessary. On my knees I beg
That you'll vouchsafe me raiment, bed, and food."
Reg. Good sir, no more; these are unsightly tricks.
Return you to my sister.
Lear. [*Rising*] Never, Regan. 160
She hath abated me of half my train;

136. *naught:* worthless. 141–2. *You . . . duty:* perhaps, "you are more likely to undervalue her worth than she is to fall short of her duty." The literal meaning hardly expresses Regan's intent. 142–7. *Say . . . blame.* Omitted in Q1. 146. *wholesome:* sensible. 161. *abated:* deprived.

Look'd black upon me; struck me with her tongue,
Most serpent-like, upon the very heart.
All the stored vengeances of heaven fall
On her ingrateful top! Strike her young bones,
You taking airs, with lameness!

Corn. Fie, sir, fie!

Lear. You nimble lightnings, dart your blinding flames
Into her scornful eyes! Infect her beauty,
You fen-suck'd fogs, drawn by the powerful sun,
To fall and blast her pride! 170

Reg. O the blest gods! So will you wish on me,
When the rash mood is on.

Lear. No, Regan, thou shalt never have my curse;
Thy tender-hefted nature shall not give
Thee o'er to harshness. Her eyes are fierce; but thine
Do comfort and not burn. 'Tis not in thee
To grudge my pleasures, to cut off my train,
To bandy hasty words, to scant my sizes,
And in conclusion to oppose the bolt
Against my coming in. Thou better know'st 180
The offices of nature, bond of childhood,
Effects of courtesy, dues of gratitude;
Thy half o' the kingdom hast thou not forgot,
Wherein I thee endow'd.

Reg. Good sir, to the purpose.

Lear. Who put my man i' the stocks? [*A tucket sounds.*

Corn. What trumpet's that?

Reg. I know't, my sister's; this approves her letter,
That she would soon be here.

Enter OSWALD.

Is your lady come?

Lear. This is a slave, whose easy-borrow'd pride

165. *top:* head. 166. *taking:* blasting, blighting. 174. *tender-hefted:* "set in a delicate bodily frame" (Wright); hence, gentle. *Heft* means "handle." 178. *scant my sizes:* reduce my allowances. 182. *Effects:* outward signs. 186. *approves:* confirms.

Dwells in the fickle grace of her he follows.
Out, varlet, from my sight!
Corn. What means your Grace? 190

Enter GONERIL.

Lear. Who stock'd my servant? Regan, I have good hope
Thou didst not know on't. Who comes here? O heavens,
If you do love old men, if your sweet sway
Allow obedience, if yourselves are old,
Make it your cause; send down, and take my part!
[*To Goneril.*] Art not ashamed to look upon this beard?
O Regan, wilt thou take her by the hand?
Gon. Why not by the hand, sir? How have I offended?
All's not offense that indiscretion finds,
And dotage terms so.
Lear. O sides, you are too tough; 200
Will you yet hold? How came my man i' the stocks?
Corn. I set him there, sir; but his own disorders
Deserved much less advancement.
Lear. You? Did you?
Reg. I pray you, father, being weak, seem so.
If, till the expiration of your month,
You will return and sojourn with my sister,
Dismissing half your train, come then to me.
I am now from home, and out of that provision
Which shall be needful for your entertainment.
Lear. Return to her? And fifty men dismiss'd? 210
No, rather I abjure all roofs, and choose
To wage against the enmity o' the air;
To be a comrade with the wolf and owl—
Necessity's sharp pinch! Return with her?
Why, the hot-blooded France, that dowerless took
Our youngest born, I could as well be brought
To knee his throne, and, squire-like, pension beg
To keep base life afoot. Return with her?

189. *fickle.* F_1 reads *sickly.* 194. *Allow:* sanction.

Persuade me rather to be slave and sumpter
To this detested groom. [*Pointing at Oswald.*

Gon. At your choice, sir. 220

Lear. I prithee, daughter, do not make me mad.
I will not trouble thee, my child; farewell.
We'll no more meet, no more see one another.
But yet thou art my flesh, my blood, my daughter;
Or rather a disease that's in my flesh,
Which I must needs call mine. Thou art a boil,
A plague-sore, an embossed carbuncle,
In my corrupted blood. But I'll not chide thee.
Let shame come when it will, I do not call it.
I do not bid the thunder-bearer shoot, 230
Nor tell tales of thee to high-judging Jove.
Mend when thou canst; be better at thy leisure.
I can be patient; I can stay with Regan,
I and my hundred knights.

Reg. Not altogether so.
I look'd not for you yet, nor am provided
For your fit welcome. Give ear, sir, to my sister;
For those that mingle reason with your passion
Must be content to think you old, and so—
But she knows what she does.

Lear. Is this well spoken?

Reg. I dare avouch it, sir. What, fifty followers? 240
Is it not well? What should you need of more?
Yea, or so many, sith that both charge and danger
Speak 'gainst so great a number? How, in one house,
Should many people, under two commands,
Hold amity? 'Tis hard, almost impossible.

Gon. Why might not you, my lord, receive attendance
From those that she calls servants or from mine?

Reg. Why not, my lord? If then they chanced to slack you,
We could control them. If you will come to me—

219. *sumpter:* pack-horse, drudge. 227. *embossed:* swollen, tumid. 230. *thunder-bearer:* Jupiter. 242. *charge:* expense. 248. *slack:* neglect.

For now I spy a danger—I entreat you 250
To bring but five and twenty; to no more
Will I give place or notice.

Lear. I gave you all.

Reg. And in good time you gave it.

Lear. Made you my guardians, my depositaries;
But kept a reservation to be follow'd
With such a number. What, must I come to you
With five and twenty? Regan, said you so?

Reg. And speak't again, my lord; no more with me.

Lear. Those wicked creatures yet do look well-favour'd
When others are more wicked; not being the worst 260
Stands in some rank of praise. [*To Goneril.*] I'll go with thee;
Thy fifty yet doth double five-and-twenty,
And thou art twice her love.

Gon. Hear me, my lord;
What need you five-and-twenty, ten, or five,
To follow in a house where twice so many
Have a command to tend you?

Reg. What need one?

Lear. O, reason not the need. Our basest beggars
Are in the poorest thing superfluous.
Allow not nature more than nature needs,
Man's life's as cheap as beast's. Thou art a lady; 270
If only to go warm were gorgeous,
Why, nature needs not what thou gorgeous wear'st,
Which scarcely keeps thee warm. But, for true need—
You heavens, give me that patience, patience I need!
You see me here, you gods, a poor old man,
As full of grief as age; wretched in both!
If it be you that stir these daughters' hearts
Against their father, fool me not so much
To bear it tamely; touch me with noble anger,
And let not women's weapons, water-drops, 280

267 ff. The very verse and the broken sentences here express the incoherence of Lear's rage. 268. *superfluous:* i.e., have more than enough.

Stain my man's cheeks! No, you unnatural hags,
I will have such revenges on you both,
That all the world shall—I will do such things—
What they are, yet I know not; but they shall be
The terrors of the earth. You think I'll weep;
No, I'll not weep. [*Storm and tempest.*
I have full cause of weeping, but this heart
Shall break into a hundred thousand flaws
Or ere I'll weep. O fool, I shall go mad!
[*Exeunt Lear, Gloucester, Kent, and Fool.*

Corn. Let us withdraw; 'twill be a storm. 290

Reg. This house is little; the old man and his people
Cannot be well bestow'd.

Gon. 'Tis his own blame; hath put himself from rest,
And must needs taste his folly.

Reg. For his particular, I'll receive him gladly,
But not one follower.

Gon. So am I purposed.
Where is my lord of Gloucester?

Re-enter GLOUCESTER.

Corn. Follow'd the old man forth; he is return'd.

Glou. The king is in high rage.

Corn. Whither is he going?

Glou. He calls to horse; but will I know not whither. 300

Corn. 'Tis best to give him way; he leads himself.

Gon. My lord, entreat him by no means to stay.

Glou. Alack, the night comes on, and the bleak winds
Do sorely ruffle; for many miles about
There's scarce a bush.

Reg. O, sir, to wilful men,
The injuries that they themselves procure
Must be their schoolmasters. Shut up your doors;
He is attended with a desperate train,

288. *flaws:* bits; literally, cracks. 289. *Or ere:* before. 295. *particular:* personal interest or concern. 304. *ruffle:* bluster. Q_1 reads *russel.*

And what they may incense him to, being apt
To have his ear abused, wisdom bids fear. 310
Corn. Shut up your doors, my lord; 'tis a wild night;
My Regan counsels well. Come out o' the storm. [*Exeunt.*

ACT III

SCENE I. *A heath near* GLOUCESTER'S *castle.*

Storm still. Enter KENT *and a* Gentleman, *meeting.*

Kent. Who's there, besides foul weather?
Gent. One minded like the weather, most unquietly.
Kent. I know you. Where's the king?
Gent. Contending with the fretful element;
Bids the wind blow the earth into the sea,
Or swell the curled waters 'bove the main,
That things might change or cease; tears his white hair,
Which the impetuous blasts, with eyeless rage,
Catch in their fury, and make nothing of;
Strives in his little world of man to out-scorn 10
The to-and-fro-conflicting wind and rain.
This night, wherein the cub-drawn bear would couch,
The lion and the belly-pinched wolf
Keep their fur dry, unbonneted he runs,
And bids what will take all.
Kent. But who is with him?
Gent. None but the fool, who labours to out-jest
His heart-struck injuries.
Kent. Sir, I do know you;

309. *incense:* provoke. *apt:* prepared, willing. 310. *abused:* imposed upon. 312. *counsels:* advises.

[III. i] 6. *main:* mainland. 7–15. *tears . . . all.* Omitted in F_1. 10. *little world of man:* a reference to the idea of the astrologers that Man represented a microcosm which contained in miniature all of the elements of the macrocosm, or universe. 12. *cub-drawn bear:* a bear whose dugs were drawn dry by its young. Even hunger and the support of its young could not induce a bear to leave its shelter on such a night.

And dare, upon the warrant of my note,
Commend a dear thing to you. There is division
(Although as yet the face of it be cover'd 20
With mutual cunning) 'twixt Albany and Cornwall;
Who have—as who have not, that their great stars
Throned and set high?—servants, who seem no less,
Which are to France the spies and speculations
Intelligent of our state. What hath been seen,
Either in snuffs and packings of the dukes,
Or the hard rein which both of them have borne
Against the old kind king; or something deeper,
Whereof perchance these are but furnishings;
But, true it is, from France there comes a power 30
Into this scatter'd kingdom, who already,
Wise in our negligence, have secret feet
In some of our best ports, and are at point
To show their open banner. Now to you.
If on my credit you dare build so far
To make your speed to Dover, you shall find
Some that will thank you, making just report
Of how unnatural and bemadding sorrow
The king hath cause to plain.
I am a gentleman of blood and breeding, 40
And from some knowledge and assurance offer
This office to you.

Gent. I will talk further with you.

Kent. No, do not.
For confirmation that I am much more
Than my out-wall, open this purse, and take
What it contains. If you shall see Cordelia—

18. *warrant . . . note:* strength of my information. 19. *dear:* important. *division:* dissension. 22–9. *Who . . . furnishings.* Omitted in Q1. 24. *speculations:* scouts. 25. *Intelligent:* bearing information. 26. *snuffs:* quarrels. *packings:* plottings. 29. *furnishings:* outward signs. 30–42. *But . . . you.* Omitted in F1. 30. *power:* army. 31. *scatter'd:* unsettled. 33. *at point:* ready. 35. *credit:* report. 39. *plain:* complain. 43. *I . . . you.* This is a polite evasion, but Kent will not be put off. 45. *out-wall:* exterior.

As fear not but you shall—show her this ring;
And she will tell you who your fellow is
That yet you do not know. Fie on this storm!
I will go seek the king.

Gent. Give me your hand; have you no more to say? 50

Kent. Few words, but, to effect, more than all yet;
That, when we have found the king—in which your pain
That way, I'll this—he that first lights on him
Holla the other. [*Exeunt severally.*

SCENE II. *Another part of the heath. Storm still.*

Enter LEAR *and* Fool.

Lear. Blow, winds, and crack your cheeks! Rage! Blow!
You cataracts and hurricanoes, spout
Till you have drench'd our steeples, drown'd the cocks!
You sulphurous and thought-executing fires,
Vaunt-couriers to oak-cleaving thunderbolts,
Singe my white head! And thou, all-shaking thunder,
Smite flat the thick rotundity o' the world!
Crack nature's moulds, all germens spill at once,
That make ingrateful man! 9

Fool. O nuncle, court holy-water in a dry house is better than this rain-water out o' door. Good nuncle, in, and ask thy daughters' blessing; here's a night pities neither wise man nor fool.

Lear. Rumble thy bellyful! Spit, fire! Spout, rain!
Nor rain, wind, thunder, fire, are my daughters.
I tax not you, you elements, with unkindness;
I never gave you kingdom, call'd you children,
You owe me no subscription. Then let fall
Your horrible pleasure. Here I stand, your slave,
A poor, infirm, weak, and despised old man. 20

[ii] 2. *hurricanoes:* waterspouts. 3. *cocks:* weathercocks, vanes. 4. *thought-executing:* doing execution with the rapidity of thought. 8. *germens:* germs, seeds. *spill:* destroy. 10. *court holy-water:* flattery. 16. *tax:* censure, blame. 18. *subscription:* submission.

But yet I call you servile ministers,
That have with two pernicious daughters join'd
Your high engender'd battles 'gainst a head
So old and white as this. O! O! 'Tis foul!

Fool. He that has a house to put 's head in has a good head-piece.

The cod-piece that will house
Before the head has any,
The head and he shall louse;
So beggars marry many. 30
The man that makes his toe
What he his heart should make
Shall of a corn cry woe,
And turn his sleep to wake.

For there was never yet fair woman but she made mouths in a glass.

Lear. No, I will be the pattern of all patience;
I will say nothing.

Enter KENT.

Kent. Who's there?

Fool. Marry, here's grace and a cod-piece; that's a wise man and a fool. 41

Kent. Alas, sir, sit you here? Things that love night
Love not such nights as these; the wrathful skies
Gallow the very wanderers of the dark,
And make them keep their caves. Since I was man,
Such sheets of fire, such bursts of horrid thunder,
Such groans of roaring wind and rain, I never
Remember to have heard. Man's nature cannot carry
The affliction nor the fear.

Lear. Let the great gods,
That keep this dreadful pudder o'er our heads, 50
Find out their enemies now. Tremble, thou wretch,
That hast within thee undivulged crimes,

23. *battles:* battalions. 44. *Gallow:* frighten. 46. *horrid:* horrible. 50. *pudder:* pother, turmoil.

Unwhipp'd of justice. Hide thee, thou bloody hand;
Thou perjured, and thou simular man of virtue
That art incestuous. Caitiff, to pieces shake
That under covert and convenient seeming
Hast practiced on man's life. Close pent-up guilts,
Rive your concealing continents, and cry
These dreadful summoners grace. I am a man
More sinn'd against than sinning.

Kent. Alack, bare-headed? 60
Gracious my lord, hard by here is a hovel;
Some friendship will it lend you 'gainst the tempest.
Repose you there; while I to this hard house—
More harder than the stones whereof 'tis raised;
Which even but now, demanding after you,
Denied me to come in—return, and force
Their scanted courtesy.

Lear. My wits begin to turn.
Come on, my boy. How dost, my boy? Art cold?
I am cold myself. Where is this straw, my fellow?
The art of our necessities is strange, 70
That can make vile things precious. Come, your hovel.
Poor fool and knave, I have one part in my heart
That's sorry yet for thee.

Fool. [*Singing*] He that has and a little tiny wit—
With hey, ho, the wind and the rain—
Must make content with his fortunes fit,
For the rain it raineth every day.

Lear. True, my good boy. Come, bring us to this hovel.
[*Exeunt Lear and Kent.*

Fool. This is a brave night to cool a courtesan.
I'll speak a prophecy ere I go: 80

54. *simular:* counterfeit. 55. *Caitiff:* wretch. 56. *convenient seeming:* expedient false appearance, hypocrisy. 57. *practiced on:* plotted against. 58. *continents:* boundaries. *cry:* beg for. 66. *Denied:* refused to permit. 74 ff. Feste in *Twelfth Night* also sings a song with this refrain. 79–96. *Fool . . . time.* Omitted in Q_1 and, hence, thought by many to be an interpolation. 79. *brave:* good, excellent.

When priests are more in word than matter;
When brewers mar their malt with water;
When nobles are their tailors' tutors,
No heretics burn'd, but wenches' suitors;
When every case in law is right,
No squire in debt, nor no poor knight;
When slanders do not live in tongues,
Nor cutpurses come not to throngs;
When usurers tell their gold i' the field,
And bawds and whores do churches build; 90
Then shall the realm of Albion
Come to great confusion.
Then comes the time, who lives to see 't,
That going shall be used with feet.
This prophecy Merlin shall make, for I live before his time.
[*Exit.*

SCENE III. GLOUCESTER'S *castle.*

Enter GLOUCESTER *and* EDMUND.

Glou. Alack, alack, Edmund, I like not this unnatural dealing. When I desired their leave that I might pity him, they took from me the use of mine own house; charged me, on pain of their perpetual displeasure, neither to speak of him, entreat for him, nor any way sustain him.

Edm. Most savage and unnatural! 7

Glou. Go to; say you nothing. There's division betwixt the dukes, and a worse matter than that. I have received a letter this night; 'tis dangerous to be spoken; I have locked the letter in my closet. These injuries the king now bears will be revenged home; there's part of a power already footed. We must incline to the king. I will seek him, and privily relieve him. Go you and maintain talk with the duke, that my charity be not of him

88. *cutpurses:* pickpockets. 89. *tell:* count. *i' the field:* in the open. 95. *Merlin:* a magician of Arthurian romance.

[iii] 9. *division:* dissension. 13. *home:* thoroughly. 14. *power:* army. *footed:* on foot.

perceived. If he ask for me, I am ill and gone to bed. Though I die for it—as no less is threatened me—the king my old master must be relieved. There is some strange thing toward, Edmund; pray you, be careful. [*Exit.*

Edm. This courtesy, forbid thee, shall the duke 22
Instantly know; and of that letter too.
This seems a fair deserving, and must draw me
That which my father loses; no less than all.
The younger rises when the old doth fall. [*Exit.*

SCENE IV. *The heath. Before a hovel.*

Enter LEAR, KENT, *and* Fool.

Kent. Here is the place, my lord; good my lord, enter.
The tyranny of the open night's too rough
For nature to endure. [*Storm still.*

Lear. Let me alone.

Kent. Good my lord, enter here.

Lear. Wilt break my heart?

Kent. I had rather break mine own. Good my lord, enter.

Lear. Thou think'st 'tis much that this contentious storm
Invades us to the skin. So 'tis to thee;
But where the greater malady is fix'd,
The lesser is scarce felt. Thou'ldst shun a bear;
But if thy flight lay toward the raging sea, 10
Thou'ldst meet the bear i' the mouth. When the mind's free,
The body's delicate. The tempest in my mind
Doth from my senses take all feeling else
Save what beats there. Filial ingratitude!
Is it not as this mouth should tear this hand
For lifting food to't? But I will punish home.
No, I will weep no more. In such a night
To shut me out? Pour on; I will endure.
In such a night as this? O Regan, Goneril!

21. *toward:* about to take place. 22. *forbid thee:* which you are forbidden to do.

[iv] 17–18. *In . . . endure.* Omitted in Q_1.

Your old kind father, whose frank heart gave all— 20
O, that way madness lies; let me shun that;
No more of that.

Kent. Good my lord, enter here.

Lear. Prithee, go in thyself; seek thine own ease.
This tempest will not give me leave to ponder
On things would hurt me more. But I'll go in.
[*To the Fool.*] In, boy; go first. You houseless poverty—
Nay, get thee in. I'll pray, and then I'll sleep. [*Fool goes in.*
Poor naked wretches, wheresoe'er you are,
That bide the pelting of this pitiless storm,
How shall your houseless heads, and unfed sides, 30
Your loop'd and window'd raggedness, defend you
From seasons such as these? O, I have ta'en
Too little care of this! Take physic, Pomp;
Expose thyself to feel what wretches feel,
That thou mayst shake the superflux to them,
And show the heavens more just.

Edg. [*Within*] Fathom and half, fathom and half! Poor Tom!
[*The Fool runs out from the hovel.*

Fool. Come not in here, nuncle, here's a spirit. Help me, help me! 40

Kent. Give me thy hand. Who's there?

Fool. A spirit, a spirit; he says his name's poor Tom.

Kent. What art thou that dost grumble there i' the straw? Come forth.

Edgar, *disguised as a madman, comes from the hovel.*

Edg. Away! The foul fiend follows me!
Through the sharp hawthorn blows the cold wind.
Hum! Go to thy cold bed, and warm thee.

Lear. Hast thou given all to thy two daughters?
And art thou come to this? 50

Edg. Who gives anything to poor Tom? Whom the foul

20. *frank:* liberal. 26–7. *In . . . sleep.* Omitted in Q1. 29. *bide:* endure. 31. *loop'd:* full of holes. 33. *physic:* medicine. 37–8. *Edg. . . . Tom.* Omitted in Q1. 38. *Poor Tom.* See note on II, iii, 14.

fiend hath led through fire and through flame, through ford and whirlpool, o'er bog and quagmire; that hath laid knives under his pillow, and halters in his pew; set ratsbane by his porridge; made him proud of heart, to ride on a bay trotting-horse over four-inched bridges, to course his own shadow for a traitor. Bless thy five wits! Tom's a-cold—O, do de, do de, do de. Bless thee from whirlwinds, star-blasting, and taking! Do poor Tom some charity, whom the foul fiend vexes. There could I have him now—and there—and there again, and there.

[*Storm still.*

Lear. What, have his daughters brought him to this pass? Couldst thou save nothing? Didst thou give them all?

Fool. Nay, he reserved a blanket, else we had been all shamed.

Lear. Now, all the plagues that in the pendulous air
Hang fated o'er men's faults light on thy daughters! 70

Kent. He hath no daughters, sir.

Lear. Death, traitor! Nothing could have subdued nature
To such a lowness but his unkind daughters.
Is it the fashion, that discarded fathers
Should have thus little mercy on their flesh?
Judicious punishment! 'Twas this flesh begot
Those pelican daughters.

Edg. Pillicock sat on Pillicock-hill,
Halloo, halloo, loo, loo! 79

Fool. This cold night will turn us all to fools and madmen.

Edg. Take heed o' the foul fiend; obey thy parents; keep thy word justly; swear not; commit not with man's sworn spouse; set not thy sweet heart on proud array. Tom's a-cold.

Lear. What hast thou been? 86

58. *course:* pursue. 59. *five wits:* not the five senses, but common wit, imagination, fantasy, estimation, and memory. 61. *taking:* malignant influence. 62. *vexes:* torments. 69. *pendulous:* hanging overhead. 73. *unkind:* unnatural. 77. *pelican:* an allusion to the popular belief that the pelican fed its young on its own heart's blood. 78. *Pillicock:* a quotation from an old song, suggested by *pelican.*

Edg. A serving-man, proud in heart and mind; that curled my hair; wore gloves in my cap; served the lust of my mistress' heart, and did the act of darkness with her. Swore as many oaths as I spake words, and broke them in the sweet face of heaven. One that slept in the contriving of lust, and waked to do it. Wine loved I deeply, dice dearly; and in woman out-paramoured the Turk. False of heart, light of ear, bloody of hand; hog in sloth, fox in stealth, wolf in greediness, dog in madness, lion in prey. Let not the creaking of shoes, nor the rustling of silks, betray thy poor heart to woman. Keep thy foot out of brothels, thy hand out of plackets, thy pen from lenders' books, and defy the foul fiend. 101

Still through the hawthorn blows the cold wind;
Says suum, mun, ha, no, nonny.

Dolphin my boy, my boy, sessa; let him trot by. [*Storm still.*

Lear. Why, thou wert better in thy grave than to answer with thy uncovered body this extremity of the skies. Is man no more than this? Consider him well. Thou owest the worm no silk, the beast no hide, the sheep no wool, the cat no perfume. Ha! Here's three on's are sophisticated! Thou art the thing itself; unaccommodated man is no more but such a poor, bare, forked animal as thou art. Off, off, you lendings! Come, unbutton here. [*Tearing off his clothes.*

Fool. Prithee, nuncle, be contented; 'tis a naughty night to swim in. Now a little fire in a wild field were like an old lecher's heart; a small spark, all the rest on's body cold. Look, here comes a walking fire. 119

Enter GLOUCESTER, *with a torch.*

Edg. This is the foul fiend Flibbertigibbet; he begins at curfew, and walks till the first cock; he gives the web and the pin,

88. *wore . . . cap:* i.e., as favors from his lady. 104. *sessa:* an interjection of doubtful import. 106. *extremity:* severity. 109. *cat:* i.e., the civet cat. 111. *sophisticated:* adulterated (Onions). 112. *unaccommodated:* unfurnished with necessaries. 115. *contented:* calm. 116. *naughty:* bad. 120. *Flibbertigibbet.* The name of this fiend and others mentioned by Edgar were taken from Harsnett's *Declaration of Egregious Popish Impostures* (1603). 122. *web and the pin:* cataract.

squints the eye, and makes the hare-lip; mildews the white wheat, and hurts the poor creature of earth.

Swithold footed thrice the old;
He met the night-mare, and her nine-fold;
Bid her alight,
And her troth plight,
And, aroint thee, witch, aroint thee!

Kent. How fares your Grace? 130

Lear. What's he?

Kent. Who's there? What is't you seek?

Glou. What are you there? Your names?

Edg. Poor Tom, that eats the swimming frog, the toad, the tadpole, the wall-newt and the water-; that in the fury of his heart, when the foul fiend rages, eats cow-dung for sallets, swallows the old rat and the ditch-dog, drinks the green mantle of the standing pool; who is whipped from tithing to tithing, and stock-punished, and imprisoned; who hath had three suits to his back, six shirts to his body, horse to ride, and weapon to wear;

But mice and rats, and such small deer, 144
Have been Tom's food for seven long year.

Beware my follower. Peace, Smulkin; peace, thou fiend!

Glou. What, hath your Grace no better company?

Edg. The prince of darkness is a gentleman.
Modo he's call'd, and Mahu.

Glou. Our flesh and blood is grown so vile, my lord, 150
That it doth hate what gets it.

Edg. Poor Tom's a-cold.

Glou. Go in with me. My duty cannot suffer
To obey in all your daughters' hard commands;
Though their injunction be to bar my doors,
And let this tyrannous night take hold upon you,
Yet have I ventured to come seek you out,
And bring you where both fire and food is ready.

125. *Swithold:* St. Vitalis, said to have been invoked in cases of nightmare. *old:* wold. 129. *aroint thee:* be gone. 135. *wall-newt:* lizard. 137. *sallets:* salads. 140. *tithing:* district. 144. *deer:* animals. 149. *Modo . . . Mahu.* Cf. IV, i, 63. 151. *gets:* begets. 153. *suffer:* permit me.

Lear. First let me talk with this philosopher.
What is the cause of thunder? 160
Kent. Good my lord, take his offer; go into the house.
Lear. I'll talk a word with this same learned Theban.
What is your study?
Edg. How to prevent the fiend, and to kill vermin.
Lear. Let me ask you one word in private.
Kent. Importune him once more to go, my lord;
His wits begin to unsettle.
Glou. Canst thou blame him? [*Storm still.*
His daughters seek his death; ah, that good Kent!
He said it would be thus, poor banish'd man!
Thou say'st the king grows mad; I'll tell thee, friend, 170
I am almost mad myself. I had a son,
Now outlaw'd from my blood; he sought my life,
But lately, very late. I loved him, friend,
No father his son dearer. True to tell thee,
The grief hath crazed my wits. What a night's this!
I do beseech your Grace—
Lear. O, cry you mercy, sir.
Noble philosopher, your company.
Edg. Tom's a-cold.
Glou. In, fellow, there, into the hovel; keep thee warm.
Lear. Come, let's in all.
Kent. This way, my lord.
Lear. With him;
I will keep still with my philosopher. 181
Kent. Good my lord, soothe him; let him take the fellow.
Glou. Take him you on.
Kent. Sirrah, come on; go along with us.
Lear. Come, good Athenian.
Glou. No words, no words; hush.

164. *prevent:* forestall. 172. *outlaw'd . . . blood.* One of the legal consequences of outlawry is corruption of blood, i.e., inability to inherit or bequeath. 175. *crazed:* cracked. 176. *cry you mercy:* I beg your pardon. 181. *still:* ever. 182. *soothe:* humor.

Edg. Childe Rowland to the dark tower came,
His word was still, "Fie, foh, and fum,
I smell the blood of a British man." [*Exeunt.*

SCENE V. GLOUCESTER'S *castle.*

Enter CORNWALL *and* EDMUND.

Corn. I will have my revenge ere I depart his house.

Edm. How, my lord, I may be censured, that nature thus gives way to loyalty, something fears me to think of.

Corn. I now perceive, it was not altogether your brother's evil disposition made him seek his death; but a provoking merit set a-work by a reprovable badness in himself. 9

Edm. How malicious is my fortune, that I must repent to be just! This is the letter he spoke of, which approves him an intelligent party to the advantages of France. O heavens, that this treason were not, or not I the detector!

Corn. Go with me to the duchess.

Edm. If the matter of this paper be certain, you have mighty business in hand.

Corn. True or false, it hath made thee earl of Gloucester. Seek out where thy father is, that he may be ready for our apprehension. 20

Edm. [*Aside*] If I find him comforting the king, it will stuff his suspicion more fully. [*To Cornwall.*] I will persevere in my course of loyalty, though the conflict be sore between that and my blood.

Corn. I will lay trust upon thee; and thou shalt find a dearer father in my love. [*Exeunt.*

187. *Childe:* knight, Sir. The passage is from an old ballad.

[v] 1. *depart:* leave. 3. *censured:* judged, criticized. 4. *something:* somewhat. *fears:* frightens. 12. *approves:* proves. *intelligent:* having information. 13. *advantages:* interests. 20. *apprehension:* arrest. 21. *comforting:* ministering relief to. 24. *blood:* natural temperament.

SCENE VI. *A room in a farmhouse adjoining* GLOUCESTER'S *castle.*

Enter GLOUCESTER, LEAR, KENT, Fool, *and* EDGAR.

Glou. Here is better than the open air; take it thankfully. I will piece out the comfort with what addition I can. I will not be long from you.

Kent. All the power of his wits have given way to his impatience. The gods reward your kindness! [*Exit Gloucester.*

Edg. Frateretto calls me, and tells me Nero is an angler in the Lake of Darkness. [*To the Fool.*] Pray, innocent, and beware the foul fiend.

Fool. Prithee, nuncle, tell me whether a madman be a gentleman or a yeoman? 11

Lear. A king, a king!

Fool. No, he's a yeoman that has a gentleman to his son; for he's a mad yeoman that sees his son a gentleman before him.

Lear. To have a thousand with red burning spits
Come hissing in upon 'em—

Edg. The foul fiend bites my back.

Fool. He's mad that trusts in the tameness of a wolf, a horse's health, a boy's love, or a whore's oath. 21

Lear. It shall be done; I will arraign them straight.
[*To Edgar.*] Come, sit thou here, most learned justicer;
[*To the Fool.*] Thou, sapient sir, sit here. Now, you she foxes—
[*Turning to two joint-stools.*

Edg. Look, where he stands and glares!
Wantest thou eyes at trial, madam?
Come o'er the bourn, Bessy, to me—

Fool. Her boat hath a leak,
And she must not speak
Why she dares not come over to thee. 30

[vi] 8. *innocent:* simpleton. 11. *yeoman:* man of the commonalty, a small freeholder. 13–15. *Fool . . . him.* Omitted in Q_1. 14. *to:* for, as. 16. *spits:* slender, pointed rods used for roasting meats. 18–59. *Edg. . . . 'scape.* Omitted in F_1. 22. *straight:* straightway. 27 ff. *Come . . . thee:* from an old ballad by William Birche. 27. *bourn:* brook.

Edg. The foul fiend haunts poor Tom in the voice of a nightingale. Hoppedance cries in Tom's belly for two white herring. Croak not, black angel; I have no food for thee.

Kent. How do you, sir? Stand you not so amazed.
Will you lie down and rest upon the cushions?

Lear. I'll see their trial first. Bring in their evidence.
[*To Edgar.*] Thou robed man of justice, take thy place;
[*To the Fool.*] And thou, his yoke-fellow of equity,
Bench by his side. [*To Kent.*] You are o' the commission, 40
Sit you too.

Edg. Let us deal justly.

Sleepest or wakest thou, jolly shepherd?
Thy sheep be in the corn;
And for one blast of thy minikin mouth,
Thy sheep shall take no harm.

Purr, the cat is gray.

Lear. Arraign her first; 'tis Goneril. I here take my oath before this honourable assembly, she kicked the poor king her father. 50

Fool. Come hither, mistress. Is your name Goneril?

Lear. She cannot deny it.

Fool. Cry you mercy, I took you for a joint-stool.

Lear. And here's another, whose warp'd looks proclaim
What store her heart is made on. Stop her there!
Arms, arms, sword, fire! Corruption in the place!
False justicer, why hast thou let her 'scape?

Edg. Bless thy five wits! 60

Kent. O pity! Sir, where is the patience now,
That you so oft have boasted to retain?

Edg. [*Aside*] My tears begin to take his part so much,
They'll mar my counterfeiting.

Lear. The little dogs and all,
Tray, Blanch, and Sweetheart; see, they bark at me.

Edg. Tom will throw his head at them.
Avaunt, you curs!

33. *white herring:* fresh herring. 45. *minikin:* shrill. 60. *five wits.* See note to III, iv, 59. 64. *counterfeiting:* dissembling, disguise.

Be thy mouth or black or white,
Tooth that poisons if it bite; 70
Mastiff, greyhound, mongrel grim,
Hound or spaniel, brach or lym,
Or bobtail tike, or trundle-tail,
Tom will make them weep and wail.
For, with throwing thus my head,
Dogs leap the hatch, and all are fled.

Do de, de, de. Sessa! Come, march to wakes and fairs and market-towns. Poor Tom, thy horn is dry. 79

Lear. Then let them anatomize Regan; see what breeds about her heart. Is there any cause in nature that makes these hard hearts? [*To Edgar.*] You, sir, I entertain for one of my hundred; only I do not like the fashion of your garments. You will say they are Persian attire; but let them be changed.

Kent. Now, good my lord, lie here and rest awhile.

Lear. Make no noise, make no noise; draw the curtains. So, so, so. We'll go to supper i' the morning. So, so, so. 91

Fool. And I'll go to bed at noon.

Re-enter GLOUCESTER.

Glou. Come hither, friend; where is the king my master?

Kent. Here, sir; but trouble him not, his wits are gone.

Glou. Good friend, I prithee, take him in thy arms;
I have o'erheard a plot of death upon him.
There is a litter ready; lay him in't,
And drive towards Dover, friend, where thou shalt meet
Both welcome and protection. Take up thy master;

72. *brach:* a female hound. *lym:* lyam-hound, bloodhound. Ff read *Hym;* the emendation is Hanmer's. 73. *bobtail tike:* curtal dog. *trundle-tail:* curly-tailed dog. 76. *hatch:* half door, gate or wicket with an open space above. 78. *horn:* the horn carried by every Tom o' Bedlam to receive food and drink. Edgar, however, is figuratively implying that he can no longer keep up his assumed role. 80. *anatomize:* dissect. 83. *entertain:* take in my service. *hundred:* company of attendants. 85. *Persian:* i.e., rich and gorgeous. 92. *Fool . . . noon.* Omitted in Q1. One of J. Heywood's *Proverbs* (1546) reads: "It seemeth ye would make me go to bed at noon."

If thou shouldst dally half an hour, his life, 100
With thine, and all that offer to defend him,
Stand in assured loss. Take up, take up;
And follow me, that will to some provision
Give thee quick conduct.

Kent. Oppressed nature sleeps;
This rest might yet have balm'd thy broken sinews,
Which, if convenience will not allow,
Stand in hard cure. [*To the Fool.*] Come, help to bear thy master;
Thou must not stay behind.

Glou. Come, come, away.

[*Exeunt all but Edgar.*

Edg. When we our betters see bearing our woes,
We scarcely think our miseries our foes. 110
Who alone suffers, suffers most i' the mind,
Leaving free things and happy shows behind.
But then the mind much sufferance doth o'er-skip,
When Grief hath mates, and Bearing fellowship.
How light and portable my pain seems now,
When that which makes me bend makes the king bow.
He childed as I father'd! Tom, away!
Mark the high noises, and thyself bewray
When false opinion, whose wrong thought defiles thee,
In thy just proof repeals and reconciles thee. 120
What will hap more tonight, safe 'scape the king!
Lurk, lurk.

[*Exit.*

102. *Stand in assured loss:* will assuredly be lost. 104–8. *Kent . . . behind.* Omitted in F_1. 105. *sinews:* nerves. Some editors emend to *senses.* 107. *hard:* difficult. 109–22. *Edg. . . . lurk.* Omitted in F_1. 113. *sufferance:* suffering, distress. 115. *portable:* bearable. 118. *bewray:* reveal. 120. *repeals:* calls you back to honors. 121. *What . . . king:* whatever else happens tonight, may the king escape.

SCENE VII. GLOUCESTER'S *castle.*

Enter CORNWALL, REGAN, GONERIL, EDMUND, *and* Servants.

Corn. Post speedily to my lord your husband; show him this letter. The army of France is landed. Seek out the villain Gloucester. [*Exeunt some of the Servants.*

Reg. Hang him instantly.

Gon. Pluck out his eyes.

Corn. Leave him to my displeasure Edmund, keep you our sister company; the revenges we are bound to take upon your traitorous father are not fit for your beholding. Advise the duke, where you are going, to a most festinate preparation; we are bound to the like. Our posts shall be swift and intelligent betwixt us. Farewell, dear sister; farewell, my lord of Gloucester.

Enter OSWALD.

How now? Where's the king? 14

Osw. My lord of Gloucester hath convey'd him hence.
Some five or six and thirty of his knights,
Hot questrists after him, met him at gate;
Who, with some other of the lords dependants,
Are gone with him towards Dover, where they boast
To have well-armed friends.

Corn. Get horses for your mistress. 20

Gon. Farewell, sweet lord, and sister.

Corn. Edmund, farewell.

[*Exeunt Goneril, Edmund, and Oswald.*

Go seek the traitor Gloucester,
Pinion him like a thief, bring him before us.

[*Exeunt other Servants.*

Though well we may not pass upon his life
Without the form of justice, yet our power
Shall do a curtsy to our wrath, which men
May blame, but not control. Who's there? The traitor?

[vii] 1. *Post:* hasten. 10. *festinate:* hasty. 11. *posts:* couriers. 12. *intelligent:* informing. 17. *questrists:* seekers.

Enter GLOUCESTER, *brought in by two or three.*

Reg. Ingrateful fox! 'Tis he.

Corn. Bind fast his corky arms.

Glou. What mean your Graces? Good my friends, consider
You are my guests; do me no foul play, friends. 31

Corn. Bind him, I say. [*Servants bind him.*

Reg. Hard, hard. O filthy traitor!

Glou. Unmerciful lady as you are, I'm none.

Corn. To this chair bind him. Villain, thou shalt find—
[*Regan plucks his beard.*

Glou. By the kind gods, 'tis most ignobly done
To pluck me by the beard.

Reg. So white, and such a traitor?

Glou. Naughty lady,
These hairs, which thou dost ravish from my chin,
Will quicken, and accuse thee. I am your host;
With robbers' hands my hospitable favours 40
You should not ruffle thus. What will you do?

Corn. Come, sir, what letters had you late from France?

Reg. Be simple answerer, for we know the truth.

Corn. And what confederacy have you with the traitors
Late footed in the kingdom?

Reg. To whose hands have you sent the lunatic king?
Speak.

Glou. I have a letter guessingly set down,
Which came from one that's of a neutral heart,
And not from one opposed.

Corn. Cunning.

Reg. And false.

Corn. Where hast thou sent the king? 50

Glou. To Dover.

Reg. Wherefore to Dover? Wast thou not charged at peril—

29. *corky:* withered. 37. *Naughty:* worthless. 39. *quicken:* come to life. 40. *favours:* features. 41. *ruffle:* outrage. 43. *simple:* plain. 44. *confederacy:* alliance. 45. *footed:* landed. 47. *guessingly:* by conjecture. *set down:* written.

Corn. Wherefore to Dover? Let him first answer that.
Glou. I am tied to the stake, and I must stand the course.
Reg. Wherefore to Dover, sir?
Glou. Because I would not see thy cruel nails
Pluck out his poor old eyes; nor thy fierce sister
In his anointed flesh stick boarish fangs.
The sea, with such a storm as his bare head
In hell-black night endured, would have buoy'd up, 60
And quench'd the stelled fires.
Yet, poor old heart, he holp the heavens to rain.
If wolves had at thy gate howl'd that stern time,
Thou shouldst have said, "Good porter, turn the key,"
All cruels else subscribed. But I shall see
The winged vengeance overtake such children.
Corn. See't shalt thou never. Fellows, hold the chair.
Upon these eyes of thine I'll set my foot.
Glou. He that will think to live till he be old,
Give me some help—[*One eye is plucked out.*] O cruel! O you gods! 70
Reg. One side will mock another; the other, too.
Corn. If you see vengeance—
First Serv. Hold your hand, my lord.
I have served you ever since I was a child;
But better service have I never done you
Than now to bid you hold.
Reg. How now, you dog!
First Serv. If you did wear a beard upon your chin,
I'd shake it on this quarrel. What do you mean?
Corn. My villain? [*They draw and fight.*
First Serv. Nay, then, come on, and take the chance of anger.
Reg. Give me thy sword. A peasant stand up thus? 80
[*Takes a sword from an Attendant, and runs at him behind.*

54. *tied to the stake:* an allusion to bear-baiting. *course:* one of a succession of attacks. 57. *Pluck . . . eyes:* a striking instance of dramatic irony; Gloucester mentions his own fate. 61. *stelled fires:* stars. 62. *holp:* helped. *rain.* Q_1 reads *rage.* 65. *cruels:* cruelties. *subscribed:* assented to.

First Serv. O, I am slain! My lord, you have one eye left
To see some mischief on him. O! [*Dies.*

Corn. Lest it see more, prevent it. Out, vile jelly!
[*Plucks out the second eye.*
Where is thy lustre now?

Glou. All dark and comfortless. Where's my son Edmund?
Edmund, enkindle all the sparks of nature,
To quit this horrid act.

Reg. Out, treacherous villain!
Thou call'st on him that hates thee. It was he
That made the overture of thy treasons to us,
Who is too good to pity thee. 90

Glou. O my follies! Then Edgar was abused.
Kind gods, forgive me that, and prosper him!

Reg. Go thrust him out at gates, and let him smell
His way to Dover. [*Exit an Attendant with Gloucester.*] How is't,
my lord? How look you?

Corn. I have received a hurt. Follow me, lady.
Turn out that eyeless villain; throw this slave
Upon the dunghill. [*Servants carry out the body.*] Regan, I bleed
apace.
Untimely comes this hurt; give me your arm.
[*Exit Cornwall, led by Regan.*

Sec. Serv. I'll never care what wickedness I do,
If this man come to good.

Third Serv. If she live long, 100
And in the end meet the old course of death,
Women will all turn monsters.

Sec. Serv. Let's follow the old earl, and get the Bedlam
To lead him where he would; his roguish madness
Allows itself to anything.

82. *mischief:* misfortune, punishment. 87. *quit:* make a return, requite. *horrid:* horrible. 89. *overture:* disclosure. 91. *abused:* unjustly treated. 97. *apace:* freely. 99–107. *Sec. Serv. . . . him.* Omitted in F_1. 101. *old . . . death:* natural death. 103. *Bedlam:* i.e., Poor Tom (Edgar). 104. *roguish:* vagrant. From Q_2; omitted in Q_1. 105. *Allows:* lends.

Third Serv. Go thou; I'll fetch some flax and whites of eggs
To apply to his bleeding face. Now, heaven help him!
[*Exeunt severally.*

ACT IV

SCENE I. *The heath.*

Enter EDGAR, *disguised still as Tom o' Bedlam.*

Edg. Yet better thus, and known to be contemn'd,
Than still contemn'd and flatter'd. To be worst,
The lowest and most dejected thing of fortune,
Stands still in esperance, lives not in fear.
The lamentable change is from the best;
The worst returns to laughter. Welcome, then,
Thou unsubstantial air that I embrace!
The wretch that thou hast blown unto the worst
Owes nothing to thy blasts. But who comes here?

Enter GLOUCESTER, *led by an* Old Man.

My father, poorly led? World, world, O world! 10
But that thy strange mutations make us hate thee,
Life would not yield to age.

Old Man. O, my good lord, I have been your tenant, and your father's tenant, these fourscore years.

Glou. Away, get thee away; good friend, be gone.
Thy comforts can do me no good at all;
Thee they may hurt.

Old Man. Alack, sir, you cannot see your way.

Glou. I have no way, and therefore want no eyes. 20
I stumbled when I saw. Full oft 'tis seen,
Our means secure us, and our mere defects
Prove our commodities. O dear son Edgar,
The food of thy abused father's wrath!

[IV. i] 4. *still:* ever. *esperance:* hope. 6–9. *Welcome . . . blasts.* Omitted in Q1. 6. *laughter:* i.e., a happy state. 22. *mere:* very, sheer. 23. *commodities:* advantages. 24. *abused:* imposed upon, deceived.

Might I but live to see thee in my touch,
I'ld say I had eyes again!

Old Man. How now? Who's there?

Edg. [*Aside*] O gods! Who is't can say, "I am at the worst"?
I am worse than e'er I was.

Old Man. 'Tis poor mad Tom.

Edg. [*Aside*] And worse I may be yet; the worst is not
So long as we can say, "This is the worst." 30

Old Man. Fellow, where goest?

Glou. Is it a beggar-man?

Old Man. Madman, and beggar too.

Glou. He has some reason, else he could not beg.
I' the last night's storm I such a fellow saw,
Which made me think a man a worm. My son
Came then into my mind, and yet my mind
Was then scarce friends with him. I have heard more since.
As flies to wanton boys, are we to the gods;
They kill us for their sport.

Edg. [*Aside*] How should this be?
Bad is the trade that must play fool to Sorrow, 40
Angering itself and others.—Bless thee, master!

Glou. Is that the naked fellow?

Old Man. Ay, my lord.

Glou. Then, prithee, get thee gone. If, for my sake,
Thou wilt o'ertake us hence a mile or twain,
I' the way toward Dover, do it for ancient love;
And bring some covering for this naked soul,
Who I'll entreat to lead me.

Old Man. Alack, sir, he is mad.

Glou. 'Tis the times' plague, when madmen lead the blind.
Do as I bid thee, or rather do thy pleasure;
Above the rest, be gone. 50

Old Man. I'll bring him the best 'parel that I have,
Come on't what will. [*Exit.*

Glou. Sirrah, naked fellow—

38. *wanton:* irresponsible, unrestrained. 39. *kill.* Q_1 reads *bite.*
45. *ancient love:* old times' sake.

Edg. Poor Tom's a-cold. [*Aside.*] I cannot daub it further.

Glou. Come hither, fellow.

Edg. [*Aside*] And yet I must. Bless thy sweet eyes, they bleed.

Glou. Know'st thou the way to Dover? 57

Edg. Both stile and gate, horse-way and foot-path. Poor Tom hath been scared out of his good wits. Bless thee, good man's son, from the foul fiend! Five fiends have been in poor Tom at once; of lust, as Obidicut; Hobbididance, prince of dumbness; Mahu, of stealing; Modo, of murder; Flibbertigibbet, of mopping and mowing, who since possesses chambermaids and waiting-women. So, bless thee, master!

Glou. [*Giving him money*] Here, take this purse, thou whom the heavens' plagues
Have humbled to all strokes. That I am wretched
Makes thee the happier; heavens, deal so still!
Let the superfluous and lust-dieted man, 70
That slaves your ordinance, that will not see
Because he doth not feel, feel your power quickly;
So distribution should undo excess,
And each man have enough. Dost thou know Dover?

Edg. Ay, master.

Glou. There is a cliff, whose high and bending head
Looks fearfully in the confined deep.
Bring me but to the very brim of it,
And I'll repair the misery thou dost bear
With something rich about me. From that place 80
I shall no leading need.

Edg. Give me thy arm;
Poor Tom shall lead thee. [*Exeunt.*

54. *daub:* dissemble. Q1 reads *dance.* 61–6. *Five . . . master.* Omitted in F1. 64. *mopping and mowing:* making faces. 69. *happier:* more fortunate, richer. 70. *superfluous:* having more than enough. 71. *slaves:* makes himself subservient to. *ordinance:* decree. 73. *undo:* be a bar to.

SCENE II. *Before the* DUKE OF ALBANY'S *palace.*

Enter GONERIL *and* EDMUND.

Gon. Welcome, my lord; I marvel our mild husband
Not met us on the way.

Enter OSWALD.

Now, where's your master?
Osw. Madam, within; but never man so changed.
I told him of the army that was landed.
He smiled at it. I told him you were coming;
His answer was, "The worse." Of Gloucester's treachery,
And of the loyal service of his son,
When I inform'd him, then he call'd me sot,
And told me I had turn'd the wrong side out.
What most he should dislike seems pleasant to him; 10
What like, offensive.
Gon. [*To Edmund*] Then shall you go no further.
It is the cowish terror of his spirit,
That dares not undertake. He'll not feel wrongs
Which tie him to an answer. Our wishes on the way
May prove effects. Back, Edmund, to my brother;
Hasten his musters and conduct his powers.
I must change arms at home and give the distaff
Into my husband's hands. This trusty servant
Shall pass between us. Ere long you are like to hear,
If you dare venture in your own behalf, 20
A mistress's command. Wear this; spare speech;
[*Giving a favour.*
Decline your head. [*Kissing him.*] This kiss, if it durst speak,
Would stretch thy spirits up into the air.
Conceive, and fare thee well.
Edm. Yours in the ranks of death.
Gon. My most dear Gloucester!
[*Exit Edmund.*

[ii] 8. *sot:* fool. 15. *prove effects:* i.e., be realized. 16. *conduct:* lead. *powers:* armies. 17. *distaff:* the symbol of woman's occupation. 24. *Conceive:* understand.

O, the difference of man and man!
To thee a woman's services are due;
My fool usurps my body.

Osw. Madam, here comes my lord. [*Exit.*

Enter ALBANY.

Gon. I have been worth the whistle.

Alb. O Goneril!
You are not worth the dust which the rude wind 30
Blows in your face. I fear your disposition;
That nature, which contemns it origin,
Cannot be border'd certain in itself.
She that herself will sliver and disbranch
From her material sap, perforce must wither
And come to deadly use.

Gon. No more; the text is foolish.

Alb. Wisdom and goodness to the vile seem vile;
Filths savour but themselves. What have you done?
Tigers, not daughters, what have you perform'd? 40
A father, and a gracious aged man,
Whose reverence even the head-lugg'd bear would lick,
Most barbarous, most degenerate, have you madded.
Could my good brother suffer you to do it?
A man, a prince, by him so benefited!
If that the heavens do not their visible spirits
Send quickly down to tame these vile offenses,
It will come,
Humanity must perforce prey on itself,
Like monsters of the deep.

Gon. Milk-liver'd man! 50
That bear'st a cheek for blows, a head for wrongs,

26. *O . . . man.* Omitted in Q_1. 28. *My . . . body.* So Ff. Qq give three distinct readings: some copies of Q_1 read *My foot usurps my body;* others, corrected, read *A fool usurps my bed;* and Q_2 reads *My foot usurps my head.* 31–50. *I fear . . . deep.* Omitted in F_1. 32. *it:* its. 33. *border'd certain:* surely kept within bounds. 39. *savour:* care for, like. 42. *head-lugg'd:* dragged by the head. 43. *madded:* maddened. 50. *Milk-liver'd:* cowardly.

Who hast not in thy brows an eye discerning
Thine honour from thy suffering; that not know'st
Fools do those villains pity who are punish'd
Ere they have done their mischief. Where's thy drum?
France spreads his banners in our noiseless land,
With plumed helm thy state begins to threat,
Whiles thou, a moral fool, sit'st still, and criest,
"Alack, why does he so?"

Alb. See thyself, devil!
Proper deformity seems not in the fiend 60
So horrid as in woman.

Gon. O vain fool!

Alb. Thou changed and self-cover'd thing, for shame,
Be-monster not thy feature. Were't my fitness
To let these hands obey my blood,
They are apt enough to dislocate and tear
Thy flesh and bones. Howe'er thou art a fiend,
A woman's shape doth shield thee.

Gon. Marry, your manhood—mew!

Enter a Messenger.

Alb. What news?

Mess. O, my good lord, the Duke of Cornwall's dead, 70
Slain by his servant, going to put out
The other eye of Gloucester.

Alb. Gloucester's eyes?

Mess. A servant that he bred, thrill'd with remorse,
Opposed against the act, bending his sword

53–9. *that . . . so.* Omitted in F_1. 56. *France:* i.e., the King of France. *noiseless:* rumorless. 58. *moral:* moralizing. 60. *Proper:* thorough. 61. *horrid:* horrible. 62–9. *Alb. . . . news.* Omitted in F_1. 62. *self-cover'd:* having the real self concealed. 63. *Be-monster:* make monstrous. *Were 't my fitness:* were it fit for me, a man. 64. *blood:* anger. 65. *apt:* ready. 68. *mew.* The uncorrected sheets of Q_1 and Q_2 read *now;* the corrected sheets *mew*—. Most editors, therefore, take *mew* as a verb, "coop up, as a hawk," and the line to mean, "don't let your manhood get out of control." 73. *remorse:* pity, compassion.

To his great master; who, thereat enraged,
Flew on him, and amongst them fell'd him dead;
But not without that harmful stroke which since
Hath pluck'd him after.

Alb. This shows you are above,
You justicers, that these our nether crimes
So speedily can venge! But, O poor Gloucester! 80
Lost he his other eye?

Mess. Both, both, my lord.
This letter, madam, craves a speedy answer;
'Tis from your sister.

Gon. [*Aside*] One way I like this well;
But being widow, and my Gloucester with her,
May all the building in my fancy pluck
Upon my hateful life. Another way,
The news is not so tart. I'll read, and answer. [*Exit.*

Alb. Where was his son when they did take his eyes?

Mess. Come with my lady hither.

Alb. He is not here. 90

Mess. No, my good lord; I met him back again.

Alb. Knows he the wickedness?

Mess. Ay, my good lord; 'twas he inform'd against him,
And quit the house on purpose, that their punishment
Might have the freer course.

Alb. Gloucester, I live
To thank thee for the love thou show'dst the king,
And to revenge thine eyes. Come hither, friend,
Tell me what more thou know'st. [*Exeunt.*

Scene III. *The French camp near Dover.*

Enter Kent *and a* Gentleman.

Kent. Why the King of France is so suddenly gone back, know you the reason?

79. *nether:* earthly. 85. *building . . . fancy:* castles in the air. 87. *tart:* painful, grievous. 91. *back:* i.e., going back. 94. *quit:* left.
[iii] This entire scene is omitted in F_1.

Gent. Something he left imperfect in the state, which since his coming forth is thought of; which imports to the kingdom so much fear and danger, that his personal return was most required and necessary.

Kent. Who hath he left behind him general?

Gent. The Marshal of France, Monsieur La Far. 10

Kent. Did your letters pierce the queen to any demonstration of grief?

Gent. Ay, sir; she took them, read them in my presence,
And now and then an ample tear trill'd down
Her delicate cheek. It seem'd she was a queen
Over her passion, who, most rebel-like,
Sought to be king o'er her.

Kent. O, then it moved her.

Gent. Not to a rage; patience and sorrow strove
Who should express her goodliest. You have seen
Sunshine and rain at once. Her smiles and tears 20
Were like a better way; those happy smilets,
That play'd on her ripe lip, seem'd not to know
What guests were in her eyes, which parted thence,
As pearls from diamonds dropp'd. In brief,
Sorrow would be a rarity most beloved,
If all could so become it.

Kent. Made she no verbal question?

Gent. 'Faith, once or twice she heaved the name of "father"
Pantingly forth, as if it press'd her heart;
Cried "Sisters! Sisters! Shame of ladies! Sisters!
Kent! Father! Sisters! What, i' the storm? I' the night? 30
Let pity not be believed!" There she shook
The holy water from her heavenly eyes,
And clamour moisten'd. Then away she started
To deal with grief alone.

Kent. It is the stars,
The stars above us, govern our conditions;

14. *trill'd:* trickled, rolled. 21. *smilets:* little smiles (a Shakespearean coinage). 26. *question:* comment. 33. *clamour moisten'd:* i.e., moistened her cries with tears.

Else one self mate and mate could not beget
Such different issues. You spoke not with her since?

Gent. No.

Kent. Was this before the king return'd?

Gent. No, since.

Kent. Well, sir, the poor distressed Lear's i' the town; 40
Who sometime, in his better tune, remembers
What we are come about, and by no means
Will yield to see his daughter.

Gent. Why, good sir?

Kent. A sovereign shame so elbows him. His own unkindness,
That stripp'd her from his benediction, turn'd her
To foreign casualties, gave her dear rights
To his dog-hearted daughters—these things sting
His mind so venomously that burning shame
Detains him from Cordelia.

Gent. Alack, poor gentleman! 49

Kent. Of Albany's and Cornwall's powers you heard not?

Gent. 'Tis so, they are afoot.

Kent. Well, sir, I'll bring you to our master Lear,
And leave you to attend him. Some dear cause
Will in concealment wrap me up awhile;
When I am known aright, you shall not grieve
Lending me this acquaintance. I pray you, go
Along with me. [*Exeunt.*

Scene iv. *The same. A tent.*

Enter, with drum and colours, Cordelia, Doctor, *and* Soldiers.

Cor. Alack, 'tis he. Why, he was met even now
As mad as the vex'd sea, singing aloud,

36. *self mate and mate:* selfsame parents. 40–9. *Well . . . Cordelia.* In the old *King Leir* Cordelia secretly relieves her father's want so that he will not be ashamed to come to her court. 44. *elbows:* jogs. 46. *casualties:* chances. 53. *dear:* important.
[iv] 2. *vex'd:* disturbed, agitated.

Crown'd with rank fumiter and furrow-weeds,
With bur-docks, hemlock, nettles, cuckoo-flowers,
Darnel, and all the idle weeds that grow
In our sustaining corn. A century send forth;
Search every acre in the high-grown field,
And bring him to our eye. [*Exit an Officer.*] What can man's wisdom
In the restoring his bereaved sense?
He that helps him take all my outward worth. 10

Doct. There is means, madam.
Our foster-nurse of nature is repose,
The which he lacks; that to provoke in him,
Are many simples operative, whose power
Will close the eye of anguish.

Cor. All blest secrets,
All you unpublish'd virtues of the earth,
Spring with my tears! Be aidant and remediate
In the good man's distress! Seek, seek for him;
Lest his ungovern'd rage dissolve the life
That wants the means to lead it.

Enter a Messenger.

Mess. News, madam; 20
The British powers are marching hitherward.

Cor. 'Tis known before; our preparation stands
In expectation of them. O dear father,
It is thy business that I go about;
Therefore great France
My mourning and important tears hath pitied.
No blown ambition doth our arms incite,
But love, dear love, and our aged father's right.
Soon may I hear and see him! [*Exeunt.*

3. *fumiter:* fumaria. *furrow-weeds:* weeds that grow on arable land. 4. *bur-docks.* Qq read *hor-docks;* F1 reads *hardokes. cuckoo-flowers.* Not identified. 5. *Darnel:* a kind of grass. *idle:* worthless. 6. *corn:* grain. *century:* a hundred soldiers (but the spelling of F1, *centery*, suggests *sentry*). 8. *can:* i.e., can do. 14. *simples:* medicinal herbs. 17. *remediate:* remedial. 26. *important:* importunate, urgent.

SCENE V. GLOUCESTER'S *castle.*

Enter REGAN *and* OSWALD.

Reg. But are my brother's powers set forth?
Osw. Ay, madam.
Reg. Himself in person there?
Osw. Madam, with much ado;
Your sister is the better soldier.
Reg. Lord Edmund spake not with your lord at home?
Osw. No, madam.
Reg. What might import my sister's letter to him?
Osw. I know not, lady.
Reg. 'Faith, he is posted hence on serious matter.
It was great ignorance, Gloucester's eyes being out,
To let him live. Where he arrives he moves 10
All hearts against us. Edmund, I think, is gone,
In pity of his misery, to dispatch
His nighted life; moreover, to descry
The strength o' the enemy.
Osw. I must needs after him, madam, with my letter.
Reg. Our troops set forth tomorrow. Stay with us;
The ways are dangerous.
Osw. I may not, madam;
My lady charged my duty in this business.
Reg. Why should she write to Edmund? Might not you
Transport her purposes by word? Belike, 20
Something—I know not what. I'll love thee much,
Let me unseal the letter.
Osw. Madam, I had rather—
Reg. I know your lady does not love her husband;
I am sure of that; and at her late being here
She gave strange œillades and most speaking looks
To noble Edmund. I know you are of her bosom.
Osw. I, madam?

[v] 8. *posted:* speeded. 12. *dispatch:* deprive him of. 13. *nighted:* dark, black as night. 25. *œillades:* amorous looks, "sheep's eyes." 26. *of her bosom:* in her confidence.

Reg. I speak in understanding; you are, I know 't.
Therefore I do advise you, take this note.
My lord is dead; Edmund and I have talk'd; 30
And more convenient is he for my hand
Than for your lady's. You may gather more.
If you do find him, pray you, give him this;
[*Giving him a favour.*
And when your mistress hears thus much from you,
I pray, desire her call her wisdom to her.
So, fare you well.
If you do chance to hear of that blind traitor,
Preferment falls on him that cuts him off.

Osw. Would I could meet him, madam! I should show
What party I do follow.

Reg. Fare thee well. [*Exeunt.* 40

SCENE VI. *Fields near Dover.*

Enter GLOUCESTER, *and* EDGAR *dressed like a peasant.*

Glou. When shall we come to the top of that same hill?

Edg. You do climb up it now; look, how we labour.

Glou. Methinks the ground is even.

Edg. Horrible steep.
Hark, do you hear the sea?

Glou. No, truly.

Edg. Why, then, your other senses grow imperfect
By your eyes' anguish.

Glou. So may it be, indeed.
Methinks thy voice is alter'd; and thou speak'st
In better phrase and matter than thou didst.

Edg. You're much deceived; in nothing am I changed
But in my garments.

Glou. Methinks you're better spoken. 10

Edg. Come on, sir; here's the place. Stand still. How fearful
And dizzy 'tis, to cast one's eyes so low!

29. *take this note:* take note of this.
[vi] 7. *Methinks:* it seems to me.

The crows and choughs that wing the midway air
Show scarce so gross as beetles. Half way down
Hangs one that gathers samphire, dreadful trade!
Methinks he seems no bigger than his head.
The fishermen, that walk upon the beach,
Appear like mice; and yond tall anchoring bark,
Diminish'd to her cock; her cock, a buoy
Almost too small for sight. The murmuring surge, 20
That on the unnumber'd idle pebbles chafes,
Cannot be heard so high. I'll look no more;
Lest my brain turn, and the deficient sight
Topple down headlong.

Glou. Set me where you stand.

Edg. Give me your hand. You are now within a foot
Of the extreme verge; for all beneath the moon
Would I not leap upright.

Glou. Let go my hand.
Here, friend, 's another purse; in it a jewel
Well worth a poor man's taking. Fairies and gods
Prosper it with thee! Go thou farther off; 30
Bid me farewell, and let me hear thee going.

Edg. Now fare you well, good sir.

Glou. With all my heart.

Edg. [*Aside*] Why I do trifle thus with his despair
Is done to cure it.

Glou. [*Kneeling*] O you mighty gods!
This world I do renounce, and, in your sights,
Shake patiently my great affliction off.
If I could bear it longer and not fall
To quarrel with your great opposeless wills,
My snuff and loathed part of nature should
Burn itself out. If Edgar live, O, bless him! 40
Now, fellow, fare thee well. [*He falls forward.*

13. *choughs:* jackdaws. 14. *gross:* big. 15. *samphire:* sea-fennel, an herb growing on the side of cliffs and much valued for pickling. 19. *cock:* cock-boat. 21. *unnumber'd:* numberless. 39. *snuff:* a smoking wick of a candle; hence, a useless remnant of life.

Photograph by The Topical Press Agency, London

SHAKESPEARE CLIFFS, DOVER

Edg. Gone, sir; farewell.
And yet I know not how conceit may rob
The treasury of life, when life itself
Yields to the theft. Had he been where he thought,
By this had thought been past. Alive or dead?
Ho, you sir! Friend! Hear you, sir! Speak!
Thus might he pass indeed; yet he revives.
What are you, sir?
Glou. Away, and let me die.
Edg. Hadst thou been aught but gossamer, feathers, air,
So many fathom down precipitating, 50
Thou'dst shiver'd like an egg. But thou dost breathe;
Hast heavy substance; bleed'st not; speak'st; art sound.
Ten masts at each make not the altitude
Which thou hast perpendicularly fell.
Thy life's a miracle. Speak yet again.
Glou. But have I fall'n, or no?
Edg. From the dread summit of this chalky bourn.
Look up a-height; the shrill-gorged lark so far
Cannot be seen or heard. Do but look up.
Glou. Alack, I have no eyes. 60
Is wretchedness deprived that benefit,
To end itself by death? 'Twas yet some comfort,
When misery could beguile the tyrant's rage,
And frustrate his proud will.
Edg. [*Assisting him*] Give me your arm.
Up, so. How is 't? Feel you your legs? You stand.
Glou. Too well, too well.
Edg. This is above all strangeness.
Upon the crown o' the cliff, what thing was that
Which parted from you?
Glou. A poor unfortunate beggar.

42. *conceit:* thought, belief. 43–4. *when . . . theft:* when one is willing to die. 46 ff. Edgar's speech must now change with the new role he has assumed. 49. *gossamer:* a film of cobwebs. 53. *at each:* i.e., placed end to end. 57. *bourn:* boundary. 58. *a-height:* on high. *shrill-gorged:* high-voiced.

Edg. As I stood here below, methought his eyes
Were two full moons; he had a thousand noses, 70
Horns whelk'd and waved like the enridged sea.
It was some fiend; therefore, thou happy father,
Think that the clearest gods, who make them honours
Of men's impossibilities, have preserved thee.
Glou. I do remember now; henceforth I'll bear
Affliction till it do cry out itself,
"Enough, enough," and die. That thing you speak of,
I took it for a man; often 'twould say,
"The fiend, the fiend." He led me to that place.
Edg. Bear free and patient thoughts. But who comes here?

Enter LEAR, *fantastically dressed with wild flowers.*

The safer sense will ne'er accommodate 81
His master thus.
Lear. No, they cannot touch me for coining;
I am the king himself.
Edg. O thou side-piercing sight!
Lear. Nature's above art in that respect. There's your press-money. That fellow handles his bow like a crow-keeper; draw me a clothier's yard. Look, look, a mouse! Peace, peace; this piece of toasted cheese will do 't. There's my gauntlet; I'll prove it on a giant. Bring up the brown bills. O, well flown, bird! I' the clout, i' the clout. Hewgh! Give the word. 93

71. *whelk'd:* twisted, convolved. *enridged.* Q_1 reads *enraged.* 72. *father:* old man. 73. *clearest:* most illustrious. 81. *safer sense:* the more sound mind. *accommodate:* equip, dress. 83 ff. Lear's wandering mind ranges from recruiting to archery, then to mousing, then to battle and challenges, then back again to falconry and archery, and then to sentry duty. 83. *coining:* counterfeiting money. F_1 reads *crying.* 87. *press-money:* money paid a soldier or sailor upon his being impressed into service. 88. *crow-keeper:* scarecrow. *clothier's yard:* "cloth-yard shaft," an arrow used with the long bow. 91. *gauntlet:* the glove thrown down in challenge. *prove:* establish as true. *on:* against. 92. *brown bills:* military weapons consisting of a long wooden handle having a painted blade- or axe-shaped head. 93. *clout:* a square piece of canvas at the archery butts, which was the mark aimed at.

Edg. Sweet marjoram.

Lear. Pass.

Glou. I know that voice.

Lear. Ha! Goneril, with a white beard? They flattered me like a dog, and told me I had white hairs in my beard ere the black ones were there. To say "ay" and "no" to everything that I said! "Ay" and "no" too was no good divinity. When the rain came to wet me once, and the wind to make me chatter; when the thunder would not peace at my bidding; there I found 'em, there I smelt 'em out. Go to, they are not men o' their words. They told me I was everything; 'tis a lie, I am not ague-proof.

Glou. The trick of that voice I do well remember;
Is't not the king?

Lear. Ay, every inch a king.
When I do stare, see how the subject quakes. 110
I pardon that man's life. What was thy cause?
Adultery?
Thou shalt not die—die for adultery? No.
The wren goes to 't, and the small gilded fly
Does lecher in my sight.
Let copulation thrive; for Gloucester's bastard son
Was kinder to his father than my daughters
Got 'tween the lawful sheets.
To 't, luxury, pell-mell, for I lack soldiers.
Behold yond simpering dame, 120
Whose face between her forks presages snow;
That minces virtue, and does shake the head
To hear of pleasure's name;
The fitchew, nor the soiled horse, goes to 't
With a more riotous appetite.
Down from the waist they are Centaurs,

98–100. *I had . . . there:* I had the wisdom of age while still a boy. 107. *ague-proof:* chill-proof. 111. *cause:* charge, accusation. 119. *luxury:* lust. 121. *forks:* legs. *presages snow:* indicates chastity. 124. *fitchew:* polecat. *soiled:* high-fed (dialectal). 126. *Centaurs:* arch examples of lust.

Though women all above.
But to the girdle do the gods inherit,
Beneath is all the Fiend's;
There's hell, there's darkness, there's the sulphurous pit, 130
Burning, scalding, stench, consumption; fie, fie, fie! Pah, pah!
Give me an ounce of civet, good apothecary, to sweeten my imagination; there's money for thee.

Glou. O, let me kiss that hand!

Lear. Let me wipe it first; it smells of mortality.

Glou. O ruin'd piece of nature! This great world
Shall so wear out to nought. Dost thou know me?

Lear. I remember thine eyes well enough. Dost thou squiny at me? No, do thy worst, blind Cupid; I'll not love. Read thou this challenge; mark but the penning of it.

[*Holding out a paper.*

Glou. Were all the letters suns, I could not see one. 143

Edg. I would not take this from report; it is,
And my heart breaks at it.

Lear. Read.

Glou. What, with the case of eyes?

Lear. O, ho, are you there with me? No eyes in your head, nor no money in your purse? Your eyes are in a heavy case, your purse in a light, yet you see how this world goes. 151

Glou. I see it feelingly.

Lear. What, art mad? A man may see how this world goes with no eyes. Look with thine ears; see how yond justice rails upon yond simple thief. Hark, in thine ear. [*Whispers.*] Change places, and, handy-dandy, which is the justice, which is the thief? Thou hast seen a farmer's dog bark at a beggar?

Glou. Ay, sir. 160

Lear. And the creature run from the cur? There thou mightst behold the great image of authority; a dog's obeyed in office.

131. *consumption.* Q_1 reads *consummation.* 132. *civet:* perfume derived from the civet cat. 144. *take:* accept as true, believe. 148. *are . . . me:* is that what you mean? 150. *heavy:* sad. 157. *handy-dandy:* a children's game: "Which hand will you have?"

Thou rascal beadle, hold thy bloody hand!
Why dost thou lash that whore? Strip thine own back;
Thou hotly lust'st to use her in that kind
For which thou whipp'st her. The usurer hangs the cozener.
Through tatter'd clothes small vices do appear;
Robes and furr'd gowns hide all. Plate sin with gold,
And the strong lance of justice hurtless breaks; 170
Arm it in rags, a pigmy's straw does pierce it.
None does offend, none, I say, none; I'll able 'em;
Take that of me, my friend, who have the power
To seal the accuser's lips. Get thee glass eyes;
And, like a scurvy politician, seem
To see the things thou dost not. Now, now, now, now.
Pull off my boots; harder, harder; so.

Edg. O, matter and impertinency mix'd!
Reason in madness!

Lear. If thou wilt weep my fortunes, take my eyes. 180
I know thee well enough; thy name is Gloucester.
Thou must be patient; we came crying hither.
Thou know'st, the first time that we smell the air,
We wawl and cry. I will preach to thee—mark.

Glou. Alack, alack the day!

Lear. When we are born, we cry that we are come
To this great stage of fools. [*Noticing his hat.*] This' a good block;
It were a delicate stratagem to shoe
A troop of horse with felt. I'll put't in proof;
And when I have stol'n upon these son-in-laws, 190
Then, kill, kill, kill, kill, kill, kill!

Enter a Gentleman, *with* Attendants.

Gent. O, here he is; lay hand upon him. Sir,
Your most dear daughter—

164. *beadle:* a minor parish officer who might punish petty offenders. 166. *kind:* way. 167. *cozener:* imposter, cheater. 168. *small.* F_1 reads *great.* 169–74. *Plate . . . lips.* Omitted in Q_1. 169. *Plate.* F_1 reads *place.* 170. *hurtless:* i.e., without doing hurt. 172. *able:* vouch for. 178. *impertinency:* irrelevancy. 180. *weep:* beweep, weep for. 187. *block:* shape. 189. *put 't in proof:* try it.

Lear. No rescue? What, a prisoner? I am even
The natural fool of Fortune. Use me well;
You shall have ransom. Let me have surgeons;
I am cut to the brains.

Gent. You shall have anything.

Lear. No seconds? All myself?
Why, this would make a man a man of salt,
To use his eyes for garden water-pots, 200
Ay, and laying autumn's dust.

Gent. Good sir—

Lear. I will die bravely, like a smug bridegroom. What?
I will be jovial. Come, come; I am a king,
My masters, know you that.

Gent. You are a royal one, and we obey you.

Lear. Then there's life in 't. Nay, if you get it, you shall get it with running. Sa, sa, sa, sa. [*Exit running; Attendants follow.*

Gent. A sight most pitiful in the meanest wretch,
Past speaking of in a king! Thou hast one daughter,
Who redeems nature from the general curse 210
Which twain have brought her to.

Edg. Hail, gentle sir.

Gent. Sir, speed you; what's your will?

Edg. Do you hear aught, sir, of a battle toward?

Gent. Most sure and vulgar; every one hears that,
Which can distinguish sound.

Edg. But, by your favour,
How near's the other army?

Gent. Near and on speedy foot; the main descry
Stands on the hourly thought.

Edg. I thank you, sir; that's all.

Gent. Though that the queen on special cause is here,
Her army is moved on.

Edg. I thank you, sir. [*Exit Gentleman.*

Glou. You ever-gentle gods, take my breath from me; 221

201. *Ay . . . sir.* Omitted in F1. 202. *smug:* neat, spruce. 213. *toward:* in preparation. 214. *vulgar:* commonly known. 217. *descry:* reconnoitre.

Let not my worser spirit tempt me again
To die before you please!

Edg. Well pray you, father.

Glou. Now, good sir, what are you?

Edg. A most poor man, made tame to Fortune's blows;
Who, by the art of known and feeling sorrows,
Am pregnant to good pity. Give me your hand,
I'll lead you to some biding.

Glou. Hearty thanks;
The bounty and the benison of heaven
To boot, and boot!

Enter Oswald.

Osw. A proclaim'd prize! Most happy! 230
That eyeless head of thine was first framed flesh
To raise my fortunes. [*Drawing his sword.*] Thou old unhappy traitor,
Briefly thyself remember; the sword is out
That must destroy thee.

Glou. Now let thy friendly hand
Put strength enough to 't. [*Edgar interposes.*

Osw. Wherefore, bold peasant,
Darest thou support a publish'd traitor? Hence;
Lest that the infection of his fortune take
Like hold on thee. Let go his arm.

Edg. Chill not let go, zir, without vurther 'casion. 240

Osw. Let go, slave, or thou diest!

Edg. Good gentleman, go your gait, and let poor volk pass. An chud ha' bin zwaggered out of my life, 'twould not ha' bin zo long as 'tis by a vortnight. Nay, come not near th' old man;

223. *father:* old man. 226. *feeling:* heartfelt. 227. *pregnant:* disposed, inclined. 228. *biding:* abode, place of shelter. 230. *proclaim'd prize:* a criminal with a price on his head. 231. *framed:* made. 233. *remember:* reflect upon (Onions); or, perhaps, confess and make your peace with heaven. 240 ff. Edgar's dialect is South-western, in which *z* for *s* and *v* for *f* are distinguishing characteristics. *Chill* and *chud* stand for *ich* (I) *will* and *ich would; Ise* is *I shall;* and *che vor ye* means *I warn you.*

keep out, che vor ye, or Ise try whether your costard or my ballow be the harder; chill be plain with you.

Osw. Out, dunghill!

Edg. Chill pick your teeth, zir. Come; no matter vor your foins. 251

[*They fight, and Edgar knocks him down with his cudgel.*

Osw. Slave, thou hast slain me. Villain, take my purse;
If ever thou wilt thrive, bury my body;
And give the letters which thou find'st about me
To Edmund, Earl of Gloucester; seek him out
Upon the British party. O, untimely death! [*Dies.*

Edg. I know thee well; a serviceable villain,
As duteous to the vices of thy mistress
As badness would desire.

Glou. What, is he dead?

Edg. Sit you down, father; rest you. 260
Let's see these pockets; [*Searching Oswald.*] the letters that he speaks of
May be my friends. He's dead; I am only sorry
He had no other death's-man. Let us see.

[*He finds a letter and breaks the seal.*

Leave, gentle wax; and, manners, blame us not.
To know our enemies' minds, we'ld rip their hearts;
Their papers, is more lawful.

[*Reads*] "Let our reciprocal vows be remembered. You have many opportunities to cut him off; if your will want not, time and place will be fruitfully offered. There is nothing done. If he return the conqueror, then am I the prisoner, and his bed my gaol, from the loathed warmth whereof deliver me, and supply the place for your labour. 274

"Your—wife, so I would say—
"Affectionate servant,
"GONERIL."

247. *costard:* head; literally, a large apple. *ballow:* club, cudgel (dialectal). 251. *foins:* fencing thrusts. 256. *British.* F_1 reads *English.* 257. *serviceable:* diligent in service. 268. *cut him off:* kill him. 269. *want:* lack. 276. *servant:* i.e., lover.

O undistinguish'd space of woman's will!
A plot upon her virtuous husband's life,
And the exchange my brother! Here, in the sands, 280
Thee I'll rake up, the post unsanctified
Of murderous lechers, and in the mature time
With this ungracious paper strike the sight
Of the death-practiced duke. For him 'tis well
That of thy death and business I can tell. [*Covering the body.*

Glou. The king is mad; how stiff is my vile sense,
That I stand up, and have ingenious feeling
Of my huge sorrows! Better I were distract;
So should my thoughts be sever'd from my griefs, 289
And woes by wrong imaginations lose [*Drum afar off.*
The knowledge of themselves.

Edg. Give me your hand.
Far off, methinks, I hear the beaten drum.
Come, father, I'll bestow you with a friend. [*Exeunt.*

SCENE VII. *A tent in the French camp.* LEAR *on a bed asleep, soft music playing;* Gentleman, *and others attending.*

Enter CORDELIA, KENT, *and* Doctor.

Cor. O thou good Kent, how shall I live and work,
To match thy goodness? My life will be too short,
And every measure fail me.

Kent. To be acknowledged, madam, is o'erpaid.
All my reports go with the modest truth;
Nor more nor clipp'd, but so.

Cor. Be better suited;
These weeds are memories of those worser hours.
I prithee, put them off.

278. *undistinguish'd:* indefinable. 281. *rake up:* cover up. *post:* messenger. *unsanctified:* unholy. 284. *death-practiced:* whose death is plotted. 287. *ingenious:* intelligent, quick of apprehension. 288. *distract:* crazy, mad.

[vii] 6. *Nor . . . nor:* neither . . . nor. *clipped:* abbreviated. *suited:* clothed. 7. *weeds:* garments. *memories:* memorials.

Kent. Pardon me, dear madam;
Yet to be known shortens my made intent.
My boon I make it, that you know me not 10
Till time and I think meet.

Cor. Then be't so, my good lord. [*To the Doctor.*] How does the king?

Doct. Madam, sleeps still.

Cor. O you kind gods,
Cure this great breach in his abused nature!
The untuned and jarring senses, O, wind up
Of this child-changed father!

Doct. So please your Majesty
That we may wake the king? He hath slept long.

Cor. Be govern'd by your knowledge, and proceed
I' the sway of your own will. Is he array'd? 20

Gent. Ay, madam; in the heaviness of his sleep
We put fresh garments on him.

Doct. Be by, good madam, when we do awake him;
I doubt not of his temperance.

Cor. Very well.

Doct. Please you, draw near. Louder the music there!

Cor. O my dear father! Restoration hang
Thy medicine on my lips, and let this kiss
Repair those violent harms that my two sisters
Have in thy reverence made!

Kent. Kind and dear princess!

Cor. Had you not been their father, these white flakes 30
Had challenged pity of them. Was this a face
To be opposed against the warring winds?
To stand against the deep dread-bolted thunder?
In the most terrible and nimble stroke

9. *Yet . . . intent:* to reveal my identity would interfere with the plans I have made. 11. *meet:* suitable. 15. *breach:* break. *abused:* ill-used. 17. *child-changed:* changed by his children. 24. *I . . . temperance:* I have no doubt that he will be calm. *not.* Omitted in F_1. 24–5. *Cor. . . . there.* Omitted in F_1. 32. *opposed.* Q_1 reads *exposed. warring.* F_1 reads *jarring.* 33–6. *To . . . helm.* Omitted in F_1. 33. *dread-bolted:* fearful-bolted.

Of quick, cross lightning? To watch—poor perdu—
With this thin helm? Mine enemy's dog,
Though he had bit me, should have stood that night
Against my fire; and wast thou fain, poor father,
To hovel thee with swine and rogues forlorn,
In short and musty straw? Alack, alack! 40
'Tis wonder that thy life and wits at once
Had not concluded all. He wakes; speak to him.

Doct. Madam, do you; 'tis fittest.

Cor. How does my royal lord? How fares your Majesty?

Lear. You do me wrong to take me out o' the grave;
Thou art a soul in bliss, but I am bound
Upon a wheel of fire, that mine own tears
Do scald like molten lead.

Cor. Sir, do you know me?

Lear. You are a spirit, I know; when did you die?

Cor. Still, still, far wide. 50

Doct. He's scarce awake; let him alone awhile.

Lear. Where have I been? Where am I? Fair daylight?
I am mightily abused; I should e'en die with pity
To see another thus. I know not what to say.
[*Holding out his hands.*] I will not swear these are my hands.
Let's see; [*Pricking himself with a pin.*
I feel this pin prick. Would I were assured
Of my condition!

Cor. O, look upon me, sir,
And hold your hands in benediction o'er me—
[*Lear is about to kneel.*
No, sir, you must not kneel.

Lear. Pray, do not mock me;
I am a very foolish fond old man, 60
Fourscore and upward, not an hour more nor less;

35. *perdu:* soldier placed in a position of special danger. 36. *enemy's.* Q_1 reads *injurious.* 38. *Against:* before. 39. *forlorn:* wretched. 42. *all:* altogether. 47. *that:* so that. 49. *when.* So Q_2; Q_1 and F_1 read *where.* 53. *abused:* deceived, ill-used. 60. *fond:* foolish. 61. *not . . . less.* Omitted in Q_1.

And, to deal plainly,
I fear I am not in my perfect mind.
Methinks I should know you, and know this man;
Yet I am doubtful, for I am mainly ignorant
What place this is. And all the skill I have
Remembers not these garments, nor I know not
Where I did lodge last night. Do not laugh at me;
For, as I am a man, I think this lady
To be my child Cordelia.

Cor. And so I am, I am! 70

Lear. Be your tears wet? Yes, 'faith. I pray, weep not.
If you have poison for me, I will drink it.
I know you do not love me; for your sisters
Have, as I do remember, done me wrong.
You have some cause, they have not.

Cor. No cause, no cause.

Lear. Am I in France?

Kent. In your own kingdom, sir.

Lear. Do not abuse me.

Doct. Be comforted, good madam; the great rage,
You see, is kill'd in him. And yet it is danger
To make him even o'er the time he has lost. 80
Desire him to go in; trouble him no more
Till further settling.

Cor. Will't please your Highness walk?

Lear. You must bear with me.
Pray you now, forget and forgive; I am old and foolish.

[*Exeunt all but Kent and Gentleman.*

Gent. Holds it true, sir, that the Duke of Cornwall was so slain?

Kent. Most certain, sir.

Gent. Who is conductor of his people?

Kent. As 'tis said, the bastard son of Gloucester.

Gent. They say Edgar, his banished son, is with the Earl of Kent in Germany. 91

65. *mainly:* entirely, perfectly. 77. *abuse:* deceive. 79. *kill'd.* Q_1 reads *cured.* 79–80. *And . . . lost.* Omitted in F_1. 80. *even o'er:* account for, fill in fully. 85–99. *Gent. . . . fought.* Omitted in F_1.

Kent. Report is changeable. 'Tis time to look about; the powers of the kingdom approach apace.

Gent. The arbitrement is like to be bloody. Fare you well, sir. [*Exit.*

Kent. My point and period will be throughly wrought,
Or well or ill, as this day's battle's fought. [*Exit.*

ACT V

SCENE I. *The British camp, near Dover.*

Enter, with drum and colours, EDMUND, REGAN, Gentlemen, *and* Soldiers.

Edm. Know of the duke if his last purpose hold,
Or whether since he is advised by aught
To change the course. He's full of alteration
And self-reproving. Bring his constant pleasure.
[*To a Gentleman, who goes out.*

Reg. Our sister's man is certainly miscarried.

Edm. 'Tis to be doubted, madam.

Reg. Now, sweet lord,
You know the goodness I intend upon you.
Tell me—but truly—but then speak the truth,
Do you not love my sister?

Edm. In honour'd love.

Reg. But have you never found my brother's way 10
To the forfended place?

Edm. That thought abuses you.

Reg. I am doubtful that you have been conjunct
And bosom'd with her, as far as we call hers.

Edm. No, by mine honour, madam.

93. *powers:* armies. 95. *arbitrement:* test, conflict that decides. 97. *period:* end. 98. *Or . . . or:* either . . . or.

[V. i] 2. *advised by aught:* i.e., anything has caused him. 3. *alteration.* Q1 reads *abdication.* 4. *constant pleasure:* settled wishes. 5. *miscarried:* come to grief. 6. *doubted:* suspected, feared. 11. *forfended:* forbidden. *abuses:* deceives, worries. 11–13. *Edm. . . . hers.* Omitted in F1. 12. *doubtful:* suspicious. 13. *bosom'd:* intimate; literally, "taken to her bosom."

Reg. I never shall endure her; dear my lord,
Be not familiar with her.

Edm. Fear me not.
She and the duke her husband!

Enter, with drum and colours, ALBANY, GONERIL, *and* Soldiers.

Gon. [*Aside*] I had rather lose the battle than that sister
Should loosen him and me.

Alb. Our very loving sister, well be-met. 20
Sir, this I hear: the king is come to his daughter,
With others whom the rigour of our state
Forced to cry out. Where I could not be honest,
I never yet was valiant. For this business,
It touches us, as France invades our land,
Not bolds the king, with others whom, I fear,
Most just and heavy causes make oppose.

Edm. Sir, you speak nobly.

Reg. Why is this reason'd?

Gon. Combine together 'gainst the enemy;
For these domestic and particular broils 30
Are not the question here.

Alb. Let's then determine
With the ancient of war on our proceedings.

Edm. I shall attend you presently at your tent.

Reg. Sister, you'll go with us?

Gon. No.

Reg. 'Tis most convenient; pray you, go with us.

Gon. [*Aside*] O, ho, I know the riddle.—I will go.

As they are going out, enter EDGAR *disguised.*

Edg. If e'er your Grace had speech with man so poor,
Hear me one word.

Alb. [*To the others*] I'll overtake you. [*To Edgar.*] Speak.

[*Exeunt all but Albany and Edgar.*

18–19. *Gon. . . . me.* Omitted in F_1. 19. *loosen:* make a breach between. 23. *cry out:* decry. 23–8. *Where . . . nobly.* Omitted in F_1. 26. *bolds:* emboldens, supports. 32. *ancient of war:* veterans. 33. *Edm. . . . tent.* Omitted in F_1. 36. *convenient:* fitting, proper.

Edg. [*Giving him a letter*] Before you fight the battle, ope this letter. 40
If you have victory, let the trumpet sound
For him that brought it. Wretched though I seem,
I can produce a champion that will prove
What is avouched there. If you miscarry,
Your business of the world hath so an end,
And machination ceases. Fortune love you!

Alb. Stay till I have read the letter.

Edg. I was forbid it.
When time shall serve, let but the herald cry,
And I'll appear again.

Alb. Why, fare thee well; I will o'erlook thy paper. 50
[*Exit Edgar.*

Re-enter EDMUND.

Edm. The enemy's in view; draw up your powers.
Here is the guess of their true strength and forces
By diligent discovery; but your haste
Is now urged on you.

Alb. We will greet the time. [*Exit.*

Edm. To both these sisters have I sworn my love;
Each jealous of the other, as the stung
Are of the adder. Which of them shall I take?
Both? One? Or neither? Neither can be enjoy'd,
If both remain alive. To take the widow
Exasperates, makes mad, her sister Goneril; 60
And hardly shall I carry out my side,
Her husband being alive. Now then, we'll use
His countenance for the battle, which being done,
Let her who would be rid of him devise
His speedy taking off. As for the mercy
Which he intends to Lear and to Cordelia,

44. *avouched:* avowed. 46. *And . . . ceases.* Omitted in Q1. 50. *o'erlook:* look over. 51. *powers:* army. 52. *guess:* rough estimate. 53. *discovery:* reconnoitring. 54. *greet the time:* be ready. 56. *jealous:* suspicious, apprehensive of evil. 63. *countenance:* aid, patronage.

The battle done, and they within our power,
Shall never see his pardon; for my state
Stands on me to defend, not to debate. [*Exit.*

SCENE II. *A field between the two camps.*

Alarum within. With drum and colours, the powers of France march over the stage, CORDELIA *leading* LEAR *by the hand.*

Enter EDGAR *and* GLOUCESTER.

Edg. Here, father, take the shadow of this tree
For your good host. Pray that the right may thrive;
If ever I return to you again,
I'll bring you comfort.
Glou. Grace go with you, sir! [*Exit Edgar.*

Alarum and retreat within. Re-enter EDGAR.

Edg. Away, old man; give me thy hand; away!
King Lear hath lost, he and his daughter ta'en.
Give me thy hand; come on.
Glou. No farther, sir; a man may rot even here.
Edg. What, in ill thoughts again? Men must endure
Their going hence, even as their coming hither; 10
Ripeness is all. Come on.
Glou. And that's true too. [*Exeunt.*

SCENE III. *The British camp near Dover.*

Enter, in conquest, with drum and colours, EDMUND; LEAR *and* CORDELIA, *prisoners;* Captain, Soldiers, *&c.*

Edm. Some officers take them away; good guard,
Until their greater pleasures first be known
That are to censure them.

69. *Stands on me:* requires me.
[ii] 6. *ta'en:* taken prisoner. 9. *endure:* await patiently. 11. *Glou. . . . too.* Omitted in Q1.
[iii] 2. *greater pleasures:* the wishes of the greater persons 3. *censure:* pass sentence upon.

Cor. We are not the first
Who, with best meaning, have incurr'd the worst.
For thee, oppressed king, am I cast down;
Myself could else out-frown false Fortune's frown.
Shall we not see these daughters and these sisters?

Lear. No, no, no, no! Come, let's away to prison;
We two alone will sing like birds i' the cage.
When thou dost ask me blessing, I'll kneel down, 10
And ask of thee forgiveness. So we'll live,
And pray, and sing, and tell old tales, and laugh
At gilded butterflies, and hear poor rogues
Talk of court news; and we'll talk with them too,
Who loses and who wins; who's in, who's out;
And take upon's the mystery of things,
As if we were God's spies. And we'll wear out,
In a wall'd prison, packs and sects of great ones,
That ebb and flow by the moon.

Edm. Take them away.

Lear. Upon such sacrifices, my Cordelia, 20
The gods themselves throw incense. Have I caught thee?
He that parts us shall bring a brand from heaven,
And fire us hence like foxes. Wipe thine eyes;
The good-years shall devour them, flesh and fell,
Ere they shall make us weep. We'll see 'em starve first.
Come. [*Exeunt Lear and Cordelia, guarded.*

Edm. Come hither, captain; hark.
Take thou this note; [*Giving a paper.*] go follow them to prison.
One step I have advanced thee; if thou dost
As this instructs thee, thou dost make thy way
To noble fortunes. [*The Captain hesitates.*] Know thou this, that men 30
Are as the time is; to be tender-minded
Does not become a sword. Thy great employment

18. *packs:* large numbers. *sects:* parties. 22. *brand:* torch.
23. *foxes:* an allusion to the method of driving foxes from their dens.
24. *good-years:* some undefined malefic influence. *fell:* skin, hide.
32. *employment:* business.

Will not bear question; either say thou'lt do't,
Or thrive by other means.

Capt. I'll do't, my lord.

Edm. About it, and write happy when thou hast done.
Mark, I say, instantly; and carry it so
As I have set it down.

Capt. I cannot draw a cart, nor eat dried oats;
If it be man's work, I'll do it. [*Exit.*

Flourish. Enter ALBANY, GONERIL, REGAN, *another* Captain, *and* Soldiers.

Alb. Sir, you have showed today your valiant strain, 40
And Fortune led you well; you have the captives
That were the opposites of this day's strife.
We do require them of you, so to use them
As we shall find their merits and our safety
May equally determine.

Edm. Sir, I thought it fit
To send the old and miserable king
To some retention and appointed guard;
Whose age has charms in it, whose title more,
To pluck the common bosom on his side,
And turn our impress'd lances in our eyes 50
Which do command them. With him I sent the queen,
My reason all the same; and they are ready
Tomorrow, or at further space, to appear
Where you shall hold your session. At this time
We sweat and bleed; the friend hath lost his friend;
And the best quarrels, in the heat, are cursed
By those that feel their sharpness.
The question of Cordelia and her father
Requires a fitter place.

33. *question:* talking about. 35. *write happy:* call yourself happy. 38–9. *Capt. . . . do it.* Omitted in F_1. 47. *and appointed guard.* So Q_2; omitted in Q_1 and Ff. 53. *at further space:* later. 54. *session:* court, judicial proceedings. 54–9. *At . . . place.* Omitted in F_1.

Alb. Sir, by your patience,
I hold you but a subject of this war, 60
Not as a brother.
Reg. That's as we list to grace him.
Methinks our pleasure might have been demanded,
Ere you had spoke so far. He led our powers,
Bore the commission of my place and person,
The which immediacy may well stand up
And call itself your brother.
Gon. Not so hot;
In his own grace he doth exalt himself,
More than in your addition.
Reg. In my rights,
By me invested, he compeers the best.
Gon. That were the most, if he should husband you. 70
Reg. Jesters do oft prove prophets.
Gon. Holla, holla,
That eye that told you so look'd but a-squint.
Reg. Lady, I am not well; else I should answer
From a full-flowing stomach. General,
Take thou my soldiers, prisoners, patrimony;
Dispose of them, of me; the walls are thine.
Witness the world, that I create thee here
My lord and master.
Gon. Mean you to enjoy him?
Alb. [*To Goneril*] The let-alone lies not in your good will.
Edm. Nor in thine, lord.
Alb. Half-blooded fellow, yes. 80
Reg. [*To Edmund*] Let the drum strike, and prove my title thine.
Alb. Stay yet; hear reason. Edmund, I arrest thee

63. *powers:* armies. 65. *immediacy:* direct relation to a position of authority. 66. *hot:* eagerly. 68. *addition:* title. 69. *compeers:* rivals, equals. 70. *Gon.* F_1 reads *Alb.* 74. *stomach:* angry temper. 76. *Dispose . . . thine.* Omitted in Q_1. *the walls are thine:* i.e., I surrender to you completely. 79. *let-alone:* hindrance. 80. *Half-blooded:* i.e., bastard.

On capital treason; and, in thine attaint,
This gilded serpent. [*Pointing to Goneril.*] For your claim, fair
sister,
I bar it in the interest of my wife;
'Tis she is sub-contracted to this lord,
And I, her husband, contradict your banns.
If you will marry, make your love to me;
My lady is bespoke.

Gon. An interlude!

Alb. Thou art arm'd, Gloucester. Let the trumpet sound; 90
If none appear to prove upon thy head
Thy heinous, manifest, and many treasons,
There is my pledge; [*Throwing down a glove.*] I'll prove it on thy
heart,
Ere I taste bread, thou art in nothing less
Than I have here proclaim'd thee.

Reg. Sick, O, sick!

Gon. [*Aside*] If not, I'll ne'er trust medicine.

Edm. There's my exchange. [*Throwing down a glove.*] What
in the world he is
That names me traitor, villain-like he lies.
Call by thy trumpet. He that dares approach,
On him—on you—who not—I will maintain 100
My truth and honour firmly.

Alb. A herald, ho!

Edm. A herald, ho, a herald!

Alb. Trust to thy single virtue; for thy soldiers,
All levied in my name, have in my name
Took their discharge.

Reg. My sickness grows upon me.

Alb. She is not well; convey her to my tent.

[*Exit Regan, led.*

83. *attaint:* impeachment. F_1 reads *thy arrest.* 87. *banns:* announcement of a proposed marriage. 89. *interlude:* play, farce. The speech is omitted in Q_1. 90. *Let . . . sound.* Omitted in Q_1. 91. *head.* F_1 reads *person.* 93. *prove.* F_1 reads *make.* 94. *thou:* that thou. 96. *medicine.* Q_1 reads *poison.* 102. *Edm. . . . herald.* Omitted in F_1. 103. *single:* own. *virtue:* valor, bravery.

Enter a Herald.

Come hither, herald. Let the trumpet sound,
And read out this. 108

Capt. Sound, trumpet! [*A trumpet sounds.*

Her. [*Reads*] "If any man of quality or degree within the lists of the army will maintain upon Edmund, supposed Earl of Gloucester, that he is a manifold traitor, let him appear by the third sound of the trumpet. He is bold in his defense."

Edm. Sound! [*First trumpet.*

Her. Again! [*Second trumpet.*

Her. Again! [*Third trumpet.*

[*Trumpet answers in the distance.*

Enter EDGAR, *at the third sound, armed, with a trumpet before him.*

Alb. Ask him his purposes, why he appears
Upon this call o' the trumpet.

Her. What are you?
Your name, your quality? And why you answer 120
This present summons?

Edg. Know, my name is lost,
By Treason's tooth bare-gnawn and canker-bit;
Yet am I noble as the adversary
I come to cope.

Alb. Which is that adversary?

Edg. What's he that speaks for Edmund, Earl of Gloucester?

Edm. Himself; what say'st thou to him?

Edg. Draw thy sword,
That, if my speech offend a noble heart,
Thy arm may do thee justice. Here is mine.
Behold, it is the privilege of mine honours,
My oath, and my profession. I protest, 130
Maugre thy strength, youth, place, and eminence,

110. *quality or degree:* rank. 113. *manifold:* many times over. 120. *quality:* rank. 122. *canker-bit:* worm-eaten. 124. *cope:* encounter. 129. *it . . . honours:* i.e., as a knight. *honours.* Q_1 reads *tongue.* 131. *Maugre:* in spite of.

Despite thy victor-sword and fire-new fortune,
Thy valour and thy heart, thou art a traitor,
False to thy gods, thy brother, and thy father;
Conspirant 'gainst this high-illustrious prince;
And, from the extremest upward of thy head
To the descent and dust below thy foot,
A most toad-spotted traitor. Say thou "No,"
This sword, this arm, and my best spirits, are bent
To prove upon thy heart, whereto I speak, 140
Thou liest.

Edm. In wisdom I should ask thy name;
But, since thy outside looks so fair and warlike,
And that thy tongue some say of breeding breathes,
What safe and nicely I might well delay
By rule of knighthood, I disdain and spurn.
Back do I toss these treasons to thy head;
With the hell-hated lie o'erwhelm thy heart;
Which, for they yet glance by and scarcely bruise,
This sword of mine shall give them instant way,
Where they shall rest for ever. Trumpets, speak! 150

[*Alarums. They fight. Edmund falls.*

Alb. Save him, save him!

Gon. This is practice, Gloucester.
By the law of arms thou wast not bound to answer
An unknown opposite; thou art not vanquish'd,
But cozen'd and beguiled.

Alb. [*Producing Goneril's letter*] Shut your mouth, dame,
Or with this paper shall I stop it. [*To Edmund.*] Hold, sir;
Thou worse than any name, read thine own evil.

[*Goneril snatches at it.*

No tearing, lady; I perceive you know it.

[*Gives the letter to Edmund.*

143. *say:* evidence. 144. *What . . . delay.* Omitted in Q1. *safe:* i.e., safely. *nicely:* scrupulously. 147. *hell-hated:* hated as hell. 151. *Save him.* Albany is concerned only that Edmund shall not be killed before he has time to make a statement. *practice:* treachery. 152. *arms.* Q1 reads *war.* 153. *opposite:* opponent. 154. *cozen'd:* cheated.

Gon. Say, if I do, the laws are mine, not thine.
Who can arraign me for't? [*Exit.*

Alb. Most monstrous! Oh,
Know'st thou this paper?

Edm. Ask me not what I know. 160

Alb. [*To an Attendant*] Go after her, she's desperate; govern her.

Edm. What you have charged me with, that have I done,
And more, much more; the time will bring it out.
'Tis past, and so am I. But what art thou
That hast this fortune on me? If thou'rt noble,
I do forgive thee.

Edg. Let's exchange charity.
I am no less in blood than thou art, Edmund;
If more, the more thou hast wrong'd me.
My name is Edgar, and thy father's son.
The gods are just, and of our pleasant vices 170
Make instruments to plague us;
The dark and vicious place where thee he got
Cost him his eyes.

Edm. Thou hast spoken right, 'tis true;
The wheel is come full circle; I am here.

Alb. Methought thy very gait did prophesy
A royal nobleness. I must embrace thee;
Let sorrow split my heart, if ever I
Did hate thee or thy father! [*Embracing him.*

Edg. Worthy prince, I know't.

Alb. Where have you hid yourself?
How have you known the miseries of your father? 180

Edg. By nursing them, my lord. List a brief tale;
And when 'tis told, O, that my heart would burst!
The bloody proclamation to escape,
That follow'd me so near—O, our lives' sweetness!
That we the pain of death would hourly die

160. *Edm.* Q1 gives this speech to Goneril. 170. *pleasant vices:* an allusion to Gloucester's guilt in begetting Edmund. Q1 reads *virtues.* 171. *plague.* Q1 reads *scourge.* 181. *List:* hear.

Rather than die at once!—taught me to shift
Into a madman's rags, to assume a semblance
That very dogs disdain'd; and in this habit
Met I my father with his bleeding rings,
Their precious stones new lost; became his guide, 190
Led him, begg'd for him, saved him from despair;
Never—O fault!—reveal'd myself unto him,
Until some half-hour past, when I was arm'd.
Not sure, though hoping, of this good success,
I ask'd his blessing, and from first to last
Told him my pilgrimage. But his flaw'd heart
(Alack, too weak the conflict to support!)
'Twixt two extremes of passion, joy and grief,
Burst smilingly.

Edm. This speech of yours hath moved me,
And shall perchance do good. But speak you on; 200
You look as you had something more to say.

Alb. If there be more, more woeful, hold it in;
For I am almost ready to dissolve,
Hearing of this.

Edg. This would have seem'd a period
To such as love not sorrow; but another,
To amplify too much, would make much more,
And top extremity.
Whilst I was big in clamour came there in a man,
Who, having seen me in my worst estate,
Shunn'd my abhorr'd society; but then, finding 210
Who 'twas that so endured, with his strong arms
He fasten'd on my neck, and bellow'd out
As he'ld burst heaven, threw him on my father,
Told the most piteous tale of Lear and him
That ever ear received, which in recounting

194. *success:* outcome. 196. *flaw'd:* cracked. 198. *passion:* emotion. 203. *dissolve:* i.e., in tears. 204–21. *Edg. . . . slave.* Omitted in F_1. 204. *period:* end. 205–7. *but . . . extremity:* but one more such circumstance, by amplifying what is already too much, would augment it, and so exceed the extreme of sorrow.

His grief grew puissant, and the strings of life
Began to crack. Twice then the trumpets sounded,
And there I left him tranced.
Alb. But who was this?
Edg. Kent, sir, the banish'd Kent; who in disguise
Follow'd his enemy king and did him service 220
Improper for a slave.

Enter a Gentleman, *with a bloody knife.*

Gent. Help, help, O, help!
Edg. What kind of help?
Alb. Speak, man.
Edg. What means that bloody knife?
Gent. 'Tis hot, it smokes;
It came even from the heart of—O, she's dead!
Alb. Who dead? Speak, man.
Gent. Your lady, sir, your lady. And her sister
By her is poisoned; she hath confess'd it.
Edm. I was contracted to them both; all three
Now marry in an instant.
Edg. Here comes Kent.
Alb. Produce their bodies, be they alive or dead. 230
This judgment of the heavens, that makes us tremble,
Touches us not with pity. [*Exit Gentleman.*

Enter Kent.

O, is this he?
The time will not allow the compliment
Which very manners urges. [*Embracing him.*
Kent. I am come
To bid my king and master aye good night.
Is he not here?
Alb. Great thing of us forgot!
Speak, Edmund, where's the king? And where's Cordelia?
See'st thou this object, Kent?
[*The bodies of Goneril and Regan are brought in.*

218. *tranced:* in a trance. 231. *judgment.* Q_1 reads *justice.*

Kent. Alack, why thus?
Edm. Yet Edmund was beloved;
The one the other poison'd for my sake, 240
And after slew herself.
Alb. Even so. Cover their faces.
Edm. I pant for life. Some good I mean to do,
Despite of mine own nature. Quickly send,
Be brief in it, to the castle; for my writ
Is on the life of Lear and on Cordelia.
Nay, send in time.
Alb. Run, run, O, run!
Edg. To who, my lord? Who hath the office? Send
Thy token of reprieve.
Edm. Well thought on; take my sword—the captain— 250
Give it the captain.
Alb. Haste thee, for thy life. [*Exit Edgar.*
Edm. He hath commission from thy wife and me
To hang Cordelia in the prison and
To lay the blame upon her own despair
That she fordid herself.
Alb. The gods defend her! Bear him hence awhile.
[*Edmund is borne off.*

Re-enter LEAR, *with* CORDELIA *dead in his arms;* EDGAR, Captain, *and others following.*

Lear. Howl, howl, howl, howl! O, you are men of stones!
Had I your tongues and eyes, I'ld use them so
That heaven's vault should crack. She's gone forever!
I know when one is dead, and when one lives; 260
She's dead as earth. Lend me a looking-glass;
If that her breath will mist or stain the stone,
Why, then she lives.
Kent. Is this the promised end?
Edg. Or image of that horror?

250. *the captain.* So Q1; omitted in other versions. 255. *fordid:* killed. 262. *the stone:* the glass. 263. *promised end:* Day of Judgment.

Alb. Fall, and cease!
Lear. This feather stirs; she lives! If it be so,
It is a chance which does redeem all sorrows
That ever I have felt.
Kent. [*Kneeling*] O my good master!
Lear. Prithee, away.
Edg. 'Tis noble Kent, your friend.
Lear. A plague upon you, murderers, traitors all!
I might have saved her; now she's gone forever! 270
Cordelia, Cordelia! Stay a little. Ha!
What is't thou say'st? Her voice was ever soft,
Gentle, and low, an excellent thing in woman.
I kill'd the slave that was a-hanging thee.
Capt. 'Tis true, my lords, he did.
Lear. Did I not, fellow?
I have seen the day, with my good biting falchion
I would have made them skip. I am old now,
And these same crosses spoil me. Who are you?
Mine eyes are not o' the best; I'll tell you straight.
Kent. If Fortune brag of two she loved and hated, 280
One of them we behold.
Lear. This is a dull sight. Are you not Kent?
Kent. The same,
Your servant Kent. Where is your servant Caius?
Lear. He's a good fellow, I can tell you that;
He'll strike, and quickly too. He's dead and rotten.
Kent. No, my good lord; I am the very man—
Lear. I'll see that straight.
Kent. That, from your first of difference and decay,
Have follow'd your sad steps.
Lear. You are welcome hither.
Kent. Nor no man else. All's cheerless, dark, and deadly.
Your eldest daughters have fordone themselves, 291
And desperately are dead.

276. *falchion:* sword with a curved blade. 278. *crosses:* adversities. 282. *This . . . sight.* Omitted in Q_1. 288. *first:* beginning, outset. Q_1 reads *life.* 291. *fordone:* killed.

Lear. Ay, so I think.
Alb. He knows not what he says, and vain it is
That we present us to him.
Edg. Very bootless.

Enter a Captain.

Capt. Edmund is dead, my lord.
Alb. That's but a trifle here.
You lords and noble friends, know our intent.
What comfort to this great decay may come
Shall be applied. For us, we will resign,
During the life of this old Majesty,
To him our absolute power; [*To Edgar and Kent.*] you, to your rights, 300
With boot, and such addition as your honours
Have more than merited. All friends shall taste
The wages of their virtue, and all foes
The cup of their deservings. O, see, see! [*They turn to Lear.*
Lear. And my poor fool is hang'd! No, no, no life!
Why should a dog, a horse, a rat, have life,
And thou no breath at all? Thou'lt come no more,
Never, never, never, never, never!
Pray you, undo this button. Thank you, sir.
Do you see this? Look on her, look, her lips, 310
Look there, look there! [*Dies.*
Edg. He faints! My lord, my lord!
Kent. Break, heart; I prithee, break!
Edg. Look up, my lord.
Kent. Vex not his ghost. O, let him pass! He hates him much
That would upon the rack of this tough world
Stretch him out longer.
Edg. He is gone, indeed.
Kent. The wonder is, he hath endured so long;
He but usurp'd his life.

294. *bootless:* vain. 301. *boot:* addition. *addition:* title. 305. *fool:* i.e., Cordelia; a term of endearment. 313. *much.* So Q_2; omitted in F_1 and Q_1. 314. *rack:* instrument of torture.

Alb. Bear them from hence. Our present business
Is general woe. [*To Kent and Edgar.*] Friends of my soul, you
twain,
Rule in this realm, and the gored state sustain. 320

Kent. I have a journey, sir, shortly to go;
My master calls me, I must not say no.

Edg. The weight of this sad time we must obey;
Speak what we feel, not what we ought to say.
The oldest hath borne most; we that are young
Shall never see so much, nor live so long.

[*Exeunt, with a dead march, the bodies borne before them.*

322. *master:* i.e., Lear. 323. *Edg.* Q_1 assigns this speech to Albany.
325–6. *The oldest . . . long.* The king has endured fullness of sorrows; we who come after, even if we live as long, will never see days as evil as those which he has seen.

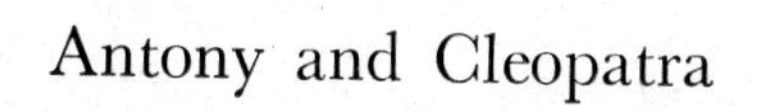

Antony and Cleopatra

Introduction

Source

Shakespeare's source for *Antony and Cleopatra* is "The Life of Marcus Antonius," which he read in Sir Thomas North's translation of Plutarch's *Lives of the Noble Grecians and Romans*, a rich storehouse from which Shakespeare obtained material for three other plays: *Julius Cæsar*, *Timon of Athens*, and *Coriolanus*. In *Julius Cæsar* (1599) he had built a drama around the assassination of Cæsar and its immediate consequences—the fall of Brutus and the rise of Mark Antony. In *Antony and Cleopatra*, eight years later, he took up the story almost where he had left it. Cæsar's death left the Roman empire divided among three men: Lepidus, Antony, and Octavius Cæsar. The breaking-up of this triumvirate, culminating in the overthrow of Antony and the ascendancy of Octavius, is the background in *Antony and Cleopatra*, a spacious and magnificent background against which is enacted the drama of the great soldier's tragic love for the glamorous queen.

To North's simple, fresh, vigorous prose Shakespeare's direct debt is great. Some passages follow North very closely, even to the extent of verbal borrowing, as in the famous description of Cleopatra's barge (II, ii, 195 ff.) and in the memorable last words of Antony (IV, xv, 45–58). A comparison of these two passages with North's prose reveals not only how much Shakespeare owes to North but also how marvelously he refashions North's account. He makes of the prose not merely admirable blank verse but, in the second passage, powerful and effective dramatic speech.

"The poop . . . was of gold, the sails of purple, and the oars of silver, which kept stroke in rowing after the sound of the music of flutes, hautboys, citherns, viols, and such other instruments as they played upon in the barge. And now for the person of herself: she was laid under a pavilion of cloth of gold of tissue, apparelled and attired like the goddess Venus, commonly drawn in picture; and hard by her, on either hand of her, pretty fair boys apparelled as painters do set forth god Cupid, with little fans in their hands, with the which they fanned wind upon her. Her ladies and gentlewomen also, the fairest of them, were apparelled like the nymphs Nereids (which are the mermaids of the waters) and like the Graces, some steering the helm, others tending the tackle and ropes of the barge, out of the which there came a wonderful passing sweet savour of perfumes, that perfumed the wharf's side, pestered with innumerable multitudes of people."

"He earnestly prayed her, and persuaded her, that she would seek to save her life, if she could possibly without reproach and dishonour; and that chiefly she should trust Proculeius above any man else about Cæsar; and, as for himself, that she should not lament nor sorrow for the miserable change of his fortune at the end of his days, but rather that she should think him the more fortunate for the former triumphs and honours he had received, considering that while he lived he was the noblest and greatest prince of the world, and that now he was overcome not cowardly, but valiantly, a Roman by another Roman."

For his plot, Shakespeare in the main follows Plutarch. Like Plutarch, he takes his reader over the vast extent of the Roman empire, and in his forty-two scenes turns from one group of characters to another with a speed that is sometimes bewildering. The historic time covered is about ten years (41–30 B.C.), but in the play the action occurs on twelve days, with intervals that total about a year. Plutarch's mastery of vivid narrative and his interest in details that reveal character are merits that Shakespeare recognizes and transfers to his play. Shakespeare transforms Plutarch's account by throwing over it a glow of poetry that gives to the old story of Antony and Cleopatra a new beauty and at the close even a touch of sublimity. But Shakespeare's Antony is not the Antony of Plutarch; the dramatist conceals many of his faults, emphasizes his virtues, and makes both him and Cleopatra more attractive, more worthy of sympathy and pity.

The Characters

Antony is not a typical hero of Shakespearean tragedy. He is not, like Hamlet and Macbeth, introspective; he does not, like Othello and Lear, question the ways of Providence; he is, in North's phrase, "a plain man, without subtlety." Despite what Hazlitt calls "the irregular grandeur" of his soul, he does not possess—as do Brutus and Hamlet and Othello—such beauty or nobility of character as commands our unreserved admiration or love. Greatness of a kind he has: "the triple pillar of the world," he is a leader adored by his soldiers, a man of a rich, enjoying nature, frank, generous, warmhearted. When the play opens, he is already caught in the trap that will hold and destroy him, and he hardly struggles to free himself from the witchery of the ever-changing queen. He knows, and we know, that he will return to her and persuade himself that "the nobleness of life is to do thus." As the catastrophe approaches, his honesty and courage grow more apparent, and at the last the completeness of his love for Cleopatra has in it a touch of the sublime. Knowing that she has destroyed him, knowing all her faults and her final deceit in sending him word of her death, he has for her nothing of blame or reproach, nothing but tenderness and unselfish thought for her future. The "irregular grandeur" of his soul is nowhere more striking than in his death.

Cleopatra, too, does not wholly win our admiration or our love. In the first half of the play she is an alluring and mysterious barbaric queen, capricious, violent, selfish, vain. As the play progresses, she acquires a certain beauty of spirit. "She has," Hazlitt observes, "great and unpardonable faults, but the grandeur of her death almost redeems them." "Almost redeems them"—for her death, despite its splendor, is not quite heroic. After Antony's death there is for her "nothing left remarkable beneath the visiting moon," and she dies to join him, but she dies also to escape humiliation by Octavius. To the last she remains the selfish, vain, mysterious, fascinating queen.

Among the minor characters Enobarbus is certainly the most interesting. Throughout the play he is the blunt truth-teller who exposes the follies and pretensions of those about him. A steadfast admirer of Antony's soldierly virtues, he understands but condemns his leader's fatal attachment. When he believes Antony's cause irretrievably lost, he deserts him:

> The loyalty well held to fools does make
> Our faith mere folly.

But he repents his treachery and dies brokenhearted, ruled, like Antony, by emotion rather than by reason.

Octavius serves as little more than a foil to Antony. In every respect he is the direct opposite of his fiery and magnanimous rival. Cold, selfish, crafty, he is the successful opportunist who never errs, and who never loses his self-control. "His figure," as Professor A. C. Bradley points out, "is invested with a certain tragic dignity, because he is felt to be the Man of Destiny, the agent of forces against which the intentions of an individual avail nothing."

Relation to Other Shakespearean Plays

To Shakespeare's other plays *Antony and Cleopatra* presents some obvious but illuminating contrasts. In theme, in style, in structure, in substance, in the nature of the tragic conflict, in the tragic impression produced, and in mood it differs from the plays that precede and follow it.

In one other play, *Romeo and Juliet*, Shakespeare chose love as a theme for tragedy. In the earlier play the youthful lovers are strengthened and ennobled by their love. *Antony and Cleo-*

patra, written at least a decade later, reveals the great soldier and the barbaric queen—both of whom are no longer young, both scarred by experience—enslaved by an overpowering passion which destroys them, but which at times (especially in their deaths) colors their actions with beauty and nobility. The difference between the two tragedies is a difference inherent in the stories and is not referable to any change in Shakespeare or in his conception of love as a force in human life.

The style of *Antony and Cleopatra* is distinctive. It lacks the decoration, the exuberance, the "honey-tongued" sweetness of his early manner, and it has lost the clarity and flowing eloquence of *Henry V* and *Julius Cæsar*. It marks the culmination of that style which Shakespeare had been developing in the great tragedies—especially in *Othello*, *King Lear*, and *Macbeth*—a style notable for intense compression, a rapid, concentrated style, in construction often irregular and elliptical, and consequently not always clear. It has, however, striking merits: it is extremely vigorous, dramatic, and, in passages of heightened emotion, productive of sudden and amazing effects. But it lacks the sustained lucidity and ease of his style in the romances that follow—*Cymbeline*, *The Winter's Tale*, and *The Tempest*.

In structure *Antony and Cleopatra* differs from the great tragedies that precede it—*Hamlet*, *Othello*, *King Lear*, *Macbeth*. The structure of *Antony and Cleopatra* is that of the old chronicle-history. Thirty-four characters move through the forty-two loosely connected scenes of the play, and such unity as the episodic plan has is given it by character rather than by action. The play lacks, consequently, the growing tension so notable in the earlier tragedies, a tension produced by the steady and exciting movement of conflicting forces toward the catastrophe. In the earlier acts, the play lacks, too, those scenes which, in *Hamlet*, *Othello*, *King Lear*, and *Macbeth*, so stir the audience with painful expectation or actual terror.

In substance, too, *Antony and Cleopatra* differs from Shakespeare's other tragedies. Evil in its more appalling forms is absent: there is here no Iago, no Regan, no Goneril. Nor does the destruction of evil involve the destruction of innocence and goodness and beauty: there is here no Juliet, no Desdemona, no Cordelia. Shakespeare does not, as in the earlier tragedies, explore and reveal the more terrifying depths of the soul. Nor are the principal characters torn by a painful inner conflict. Although Antony knows that he is pursuing the worse of two courses, he is tortured by no struggle between the forces of good and evil in his own nature. He does not suffer the agonies of Lear, of Othello, of Lady Macbeth.

As a result of these differences *Antony and Cleopatra* produces tragic impressions different from those of the earlier tragedies. The errors of the principal characters, the decline of their fortunes, the approach of their doom—these move us less powerfully than in the tragedies from *Hamlet* to *Macbeth*. Poignant and beautiful as the closing scenes are, we do not feel that sense of loss, of waste, that so oppresses us in *Hamlet*, *Othello*, and *King Lear*. We feel instead that the love of Antony and Cleopatra has ennobled them as nothing else could, that for them death is a kind of victory, that since fate has decreed the fall of Antony we must "let determined things to destiny hold unbewailed their way."

Perhaps it is not fanciful to imagine in *Antony and Cleopatra* a change in Shakespeare's mood. As Barrett Wendell observes, "The profound emotional impulse which has surged beneath the great tragedies seems here to slacken." He appears to write here with less tension than in the earlier tragedies, with less dark questioning of Providence; there is here more of detachment, something even of "that serene and blessed mood" that he was soon to reveal in *The Tempest*. In one great passage, indeed, we are in the atmosphere of *The Tempest*, and we hear the voice of Prospero. Antony, when he knows the end is near, talks with Eros:

Antony. Sometime we see a cloud that's dragonish,
A vapour sometime like a bear or lion,
A tower'd citadel, a pendent rock,
A forked mountain, or blue promontory
With trees upon 't that nod unto the world
And mock our eyes with air. Thou hast seen these signs;
They are black vesper's pageants.

Eros. Ay, my lord.

Antony. That which is now a horse, even with a thought
The rack dislimns, and makes it indistinct
As water is in water.

Eros. It does, my lord.

Antony. My good knave Eros, now thy captain is
Even such a body. Here I am Antony,
Yet cannot hold this visible shape, my knave.

To Prospero when he had ended his revels and finished his work, to Antony in this scene, as perhaps to Shakespeare as he grew older, life seemed a mere passing pageant and men themselves but dreams.

Date and Text

A book called *Antony and Cleopatra*, presumably Shakespeare's play, was entered in the Stationers' Register, May 20, 1608. The earliest known edition of the play is that included in the First Folio of 1623. This is, of course, the basis of all modern texts.

The play was probably written and produced in 1606 or early in 1607. In the latter year Samuel Daniel issued a new edition of his *Certain Small Workes*, and therein made changes in his *Cleopatra* of 1594, which, in the opinion of Sir Edmund Chambers, show clearly the influence of Shakespeare's play.

DRAMATIS PERSONÆ

CLEOPATRA, Queen of Egypt.
MARK ANTONY, OCTAVIUS CÆSAR, M. ÆMILIUS LEPIDUS — Triumvirs.
SEXTUS POMPEIUS.
OCTAVIA, sister of Octavius Cæsar.
CANIDIUS, lieutenant-general under Antony.
DOMITIUS ENOBARBUS, VENTIDIUS, EROS, SCARUS, DERCETUS, DEMETRIUS, PHILO — friends of Antony.
TAURUS, lieutenant-general under Octavius Cæsar.
MECÆNAS, AGRIPPA, DOLABELLA, PROCULEIUS, THYREUS, GALLUS — friends of Octavius Cæsar.
MENAS, MENECRATES, VARRIUS — friends of Pompey.
CHARMIAN, IRAS — maids-of-honor attending Cleopatra.
ALEXAS, MARDIAN, a eunuch, SELEUCUS, DIOMEDES — attendants upon Cleopatra.
SILIUS, an officer in Ventidius' army.
EUPHRONIUS, a schoolmaster, ambassador from Antony to Cæsar.
A SOOTHSAYER.
A CLOWNISH COUNTRYMAN.
Officers, Soldiers, Messengers, Attendants.

Scene of the Action: Alexandria, Rome, Athens, and various other parts of the Roman Empire.

Time: 41 B.C. to 30 B.C.

Antony and Cleopatra

ACT I

SCENE I. *Alexandria. A room in* CLEOPATRA'S *palace.*

Enter DEMETRIUS *and* PHILO.

Phi. Nay, but this dotage of our general's
O'erflows the measure. Those his goodly eyes,
That o'er the files and musters of the war
Have glow'd like plated Mars, now bend, now turn
The office and devotion of their view
Upon a tawny front. His captain's heart,
Which in the scuffles of great fights hath burst
The buckles on his breast, reneges all temper
And is become the bellows and the fan
To cool a gipsy's lust.

Flourish. Enter ANTONY, CLEOPATRA, *her Ladies, the train, with Eunuchs fanning her.*

Look, where they come. 10
Take but good note, and you shall see in him
The triple pillar of the world transform'd
Into a strumpet's fool. Behold and see.
Cleo. If it be love indeed, tell me how much.
Ant. There's beggary in the love that can be reckon'd.
Cleo. I'll set a bourn how far to be beloved.
Ant. Then must thou needs find out new heaven, new earth.

[I. i] 3. *files . . . war:* troops in battle formation. 4. *plated:* armored. 5. *office and devotion:* devoted office (hendiadys). 6. *front:* forehead, face. 8. *reneges all temper:* renounces all self-control (with pun on "temper" of steel). 10. *gipsy's.* Cleopatra was of Greek blood, though he calls her *tawny*. His sneer gains point from the fact that *gipsy* is derived from *Egyptian*, and that gipsies were believed to be descended from Egyptians. 12. *triple pillar:* i.e., one of the triumvirs. 15. *beggary:* beggarliness. 16. *bourn:* limit.

Enter an Attendant.

Att. News, my good lord, from Rome.
Ant. Grates me—the sum.
Cleo. Nay, hear them, Antony.
Fulvia perchance is angry; or who knows 20
If the scarce-bearded Cæsar have not sent
His powerful mandate to you, "Do this, or this;
Take in that kingdom, and enfranchise that.
Perform 't, or else we damn thee."
Ant. How, my love?
Cleo. Perchance? Nay, and most like.
You must not stay here longer; your dismission
Is come from Cæsar; therefore hear it, Antony.
Where's Fulvia's process? Cæsar's, I would say? Both?
Call in the messengers. As I am Egypt's queen,
Thou blushest, Antony, and that blood of thine 30
Is Cæsar's homager; else so thy cheek pays shame
When shrill-tongued Fulvia scolds. The messengers!
Ant. Let Rome in Tiber melt, and the wide arch
Of the ranged empire fall! Here is my space.
Kingdoms are clay. Our dungy earth alike
Feeds beast as man. The nobleness of life
Is to do thus, when such a mutual pair [*Embracing.*
And such a twain can do 't, in which I bind,
On pain of punishment, the world to weet
We stand up peerless.
Cleo. Excellent falsehood! 40
Why did he marry Fulvia, and not love her?

18. *Grates . . . sum:* it annoys me; tell me the gist of the news. 19. *them:* i.e., the news, here, as often, regarded as plural. 20. *Fulvia:* Antony's wife, who with the consul Lucius, her brother, was waging war against Octavius. 21. *scarce-bearded.* In 41 B.C., when the play opens, Octavius Cæsar was twenty-three years old, and Antony about forty-three. 23. *Take in:* conquer. *enfranchise:* set free. 26. *dismission:* discharge. 28. *process:* formal summons. 31. *homager:* humble servant. *else so:* so at other times. 34. *ranged:* ordered. 37. *mutual:* intimate. 39. *weet:* know.

I'll seem the fool I am not. Antony
Will be himself.

Ant. But stirr'd by Cleopatra.
Now, for the love of Love and her soft hours,
Let's not confound the time with conference harsh.
There's not a minute of our lives should stretch
Without some pleasure now. What sport tonight?

Cleo. Hear the ambassadors.

Ant. Fie, wrangling queen;
Whom everything becomes, to chide, to laugh,
To weep; whose every passion fully strives 50
To make itself, in thee, fair and admired!
No messenger but thine, and all alone
Tonight we'll wander through the streets and note
The qualities of people. Come, my queen;
Last night you did desire it.—Speak not to us.

[*Exeunt Antony and Cleopatra with their train.*

Dem. Is Cæsar with Antonius prized so slight?

Phi. Sir, sometimes, when he is not Antony,
He comes too short of that great property
Which still should go with Antony.

Dem. I am full sorry
That he approves the common liar, who 60
Thus speaks of him at Rome; but I will hope
Of better deeds tomorrow. Rest you happy! [*Exeunt.*

SCENE II. *Another room in* CLEOPATRA'S *palace.*

Enter CHARMIAN, IRAS, ALEXAS, *and a* Soothsayer.

Char. Lord Alexas, sweet Alexas, most anything Alexas, almost most absolute Alexas, where's the soothsayer that you

42–3. *I'll . . . himself:* i.e., if I believe you, I'll seem more foolish than I am. Antony will always be fickle. 43. *stirr'd:* moved, inspired. 45. *confound:* waste. 46. *stretch:* extend. 50. *passion:* passionate outburst. 54. *qualities:* characteristics. 58. *property:* behavior. 59. *still:* always. 60. *approves:* proves true.
[ii] 2. *absolute:* perfect.

praised so to the queen? O that I knew this husband, which, you say, must charge his horns with garlands!

Alex. Soothsayer!

Sooth. Your will?

Char. Is this the man? Is 't you, sir, that know things?

Sooth. In Nature's infinite book of secrecy
A little I can read.

Alex. Show him your hand. 10

Enter ENOBARBUS.

Eno. Bring in the banquet quickly; wine enough
Cleopatra's health to drink.

Char. Good sir, give me good fortune.

Sooth. I make not, but foresee.

Char. Pray, then, foresee me one.

Sooth. You shall be yet far fairer than you are.

Char. He means in flesh.

Iras. No, you shall paint when you are old.

Char. Wrinkles forbid!

Alex. Vex not his prescience; be attentive. 20

Char. Hush!

Sooth. You shall be more beloving than beloved.

Char. I had rather heat my liver with drinking.

Alex. Nay, hear him.

Char. Good now, some excellent fortune! Let me be married to three kings in a forenoon, and widow them all. Let me have a child at fifty, to whom Herod of Jewry may do homage. Find me to marry me with Octavius Cæsar, and companion me with my mistress. 30

Sooth. You shall outlive the lady whom you serve.

Char. O excellent! I love long life better than figs.

5. *charge:* load, adorn. The reference is either to adorning a bull for sacrifice or to putting on a marriage wreath (with an allusion to the mythical horns worn by a deceived husband). 11. *banquet:* dessert. 23. *with drinking:* i.e., rather than with love. The liver was believed to be the seat of love. 28. *Herod.* See Matthew 2 : 8. *Find me:* i.e., by examining my hand. 30. *companion me with:* make me equal to.

Sooth. You have seen and proved a fairer former fortune
Than that which is to approach.

Char. Then belike my children shall have no names. Prithee, how many boys and wenches must I have?

Sooth. If every of your wishes had a womb,
And fertile every wish, a million.

Char. Out, fool! I forgive thee for a witch. 40

Alex. You think none but your sheets are privy to your wishes.

Char. Nay, come, tell Iras hers.

Alex. We'll know all our fortunes.

Eno. Mine, and most of our fortunes, tonight, shall be—drunk to bed.

Iras. There's a palm presages chastity, if nothing else.

Char. E'en as the o'erflowing Nilus presageth famine. 50

Iras. Go, you wild bedfellow, you cannot soothsay.

Char. Nay, if an oily palm be not a fruitful prognostication, I cannot scratch mine ear. Prithee tell her but a worky-day fortune.

Sooth. Your fortunes are alike.

Iras. But how, but how? Give me particulars.

Sooth. I have said.

Iras. Am I not an inch of fortune better than she? 60

Char. Well, if you were but an inch of fortune better than I, where would you choose it?

Iras. Not in my husband's nose.

Char. Our worser thoughts heavens mend! Alexas, come, his fortune, his fortune! O, let him marry a woman that cannot go, sweet Isis, I beseech thee! And let her die too, and give him a worse! And let worse follow worse, till the worst of all follow him laughing to his grave, fifty-fold a cuckold! Good Isis, hear me this prayer, though thou deny me a matter of more weight. Good Isis, I beseech thee! 72

39. *fertile:* the emendation of Theobald and Warburton; F_1 reads *foretell.* 40. *for:* as. 47. *There's . . . chastity:* i.e., because dry and cool. 55. *worky-day:* commonplace. 66. *go:* bear children. *Isis:* chief goddess of Egypt. 70. *cuckold:* deceived husband.

Iras. Amen. Dear goddess, hear that prayer of the people, for, as it is a heart-breaking to see a handsome man loose-wived, so it is a deadly sorrow to behold a foul knave uncuckolded. Therefore, dear Isis, keep decorum, and fortune him accordingly!

Char. Amen. 79

Alex. Lo, now, if it lay in their hands to make me a cuckold, they would make themselves whores, but they 'ld do 't!

Eno. Hush! Here comes Antony.

Char. Not he; the queen.

Enter CLEOPATRA.

Cleo. Saw you my lord?

Eno. No, lady.

Cleo. Was he not here?

Char. No, madam.

Cleo. He was disposed to mirth, but on the sudden
A Roman thought hath struck him. Enobarbus!

Eno. Madam?

Cleo. Seek him, and bring him hither. Where's Alexas?

Alex. Here, at your service. My lord approaches. 90

Cleo. We will not look upon him. Go with us. [*Exeunt.*

Enter ANTONY *with a* Messenger *and* Attendants.

Mess. Fulvia thy wife first came into the field.

Ant. Against my brother Lucius?

Mess. Ay.
But soon that war had end, and the time's state
Made friends of them, jointing their force 'gainst Cæsar,
Whose better issue in the war, from Italy,
Upon the first encounter, drave them.

Ant. Well, what worst?

Mess. The nature of bad news infects the teller.

Ant. When it concerns the fool or coward. On! 100
Things that are past are done with me. 'Tis thus:
Who tells me true, though in his tale lie death,
I hear him as he flatter'd.

103. *as:* as though.

Mess. Labienus—
This is stiff news—hath, with his Parthian force,
Extended Asia from Euphrates;
His conquering banner shook from Syria
To Lydia and to Ionia,
Whilst—

Ant. Antony, thou wouldst say—

Mess. O, my lord!

Ant. Speak to me home; mince not the general tongue;
Name Cleopatra as she is call'd in Rome; 110
Rail thou in Fulvia's phrase; and taunt my faults
With such full license as both truth and malice
Have power to utter. O, then we bring forth weeds,
When our quick minds lie still; and our ills told us
Is as our earing. Fare thee well awhile.

Mess. At your noble pleasure. [*Exit.*

Ant. From Sicyon, ho, the news! Speak there!

First Att. The man from Sicyon—is there such an one?

Sec. Att. He stays upon your will.

Ant. Let him appear.
These strong Egyptian fetters I must break 120
Or lose myself in dotage.

Enter another Messenger.

What are you?

Sec. Mess. Fulvia thy wife is dead.

Ant. Where died she?

Sec. Mess. In Sicyon.
Her length of sickness, with what else more serious
Importeth thee to know, this bears. [*Gives a letter.*

Ant. Forbear me.

[*Exit Second Messenger.*

There's a great spirit gone! Thus did I desire it.

105. *Extended:* seized upon (a legal phrase). 109. *home:* plainly. *mince . . . tongue:* soften not the common report. 111. *Fulvia's phrase.* Plutarch writes that Fulvia was of a "peevish, crooked, and troublesome nature." 115. *earing:* plowing. 117. *Sicyon:* a city in Greece. 119. *stays upon:* awaits. 125. *Forbear:* leave.

What our contempt doth often hurl from us,
We wish it ours again. The present pleasure,
By revolution lowering, does become
The opposite of itself. She's good, being gone; 130
The hand could pluck her back that shoved her on.
I must from this enchanting queen break off.
Ten thousand harms, more than the ills I know,
My idleness doth hatch. How now, Enobarbus!

Re-enter ENOBARBUS.

Eno. What's your pleasure, sir?

Ant. I must with haste from hence.

Eno. Why, then we kill all our women. We see how mortal an unkindness is to them. If they suffer our departure, death's the word.

Ant. I must be gone. 140

Eno. Under a compelling occasion, let women die. It were pity to cast them away for nothing; though, between them and a great cause, they should be esteemed nothing. Cleopatra, catching but the least noise of this, dies instantly. I have seen her die twenty times upon far poorer moment. I do think there is mettle in death, which commits some loving act upon her, she hath such a celerity in dying.

Ant. She is cunning past man's thought. 150

Eno. Alack, sir, no; her passions are made of nothing but the finest part of pure love. We cannot call her winds and waters sighs and tears; they are greater storms and tempests than almanacs can report. This cannot be cunning in her; if it be, she makes a shower of rain as well as Jove.

Ant. Would I had never seen her!

Eno. O, sir, you had then left unseen a wonderful piece of work, which not to have been blest withal would have discredited your travel. 161

129. *By revolution lowering:* decreasing by change. 131. *could:* would be willing to. 141. *occasion:* cause. 147. *moment:* cause. *mettle:* ardor. 161. *withal:* with. *discredited your travel:* proved you had seen little.

Ant. Fulvia is dead.

Eno. Sir?

Ant. Fulvia is dead.

Eno. Fulvia!

Ant. Dead.

Eno. Why, sir, give the gods a thankful sacrifice. When it pleaseth their deities to take the wife of a man from him, it shows to man the tailors of the earth; comforting therein, that when old robes are worn out, there are members to make new. If there were no more women but Fulvia, then had you indeed a cut, and the case to be lamented. This grief is crowned with consolation; your old smock brings forth a new petticoat; and indeed the tears live in an onion that should water this sorrow.

Ant. The business she hath broached in the state
Cannot endure my absence. 179

Eno. And the business you have broached here cannot be without you; especially that of Cleopatra's, which wholly depends on your abode.

Ant. No more light answers. Let our officers
Have notice what we purpose. I shall break
The cause of our expedience to the queen,
And get her leave to part. For not alone
The death of Fulvia, with more urgent touches,
Do strongly speak to us, but the letters too
Of many our contriving friends in Rome
Petition us at home. Sextus Pompeius 190
Hath given the dare to Cæsar, and commands
The empire of the sea. Our slippery people,
Whose love is never link'd to the deserver
Till his deserts are past, begin to throw
Pompey the Great and all his dignities

169–70. *it shows . . . earth:* i.e., the gods are like tailors. 171. *members:* i.e., tailors. 173. *cut:* (a) blow, (b) cut of a garment. 176–7. *the tears . . . sorrow:* i.e., real tears are unnecessary. 182. *abode:* staying. 185. *expedience:* enterprise. 187. *touches:* reasons. 190. *at home:* i.e., to come home. *Sextus Pompeius:* son of Pompey the Great. 194–6. *throw . . . son:* bestow the honors of Pompey the Great, including his title, upon his son.

Upon his son; who, high in name and power,
Higher than both in blood and life, stands up
For the main soldier; whose quality, going on,
The sides o' the world may danger. Much is breeding
Which, like the courser's hair, hath yet but life 200
And not a serpent's poison. Say, our pleasure,
To such whose place is under us, requires
Our quick remove from hence.

Eno. I shall do 't. [*Exeunt.*

SCENE III. *A room in* CLEOPATRA'S *palace.*

Enter CLEOPATRA, CHARMIAN, IRAS, *and* ALEXAS.

Cleo. Where is he?

Char. I did not see him since.

Cleo. See where he is, who's with him, what he does.
I did not send you. If you find him sad,
Say I am dancing; if in mirth, report
That I am sudden sick. Quick, and return. [*Exit Alexas.*

Char. Madam, methinks, if you did love him dearly,
You do not hold the method to enforce
The like from him.

Cleo. What should I do, I do not?

Char. In each thing give him way; cross him in nothing.

Cleo. Thou teachest like a fool. The way to lose him! 10

Char. Tempt him not so too far; I wish, forbear;
In time we hate that which we often fear.
But here comes Antony.

Enter ANTONY.

Cleo. I am sick and sullen.

Ant. I am sorry to give breathing to my purpose—

Cleo. Help me away, dear Charmian; I shall fall.

197. *blood and life:* spirit and vigor. 197–8. *stands up . . . soldier:* takes his stand as the chief soldier. 198–9. *whose . . . danger:* whose power, increasing, may endanger the ends of the Roman world. 200–1. *courser's . . . poison.* It was believed that a horse's hair kept in water turned into a snake.

[iii] 13. *sullen:* melancholy. 14. *breathing:* utterance.

It cannot be thus long; the sides of nature
Will not sustain it.

Ant. Now, my dearest queen—

Cleo. Pray you, stand farther from me.

Ant. What's the matter?

Cleo. I know, by that same eye, there's some good news.
What says the married woman? You may go; 20
Would she had never given you leave to come!
Let her not say 'tis I that keep you here;
I have no power upon you; hers you are.

Ant. The gods best know—

Cleo. O, never was there queen
So mightily betray'd! Yet at the first
I saw the treasons planted.

Ant. Cleopatra—

Cleo. Why should I think you can be mine and true,
Though you in swearing shake the throned gods,
Who have been false to Fulvia? Riotous madness
To be entangled with those mouth-made vows 30
Which break themselves in swearing!

Ant. Most sweet queen—

Cleo. Nay, pray you, seek no colour for your going,
But bid farewell, and go. When you sued staying,
Then was the time for words. No going then!
Eternity was in our lips and eyes,
Bliss in our brows' bent, none our parts so poor
But was a race of heaven. They are so still,
Or thou, the greatest soldier of the world,
Art turn'd the greatest liar.

Ant. How now, lady?

Cleo. I would I had thy inches! Thou shouldst know 40
There were a heart in Egypt.

Ant. Hear me, queen.

16. *the sides of nature:* the body. 20. *married woman:* Fulvia. 32. *colour:* pretext, excuse. 33. *sued staying:* asked permission to stay. 36. *bent:* arch, expression. *so poor:* however poor. 37. *a race:* an inheritance.

The strong necessity of time commands
Our services awhile; but my full heart
Remains in use with you. Our Italy
Shines o'er with civil swords; Sextus Pompeius
Makes his approaches to the port of Rome.
Equality of two domestic powers
Breed scrupulous faction. The hated, grown to strength,
Are newly grown to love. The condemn'd Pompey,
Rich in his father's honour, creeps apace 50
Into the hearts of such as have not thrived
Upon the present state, whose numbers threaten;
And quietness, grown sick of rest, would purge
By any desperate change. My more particular,
And that which most with you should safe my going,
Is Fulvia's death.

Cleo. Though age from folly could not give me freedom,
It does from childishness. Can Fulvia die?

Ant. She's dead, my queen.
Look here, and at thy sovereign leisure read 60
The garboils she awaked. At the last, best,
See when and where she died.

Cleo. O most false love!
Where be the sacred vials thou shouldst fill
With sorrowful water? Now I see, I see,
In Fulvia's death, how mine received shall be.

Ant. Quarrel no more, but be prepared to know
The purposes I bear; which are, or cease,
As you shall give the advice. By the fire
That quickens Nilus' slime, I go from hence
Thy soldier, servant, making peace or war 70
As thou affect'st.

44. *use:* trust. 45. *civil swords:* swords used in civil war. 46. *port:* gate. 48. *scrupulous faction:* cautious dissension. 49. *condemn'd.* After the assassination of Julius Cæsar, the triumvirs had condemned Sextus Pompeius to death. 53. *purge:* seek cure. 54. *particular:* personal concern. 55. *safe:* make safe. 61. *garboils:* disturbances. *best:* i.e., the best news. 68. *fire:* i.e., the sun. 71. *affect'st:* wishest.

Cleo. Cut my lace, Charmian, come!
But let it be. I am quickly ill, and well—
So Antony loves.
Ant. My precious queen, forbear,
And give true evidence to his love, which stands
An honourable trial.
Cleo. So Fulvia told me.
I prithee, turn aside and weep for her;
Then bid adieu to me, and say the tears
Belong to Egypt. Good now, play one scene
Of excellent dissembling, and let it look
Like perfect honour.
Ant. You'll heat my blood. No more! 80
Cleo. You can do better yet; but this is meetly.
Ant. Now, by my sword—
Cleo. And target. Still he mends;
But this is not the best. Look, prithee, Charmian,
How this Herculean Roman does become
The carriage of his chafe.
Ant. I'll leave you, lady.
Cleo. Courteous lord, one word.
Sir, you and I must part, but that's not it;
Sir, you and I have loved, but there's not it;
That you know well. Something it is I would—
O, my oblivion is a very Antony, 90
And I am all forgotten!
Ant. But that your royalty
Holds idleness your subject, I should take you
For idleness itself.

71. *lace:* cord that fastens stays. 73. *So . . . loves:* i.e., his love is as changeable as my health. 73–4. *forbear . . . love:* i.e., stop taunting me, and show by your conduct that you appreciate my love. 78. *Egypt:* the queen of Egypt. 81. *meetly:* fairly good. 82. *target:* shield. *mends:* improves. 84–5. *How . . . chafe:* how becomingly this descendant of Hercules displays his anger. 90–1. *my oblivion . . . forgotten:* my forgetfulness is like Antony (i.e., utterly forgetful), and I have forgotten all. 91–3. *But . . . itself:* if you were not the queen of frivolity, I should think you were ruled by it.

Cleo. 'Tis sweating labour
To bear such idleness so near the heart
As Cleopatra this. But, sir, forgive me;
Since my becomings kill me when they do not
Eye well to you. Your honour calls you hence;
Therefore be deaf to my unpitied folly,
And all the gods go with you! Upon your sword
Sit laurel victory! And smooth success 100
Be strew'd before your feet!
Ant. Let us go. Come;
Our separation so abides and flies
That thou, residing here, go'st yet with me,
And I, hence fleeting, here remain with thee.
Away! [*Exeunt.*

SCENE IV. *Rome. A room in* CÆSAR'S *house.*

Enter OCTAVIUS CÆSAR, *reading a letter*, LEPIDUS, *and their train.*

Cæs. You may see, Lepidus, and henceforth know
It is not Cæsar's natural vice to hate
Our great competitor. From Alexandria
This is the news: he fishes, drinks, and wastes
The lamps of night in revel; is not more man-like
Than Cleopatra, nor the queen of Ptolemy
More womanly than he; hardly gave audience, or
Vouchsafed to think he had partners. You shall find there
A man who is the abstract of all faults
That all men follow.
Lep. I must not think there are 10
Evils enow to darken all his goodness.
His faults, in him, seem as the spots of heaven,
More fiery by night's blackness; hereditary,
Rather than purchased; what he cannot change,
Than what he chooses.

96. *becomings:* graces. 97. *Eye:* look.
[iv] 3. *competitor:* partner. 6. *Ptolemy:* Cleopatra's late husband. 9. *abstract:* epitome. 11. *enow:* enough. 14. *purchased:* acquired.

Cæs. You are too indulgent. Let's grant, it is not
Amiss to tumble on the bed of Ptolemy,
To give a kingdom for a mirth, to sit
And keep the turn of tippling with a slave,
To reel the streets at noon, and stand the buffet 20
With knaves that smell of sweat. Say this becomes him—
As his composure must be rare indeed
Whom these things cannot blemish—yet must Antony
No way excuse his foils when we do bear
So great weight in his lightness. If he fill'd
His vacancy with his voluptuousness,
Full surfeits and the dryness of his bones
Call on him for 't! But to confound such time
That drums him from his sport and speaks as loud
As his own state and ours—'tis to be chid 30
As we rate boys who, being mature in knowledge,
Pawn their experience to their present pleasure
And so rebel to judgment.

Enter a Messenger.

Lep. Here's more news.
Mess. Thy biddings have been done, and every hour,
Most noble Cæsar, shalt thou have report
How 'tis abroad. Pompey is strong at sea,
And it appears he is beloved of those
That only have fear'd Cæsar. To the ports
The discontents repair, and men's reports
Give him much wrong'd.
Cæs. I should have known no less. 40
It hath been taught us from the primal state

19. *keep . . . of:* take turns at. 20. *stand the buffet:* exchange blows. 22. *As . . . rare:* as may be true, although his composition must be rare. 24. *foils:* blemishes. 25. *in his lightness:* because of his levity (with pun on the literal meaning). 25–8. *If . . . for 't:* if he filled his idle hours with voluptuousness, gluttony, and ill health, call him to account for it. 28. *confound:* waste. 31. *rate:* scold. 33. *rebel to judgment:* rebel against good sense. 40. *Give him:* represent him as. 41. *primal:* primeval.

That he which is was wish'd until he were,
And the ebb'd man, ne'er loved till ne'er worth love,
Comes dear'd by being lack'd. This common body,
Like to a vagabond flag upon the stream,
Goes to and back, lackeying the varying tide,
To rot itself with motion.

Mess. Cæsar, I bring thee word
Menecrates and Menas, famous pirates,
Make the sea serve them, which they ear and wound
With keels of every kind. Many hot inroads 50
They make in Italy; the borders maritime
Lack blood to think on 't, and flush youth revolt.
No vessel can peep forth but 'tis as soon
Taken as seen; for Pompey's name strikes more
Than could his war resisted.

Cæs. Antony,
Leave thy lascivious wassails. When thou once
Wast beaten from Modena, where thou slew'st
Hirtius and Pansa, consuls, at thy heel
Did Famine follow; whom thou fought'st against,
Though daintily brought up, with patience more 60
Than savages could suffer. Thou didst drink
The stale of horses and the gilded puddle
Which beasts would cough at. Thy palate then did deign
The roughest berry on the rudest hedge.
Yea, like the stag, when snow the pasture sheets,
The barks of trees thou brows'd. On the Alps
It is reported thou didst eat strange flesh,
Which some did die to look on. And all this—

42. *That . . . were:* that the man now in power was desired until he became powerful. 43. *ebb'd:* decayed in fortune. 44. *Comes dear'd:* becomes prized. 45. *flag:* iris. 46. *lackeying:* following like a lackey. This is Theobald's emendation; F1 reads *lacking.* 49. *ear:* plow. 52. *Lack blood:* turn pale. *flush:* vigorous. 54. *strikes:* destroys by malign influence. 56. *wassails:* revels. This is Pope's perhaps unnecessary emendation of the F1 reading, *Vassailes* (vassals). 62. *stale:* urine. 63. *deign:* condescend to take.

It wounds thine honour that I speak it now—
Was borne so like a soldier that thy cheek 70
So much as lank'd not.

Lep. 'Tis pity of him.

Cæs. Let his shames quickly
Drive him to Rome. 'Tis time we twain
Did show ourselves i' the field; and to that end
Assemble we immediate council. Pompey
Thrives in our idleness.

Lep. Tomorrow, Cæsar,
I shall be furnish'd to inform you rightly
Both what by sea and land I can be able
To front this present time.

Cæs. Till which encounter,
It is my business too. Farewell. 80

Lep. Farewell, my lord. What you shall know meantime
Of stirs abroad, I shall beseech you, sir,
To let me be partaker.

Cæs. Doubt not, sir;
I knew it for my bond. [*Exeunt.*

SCENE V. *Alexandria. A room in* CLEOPATRA'S *palace.*

Enter CLEOPATRA, CHARMIAN, IRAS, *and* MARDIAN.

Cleo. Charmian!

Char. Madam?

Cleo. Ha, ha!
Give me to drink mandragora.

Char. Why, madam?

Cleo. That I might sleep out this great gap of time
My Antony is away.

Char. You think of him too much.

Cleo. O, 'tis treason!

Char. Madam, I trust, not so.

71. *lank'd:* grew thin. *of:* about. 79. *front:* confront. 84. *bond:* duty.
[v] 4. *mandragora:* a narcotic.

Cleo. Thou, eunuch Mardian!
Mar. What's your Highness' pleasure?
Cleo. Not now to hear thee sing; I take no pleasure
In aught an eunuch has. 'Tis well for thee 10
That, being unseminar'd, thy freer thoughts
May not fly forth of Egypt. Hast thou affections?
Mar. Yes, gracious madam.
Cleo. Indeed?
Mar. Not in deed, madam; for I can do nothing
But what indeed is honest to be done;
Yet have I fierce affections, and think
What Venus did with Mars.
Cleo. O Charmian,
Where think'st thou he is now? Stands he, or sits he?
Or does he walk? Or is he on his horse? 20
O happy horse, to bear the weight of Antony!
Do bravely, horse! For wot'st thou whom thou movest?
The demi-Atlas of this earth, the arm
And burgonet of men. He's speaking now,
Or murmuring, "Where's my serpent of old Nile?"
For so he calls me. Now I feed myself
With most delicious poison. Think on me,
That am with Phœbus' amorous pinches black,
And wrinkled deep in time. Broad-fronted Cæsar,
When thou wast here above the ground, I was 30
A morsel for a monarch, and great Pompey
Would stand and make his eyes grow in my brow;
There would he anchor his aspect and die
With looking on his life.

Enter Alexas.

Alex. Sovereign of Egypt, hail!
Cleo. How much unlike art thou Mark Antony!

11. *unseminar'd:* unsexed. 22. *wot'st:* knowest. 24. *burgonet:* helmet, an allusion to the heraldic crest of the arm and helmet. 28. *with . . . black:* sunburned. 29. *Broad-fronted:* broad-browed. 33. *aspect:* look.

Yet, coming from him, that great medicine hath
With his tinct gilded thee.
How goes it with my brave Mark Antony?
Alex. Last thing he did, dear queen,
He kiss'd—the last of many doubled kisses— 40
This orient pearl. His speech sticks in my heart.
Cleo. Mine ear must pluck it thence.
Alex. "Good friend," quoth he,
"Say the firm Roman to great Egypt sends
This treasure of an oyster; at whose foot,
To mend the petty present, I will piece
Her opulent throne with kingdoms. All the east,
Say thou, shall call her mistress." So he nodded,
And soberly did mount an arm-gaunt steed,
Who neigh'd so high that what I would have spoke
Was beastly dumb'd by him.
Cleo. What, was he sad or merry? 50
Alex. Like to the time o' the year between the extremes
Of hot and cold, he was nor sad nor merry.
Cleo. O well-divided disposition! Note him,
Note him, good Charmian; 'tis the man; but note him!
He was not sad, for he would shine on those
That make their looks by his; he was not merry,
Which seem'd to tell them his remembrance lay
In Egypt with his joy; but between both.
O heavenly mingle! Be'st thou sad or merry,
The violence of either thee becomes, 60
So does it no man else.—Met'st thou my posts?
Alex. Ay, madam, twenty several messengers.
Why do you send so thick?
Cleo. Who's born that day
When I forget to send to Antony

36. *medicine:* physician. 37. *tinct:* the alchemists' elixir, a compound believed to transmute base metals into gold. 44. *at whose foot:* after which. 45. *piece:* add to. 48. *arm-gaunt:* gaunt from warfare (?). 50. *beastly dumb'd:* silenced by a beast, or made silent as a beast. 61. *posts:* messengers.

Shall die a beggar. Ink and paper, Charmian.
Welcome, my good Alexas. Did I, Charmian,
Ever love Cæsar so?

Char. O that brave Cæsar!

Cleo. Be choked with such another emphasis!
Say "the brave Antony."

Char. The valiant Cæsar!

Cleo. By Isis, I will give thee bloody teeth 70
If thou with Cæsar paragon again
My man of men.

Char. By your most gracious pardon,
I sing but after you.

Cleo. My salad days,
When I was green in judgment, cold in blood,
To say as I said then! But come, away;
Get me ink and paper.
He shall have every day a several greeting,
Or I'll unpeople Egypt. [*Exeunt.*

ACT II

Scene i. *Messina. A room in* Pompey's *house.*

Enter Pompey, Menecrates, *and* Menas, *in warlike manner.*

Pom. If the great gods be just, they shall assist
The deeds of justest men.

Mene. Know, worthy Pompey,
That what they do delay, they not deny.

Pom. Whiles we are suitors to their throne, decays
The thing we sue for.

Mene. We, ignorant of ourselves,
Beg often our own harms, which the wise powers
Deny us for our good; so find we profit
By losing of our prayers.

Pom. I shall do well.
The people love me, and the sea is mine;

71. *paragon:* compare. 73. *salad days:* days of youthful inexperience. 78. *Or I'll:* though I must.

My powers are crescent, and my auguring hope   10
Says it will come to the full. Mark Antony
In Egypt sits at dinner, and will make
No wars without doors. Cæsar gets money where
He loses hearts. Lepidus flatters both,
Of both is flatter'd; but he neither loves,
Nor either cares for him.

Men. Cæsar and Lepidus
Are in the field; a mighty strength they carry.

Pom. Where have you this? 'Tis false.

Men. From Silvius, sir.

Pom. He dreams. I know they are in Rome together,
Looking for Antony. But all the charms of love,   20
Salt Cleopatra, soften thy waned lip!
Let witchcraft join with beauty, lust with both!
Tie up the libertine in a field of feasts;
Keep his brain fuming; Epicurean cooks
Sharpen with cloyless sauce his appetite,
That sleep and feeding may prorogue his honour
Even till a Lethe'd dulness!

Enter VARRIUS.

How now, Varrius!

Var. This is most certain that I shall deliver:
Mark Antony is every hour in Rome
Expected. Since he went from Egypt 'tis   30
A space for further travel.

Pom. I could have given less matter
A better ear. Menas, I did not think
This amorous surfeiter would have donn'd his helm
For such a petty war. His soldiership
Is twice the other twain. But let us rear
The higher our opinion, that our stirring

[II. i] 10. *crescent:* growing (like the crescent moon). *auguring:* prophesying. 11. *it:* i.e., powers. 21. *Salt:* wanton. 25. *cloyless:* that does not satiate. 26. *prorogue:* prolong. 27. *Lethe'd:* oblivious. 31. *space:* time. 36. *opinion:* self-confidence.

Can from the lap of Egypt's widow pluck
The ne'er-lust-wearied Antony.

Men. I cannot hope
Cæsar and Antony shall well greet together.
His wife that's dead did trespasses to Cæsar; 40
His brother warr'd upon him, although, I think,
Not moved by Antony.

Pom. I know not, Menas,
How lesser enmities may give way to greater.
Were't not that we stand up against them all,
'Twere pregnant they should square between themselves,
For they have entertained cause enough
To draw their swords; but how the fear of us
May cement their divisions and bind up
The petty difference, we yet not know.
Be 't as our gods will have 't! It only stands 50
Our lives upon to use our strongest hands.
Come, Menas. [*Exeunt.*

SCENE II. *Rome. A room in the house of* LEPIDUS.

Enter ENOBARBUS *and* LEPIDUS.

Lep. Good Enobarbus, 'tis a worthy deed,
And shall become you well, to entreat your captain
To soft and gentle speech.

Eno. I shall entreat him
To answer like himself. If Cæsar move him,
Let Antony look over Cæsar's head
And speak as loud as Mars. By Jupiter,
Were I the wearer of Antonius' beard,
I would not shave 't today!

Lep. 'Tis not a time
For private stomaching.

45. *pregnant:* obvious. *square:* quarrel. 46. *entertained:* received.
50–1. *It . . . use:* our lives depend upon our using.
[ii] 4. *move:* exasperate. 7–8. *I . . . shave:* i.e., I would let Cæsar "beard me" (defy me) if he dared. 9. *stomaching:* resentment.

Eno. Every time
Serves for the matter that is then born in 't. 10
Lep. But small to greater matters must give way.
Eno. Not if the small come first.
Lep. Your speech is passion;
But, pray you, stir no embers up. Here comes
The noble Antony.

Enter ANTONY *and* VENTIDIUS.

Eno. And yonder, Cæsar.

Enter CÆSAR, MECÆNAS, *and* AGRIPPA.

Ant. If we compose well here, to Parthia.
Hark, Ventidius.
Cæs. I do not know,
Mecænas. Ask Agrippa.
Lep. Noble friends,
That which combined us was most great, and let not
A leaner action rend us. What's amiss,
May it be gently heard. When we debate 20
Our trivial difference loud, we do commit
Murder in healing wounds. Then, noble partners,
The rather for I earnestly beseech,
Touch you the sourest points with sweetest terms,
Nor curstness grow to the matter.
Ant. 'Tis spoken well.
Were we before our armies, and to fight,
I should do thus. [*Flourish.*
Cæs. Welcome to Rome.
Ant. Thank you.
Cæs. Sit.
Ant. Sit, sir.
Cæs. Nay, then.
Ant. I learn you take things ill which are not so,
Or being, concern you not.

12. *passion:* anger. 15. *compose:* agree. *to Parthia:* I shall go to Parthia. 25. *Nor . . . matter:* and do not let ill-humor be added to the matter for consideration.

Cæs. I must be laugh'd at, 30
If, or for nothing or a little, I
Should say myself offended, and with you
Chiefly i' the world; more laugh'd at that I should
Once name you derogately when to sound your name
It not concern'd me.
Ant. My being in Egypt, Cæsar,
What was 't to you?
Cæs. No more than my residing here at Rome
Might be to you in Egypt; yet, if you there
Did practice on my state, your being in Egypt
Might be my question.
Ant. How intend you, "practiced"? 40
Cæs. You may be pleased to catch at mine intent
By what did here befall me. Your wife and brother
Made wars upon me, and their contestation
Was theme for you; you were the word of war.
Ant. You do mistake your business. My brother never
Did urge me in his act; I did inquire it,
And have my learning from some true reports
That drew their swords with you. Did he not rather
Discredit my authority with yours,
And make the wars alike against my stomach, 50
Having alike your cause? Of this my letters
Before did satisfy you. If you'll patch a quarrel—
As matter whole you have not to make it with—
It must not be with this.
Cæs. You praise yourself
By laying defects of judgment to me; but
You patch'd up your excuses.
Ant. Not so, not so!
I know you could not lack—I am certain on 't—

34. *derogately:* disparagingly. 39. *practice . . . state:* plot against my power. 40. *question:* reason for quarrel. *intend:* mean. 44. *Was theme for you.* Perhaps *theme* should read *then,* or perhaps the passage means "you were the theme, the cause, of their war." 46. *urge . . . act:* i.e., insist that he was fighting for me. 47. *reports:* reporters. 50. *stomach:* inclination. 52. *patch:* devise, invent. 53. *As:* since.

Very necessity of this thought, that I,
Your partner in the cause 'gainst which he fought,
Could not with graceful eyes attend those wars 60
Which fronted mine own peace. As for my wife,
I would you had her spirit in such another!
The third o' the world is yours, which with a snaffle
You may pace easy, but not such a wife.

Eno. Would we had all such wives, that the men might go to wars with the women!

Ant. So much uncurbable, her garboils, Cæsar,
Made out of her impatience, which not wanted
Shrewdness of policy too, I grieving grant
Did you too much disquiet. For that you must 70
But say I could not help it.

Cæs. I wrote to you
When rioting in Alexandria. You
Did pocket up my letters, and with taunts
Did gibe my missive out of audience.

Ant. Sir,
He fell upon me ere admitted. Then
Three kings I had newly feasted, and did want
Of what I was i' the morning. But next day
I told him of myself, which was as much
As to have ask'd him pardon. Let this fellow
Be nothing of our strife; if we contend, 80
Out of our question wipe him.

Cæs. You have broken
The article of your oath, which you shall never
Have tongue to charge me with.

Lep. Soft, Cæsar!

Ant. No,
Lepidus, let him speak.

58. *Very . . . thought:* this inevitable thought. 60. *with . . . attend:* regard favorably. 61. *fronted:* opposed. 63–4. *with . . . easy:* with a bridle you may easily control. 67. *garboils:* disturbances. 68. *wanted:* lacked. 74. *missive:* messenger. 78. *of myself:* of my condition. 81. *question:* talk.

The honour is sacred which he talks on now,
Supposing that I lack'd it. But, on, Cæsar;
The article of my oath—

Cæs. To lend me arms and aid when I required them,
The which you both denied.

Ant. Neglected, rather;
And then when poison'd hours had bound me up 90
From mine own knowledge. As nearly as I may,
I'll play the penitent to you; but mine honesty
Shall not make poor my greatness, nor my power
Work without it. Truth is, that Fulvia,
To have me out of Egypt, made wars here;
For which myself, the ignorant motive, do
So far ask pardon as befits mine honour
To stoop in such a case.

Lep. 'Tis noble spoken.

Mec. If it might please you to enforce no further
The griefs between ye, to forget them quite 100
Were to remember that the present need
Speaks to atone you.

Lep. Worthily spoken, Mecænas.

Eno. Or, if you borrow one another's love for the instant, you may, when you hear no more words of Pompey, return it again. You shall have time to wrangle in when you have nothing else to do.

Ant. Thou art a soldier only; speak no more.

Eno. That truth should be silent I had almost forgot. 110

Ant. You wrong this presence; therefore speak no more.

Eno. Go to, then; your considerate stone.

Cæs. I do not much dislike the matter but
The manner of his speech, for 't cannot be

89. *The . . . denied:* both of which you denied. 92–4. *but . . . it:* i.e., in confessing my faults, I will not belittle myself, nor shall my power work without honesty. 100. *griefs:* grievances. 102. *atone:* reconcile. 112. *your . . . stone:* i.e., I shall be silently critical. 113–14. *I . . . speech.* This refers to Antony, not to Enobarbus, and answers Mecænas' suggestion, lines 99–102.

We shall remain in friendship, our conditions
So differing in their acts. Yet if I knew
What hoop should hold us stanch, from edge to edge
O' the world I would pursue it.

Agr. Give me leave, Cæsar.

Cæs. Speak, Agrippa.

Agr. Thou hast a sister by the mother's side, 120
Admired Octavia. Great Mark Antony
Is now a widower.

Cæs. Say not so, Agrippa.
If Cleopatra heard you, your reproof
Were well deserved of rashness.

Ant. I am not married, Cæsar. Let me hear
Agrippa further speak.

Agr. To hold you in perpetual amity,
To make you brothers, and to knit your hearts
With an unslipping knot, take Antony
Octavia to his wife, whose beauty claims 130
No worse a husband than the best of men,
Whose virtue and whose general graces speak
That which none else can utter. By this marriage
All little jealousies, which now seem great,
And all great fears, which now import their dangers,
Would then be nothing. Truths would be tales,
Where now half tales be truths. Her love to both
Would each to other, and all loves to both,
Draw after her. Pardon what I have spoke,
For 'tis a studied, not a present thought, 140
By duty ruminated.

Ant. Will Cæsar speak?

Cæs. Not till he hears how Antony is touch'd
With what is spoke already.

Ant. What power is in Agrippa,

115. *conditions:* characters. 117. *stanch:* firm. 121. *Octavia:* the full sister, not the half-sister, of Octavius. 124. *of:* because of. 135. *import:* carry with them. 137. *half . . . truths:* rumors are accepted as truths.

If I would say, "Agrippa, be it so,"
To make this good?
Cæs. The power of Cæsar, and
His power unto Octavia.
Ant. May I never
To this good purpose, that so fairly shows,
Dream of impediment! Let me have thy hand!
Further this act of grace; and from this hour
The heart of brothers govern in our loves 150
And sway our great designs!
Cæs. There is my hand.
A sister I bequeath you, whom no brother
Did ever love so dearly. Let her live
To join our kingdoms and our hearts; and never
Fly off our loves again!
Lep. Happily, amen!
Ant. I did not think to draw my sword 'gainst Pompey,
For he hath laid strange courtesies and great
Of late upon me. I must thank him only,
Lest my remembrance suffer ill report;
At heel of that, defy him.
Lep. Time calls upon 's. 160
Of us must Pompey presently be sought,
Or else he seeks out us.
Ant. Where lies he?
Cæs. About the Mount Misenum.
Ant. What is his strength by land?
Cæs. Great and increasing; but by sea
He is an absolute master.
Ant. So is the fame.
Would we had spoke together! Haste we for it.
Yet, ere we put ourselves in arms, dispatch we
The business we have talk'd of.

146. *unto:* over. 154–5. *never . . . again:* may our friendship never again be broken. 160. *At heel of:* immediately after. 161. *presently:* at once. 163. *the Mount Misenum:* a promontory on the bay of Naples. 166. *fame:* rumor. 167. *spoke together:* met in battle.

Cæs. With most gladness;
And do invite you to my sister's view, 170
Whither straight I'll lead you.

Ant. Let us, Lepidus,
Not lack your company.

Lep. Noble Antony,
Not sickness should detain me.

[*Flourish. Exeunt Cæsar, Antony, and Lepidus.*

Mec. Welcome from Egypt, sir.

Eno. Half the heart of Cæsar, worthy Mecænas! My honourable friend, Agrippa!

Agr. Good Enobarbus!

Mec. We have cause to be glad that matters are so well digested. You stayed well by 't in Egypt. 180

Eno. Ay, sir; we did sleep day out of countenance, and made the night light with drinking.

Mec. Eight wild-boars roasted whole at a breakfast, and but twelve persons there. Is this true?

Eno. This was but as a fly by an eagle. We had much more monstrous matter of feast, which worthily deserved noting.

Mec. She's a most triumphant lady, if report be square to her. 190

Eno. When she first met Mark Antony, she pursed up his heart, upon the river of Cydnus.

Agr. There she appeared indeed; or my reporter devised well for her.

Eno. I will tell you.
The barge she sat in, like a burnish'd throne,
Burn'd on the water. The poop was beaten gold;
Purple the sails, and so perfumed that
The winds were love-sick with them. The oars were silver,
Which to the tune of flutes kept stroke, and made 200
The water which they beat to follow faster,
As amorous of their strokes. For her own person,

170. *to . . . view:* to see my sister. 179. *stayed well by 't:* "stuck to it well" or "kept things going." 190. *square:* just. 192. *pursed up:* took possession of. 194. *devised:* imagined.

It beggar'd all description. She did lie
In her pavilion—cloth-of-gold of tissue—
O'er-picturing that Venus where we see
The fancy outwork nature. On each side her
Stood pretty dimpled boys, like smiling Cupids,
With divers-colour'd fans, whose wind did seem
To glow the delicate cheeks which they did cool,
And what they undid did.

Agr. O, rare for Antony! 210

Eno. Her gentlewomen, like the Nereides,
So many mermaids, tended her i' the eyes,
And made their bends adornings. At the helm
A seeming mermaid steers. The silken tackle
Swell with the touches of those flower-soft hands
That yarely frame the office. From the barge
A strange invisible perfume hits the sense
Of the adjacent wharfs. The city cast
Her people out upon her; and Antony,
Enthroned i' the market-place, did sit alone, 220
Whistling to the air, which, but for vacancy,
Had gone to gaze on Cleopatra too
And made a gap in nature.

Agr. Rare Egyptian!

Eno. Upon her landing, Antony sent to her,
Invited her to supper. She replied,
It should be better he became her guest,
Which she entreated. Our courteous Antony,
Whom ne'er the word of "no" woman heard speak,
Being barber'd ten times o'er, goes to the feast,
And for his ordinary pays his heart 230
For what his eyes eat only.

204. *cloth-of-gold of tissue:* cloth made of gold thread and silk. 205. *O'er-picturing:* surpassing the picture of. 206. *outwork:* excel. 209. *glow:* cause to glow. 211. *Nereides:* sea-nymphs. 212–13. *tended . . . adornings:* attended her, and their glances and bows added beauty to the picture. 216. *yarely . . . office:* easily do the work. 218. *wharfs:* banks. 221–2. *but . . . gone:* but for leaving a vacuum, would have gone. 230. *ordinary:* meal.

Agr. Royal wench!
She made great Cæsar lay his sword to bed.
He plough'd her, and she cropp'd.
Eno. I saw her once
Hop forty paces through the public street;
And having lost her breath, she spoke, and panted,
That she did make defect perfection,
And, breathless, power breathe forth.
Mec. Now Antony must leave her utterly.
Eno. Never! He will not.
Age cannot wither her, nor custom stale 240
Her infinite variety. Other women cloy
The appetites they feed, but she makes hungry
Where most she satisfies; for vilest things
Become themselves in her, that the holy priests
Bless her when she is riggish.
Mec. If beauty, wisdom, modesty can settle
The heart of Antony, Octavia is
A blessed lottery to him.
Agr. Let us go.
Good Enobarbus, make yourself my guest 249
Whilst you abide here.
Eno. Humbly, sir, I thank you. [*Exeunt.*

SCENE III. *Rome. A room in* CÆSAR'S *house.*

Enter ANTONY, CÆSAR, OCTAVIA *between them, and* Attendants.

Ant. The world and my great office will sometimes
Divide me from your bosom.
Oct. All which time
Before the gods my knee shall bow my prayers
To them for you.
Ant. Good night, sir. My Octavia,

232. *Cæsar:* Julius Cæsar. 233. *cropp'd:* produced a crop. 236. *That:* so that. 237. *power:* i.e., of her beauty. 244. *Become themselves:* are themselves becoming. 245. *riggish:* wanton. 248. *lottery:* prize.

Read not my blemishes in the world's report.
I have not kept my square, but that to come
Shall all be done by the rule. Good night, dear lady.
Good night, sir.

Cæs. Good night. [*Exeunt Cæsar and Octavia.*

Enter Soothsayer.

Ant. Now, sirrah, you do wish yourself in Egypt? 10

Sooth. Would I had never come from thence, nor you
Thither!

Ant. If you can, your reason?

Sooth. I see it in
My motion, have it not in my tongue. But yet
Hie you to Egypt again.

Ant. Say to me
Whose fortunes shall rise higher, Cæsar's or mine?

Sooth. Cæsar's.
Therefore, O Antony, stay not by his side.
Thy demon—that thy spirit which keeps thee—is
Noble, courageous, high, unmatchable, 20
Where Cæsar's is not; but, near him, thy angel
Becomes afeard, as being o'erpower'd. Therefore
Make space enough between you.

Ant. Speak this no more.

Sooth. To none but thee; no more but when to thee.
If thou dost play with him at any game,
Thou art sure to lose; and, of that natural luck,
He beats thee 'gainst the odds. Thy lustre thickens
When he shines by. I say again, thy spirit
Is all afraid to govern thee near him;
But, he away, 'tis noble.

Ant. Get thee gone. 30
Say to Ventidius I would speak with him; [*Exit Soothsayer.*
He shall to Parthia.—Be it art or hap,

[iii] 6. *square:* due bounds (metaphor from carpentry). 14. *motion:* inward prompting. 19. *demon:* attendant spirit. 22. *afeard:* afraid. The F_1 reading is *a feare*. Cf. II, v, 81: *afeard*. 26. *of:* because of. 27. *thickens:* grows dim. 32. *hap:* chance.

He hath spoken true. The very dice obey him,
And in our sports my better cunning faints
Under his chance. If we draw lots, he speeds;
His cocks do win the battle still of mine
When it is all to nought, and his quails ever
Beat mine, inhoop'd, at odds. I will to Egypt;
And though I make this marriage for my peace,
I' the east my pleasure lies.

Enter VENTIDIUS.

O, come, Ventidius, 40
You must to Parthia. Your commission's ready;
Follow me, and receive 't. [*Exeunt.*

SCENE IV. *Rome. A street.*

Enter LEPIDUS, MECÆNAS, *and* AGRIPPA.

Lep. Trouble yourselves no further. Pray you, hasten
Your generals after.
Agr. Sir, Mark Antony
Will e'en but kiss Octavia, and we'll follow.
Lep. Till I shall see you in your soldier's dress,
Which will become you both, farewell.
Mec. We shall,
As I conceive the journey, be at the Mount
Before you, Lepidus.
Lep. Your way is shorter;
My purposes do draw me much about.
You'll win two days upon me.
Mec. } *Agr.* } Sir, good success! 9
Lep. Farewell. [*Exeunt.*

34. *cunning:* skill. 35. *chance:* good luck. *speeds:* wins. 36. *still:* always. 38. *inhoop'd:* placed within the hoop or circle for fighting. *at odds:* i.e., even when the odds are against them.

[iv] 2. *Your . . . after:* after your generals. 6. *the Mount.* See II, ii, 163.

SCENE V. *Alexandria. A room in* CLEOPATRA'S *palace.*

Enter CLEOPATRA, CHARMIAN, IRAS, *and* ALEXAS.

Cleo. Give me some music—music, moody food
Of us that trade in love.
Omnes. The music, ho!

Enter MARDIAN.

Cleo. Let it alone. Let's to billiards. Come, Charmian.
Char. My arm is sore; best play with Mardian.
Cleo. As well a woman with an eunuch play'd
As with a woman. Come, you'll play with me, sir?
Mar. As well as I can, madam.
Cleo. And when good will is show'd, though 't come too short,
The actor may plead pardon. I'll none now.
Give me mine angle; we'll to the river. There, 10
My music playing far off, I will betray
Tawny-finn'd fishes. My bended hook shall pierce
Their slimy jaws; and, as I draw them up,
I'll think them every one an Antony,
And say, "Ah, ha, you're caught!"
Char. 'Twas merry when
You wager'd on your angling, when your diver
Did hang a salt-fish on his hook, which he
With fervency drew up.
Cleo. That time—O times!—
I laugh'd him out of patience; and that night
I laugh'd him into patience; and next morn, 20
Ere the ninth hour, I drunk him to his bed,
Then put my tires and mantles on him, whilst
I wore his sword Philippan.

[v] 10. *angle:* fishing tackle. 18. *fervency:* eagerness. 22. *tires:* headdress. 23. *Philippan;* i.e., the sword Antony wore at Philippi, where he defeated Brutus and Cassius; perhaps the name of the sword.

Enter a Messenger.

O, from Italy!
Ram thou thy fruitful tidings in mine ears,
That long time have been barren.

Mess. Madam, madam—

Cleo. Antonius dead!—If thou say so, villain,
Thou kill'st thy mistress; but well and free,
If thou so yield him, there is gold, and here
My bluest veins to kiss—a hand that kings
Have lipp'd, and trembled kissing. 30

Mess. First, madam, he is well.

Cleo. Why, there's more gold.
But, sirrah, mark, we use
To say the dead are well. Bring it to that,
The gold I give thee will I melt and pour
Down thy ill-uttering throat.

Mess. Good madam, hear me.

Cleo. Well, go to, I will;
But there's no goodness in thy face. If Antony
Be free and healthful—so tart a favour
To trumpet such good tidings? If not well,
Thou shouldst come like a Fury crown'd with snakes, 40
Not like a formal man.

Mess. Will 't please you hear me?

Cleo. I have a mind to strike thee ere thou speak'st.
Yet, if thou say Antony lives, is well,
Or friends with Cæsar, or not captive to him,
I'll set thee in a shower of gold, and hail
Rich pearls upon thee.

Mess. Madam, he's well.

Cleo. Well said.

Mess. And friends with Cæsar.

Cleo. Thou 'rt an honest man.

Mess. Cæsar and he are greater friends than ever.

Cleo. Make thee a fortune from me!

28. *yield:* report. 32. *use:* are accustomed. 38. *favour:* face.
41. *formal:* normal.

Mess. But yet, madam—
Cleo. I do not like "but yet"; it does allay 50
The good precedence; fie upon "but yet"!
"But yet" is as a gaoler to bring forth
Some monstrous malefactor. Prithee, friend,
Pour out the pack of matter to mine ear,
The good and bad together. He's friends with Cæsar;
In state of health thou say'st; and thou say'st free.
Mess. Free, madam! No; I made no such report.
He's bound unto Octavia.
Cleo. For what good turn?
Mess. For the best turn i' the bed.
Cleo. I am pale, Charmian.
Mess. Madam, he's married to Octavia. 60
Cleo. The most infectious pestilence upon thee!
[*Strikes him down.*
Mess. Good madam, patience.
Cleo. What say you? Hence,
[*Strikes him again.*
Horrible villain, or I'll spurn thine eyes
Like balls before me! I'll unhair thy head!
[*She hales him up and down.*
Thou shalt be whipp'd with wire, and stew'd in brine,
Smarting in lingering pickle!
Mess. Gracious madam,
I that do bring the news made not the match.
Cleo. Say 'tis not so, a province I will give thee
And make thy fortunes proud. The blow thou hadst
Shall make thy peace for moving me to rage; 70
And I will boot thee with what gift beside
Thy modesty can beg.
Mess. He's married, madam.
Cleo. Rogue, thou hast lived too long. [*Draws a knife.*
Mess. Nay, then I'll run.
What mean you, madam? I have made no fault. [*Exit.*

51. *precedence:* what has preceded. 63. *spurn:* kick. 71. *boot:* reward. 72. *modesty:* moderation.

Char. Good madam, keep yourself within yourself.
The man is innocent.
Cleo. Some innocents 'scape not the thunderbolt.
Melt Egypt into Nile! And kindly creatures
Turn all to serpents! Call the slave again.
Though I am mad, I will not bite him. Call! 80
Char. He is afeard to come.
Cleo. I will not hurt him.
[*Exit Charmian.*
These hands do lack nobility, that they strike
A meaner than myself, since I myself
Have given myself the cause.

Re-enter CHARMIAN *and* Messenger.

Come hither, sir.
Though it be honest, it is never good
To bring bad news. Give to a gracious message
An host of tongues, but let ill tidings tell
Themselves when they be felt.
Mess. I have done my duty.
Cleo. Is he married?
I cannot hate thee worser than I do, 90
If thou again say "yes."
Mess. He's married, madam.
Cleo. The gods confound thee! Dost thou hold there still?
Mess. Should I lie, madam?
Cleo. O, I would thou didst,
So half my Egypt were submerged and made
A cistern for scaled snakes! Go, get thee hence!
Hadst thou Narcissus in thy face, to me
Thou wouldst appear most ugly. He is married?
Mess. I crave your Highness' pardon.
Cleo. He is married?

92. *Dost . . . still:* i.e., will you not deny that Antony is married?
94. *So:* even if. 96. *Narcissus:* a beautiful boy of Greek mythology.

Mess. Take no offense that I would not offend you.
To punish me for what you make me do 100
Seems much unequal. He's married to Octavia.

Cleo. O, that his fault should make a knave of thee,
That art not what thou 'rt sure of! Get thee hence.
The merchandise which thou hast brought from Rome
Are all too dear for me. Lie they upon thy hand,
And be undone by 'em! [*Exit Messenger.*

Char. Good your Highness, patience.

Cleo. In praising Antony, I have dispraised Cæsar.

Char. Many times, madam.

Cleo. I am paid for 't now.
Lead me from hence;
I faint. O Iras, Charmian! 'Tis no matter. 110
Go to the fellow, good Alexas; bid him
Report the feature of Octavia, her years,
Her inclination; let him not leave out
The colour of her hair. Bring me word quickly. [*Exit Alexas.*
Let him forever go—let him not!—Charmian,
Though he be painted one way like a Gorgon,
The other way 's a Mars. [*To Mardian.*] Bid you Alexas
Bring me word how tall she is. Pity me, Charmian,
But do not speak to me. Lead me to my chamber. [*Exeunt.*

Scene vi. *Near Misenum.*

Flourish. Enter Pompey *and* Menas *at one door, with drum and trumpet; at another,* Cæsar, Antony, Lepidus, Enobarbus, Mecænas, *with* Soldiers *marching.*

Pom. Your hostages I have, so have you mine;
And we shall talk before we fight.

99. *that . . . you:* i.e., by repeating unwelcome news. 101. *unequal:* unjust. 103. *what . . . of:* i.e., the news, or, perhaps, Antony's deceitfulness. 105. *they:* i.e., the merchandise, the news. 112. *feature:* appearance. 113. *inclination:* disposition. 115. *Let him:* i.e., Antony. 116–17. *Though . . . Mars:* i.e., as in a "perspective," which would from one angle reveal a Gorgon, from another angle, Mars.

Cæs. Most meet
That first we come to words; and therefore have we
Our written purposes before us sent,
Which, if thou hast consider'd, let us know
If 'twill tie up thy discontented sword,
And carry back to Sicily much tall youth
That else must perish here.
Pom. To you all three,
The senators alone of this great world,
Chief factors for the gods, I do not know 10
Wherefore my father should revengers want,
Having a son and friends, since Julius Cæsar,
Who at Philippi the good Brutus ghosted,
There saw you labouring for him. What was 't
That moved pale Cassius to conspire? And what
Made the all-honour'd, honest Roman, Brutus,
With the arm'd rest, courtiers of beauteous freedom,
To drench the Capitol, but that they would
Have one man but a man? And that is it
Hath made me rig my navy, at whose burden 20
The anger'd ocean foams; with which I meant
To scourge the ingratitude that despiteful Rome
Cast on my noble father.
Cæs. Take your time.
Ant. Thou canst not fear us, Pompey, with thy sails.
We'll speak with thee at sea. At land, thou know'st
How much we do o'er-count thee.
Pom. At land, indeed,
Thou dost o'er-count me of my father's house!
But, since the cuckoo builds not for himself,
Remain in 't as thou mayst.

[vi] 7. *tall:* valiant. 10. *factors:* agents. 11. *want:* lack. 13. *ghosted:* appeared as ghost to. 19. *Have . . . a man:* i.e., prevent his being more than a man, i.e., a god. 24. *fear:* frighten. 26. *o'er-count:* outnumber. 27. *o'er-count:* cheat. According to Plutarch, Antony bought the elder Pompey's house and later refused to pay for it.

Lep. Be pleased to tell us—
For this is from the present—how you take 30
The offers we have sent you.
Cæs. There's the point.
Ant. Which do not be entreated to, but weigh
What it is worth embraced.
Cæs. And what may follow,
To try a larger fortune.
Pom. You have made me offer
Of Sicily, Sardinia; and I must
Rid all the sea of pirates; then, to send
Measures of wheat to Rome; this 'greed upon,
To part with unhack'd edges and bear back
Our targes undinted.
Cæs. Ant. Lep. That's our offer.
Pom. Know, then, 40
I came before you here a man prepared
To take this offer, but Mark Antony
Put me to some impatience. Though I lose
The praise of it by telling, you must know,
When Cæsar and your brother were at blows,
Your mother came to Sicily and did find
Her welcome friendly.
Ant. I have heard it, Pompey,
And am well studied for a liberal thanks
Which I do owe you.
Pom. Let me have your hand.
I did not think, sir, to have met you here. 50
Ant. The beds i' the east are soft; and thanks to you,
That call'd me timelier than my purpose hither,
For I have gain'd by 't.
Cæs. Since I saw you last,
There is a change upon you.
Pom. Well, I know not

30. *from the present:* beside the point. 34. *To try:* if you try.
38. *edges:* swords. 39. *targes:* shields. 48. *studied:* inclined.
52. *timelier:* earlier.

What counts harsh Fortune casts upon my face,
But in my bosom shall she never come
To make my heart her vassal.

Lep. Well met here.

Pom. I hope so, Lepidus. Thus we are agreed.
I crave our composition may be written
And seal'd between us.

Cæs. That's the next to do. 60

Pom. We'll feast each other ere we part, and let's
Draw lots who shall begin.

Ant. That will I, Pompey.

Pom. No, Antony, take the lot; but, first
Or last, your fine Egyptian cookery
Shall have the fame. I have heard that Julius Cæsar
Grew fat with feasting there.

Ant. You have heard much.

Pom. I have fair meanings, sir.

Ant. And fair words to them.

Pom. Then so much have I heard.
And I have heard Apollodorus carried—

Eno. No more of that! He did so.

Pom. What, I pray you? 70

Eno. A certain queen to Cæsar in a mattress.

Pom. I know thee now. How farest thou, soldier?

Eno. Well;
And well am like to do, for I perceive
Four feasts are toward.

Pom. Let me shake thy hand.
I never hated thee. I have seen thee fight
When I have envied thy behaviour.

Eno. Sir,
I never loved you much; but I ha' praised ye

55. *counts:* accounts. *casts:* calculates, draws up. 59. *composition:* agreement. 69–71. *Apollodorus . . . mattress.* This story, told by Plutarch, is included in G. B. Shaw's *Cæsar and Cleopatra.* 74. *toward:* in preparation.

When you have well deserved ten times as much
As I have said you did.

Pom. Enjoy thy plainness; 80
It nothing ill becomes thee.
Aboard my galley I invite you all.
Will you lead, lords?

Cæs. Ant. Lep. Show us the way, sir.

Pom. Come.

[*Exeunt all but Menas and Enobarbus.*

Men. [*Aside*] Thy father, Pompey, would ne'er have made this treaty.—You and I have known, sir.

Eno. At sea, I think.

Men. We have, sir.

Eno. You have done well by water.

Men. And you by land. 90

Eno. I will praise any man that will praise me, though it cannot be denied what I have done by land.

Men. Nor what I have done by water.

Eno. Yes, something you can deny for your own safety. You have been a great thief by sea.

Men. And you by land.

Eno. There I deny my land service. But give me your hand, Menas. If our eyes had authority, here they might take two thieves kissing. 101

Men. All men's faces are true, whatsome'er their hands are.

Eno. But there is never a fair woman has a true face.

Men. No slander; they steal hearts.

Eno. We came hither to fight with you.

Men. For my part, I am sorry it is turned to a drinking. Pompey doth this day laugh away his fortune. 110

Eno. If he do, sure, he cannot weep 't back again.

Men. You've said, sir. We looked not for Mark Antony here. Pray you, is he married to Cleopatra?

Eno. Cæsar's sister is called Octavia.

Men. True, sir. She was the wife of Caius Marcellus.

Eno. But she is now the wife of Marcus Antonius.

86. *known:* met. 100. *take:* arrest.

Men. Pray ye, sir? 120

Eno. 'Tis true.

Men. Then is Cæsar and he forever knit together.

Eno. If I were bound to divine of this unity, I would not prophesy so.

Men. I think the policy of that purpose made more in the marriage than the love of the parties.

Eno. I think so too. But you shall find the band that seems to tie their friendship together will be the very strangler of their amity. Octavia is of a holy, cold, and still conversation. 131

Men. Who would not have his wife so?

Eno. Not he that himself is not so, which is Mark Antony. He will to his Egyptian dish again. Then shall the sighs of Octavia blow the fire up in Cæsar; and, as I said before, that which is the strength of their amity shall prove the immediate author of their variance. Antony will use his affection where it is. He married but his occasion here. 140

Men. And thus it may be. Come, sir, will you aboard? I have a health for you.

Eno. I shall take it, sir. We have used our throats in Egypt.

Men. Come, let's away. [*Exeunt.*

SCENE VII. *On board* POMPEY'S *galley, off Misenum.*

Music plays. Enter two or three Servants *with a banquet.*

First Serv. Here they'll be, man. Some o' their plants are ill-rooted already; the least wind i' the world will blow them down.

Sec. Serv. Lepidus is high-coloured.

First Serv. They have made him drink alms-drink. 6

Sec. Serv. As they pinch one another by the disposition, he cries out, "No more!" reconciles them to his entreaty, and himself to the drink.

124. *divine of:* prophesy about. 131. *still conversation:* quiet conduct. 140. *occasion:* opportunity.

[vii] S. D. *banquet:* sweetmeats, fruit, and wine. 2. *plants:* soles of the feet (with pun). 6. *alms-drink:* leavings (in addition to his own share). 7. *pinch:* annoy (by their conflicting moods).

First Serv. But it raises the greater war between him and his discretion.

Sec. Serv. Why, this it is to have a name in great men's fellowship. I had as lief have a reed that will do me no service as a partisan I could not heave.

First Serv. To be called into a huge sphere, and not to be seen to move in't, are the holes where eyes should be, which pitifully disaster the cheeks.

A sennet sounded. Enter Cæsar, Antony, Lepidus, Pompey, Agrippa, Mecænas, Enobarbus, Menas, *with other captains.*

Ant. [*To Cæsar*] Thus do they, sir; they take the flow o' the
Nile 20
By certain scales i' the pyramid. They know
By the height, the lowness, or the mean, if dearth
Or foison follow. The higher Nilus swells,
The more it promises. As it ebbs, the seedsman
Upon the slime and ooze scatters his grain,
And shortly comes to harvest.

Lep. You've strange serpents there.

Ant. Ay, Lepidus.

Lep. Your serpent of Egypt is bred now of your mud by the operation of your sun; so is your crocodile. 31

Ant. They are so.

Pom. Sit—and some wine! A health to Lepidus!

Lep. I am not so well as I should be, but I'll ne'er out.

Eno. Not till you have slept; I fear me you'll be in till then.

Lep. Nay, certainly, I have heard the Ptolemies' pyramises are very goodly things; without contradiction, I have heard that. 41

Men. [*Aside to Pompey*] Pompey, a word.

Pom. [*Aside to Menas*] Say in mine ear: what is't?

14. *partisan:* halberd. 15. *heave:* lift. 18. *disaster:* injure, ruin (an astrological term). S. D. *sennet:* trumpet call announcing the approach and departure of processions. 23. *foison:* plenty. 29. *Your.* Used impersonally. 36. *I'll ne'er out:* I'll not stop. 38. *in:* intoxicated. 40. *pyramises:* a sixteenth-century variant spelling of *pyramids*.

Men. [*Aside to Pompey*] Forsake thy seat, I do beseech thee, captain,
And hear me speak a word.

Pom. [*Aside to Menas*] Forbear me till anon.
This wine for Lepidus!

Lep. What manner o' thing is your crocodile?

Ant. It is shaped, sir, like itself, and it is as broad as it hath breadth. It is just so high as it is, and moves with it own organs. It lives by that which nourisheth it, and the elements once out of it, it transmigrates. 51

Lep. What colour is it of?

Ant. Of it own colour too.

Lep. 'Tis a strange serpent.

Ant. 'Tis so. And the tears of it are wet.

Cæs. Will this description satisfy him?

Ant. With the health that Pompey gives him; else he is a very epicure.

Pom. [*Aside to Menas*] Go hang, sir, hang! Tell me of that? Away!
Do as I bid you.—Where's this cup I call'd for? 60

Men. [*Aside to Pompey*] If for the sake of merit thou wilt hear me,
Rise from thy stool.

Pom. [*Aside to Menas*] I think thou'rt mad. The matter?
[*Rises, and walks aside.*

Men. I have ever held my cap off to thy fortunes.

Pom. Thou hast served me with much faith. What's else to say?—
Be jolly, lords.

Ant. These quick-sands, Lepidus,
Keep off them, for you sink.

Men. Wilt thou be lord of all the world?

Pom. What say'st thou?

44. *Forbear . . . anon:* leave me for a while. 49. *it own:* its own. 50. *elements:* vital elements. 51. *it transmigrates:* its soul enters another body. 55. *tears.* The crocodile was believed to weep while devouring its victim. 63. *held my cap off:* been a good servant.

Men. Wilt thou be lord of the whole world? That's twice.
Pom. How should that be?
Men. But entertain it,
And, though thou think me poor, I am the man 70
Will give thee all the world.
Pom. Hast thou drunk well?
Men. No, Pompey, I have kept me from the cup.
Thou art, if thou darest be, the earthly Jove.
Whate'er the ocean pales, or sky inclips,
Is thine, if thou wilt ha't.
Pom. Show me which way.
Men. These three world-sharers, these competitors,
Are in thy vessel. Let me cut the cable;
And, when we are put off, fall to their throats.
All there is thine.
Pom. Ah, this thou shouldst have done,
And not have spoke on't! In me 'tis villainy; 80
In thee't had been good service. Thou must know
'Tis not my profit that does lead mine honour;
Mine honour, it. Repent that e'er thy tongue
Hath so betray'd thine act. Being done unknown,
I should have found it afterwards well done,
But must condemn it now. Desist and drink.
Men. [*Aside*] For this,
I'll never follow thy pall'd fortunes more.
Who seeks, and will not take when once 'tis offer'd,
Shall never find it more.
Pom. This health to Lepidus! 90
Ant. Bear him ashore. I'll pledge it for him, Pompey.
Eno. Here's to thee, Menas!
Men. Enobarbus, welcome!
Pom. Fill till the cup be hid.
Eno. There's a strong fellow, Menas.
[*Pointing to the Attendant who carries off Lepidus.*
Men. Why?

69. *But . . . it:* only receive it. 74. *pales:* encloses. *inclips:* embraces. 76. *competitors:* partners. 88. *pall'd:* weakened.

Eno. A' bears the third part of the world, man; see'st not?

Men. The third part, then, is drunk. Would it were all,
That it might go on wheels!

Eno. Drink thou; increase the reels. 100

Men. Come.

Pom. This is not yet an Alexandrian feast.

Ant. It ripens towards it. Strike the vessels, ho!
Here is to Cæsar!

Cæs. I could well forbear't.
It's monstrous labour when I wash my brain
And it grows fouler.

Ant. Be a child o' the time.

Cæs. Possess it; I'll make answer.
But I had rather fast from all four days
Than drink so much in one.

Eno. [*To Antony*] Ha, my brave emperor!
Shall we dance now the Egyptian Bacchanals, 110
And celebrate our drink?

Pom. Let's ha't, good soldier.

Ant. Come, let's all take hands,
Till that the conquering wine hath steep'd our sense
In soft and delicate Lethe.

Eno. All take hands.
Make battery to our ears with the loud music.
The while I'll place you; then the boy shall sing.
The holding every man shall bear as loud
As his strong sides can volley.

[*Music plays. Enobarbus places them hand in hand.*

99. *on wheels:* i.e., easily and pleasantly. 100. *reels:* revels. 103. *Strike the vessels:* tap the casks, or perhaps "clink the cups." 105. *wash my brain:* drink freely. 106. *fouler:* (a) dirtier, (b) cloudier, duller. *Be . . . time:* lend yourself to the spirit of the present moment. 107. *Possess . . . answer.* Perhaps he means, "Be the master, not the slave, of the moment; that's my answer." It is more probable that he means, "Proceed with your toast; I'll reply." 108. *from all:* from all food. 115. *battery to:* assault on. 117. *holding:* burden, refrain.

The Song.

Come, thou monarch of the vine, 120
Plumpy Bacchus with pink eyne!
In thy fats our cares be drown'd,
With thy grapes our hairs be crown'd.
Cup us, till the world go round,
Cup us, till the world go round!

Cæs. What would you more? Pompey, good night. Good brother,
Let me request you off. Our graver business
Frowns at this levity. Gentle lords, let's part.
You see we have burnt our cheeks. Strong Enobarb
Is weaker than the wine, and mine own tongue 130
Splits what it speaks. The wild disguise hath almost
Antick'd us all. What needs more words? Good night.
Good Antony, your hand.

Pom. I'll try you on the shore.

Ant. And shall, sir.—Give's your hand.

Pom. O Antony,
You have my father's house—but what? We are friends!
Come down into the boat.

Eno. Take heed you fall not.

[*Exeunt all but Enobarbus and Menas.*

Menas, I'll not on shore.

Men. No, to my cabin.
These drums! These trumpets, flutes! What!
Let Neptune hear we bid a loud farewell
To these great fellows. Sound and be hang'd; sound out!

[*Sound a flourish, with drums.*

Eno. Ho, says a'. There's my cap. 141

Men. Ho! Noble captain, come. [*Exeunt.*

121. *pink eyne:* half-shut eyes. 122. *fats:* wine vats. 127. *off:* to leave. 131. *disguise:* drunkenness. 132. *Antick'd:* made fools of. 133. *try you:* try conclusions with you.

ACT III

SCENE I. *A plain in Syria.*

Enter VENTIDIUS *as it were in triumph, with* SILIUS *and other* Romans, Officers, *and* Soldiers; *the dead body of Pacorus borne before him.*

Ven. Now, darting Parthia, art thou struck, and now
Pleased Fortune does of Marcus Crassus' death
Make me revenger. Bear the king's son's body
Before our army. Thy Pacorus, Orodes,
Pays this for Marcus Crassus.
Sil. Noble Ventidius,
Whilst yet with Parthian blood thy sword is warm,
The fugitive Parthians follow. Spur through Media,
Mesopotamia, and the shelters whither
The routed fly. So thy grand captain Antony
Shall set thee on triumphant chariots and 10
Put garlands on thy head.
Ven. O Silius, Silius,
I have done enough. A lower place, note well,
May make too great an act; for learn this, Silius:
Better to leave undone than by our deed
Acquire too high a fame when him we serve's away.
Cæsar and Antony have ever won
More in their officer than person. Sossius,
One of my place in Syria, his lieutenant,
For quick accumulation of renown,
Which he achieved by the minute, lost his favour. 20
Who does i' the wars more than his captain can
Becomes his captain's captain; and ambition,
The soldier's virtue, rather makes choice of loss,

[III. i] 1. *darting:* shooting darts. The Parthians were famous for archery, especially when they were retreating. *Parthia:* Orodes, king of Parthia. In 53 B.C. he defeated and killed the Roman proconsul, Marcus Crassus. Pacorus was the son of Orodes. 12. *A lower place:* one of lower rank. 17. *in their officer:* through their subordinates. 20. *by the minute:* every moment.

Than gain which darkens him.
I could do more to do Antonius good,
But 'twould offend him; and in his offense
Should my performance perish.
Sil. Thou hast, Ventidius, that
Without the which a soldier and his sword
Grants scarce distinction. Thou wilt write to Antony?
Ven. I'll humbly signify what in his name, 30
That magical word of war, we have effected,
How, with his banners and his well-paid ranks,
The ne'er-yet-beaten horse of Parthia
We have jaded out o' the field.
Sil. Where is he now?
Ven. He purposeth to Athens, whither, with what haste
The weight we must convey with's will permit,
We shall appear before him. On, there; pass along! [*Exeunt.*

SCENE II. *Rome. An ante-chamber in* CÆSAR'S *house.*

Enter AGRIPPA *at one door*, ENOBARBUS *at another.*

Agr. What, are the brothers parted?
Eno. They have dispatch'd with Pompey; he is gone;
The other three are sealing. Octavia weeps
To part from Rome; Cæsar is sad; and Lepidus,
Since Pompey's feast, as Menas says, is troubled
With the green sickness.
Agr. 'Tis a noble Lepidus.
Eno. A very fine one! O, how he loves Cæsar!
Agr. Nay, but how dearly he adores Mark Antony!
Eno. Cæsar? Why, he's the Jupiter of men.
Agr. What's Antony? The god of Jupiter. 10
Eno. Spake you of Cæsar? How! The nonpareil!

24. *darkens:* obscures. 27. *that:* i.e., judgment. 29. *Grants scarce distinction:* can scarcely be distinguished. 34. *jaded:* driven exhausted. 36. *with 's:* with us.

[ii] 2. *dispatch'd:* settled (the matter). 3. *sealing:* i.e., their agreement. 6. *green sickness:* anemia.

Agr. O Antony! O thou Arabian bird!
Eno. Would you praise Cæsar, say "Cæsar." Go no further.
Agr. Indeed, he plied them both with excellent praises.
Eno. But he loves Cæsar best; yet he loves Antony.
Ho! Hearts, tongues, figures, scribes, bards, poets, cannot
Think, speak, cast, write, sing, number—ho!—
His love to Antony. But as for Cæsar,
Kneel down, kneel down, and wonder.
Agr. Both he loves.
Eno. They are his shards, and he their beetle. [*Trumpets within.*] So— 20
This is to horse. Adieu, noble Agrippa.
Agr. Good fortune, worthy soldier; and farewell!

Enter CÆSAR, ANTONY, LEPIDUS, *and* OCTAVIA.

Ant. No further, sir.
Cæs. You take from me a great part of myself;
Use me well in't. Sister, prove such a wife
As my thoughts make thee, and as my farthest band
Shall pass on thy approof. Most noble Antony,
Let not the piece of virtue which is set
Betwixt us as the cement of our love
To keep it builded, be the ram to batter 30
The fortress of it, for better might we
Have loved without this mean, if on both parts
This be not cherish'd.
Ant. Make me not offended
In your distrust.
Cæs. I have said.
Ant. You shall not find,
Though you be therein curious, the least cause
For what you seem to fear. So, the gods keep you,

12. *Arabian bird:* the phoenix. 17. *cast:* calculate. *number:* versify. 20. *shards:* wings. 26–7. *and as . . . approof:* and as my utmost bond shall be pledged on the trial of thy conduct. 28. *piece of virtue:* virtuous one (Octavia). 32. *mean:* means. 35. *curious:* extremely particular.

And make the hearts of Romans serve your ends!
We will here part.

Cæs. Farewell, my dearest sister, fare thee well!
The elements be kind to thee, and make 40
Thy spirits all of comfort! Fare thee well!

Oct. My noble brother!

Ant. The April's in her eyes. It is love's spring,
And these the showers to bring it on. Be cheerful.

Oct. Sir, look well to my husband's house, and—

Cæs. What,
Octavia?

Oct. I'll tell you in your ear. [*She whispers to Cæsar.*

Ant. Her tongue will not obey her heart, nor can
Her heart inform her tongue—swan's-down feather
That stands upon the swell at full of tide
And neither way inclines.

Eno. [*Aside to Agrippa*] Will Cæsar weep? 50

Agr. [*Aside to Enobarbus*] He has a cloud in 's face.

Eno. [*Aside to Agrippa*] He were the worse for that, were he a horse;
So he is, being a man.

Agr. [*Aside to Enobarbus*] Why, Enobarbus,
When Antony found Julius Cæsar dead,
He cried almost to roaring; and he wept
When at Philippi he found Brutus slain.

Eno. [*Aside to Agrippa*] That year indeed he was troubled with a rheum.
What willingly he did confound he wail'd,
Believe 't, till I wept too.

Cæs. No, sweet Octavia,
You shall hear from me still. The time shall not 60
Outgo my thinking on you.

Ant. Come, sir, come.

51. *cloud in 's face.* A horse lacking a white mark on his forehead was said to have a cloud in his face, and to be bad-tempered. 57. *rheum:* cold that caused his eyes to water. 58. *confound:* destroy. *wail'd:* bewailed. 61. *Outgo:* last longer than.

I'll wrestle with you in my strength of love.
Look, here I have you; thus I let you go,
And give you to the gods.

Cæs. Adieu; be happy!

Lep. Let all the number of the stars give light
To thy fair way!

Cæs. Farewell, farewell! [*Kisses Octavia.*

Ant. Farewell!

[*Trumpets sound. Exeunt.*

SCENE III. *Alexandria. A room in* CLEOPATRA'S *palace.*

Enter CLEOPATRA, CHARMIAN, IRAS, *and* ALEXAS.

Cleo. Where is the fellow?

Alex. Half afeard to come.

Cleo. Go to, go to!

Enter the Messenger *as before.*

Come hither, sir.

Alex. Good Majesty,
Herod of Jewry dare not look upon you
But when you are well pleased.

Cleo. That Herod's head
I'll have! But how, when Antony is gone
Through whom I might command it? Come thou near.

Mess. Most gracious Majesty—

Cleo. Didst thou behold Octavia?

Mess. Ay, dread queen.

Cleo. Where? 10

Mess. Madam, in Rome.
I look'd her in the face, and saw her led
Between her brother and Mark Antony.

Cleo. Is she as tall as me?

Mess. She is not, madam.

Cleo. Didst hear her speak? Is she shrill-tongued or low?

Mess. Madam, I heard her speak; she is low-voiced.

[iii] 1. *afeard:* afraid.

Cleo. That's not so good. He cannot like her long.
Char. Like her! O Isis, 'tis impossible.
Cleo. I think so, Charmian. Dull of tongue, and dwarfish!
What majesty is in her gait? Remember, 20
If e'er thou look'dst on majesty.
Mess. She creeps.
Her motion and her station are as one.
She shows a body rather than a life,
A statue than a breather.
Cleo. Is this certain?
Mess. Or I have no observance.
Char. Three in Egypt
Cannot make better note.
Cleo. He's very knowing;
I do perceive 't. There's nothing in her yet.
The fellow has good judgment.
Char. Excellent.
Cleo. Guess at her years, I prithee.
Mess. Madam,
She was a widow—
Cleo. Widow! Charmian, hark. 30
Mess. And I do think she's thirty.
Cleo. Bear'st thou her face in mind? Is't long or round?
Mess. Round even to faultiness.
Cleo. For the most part, too, they are foolish that are so.
Her hair, what colour?
Mess. Brown, madam; and her forehead
As low as she would wish it.
Cleo. There's gold for thee.
Thou must not take my former sharpness ill.
I will employ thee back again; I find thee
Most fit for business. Go make thee ready; 40
Our letters are prepared. [*Exit Messenger.*
Char. A proper man.

22. *station:* manner of standing. 25. *observance:* ability to observe. 37. *low.* Low foreheads were considered ugly. 41. *proper:* handsome.

Cleo. Indeed he is so. I repent me much
That so I harried him. Why, methinks, by him,
This creature's no such thing.

Char. Nothing, madam.

Cleo. The man hath seen some majesty, and should know.

Char. Hath he seen majesty? Isis else defend,
And serving you so long!

Cleo. I have one thing more to ask him yet, good Charmian—
But 'tis no matter; thou shalt bring him to me
Where I will write. All may be well enough. 50

Char. I warrant you, madam. [*Exeunt.*

SCENE IV. *Athens. A room in* ANTONY'S *house.*

Enter ANTONY *and* OCTAVIA.

Ant. Nay, nay, Octavia, not only that—
That were excusable, that, and thousands more
Of semblable import—but he hath waged
New wars 'gainst Pompey; made his will, and read it
To public ear;
Spoke scantly of me; when perforce he could not
But pay me terms of honour, cold and sickly
He vented them; most narrow measure lent me;
When the best hint was given him, he not took't,
Or did it from his teeth.

Oct. O my good lord, 10
Believe not all; or, if you must believe,

44. *such:* very remarkable. 46. *defend:* forbid.
[iv] S. D. *Athens.* Antony married Octavia in 40 B.C. When, eight years later, he divorced her, Octavius declared war against Cleopatra. The battle of Actium occurred in 31 B.C., the capture of Alexandria and the deaths of Antony and Cleopatra in 30 B.C. There is, then, an interval of eight years between II, ii, and III, iv. 3. *semblable import:* similar purpose. 4–5. *made . . . ear.* Plutarch states that it was Antony's will that Octavius read publicly and criticized. 6. *scantly:* disparagingly. 8. *vented:* uttered. 9. *hint:* opportunity. 10. *from his teeth:* i.e., outwardly, not from the heart.

Stomach not all. A more unhappy lady,
If this division chance, ne'er stood between,
Praying for both parts.
The good gods will mock me presently
When I shall pray, "O, bless my lord and husband!"
Undo that prayer by crying out as loud,
"O, bless my brother!" Husband win, win brother,
Prays, and destroys the prayer; no midway
'Twixt these extremes at all.

Ant. Gentle Octavia, 20
Let your best love draw to that point which seeks
Best to preserve it. If I lose mine honour,
I lose myself. Better I were not yours
Than yours so branchless. But, as you requested,
Yourself shall go between's. The mean time, lady,
I'll raise the preparation of a war
Shall stain your brother. Make your soonest haste;
So your desires are yours.

Oct. Thanks to my lord.
The Jove of power make me most weak, most weak,
Your reconciler! Wars 'twixt you twain would be 30
As if the world should cleave, and that slain men
Should solder up the rift.

Ant. When it appears to you where this begins,
Turn your displeasure that way, for our faults
Can never be so equal that your love
Can equally move with them. Provide your going,
Choose your own company, and command what cost
Your heart has mind to. [*Exeunt.*

SCENE V. *Another room in* ANTONY'S *house.*

Enter ENOBARBUS *and* EROS, *meeting.*

Eno. How now, friend Eros?

Eros. There's strange news come, sir.

12. *Stomach:* resent. 13. *chance:* occur, happen. 14. *parts:* sides. 24. *branchless:* destitute. 27. *stain:* make dim. 36. *Provide:* prepare.

Eno. What, man?

Eros. Cæsar and Lepidus have made wars upon Pompey.

Eno. This is old. What is the success?

Eros. Cæsar, having made use of him in the wars 'gainst Pompey, presently denied him rivality; would not let him partake in the glory of the action; and, not resting here, accuses him of letters he had formerly wrote to Pompey; upon his own appeal, seizes him. So the poor third is up, till death enlarge his confine. 13

Eno. Then, world, thou hast a pair of chaps, no more;
And throw between them all the food thou hast,
They'll grind the one the other. Where's Antony?

Eros. He's walking in the garden—thus; and spurns
The rush that lies before him; cries, "Fool Lepidus!"
And threats the throat of that his officer
That murder'd Pompey.

Eno. Our great navy's rigg'd. 20

Eros. For Italy and Cæsar. More, Domitius;
My lord desires you presently. My news
I might have told hereafter.

Eno. 'Twill be naught,
But let it be. Bring me to Antony.

Eros. Come, sir. [*Exeunt.*

SCENE VI. *Rome. A room in* CÆSAR'S *house.*

Enter CÆSAR, AGRIPPA, *and* MECÆNAS.

Cæs. Contemning Rome, he has done all this and more
In Alexandria. Here's the manner of 't:
I' the market-place, on a tribunal silver'd,

[v] 6. *success:* outcome. 8. *rivality:* partnership. 12. *his own appeal:* Cæsar's own accusation. 13. *the poor . . . confine:* the weak third member of the triumvirate is imprisoned, until death free him. 14. *chaps:* jaws. 17. *spurns:* kicks. 20. *Pompey.* In 35 B.C., he surrendered to Antony and was executed, presumably with Antony's consent. 22. *presently:* at once.

[vi] 1. *Contemning:* scorning. 3. *tribunal:* raised platform.

Cleopatra and himself in chairs of gold
Were publicly enthroned. At the feet sat
Cæsarion, whom they call my father's son,
And all the unlawful issue that their lust
Since then hath made between them. Unto her
He gave the stablishment of Egypt; made her
Of lower Syria, Cyprus, Lydia, 10
Absolute queen.

Mec. This in the public eye?

Cæs. I' the common show-place, where they exercise.
His sons he there proclaim'd the kings of kings.
Great Media, Parthia, and Armenia,
He gave to Alexander; to Ptolemy he assign'd
Syria, Cilicia, and Phœnicia. She
In the habiliments of the goddess Isis
That day appear'd; and oft before gave audience,
As 'tis reported, so.

Mec. Let Rome be thus
Inform'd.

Agr. Who, queasy with his insolence 20
Already, will their good thoughts call from him.

Cæs. The people know it, and have now received
His accusations.

Agr. Who does he accuse?

Cæs. Cæsar; and that, having in Sicily
Sextus Pompeius spoil'd, we had not rated him
His part o' the isle. Then does he say, he lent me
Some shipping unrestored. Lastly, he frets
That Lepidus of the triumvirate
Should be deposed; and, being, that we detain
All his revenue.

6. *Cæsarion.* He was the son of Julius Cæsar and Cleopatra. Octavius, Cæsar's adopted son, was actually his sister's grandson. 9. *stablishment:* settled occupation. 10. *Lydia:* a Roman province in Asia Minor. 19. *Rome:* the Roman people. 20. *queasy:* disgusted. 25. *spoil'd:* plundered. *rated:* assigned. 27. *unrestored:* i.e., which has not been returned. 29. *being:* i.e., being deposed. *we:* Cæsar.

Agr. Sir, this should be answer'd. 30
Cæs. 'Tis done already, and the messenger gone.
I have told him Lepidus was grown too cruel;
That he his high authority abused,
And did deserve his change. For what I have conquer'd,
I grant him part; but then in his Armenia,
And other of his conquer'd kingdoms, I
Demand the like.
Mec. He'll never yield to that.
Cæs. Nor must not then be yielded to in this.

Enter OCTAVIA *with her train.*

Oct. Hail, Cæsar, and my lord! Hail, most dear Cæsar!
Cæs. That ever I should call thee castaway! 40
Oct. You have not call'd me so, nor have you cause.
Cæs. Why have you stol'n upon us thus? You come not
Like Cæsar's sister. The wife of Antony
Should have an army for an usher, and
The neighs of horse to tell of her approach
Long ere she did appear. The trees by the way
Should have borne men, and expectation fainted,
Longing for what it had not. Nay, the dust
Should have ascended to the roof of heaven,
Raised by your populous troops. But you are come 50
A market-maid to Rome, and have prevented
The ostentation of our love, which, left unshown,
Is often left unloved. We should have met you
By sea and land, supplying every stage
With an augmented greeting.
Oct. Good my lord,
To come thus was I not constrain'd, but did it
On my free will. My lord, Mark Antony,
Hearing that you prepared for war, acquainted

40 ff. Cæsar puts the worst possible construction upon Antony's acts, and imagines a slight which at the time was not intended. Cf. III, iv, 27–8. 50. *populous:* numerous. 51–2. *prevented . . . ostentation:* forestalled the demonstration.

My grieved ear withal, whereon I begg'd
His pardon for return.
Cæs. Which soon he granted, 60
Being an abstract 'tween his lust and him.
Oct. Do not say so, my lord.
Cæs. I have eyes upon him,
And his affairs come to me on the wind.
Where is he now?
Oct. My lord, in Athens.
Cæs. No, my most wronged sister; Cleopatra
Hath nodded him to her. He hath given his empire
Up to a whore, who now are levying
The kings o' the earth for war. He hath assembled
Bocchus, the king of Libya; Archelaus,
Of Cappadocia; Philadelphos, king 70
Of Paphlagonia; the Thracian king, Adallas;
King Malchus of Arabia; King of Pont;
Herod of Jewry; Mithridates, king
Of Comagene; Polemon and Amyntas,
The kings of Mede and Lycaonia,
With a more larger list of sceptres.
Oct. Ay me, most wretched,
That have my heart parted betwixt two friends
That do afflict each other!
Cæs. Welcome hither!
Your letters did withhold our breaking forth,
Till we perceived both how you were wrong led 80
And we in negligent danger. Cheer your heart!
Be you not troubled with the time, which drives
O'er your content these strong necessities,
But let determined things to destiny
Hold unbewail'd their way. Welcome to Rome;

60. *pardon:* permission. 61. *abstract:* abbreviation (i.e., her departure shortened the interval between Cleopatra and Antony). Many editors accept Theobald's emendation, *obstruct* (impediment, bar), a word elsewhere unknown. 67. *levying:* assembling. 80. *wrong led:* deluded. 81. *negligent danger:* danger through negligence.

Nothing more dear to me! You are abused
Beyond the mark of thought; and the high gods,
To do you justice, make them ministers
Of us and those that love you. Best of comfort;
And ever welcome to us!

Agr. Welcome, lady. 90

Mec. Welcome, dear madam.
Each heart in Rome does love and pity you.
Only the adulterous Antony, most large
In his abominations, turns you off
And gives his potent regiment to a trull
That noises it against us.

Oct. Is it so, sir?

Cæs. Most certain. Sister, welcome! Pray you
Be ever known to patience. My dear'st sister! [*Exeunt.*

SCENE VII. *Near Actium.* ANTONY'S *camp.*

Enter CLEOPATRA *and* ENOBARBUS.

Cleo. I will be even with thee; doubt it not.

Eno. But why, why, why?

Cleo. Thou hast forspoke my being in these wars,
And say'st it is not fit.

Eno. Well, is it, is it?

Cleo. Is 't not denounced against us? Why should not we
Be there in person?

Eno. [*Aside*] Well, I could reply:
If we should serve with horse and mares together,
The horse were merely lost; the mares would bear
A soldier and his horse.

Cleo. What is 't you say? 10

Eno. Your presence needs must puzzle Antony;

87. *mark:* reach. 88. *make them:* Capell's emendation; F1 reads *makes his. them:* for themselves. 93. *large:* free. 95. *regiment:* government. 96. *noises it:* is clamorous.

[vii] S. D. *Actium:* on the west coast of Greece. 3. *forspoke:* opposed. 5. *Is 't not.* Hanmer's emendation; F1 reads *If not.* 9. *merely:* utterly. 11. *puzzle:* embarrass.

Take from his heart, take from his brain, from's time,
What should not then be spared. He is already
Traduced for levity, and 'tis said in Rome
That Photinus, an eunuch, and your maids
Manage this war.

Cleo. Sink Rome, and their tongues rot
That speak against us! A charge we bear i' the war,
And, as the president of my kingdom, will
Appear there for a man. Speak not against it;
I will not stay behind!

Enter Antony *and* Canidius.

Eno. Nay, I have done. 20
Here comes the emperor.

Ant. Is it not strange, Canidius,
That from Tarentum and Brundusium
He could so quickly cut the Ionian sea
And take in Toryne? You have heard on 't, sweet?

Cleo. Celerity is never more admired
Than by the negligent.

Ant. A good rebuke,
Which might have well becomed the best of men,
To taunt at slackness. Canidius, we
Will fight with him by sea.

Cleo. By sea? What else?

Can. Why will my lord do so?

Ant. For that he dares us to 't.

Eno. So hath my lord dared him to single fight. 31

Can. Ay, and to wage this battle at Pharsalia,
Where Cæsar fought with Pompey; but these offers,
Which serve not for his vantage, he shakes off;
And so should you.

Eno. Your ships are not well mann'd;
Your mariners are muleters, reapers, people

14. *Traduced:* blamed. 15. *eunuch:* i.e., Mardian. 17. *charge:* military command, or, perhaps, part of the cost. 19. *for a man:* as a man. 24. *take in:* capture.

Ingross'd by swift impress. In Cæsar's fleet
Are those that often have 'gainst Pompey fought;
Their ships are yare; yours, heavy. No disgrace
Shall fall you for refusing him at sea, 40
Being prepared for land.

Ant. By sea, by sea!

Eno. Most worthy sir, you therein throw away
The absolute soldiership you have by land;
Distract your army, which doth most consist
Of war-mark'd footmen; leave unexecuted
Your own renowned knowledge; quite forego
The way which promises assurance; and
Give up yourself merely to chance and hazard,
From firm security.

Ant. I'll fight at sea.

Cleo. I have sixty sails, Cæsar none better. 50

Ant. Our overplus of shipping will we burn,
And, with the rest full-mann'd, from the head of Actium
Beat the approaching Cæsar. But if we fail,
We then can do 't at land.

Enter a Messenger.

Thy business?

Mess. The news is true, my lord. He is descried;
Cæsar has taken Toryne.

Ant. Can he be there in person? 'Tis impossible;
Strange that his power should be! Canidius,
Our nineteen legions thou shalt hold by land
And our twelve thousand horse. We'll to our ship. 60
Away, my Thetis!

Enter a Soldier.

How now, worthy soldier?

Sold. O noble emperor, do not fight by sea;

37. *Ingross'd:* recruited. *impress:* enforced levy. 39. *yare:* easily managed. 40. *fall:* befall. 43. *absolute:* perfect. 44. *Distract:* divide, scatter. 45. *unexecuted:* unused. 48. *merely:* completely. 52. *head:* headland. 58. *power:* army. 61. *Thetis:* a sea-nymph, mother of Achilles.

Trust not to rotten planks. Do you misdoubt
This sword and these my wounds? Let the Egyptians
And the Phœnicians go a-ducking; we
Have used to conquer, standing on the earth,
And fighting foot to foot.

Ant. Well, well; away!

[*Exeunt Antony, Cleopatra, and Enobarbus.*

Sold. By Hercules, I think I am i' the right.

Can. Soldier, thou art. But his whole action grows
Not in the power on 't; so our leader's led, 70
And we are women's men.

Sold. You keep by land
The legions and the horse whole, do you not?

Can. Marcus Octavius, Marcus Justeius,
Publicola, and Cælius, are for sea,
But we keep whole by land. This speed of Cæsar's
Carries beyond belief.

Sold. While he was yet in Rome,
His power went out in such distractions as
Beguiled all spies.

Can. Who's his lieutenant, hear you?

Sold. They say, one Taurus.

Can. Well I know the man.

Enter a Messenger.

Mess. The emperor calls Canidius. 80

Can. With news the time's with labour, and throes forth
Each minute some. [*Exeunt.*

Scene viii. *A plain near Actium.*

Enter Cæsar *and* Taurus, *with his army, marching.*

Cæs. Taurus!

Taur. My lord?

63. *misdoubt:* distrust. 69–70. *his . . . on 't:* his whole enterprise moves not in the best direction. 77. *power:* forces. *distractions:* small detachments. 81. *throes forth:* gives painful birth to.

Cæs. Strike not by land; keep whole; provoke not battle
Till we have done at sea. Do not exceed
The prescript of this scroll. Our fortune lies
Upon this jump. [*Exeunt.*

SCENE IX. *Another part of the plain.*

Enter ANTONY *and* ENOBARBUS.

Ant. Set we our squadrons on yond side o' the hill
In eye of Cæsar's battle, from which place
We may the number of the ships behold,
And so proceed accordingly. [*Exeunt.*

SCENE X. *Another part of the plain.*

CANIDIUS *marches with his land army one way over the stage, and* TAURUS, *the lieutenant of* CÆSAR, *the other way. After their going in, is heard the noise of a sea-fight.*

Alarum. Enter ENOBARBUS.

Eno. Naught, naught, all naught! I can behold no longer.
The Antoniad, the Egyptian admiral,
With all their sixty, fly and turn the rudder.
To see 't mine eyes are blasted.

Enter SCARUS.

Scar. Gods and goddesses,
All the whole synod of them!
Eno. What's thy passion?
Scar. The greater cantle of the world is lost
With very ignorance. We have kiss'd away
Kingdoms and provinces.

[viii] 5. *prescript:* instructions. 6. *jump:* hazard; or *jump* may be an adverb, "exactly," "precisely."
[ix] 2. *In eye:* in sight. *battle:* battle array.
[x] 2. *Antoniad:* the name of Cleopatra's admiral or flagship. 5. *synod:* assembly of the gods. 6. *cantle:* part.

Eno. How appears the fight?
Scar. On our side like the token'd pestilence,
Where death is sure. Yon ribaudred nag of Egypt— 10
Whom leprosy o'ertake!—i' the midst o' the fight,
When vantage like a pair of twins appear'd,
Both as the same, or rather ours the elder,
The breese upon her, like a cow in June,
Hoists sails and flies.
Eno. That I beheld.
Mine eyes did sicken at the sight and could not
Endure a further view.
Scar. She once being loof'd,
The noble ruin of her magic, Antony,
Claps on his sea-wing, and, like a doting mallard, 20
Leaving the fight in height, flies after her.
I never saw an action of such shame.
Experience, manhood, honour, ne'er before
Did violate so itself.
Eno. Alack, alack!

Enter Canidius.

Can. Our fortune on the sea is out of breath
And sinks most lamentably. Had our general
Been what he knew himself, it had gone well.
O, he has given example for our flight
Most grossly by his own!
Eno. Ay, are you thereabouts?
Why, then, good night indeed. 30
Can. Toward Peloponnesus are they fled.
Scar. 'Tis easy to 't; and there I will attend
What further comes.
Can. To Cæsar will I render

9. *token'd:* indicated by "tokens" (marks on the skin of the plague-smitten). 10. *ribaudred:* lewd, wanton (?). 12. *vantage:* opportunity. 14. *breese:* gadfly. 18. *loof'd:* luffed, brought head around in the wind. 20. *mallard:* male of the wild duck. 29. *thereabouts:* thinking of that. 32. *to 't:* to reach it. *attend:* await.

My legions and my horse. Six kings already
Show me the way of yielding.
Eno. I'll yet follow
The wounded chance of Antony, though my reason
Sits in the wind against me. [*Exeunt.*

SCENE XI. *Alexandria. A room in* CLEOPATRA'S *palace.*

Enter ANTONY *with* Attendants.

Ant. Hark! The land bids me tread no more upon 't;
It is ashamed to bear me! Friends, come hither!
I am so lated in the world that I
Have lost my way for ever. I have a ship
Laden with gold; take that, divide it. Fly,
And make your peace with Cæsar.
All. Fly? Not we!
Ant. I have fled myself, and have instructed cowards
To run and show their shoulders. Friends, be gone.
I have myself resolved upon a course
Which has no need of you. Be gone. 10
My treasure's in the harbour. Take it! O,
I follow'd that I blush to look upon.
My very hairs do mutiny, for the white
Reprove the brown for rashness, and they them
For fear and doting. Friends, be gone. You shall
Have letters from me to some friends that will
Sweep your way for you. Pray you look not sad
Nor make replies of loathness. Take the hint
Which my despair proclaims. Let that be left
Which leaves itself. To the sea-side straightway! 20
I will possess you of that ship and treasure.
Leave me, I pray, a little; pray you now!
Nay, do so, for indeed I have lost command;
Therefore I pray you. I'll see you by and by. [*Sits down.*

36. *wounded chance:* broken fortunes.
[xi] 3. *lated:* belated. 7. *instructed:* i.e., by my own flight.
18. *loathness:* unwillingness. *hint:* opportunity.

Enter CLEOPATRA *led by* CHARMIAN *and* IRAS,
EROS *following.*

Eros. Nay, gentle madam, to him! Comfort him!
Iras. Do, most dear queen.
Char. Do! Why, what else?
Cleo. Let me sit down. O Juno!
Ant. No, no, no, no, no!
Eros. See you here, sir? 30
Ant. O fie, fie, fie!
Char. Madam!
Iras. Madam, O good empress!
Eros. Sir, sir—
Ant. Yes, my lord, yes! He at Philippi kept
His sword e'en like a dancer, while I struck
The lean and wrinkled Cassius; and 'twas I
That the mad Brutus ended. He alone
Dealt on lieutenantry, and no practice had
In the brave squares of war. Yet now—no matter. 40
Cleo. Ah, stand by.
Eros. The queen, my lord, the queen!
Iras. Go to him, madam, speak to him.
He is unqualitied with very shame.
Cleo. Well then, sustain me. O!
Eros. Most noble sir, arise; the queen approaches.
Her head's declined, and death will seize her, but
Your comfort makes the rescue.
Ant. I have offended reputation—
A most unnoble swerving.
Eros. Sir, the queen. 50
Ant. O, whither hast thou led me, Egypt? See

35. *my lord.* Perhaps addressed to Octavius, or, more probably, to Eros. *He:* i.e., Octavius. 36. *like a dancer:* i.e., for ornament only. 39. *on lieutenantry:* by deputy. *practice:* part, experience. 40. *squares:* quarrels, or, perhaps, squadrons. 44. *unqualitied:* deprived of his (manly) qualities. 45. *sustain:* support, strengthen. 47. *but:* unless.

How I convey my shame out of thine eyes
By looking back what I have left behind
'Stroy'd in dishonour.

Cleo. O my lord, my lord,
Forgive my fearful sails! I little thought
You would have follow'd.

Ant. Egypt, thou knew'st too well
My heart was to thy rudder tied by the strings,
And thou shouldst tow me after. O'er my spirit
Thy full supremacy thou knew'st, and that
Thy beck might from the bidding of the gods 60
Command me.

Cleo. O, my pardon!

Ant. Now I must
To the young man send humble treaties, dodge
And palter in the shifts of lowness, who
With half the bulk o' the world play'd as I pleased,
Making and marring fortunes. You did know
How much you were my conqueror, and that
My sword, made weak by my affection, would
Obey it on all cause.

Cleo. Pardon, pardon!

Ant. Fall not a tear, I say; one of them rates
All that is won and lost. Give me a kiss; 70
Even this repays me. We sent our schoolmaster;
Is he come back? Love, I am full of lead.
Some wine, within there, and our viands! Fortune knows
We scorn her most when most she offers blows. [*Exeunt.*

52–3. *How . . . behind:* how I hide my shame from you by reflecting on my ruined fortunes. 55. *fearful:* terrified. 57. *strings:* heartstrings. 60. *from:* contrary to. 62. *treaties:* negotiations. 63. *palter:* use trickery. *in . . . lowness:* with mean subterfuges. 69. *Fall:* let fall. *rates:* is worth (?). 71. *schoolmaster:* Euphronius. 72. *full of lead:* heavy, sad.

Scene xii. *Egypt.* Cæsar's *camp.*

Enter Cæsar, Dolabella, *and* Thyreus, *with others.*

Cæs. Let him appear that's come from Antony.
Know you him?
Dol. Cæsar, 'tis his schoolmaster—
An argument that he is pluck'd, when hither
He sends so poor a pinion of his wing,
Which had superfluous kings for messengers
Not many moons gone by.

Enter Euphronius, *ambassador from* Antony.

Cæs. Approach and speak.
Euph. Such as I am, I come from Antony.
I was of late as petty to his ends
As is the morn-dew on the myrtle-leaf
To his grand sea.
Cæs. Be't so. Declare thine office. 10
Euph. Lord of his fortunes he salutes thee, and
Requires to live in Egypt; which not granted,
He lessens his requests and to thee sues
To let him breathe between the heavens and earth,
A private man in Athens. This for him.
Next, Cleopatra does confess thy greatness,
Submits her to thy might, and of thee craves
The circle of the Ptolemies for her heirs,
Now hazarded to thy grace.
Cæs. For Antony,
I have no ears to his request. The queen 20
Of audience nor desire shall fail, so she
From Egypt drive her all-disgraced friend
Or take his life there. This if she perform,
She shall not sue unheard. So to them both.
Euph. Fortune pursue thee! [*Exit Euphronius.*

[xii] 3. *argument:* proof. 12. *Requires:* asks. 16. *confess:* acknowledge. 18. *circle:* crown. 19. *hazarded . . . grace:* staked on thy favor. 22. *friend:* lover.

Cæs. Bring him through the bands.
[*To Thyreus.*] To try thy eloquence, now 'tis time. Dispatch!
From Antony win Cleopatra. Promise,
And in our name, what she requires. Add more,
From thine invention, offers. Women are not
In their best fortunes strong, but want will perjure 30
The ne'er-touch'd vestal. Try thy cunning, Thyreus;
Make thine own edict for thy pains, which we
Will answer as a law.

Thyr. Cæsar, I go.

Cæs. Observe how Antony becomes his flaw,
And what thou think'st his very action speaks
In every power that moves.

Thyr. Cæsar, I shall. [*Exeunt.*

SCENE XIII. *Alexandria. A room in* CLEOPATRA'S *palace.*

Enter CLEOPATRA, ENOBARBUS, CHARMIAN, *and* IRAS.

Cleo. What shall we do, Enobarbus?

Eno. Think—and die.

Cleo. Is Antony or we in fault for this?

Eno. Antony only, that would make his will
Lord of his reason. What though you fled
From that great face of war, whose several ranges
Frighted each other? Why should he follow?
The itch of his affection should not then
Have nick'd his captainship, at such a point,
When half to half the world opposed, he being
The mered question. 'Twas a shame no less 10
Than was his loss, to course your flying flags,
And leave his navy gazing.

25. *bands:* troops. 31. *ne'er-touch'd:* unsullied. *vestal:* virgin. 32. *Make . . . pains:* decree thine own reward. 33. *answer:* obey. 34. *becomes his flaw:* adapts himself to his disaster. 35–6. *speaks . . . moves:* reveals in every one of his movements.

[xiii] 1. *Think:* have melancholy thoughts. 3. *will:* carnal appetite. 5. *ranges:* ranks. 8. *nick'd:* cut short. 10. *mered question:* sole matter of dispute. 11. *course:* follow.

Cleo. Prithee, peace!

Enter Antony *with* Euphronius, *the ambassador.*

Ant. Is that his answer?
Euph. Ay, my lord.
Ant. The queen shall then have courtesy, so she
Will yield us up.
Euph. He says so.
Ant. Let her know't.
To the boy Cæsar send this grizzled head,
And he will fill thy wishes to the brim
With principalities.
Cleo. That head, my lord?
Ant. To him again! Tell him he wears the rose 20
Of youth upon him, from which the world should note
Something particular. His coin, ships, legions
May be a coward's, whose ministers would prevail
Under the service of a child as soon
As i' the command of Cæsar. I dare him therefore
To lay his gay comparisons apart,
And answer me declined, sword against sword,
Ourselves alone. I'll write it. Follow me.
[*Exeunt Antony and Euphronius.*
Eno. [*Aside*] Yes, like enough, high-battled Cæsar will
Unstate his happiness and be staged to the show 30
Against a sworder! I see men's judgments are
A parcel of their fortunes, and things outward
Do draw the inward quality after them
To suffer all alike. That he should dream,
Knowing all measures, the full Cæsar will

15. *so:* if. 22. *particular:* personal, outstanding. 26. *his gay comparisons:* advantages that appear when we are compared. 27. *declined:* i.e., in fortune and strength. 29. *high-battled:* aided by powerful armies. 30. *Unstate his happiness:* lay aside the dignity of his good fortune. *staged:* exhibited publicly. 31. *sworder:* gladiator. 32. *parcel:* part. 35. *Knowing all measures:* having experienced every measure of fortune.

Answer his emptiness! Cæsar, thou hast subdued
His judgment too.

Enter an Attendant.

Att. A messenger from Cæsar.

Cleo. What, no more ceremony? See, my women!
Against the blown rose may they stop their nose
That kneel'd unto the buds. Admit him, sir. [*Exit Attendant.*

Eno. [*Aside*] Mine honesty and I begin to square. 41
The loyalty well held to fools does make
Our faith mere folly; yet he that can endure
To follow with allegiance a fall'n lord
Does conquer him that did his master conquer,
And earns a place i' the story.

Enter THYREUS.

Cleo. Cæsar's will?

Thyr. Hear it apart.

Cleo. None but friends. Say boldly.

Thyr. So haply are they friends to Antony.

Eno. He needs as many, sir, as Cæsar has,
Or needs not us. If Cæsar please, our master 50
Will leap to be his friend. For us, you know
Whose he is we are, and that is Cæsar's.

Thyr. So.
Thus then, thou most renown'd: Cæsar entreats
Not to consider in what case thou stand'st
Further than he is Cæsar.

Cleo. Go on. Right royal!

Thyr. He knows that you embrace not Antony
As you did love, but as you fear'd him.

Cleo. O!

Thyr. The scars upon your honour, therefore, he
Does pity, as constrained blemishes,
Not as deserved.

39. *blown:* blossomed. 41. *square:* quarrel. 48. *haply:* perhaps. 54. *case:* circumstances. 55. *Further . . . Cæsar:* i.e., not an emperor but a kindly man. 56. *embrace:* cherish, cling to. 59. *constrained:* produced by compulsion.

Cleo. He is a god, and knows 60
What is most right. Mine honour was not yielded,
But conquer'd merely.

Eno. [*Aside*] To be sure of that,
I will ask Antony. Sir, sir, thou art so leaky
That we must leave thee to thy sinking, for
Thy dearest quit thee. [*Exit.*

Thyr. Shall I say to Cæsar
What you require of him, for he partly begs
To be desired to give? It much would please him
That of his fortunes you should make a staff
To lean upon; but it would warm his spirits,
To hear from me you had left Antony, 70
And put yourself under his shroud,
The universal landlord.

Cleo. What's your name?

Thyr. My name is Thyreus.

Cleo. Most kind messenger,
Say to great Cæsar this: in deputation
I kiss his conquering hand. Tell him I am prompt
To lay my crown at 's feet, and there to kneel.
Tell him, from his all-obeying breath, I hear
The doom of Egypt.

Thyr. 'Tis your noblest course.
Wisdom and fortune combating together,
If that the former dare but what it can, 80
No chance may shake it. Give me grace to lay
My duty on your hand.

Cleo. Your Cæsar's father oft,
When he hath mused of taking kingdoms in,
Bestow'd his lips on that unworthy place,
As it rain'd kisses.

Re-enter ANTONY *and* ENOBARBUS.

Ant. Favours, by Jove that thunders!
What art thou, fellow?

62. *merely:* entirely. 71. *shroud:* protection. 74. *in deputation:* by deputy. 78. *Egypt:* the queen of Egypt.

Thyr. One that but performs
The bidding of the fullest man, and worthiest
To have command obey'd.
Eno. [*Aside*] You will be whipp'd.
Ant. Approach, there! Ah, you kite! Now, gods and devils!
Authority melts from me. Of late, when I cried "Ho!" 90
Like boys unto a muss, kings would start forth,
And cry "Your will?" Have you no ears? I am
Antony yet.

Enter Attendants.

Take hence this Jack, and whip him.
Eno. [*Aside*] 'Tis better playing with a lion's whelp
Than with an old one dying.
Ant. Moon and stars!
Whip him. Were 't twenty of the greatest tributaries
That do acknowledge Cæsar, should I find them
So saucy with the hand of she here—what's her name
Since she was Cleopatra? Whip him, fellows,
Till, like a boy, you see him cringe his face 100
And whine aloud for mercy. Take him hence.
Thyr. Mark Antony!
Ant. Tug him away. Being whipp'd,
Bring him again. This Jack of Cæsar's shall
Bear us an errand to him. [*Exeunt Attendants with Thyreus.*
You were half blasted ere I knew you, ha!
Have I my pillow left unpress'd in Rome,
Forborne the getting of a lawful race,
And by a gem of women, to be abused
By one that looks on feeders?
Cleo. Good my lord—
Ant. You have been a boggler ever, 110
But when we in our viciousness grow hard—
O misery on 't!—the wise gods seel our eyes,

87. *fullest:* most complete. 91. *muss:* scramble. 93. *Jack:* rogue. 105. *blasted:* withered. 108. *abused:* deceived. 109. *feeders:* servants. 110. *boggler:* waverer. 112. *seel:* close (sew shut the eyes of hawks).

In our own filth drop our clear judgments, make us
Adore our errors, laugh at 's, while we strut
To our confusion.

Cleo. O, is't come to this?

Ant. I found you as a morsel cold upon
Dead Cæsar's trencher. Nay, you were a fragment
Of Cneius Pompey's, besides what hotter hours,
Unregister'd in vulgar fame, you have
Luxuriously pick'd out; for, I am sure, 120
Though you can guess what temperance should be,
You know not what it is.

Cleo. Wherefore is this?

Ant. To let a fellow that will take rewards
And say "God quit you!" be familiar with
My playfellow, your hand, this kingly seal
And plighter of high hearts! O, that I were
Upon the hill of Bashan, to outroar
The horned herd! For I have savage cause,
And to proclaim it civilly were like
A halter'd neck which does the hangman thank 130
For being yare about him.

Re-enter Attendants *with* Thyreus.

Is he whipp'd?

First Att. Soundly, my lord.

Ant. Cried he? And begg'd a' pardon?

First Att. He did ask favour.

Ant. If that thy father live, let him repent
Thou wast not made his daughter; and be thou sorry
To follow Cæsar in his triumph, since
Thou hast been whipp'd for following him. Henceforth
The white hand of a lady fever thee!
Shake thou to look on't! Get thee back to Cæsar;

117. *trencher:* plate. 119. *vulgar fame:* common rumor. 120. *Luxuriously:* lustfully. 121. *temperance:* chastity. 124. *quit:* requite. 127. *Bashan:* a land famous for its bulls. See Psalms 22:12, and 68:15. 128. *horned:* cuckolded. 131. *yare:* nimble, brisk. 138. *fever:* throw into a fever.

Tell him thy entertainment. Look thou say 140
He makes me angry with him, for he seems
Proud and disdainful, harping on what I am,
Not what he knew I was. He makes me angry,
And at this time most easy 'tis to do 't,
When my good stars, that were my former guides,
Have empty left their orbs and shot their fires
Into the abysm of hell. If he mislike
My speech and what is done, tell him he has
Hipparchus, my enfranched bondman, whom
He may at pleasure whip or hang or torture, 150
As he shall like, to quit me. Urge it thou.
Hence with thy stripes! Be gone! [*Exit Thyreus.*

Cleo. Have you done yet?

Ant. Alack, our terrene moon
Is now eclipsed, and it portends alone
The fall of Antony!

Cleo. I must stay his time.

Ant. To flatter Cæsar, would you mingle eyes
With one that ties his points?

Cleo. Not know me yet?

Ant. Cold-hearted toward me?

Cleo. Ah, dear, if I be so,
From my cold heart let heaven engender hail,
And poison it in the source, and the first stone 160
Drop in my neck. As it determines, so
Dissolve my life! The next Cæsarion smite!
Till by degrees the memory of my womb,
Together with my brave Egyptians all,
By the discandying of this pelleted storm,
Lie graveless, till the flies and gnats of Nile
Have buried them for prey!

146. *orbs:* spheres. 149. *enfranched:* enfranchised. 151. *quit:* requite. 153. *terrene moon:* terrestrial moon, i.e., Cleopatra. 157. *points:* tagged laces for attaching hose to the doublet. 161. *determines:* ends, i.e., melts. 162. *Cæsarion:* son of Julius Cæsar and Cleopatra. 163. *memory:* memorials, i.e., children. 165. *discandying:* melting. *pelleted:* falling in pellets.

Ant. I am satisfied.
Cæsar sits down in Alexandria, where
I will oppose his fate. Our force by land
Hath nobly held; our sever'd navy too 170
Have knit again, and fleet, threatening most sea-like.
Where hast thou been, my heart? Dost thou hear, lady?
If from the field I shall return once more
To kiss these lips, I will appear in blood.
I and my sword will earn our chronicle.
There's hope in 't yet.

Cleo. That's my brave lord!

Ant. I will be treble-sinew'd, hearted, breathed,
And fight maliciously; for when mine hours
Were nice and lucky, men did ransom lives 180
Of me for jests; but now I'll set my teeth
And send to darkness all that stop me. Come,
Let's have one other gaudy night. Call to me
All my sad captains; fill our bowls once more.
Let's mock the midnight bell.

Cleo. It is my birthday.
I had thought to have held it poor; but, since my lord
Is Antony again, I will be Cleopatra.

Ant. We will yet do well.

Cleo. Call all his noble captains to my lord.

Ant. Do so, we'll speak to them; and tonight I'll force 190
The wine peep through their scars. Come on, my queen;
There's sap in't yet. The next time I do fight
I'll make Death love me, for I will contend
Even with his pestilent scythe. [*Exeunt all but Enobarbus.*

Eno. Now he'll outstare the lightning. To be furious
Is to be frighted out of fear, and in that mood
The dove will peck the estridge; and I see still

171. *fleet:* float. *sea-like:* in seagoing trim. 174. *in blood:* (a) in health, (b) blood-spattered. 178. *breathed:* trained, inured. 180. *nice and lucky:* indolent and heedless. 183. *gaudy night:* night of rejoicing. 193. *contend:* compete. 194. *pestilent:* pestilential. 197. *estridge:* ostrich, or, perhaps, falcon.

A diminution in our captain's brain
Restores his heart. When valour preys on reason,
It eats the sword it fights with. I will seek 200
Some way to leave him. [*Exit.*

ACT IV

SCENE I. *Before Alexandria.* CÆSAR'S *camp.*

Enter CÆSAR, AGRIPPA, *and* MECÆNAS, *with his army;* CÆSAR *reading a letter.*

Cæs. He calls me boy, and chides as he had power
To beat me out of Egypt. My messenger
He hath whipp'd with rods; dares me to personal combat,
Cæsar to Antony. Let the old ruffian know
I have many other ways to die; meantime
Laugh at his challenge.
Mec. Cæsar must think,
When one so great begins to rage, he's hunted
Even to falling. Give him no breath, but now
Make boot of his distraction. Never anger
Made good guard for itself.
Cæs. Let our best heads 10
Know that tomorrow the last of many battles
We mean to fight. Within our files there are,
Of those that served Mark Antony but late,
Enough to fetch him in. See it done.
And feast the army; we have store to do 't,
And they have earn'd the waste. Poor Antony! [*Exeunt.*

SCENE II. *Alexandria. A room in* CLEOPATRA'S *palace.*

Enter ANTONY, CLEOPATRA, ENOBARBUS, CHARMIAN, IRAS, ALEXAS, *with others.*

Ant. He will not fight with me, Domitius?
Eno. No.

198. *diminution:* impairment.
[IV. i] 9. *boot:* profit. *distraction:* bewilderment. 14. *fetch him in:* surround him, capture him.

Ant. Why should he not?
Eno. He thinks, being twenty times of better fortune,
He is twenty men to one.
Ant. Tomorrow, soldier,
By sea and land I'll fight. Or I will live,
Or bathe my dying honour in the blood
Shall make it live again. Woo 't thou fight well?
Eno. I'll strike and cry, "Take all."
Ant. Well said. Come on.
Call forth my household servants. Let's tonight
Be bounteous at our meal.

Enter three or four Servitors.

Give me thy hand; 10
Thou hast been rightly honest. So hast thou—
Thou—and thou—and thou. You have served me well,
And kings have been your fellows.
Cleo. [*Aside to Enobarbus*] What means this?
Eno. [*Aside to Cleopatra*] 'Tis one of those odd tricks which sorrow shoots
Out of the mind.
Ant. And thou art honest too.
I wish I could be made so many men,
And all of you clapp'd up together in
An Antony, that I might do you service
So good as you have done.
All. The gods forbid!
Ant. Well, my good fellows, wait on me tonight. 20
Scant not my cups, and make as much of me
As when mine empire was your fellow too
And suffer'd my command.
Cleo. [*Aside to Enobarbus*] What does he mean?
Eno. [*Aside to Cleopatra*] To make his followers weep.
Ant. Tend me tonight.
May be it is the period of your duty.

[ii] 5. *Or:* either. 7. *Woo 't:* wilt. 8. "*Take all*": let the winner take all. 17. *clapp'd up:* shut up. 25. *period:* end.

Haply you shall not see me more; or if,
A mangled shadow. Perchance tomorrow
You'll serve another master. I look on you
As one that takes his leave. Mine honest friends,
I turn you not away; but, like a master 30
Married to your good service, stay till death.
Tend me tonight two hours; I ask no more,
And the gods yield you for 't!

Eno. What mean you, sir,
To give them this discomfort? Look, they weep;
And I, an ass, am onion-eyed. For shame!
Transform us not to women.

Ant. Ho, ho, ho!
Now the witch take me if I meant it thus!
Grace grow where those drops fall! My hearty friends,
You take me in too dolorous a sense,
For I spake to you for your comfort, did desire you 40
To burn this night with torches. Know, my hearts,
I hope well of tomorrow, and will lead you
Where rather I'll expect victorious life
Than death and honour. Let's to supper; come
And drown consideration. [*Exeunt.*

SCENE III. *Alexandria. Before* CLEOPATRA'S *palace.*

Enter two Soldiers *to their guard.*

First Sold. Brother, good night. Tomorrow is the day.

Sec. Sold. It will determine one way. Fare you well.
Heard you of nothing strange about the streets?

First Sold. Nothing. What news?

Sec. Sold. Belike 'tis but a rumour. Good night to you.

First Sold. Well, sir, good night.

33. *yield:* reward.
[iii] 2. *determine one way:* decide one way or the other.

Enter two other Soldiers.

Sec. Sold. Soldiers, have careful watch.
Third Sold. And you. Good night, good night.
[*They place themselves in every corner of the stage.*
Fourth Sold. Here we; and if tomorrow
Our navy thrive, I have an absolute hope 10
Our landmen will stand up.
Third Sold. 'Tis a brave army,
And full of purpose. [*Music of the hautboys as under the stage.*
Fourth Sold. Peace! What noise?
First Sold. List, list!
Sec. Sold. Hark!
First Sold. Music i' the air.
Third Sold. Under the earth.
Fourth Sold. It signs well, does it not?
Third Sold. No.
First Sold. Peace, I say!
What should this mean?
Sec. Sold. 'Tis the god Hercules, whom Antony loved,
Now leaves him.
First Sold. Walk. Let's see if other watchmen
Do hear what we do. [*They advance to another post.*
Sec. Sold. How now, masters?
Omnes. [*Speaking together*] How now?
How now? Do you hear this?
First Sold. Ay. Is 't not strange? 20
Third Sold. Do you hear, masters? Do you hear?
First Sold. Follow the noise so far as we have quarter.
Let's see how it will give off.
Omnes. Content. 'Tis strange. [*Exeunt.*

10. *absolute:* perfectly certain. S. D. *hautboys:* oboes. 13. *Music . . . earth.* In Plutarch the music symbolizes the departure of Bacchus, the god of Antony's "singular devotion." Shakespeare substitutes Hercules, whom Antony claimed as an ancestor. 14. *signs:* bodes. 22. *noise:* music. *have quarter:* occupy positions. 23. *give off:* cease.

SCENE IV. *The same. A room in* CLEOPATRA'S *palace.*

Enter ANTONY *and* CLEOPATRA, CHARMIAN, *and others attending.*

Ant. Eros! Mine armour, Eros!
Cleo. Sleep a little.
Ant. No, my chuck. Eros, come; mine armour, Eros!

Enter EROS *with armour.*

Come, good fellow, put mine iron on.
If fortune be not ours today, it is
Because we brave her. Come.
Cleo. Nay, I'll help too.
What's this for?
Ant. Ah, let be, let be! Thou art
The armourer of my heart.—False, false! This, this!
Cleo. Sooth, la, I'll help. Thus it must be.
Ant. Well, well.
We shall thrive now. Seest thou, my good fellow?
Go put on thy defenses.
Eros. Briefly, sir. 10
Cleo. Is not this buckled well?
Ant. Rarely, rarely!
He that unbuckles this, till we do please
To daff 't for our repose, shall hear a storm.
Thou fumblest, Eros, and my queen's a squire
More tight at this than thou. Dispatch. O love,
That thou couldst see my wars today, and knew'st
The royal occupation! Thou shouldst see
A workman in 't.

Enter an armed Soldier.

Good morrow to thee! Welcome.
Thou look'st like him that knows a warlike charge.

[iv] 2. *chuck:* chick. 5. *brave:* defy too boldly. 7. *False:* wrong. 10. *Briefly:* quickly. 11. *Rarely:* excellently. 13. *daff 't:* take it off. 15. *tight:* dextrous. *Dispatch:* make haste. 19. *warlike charge:* military duty.

To business that we love we rise betime 20
And go to 't with delight.
Sold. A thousand, sir,
Early though 't be, have on their riveted trim,
And at the port expect you. [*Shout. Trumpets flourish.*

Enter Captains *and* Soldiers.

Capt. The morn is fair. Good morrow, general.
Omnes. Good morrow, general.
Ant. 'Tis well blown, lads.
This morning, like the spirit of a youth
That means to be of note, begins betimes.
So, so. Come, give me that! This way!—Well said.
Fare thee well, dame, whate'er becomes of me. 29
This is a soldier's kiss. Rebukable [*Kisses her.*
And worthy shameful check it were to stand
On more mechanic compliment. I'll leave thee
Now, like a man of steel. You that will fight,
Follow me close; I'll bring you to 't. Adieu.
[*Exeunt Antony, Eros, Captains, and Soldiers.*
Char. Please you, retire to your chamber.
Cleo. Lead me.
He goes forth gallantly. That he and Cæsar might
Determine this great war in single fight!
Then, Antony—but now—Well, on! [*Exeunt.*

SCENE V. *Alexandria.* ANTONY'S *camp.*

Trumpets sound. Enter ANTONY *and* EROS,
a Soldier *meeting them.*

Sold. The gods make this a happy day to Antony!
Ant. Would thou and those thy scars had once prevail'd
To make me fight at land!
Sold. Hadst thou done so,
The kings that have revolted and the soldier

22. *riveted trim:* armor. 23. *port:* gate. 31. *check:* censure. *stand:* insist. 32. *mechanic:* befitting a mechanic, vulgar, overdemonstrative.

That has this morning left thee would have still
Follow'd thy heels.

Ant. Who's gone this morning?

Sold. Who?
One ever near thee. Call for Enobarbus,
He shall not hear thee, or from Cæsar's camp
Say, "I am none of thine."

Ant. What say'st thou?

Sold. Sir,
He is with Cæsar.

Eros. Sir, his chests and treasure 10
He has not with him.

Ant. Is he gone?

Sold. Most certain.

Ant. Go, Eros, send his treasure after. Do it.
Detain no jot, I charge thee. Write to him—
I will subscribe—gentle adieus and greetings.
Say that I wish he never find more cause
To change a master. O, my fortunes have
Corrupted honest men! Dispatch.—Enobarbus! [*Exeunt.*

SCENE VI. *Alexandria.* CÆSAR'S *camp.*

Flourish. Enter CÆSAR *with* AGRIPPA, ENOBARBUS, *and others.*

Cæs. Go forth, Agrippa, and begin the fight.
Our will is Antony be took alive.
Make it so known.

Agr. Cæsar, I shall. [*Exit.*

Cæs. The time of universal peace is near.
Prove this a prosperous day, the three-nook'd world
Shall bear the olive freely.

Enter a Messenger.

Mess. Antony
Is come into the field.

[v] 14. *subscribe:* sign.
[vi] 6. *three-nook'd:* three-cornered, i.e., consisting of Europe, Asia, and Africa (?).

Cæs. Go charge Agrippa
Plant those that have revolted in the van,
That Antony may seem to spend his fury 10
Upon himself. [*Exeunt all but Enobarbus.*

Eno. Alexas did revolt, and went to Jewry on
Affairs of Antony; there did dissuade
Great Herod to incline himself to Cæsar
And leave his master Antony. For this pains
Cæsar hath hang'd him. Canidius and the rest
That fell away have entertainment, but
No honourable trust. I have done ill,
Of which I do accuse myself so sorely
That I will joy no more.

Enter a Soldier *of* Cæsar's.

Sold. Enobarbus, Antony 20
Hath after thee sent all thy treasure, with
His bounty overplus. The messenger
Came on my guard, and at thy tent is now
Unloading of his mules.

Eno. I give it you!

Sold. Mock not, Enobarbus.
I tell you true. Best you safed the bringer
Out of the host; I must attend mine office,
Or would have done 't myself. Your emperor
Continues still a Jove. [*Exit.*

Eno. I am alone the villain of the earth, 30
And feel I am so most. O Antony,
Thou mine of bounty, how wouldst thou have paid
My better service, when my turpitude
Thou dost so crown with gold! This blows my heart.
If swift thought break it not, a swifter mean
Shall outstrike thought; but thought will do 't, I feel.

13. *dissuade:* persuade (from his allegiance to Antony). 17. *entertainment:* employment. 22. *bounty overplus:* gift in addition. 26. *safed:* escorted. 34. *blows:* swells. 35. *thought:* sorrow, regret. *mean:* means.

I fight against thee? No! I will go seek
Some ditch wherein to die; the foul'st best fits
My latter part of life. [*Exit.*

SCENE VII. *Field of battle between the camps.*

Alarum. Drums and trumpets. Enter AGRIPPA *and others.*

Agr. Retire. We have engaged ourselves too far.
Cæsar himself has work, and our oppression
Exceeds what we expected. [*Exeunt.*

Alarums. Enter ANTONY, *and* SCARUS *wounded.*

Scar. O my brave emperor, this is fought indeed!
Had we done so at first, we had droven them home
With clouts about their heads.
Ant. Thou bleed'st apace.
Scar. I had a wound here that was like a T,
But now 'tis made an H.
Ant. They do retire.
Scar. We'll beat 'em into bench-holes. I have yet
Room for six scotches more. 10

Enter EROS.

Eros. They are beaten, sir, and our advantage serves
For a fair victory.
Scar. Let us score their backs
And snatch 'em up, as we take hares, behind!
'Tis sport to maul a runner.
Ant. I will reward thee
Once for thy spritely comfort, and ten-fold
For thy good valour. Come thee on!
Scar. I'll halt after. [*Exeunt.*

[vii] 2. *work:* difficulty. *oppression:* opposition. 6. *clouts:* bandages. 8. *an H:* i.e., an ache (pronounced like the letter *h*). 9. *bench-holes:* privies. 10. *scotches:* cuts. 15. *spritely:* spirited, cheerful. 16. *halt:* limp.

SCENE VIII. *Under the walls of Alexandria.*

Alarum. Enter ANTONY *in a march;* SCARUS, *with others.*

Ant. We have beat him to his camp. Run one before
And let the queen know of our gests. Tomorrow,
Before the sun shall see 's, we'll spill the blood
That has today escaped. I thank you all,
For doughty-handed are you, and have fought
Not as you served the cause, but as 't had been
Each man's like mine. You have shown all Hectors.
Enter the city; clip your wives, your friends;
Tell them your feats, whilst they with joyful tears
Wash the congealment from your wounds, and kiss 10
The honour'd gashes whole. [*To Scarus.*] Give me thy hand.

Enter CLEOPATRA, *attended.*

To this great fairy I'll commend thy acts,
Make her thanks bless thee. [*To Cleopatra.*] O thou day o' the
world,
Chain mine arm'd neck! Leap thou, attire and all,
Through proof of harness to my heart, and there
Ride on the pants triumphing!

Cleo. Lord of lords!
O infinite virtue, comest thou smiling from
The world's great snare uncaught?

Ant. My nightingale,
We have beat them to their beds. What, girl! Though grey
Do something mingle with our younger brown, yet ha' we 20
A brain that nourishes our nerves, and can
Get goal for goal of youth. Behold this man.

[viii] 2. *gests:* deeds. 6. *as 't:* as if it. 7. *shown all Hectors:* all shown yourselves to be valiant warriors. The Elizabethans did not always account Hector a brave man. Cf. *Much Ado,* II, iii, 196. 8. *clip:* embrace. 10. *congealment:* clotted blood. 12. *fairy:* enchantress. 14. *Chain:* embrace, encircle as with a chain. 15. *proof of harness:* impenetrable armor. 16. *pants:* heartbeats. 17. *virtue:* valor. 20. *something:* somewhat. 22. *Get . . . youth:* play on even terms with youth.

Commend unto his lips thy favouring hand.—
Kiss it, my warrior! He hath fought today
As if a god, in hate of mankind, had
Destroy'd in such a shape.

Cleo. I'll give thee, friend,
An armour all of gold. It was a king's.

Ant. He has deserved it, were it carbuncled
Like holy Phœbus' car. Give me thy hand.
Through Alexandria make a jolly march; 30
Bear our hack'd targets like the men that owe them.
Had our great palace the capacity
To camp this host, we all would sup together
And drink carouses to the next day's fate,
Which promises royal peril. Trumpeters,
With brazen din blast you the city's ear;
Make mingle with our rattling tabourines,
That heaven and earth may strike their sounds together,
Applauding our approach. [*Exeunt.*

SCENE IX. CÆSAR'S *camp.*

Sentinels *at their post.*

First Sold. If we be not relieved within this hour,
We must return to the court of guard. The night
Is shiny, and they say we shall embattle
By the second hour i' the morn.

Sec. Sold. This last day was
A shrewd one to 's.

Enter ENOBARBUS.

Eno. O, bear me witness, night—

Third Sold. What man is this?

Sec. Sold. Stand close, and list him.

Eno. Be witness to me, O thou blessed moon,
When men revolted shall upon record

28. *carbuncled:* set with carbuncles, bejewelled. 31. *targets:* shields. *owe:* own. 37. *mingle:* mingling. *tabourines:* drums.

[ix] 2. *court of guard:* guardroom. 3. *embattle:* be drawn up in battle array. 5. *shrewd:* grievous. 6. *list:* listen to.

Bear hateful memory, poor Enobarbus did
Before thy face repent!

First Sold. Enobarbus!

Third Sold. Peace! 10
Hark further.

Eno. O sovereign mistress of true melancholy,
The poisonous damp of night disponge upon me,
That life, a very rebel to my will,
May hang no longer on me! Throw my heart
Against the flint and hardness of my fault,
Which, being dried with grief, will break to powder,
And finish all foul thoughts. O Antony,
Nobler than my revolt is infamous,
Forgive me in thine own particular, 20
But let the world rank me in register
A master-leaver and a fugitive!
O Antony! O Antony! [*Dies.*

Sec. Sold. Let's speak
To him.

First Sold. Let's hear him, for the things he speaks
May concern Cæsar.

Third Sold. Let's do so. But he sleeps.

First Sold. Swoons rather, for so bad a prayer as his
Was never yet for sleep.

Sec. Sold. Go we to him.

Third Sold. Awake, sir, awake! Speak to us!

Sec. Sold. Hear you, sir?

First Sold. The hand of death hath raught him. [*Drums afar off.*] Hark! The drums 30
Demurely wake the sleepers. Let us bear him
To the court of guard. He is of note. Our hour
Is fully out.

Third Sold. Come on then.
He may recover yet. [*Exeunt with the body.*

9. *bear . . . memory:* be remembered with hatred. 13. *disponge:* pour down. 17. *Which:* i.e., the heart. 20. *in . . . particular:* thyself. 30. *raught:* snatched. 31. *Demurely:* with subdued sound.

SCENE X. *Between the two camps.*

Enter ANTONY *and* SCARUS, *with their Army.*

Ant. Their preparation is today by sea;
We please them not by land.
Scar. For both, my lord.
Ant. I would they 'ld fight i' the fire or i' the air;
We 'ld fight there too. But this it is: our foot
Upon the hills adjoining to the city
Shall stay with us. Order for sea is given.
They have put forth the haven. Let us go
Where their appointment we may best discover
And look on their endeavour. [*Exeunt.*

SCENE XI. *Another part of the same.*

Enter CÆSAR *and his Army.*

Cæs. But being charged, we will be still by land,
Which, as I take 't, we shall; for his best force
Is forth to man his galleys. To the vales,
And hold our best advantage. [*Exeunt.*

SCENE XII. *Another part of the same.*

Enter ANTONY *and* SCARUS.

Ant. Yet they are not join'd. Where yond pine does stand
I shall discover all. I'll bring thee word
Straight how 'tis like to go. [*Exit.*
Scar. Swallows have built
In Cleopatra's sails their nests. The augurers
Say they know not, they cannot tell, look grimly,
And dare not speak their knowledge. Antony
Is valiant and dejected; and by starts

[x] 7. *forth:* forth from. *Let us go.* Omitted in F_1.
[xi] 1. *But . . . land:* unless attacked, we will keep our land forces inactive.
[xii] 1. *join'd:* i.e., in battle. 7. *starts:* sudden fits or impulses.

His fretted fortunes give him hope and fear
Of what he has and has not.
[*Alarum afar off, as at a sea-fight.*

Re-enter Antony.

Ant. All is lost!
This foul Egyptian hath betrayed me! 10
My fleet hath yielded to the foe, and yonder
They cast their caps up and carouse together
Like friends long lost. Triple-turn'd whore! 'Tis thou
Hast sold me to this novice, and my heart
Makes only wars on thee. Bid them all fly,
For when I am revenged upon my charm,
I have done all. Bid them all fly. Be gone! [*Exit Scarus.*
O sun, thy uprise shall I see no more.
Fortune and Antony part here; even here
Do we shake hands. All come to this? The hearts 20
That spaniel'd me at heels, to whom I gave
Their wishes, do discandy, melt their sweets
On blossoming Cæsar; and this pine is bark'd,
That overtopp'd them all. Betray'd I am.
O this false soul of Egypt! This grave charm—
Whose eye beck'd forth my wars and call'd them home,
Whose bosom was my crownet, my chief end—
Like a right gipsy, hath at fast and loose
Beguiled me to the very heart of loss.
What, Eros, Eros!

Enter Cleopatra.

Ah, thou spell! Avaunt! 30

Cleo. Why is my lord enraged against his love?

Ant. Vanish, or I shall give thee thy deserving

8. *fretted:* checkered, worn. 13. *Triple-turn'd:* thrice-faithless. 16. *charm:* enchantress. 21. *spaniel'd:* followed doglike. 22. *discandy:* melt. 23. *bark'd:* stripped. 25. *grave charm:* destructive enchantress. 26. *beck'd:* beckoned. 27. *crownet:* coronet. 28. *right:* true. *fast and loose:* a trick played by the gipsies of Shakespeare's day. A girdle or handkerchief was tied into a knot which could be loosened by pulling the ends.

And blemish Cæsar's triumph. Let him take thee
And hoist thee up to the shouting plebeians.
Follow his chariot, like the greatest spot
Of all thy sex; most monster-like, be shown
For poor'st diminutives, for dolts; and let
Patient Octavia plough thy visage up
With her prepared nails. [*Exit Cleopatra.*] 'Tis well thou 'rt gone,
If it be well to live; but better 'twere 40
Thou fell'st into my fury, for one death
Might have prevented many. Eros, ho!
The shirt of Nessus is upon me. Teach me,
Alcides, thou mine ancestor, thy rage.
Let me lodge Lichas on the horns o' the moon
And with those hands that grasp'd the heaviest club
Subdue my worthiest self. The witch shall die.
To the young Roman boy she hath sold me, and I fall
Under this plot. She dies for 't. Eros, ho! [*Exit.*

SCENE XIII. *Alexandria. A room in* CLEOPATRA'S *palace.*

Enter CLEOPATRA, CHARMIAN, IRAS, *and* MARDIAN.

Cleo. Help me, my women! O, he is more mad
Than Telamon for his shield. The boar of Thessaly
Was never so emboss'd.
Char. To the monument!
There lock yourself, and send him word you are dead.
The soul and body rive not more in parting
Than greatness going off.

35. *spot:* stain, disgrace. 36. *shown:* exhibited. 37. *For . . . diminutives:* to poorest weaklings. *dolts.* This is the F_1 reading. Most modern editors accept Warburton's emendation, *doits,* i.e., small coins. 43. *shirt of Nessus:* the poisoned shirt that killed Hercules (Alcides). 45. *Lichas:* Hercules' companion whom he cast into the sea.

[xiii] 2. *Telamon:* Ajax Telamon, who went mad because he did not receive the armor of Achilles. *boar of Thessaly:* the boar that Diana sent to ravage the fields of Calydon. 3. *emboss'd:* foaming with rage, or, perhaps, driven to extremity. *monument:* tomb. 5. *rive:* are torn.

Cleo. To the monument!
Mardian, go tell him I have slain myself.
Say that the last I spoke was "Antony,"
And word it, prithee, piteously. Hence, Mardian,
And bring me how he takes my death. To the monument! 10
[*Exeunt.*

SCENE XIV. *Another room in* CLEOPATRA'S *palace.*

Enter ANTONY *and* EROS.

Ant. Eros, thou yet behold'st me?
Eros. Ay, noble lord.
Ant. Sometime we see a cloud that's dragonish,
A vapour sometime like a bear or lion,
A tower'd citadel, a pendent rock,
A forked mountain, or blue promontory
With trees upon 't that nod unto the world
And mock our eyes with air. Thou hast seen these signs;
They are black vesper's pageants.
Eros. Ay, my lord.
Ant. That which is now a horse, even with a thought
The rack dislimns, and makes it indistinct 10
As water is in water.
Eros. It does, my lord.
Ant. My good knave Eros, now thy captain is
Even such a body. Here I am Antony,
Yet cannot hold this visible shape, my knave.
I made these wars for Egypt; and the queen—
Whose heart I thought I had, for she had mine,
Which, whilst it was mine, had annex'd unto 't
A million more, now lost—she, Eros, has
Pack'd cards with Cæsar and false-play'd my glory
Unto an enemy's triumph. 20

10. *bring me:* bring me word.
[xiv] 8. *vesper's:* evening's. 10. *rack dislimns:* the cloud-drift blots out. 12. *knave:* boy. 19. *Pack'd cards:* cheated. 20. *triumph:* (a) trump card, (b) victory.

Nay, weep not, gentle Eros. There is left us
Ourselves to end ourselves.

Enter MARDIAN.

O, thy vile lady!
She has robb'd me of my sword.

Mar. No, Antony.
My mistress loved thee, and her fortunes mingled
With thine entirely.

Ant. Hence, saucy eunuch! Peace!
She hath betray'd me and shall die the death.

Mar. Death of one person can be paid but once,
And that she has discharged. What thou wouldst do
Is done unto thy hand. The last she spake
Was "Antony! Most noble Antony!" 30
Then in the midst a tearing groan did break
The name of Antony; it was divided
Between her heart and lips. She render'd life,
Thy name so buried in her.

Ant. Dead, then?

Mar. Dead.

Ant. Unarm, Eros. The long day's task is done,
And we must sleep. [*To Mardian.*] That thou depart'st hence safe,
Does pay thy labour richly. Go. [*Exit Mardian.*] Off, pluck off!
The seven-fold shield of Ajax cannot keep
The battery from my heart. O, cleave, my sides!
Heart, once be stronger than thy continent; 40
Crack thy frail case!—Apace, Eros, apace.—
No more a soldier. Bruised pieces, go;
You have been nobly borne.—From me awhile. [*Exit Eros.*
I will o'ertake thee, Cleopatra, and
Weep for my pardon. So it must be, for now
All length is torture. Since the torch is out,
Lie down, and stray no farther. Now all labour

29. *unto thy hand:* ready for thee. 33. *render'd:* gave up. 38. *seven-fold:* reinforced with seven thicknesses of oxhide. 39. *battery:* assault. *cleave:* burst. 40. *continent:* container. 46. *length:* delay.

Mars what it does; yea, very force entangles
Itself with strength. Seal then, and all is done.
Eros!—I come, my queen.—Eros!—Stay for me. 50
Where souls do couch on flowers, we'll hand in hand,
And with our sprightly port make the ghosts gaze.
Dido and her Æneas shall want troops,
And all the haunt be ours.—Come, Eros, Eros!

Re-enter Eros.

Eros. What would my lord?

Ant. Since Cleopatra died,
I have lived in such dishonour that the gods
Detest my baseness. I, that with my sword
Quarter'd the world and o'er green Neptune's back
With ships made cities, condemn myself to lack
The courage of a woman—less noble mind 60
Than she which by her death our Cæsar tells,
"I am conqueror of myself." Thou art sworn, Eros,
That, when the exigent should come—which now
Is come indeed—when I should see behind me
The inevitable prosecution of
Disgrace and horror, that, on my command,
Thou then wouldst kill me. Do 't; the time is come.
Thou strikest not me; 'tis Cæsar thou defeat'st.
Put colour in thy cheek.

Eros. The gods withhold me!
Shall I do that which all the Parthian darts, 70
Though enemy, lost aim and could not?

Ant. Eros,
Wouldst thou be window'd in great Rome and see
Thy master thus with pleach'd arms, bending down
His corrigible neck, his face subdued

48–9. *force . . . strength:* i.e., strength defeats itself. 49. *Seal:* finish. 51. *couch:* lie. 52. *port:* bearing. 53. *want troops:* lack retinue, followers. 54. *haunt:* popularity. 60. *less noble mind:* i.e., I have a mind less noble. 63. *exigent:* need. 65. *prosecution:* pursuit. 72. *window'd:* in a window to watch a spectacle. 73. *pleach'd:* folded. 74. *corrigible:* submissive.

To penetrative shame, whilst the wheel'd seat
Of fortunate Cæsar, drawn before him, branded
His baseness that ensued?

Eros. I would not see 't.

Ant. Come then, for with a wound I must be cured.
Draw that thy honest sword, which thou hast worn
Most useful for thy country.

Eros. O, sir, pardon me! 80

Ant. When I did make thee free, sworest thou not then
To do this when I bade thee? Do it at once,
Or thy precedent services are all
But accidents unpurposed. Draw and come.

Eros. Turn from me, then, that noble countenance
Wherein the worship of the whole world lies.

Ant. Lo thee! [*Turning from him.*

Eros. My sword is drawn.

Ant. Then let it do at once
The thing why thou hast drawn it.

Eros. My dear master,
My captain, and my emperor, let me say, 90
Before I strike this bloody stroke, farewell.

Ant. 'Tis said, man; and farewell.

Eros. Farewell, great chief. Shall I strike now?

Ant. Now, Eros.

Eros. Why, there then. [*Kills himself.*] Thus I do escape the sorrow
Of Antony's death.

Ant. Thrice-nobler than myself!
Thou teachest me, O valiant Eros, what
I should, and thou couldst not. My queen and Eros
Have by their brave instruction got upon me
A nobleness in record. But I will be
A bridegroom in my death and run into 't 100

75. *penetrative:* penetrating. 76–7. *branded . . . ensued:* made conspicuous as by a brand the disgrace of him who followed. 83. *precedent:* former. 86. *worship:* honor. 98–9. *got . . . record:* gained an advantage over me in the record of noble deeds.

As to a lover's bed. Come then; and, Eros,
Thy master dies thy scholar. To do thus [*Falls on his sword.*
I learn'd of thee. How? Not dead? Not dead?
The guard, ho! O, dispatch me!

Enter Dercetas *and* Guard.

First Guard. What's the noise?
Ant. I have done my work ill, friends. O, make an end
Of what I have begun.
Sec. Guard. The star is fall'n.
First Guard. And time is at his period.
All. Alas, and woe!
Ant. Let him that loves me strike me dead.
First Guard. Not I.
Sec. Guard. Nor I.
Third Guard. Nor any one. [*Exeunt Guard.*
Der. Thy death and fortunes bid thy followers fly. 111
This sword but shown to Cæsar, with this tidings,
Shall enter me with him.

Enter Diomedes.

Dio. Where's Antony?
Der. There, Diomed, there.
Dio. Lives he?
Wilt thou not answer, man? [*Exit Dercetas.*
Ant. Art thou there, Diomed? Draw thy sword, and give me
Sufficing strokes for death.
Dio. Most absolute lord,
My mistress Cleopatra sent me to thee.
Ant. When did she send thee?
Dio. Now, my lord.
Ant. Where is she?
Dio. Lock'd in her monument. She had a prophesying fear
Of what hath come to pass, for when she saw— 121

104. *dispatch:* kill. 107. *his period:* its end. 113. *enter me with:* recommend me with.

Which never shall be found—you did suspect
She had disposed with Cæsar, and that your rage
Would not be purged, she sent you word she was dead;
But, fearing since how it might work, hath sent
Me to proclaim the truth; and I am come,
I dread, too late.

Ant. Too late, good Diomed. Call my guard, I prithee.

Dio. What, ho! The emperor's guard! The guard, what, ho!
Come, your lord calls! 130

Enter four or five of the Guard *of* ANTONY.

Ant. Bear me, good friends, where Cleopatra bides.
'Tis the last service that I shall command you.

First Guard. Woe, woe are we, sir, you may not live to wear
All your true followers out.

All. Most heavy day!

Ant. Nay, good my fellows, do not please sharp fate
To grace it with your sorrows. Bid that welcome
Which comes to punish us, and we punish it
Seeming to bear it lightly. Take me up.
I have led you oft; carry me now, good friends, 139
And have my thanks for all. [*Exeunt, bearing Antony.*

SCENE XV. *Alexandria. A monument.*

Enter CLEOPATRA *and her maids aloft, with* CHARMIAN *and* IRAS.

Cleo. O Charmian, I will never go from hence.

Char. Be comforted, dear madam.

Cleo. No, I will not.
All strange and terrible events are welcome,
But comforts we despise. Our size of sorrow,
Proportion'd to our cause, must be as great
As that which makes it.

122. *found:* i.e., found true. 123. *disposed:* come to terms.
124. *purged:* cleared away. 136. *To grace:* by gracing.
[xv] 4. *Our . . . sorrow:* the extent of our sorrow.

Enter, below, DIOMEDES.

How now? Is he dead?

Dio. His death's upon him, but not dead.
Look out o' the other side your monument.
His guard have brought him thither.

Enter, below, ANTONY, *borne by the* Guard.

Cleo. O sun,
Burn the great sphere thou movest in! Darkling stand 10
The varying shore o' the world! O Antony,
Antony, Antony! Help, Charmian; help, Iras; help!
Help, friends below! Let's draw him hither.

Ant. Peace!
Not Cæsar's valour hath o'erthrown Antony,
But Antony's hath triumph'd on itself.

Cleo. So it should be, that none but Antony
Should conquer Antony; but woe 'tis so!

Ant. I am dying, Egypt, dying. Only
I here importune Death awhile, until
Of many thousand kisses the poor last 20
I lay upon thy lips.

Cleo. I dare not, dear—
Dear my lord, pardon—I dare not,
Lest I be taken. Not the imperious show
Of the full-fortuned Cæsar ever shall
Be brooch'd with me! If knife, drugs, serpents have
Edge, sting, or operation, I am safe.
Your wife Octavia, with her modest eyes
And still conclusion, shall acquire no honour
Demuring upon me. But come, come, Antony—

10. *sphere.* According to the Ptolemaic system, the sun was fixed in a great sphere with which it revolved around the earth. *Darkling:* in darkness. 11. *shore.* Staunton's beautiful but unnecessary emendation *star* (i.e., the moon) has been adopted by some editors. 19. *importune:* trouble with a request. 21. *I dare not:* i.e., descend from the monument. 23. *imperious:* imperial. 25. *brooch'd:* adorned. 28. *still conclusion:* sedate judgment. 29. *Demuring:* looking demurely. Furness suggests *demurring*, looking doubtfully.

Help me, my women—we must draw thee up. 30
Assist, good friends.

Ant. O, quick, or I am gone.

Cleo. Here's sport indeed! How heavy weighs my lord!
Our strength is all gone into heaviness;
That makes the weight. Had I great Juno's power,
The strong-wing'd Mercury should fetch thee up,
And set thee by Jove's side. Yet come a little—
Wishers were ever fools—O, come, come, come!

[*They heave Antony aloft to Cleopatra.*

And welcome, welcome! Die where thou hast lived.
Quicken with kissing. Had my lips that power,
Thus would I wear them out.

All. A heavy sight! 40

Ant. I am dying, Egypt, dying.
Give me some wine, and let me speak a little.

Cleo. No, let me speak, and let me rail so high
That the false housewife Fortune break her wheel,
Provoked by my offense.

Ant. One word, sweet queen.
Of Cæsar seek your honour, with your safety. O!

Cleo. They do not go together.

Ant. Gentle, hear me.
None about Cæsar trust but Proculeius.

Cleo. My resolution and my hands I'll trust;
None about Cæsar. 50

Ant. The miserable change now at my end
Lament nor sorrow at; but please your thoughts
In feeding them with those my former fortunes
Wherein I lived, the greatest prince o' the world,
The noblest; and do now not basely die,
Not cowardly put off my helmet to
My countryman—a Roman by a Roman
Valiantly vanquish'd. Now my spirit is going;
I can no more.

32. *sport:* i.e., angling. 33. *heaviness:* (a) sorrow, (b) weight.
39. *Quicken:* gain life. 44. *housewife:* hussy.

Cleo. Noblest of men, woo 't die?
Hast thou no care of me? Shall I abide 60
In this dull world, which in thy absence is
No better than a sty? O, see, my women, [*Antony dies.*
The crown o' the earth doth melt. My lord!
O, wither'd is the garland of the war;
The soldier's pole is fall'n! Young boys and girls
Are level now with men. The odds is gone,
And there is nothing left remarkable
Beneath the visiting moon. [*Faints.*
Char. O, quietness, lady!
Iras. She is dead too, our sovereign.
Char. Lady!
Iras. Madam!
Char. O madam, madam, madam!
Iras. Royal Egypt! 70
Empress!
Char. Peace, peace, Iras!
Cleo. No more, but e'en a woman, and commanded
By such poor passion as the maid that milks
And does the meanest chares. It were for me
To throw my sceptre at the injurious gods,
To tell them that this world did equal theirs
Till they had stol'n our jewel. All's but naught,
Patience is sottish, and impatience does
Become a dog that's mad. Then is it sin 80
To rush into the secret house of Death,
Ere Death dare come to us? How do you, women?
What, what! Good cheer! Why, how now, Charmian?
My noble girls! Ah, women, women, look!
Our lamp is spent, it's out! Good sirs, take heart.
We'll bury him; and then, what's brave, what's noble,
Let's do it after the high Roman fashion,

59. *woo 't:* wouldst thou. 64. *garland:* glory. 65. *pole:* guiding star, or, perhaps, standard. 66. *odds:* superiority. 67. *remarkable:* noteworthy. 74. *passion:* emotion, sorrow. 75. *chares:* chores. 79. *sottish:* stupid. 80. *Become:* suit.

And make Death proud to take us. Come away!
This case of that huge spirit now is cold.
Ah, women, women! Come; we have no friend 90
But resolution and the briefest end.
[*Exeunt, those above bearing off Antony's body.*

ACT V

SCENE I. *Alexandria.* CÆSAR'S *camp.*

Enter CÆSAR, AGRIPPA, DOLABELLA, MECÆNAS, GALLUS, PROCULEIUS, *and others, his council of war.*

Cæs. Go to him, Dolabella, bid him yield.
Being so frustrate, tell him he mocks
The pauses that he makes.
Dol. Cæsar, I shall. [*Exit.*

Enter DERCETAS, *with the sword of* ANTONY.

Cæs. Wherefore is that? And what art thou that darest
Appear thus to us?
Der. I am call'd Dercetas.
Mark Antony I served, who best was worthy
Best to be served. Whilst he stood up and spoke,
He was my master, and I wore my life
To spend upon his haters. If thou please
To take me to thee, as I was to him 10
I'll be to Cæsar. If thou pleasest not,
I yield thee up my life.
Cæs. What is 't thou say'st?
Der. I say, O Cæsar, Antony is dead.
Cæs. The breaking of so great a thing should make
A greater crack. The round world
Should have shook lions into civil streets,
And citizens to their dens. The death of Antony

89. *case:* the body, as containing the soul.
[V. i] 2. *frustrate:* baffled. 2–3. *he . . . makes:* he makes a mere pretense of delay. 16. *civil:* orderly.

Is not a single doom; in the name lay
A moiety of the world.
Der. He is dead, Cæsar,
Not by a public minister of justice, 20
Nor by a hired knife; but that self hand
Which writ his honour in the acts it did
Hath, with the courage which the heart did lend it,
Splitted the heart. This is his sword.
I robb'd his wound of it. Behold it stain'd
With his most noble blood.
Cæs. Look you sad, friends?
The gods rebuke me, but it is tidings
To wash the eyes of kings!
Agr. And strange it is
That nature must compel us to lament
Our most persisted deeds.
Mec. His taints and honours 30
Waged equal with him.
Agr. A rarer spirit never
Did steer humanity; but you gods will give us
Some faults to make us men. Cæsar is touch'd.
Mec. When such a spacious mirror's set before him,
He needs must see himself.
Cæs. O Antony!
I have follow'd thee to this. But we do lance
Diseases in our bodies. I must perforce
Have shown to thee such a declining day,
Or look on thine; we could not stall together
In the whole world. But yet let me lament, 40
With tears as sovereign as the blood of hearts,
That thou, my brother, my competitor
In top of all design, my mate in empire,

19. *moiety:* half. 27. *but it is:* if it be not. 30. *persisted:* persistently desired. 31. *Waged . . . him:* contended on equal terms within him. 32. *humanity:* human nature. 36. *follow'd:* pursued, driven. 39. *stall:* dwell. 41. *sovereign:* excellent. 42. *competitor:* partner. 43. *top . . . design:* all high ambitions.

Friend and companion in the front of war,
The arm of mine own body, and the heart
Where mine his thoughts did kindle—that our stars,
Unreconciliable, should divide
Our equalness to this. Hear me, good friends—
But I will tell you at some meeter season.

Enter an Egyptian.

The business of this man looks out of him; 50
We'll hear him what he says. Whence are you?
Egyp. A poor Egyptian yet. The queen my mistress,
Confined in all she has, her monument,
Of thy intents desires instruction,
That she preparedly may frame herself
To the way she's forced to.
Cæs. Bid her have good heart.
She soon shall know of us, by some of ours,
How honourable and how kindly we
Determine for her, for Cæsar cannot live 59
To be ungentle.
Egyp. So the gods preserve thee! [*Exit.*
Cæs. Come hither, Proculeius. Go and say
We purpose her no shame. Give her what comforts
The quality of her passion shall require,
Lest, in her greatness, by some mortal stroke
She do defeat us, for her life in Rome
Would be eternal in our triumph. Go,
And with your speediest bring us what she says,
And how you find of her.
Pro. Cæsar, I shall. [*Exit.*
Cæs. Gallus, go you along. [*Exit Gallus.*] Where's Dolabella,
To second Proculeius?
All. Dolabella! 70
Cæs. Let him alone, for I remember now

46. *his:* its. 55. *frame:* adjust, conform. 63. *passion:* sorrow.
65–6. *her . . . triumph:* her presence in Rome would add eternal glory to our triumphal festivities.

How he's employ'd. He shall in time be ready.
Go with me to my tent, where you shall see
How hardly I was drawn into this war,
How calm and gentle I proceeded still
In all my writings. Go with me, and see
What I can show in this. [*Exeunt.*

SCENE II. *Alexandria. A room in the monument.*

Enter CLEOPATRA, CHARMIAN, *and* IRAS.

Cleo. My desolation does begin to make
A better life. 'Tis paltry to be Cæsar.
Not being Fortune, he's but Fortune's knave,
A minister of her will. And it is great
To do that thing that ends all other deeds;
Which shackles accidents and bolts up change;
Which sleeps, and never palates more the dung,
The beggar's nurse and Cæsar's.

Enter, to the gates of the monument, PROCULEIUS, GALLUS, *and* Soldiers.

Pro. Cæsar sends greeting to the Queen of Egypt,
And bids thee study on what fair demands 10
Thou mean'st to have him grant thee.
Cleo. What's thy name?
Pro. My name is Proculeius.
Cleo. Antony
Did tell me of you, bade me trust you; but
I do not greatly care to be deceived,
That have no use for trusting. If your master
Would have a queen his beggar, you must tell him
That majesty, to keep decorum, must
No less beg than a kingdom. If he please

74. *hardly:* with difficulty. 75. *still:* always.
[ii] 3. *knave:* servant. 6. *bolts up:* locks up, i.e., ends. 7. *dung:* i.e., life's gross food. See I, i, 35. 14. *to be deceived:* whether I am deceived.

To give me conquer'd Egypt for my son,
He gives me so much of mine own as I 20
Will kneel to him with thanks.

Pro. Be of good cheer.
You're fall'n into a princely hand; fear nothing.
Make your full reference freely to my lord,
Who is so full of grace that it flows over
On all that need. Let me report to him
Your sweet dependency, and you shall find
A conqueror that will pray in aid for kindness,
Where he for grace is kneel'd to.

Cleo. Pray you tell him
I am his fortune's vassal, and I send him
The greatness he has got. I hourly learn 30
A doctrine of obedience, and would gladly
Look him i' the face.

Pro. This I'll report, dear lady.
Have comfort, for I know your plight is pitied
Of him that caused it.

Gal. You see how easily she may be surprised.

[*Here Proculeius and two of the Guard ascend the monument by a ladder placed against a window, and come behind Cleopatra. Some of the Guard unbar and open the gates.*]

[*To Proculeius and the Guard.*] Guard her till Cæsar come. [*Exit.*

Iras. Royal queen!

Char. O Cleopatra! Thou art taken, queen.

Cleo. Quick, quick, good hands! [*Draws a dagger.*

Pro. Hold, worthy lady, hold!
[*Disarms her.*
Do not yourself such wrong, who are in this 40
Relieved, but not betray'd.

Cleo. What, of death too,
That rids our dogs of languish?

Pro. Cleopatra,

23. *reference:* submission. 27. *pray in aid:* call in help from others (a legal phrase). 29–30. *I send . . . got:* I acknowledge the greatness that he has already won. 42. *languish:* lingering disease.

Do not abuse my master's bounty by
The undoing of yourself. Let the world see
His nobleness well acted, which your death
Will never let come forth.

Cleo. Where art thou, Death?
Come hither, come! Come, come, and take a queen
Worth many babes and beggars!

Pro. O, temperance, lady!

Cleo. Sir, I will eat no meat, I'll not drink, sir—
If idle talk will once be necessary— 50
I'll not sleep neither. This mortal house I'll ruin,
Do Cæsar what he can. Know, sir, that I
Will not wait pinion'd at your master's court,
Nor once be chastised with the sober eye
Of dull Octavia. Shall they hoist me up
And show me to the shouting varletry
Of censuring Rome? Rather a ditch in Egypt
Be gentle grave unto me! Rather on Nilus' mud
Lay me stark naked, and let the water-flies
Blow me into abhorring! Rather make 60
My country's high pyramides my gibbet,
And hang me up in chains!

Pro. You do extend
These thoughts of horror further than you shall
Find cause in Cæsar.

Enter DOLABELLA.

Dol. Proculeius,
What thou hast done thy master Cæsar knows,
And he hath sent for thee. For the queen,
I'll take her to my guard.

Pro. So, Dolabella,

44. *undoing:* destruction. 48. *temperance:* moderation. 49. *meat:* food. 50. *If . . . necessary:* if I must talk idly. 53. *pinion'd:* bound. 56. *varletry:* rabble. 60. *Blow:* befoul. *abhorring:* an object to be abhorred. 62. *chains.* In Shakespeare's London the bodies of executed criminals were hung in chains as a warning to evildoers.

It shall content me best. Be gentle to her.
[*To Cleopatra.*] To Cæsar I will speak what you shall please,
If you'll employ me to him.

Cleo. Say, I would die. 70

[*Exeunt Proculeius and Soldiers.*

Dol. Most noble empress, you have heard of me?

Cleo. I cannot tell.

Dol. Assuredly you know me.

Cleo. No matter, sir, what I have heard or known.
You laugh when boys or women tell their dreams.
Is't not your trick?

Dol. I understand not, madam.

Cleo. I dream'd there was an Emperor Antony.
O, such another sleep, that I might see
But such another man!

Dol. If it might please ye—

Cleo. His face was as the heavens, and therein stuck
A sun and moon, which kept their course and lighted 80
The little O, the earth.

Dol. Most sovereign creature—

Cleo. His legs bestrid the ocean; his rear'd arm
Crested the world. His voice was propertied
As all the tuned spheres, and that to friends;
But when he meant to quail and shake the orb,
He was as rattling thunder. For his bounty,
There was no winter in 't; an autumn 'twas
That grew the more by reaping. His delights
Were dolphin-like; they show'd his back above
The element they lived in. In his livery 90
Walk'd crowns and crownets. Realms and islands were
As plates dropp'd from his pocket.

Dol. Cleopatra—

76–94. Cf. *Romeo and Juliet*, I, iii, 81–94, and note. 83. *Crested:* formed a crest for. In heraldry, a raised arm was often used for a crest. 83–4. *His voice . . . friends:* to his friends the quality of his voice was as the music of the spheres. 85. *quail:* frighten. *orb:* earth. 87. *an autumn 'twas:* Theobald's emendation; F_1 reads *an Anthony it was.* 92. *plates:* coins.

Cleo. Think you there was or might be such a man
As this I dream'd of?
Dol. Gentle madam, no.
Cleo. You lie, up to the hearing of the gods!
But, if there be or ever were one such,
It's past the size of dreaming. Nature wants stuff
To vie strange forms with fancy; yet, to imagine
An Antony, were Nature's piece 'gainst fancy,
Condemning shadows quite.
Dol. Hear me, good madam. 100
Your loss is as yourself, great; and you bear it
As answering to the weight. Would I might never
O'ertake pursued success but I do feel,
By the rebound of yours, a grief that smites
My very heart at root.
Cleo. I thank you, sir.
Know you what Cæsar means to do with me?
Dol. I am loath to tell you what I would you knew.
Cleo. Nay, pray you, sir—
Dol. Though he be honourable—
Cleo. He'll lead me, then, in triumph?
Dol. Madam, he will. I know 't. 110
[*Flourish and shout within,* "Make way there! Cæsar!"

Enter CÆSAR, GALLUS, PROCULEIUS, MECÆNAS, SELEUCUS, *and others of his train.*

Cæs. Which is the Queen of Egypt?
Dol. It is the emperor, madam. [*Cleopatra kneels.*
Cæs. Arise! You shall not kneel.
I pray you, rise; rise, Egypt.
Cleo. Sir, the gods
Will have it thus! My master and my lord
I must obey.
Cæs. Take to you no hard thoughts.

97–100. *Nature . . . quite:* Nature ordinarily lacks materials with which to rival fancy; but for nature to imagine an Antony would be to make a masterpiece in competition with fancy, quite discrediting the products of fancy. 103. *but I do:* if I do not.

The record of what injuries you did us,
Though written in our flesh, we shall remember
As things but done by chance.
Cleo. Sole sir o' the world, 120
I cannot project mine own cause so well
To make it clear, but do confess I have
Been laden with like frailties which before
Have often shamed our sex.
Cæs. Cleopatra, know
We will extenuate rather than enforce.
If you apply yourself to our intents,
Which towards you are most gentle, you shall find
A benefit in this change; but if you seek
To lay on me a cruelty by taking
Antony's course, you shall bereave yourself 130
Of my good purposes, and put your children
To that destruction which I'll guard them from,
If thereon you rely. I'll take my leave.
Cleo. And may, through all the world! 'Tis yours; and we,
Your scutcheons and your signs of conquest, shall
Hang in what place you please. Here, my good lord.
Cæs. You shall advise me in all for Cleopatra.
Cleo. This is the brief of money, plate, and jewels,
I am possess'd of. 'Tis exactly valued;
Not petty things admitted. Where's Seleucus? 140
Sel. Here, madam.
Cleo. This is my treasurer. Let him speak, my lord,
Upon his peril, that I have reserved
To myself nothing. Speak the truth, Seleucus.
Sel. Madam,
I had rather seal my lips than to my peril
Speak that which is not.
Cleo. What have I kept back?

121. *project:* exhibit. 125. *enforce:* lay stress upon (them). 126. *If . . . intents:* if you accept my plans. 130. *bereave:* deprive. 135. *scutcheons:* shields displaying armorial bearings. 138. *brief:* list. 140. *Not . . . admitted:* trifles excluded.

Sel. Enough to purchase what you have made known.
Cæs. Nay, blush not, Cleopatra. I approve
Your wisdom in the deed.
Cleo. See, Cæsar! O, behold, 150
How pomp is follow'd! Mine will now be yours;
And, should we shift estates, yours would be mine.
The ingratitude of this Seleucus does
Even make me wild. O slave, of no more trust
Than love that's hired! What, goest thou back? Thou shalt
Go back, I warrant thee; but I'll catch thine eyes,
Though they had wings. Slave, soulless villain, dog!
O rarely base!
Cæs. Good queen, let us entreat you.
Cleo. O Cæsar, what a wounding shame is this,
That thou, vouchsafing here to visit me, 160
Doing the honour of thy lordliness
To one so meek, that mine own servant should
Parcel the sum of my disgraces by
Addition of his envy! Say, good Cæsar,
That I some lady trifles have reserved,
Immoment toys, things of such dignity
As we greet modern friends withal; and say
Some nobler token I have kept apart
For Livia and Octavia, to induce
Their mediation. Must I be unfolded 170
With one that I have bred? The gods! It smites me
Beneath the fall I have. [*To Seleucus.*] Prithee go hence,
Or I shall show the cinders of my spirits
Through the ashes of my chance. Wert thou a man,
Thou wouldst have mercy on me.
Cæs. Forbear, Seleucus.
[*Exit Seleucus.*

151. *Mine:* my followers, my servants. 160. *vouchsafing:* condescending. 163. *Parcel:* add an item to, or, perhaps, make a parcel of. 164. *envy:* malice. 165. *lady:* feminine. 166. *Immoment toys:* unimportant trifles. 167. *modern:* ordinary. 169. *Livia:* Cæsar's wife. 170–1. *unfolded With:* exposed by. 174. *chance:* misfortunes. 175. *Forbear:* withdraw.

Cleo. Be it known that we, the greatest, are misthought
For things that others do; and when we fall
We answer others' merits in our name,
Are therefore to be pitied.
Cæs. Cleopatra,
Not what you have reserved, nor what acknowledged, 180
Put we i' the roll of conquest. Still be't yours;
Bestow it at your pleasure; and believe,
Cæsar's no merchant, to make prize with you
Of things that merchants sold. Therefore be cheer'd;
Make not your thoughts your prisons. No, dear queen,
For we intend so to dispose you as
Yourself shall give us counsel. Feed and sleep.
Our care and pity is so much upon you
That we remain your friend; and so, adieu.
Cleo. My master and my lord!
Cæs. Not so. Adieu. 190
[*Flourish. Exeunt Cæsar and his train.*
Cleo. He words me, girls; he words me, that I should not
Be noble to myself. But, hark thee, Charmian.
[*Whispers Charmian.*
Iras. Finish, good lady. The bright day is done,
And we are for the dark.
Cleo. Hie thee again.
I have spoke already, and it is provided;
Go put it to the haste.
Char. Madam, I will.

Re-enter DOLABELLA.

Dol. Where is the queen?
Char. Behold, sir. [*Exit.*

176. *misthought:* misjudged. 178. *We . . . name:* i.e., because of our greatness, we are held responsible for the misdeeds of others. 183. *prize:* appraisal. 186. *dispose:* dispose of. 191. *He words me:* he tries to deceive me with words. In order to make Cæsar believe that she no longer plans suicide, Cleopatra—probably with the connivance of Seleucus—pretends to desire her wealth. Plutarch concludes: "So he (Cæsar) took his leave of her, supposing he had deceived her, but indeed he was deceived himself." 193. *Finish:* die. 195. *it:* i.e., the asp. 196. *put . . . haste:* make haste.

Cleo. Dolabella!

Dol. Madam, as thereto sworn, by your command—
Which my love makes religion to obey—
I tell you this: Cæsar through Syria 200
Intends his journey, and within three days
You with your children will he send before.
Make your best use of this. I have perform'd
Your pleasure and my promise.

Cleo. Dolabella,
I shall remain your debtor.

Dol. I your servant.
Adieu, good queen. I must attend on Cæsar.

Cleo. Farewell, and thanks. [*Exit Dolabella.*] Now, Iras, what think'st thou?
Thou, an Egyptian puppet, shalt be shown
In Rome, as well as I. Mechanic slaves,
With greasy aprons, rules, and hammers, shall 210
Uplift us to the view. In their thick breaths,
Rank of gross diet, shall we be enclouded,
And forced to drink their vapour.

Iras. The gods forbid!

Cleo. Nay, 'tis most certain, Iras. Saucy lictors
Will catch at us like strumpets, and scald rhymers
Ballad us out o' tune. The quick comedians
Extemporally will stage us and present
Our Alexandrian revels. Antony
Shall be brought drunken forth, and I shall see
Some squeaking Cleopatra boy my greatness 220
I' the posture of a whore.

Iras. O the good gods!

Cleo. Nay, that's certain.

Iras. I'll never see 't, for, I am sure, my nails
Are stronger than mine eyes.

214. *lictors:* consuls' officers. 215. *scald:* mean, petty. 216. *Ballad us:* sing ballads about us. *quick:* quick-witted. 220. *boy.* In the Elizabethan theatre boys acted the women's parts. *Boy* is here a verb. 221. *posture:* behavior.

Cleo. Why, that's the way
To fool their preparation and to conquer
Their most absurd intents.

Re-enter CHARMIAN.

Now, Charmian!
Show me, my women, like a queen. Go fetch
My best attires. I am again for Cydnus,
To meet Mark Antony. Sirrah, Iras, go.
Now, noble Charmian, we'll dispatch indeed; 230
And, when thou hast done this chare, I'll give thee leave
To play till doomsday. Bring our crown and all.
Wherefore's this noise? [*Exit Iras. A noise within.*

Enter a Guardsman.

Guard. Here is a rural fellow
That will not be denied your Highness' presence.
He brings you figs.

Cleo. Let him come in. [*Exit Guardsman.*] What poor an instrument
May do a noble deed! He brings me liberty.
My resolution's placed, and I have nothing
Of woman in me. Now from head to foot
I am marble-constant. Now the fleeting moon 240
No planet is of mine.

Re-enter Guardsman, *with* Clown *carrying a basket.*

Guard. This is the man.

Cleo. Avoid, and leave him. [*Exit Guardsman.*
Hast thou the pretty worm of Nilus there
That kills and pains not?

Clown. Truly, I have him, but I would not be the party that should desire you to touch him, for his biting is immortal. Those that do die of it do seldom or never recover.

Cleo. Rememberest thou any that have died on't? 249

226. *absurd:* rude, outrageous. 230. *dispatch:* make haste. 231. *chare:* chore. 236. *What:* how. 238. *placed:* fixed. 240. *marble-constant:* firm as marble. *fleeting:* changeable. 242. *Avoid:* withdraw. 243. *worm:* snake. 247. *immortal.* Blunder for *mortal.*

Clown. Very many, men and women too. I heard of one of them no longer than yesterday—a very honest woman, but something given to lie, as a woman should not do but in the way of honesty—how she died of the biting of it, what pain she felt. Truly, she makes a very good report o' the worm. But he that will believe all that they say shall never be saved by half that they do. But this is most fallible: the worm's an odd worm.

Cleo. Get thee hence. Farewell. 260

Clown. I wish you all joy of the worm.

[*Sets down his basket.*

Cleo. Farewell.

Clown. You must think this, look you, that the worm will do his kind.

Cleo. Ay, ay. Farewell.

Clown. Look you, the worm is not to be trusted but in the keeping of wise people, for indeed there is no goodness in the worm.

Cleo. Take thou no care; it shall be heeded.

Clown. Very good. Give it nothing, I pray you, for it is not worth the feeding. 271

Cleo. Will it eat me?

Clown. You must not think I am so simple but I know the Devil himself will not eat a woman. I know that a woman is a dish for the gods, if the Devil dress her not. But, truly, these same whoreson devils do the gods great harm in their women, for, in every ten that they make, the devils mar five.

Cleo. Well, get thee gone. Farewell. 280

Clown. Yes, forsooth. I wish you joy o' the worm. [*Exit.*

Re-enter Iras *with a robe, crown, &c.*

Cleo. Give me my robe; put on my crown; I have
Immortal longings in me. Now no more
The juice of Egypt's grape shall moist this lip.

258. *fallible.* Blunder for *infallible.* 264. *do his kind:* act according to its nature. 276. *dress:* season, prepare. 284. *Immortal longings:* longing for immortality.

Yare, yare, good Iras; quick. Methinks I hear
Antony call; I see him rouse himself
To praise my noble act; I hear him mock
The luck of Cæsar, which the gods give men
To excuse their after wrath. Husband, I come! 290
Now to that name my courage prove my title!
I am fire and air; my other elements
I give to baser life. So—have you done?
Come, then, and take the last warmth of my lips.
Farewell, kind Charmian. Iras, long farewell.
[*Kisses them. Iras falls and dies.*
Have I the aspic in my lips? Dost fall?
If thou and nature can so gently part,
The stroke of Death is as a lover's pinch,
Which hurts, and is desired. Dost thou lie still?
If thus thou vanishest, thou tell'st the world 300
It is not worth leave-taking.

Char. Dissolve, thick cloud, and rain, that I may say,
The gods themselves do weep!

Cleo. This proves me base.
If she first meet the curled Antony,
He'll make demand of her, and spend that kiss
Which is my heaven to have. Come, thou mortal wretch,
[*To an asp, which she applies to her breast.*
With thy sharp teeth this knot intrinsicate
Of life at once untie. Poor venomous fool,
Be angry, and dispatch. O, couldst thou speak,
That I might hear thee call great Cæsar ass 310
Unpolicied!

Char. O eastern star!

Cleo. Peace, peace!

286. *Yare:* quick. 292. *my other elements:* i.e., earth and water. 296. *aspic:* the poison of the asp. 305. *He'll . . . kiss:* i.e., he will question her about me, and kiss her for telling him. 306. *mortal:* deadly. *wretch.* Used as a term of endearment. 307. *intrinsicate:* intricate. 309. *dispatch:* make haste. 311. *Unpolicied:* devoid of cunning.

Dost thou not see my baby at my breast,
That sucks the nurse asleep?

Char. O, break! O, break!

Cleo. As sweet as balm, as soft as air, as gentle—
O Antony!—Nay, I will take thee too.

[*Applying another asp to her arm.*

What should I stay— [*Dies.*

Char. In this wild world? So, fare thee well.
Now boast thee, Death, in thy possession lies
A lass unparallel'd. Downy windows, close;
And golden Phœbus never be beheld 320
Of eyes again so royal! Your crown's awry.
I'll mend it, and then play.

Enter the Guard, *rushing in.*

First Guard. Where is the queen?

Char. Speak softly. Wake her not.

First Guard. Cæsar hath sent—

Char. Too slow a messenger.

[*Applies an asp.*

O, come apace, dispatch! I partly feel thee.

First Guard. Approach, ho! All's not well. Cæsar's beguiled.

Sec. Guard. There's Dolabella sent from Cæsar. Call him.

First Guard. What work is here? Charmian, is this well done?

Char. It is well done, and fitting for a princess
Descended of so many royal kings. 330
Ah, soldier! [*Dies.*

Re-enter DOLABELLA.

Dol. How goes it here?

Sec. Guard. All dead.

Dol. Cæsar, thy thoughts
Touch their effects in this. Thyself art coming

316. *What:* why. 321. *crown's awry.* Pope's emendation; F_1 reads *Crownes away.* 326. *beguiled:* cheated. 332–3. *thoughts . . . effects:* fears are realized.

To see perform'd the dreaded act which thou
So sought'st to hinder.

[*Within*, "A way there, a way for Cæsar!"

Re-enter CÆSAR *and all his train.*

Dol. O sir, you are too sure an augurer.
That you did fear is done.

Cæs. Bravest at the last!
She levell'd at our purposes, and, being royal,
Took her own way. The manner of their deaths? 340
I do not see them bleed.

Dol. Who was last with them?

First Guard. A simple countryman that brought her figs.
This was his basket.

Cæs. Poison'd, then.

First Guard. O Cæsar,
This Charmian lived but now. She stood and spake.
I found her trimming up the diadem
On her dead mistress. Tremblingly she stood
And on the sudden dropp'd.

Cæs. O noble weakness!
If they had swallow'd poison, 'twould appear
By external swelling, but she looks like sleep,
As she would catch another Antony 350
In her strong toil of grace.

Dol. Here on her breast
There is a vent of blood and something blown.
The like is on her arm.

First Guard. This is an aspic's trail, and these fig-leaves
Have slime upon them, such as the aspic leaves
Upon the caves of Nile.

Cæs. Most probable
That so she died, for her physician tells me
She hath pursued conclusions infinite

337. *augurer:* one who predicts future events. 339. *levell'd at:* aimed at, guessed. 351. *toil:* net, snare. 352. *vent:* discharge. *blown:* swollen. 358. *pursued conclusions:* tried experiments.

Of easy ways to die. Take up her bed,
And bear her women from the monument. 360
She shall be buried by her Antony.
No grave upon the earth shall clip in it
A pair so famous. High events as these
Strike those that make them, and their story is
No less in pity than his glory which
Brought them to be lamented. Our army shall
In solemn show attend this funeral—
And then to Rome. Come, Dolabella; see
High order in this great solemnity. [*Exeunt.*

362. *clip:* enfold. 363–6. *High . . . lamented:* great calamities involve those who cause them, and history records the pitiable tale of the victims as well as the glory of the conqueror. 369. *solemnity:* ceremony.

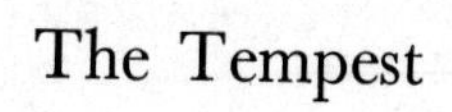
The Tempest

Introduction

Relation to Other Shakespearean Plays

The Tempest among Shakespeare's later plays is the counterpart of *A Midsummer Night's Dream*, produced in his youth. Both are fairy tales in which the interest lies less in the dramatic appeal to the emotions than in an indefinable romantic charm to which setting, characters, lyric beauty, and, above all, mood, contribute. Both make use of the supernatural, but in the more mature play the otherworldliness supplies more than a dreamlike explanation for the perplexities of a night. *The Tempest* creates a new mythology; the good-natured and mischievous fairies of popular belief are replaced by spirits which symbolize the forces that rule human life. Instead of Oberon, there is Prospero, controlling the action by his magic art and symbolizing for the time being the mysteries of Destiny and an overruling Providence. In place of the merry Puck, there are Ariel, a beautiful being of air and fire, and Caliban, "a freckled whelp, hag-born," akin to earth and water, both of them subdued to the purposes of man. For a few short hours, a supreme controller of the elements—acting only in care of his matchless daughter—gathers his foes within the circle of his power, avenges a wrong done years before by returning good for evil, and then abjures his art by breaking his staff and "deeper than did ever plummet sound" drowning his magic book. The element of earnestness is deeper in this play than it had been in the youthful comedy, and if, in consequence, there is some lack of tolerant fun at the expense of foolish mortals, it is amply atoned for by wisdom and mellowness. Indeed, from some points of view, *The Tempest* is hardly a comedy at all, but its mood of serene optimism and tender forgiveness places it with the so-called "romances" or "reconciliation dramas"—*Cymbeline*, *Pericles*, and *The Winter's Tale*. This spirit perhaps accounts for the lasting appeal which the play has had, and for the fact that in Prospero, as in Hamlet, many readers believe they have found the mouthpiece of the dramatist himself.

In style, as well as in mood, *The Tempest*, together with these later plays, presents an interesting departure from the early comedies. From the beginning Shakespeare had been a lover of fresh and flexible language, delighting in tricks of phrase, adorning his themes "with many holiday and lady terms,"

> Taffeta phrases, silken terms precise,
> Three-piled hyperboles, spruce affectation,
> Figures pedantical,
>
> (*Love's Labor's Lost*, V, ii, 406 ff.)

and proving, with Feste, that "a sentence is but a cheveril glove to a good wit. How quickly the wrong side may be turned outward!" In the maturer comedies like *The Tempest*, verbal quibbling is less frequent and less exuberant than in the earlier, and the style in general is more like that of the great tragedies. The thought is richer and fills the language to overflowing; the dramatist's interest in ideas is greater than his interest in phrasing; his expression is more varied, and, as thought crowds upon thought, constructions are mixed, and the patterns of his verse are more and more broken by the patterns of his thought. Leontes' disordered mind in *The Winter's Tale* is reflected in his disordered speculations; Imogen's devotion and pain in *Cymbeline* are revealed in her broken questions to Pisanio; and Prospero's deep emotion in this play breaks through his narratives to Miranda and to Ariel. The mature Shakespeare is more than the master of his dramatic medium,

Source

No satisfactory literary source of *The Tempest* is known, but the similarity of the theme to other romantic stories and the existence of analogues to it in Italian, Spanish, German, and other literatures suggest the possibility of a source which is lost or has escaped detection. Passages in the drama suggest a number of minor sources, notably Montaigne's *Essais*, translated into English by John Florio (1603), which may have suggested the character of Caliban and certainly Gonzalo's description of an ideal commonwealth (II, i, 147 ff.). But travelers' tales, contemporary events, and, particularly, several pamphlets describing the wreck of a shipload of colonists on the Bermudas in 1609, seem to have contributed the background of the play as well as some of the details.

Early in June, 1609, a fleet of nine vessels under the leadership of Sir George Sommers, Sir Thomas Gates, and Captain Christopher Newport, set sail from Plymouth with settlers and provisions for the new colony in Virginia. When near the end of the voyage, on July 25, the fleet was scattered by a terrific storm, and three days later the flagship, called the *Sea-Adventure*, managed to make shore on the Bermudas. There the voyagers —about a hundred and fifty in all—found an uninhabited island, "the richest, healthfulest, and pleasing land . . . as ever man set foot upon," which, however, had the reputation of a "prodigious and enchanted place." For some nine months the colonists remained here in comparative comfort, except for "some dangerous and secret discontents nourished amongst us," when they made their way to Virginia and there rejoined their fellows, who, with the loss of but one other ship, had reached their destination safely.

Some anxiety had been felt in England for the *Sea-Adventure* and its passengers who were supposed to be lost, and, accordingly, several pamphlets appeared giving an account of the disaster. By October of 1610 some of the survivors had reached England, and one of them, Sylvester Jourdan, wrote *A Discovery of the Bermudas, otherwise called the Isle of Devils* (London, 1610). Another, William Strachey, wrote a long letter entitled *A True Repertory of the Wrack and Redemption of Sir Thomas Gates Knight; upon, and from, the Islands of the Bermudas* (dated July 15, 1610, but first printed in Purchas's *Pilgrims*, 1625), while toward the end of the year the Council of Virginia published *A True Declaration of the Estate of the Colony in Virginia*, based upon Strachey's account, to set fears at rest and to confute the scandalous reports which had been circulating. From the talk of these events that Shakespeare must have heard in the taverns and ordinaries of London—and perhaps from the pamphlets themselves—he received hints for the background of *The Tempest*—the storm and the shipwreck on an island which seems to be inhabited only by devils.

The possibility, suggested by the marriage-masque in Act IV, that the play was composed or revised for the festivities during the winter of 1612–13 attending the betrothal of the incomparable Queen of Hearts, the Princess Elizabeth, to Frederick V, the Elector Palatine, makes it attractive to suppose that Shakespeare was utilizing this very occasion as subject matter for his romantic plot—the island princess who has never left her home, the prince who comes from beyond the sea and woos her, the wise father who brings about a happy conclusion by his policy. Some have even seen, in Alonso's mourning for the supposed loss of Ferdinand, a tender and a tactful allusion to the death of Prince Henry (1612), which for a time interrupted the wedding plans. Also, because *The Tempest* is perhaps the last play which Shakespeare wrote alone, some readers perceive in the lines beginning, "Our revels now are ended" (IV, i, 148 ff.) and in the passage in which Prospero speaks of abjuring his rough magic, breaking his staff, and drowning his book, if not an actual farewell to the stage, at least a presentiment of his retirement from active life. It is, of course, possible to push fancied analogies too far, but, whatever is true, in *The Tempest*, as in *Love's Labor's Lost*, the dramatist appears to have made some use at least of contemporary happenings.

Dramatic Structure

The Tempest has been called the most masque-like of all of Shakespeare's plays, not merely because as court entertainment it introduced songs, dances, lyricism, and spectacle, but because its very structure seems patterned upon the balance of masque and antimasque which is found in many a dramatic setting for a court ball. The play abounds in parallels and contrasts. Variations on the central theme of the wrongs of Prospero may be seen in similar conspiracies in each of the groups cast up on the island—that of the arch-plotters against Alonso is balanced by a comic parallel in the designs of Stephano, Trinculo, and Caliban against Prospero, and, "lest too light winning make the prize light," even the love story is complicated by Prospero's pretense that Ferdinand is a spy. The characters, also, are presented in pairs, the members of which set one another off by both similarities and contrasts—the two servants of Prospero, who seek different ways to gain their freedom; the good and the bad pupils of the magician, neither of whom has seen any other person of the opposite sex and is amazed at the "brave new world" that is opened to them; the two lovers of Miranda, savage brute and ideal gentleman—each pair reinforcing the belief, repeatedly expressed by the child of Nature, in the connection of beauty and goodness, ugliness and evil. More important—and more daring in an age which still believed in magic—is the contrast between the two sorcerers Sycorax and Prospero—workers in "black magic" and "white"—and the implication that not power and learning alone, but character and spirit are of prime importance. The details of these comparisons will occur to every reader of the play.

The Play since Shakespeare

As might be expected, the symbolical character of *The Tempest* has encouraged frequent allegorical interpretations of the play. To some readers Prospero must stand for imagination, the artist, the aristocratic spirit; Miranda for womanhood, art, love; Ferdinand for youth, the soul, mankind; Ariel for fancy, the Hellenic spirit of love and beauty, faithful and imaginative labor; and Caliban for brute understanding, the grosser passions, democracy, or rebellious and slavish labor. To others the play is a sustained philosophical, social, or religious tract, a kind of dramatic sermon rather than a work of art.

More significant is the attraction which *The Tempest* has had for dramatists and poets. Reminiscences may be found as early as John Fletcher's *The Sea Voyage* (1622) and Sir John Suckling's *The Goblins* (1638). *The Tempest, or the Enchanted Island* (1670), by Sir William Davenant and John Dryden, is a complete perversion of Shakespeare's poetic fantasy into a salty Restoration comedy, which was made into an opera by Thomas Shadwell in 1673 and in one form or another held the stage until the early nineteenth century. A sequel to the play is F. G. Waldron's *The Virgin Queen* (1797). Some of the works based upon *The Tempest* also imply an allegorical interpretation. Robert Browning's *Caliban upon Setebos; or Natural Theology in the Island* (1864) is a philosophical dramatic monologue in which Caliban, the aboriginal, ponders upon the existence of an overruling power, the problem of evil, and the government of the world. Caliban's speculations about Setebos are Browning's satire upon the conception of an anthropomorphic god. In Ernest Renan's *Caliban, un drame philosophique* (1878), also a continuation of Shakespeare's play, the material is given social significance. After his migration to Milan with Prospero, Caliban becomes a red republican, not unlike Jack Cade, and leads a revolution against his bookish master; but instead of destroying the magician, he patronizes him and carries out his benevolent policies for the glory of his own reign. Percy MacKaye's *Caliban by the Golden Sands* (1916), written to commemorate the tercentenary of Shakespeare's death, is a symbolic masque on the art of the theatre which liberates the imagination of mankind, personified in Caliban.

Date and Text

The Tempest stands first in the Folio of 1623, but scholars generally agree that it is one of the last of Shakespeare's plays. Its exact date, however, is still in dispute. In the Revels Accounts, the authenticity of which is doubted by some scholars, there is mention of a performance of the play at court on November 1, 1611. A record in the Chamber Accounts, which is unquestioned, lists the play as having been performed during the winter festivities of 1612–13. So suitable is *The Tempest* as a betrothal play, that, even if the early date is accepted, the drama as we have it may represent a revision for this special occasion. Be that as it may, the date usually assigned to it is 1611–12, and some read in Act V, i, 33 ff. and in the Epilogue the poet's farewell to the theatre and the announcement of his retirement.

Only one text of *The Tempest* exists, that of the First Folio of 1623 (F_1), and upon it all other editions are based. With the exception of *The Comedy of Errors* it is the shortest of the plays.

DRAMATIS PERSONÆ

PROSPERO, rightful Duke of Milan, a magician.

ARIEL, a spirit, Prospero's servant, and the symbol of his control of the upper elements of air and fire.

CALIBAN, a deformed monster, Prospero's slave, and the symbol of his control of the lower elements of earth and water.

MIRANDA, daughter of Prospero.

FERDINAND, son of the King of Naples.

ANTONIO, brother of Prospero, and usurping Duke of Milan.

ALONSO, King of Naples.

SEBASTIAN, brother of Alonso.

GONZALO, an honest old counsellor.

ADRIAN, FRANCISCO } lords attending the King of Naples.

TRINCULO, jester from the court of Naples.

STEPHANO, a drunken Neapolitan butler.

A Ship-Master.

A Boatswain.

Mariners.

IRIS, CERES, JUNO, NYMPHS, REAPERS } roles assumed by spirits in Prospero's masque.

Other spirits and grotesque shapes assisting Ariel.

Scene of the Action: A ship at sea, and an enchanted island.

The Tempest

ACT I

SCENE I. *On a ship at sea: a tempestuous noise of thunder and lightning heard. As the storm increases, balls of St. Elmo's fire flame along the rigging, adding to the terror and confusion.*

A Ship-Master *and a* Boatswain *meet.*

Mast. Boatswain!

Boats. Here, master; what cheer?

Mast. Good, speak to the mariners; fall to't, yarely, or we run ourselves aground. Bestir, bestir! [*Exit, blowing his whistle.*

Enter Mariners.

Boats. Heigh, my hearts! Cheerly, cheerly, my hearts! Yare, yare! Take in the topsail. Tend to the master's whistle. [*To the storm.*] Blow, till thou burst thy wind, if room enough!

Enter ALONSO, SEBASTIAN, ANTONIO, FERDINAND, GONZALO, *and others from below decks.*

Alon. Good boatswain, have care. Where's the master? Play the men. 11

Boats. I pray now, keep below.

Ant. Where is the master, boatswain?

Boats. Do you not hear him? You mar our labour. Keep your cabins! You do assist the storm.

Gon. Nay, good, be patient.

Boats. When the sea is. Hence! What cares these roarers for the name of king? To cabin! Silence! Trouble us not.

[I. i] S. D. Cf. I, ii, 196 ff. 3. *Good:* hardly an answer to the question, *What cheer?* but an expression of satisfaction that the boatswain was there. 4. *yarely:* nimbly, briskly. 6. *hearts:* "hearties." 8. *Tend:* pay attention to. 9. *room:* i.e., in which to navigate. 11. *Play the men:* i.e., be men. 18. *these roarers:* these waves as contrasted with the "roaring boys" or roisterers of the king's train.

Gon. Good, yet remember whom thou hast aboard. 21

Boats. None that I more love than myself. You are a counsellor; if you can command these elements to silence, and work the peace of the present, we will not hand a rope more; use your authority. If you cannot, give thanks you have lived so long, and make yourself ready in your cabin for the mischance of the hour, if it so hap.—Cheerly, good hearts!—Out of our way, I say! [*Exit.*

Gon. I have great comfort from this fellow. Methinks he hath no drowning mark upon him; his complexion is perfect gallows. Stand fast, good Fate, to his hanging; make the rope of his destiny our cable, for our own doth little advantage. If he be not born to be hanged, our case is miserable.

[*They go below.*

Re-enter Boatswain.

Boats. Down with the topmast! Yare! Lower, lower! Bring her to try wi' th' main-course. [*A cry is heard below.*] A plague upon this howling! They are louder than the weather or our office. 40

Re-enter SEBASTIAN, ANTONIO, *and* GONZALO.

Yet again? What do you here? Shall we give o'er and drown? Have you a mind to sink?

Seb. A pox o' your throat, you bawling, blasphemous, incharitable dog!

Boats. Work you, then.

Ant. Hang, cur! Hang, you whoreson, insolent noisemaker! We are less afraid to be drowned than thou art. 48

Gon. I'll warrant him for drowning, though the ship were no stronger than a nutshell and as leaky as an unstanched wench.

25. *hand:* handle. 28. *hap:* happen. 32. *gallows:* an allusion to the proverb, "He that's born to be hanged needs fear no drowning." 33. *rope of his destiny:* the hangman's rope. 34. *doth . . . advantage:* is of little benefit (*advantage* is a verb). 38. *Bring . . . main-course:* keep her close to the wind with the mainsail. 40. *office:* i.e., shouted orders. 41. *give o'er:* give up. 43. *pox:* plague. 49. *warrant:* guarantee. *for:* against.

Boats. Lay her a-hold, a-hold! Set her two courses off to sea again; lay her off.

Enter Mariners, *wet.*

Mariners. All lost! To prayers, to prayers! All lost!
Boats. What, must our mouths be cold?
Gon. The king and prince at prayers! Let's assist them,
For our case is as theirs.
Seb. I'm out of patience.
Ant. We are merely cheated of our lives by drunkards.
This wide-chapp'd rascal—would thou mightst lie drowning 60
The washing of ten tides!
Gon. He'll be hang'd yet,
Though every drop of water swear against it
And gape at wid'st to glut him.
A confused noise below: "Mercy on us!"—
"We split, we split!"—"Farewell my wife and children!"—
"Farewell, brother!"—"We split, we split, we split!"
Ant. Let's all sink wi' th' king.
Seb. Let's take leave of him. [*Exeunt Antonio and Sebastian.*
Gon. Now would I give a thousand furlongs of sea for an acre of barren ground, long heath, brown furze, anything. The wills above be done, but I would fain die a dry death. 72
[*In a frenzy the courtiers, headed by Ferdinand, come from below and rush to the rail and plunge overboard.*

52. *a-hold:* close to the wind. 53. *courses:* sails. *lay her off:* steer her away from shore. 59. *merely:* absolutely, entirely. 60. *wide-chapp'd:* wide-jawed; here, perhaps, loud-mouthed. 61. *washing of ten tides.* "Pirates and robbers by sea are . . . hanged on the shore at low water mark, where they are left till three tides have over-washed them" (Harrison, *Description of England,* 1577). Ten tide-washings are not enough for this fellow. 63. *glut:* swallow. 70. *long heath:* common heath, or heather. 71. *furze:* a spiny shrub; gorse. F_1 reads *firs;* the emendation is Rowe's. 72. S. D. Cf. I, ii, 209 ff.

Scene ii. *The island. Before* Prospero's *cell.*

Prospero, *clad as a magician, and* Miranda, *looking out to sea.*

Mir. If by your art, my dearest father, you have
Put the wild waters in this roar, allay them.
The sky, it seems, would pour down stinking pitch,
But that the sea, mounting to the welkin's cheek,
Dashes the fire out. O, I have suffer'd
With those that I saw suffer—a brave vessel
(Who had, no doubt, some noble creature in her)
Dash'd all to pieces. O, the cry did knock
Against my very heart. Poor souls, they perish'd.
Had I been any god of power, I would 10
Have sunk the sea within the earth or ere
It should the good ship so have swallow'd and
The fraughting souls within her.

Pros. Be collected,
No more amazement. Tell your piteous heart
There's no harm done.

Mir. O, woe the day!

Pros. No harm.
I have done nothing but in care of thee,
Of thee, my dear one, thee, my daughter, who
Art ignorant of what thou art, nought knowing
Of whence I am, nor that I am more better
Than Prospero, master of a full poor cell, 20
And thy no greater father.

Mir. More to know
Did never meddle with my thoughts.

Pros. 'Tis time
I should inform thee farther. Lend thy hand,
And pluck my magic garment from me. So,
[*Lays down his mantle.*

[ii] 4. *welkin's:* sky's. *cheek:* (a) face, (b) sidepiece of a grate or stove (*New English Dictionary*). Cf. *stinking pitch* in line 3. 6. *brave:* fine, splendid. 10. *god of power:* powerful god. 11. *or ere:* before. 13. *fraughting:* forming the cargo. 14. *amazement:* bewildering terror. *piteous:* pitying. 20. *full:* very. 22. *meddle with:* mingle with, engage.

Lie there, my art. Wipe thou thine eyes; have comfort.
The direful spectacle of the wrack, which touch'd
The very virtue of compassion in thee,
I have with such provision in mine art
So safely ordered that there is no soul—
No, not so much perdition as an hair 30
Betid to any creature in the vessel
Which thou heard'st cry, which thou saw'st sink. Sit down,
For thou must now know farther.

Mir. You have often
Begun to tell me what I am, but stopp'd
And left me to a bootless inquisition,
Concluding "Stay; not yet."

Pros. The hour's now come;
The very minute bids thee ope thine ear;
Obey and be attentive. [*They sit.*] Canst thou remember
A time before we came unto this cell?
I do not think thou canst, for then thou wast not 40
Out three years old.

Mir. Certainly, sir, I can.

Pros. By what? By any other house or person?
Of anything the image, tell me, that
Hath kept with thy remembrance?

Mir. 'Tis far off,
And rather like a dream than an assurance
That my remembrance warrants. Had I not
Four or five women once that tended me?

Pros. Thou hadst, and more, Miranda. But how is it
That this lives in thy mind? What seest thou else
In the dark backward and abysm of time? 50
If thou remember'st aught ere thou camest here,
How thou camest here thou mayst.

26–30. This short passage affords a striking illustration of the Latinity of the Elizabethan vocabulary. *Spectacle* (sight), *virtue* (essence), *compassion* (pity), *provision* (foresight), *perdition* (loss), are words derived from Latin roots in good use today, but their Shakespearean meanings are nearer to the original than their present meanings. 35. *bootless inquisition:* vain questioning. 41. *Out:* fully.

Mir. But that I do not.
Pros. Twelve year since, Miranda, twelve year since,
Thy father was the Duke of Milan and
A prince of power.
Mir. Sir, are not you my father?
Pros. Thy mother was a piece of virtue, and
She said thou wast my daughter; and thy father
Was Duke of Milan, and thou his only heir
And princess no worse issued.
Mir. O, the heavens!
What foul play had we, that we came from thence? 60
Or blessed was't we did?
Pros. Both, both, my girl.
By foul play, as thou say'st, were we heaved thence,
But blessedly holp hither.
Mir. O, my heart bleeds
To think o' the teen that I have turn'd you to,
Which is from my remembrance! Please you, farther.
Pros. My brother and thy uncle, call'd Antonio—
I pray thee, mark me—that a brother should
Be so perfidious!—he whom next thyself
Of all the world I loved and to him put
The manage of my state, as at that time 70
Through all the signories it was the first
And Prospero the prime duke, being so reputed
In dignity, and for the liberal arts
Without a parallel; those being all my study,
The government I cast upon my brother,
And to my state grew stranger, being transported
And rapt in secret studies. Thy false uncle—
Dost thou attend me?
Mir. [*Whose eye and mind are still wandering out to sea*] Sir, most heedfully.

55. *prince of power:* powerful prince. 56. *piece:* often applied to a woman or girl. 63. *holp:* helped. 64. *teen:* trouble, grief. 70. *manage:* management. 71. *signories:* city-states. 72. *prime:* first in rank or dignity. 77. *secret studies:* the study of magic.

Pros. Being once perfected how to grant suits,
How to deny them, who to advance and who 80
To trash for over-topping, new created
The creatures that were mine, I say, or changed 'em,
Or else new form'd 'em; having both the key
Of officer and office, set all hearts i' the state
To what tune pleased his ear, that now he was
The ivy which had hid my princely trunk,
And suck'd my verdure out on't. Thou attend'st not.

Mir. O, good sir, I do.

Pros. I pray thee, mark me.
I, thus neglecting worldly ends, all dedicated
To closeness and the bettering of my mind 90
With that which, but by being so retired,
O'er-prized all popular rate, in my false brother
Awaked an evil nature; and my trust,
Like a good parent, did beget of him
A falsehood in its contrary as great
As my trust was, which had indeed no limit,
A confidence sans bound. He being thus lorded,
Not only with what my revenue yielded,
But what my power might else exact, like one
Who having unto truth, by telling of it, 100
Made such a sinner of his memory
To credit his own lie, he did believe
He was indeed the duke; out o' the substitution,
And executing the outward face of royalty,
With all prerogative. Hence, his ambition growing—
Dost thou hear?

81. *trash:* a hunting term meaning to "check" by fastening a weight around the neck of a hound to prevent his outstripping the pack. 85. *that:* so that. 90. *closeness:* retirement. 92. *O'er-prized . . . rate:* was worth more than the esteem of the crowd. 94. *Like . . . parent:* "alluding to the observation that a father above the common rate of men has commonly a son below it" (Johnson). 95. *contrary:* i.e., my brother's evil nature. 97. *sans:* without. *lorded:* made a lord. 100. *unto.* F_1 reads *into.* 102. *credit:* believe. 103. *substitution:* deputyship. 104. *outward . . . royalty:* the duties of king.

Mir. Your tale, sir, would cure deafness.

Pros. To have no screen between this part he play'd
And him he play'd it for, he needs will be
Absolute Milan. Me, poor man, my library
Was dukedom large enough. Of temporal royalties 110
He thinks me now incapable; confederates—
So dry he was for sway—wi' th' King of Naples
To give him annual tribute, do him homage,
Subject his coronet to his crown, and bend
The dukedom yet unbow'd—alas, poor Milan!—
To most ignoble stooping.

Mir. O the heavens!

Pros. Mark his condition, and the event; then tell me
If this might be a brother.

Mir. I should sin
To think but nobly of my grandmother;
Good wombs have borne bad sons.

Pros. Now the condition. 120
This King of Naples, being an enemy
To me inveterate, hearkens my brother's suit;
Which was, that he, in lieu o' the premises
Of homage and I know not how much tribute,
Should presently extirpate me and mine
Out of the dukedom, and confer fair Milan
With all the honours on my brother. Whereon,
A treacherous army levied, one midnight
Fated to the purpose did Antonio open
The gates of Milan, and, i' the dead of darkness, 130
The ministers for the purpose hurried thence
Me and thy crying self.

Mir. [*Weeping*] Alack, for pity!

107–9. *To have . . . Milan:* to have no barrier between the role he had assumed and the actual rank, he was determined to be the Duke of Milan indeed. 109. *Me:* i.e., for me. 112. *dry:* thirsty. *sway:* rule, sovereignty. 117. *his . . . event:* the terms he made and the consequences. 119. *but:* otherwise than. 122. *hearkens:* listens to. 123. *in . . . premises:* in return for the stipulations. 125. *presently:* immediately. 131. *ministers:* agents.

I, not remembering how I cried out then,
Will cry it o'er again; it is a hint
That wrings mine eyes to 't.
Pros. Hear a little further
And then I'll bring thee to the present business
Which now's upon's; without the which this story
Were most impertinent.
Mir. Wherefore did they not
That hour destroy us?
Pros. Well demanded, wench;
My tale provokes that question. Dear, they durst not, 140
So dear the love my people bore me, nor set
A mark so bloody on the business, but
With colours fairer painted their foul ends.
In few, they hurried us aboard a bark,
Bore us some leagues to sea, where they prepared
A rotten carcass of a butt, not rigg'd,
Nor tackle, sail, nor mast—the very rats
Instinctively have quit it. There they hoist us,
To cry to the sea that roar'd to us; to sigh
To the winds, whose pity, sighing back again, 150
Did us but loving wrong.
Mir. Alack, what trouble
Was I then to you?
Pros. O, a cherubin
Thou wast that did preserve me! Thou didst smile,
Infused with a fortitude from heaven,
When I have deck'd the sea with drops full salt,
Under my burden groan'd; which raised in me
An undergoing stomach, to bear up
Against what should ensue.
Mir. How came we ashore?

134. *hint:* occasion. 138. *impertinent:* irrelevant. 139. *Well . . . wench:* well asked, dear. 143. *colours:* (a) pretenses, (b) paints. 144. *In few:* in few words, in short. 146. *butt:* i.e., "tub"; some editors emend to *boat.* 152. *cherubin:* the plural form. Shakespeare uses it habitually as the singular. 155. *deck'd:* sprinkled (dialectal). 157. *undergoing stomach:* enduring courage.

Pros. By Providence divine.
Some food we had, and some fresh water, that 160
A noble Neapolitan, Gonzalo,
Out of his charity, who being then appointed
Master of this design, did give us, with
Rich garments, linens, stuffs, and necessaries,
Which since have steaded much; so, of his gentleness,
Knowing I loved my books, he furnish'd me
From mine own library with volumes that
I prize above my dukedom.
Mir. Would I might
But ever see that man!
Pros. Now I arise. [*Resumes his mantle.*
Sit still, and hear the last of our sea-sorrow. 170
Here in this island we arrived; and here
Have I, thy schoolmaster, made thee more profit
Than other princess can that have more time
For vainer hours and tutors not so careful.
Mir. Heavens thank you for't! And now, I pray you, sir,
For still 'tis beating in my mind, your reason
For raising this sea-storm?
Pros. Know thus far forth:
By accident most strange, bountiful Fortune,
Now my dear lady, hath mine enemies
Brought to this shore; and by my prescience 180
I find my zenith doth depend upon
A most auspicious star, whose influence
If now I court not but omit, my fortunes
Will ever after droop. Here cease more questions.
Thou art inclined to sleep; 'tis a good dulness,
And give it way. I know thou canst not choose.
[*Miranda sleeps.*
Come away, servant, come. I am ready now.
Approach, my Ariel, come!

165. *steaded much:* stood us in good stead. 172. *profit:* proficiency. 181. *my zenith:* highest point in my fortune (an astrological term). 183. *omit:* neglect. 185. *dulness:* sleepiness.

Enter ARIEL.

Ari. All hail, great master! Grave sir, hail! I come
To answer thy best pleasure; be't to fly, 190
To swim, to dive into the fire, to ride
On the curl'd clouds, to thy strong bidding task
Ariel and all his quality.
Pros. Hast thou, spirit,
Perform'd to point the tempest that I bade thee?
Ari. To every article.
I boarded the king's ship; now on the beak,
Now in the waist, the deck, in every cabin,
I flamed amazement. Sometime I'ld divide,
And burn in many places; on the topmast,
The yards and bowsprit, would I flame distinctly, 200
Then meet and join. Jove's lightnings, the precursors
O' the dreadful thunder-claps, more momentary
And sight-outrunning were not; the fire and cracks
Of sulphurous roaring the most mighty Neptune
Seem to besiege and make his bold waves tremble,
Yea, his dread trident shake.
Pros. My brave spirit!
Who was so firm, so constant, that this coil
Would not infect his reason?
Ari. Not a soul
But felt a fever of the mad and play'd
Some tricks of desperation. All but mariners 210
Plunged in the foaming brine and quit the vessel;
Then all afire with me the king's son, Ferdinand,
With hair up-staring—then like reeds, not hair—

193. *all his quality:* his entire company of spirits; literally, "all his profession." 194. *to point:* in detail. 197. *waist:* midship. 198. *amazement:* bewilderment, terror. 200. *distinctly:* separately. 203. *cracks:* peals. 206. *brave:* splendid. 207. *constant:* steady. *coil:* uproar. 209. *of the mad:* of madmen. 212. *all afire . . . me:* i.e., bewitched. The punctuation is that of F_1; this line is usually repunctuated to make the phrase refer to the ship. 213. *up-staring:* upstanding.

Was the first man that leap'd; cried, "Hell is empty,
And all the devils are here."

Pros. Why, that's my spirit!
But was not this nigh shore?

Ari. Close by, my master.

Pros. But are they, Ariel, safe?

Ari. Not a hair perish'd;
On their sustaining garments not a blemish,
But fresher than before; and, as thou badest me,
In troops I have dispersed them 'bout the isle. 220
The king's son have I landed by himself;
Whom I left cooling of the air with sighs
In an odd angle of the isle and sitting,
His arms in this sad knot. [*He folds his arms in illustration.*

Pros. Of the king's ship
The mariners say how thou hast disposed
And all the rest o' the fleet.

Ari. Safely in harbour
Is the king's ship; in the deep nook, where once
Thou call'dst me up at midnight to fetch dew
From the still-vex'd Bermoothes, there she's hid;
The mariners all under hatches stow'd; 230
Who, with a charm join'd to their suffer'd labour,
I have left asleep. And for the rest o' the fleet,
Which I dispersed, they all have met again
And are upon the Mediterranean flote,
Bound sadly home for Naples,
Supposing that they saw the king's ship wrack'd
And his great person perish.

Pros. Ariel, thy charge
Exactly is perform'd; but there's more work.
What is the time o' the day?

Ari. Past the mid season.

Pros. At least two glasses. The time 'twixt six and now 240
Must by us both be spent most preciously.

218. *sustaining garments:* garments that bear them up on the water (Onions). 229. *still-vex'd:* constantly troubled. *Bermoothes:* Bermudas. 234. *flote:* wave, sea. 240. *glasses:* hourglasses.

Ari. Is there more toil? Since thou dost give me pains,
Let me remember thee what thou hast promised,
Which is not yet perform'd me.

Pros. How now? Moody?
What is 't thou canst demand?

Ari. My liberty.

Pros. Before the time be out? No more!

Ari. I prithee,
Remember I have done thee worthy service,
Told thee no lies, made thee no mistakings, served
Without or grudge or grumblings. Thou didst promise
To bate me a full year.

Pros. Dost thou forget 250
From what a torment I did free thee?

Ari. No.

Pros. Thou dost, and think'st it much to tread the ooze
Of the salt deep,
To run upon the sharp wind of the north,
To do me business in the veins o' the earth
When it is baked with frost.

Ari. I do not, sir.

Pros. Thou liest, malignant thing! Hast thou forgot
The foul witch Sycorax, who with age and envy
Was grown into a hoop? Hast thou forgot her? 259

Ari. No, sir.

Pros. Thou hast. Where was she born? Speak; tell me.

Ari. Sir, in Argier.

Pros. O, was she so? I must
Once in a month recount what thou hast been,
Which thou forget'st. This damn'd witch Sycorax,
For mischiefs manifold, and sorceries terrible
To enter human hearing, from Argier,
Thou know'st, was banish'd. For one thing she did
They would not take her life. Is not this true?

242. *pains:* tasks. 243. *remember:* remind. 246. *No more:* say no more. 247, 248. *thee:* for thee. 250. *bate . . . year:* remit a year of service. 252. *think'st it much:* consider it an important service. 255. *me:* for me. 261. *Argier:* Algiers.

Ari. Ay, sir.

Pros. This blue-eyed hag was hither brought with child
And here was left by the sailors. Thou, my slave, 270
As thou report'st thyself, wast then her servant;
And, for thou wast a spirit too delicate
To act her earthy and abhorr'd commands,
Refusing her grand hests, she did confine thee,
By help of her more potent ministers,
And in her most unmitigable rage,
Into a cloven pine; within which rift
Imprison'd thou didst painfully remain
A dozen years. Within which space she died
And left thee there, where thou didst vent thy groans 280
As fast as mill-wheels strike. Then was this island—
Save for the son that she did litter here,
A freckled whelp hag-born—not honour'd with
A human shape.

Ari. Yes, Caliban her son.

Pros. Dull thing, I say so; he, that Caliban
Whom now I keep in service. Thou best know'st
What torment I did find thee in; thy groans
Did make wolves howl and penetrate the breasts
Of ever-angry bears. It was a torment
To lay upon the damn'd, which Sycorax 290
Could not again undo. It was mine art,
When I arrived and heard thee, that made gape
The pine and let thee out.

Ari. I thank thee, master.

Pros. If thou more murmur'st, I will rend an oak
And peg thee in his knotty entrails till
Thou hast howl'd away twelve winters.

269. *blue-eyed.* This is probably not a reference to the actual color of the eye, but to the dark rings around it. A blue eye in this sense was supposed to be a sign of pregnancy. 271. *As . . . thyself:* as you yourself say. 273. *earthy:* i.e., gross. 274. *hests:* behests, commands. 284. *Caliban.* The suggestion that this name represents merely an anagram of *cannibal* has been generally accepted. Some derive it from Calibia, on the Moorish coast.

Ari. Pardon, master;
I will be correspondent to command
And do my spiriting gently.

Pros. Do so, and after two days
I will discharge thee.

Ari. That's my noble master!
What shall I do? Say what? What shall I do? 300

Pros. Go make thyself like a nymph o' the sea; be subject
To no sight but thine and mine, invisible
To every eyeball else. Go take this shape
And hither come in't. Go, hence with diligence!

[*Exit Ariel. Prospero turns to the sleeping Miranda.*

Awake, dear heart, awake! Thou hast slept well.
Awake!

Mir. The strangeness of your story put
Heaviness in me.

Pros. Shake it off. Come on;
We'll visit Caliban my slave, who never
Yields us kind answer.

Mir. 'Tis a villain, sir,
I do not love to look on.

Pros. But, as 'tis, 310
We cannot miss him. He does make our fire,
Fetch in our wood, and serves in offices
That profit us. What, ho! Slave! Caliban!
Thou earth, thou! Speak.

Cal. [*Within*] There's wood enough within.

Pros. Come forth, I say! There's other business for thee.
Come, thou tortoise! When?

Re-enter ARIEL, *like a water-nymph.*

Fine apparition! My quaint Ariel,
Hark in thine ear. [*Whispers.*

Ari. My lord, it shall be done. [*Exit.*

297. *correspondent:* responsive, submissive. 307. *Heaviness:* sleepiness. 308. *visit:* see after. 309. *villain:* serf, low-born creature. 311. *miss:* do without. 313. *profit us:* are advantageous to us. 317. *quaint:* beautiful, dainty.

Pros. Thou poisonous slave, got by the Devil himself
Upon thy wicked dam, come forth! 320

Enter Caliban.

Cal. As wicked dew as e'er my mother brush'd
With raven's feather from unwholesome fen
Drop on you both! A south-west blow on ye
And blister you all o'er!

Pros. For this, be sure, tonight thou shalt have cramps,
Side-stitches that shall pen thy breath up; urchins
Shall, for that vast of night that they may work,
All exercise on thee. Thou shalt be pinch'd
As thick as honeycomb, each pinch more stinging
Than bees that made 'em.

Cal. I must eat my dinner. 330
This island's mine, by Sycorax my mother,
Which thou takest from me. When thou camest first,
Thou strokedst me, and mad'st much of me, wouldst give me
Water with berries in't, and teach me how
To name the bigger light, and how the less,
That burn by day and night. And then I loved thee
And show'd thee all the qualities o' the isle,
The fresh springs, brine-pits, barren place and fertile.
Cursed be I that did so! All the charms
Of Sycorax, toads, beetles, bats, light on you! 340
For I am all the subjects that you have,
Which first was mine own king. And here you sty me
In this hard rock, whiles you do keep from me
The rest o' the island.

Pros. Thou most lying slave,
Whom stripes may move, not kindness! I have used thee,
Filth as thou art, with human care, and lodged thee
In mine own cell, till thou didst seek to violate
The honour of my child.

322. *unwholesome:* unhealthy, foul. 325. *cramps.* Physical punishment is the only kind that Caliban is capable of feeling. 326. *Side-stitches:* pains in the side. *urchins:* goblins; literally, "hedgehogs." 327. *vast:* desolate period. 342. *sty:* keep penned up as in a sty.

Cal. O ho, O ho! Would't had been done!
Thou didst prevent me; I had peopled else 350
This isle with Calibans.
Mir. Abhorred slave,
Which any print of goodness wilt not take,
Being capable of all ill! I pitied thee,
Took pains to make thee speak, taught thee each hour
One thing or other. When thou didst not, savage,
Know thine own meaning, but wouldst gabble like
A thing most brutish, I endow'd thy purposes
With words that made them known. But thy vile race
(Though thou didst learn) had that in't which good natures
Could not abide to be with; therefore wast thou 360
Deservedly confined into this rock,
Who hadst deserved more than a prison.
Cal. You taught me language; and my profit on't
Is, I know how to curse. The red plague rid you
For learning me your language!
Pros. Hag-seed, hence!
Fetch us in fuel; and be quick, thou'rt best,
To answer other business. Shrug'st thou, malice?
If thou neglect'st or dost unwillingly
What I command, I'll rack thee with old cramps,
Fill all thy bones with aches, make thee roar 370
That beasts shall tremble at thy din.
Cal. No, pray thee.
[*Aside.*] I must obey. His art is of such power,
It would control my dam's god, Setebos,
And make a vassal of him.
Pros. So, slave; hence! [*Exit Caliban.*

351 ff. Although F_1 assigns this speech to Miranda, most editors, following Dryden and Theobald, think it uncharacteristic and give it to Prospero. Caliban, however, refers to Miranda as his teacher (II, ii, 144). 358. *race:* hereditary nature. 364. *rid:* destroy. 365. *learning:* teaching. *Hag-seed:* offspring of a hag. 370. *aches:* a dissyllable, pronounced "aitches." 373. *control:* overpower. *Setebos:* mentioned in Richard Eden's *History of Travel in the East and West Indies* (1577) as a god or a devil of the Patagonians.

Re-enter ARIEL, *invisible, playing and singing;*
FERDINAND *following.*

ARIEL'S *song.*

Come unto these yellow sands,
And then take hands.
Curtsied when you have and kiss'd
The wild waves whist,
Foot it featly here and there; 380
And, sweet sprites, the burden bear.
Hark, hark!

Burden. [*Dispersedly*] Bow-wow.

Ari. The watch-dogs bark:

Burden. Bow-wow.

Ari. Hark, hark! I hear
The strain of strutting chanticleer
Cry, Cock-a-diddle-dow.

Fer. Where should this music be? I' the air or the earth?
It sounds no more. And, sure, it waits upon
Some god o' the island. Sitting on a bank,
Weeping again the king my father's wrack, 390
This music crept by me upon the waters,
Allaying both their fury and my passion
With its sweet air. Thence I have follow'd it,

376 ff., 396 ff. *Ariel's songs.* "The laughing invitation . . . has drawn Ferdinand hither from the sea, and the illusion is given of terra firma by the noise of dogs barking and cocks crowing. An echo all round the stage is almost suggested. The singing has hardly ceased when it recommences, but now in another strain and from the waters beyond the sands. Ferdinand is mocked into the belief that his father is drowned and the nymphs no more than formally grieve. The impression is given that Ariel has translated into song Ferdinand's imaginings and fears: one does not know whether the singing is real or a mere delusion of the senses" (Richmond Noble, *Shakespeare's Use of Song,* p. 100). 378. *Curtsied . . . kiss'd.* The curtsy and the kiss were customary formalities before some Elizabethan dances. 379. *whist:* silent; i.e., into silence. 380. *featly:* gracefully. 381. *burden:* refrain. 388. *waits:* attends. 392. *passion:* strong emotion, grief.

Or it hath drawn me rather. But 'tis gone.
No, it begins again.

ARIEL *sings.*

Full fathom five thy father lies;
Of his bones are coral made;
Those are pearls that were his eyes.
Nothing of him that doth fade
But doth suffer a sea-change 400
Into something rich and strange.
Sea-nymphs hourly ring his knell:

Burden. Ding-dong.

Ari. Hark! Now I hear them—

Burden. Ding-dong, bell.

Fer. The ditty does remember my drown'd father.
This is no mortal business, nor no sound
That the earth owes. I hear it now above me.

Pros. The fringed curtains of thine eye advance
And say what thou seest yond.

Mir. What is't? A spirit?
Lord, how it looks about! Believe me, sir, 410
It carries a brave form. But 'tis a spirit.

Pros. No, wench; it eats and sleeps and hath such senses
As we have, such. This gallant which thou seest
Was in the wrack; and, but he's something stain'd
With grief (that's beauty's canker), thou mightst call him
A goodly person. He hath lost his fellows
And strays about to find 'em.

Mir. I might call him
A thing divine, for nothing natural
I ever saw so noble.

Pros. [*To himself*] It goes on, I see,
As my soul prompts it. Spirit, fine spirit! I'll free thee 420
Within two days for this.

399. *that doth fade:* that is changeable. 405. *remember:* commemorate, recall to mind. 406. *mortal:* belonging to mankind, human. 407. *owes:* owns. 408. *advance:* lift up. 411. *brave:* splendid.

Fer. Most sure, the goddess
On whom these airs attend! Vouchsafe my prayer
May know if you remain upon this island;
And that you will some good instruction give
How I may bear me here. My prime request,
Which I do last pronounce, is, O you wonder,
If you be maid or no?

Mir. No wonder, sir;
But certainly a maid.

Fer. My language! Heavens!
I am the best of them that speak this speech,
Were I but where 'tis spoken.

Pros. How? The best? 430
What wert thou, if the King of Naples heard thee?

Fer. A single thing, as I am now, that wonders
To hear thee speak of Naples. He does hear me;
And that he does I weep. Myself am Naples,
Who with mine eyes, never since at ebb, beheld
The king my father wrack'd.

Mir. Alack, for mercy!

Fer. Yes, faith, and all his lords; the Duke of Milan
And his brave son being twain.

Pros. [*To himself*] The Duke of Milan
And his more braver daughter could control thee,
If now 'twere fit to do't. At the first sight 440
They have changed eyes. Delicate Ariel,
I'll set thee free for this. [*To Ferdinand.*] A word, good sir;
I fear you have done yourself some wrong. A word.

Mir. Why speaks my father so ungently? This
Is the third man that e'er I saw, the first
That e'er I sigh'd for. Pity move my father
To be inclined my way!

425. *bear me:* conduct myself. *prime:* first in importance. 429. *best:* highest in rank. 432. *single:* (a) weak, (b) solitary. 435. *at ebb:* i.e., dry of tears. 439. *control:* overpower. 441. *changed eyes:* exchanged looks of love. 443. *wrong:* i.e., by your misrepresentation that you are King of Naples.

Fer. O, if a virgin,
And your affection not gone forth, I'll make you
The Queen of Naples.

Pros. Soft, sir! One word more.
[*To himself.*] They are both in either's powers; but this swift business 450
I must uneasy make, lest too light winning
Make the prize light. [*To Ferdinand.*] One word more: I charge thee
That thou attend me. Thou dost here usurp
The name thou owest not; and hast put thyself
Upon this island as a spy, to win it
From me, the lord on't.

Fer. No, as I am a man.

Mir. There's nothing ill can dwell in such a temple.
If the ill spirit have so fair a house,
Good things will strive to dwell with't.

Pros. Follow me—
Speak not you for him; he's a traitor.—Come; 460
I'll manacle thy neck and feet together.
Sea-water shalt thou drink; thy food shall be
The fresh-brook mussels, wither'd roots, and husks
Wherein the acorn cradled. Follow.

Fer. No;
I will resist such entertainment till
Mine enemy has more power.

[*Draws, and is charmed from moving.*

Mir. O dear father,
Make not too rash a trial of him, for
He's gentle and not fearful.

Pros. What? I say,

449. *Soft:* stay, stop. 451. *uneasy:* difficult. 453. *attend:* listen to. 454. *owest:* ownest, hast a right to. 465. *entertainment:* treatment. 468. *gentle . . . fearful:* noble and not cowardly. Miranda instantly contrasts Ferdinand with Caliban, whom she has seen cringe under the severe discipline with which Prospero now threatens Ferdinand.

My foot my tutor?—Put thy sword up, traitor;
Who makest a show but darest not strike, thy conscience 470
Is so possess'd with guilt. Come from thy ward,
For I can here disarm thee with this stick
And make thy weapon drop.
[*Ferdinand's sword falls from his hand.*

Mir. [*Clinging to her father*] Beseech you, father.

Pros. Hence! Hang not on my garments.

Mir. Sir, have pity;
I'll be his surety.

Pros. Silence! One word more
Shall make me chide thee, if not hate thee. What!
An advocate for an impostor? Hush!
Thou think'st there is no more such shapes as he,
Having seen but him and Caliban. Foolish wench,
To the most of men this is a Caliban 480
And they to him are angels.

Mir. My affections
Are then most humble; I have no ambition
To see a goodlier man.

Pros. Come on; obey.
Thy nerves are in their infancy again
And have no vigour in them.

Fer. So they are;
My spirits, as in a dream, are all bound up.
My father's loss, the weakness which I feel,
The wrack of all my friends, nor this man's threats,
To whom I am subdued, are but light to me,
Might I but through my prison once a day 490
Behold this maid. All corners else o' the earth
Let liberty make use of; space enough
Have I in such a prison.

Pros. [*To himself*] It works. [*To Ferdinand.*] Come on.

469. *My . . . tutor:* i.e., one who has been subject to me now presuming to tell me what to do. 471. *ward:* guard, a posture of defense. 475. *surety:* security. 480. *To:* in comparison with. *most:* majority. 484. *nerves:* sinews. 492. *liberty:* free men.

[*To Ariel.*] Thou hast done well, fine Ariel! [*To Ferdinand.*]
Follow me.
[*To Ariel.*] Hark what thou else shalt do me.
Mir. Be of comfort;
My father's of a better nature, sir,
Than he appears by speech. This is unwonted
Which now came from him.
Pros. [*To Ariel*] Thou shalt be as free
As mountain winds. But then exactly do
All points of my command.
Ari. To the syllable. 500
Pros. Come, follow. [*To Miranda.*] Speak not for him.
[*Exeunt.*

ACT II

SCENE I. *Another part of the island.*

ALONSO, GONZALO, ADRIAN, FRANCISCO, *and others, in dejection;* SEBASTIAN *and* ANTONIO *somewhat apart from the rest.*

Gon. Beseech you, sir, be merry; you have cause,
So have we all, of joy; for our escape
Is much beyond our loss. Our hint of woe
Is common; every day some sailor's wife,
The masters of some merchant, and the merchant,
Have just our theme of woe. But for the miracle—
I mean our preservation—few in millions
Can speak like us. Then wisely, good sir, weigh
Our sorrow with our comfort.
Alon. Prithee, peace.
Seb. He receives comfort like cold porridge. 10
Ant. The visitor will not give him o'er so.
Seb. Look, he's winding up the watch of his wit; by and by it will strike.

495. *me:* for me. 497. *unwonted:* not customary.
[II. i] 3. *hint:* occasion, cause. 8–9. *weigh . . . with:* balance our sorrow against. 11. *visitor.* Gonzalo, like a visitor to the sick, is trying to console Alonso. 13. *strike.* Striking watches were not uncommon in Shakespeare's day.

Gon. Sir—

Seb. One: tell.

Gon. When every grief is entertain'd that's offer'd,
Comes to the entertainer—

Seb. A dollar.

Gon. Dolour comes to him, indeed; you have spoken truer than you purposed. 20

Seb. You have taken it wiselier than I meant you should.

Gon. Therefore, my lord—

Ant. Fie, what a spendthrift is he of his tongue!

Alon. I prithee, spare.

Gon. Well, I have done; but yet—

Seb. He will be talking.

Ant. Which, of he or Adrian, for a good wager, first begins to crow?

Seb. The old cock.

Ant. The cockerel. 30

Seb. Done. The wager?

Ant. A laughter.

Seb. A match!

Adr. Though this island seem to be desert—

Ant. Ha, ha, ha!

Seb. So, you're paid.

Adr. Uninhabitable and almost inaccessible—

Seb. Yet—

Adr. Yet—

Ant. He could not miss 't. 40

Adr. It must needs be of subtle, tender, and delicate temperance.

15. *tell:* count. 17. *entertainer:* (a) one who cherishes a feeling, (b) an innkeeper or a performer. 18. *dollar:* the German *thaler*. *Dollar* was pronounced like *dolour;* the meaning here depends upon puns on both *entertain* and *dolour*. 24. *spare:* forbear. 29. *old cock:* Gonzalo. 30. *cockerel:* Adrian. 32. *laughter:* (a) the number of eggs laid by a fowl before she is ready to sit; hence, a sitting of eggs (*N.E.D.*) (suggested by *cock* and *cockerel* above), (b) a laugh. 36. *So . . . paid.* F_1 attributes these words to Antonio and the laughter to Sebastian. 41. *subtle:* rare, delicate; in line 44, "sly." 42. *temperance:* temperature; sometimes among the Puritans used as a girl's name.

Ant. Temperance was a delicate wench.

Seb. Ay, and a subtle, as he most learnedly delivered.

Adr. The air breathes upon us here most sweetly.

Seb. As if it had lungs, and rotten ones.

Ant. Or as 'twere perfumed by a fen.

Gon. Here is everything advantageous to life.

Ant. True; save means to live. 50

Seb. Of that there's none, or little.

Gon. How lush and lusty the grass looks! How green!

Ant. The ground indeed is tawny.

Seb. With an eye of green in't.

Ant. He misses not much.

Seb. No; he doth but mistake the truth totally.

Gon. But the rarity of it is—which is indeed almost beyond credit—

Seb. As many vouched rarities are. 60

Gon. That our garments, being, as they were, drenched in the sea, hold notwithstanding their freshness and gloss, as being rather new-dyed than stained with salt water.

Ant. If but one of his pockets could speak, would it not say he lies?

Seb. Ay, or very falsely pocket up his report.

Gon. Methinks our garments are now as fresh as when we put them on first in Afric, at the marriage of the king's fair daughter Claribel to the King of Tunis. 71

Seb. 'Twas a sweet marriage, and we prosper well in our return.

Adr. Tunis was never graced before with such a paragon to their queen.

Gon. Not since widow Dido's time.

Ant. "Widow"? A pox o' that! How came that "widow" in? Widow Dido!

Seb. What if he had said "widower Æneas," too? Good Lord, how you take it! 80

45. *delivered:* remarked. 52. *lush and lusty:* luxuriant and fresh. 55. *eye:* shade, tinge. 56. *He . . . much:* he isn't far wrong. 59. *credit:* belief. 60. *vouched:* vouched for. 63. *gloss, as being.* F1 reads *glosses, being.* 67. *pocket up:* remain silent about. 75. *to:* as.

Adr. "Widow Dido," said you? You make me study of that; she was of Carthage, not of Tunis.

Gon. This Tunis, sir, was Carthage.

Adr. Carthage?

Gon. I assure you, Carthage.

Seb. His word is more than the miraculous harp; he hath raised the wall and houses too.

Ant. What impossible matter will he make easy next?

Seb. I think he will carry this island home in his pocket and give it his son for an apple. 91

Ant. And, sowing the kernels of it in the sea, bring forth more islands.

Gon. Ay.

Ant. Why, in good time—

Gon. Sir, we were talking that our garments seem now as fresh as when we were at Tunis at the marriage of your daughter, who is now queen.

Ant. And the rarest that e'er came there.

Seb. Bate, I beseech you, widow Dido. 100

Ant. O, widow Dido! Ay, widow Dido.

Gon. Is not, sir, my doublet as fresh as the first day I wore it? I mean, in a sort.

Ant. That "sort" was well fished for.

Gon. When I wore it at your daughter's marriage?

Alon. You cram these words into mine ears against
The stomach of my sense. Would I had never
Married my daughter there! For, coming thence,
My son is lost, and, in my rate, she too,
Who is so far from Italy removed 110
I ne'er again shall see her. O thou mine heir
Of Naples and of Milan, what strange fish
Hath made his meal on thee?

Fran. Sir, he may live.

86. *miraculous harp:* i.e., that of Apollo which raised the walls of Troy, or that of Amphion which raised those of Thebes. 100. *Bate:* omit, leave out. 103. *sort:* way. 107. *stomach:* appetite. 109. *rate:* opinion.

I saw him beat the surges under him,
And ride upon their backs; he trod the water,
Whose enmity he flung aside, and breasted
The surge most swoln that met him; his bold head
'Bove the contentious waves he kept, and oar'd
Himself with his good arms in lusty stroke
To the shore, that o'er his wave-worn basis bow'd, 120
As stooping to relieve him. I not doubt
He came alive to land.

Alon. No, no, he's gone.

Seb. Sir, you may thank yourself for this great loss,
That would not bless our Europe with your daughter,
But rather loose her to an African;
Where she at least is banish'd from your eye,
Who hath cause to wet the grief on 't.

Alon. Prithee, peace.

Seb. You were kneel'd to and importuned otherwise
By all of us, and the fair soul herself
Weigh'd between loathness and obedience, at 130
Which end o' the beam sh'ould bow. We have lost your son,
I fear, forever. Milan and Naples have
Moe widows in them of this business' making
Than we bring men to comfort them.
The fault's your own.

Alon. So is the dear'st o' the loss.

Gon. My lord Sebastian,
The truth you speak doth lack some gentleness
And time to speak it in. You rub the sore,
When you should bring the plaster.

Seb. Very well.

Ant. And most chirurgeonly. 140

Gon. It is foul weather in us all, good sir,
When you are cloudy.

119. *lusty:* vigorous. 125. *loose her:* i.e., let her loose. Most editors emend to *lose.* 130. *loathness:* reluctance. 131. *sh'ould:* she should (Wilson). F_1 reads *should.* 133. *Moe:* more. 135. *dear'st:* greatest, most important. 140. *chirurgeonly:* like a surgeon. 142. *cloudy:* gloomy.

Seb. Foul weather?

Ant. Very foul.

Gon. Had I plantation of this isle, my lord—

Ant. He'ld sow 't with nettle-seed.

Seb. Or docks, or mallows.

Gon. And were the king on't, what would I do?

Seb. 'Scape being drunk for want of wine.

Gon. I' the commonwealth I would, by contraries,
Execute all things; for no kind of traffic
Would I admit; no name of magistrate;
Letters should not be known; riches, poverty, 150
And use of service, none; contract, succession,
Bourn, bound of land, tilth, vineyard, none;
No use of metal, corn, or wine, or oil;
No occupation; all men idle, all;
And women too, but innocent and pure;
No sovereignty—

Seb. Yet he would be king on't.

Ant. The latter end of his commonwealth forgets the beginning.

Gon. All things in common Nature should produce
Without sweat or endeavour; treason, felony, 160
Sword, pike, knife, gun, or need of any engine,
Would I not have; but Nature should bring forth,
Of it own kind, all foison, all abundance,
To feed my innocent people.

Seb. No marrying 'mong his subjects?

Ant. None, man; all idle—whores and knaves.

Gon. I would with such perfection govern, sir,
To excel the golden age.

143. *plantation:* colonization. The scoffers quibble on the ordinary meaning of the word. 144. *mallows:* a weed. 147 ff. This description of an ideal commonwealth closely parallels a passage in Montaigne's *Essays,* "Of the Cannibals" (Book I, Ch. XXX of Florio's translation, 1603). 151. *use:* need. 152. *Bourn:* boundary. *bound of land:* district, precinct. *tilth:* cultivation. 161. *engine:* machine of war. 163. *it.* The spelling of the possessive of *it* was somewhat uncertain in Shakespeare's time. *foison:* plentiful crop, harvest.

Seb. 'Save his Majesty!

Ant. Long live Gonzalo!

Gon. And—do you mark me, sir?

Alon. Prithee, no more; thou dost talk nothing to me. 171

Gon. I do well believe your Highness; and did it to minister occasion to these gentlemen, who are of such sensible and nimble lungs that they always use to laugh at nothing.

Ant. 'Twas you we laughed at.

Gon. Who, in this kind of merry fooling, am nothing to you; so you may continue and laugh at nothing still.

Ant. What a blow was there given! 180

Seb. An it had not fallen flat-long.

Gon. You are gentlemen of brave mettle; you would lift the moon out of her sphere, if she would continue in it five weeks without changing.

Enter ARIEL, *invisible, playing solemn music.*

Seb. We would so, and then go a bat-fowling.

Ant. Nay, good my lord, be not angry.

Gon. No, I warrant you; I will not adventure my discretion so weakly. Will you laugh me asleep, for I am very heavy?

Ant. Go sleep, and hear us. 190

[*All sleep except Alonso, Sebastian, and Antonio.*

Alon. What, all so soon asleep? I wish mine eyes
Would, with themselves, shut up my thoughts. I find
They are inclined to do so.

Seb. Please you, sir,

170. *nothing:* nonsense. 173. *minister occasion:* give cues, as to a professional jester. 174. *sensible:* sensitive. 181. *flat-long:* with the flat side of the sword downward. 183. *sphere:* orbit. According to the Ptolemaic theory, the sun, moon, and planets were each set in a transparent sphere revolving around the earth as a center. 185. *bat-fowling:* (a) bird hunting, "carried on at night, when the birds, stupefied by glaring torches, were roused out of their roosting places and beaten or 'batted' down as they flew about the lights" (*Shakespeare's England,* II, 371); (b) gulling a fool. Here, the *fowl* is Gonzalo, and Sebastian would use the moon as a light. 187–8. *adventure my discretion:* risk my reputation for discretion. 189. *heavy:* sleepy. 190. *Go . . . us:* go to sleep, and we'll laugh at you.

Do not omit the heavy offer of it.
It seldom visits sorrow; when it doth,
It is a comforter.

Ant. We two, my lord,
Will guard your person while you take your rest,
And watch your safety.

Alon. Thank you. Wondrous heavy.

[*Alonso sleeps. Exit Ariel.*

Seb. What a strange drowsiness possesses them!

Ant. It is the quality o' the climate.

Seb. Why 200
Doth it not then our eyelids sink? I find not
Myself disposed to sleep.

Ant. Nor I; my spirits are nimble.
They fell together all, as by consent;
They dropp'd, as by a thunder-stroke. What might,
Worthy Sebastian? O, what might?—No more—
And yet methinks I see it in thy face,
What thou shouldst be. The occasion speaks thee, and
My strong imagination sees a crown
Dropping upon thy head.

Seb. What, art thou waking?

Ant. Do you not hear me speak?

Seb. I do, and surely 210
It is a sleepy language; and thou speak'st
Out of thy sleep. What is it thou didst say?
This is a strange repose, to be asleep
With eyes wide open; standing, speaking, moving,
And yet so fast asleep.

Ant. Noble Sebastian,
Thou let'st thy fortune sleep—die, rather—wink'st
Whiles thou art waking.

Seb. Thou dost snore distinctly;
There's meaning in thy snores.

194. *omit . . . offer:* neglect the offered opportunity of sleep. 206. *methinks:* it seems to me. 207. *shouldst:* ought to. *The occasion speaks thee:* opportunity calls to you. 216. *wink'st:* have your eyes shut.

Ant. I am more serious than my custom. You
Must be so too, if heed me; which to do 220
Trebles thee o'er.

Seb. Well, I am standing water.

Ant. I'll teach you how to flow.

Seb. Do so; to ebb
Hereditary sloth instructs me.

Ant. O,
If you but knew how you the purpose cherish
Whiles thus you mock it! How, in stripping it,
You more invest it! Ebbing men, indeed,
Most often do so near the bottom run
By their own fear or sloth.

Seb. Prithee, say on;
The setting of thine eye and cheek proclaim
A matter from thee, and a birth indeed 230
Which throes thee much to yield.

Ant. [*Indicating Gonzalo*] Thus, sir:
Although this lord of weak remembrance—this,
Who shall be of as little memory
When he is earth'd—hath here almost persuaded—
For he's a spirit of persuasion, only
Professes to persuade—the king his son's alive,
'Tis as impossible that he's undrown'd
As he that sleeps here swims.

Seb. I have no hope
That he's undrown'd.

Ant. O, out of that "no hope"
What great hope have you? No hope that way is 240
Another way so high a hope that even
Ambition cannot pierce a wink beyond,
But douts discovery there. Will you grant with me
That Ferdinand is drown'd?

221. *standing water:* i.e., neither ebbing nor flowing. 224. *purpose:* i.e., of becoming king. 229. *setting:* set expression. 231. *throes:* pains. 234. *earth'd:* buried. 236. *Professes:* practices as a profession. 242–3. *Ambition . . . there:* Ambition cannot look higher, but exhausts the power of discernment there. 243. *douts:* literally, "does out." F_1 reads *doubt;* the emendation is J. D. Wilson's.

Seb. He's gone.

Ant. Then, tell me,
Who's the next heir of Naples?

Seb. Claribel.

Ant. She that is Queen of Tunis; she that dwells
Ten leagues beyond man's life; she that from Naples
Can have no note, unless the sun were post—
The man i' the moon's too slow—till new-born chins
Be rough and razorable; she that—from whom? 250
We all were sea-swallow'd, though some cast again,
And by that destiny to perform an act
Whereof what's past is prologue, what to come
In yours and my discharge.

Seb. What stuff is this? How say you?
'Tis true, my brother's daughter's Queen of Tunis;
So is she heir of Naples; 'twixt which regions
There is some space.

Ant. A space whose every cubit
Seems to cry out, "How shall that Claribel
Measure us back to Naples? Keep in Tunis,
And let Sebastian wake." Say this were death 260
That now hath seized them; why, they were no worse
Than now they are. There be that can rule Naples
As well as he that sleeps; lords that can prate
As amply and unnecessarily
As this Gonzalo; I myself could make
A chough of as deep chat. O, that you bore
The mind that I do! What a sleep were this
For your advancement! Do you understand me?

Seb. Methinks I do.

Ant. And how does your content
Tender your own good fortune?

248. *note:* information. *post:* messenger. 251. *cast:* (a) cast up, disgorged (by the sea), (b) cast for new parts (as in a play). 254. *discharge:* performance, execution. 259–60. *Keep . . . wake:* let her remain in Tunis, and let Sebastian wake to his opportunity. 265–6. *make . . . chat:* teach a jackdaw to chatter as profoundly. 269. *content:* desire, contentment. 270. *Tender:* care for, provide for.

Seb. I remember 270
You did supplant your brother Prospero.
Ant. True.
And look how well my garments sit upon me;
Much feater than before. My brother's servants
Were then my fellows; now they are my men.
Seb. But, for your conscience?
Ant. Ay, sir; where lies that? If 'twere a kibe,
'Twould put me to my slipper. But I feel not
This deity in my bosom; twenty consciences,
That stand 'twixt me and Milan, candied be they
And melt, ere they molest! Here lies your brother, 280
No better than the earth he lies upon,
If he were that which now he's like—that's dead—
Whom I, with this obedient steel [*Touching his sword.*]—three
inches of it—
Can lay to bed for ever; whiles you, doing thus,
[*Making a stabbing motion.*
To the perpetual wink for aye might put
This ancient morsel, this Sir Prudence, who
Should not upbraid our course. For all the rest,
They'll take suggestion as a cat laps milk;
They'll tell the clock to any business that
We say befits the hour.
Seb. Thy case, dear friend, 290
Shall be my precedent; as thou got'st Milan,
I'll come by Naples. Draw thy sword; one stroke
Shall free thee from the tribute which thou payest,
And I the king shall love thee.
Ant. Draw together;
And when I rear my hand, do you the like,
To fall it on Gonzalo. [*They draw.*
Seb. O, but one word. [*They talk apart.*

273. *feater:* more neatly. 274. *fellows:* equals, associates. *men:* servants. 276. *kibe:* chilblain. 279. *candied:* frozen. 285. *wink:* closing of the eye. 288. *suggestion:* temptation, prompting to evil. 289. *tell:* count. 293. *tribute.* Cf. I, ii, 113. 296. *fall:* let fall.

Re-enter Ariel, *invisible.*

Ari. My master through his art foresees the danger
That you, his friend, are in; and sends me forth—
For else his project dies—to keep them living.
[*Sings in Gonzalo's ear.*

While you here do snoring lie, 300
Open-eyed conspiracy
His time doth take.
If of life you keep a care,
Shake off slumber, and beware.
Awake, awake!

Ant. Then let us both be sudden.
Gon. Now, good angels
Preserve the king.
[*To Antonio and Sebastian.*] Why, how now? [*Shaking Alonso.*] Ho, awake? [*To Antonio and Sebastian.*] Why are you drawn?
Wherefore this ghastly looking?
Alon. [*Awaking*] What's the matter?
Seb. Whiles we stood here securing your repose, 310
Even now, we heard a hollow burst of bellowing
Like bulls, or rather lions. Did't not wake you?
It struck mine ear most terribly.
Alon. I heard nothing.
Ant. O, 'twas a din to fright a monster's ear,
To make an earthquake! Sure, it was the roar
Of a whole herd of lions.
Alon. Heard you this, Gonzalo?
Gon. [*Significantly*] Upon mine honour, sir, I heard a humming,
(And that a strange one too) which did awake me.
I shaked you, sir, and cried; as mine eyes open'd,

302. *time:* opportunity. 306. *sudden:* speedy. 308–9. *Why .... matter.* In F_1 these speeches are assigned to Alonso and Gonzalo respectively. The context, however, supports this re-assignment. (Cf. lines 319 ff.) 310. *securing:* guarding.

I saw their weapons drawn. There was a noise, 320
That's verily. 'Tis best we stand upon our guard,
Or that we quit this place. Let's draw our weapons.

Alon. Lead off this ground, and let's make further search
For my poor son.

Gon. Heavens keep him from these beasts!
For he is, sure, i' the island.

Alon. Lead away.

Ari. Prospero my lord shall know what I have done.
So, king, go safely on to seek thy son. [*Exeunt.*

SCENE II. *Another part of the island.*

Enter CALIBAN *with a burden of wood. A noise of thunder heard.*

Cal. All the infections that the sun sucks up
From bogs, fens, flats, on Prosper fall and make him
By inch-meal a disease! His spirits hear me,
And yet I needs must curse. But they'll nor pinch,
Fright me with urchin-shows, pitch me i' the mire,
Nor lead me, like a firebrand, in the dark
Out of my way, unless he bid 'em; but
For every trifle are they set upon me;
Sometime like apes that mow and chatter at me
And after bite me, then like hedgehogs which 10
Lie tumbling in my barefoot way and mount
Their pricks at my footfall; sometime am I
All wound with adders, who with cloven tongues
Do hiss me into madness.

Enter TRINCULO.

Lo, now, lo!
Here comes a spirit of his, and to torment me

322. *quit:* leave.
[ii] 3. *inch-meal:* little by little. *disease:* discomfort, trouble. 4–6. *nor . . . Nor:* not . . . nor. 5. *urchin-shows:* goblin apparitions. 6. *firebrand:* will-o'-the-wisp. 9. *mow:* grimace, make faces.

For bringing wood in slowly. [*Lying down.*] I'll fall flat;
Perchance he will not mind me. 17

Trin. Here's neither bush nor shrub, to bear off any weather at all, and another storm brewing; I hear it sing i' the wind. Yond same black cloud, yond huge one, looks like a foul bombard that would shed his liquor. If it should thunder as it did before, I know not where to hide my head. Yond same cloud cannot choose but fall by pailfuls. What have we here? A man or a fish? Dead or alive? A fish. He smells like a fish; a very ancient and fish-like smell; a kind of not of the newest Poor-John. A strange fish! Were I in England now—as once I was—and had but this fish painted, not a holiday fool there but would give a piece of silver. There would this monster make a man; any strange beast there makes a man. When they will not give a doit to relieve a lame beggar, they will lay out ten to see a dead Indian. [*Examining Caliban more closely.*] Legged like a man! And his fins like arms! Warm, o' my troth! I do now let loose my opinion—hold it no longer—this is no fish, but an islander, that hath lately suffered by a thunderbolt. [*Thunder.*] Alas, the storm is come again! My best way is to creep under his gaberdine; there is no other shelter hereabout. Misery acquaints a man with strange bed-fellows. I will here shroud till the dregs of the storm be past. [*Creeps under Caliban's cloak.*

Enter Stephano, *singing, a bark bottle in his hand.*

Ste. I shall no more to sea, to sea,
Here shall I die ashore—

This is a very scurvy tune to sing at a man's funeral. Well, here's my comfort. [*Drinks.*

17. *mind:* pay any attention to. 21. *bombard:* leather jug for liquor, a blackjack. 28. *Poor-John:* salted and dried hake. 30. *this fish painted:* i.e., on a billboard. 32. *make a man:* i.e., make his fortune. 33. *doit:* a Dutch coin, equivalent to about half a farthing. 34. *dead Indian.* Several sixteenth-century voyagers to the New World brought home Indians and exhibited them publicly, even after the English climate had killed them. 40. *gaberdine:* cloak. 42. *shroud:* hide. *dregs:* i.e., the very last drops.

[*Sings.*]

The master, the swabber, the boatswain, and I,
The gunner, and his mate
Loved Mall, Meg, and Marian, and Margery, 50
But none of us cared for Kate;
For she had a tongue with a tang,
Would cry to a sailor, "Go hang!"
She loved not the savour of tar nor of pitch,
Yet a tailor might scratch her where'er she did itch.
Then to sea, boys, and let her go hang!

This is a scurvy tune too, but here's my comfort. [*Drinks.*

Cal. Do not torment me! Oh! 58

Ste. What's the matter? Have we devils here? Do you put tricks upon's with savages and men of Ind? Ha? I have not 'scaped drowning to be afeard now of your four legs; for it hath been said, "As proper a man as ever went on four legs cannot make him give ground"; and it shall be said so again while Stephano breathes at nostrils.

Cal. The spirit torments me! Oh!

Ste. This is some monster of the isle with four legs, who hath got, as I take it, an ague. Where the devil should he learn our language? I will give him some relief, if it be but for that. If I can recover him, and keep him tame, and get to Naples with him, he's a present for any emperor that ever trod on neat's-leather. 73

Cal. Do not torment me, prithee; I'll bring my wood home faster.

Ste. He's in his fit now and does not talk after the wisest. He shall taste of my bottle; if he have never drunk wine afore,

48 ff. *Sings.* This rough forecastle song is, with characteristic Shakespearean humor, put into the mouth of a butler, who is a thorough landsman, and who would be treated with contempt by a true sailor. This is one of the oldest sea songs in the English language. 62. *afeard:* made afraid. 63. *proper:* handsome. *four legs.* The proverb says *two* legs, but Stephano alters it to suit the occasion. 64. *give ground:* retreat. 71. *recover:* revive. 73. *neat's-leather:* cowhide.

it will go near to remove his fit. [*Fumbles about Caliban.*] If I can recover him, and keep him tame, I will not take too much for him; he shall pay for him that hath him, and that soundly. 81

Cal. Thou dost me yet but little hurt; thou wilt anon, I know it by thy trembling; now Prosper works upon thee.

Ste. Come on your ways; [*Giving him drink.*] open your mouth; here is that which will give language to you, cat. Open your mouth; this will shake your shaking, I can tell you, and that soundly. You cannot tell who's your friend. Open your chaps again. 89

Trin. I should know that voice; it should be—but he is drowned; and these are devils. O, defend me!

Ste. Four legs and two voices; a most delicate monster! His forward voice now is to speak well of his friend; his backward voice is to utter foul speeches and to detract. If all the wine in my bottle will recover him, I will help his ague. Come. Amen! I will pour some in thy other mouth.

[*Goes to the other end.*

Trin. Stephano! 100

Ste. Doth thy other mouth call me? Mercy, mercy! This is a devil, and no monster. I will leave him; I have no long spoon.

[*Starts to run away.*

Trin. Stephano! If thou beest Stephano, touch me and speak to me; for I am Trinculo—be not afeard—thy good friend Trinculo.

Ste. If thou beest Trinculo, come forth. [*Comes back and pulls him by the legs.*] I'll pull thee by the lesser legs. If any be Trinculo's legs, these are they. Thou art very Trinculo indeed! How camest thou to be the siege of this moon-calf? Can he vent Trinculos? 111

Trin. I took him to be killed with a thunder-stroke. But

79–81. *If . . . soundly.* Either Stephano's prospects of gain make him a little contradictory, or he means merely that he will take all he can get. 86. *cat.* "Good liquor will make even a cat speak" (proverb). 89. *chaps:* jaws. 103. *long spoon.* "He who would eat with the Devil must have a long spoon" (proverb). 109. *very:* really. 110. *siege:* excrement. 111. *moon-calf:* monster.

art thou not drowned, Stephano? I hope now thou art not drowned. Is the storm overblown? I hid me under the dead moon-calf's gaberdine for fear of the storm. And art thou living, Stephano? [*Embracing him.*] O Stephano, two Neapolitans 'scaped?

Ste. Prithee, do not turn me about; my stomach is not constant. 120

Cal. [*To himself*] These be fine things, an if they be not sprites.
That's a brave god and bears celestial liquor.
I will kneel to him.

Ste. [*To Trinculo*] How didst thou 'scape? How camest thou hither? Swear by this bottle how thou camest hither. I escaped upon a butt of sack which the sailors heaved o'erboard, by this bottle, which I made of the bark of a tree with mine own hands since I was cast ashore.

Cal. I'll swear upon that bottle to be thy true subject; for the liquor is not earthly. 131

Ste. [*Giving Trinculo the bottle*] Here; swear then how thou escapedst.

Trin. Swum ashore, man, like a duck. I can swim like a duck, I'll be sworn.

Ste. Here, kiss the book. [*Trinculo drinks.*] Though thou canst swim like a duck, thou art made like a goose.

Trin. O Stephano, hast any more of this?

Ste. The whole butt, man. My cellar is in a rock by the sea-side where my wine is hid. [*Seeing Caliban.*] How now, moon-calf? How does thine ague?

Cal. Hast thou not dropp'd from heaven? 140

Ste. Out o' the moon, I do assure thee. I was the man i' the moon when time was.

Cal. I have seen thee in her, and I do adore thee.
My mistress show'd me thee and thy dog and thy bush.

Ste. Come, swear to that; kiss the book. [*Giving Caliban more drink.*] I will furnish it anon with new contents. Swear.

120. *constant:* settled. 122. *brave:* splendid. 126. *butt:* cask. *sack:* a variety of sherry. 142. *when time was:* once upon a time.

Trin. By this good light, this is a very shallow monster! I afeard of him? A very weak monster! The man i' the moon? A most poor credulous monster! [*Caliban takes a long pull at the bottle.*] Well drawn, monster, in good sooth! 151

Cal. I'll show thee every fertile inch o' th' island;
And I will kiss thy foot. I prithee, be my god.

Trin. By this light, a most perfidious and drunken monster! When 's god's asleep, he'll rob his bottle.

Cal. I'll kiss thy foot; I'll swear myself thy subject.

Ste. Come on then; down, and swear. [*Caliban kneels.*

Trin. I shall laugh myself to death at this puppy-headed monster. A most scurvy monster! I could find in my heart to beat him— 160

Ste. Come, kiss.

Trin. But that the poor monster's in drink. An abominable monster!

Cal. I'll show thee the best springs; I'll pluck thee berries;
I'll fish for thee and get thee wood enough.
A plague upon the tyrant that I serve!
I'll bear him no more sticks, but follow thee,
Thou wondrous man.

Trin. A most ridiculous monster, to make a wonder of a poor drunkard! 170

Cal. I prithee, let me bring thee where crabs grow;
And I with my long nails will dig thee pig-nuts;
Show thee a jay's nest, and instruct thee how
To snare the nimble marmoset; I'll bring thee
To clustering filberts, and sometimes I'll get thee
Young scamels from the rock. Wilt thou go with me?

Ste. I prithee now, lead the way without any more talking. Trinculo, the king and all our company else being drowned, we will inherit here. Here; [*To Caliban.*] bear my bottle. Fellow Trinculo, we'll fill him by and by again. 181

163. *abominable:* not human. Spelled *abhominable* in F_1. 171. *crabs:* crab apples. 174. *marmoset:* small monkey. 176. *scamels.* This word remains unexplained, though numerous emendations have been suggested, including *chamois, sea-mews, sea-mells, staniels, mussels, conies.* 179. *inherit:* take possession. 181. *him:* it.

Cal. [*Sings drunkenly*] Farewell, master; farewell, farewell!

Trin. A howling monster; a drunken monster!

Cal. No more dams I'll make for fish;
Nor fetch in firing
At requiring;
Nor scrape trenchering, nor wash dish.
'Ban, 'Ban, Ca—Caliban
Has a new master. Get a new man.

Freedom, hey-day! Hey-day, freedom! Freedom, hey-day, freedom! 191

Ste. O brave monster! Lead the way. [*Exeunt.*

ACT III

SCENE I. *Before* PROSPERO'S *cell.*

Enter FERDINAND, *bearing a log.*

Fer. There be some sports are painful, and their labour
Delight in them sets off. Some kinds of baseness
Are nobly undergone, and most poor matters
Point to rich ends. This my mean task
Would be as heavy to me as odious, but
The mistress which I serve quickens what's dead
And makes my labours pleasures. O, she is
Ten times more gentle than her father's crabbed,
And he's composed of harshness. I must remove
Some thousands of these logs and pile them up, 10
Upon a sore injunction. My sweet mistress
Weeps when she sees me work, and says such baseness
Had never like executor. I forget— [*Resumes work.*

182 ff. *Sings.* With this song of freedom contrast that of Ariel (V, i, 88 ff.). 192. *brave:* excellent.

[III. i] 1. *painful:* laborious, toilsome. *their labour:* i.e., the labor of them. 2. *sets off:* counterbalances. 2–3. *Some . . . undergone:* i.e., it is noble to perform some humble tasks. Ferdinand bears his logs like a prince, Caliban like a slave. 5. *heavy:* burdensome. 6. *quickens:* livens. 11. *sore:* severe. 13. *executor:* performer. *forget:* i.e., my work.

But these sweet thoughts do even refresh my labours,
Most busy lest, when I do it.

Enter MIRANDA *from the cell, and* PROSPERO
at a distance, unseen.

Mir. Alas, now, pray you,
Work not so hard. I would the lightning had
Burnt up those logs that you are enjoin'd to pile!
Pray, set it down and rest you. When this burns,
'Twill weep for having wearied you. My father
Is hard at study; pray now, rest yourself; 20
He's safe for these three hours.

Fer. O most dear mistress,
The sun will set before I shall discharge
What I must strive to do.

Mir. If you'll sit down,
I'll bear your logs the while. [*Tries to take the log from him.*]
Pray, give me that;
I'll carry it to the pile.

Fer. No, precious creature;
I had rather crack my sinews, break my back,
Than you should such dishonour undergo,
While I sit lazy by.

Mir. It would become me
As well as it does you, and I should do it
With much more ease; for my good will is to it, 30
And yours it is against.

Pros. Poor worm, thou art infected!
This visitation shows it.

Mir. You look wearily.

Fer. No, noble mistress, 'tis fresh morning with me
When you are by at night. I do beseech you—

15. *Most busy lest.* This is a famous crux, still unexplained. 19. *'Twill weep:* an allusion to the moisture which oozes from unseasoned wood as it burns. 31. *worm:* creature, a term of commiseration. 32. *visitation:* affliction. Prospero uses language that is reminiscent of plague-time. *wearily:* weary.

Chiefly that I might set it in my prayers—
What is your name?
Mir. Miranda. O my father,
I have broke your hest to say so!
Fer. Admired Miranda!
Indeed the top of admiration! Worth
What's dearest to the world! Full many a lady
I have eyed with best regard and many a time 40
The harmony of their tongues hath into bondage
Brought my too diligent ear. For several virtues
Have I liked several women; never any
With so full soul, but some defect in her
Did quarrel with the noblest grace she owed
And put it to the foil. But you, O you,
So perfect and so peerless, are created
Of every creature's best!
Mir. I do not know
One of my sex; no woman's face remember,
Save, from my glass, mine own; nor have I seen 50
More that I may call men than you, good friend,
And my dear father. How features are abroad,
I am skilless of; but, by my modesty—
The jewel in my dower—I would not wish
Any companion in the world but you,
Nor can imagination form a shape,
Besides yourself, to like of. But I prattle
Something too wildly, and my father's precepts
I therein do forget.
Fer. I am in my condition
A prince, Miranda; I do think, a king— 60
I would, not so—and would no more endure
This wooden slavery than to suffer

37. *hest:* behest, command. *Admired:* admirable, wonderful. 42. *diligent:* attentive, heedful. 45. *owed:* possessed. 46. *put . . . foil:* (a) set it off by contrast, (b) defeated it (a wrestling term). 52. *How . . . abroad:* i.e., how people look elsewhere. 53. *skilless of:* unacquainted with, ignorant of. 61. *I would:* I wish.

The flesh-fly blow my mouth. Hear my soul speak.
The very instant that I saw you did
My heart fly to your service; there resides,
To make me slave to it; and for your sake
Am I this patient log-man.

Mir. Do you love me?

Fer. O heaven, O earth, bear witness to this sound
And crown what I profess with kind event
If I speak true! If hollowly, invert 70
What best is boded me to mischief! I
Beyond all limit of what else i' the world
Do love, prize, honour you.

Mir. [*Weeping*] I am a fool
To weep at what I am glad of.

Pros. Fair encounter
Of two most rare affections! Heavens rain grace
On that which breeds between 'em!

Fer. [*Comforting her*] Wherefore weep you?

Mir. At mine unworthiness that dare not offer
What I desire to give, and much less take
What I shall die to want. But this is trifling;
And all the more it seeks to hide itself, 80
The bigger bulk it shows. Hence, bashful cunning!
And prompt me, plain and holy innocence!
I am your wife, if you will marry me;
If not, I'll die your maid. To be your fellow
You may deny me; but I'll be your servant,
Whether you will or no.

Fer. [*Kneeling*] My mistress, dearest;
And I thus humble ever.

Mir. My husband, then?

Fer. Ay, with a heart as willing
As bondage e'er of freedom. Here's my hand.

[*They clasp hands.*

63. *flesh-fly:* bluebottle. 69. *kind event:* favorable outcome. 71. *boded me:* in store for me. 79. *want:* lack. 80. *it:* i.e., my love. 84. *fellow:* companion. 86. *will:* wish it.

Mir. And mine, with my heart in 't. And now farewell 90
Till half an hour hence.

Fer. A thousand thousand!

[*Exeunt Ferdinand and Miranda severally.*

Pros. So glad of this as they I cannot be,
Who are surprised withal; but my rejoicing
At nothing can be more. I'll to my book,
For yet ere supper-time must I perform
Much business appertaining. [*Exit.*

SCENE II. *Another part of the island.*

Enter CALIBAN, STEPHANO, *and* TRINCULO, *each with a bottle, drunk.*

Ste. Tell not me; when the butt is out, we will drink water; not a drop before. Therefore bear up, and board 'em. Servant-monster, drink to me.

Trin. Servant-monster? The folly of this island! They say there's but five upon this isle. We are three of them; if th' other two be brained like us, the state totters.

Ste. Drink, servant-monster, when I bid thee. Thy eyes are almost set in thy head. 10

Trin. Where should they be set else? He were a brave monster indeed if they were set in his tail.

Ste. My man-monster hath drown'd his tongue in sack. For my part, the sea cannot drown me; I swam, ere I could recover the shore, five and thirty leagues off and on. By this light, thou shalt be my lieutenant, monster, or my standard.

Trin. Your lieutenant, if you list; he's no standard. 20

Ste. We'll not run, Monsieur Monster.

Trin. Nor go neither; but you'll lie like dogs, and yet say nothing neither.

[ii] 3. *bear . . . 'em:* make another attack on the bottle. These are nautical terms which Stephano probably heard used on shipboard as drinking expressions. 10. *set:* fixed, staring (from excessive drinking). 12. *brave:* fine, rare. 20. *he's no standard:* he's no standard-bearer, i.e., he can't stand upright.

Ste. Moon-calf, speak once in thy life, if thou beest a good moon-calf.

Cal. How does thy Honour? Let me lick thy shoe.
I'll not serve him; he is not valiant.

Trin. Thou liest, most ignorant monster. I am in case to justle a constable. Why, thou deboshed fish, thou, was there ever man a coward that hath drunk so much sack as I today? Wilt thou tell a monstrous lie, being but half a fish and half a monster? 33

Cal. Lo, how he mocks me! Wilt thou let him, my lord?

Trin. "Lord," quoth he? That a monster should be such a natural!

Cal. Lo, lo, again! Bite him to death, I prithee.

Ste. Trinculo, keep a good tongue in your head. If you prove a mutineer—the next tree! The poor monster's my subject, and he shall not suffer indignity. 43

Cal. I thank my noble lord. Wilt thou be pleased to hearken once again to the suit I made to thee?

Ste. Marry, will I. Kneel and repeat it; I will stand, and so shall Trinculo.

Enter ARIEL, *invisible.*

Cal. [*Kneeling*] As I told thee before, I am subject to a tyrant, a sorcerer, that by his cunning hath cheated me of the island. 50

Ari. Thou liest.

Cal. [*To Trinculo*] Thou liest, thou jesting monkey, thou! I would my valiant master would destroy thee! I do not lie.

Ste. Trinculo, if you trouble him any more in's tale, by this hand, I will supplant some of your teeth.

Trin. Why, I said nothing.

Ste. Mum, then, and no more. Proceed.

Cal. I say, by sorcery he got this isle; 60
From me he got it. If thy greatness will

24. *Moon-calf:* monster. 29. *case:* condition. 30. *deboshed:* debauched. 37. *natural:* idiot. 40. *next tree:* nearest tree, i.e., for hanging. S. D. *invisible:* i.e., clad in some garment that to the spectators in the Elizabethan theatre symbolized invisibility. See note on *A Midsummer Night's Dream*, II, i, 186.

Revenge it on him—for I know thou darest,
But this thing dare not—

Ste. That's most certain.

Cal. Thou shalt be lord of it, and I'll serve thee.

Ste. How now shall this be compassed?
Canst thou bring me to the party?

Cal. Yea, yea, my lord; I'll yield him thee asleep,
Where thou mayst knock a nail into his head.

Ari. Thou liest; thou canst not. 70

Cal. [*To Trinculo*] What a pied ninny's this? Thou scurvy patch!
[*To Stephano.*] I do beseech thy greatness, give him blows
And take his bottle from him. When that's gone
He shall drink nought but brine; for I'll not show him
Where the quick freshes are.

Ste. Trinculo, run into no further danger; interrupt the monster one word further, and, by this hand, I'll turn my mercy out o' doors and make a stock-fish of thee. 79

Trin. Why, what did I? I did nothing. I'll go farther off. [*Withdraws.*

Ste. Didst thou not say he lied?

Ari. Thou liest.

Ste. Do I so? Take thou that. [*Strikes Trinculo.*] As you like this, give me the lie another time.

Trin. I did not give the lie. Out o' your wits and hearing too? A pox o' your bottle! This can sack and drinking do. A murrain on your monster, and the Devil take your fingers!

Cal. Ha, ha, ha! 90

Ste. [*To Caliban*] Now, forward with your tale. [*To Trinculo.*] Prithee, stand farther off.

Cal. Beat him enough; after a little time
I'll beat him too.

Ste. [*To Trinculo*] Stand farther. [*To Caliban.*] Come, proceed.

Cal. Why, as I told thee, 'tis a custom with him,

66. *compassed:* brought about. 71. *pied ninny:* fool in motley. *patch:* fool. 75. *quick freshes:* live freshets, springs. 79. *stock-fish:* dried cod, beaten before cooking. 87. *pox:* plague. 88. *murrain:* plague.

I' th' afternoon to sleep. There thou mayst brain him,
Having first seized his books, or with a log
Batter his skull, or paunch him with a stake,
Or cut his wezand with thy knife. Remember
First to possess his books; for without them 100
He's but a sot, as I am, nor hath not
One spirit to command. They all do hate him
As rootedly as I. Burn but his books.
He has brave utensils—for so he calls them—
Which, when he has a house, he'll deck withal.
And that most deeply to consider is
The beauty of his daughter. He himself
Calls her a nonpareil. I never saw a woman,
But only Sycorax my dam and she;
But she as far surpasseth Sycorax 110
As great'st does least.

Ste. Is it so brave a lass?

Cal. Ay, lord; she will become thy bed, I warrant,
And bring thee forth brave brood.

Ste. Monster, I will kill this man. His daughter and I will be king and queen—save our Graces—and Trinculo and thyself shall be viceroys. Dost thou like the plot, Trinculo?

Trin. Excellent.

Ste. Give me thy hand. I am sorry I beat thee; but, while thou livest, keep a good tongue in thy head. 121

Cal. Within this half hour will he be asleep.
Wilt thou destroy him then?

Ste. Ay, on mine honour.

Ari. This will I tell my master.

Cal. Thou makest me merry; I am full of pleasure.
Let us be jocund. Will you troll the catch
You taught me but while-ere?

Ste. At thy request, monster, I will do reason, any reason.
Come on, Trinculo, let us sing. [*Sings.*

98. *paunch him:* stab him in the belly. 99. *wezand:* windpipe. 101. *sot:* blockhead. 104. *brave:* splendid, fine. 126. *troll:* run over. *catch:* a "round" song. 127. *while-ere:* a short time ago.

Flout 'em and scout 'em 130
And scout 'em and flout 'em;
Thought is free.

Cal. That's not the tune.

[*Ariel plays the tune on a tabor and pipe.*

Ste. What is this same?

Trin. This is the tune of our catch, played by the picture of Nobody.

Ste. If thou beest a man, show thyself in thy likeness. If thou beest a devil, take 't as thou list.

Trin. O, forgive me my sins! 139

Ste. He that dies pays all debts. I defy thee. Mercy upon us!

Cal. Art thou afeard?

Ste. No, monster, not I.

Cal. Be not afeard; the isle is full of noises,
Sounds, and sweet airs that give delight and hurt not.
Sometimes a thousand twangling instruments
Will hum about mine ears, and sometime voices
That, if I then had waked after long sleep,
Will make me sleep again. And then, in dreaming,
The clouds methought would open and show riches 150
Ready to drop upon me, that, when I waked,
I cried to dream again.

Ste. This will prove a brave kingdom to me, where I shall have my music for nothing.

Cal. When Prospero is destroyed.

Ste. That shall be by and by; I remember the story.

130. *scout:* deride. S. D. *tabor:* drum. 136. *picture of Nobody.* This is probably a topical allusion. A play called *The Picture of Nobody* was entered in the Stationers' Register to John Trundell on January 8, 1606. It is doubtless identical with *Nobody and Somebody,* which was acted by the Queen's Men about the same time. On the title page there is a woodcut of a man whose breeches reach to his neck, no body being visible. J. D. Wilson suggests that the reference is to the shop-sign of John Trundell, who was a publisher of ballads and broadsides as well as a bookseller. 144. *noises:* musical sounds. 156. *by and by:* forthwith.

Trin. The sound is going away; let's follow it, and after do our work.

Ste. Lead, monster; we'll follow. I would I could see this taborer; he lays it on. 160

Trin. Wilt come? I'll follow, Stephano. [*Exeunt.*

Scene III. *Another part of the island.*

Enter Alonso, Sebastian, Antonio, Gonzalo, Adrian, Francisco, *and others.*

Gon. By 'r lakin, I can go no further, sir;
My old bones ache. Here's a maze trod indeed
Through forth-rights and meanders! By your patience,
I needs must rest me.

Alon. Old lord, I cannot blame thee,
Who am myself attach'd with weariness,
To the dulling of my spirits. Sit down, and rest.
Even here I will put off my hope and keep it
No longer for my flatterer. He is drown'd
Whom thus we stray to find, and the sea mocks
Our frustrate search on land. Well, let him go. 10

Ant. [*Drawing Sebastian aside*] I am right glad that he's so out of hope.
Do not, for one repulse, forego the purpose
That you resolved to effect.

Seb. The next advantage
Will we take throughly.

Ant. Let it be tonight;
For, now they are oppress'd with travel, they
Will not, nor cannot, use such vigilance
As when they are fresh.

Seb. I say, tonight; no more.
[*Solemn and strange music.*

160. *lays it on:* does it in good style.
[iii] 1. *By 'r lakin:* by Our Ladykin, i.e., the Virgin Mary.
3. *forth-rights and meanders:* straight paths and winding ones.
5. *attach'd:* seized. 12. *for:* because of. 13. *advantage:* opportunity.

Alon. What harmony is this? My good friends, hark!
Gon. Marvellous sweet music!

Enter PROSPERO *above, invisible; then several strange Shapes, bringing in a banquet; they dance about it with gentle actions of salutation; and, inviting the King, &c. to eat, they depart.*

Alon. Give us kind keepers, heavens! What were these? 20
Seb. A living drollery. Now I will believe
That there are unicorns, that in Arabia
There is one tree, the phœnix' throne, one phœnix
At this hour reigning there.
Ant. I'll believe both;
And what does else want credit, come to me,
And I'll be sworn 'tis true. Travellers ne'er did lie,
Though fools at home condemn 'em.
Gon. If in Naples
I should report this now, would they believe me?
If I should say, I saw such islanders—
For, certes, these are people of the island— 30
Who, though they are of monstrous shape, yet, note,
Their manners are more gentle-kind than of
Our human generation you shall find
Many—nay, almost any.
Pros. [*Aside*] Honest lord,
Thou hast said well; for some of you there present
Are worse than devils.
Alon. I cannot too much muse
Such shapes, such gesture, and such sound, expressing—
Although they want the use of tongue—a kind
Of excellent dumb discourse.
Pros. [*Aside*] Praise in departing.
Fran. They vanish'd strangely.

20. *keepers:* guardian angels. 21. *drollery:* puppet show. 23. *phœnix:* a unique mythical Arabian bird which builds its nest of aromatical herbs and spices and, when it has lived 500 years, sets the nest afire that another phoenix may rise from the ashes. 36. *muse:* marvel at. 39. *Praise in departing:* i.e., wait till the end before praising (a proverbial expression).

Seb. No matter, since 40
They have left their viands behind; for we have stomachs.
Will't please you taste of what is here?

Alon. Not I.

Gon. Faith, sir, you need not fear. When we were boys,
Who would believe that there were mountaineers
Dew-lapp'd like bulls, whose throats had hanging at 'em
Wallets of flesh? Or that there were such men
Whose heads stood in their breasts? Which now we find
Each putter-out of five for one will bring us
Good warrant of.

Alon. I will stand to and feed,
Although my last; no matter, since I feel 50
The best is past. Brother, my lord the duke,
Stand to and do as we. [*Begins to eat.*

Thunder and lightning. Enter ARIEL, *like a harpy; claps his wings upon the table; and, with a quaint device, the banquet vanishes.*

Ari. You are three men of sin, whom Destiny
(That hath to instrument this lower world
And what is in't) the never-surfeited sea
Hath caused to belch up you, and on this island,
Where man doth not inhabit—you 'mongst men
Being most unfit to live. I have made you mad;

41. *stomachs:* appetites. 45. *Dew-lapp'd:* having a fold of loose skin hanging from the throat. 47. *heads . . . breasts.* Pliny, and, through him, the Elizabethan travelers, refer to this strange race. (Cf. *Othello*, I, iii, 145.) 48. *putter-out . . . one:* gamblers upon the risks of travel. "I do intend . . . to travel, and . . . I am determined to put forth some five thousand pound to be paid me five for one upon the return of myself, my wife, and my dog from the Turk's court in Constantinople. If all or either of us miscarry in the journey, 'tis gone; if we be successful, why there will be five and twenty thousand pound to entertain time withal" (Jonson, *Every Man Out of His Humour*). S. D. *harpy:* a fabulous monster with a vulture's body and a woman's head, supposed to be the minister of divine vengeance. 53. *men of sin:* sinful men. 54. *to instrument:* as an instrument or tool.

And even with such-like valour men hang and drown
Their proper selves.

[*Alonso, Sebastian, and Antonio draw their swords, but are charmed from moving.*

You fools! I and my fellows 60
Are ministers of Fate. The elements,
Of whom your swords are temper'd, may as well
Wound the loud winds, or with bemock'd-at stabs
Kill the still-closing waters, as diminish
One dowle that's in my plume. My fellow-ministers
Are like invulnerable. If you could hurt,
Your swords are now too massy for your strengths
And will not be uplifted. But remember—
For that's my business to you—that you three
From Milan did supplant good Prospero; 70
Exposed unto the sea, which hath requit it,
Him and his innocent child, for which foul deed
The powers—delaying, not forgetting—have
Incensed the seas and shores—yea, all the creatures—
Against your peace. Thee of thy son, Alonso,
They have bereft; and do pronounce by me
Lingering perdition—worse than any death
Can be at once— shall step by step attend
You and your ways, whose wraths to guard you from—
Which here, in this most desolate isle, else falls 80
Upon your heads—is nothing but heart-sorrow
And a clear life ensuing.

He vanishes in thunder; then, to soft music, enter the Shapes again, and dance, with mocks and mows, and carrying out the table.

Pros. Bravely the figure of this harpy hast thou
Perform'd, my Ariel; a grace it had, devouring.

59. *valour:* estimate of themselves. 60. *proper:* own. 64. *still-closing:* ever-closing. 65. *dowle:* filament or fibre of a feather, down. *plume:* plumage (?) (Onions). 66. *like:* alike. 71. *requit:* requited, avenged. 77. *perdition:* destruction. 78. *at once:* i.e., any instantaneous death. 82. *clear:* innocent. S. D. *mows:* grimaces. 83. *Bravely:* splendidly.

Of my instruction hast thou nothing bated
In what thou hadst to say; so, with good life
And observation strange, my meaner ministers
Their several kinds have done. My high charms work,
And these mine enemies are all knit up
In their distractions; they now are in my power; 90
And in these fits I leave them, while I visit
Young Ferdinand, whom they suppose is drown'd,
And his and mine loved darling. [*Exit above.*

Gon. I' the name of something holy, sir, why stand you
In this strange stare?

Alon. O, it is monstrous, monstrous!
Methought the billows spoke and told me of it;
The winds did sing it to me, and the thunder—
That deep and dreadful organ-pipe—pronounced
The name of Prosper. It did bass my trespass.
Therefore my son i' the ooze is bedded, and 100
I'll seek him deeper than e'er plummet sounded
And with him there lie mudded. [*Exit.*

Seb. But one fiend at a time,
I'll fight their legions o'er.

Ant. I'll be thy second.
[*Exeunt Sebastian and Antonio.*

Gon. All three of them are desperate. Their great guilt,
Like poison given to work a great time after,
Now 'gins to bite the spirit. I do beseech you
That are of suppler joints, follow them swiftly
And hinder them from what this ecstasy
May now provoke them to.

Adr. Follow, I pray you. [*Exeunt.*

85. *bated:* abated. 86. *with good life:* in a lifelike manner. 87. *observation strange:* unusually careful attention. 89. *knit up:* perplexed. 99. *bass my trespass:* in a bass voice proclaimed my guilt. 106. *bite the spirit:* trouble the conscience. 108. *ecstasy:* madness.

ACT IV

SCENE I. *Before* PROSPERO'S *cell, later in the afternoon.*

Enter PROSPERO, FERDINAND, *and* MIRANDA.

Pros. If I have too austerely punish'd you,
Your compensation makes amends, for I
Have given you here a third of mine own life,
Or that for which I live; who once again
I tender to thy hand. All thy vexations
Were but my trials of thy love, and thou
Hast strangely stood the test. Here, afore Heaven,
I ratify this my rich gift. O Ferdinand,
Do not smile at me that I boast her off,
For thou shalt find she will outstrip all praise 10
And make it halt behind her.

Fer. I do believe it
Against an oracle.

Pros. Then, as my gift and thine own acquisition
Worthily purchased, take my daughter. But
If thou dost break her virgin-knot before
All sanctimonious ceremonies may
With full and holy rite be minister'd,
No sweet aspersion shall the heavens let fall
To make this contract grow; but barren Hate,
Sour-eyed Disdain, and Discord shall bestrew 20
The union of your bed with weeds so loathly
That you shall hate it both. Therefore take heed,
As Hymen's lamps shall light you.

Fer. As I hope
For quiet days, fair issue, and long life,

[IV. i] 3. *third.* Some editors emend to *thread.* 5. *tender:* offer. 7. *strangely:* extraordinarily. 9. *her off.* F_2; F_1 reads *her of*, and some modern editors emend to *hereof.* 13. *gift.* F_1 reads *guest;* the emendation is Rowe's. 14. *purchased:* won, gained (a legal term). 15. *virgin-knot:* an allusion to the zone or girdle worn by maidens in classical times. 16. *sanctimonious:* holy, not "hypocritically devout." 18. *aspersion:* sprinkling (of dew, as in blessing).

With such love as 'tis now, the murkiest den,
The most opportune place, the strong'st suggestion
Our worser genius can, shall never melt
Mine honour into lust, to take away
The edge of that day's celebration
When I shall think, or Phœbus' steeds are founder'd, 30
Or Night kept chain'd below.

Pros. Fairly spoke.
Sit then and talk with her; she is thine own.
What, Ariel! My industrious servant, Ariel!

Enter ARIEL.

Ari. What would my potent master? Here I am.

Pros. Thou and thy meaner fellows your last service
Did worthily perform; and I must use you
In such another trick. Go bring the rabble,
O'er whom I give thee power, here to this place.
Incite them to quick motion; for I must
Bestow upon the eyes of this young couple 40
Some vanity of mine art. It is my promise,
And they expect it from me.

Ari. Presently?

Pros. Ay, with a twink.

Ari. Before you can say "come" and "go,"
And breathe twice and cry "so, so,"
Each one, tripping on his toe,
Will be here with mop and mow.
Do you love me, master? No?

Pros. Dearly, my delicate Ariel. Do not approach 49
Till thou dost hear me call.

Ari. Well, I conceive. [*Exit.*

26. *suggestion:* temptation. 27. *worser genius:* i.e., evil genius or spirit, bad angel. 30–1. *or . . . Or:* either . . . or. 30. *Phœbus' steeds:* the four horses that draw the chariot of the sun. *founder'd:* gone lame. 37. *rabble:* company, troupe, or the *meaner fellows* (line 35). 41. *vanity:* toy, trifle. 42. *Presently:* immediately. 47. *mop and mow:* grimaces. 50. *conceive:* understand, know.

Pros. [*To Ferdinand*] Look thou be true; do not give dalliance
Too much the rein. The strongest oaths are straw
To the fire i' the blood. Be more abstemious,
Or else, good night your vow!
Fer. I warrant you, sir;
The white cold virgin snow upon my heart
Abates the ardour of my liver.
Pros. Well.
Now come, my Ariel, bring a corollary,
Rather than want a spirit. Appear, and pertly!
No tongue! All eyes! Be silent. [*Soft music.*

Enter IRIS.

Iris. Ceres, most bounteous lady, thy rich leas 60
Of wheat, rye, barley, vetches, oats, and pease;
Thy turfy mountains, where live nibbling sheep,
And flat meads thatch'd with stover, them to keep;
Thy banks with pioned and twilled brims,
Which spongy April at thy hest betrims,
To make cold nymphs chaste crowns; and thy broom-groves,
Whose shadow the dismissed bachelor loves,
Being lass-lorn; thy pole-clipt vineyard;
And thy sea-marge, sterile and rocky-hard,
Where thou thyself dost air—the queen o' the sky, 70
Whose watery arch and messenger am I,

51. *dalliance:* amorous play. 56. *liver:* believed to be the seat of the passions. 57. *corollary:* surplus. 58. *want:* lack. S. D. *Iris:* goddess of the rainbow. 60 ff. What follows is the most masque-like scene in Shakespeare. The dance of the nymphs and "sunburnt sicklemen" (134 ff.) constitutes the antimasque. 60. *Ceres:* goddess of vegetation and fertility. *leas:* pastures, grasslands. 61. *vetches:* plants used for fodder. 63. *stover:* fodder. 64. *pioned and twilled:* "trenched" and "ridged" (?). 65. *hest:* behest, command. 66. *broom-groves.* This reading of F_1 is unsatisfactory; "grove" can hardly be applied to a plant like the broom. Hanmer's emendation *brown* is often accepted today. 68. *pole-clipt:* hedged in with poles. 69. *sea-marge:* coast. 71. *watery arch:* i.e., the rainbow.

Bids thee leave these, and with her sovereign grace,
[*Juno's car appears and gradually descends.*
Here on this grass-plot, in this very place,
To come and sport. Her peacocks fly amain;
Approach, rich Ceres, her to entertain.

Enter CERES.

Cer. Hail, many-colour'd messenger, that ne'er
Dost disobey the wife of Jupiter;
Who with thy saffron wings upon my flowers
Diffusest honey-drops, refreshing showers,
And with each end of thy blue bow dost crown 80
My bosky acres and my unshrubb'd down,
Rich scarf to my proud earth; why hath thy queen
Summon'd me hither, to this short-grass'd green?
Iris. A contract of true love to celebrate,
And some donation freely to estate
On the blest lovers.
Cer. Tell me, heavenly bow,
If Venus or her son, as thou dost know,
Do now attend the queen? Since they did plot
The means that dusky Dis my daughter got,
Her and her blind boy's scandal'd company 90
I have forsworn.
Iris. Of her society
Be not afraid. I met her deity
Cutting the clouds towards Paphos, and her son
Dove-drawn with her. Here thought they to have done
Some wanton charm upon this man and maid,
Whose vows are, that no bed-rite shall be paid

74. *amain:* with strength or speed. 81. *bosky:* shrubby. *unshrubb'd down:* shrubless upland. 85. *freely:* liberally. 87. *her son:* blind Cupid. 89. *Dis:* god of the infernal regions, Pluto. He carried off Persephone, daughter of Ceres, to be his bride. 90. *scandal'd:* disreputable. 93. *Paphos:* a town in Cyprus where there was a temple of Venus. 94. *Dove-drawn.* Venus's car was drawn by a team of doves. 95. *wanton:* lascivious.

Till Hymen's torch be lighted. But in vain;
Mars's hot minion is return'd again;
Her waspish-headed son has broke his arrows,
Swears he will shoot no more but play with sparrows 100
And be a boy right out.

JUNO *alights.*

Cer. High'st queen of state,
Great Juno, comes; I know her by her gait.
Juno. How does my bounteous sister? Go with me
To bless this twain, that they may prosperous be
And honour'd in their issue. [*They sing.*

Juno. Honour, riches, marriage-blessing,
Long continuance, and increasing,
Hourly joys be still upon you!
Juno sings her blessings on you.

Cer. Earth's increase, foison plenty, 110
Barns and garners never empty,
Vines with clustering bunches growing,
Plants with goodly burden bowing;

Spring come to you at the farthest
In the very end of harvest!
Scarcity and want shall shun you;
Ceres' blessing so is on you.

Fer. This is a most majestic vision, and
Harmonious charmingly. May I be bold
To think these spirits?
Pros. Spirits, which by mine art 120
I have from their confines call'd to enact
My present fancies.

97. *Till . . . lighted:* i.e., until they be married. 98. *minion:* darling, favorite; i.e., Venus. 99. *waspish-headed:* irritable. 101. *right out:* outright. 108. *still:* ever. 110. *Ceres.* F_1 gives this whole song to Juno; the assignment to Ceres is Theobald's. *foison plenty:* plentiful harvest.

Fer. Let me live here ever;
So rare a wonder'd father and a wife
Makes this place Paradise.
[*Juno and Ceres whisper, and send Iris on employment.*
Pros. Sweet, now, silence!
Juno and Ceres whisper seriously;
There's something else to do. Hush, and be mute,
Or else our spell is marr'd.
Iris. You nymphs, call'd Naiads, of the winding brooks,
With your sedged crowns and ever-harmless looks,
Leave your crisp channels and on this green land 130
Answer your summons; Juno does command.
Come, temperate nymphs, and help to celebrate
A contract of true love; be not too late.

Enter certain Nymphs.

You sunburnt sicklemen, of August weary,
Come hither from the furrow and be merry.
Make holiday; your rye-straw hats put on
And these fresh nymphs encounter every one
In country footing.

Enter certain Reapers, properly habited; they join with the Nymphs in a graceful dance; towards the end whereof PROSPERO *starts suddenly, and speaks; after which, to a strange, hollow, and confused noise, they heavily vanish.*

Pros. [*To himself*] I had forgot that foul conspiracy
Of the beast Caliban and his confederates 140
Against my life. The minute of their plot
Is almost come. [*To the Spirits.*] Well done! Avoid; no more!
Fer. This is strange; your father's in some passion
That works him strongly.

123. *So rare a wonder'd:* performing such rare wonders. 128. *winding.* Rowe's emendation; F_1 reads *windring.* Some editors prefer *wand'ring.* 130. *crisp:* rippled. 132. *temperate:* chaste. 138. *footing:* dancing. S. D. *habited:* costumed. 142. *Avoid:* withdraw. 143. *passion:* disordering emotion. 144. *works:* affects.

Mir. Never till this day
Saw I him touch'd with anger so distemper'd.

Pros. You do look, my son, in a moved sort,
As if you were dismay'd. Be cheerful, sir.
Our revels now are ended. These our actors,
As I foretold you, were all spirits and
Are melted into air, into thin air. 150
And, like the baseless fabric of this vision,
The cloud-capp'd towers, the gorgeous palaces,
The solemn temples, the great globe itself—
Yea, all which it inherit—shall dissolve,
And, like this insubstantial pageant faded,
Leave not a rack behind. We are such stuff
As dreams are made on, and our little life
Is rounded with a sleep. Sir, I am vex'd;
Bear with my weakness; my old brain is troubled.
Be not disturb'd with my infirmity. 160
If you be pleased, retire into my cell
And there repose. A turn or two I'll walk,
To still my beating mind.

Fer., *Mir.* We wish your peace. [*Exeunt.*

Pros. Come with a thought. I thank thee, Ariel. Come.

Enter ARIEL.

Ari. Thy thoughts I cleave to. What's thy pleasure?

Pros. Spirit,
We must prepare to meet with Caliban.

Ari. Ay, my commander, when I presented Ceres,
I thought to have told thee of it, but I fear'd
Lest I might anger thee.

Pros. Say again, where didst thou leave these varlets? 170

Ari. I told you, sir, they were red-hot with drinking;

145. *distemper'd:* disordered. 149. *foretold you:* told you before. 156. *rack:* mass of cloud driven before the wind in the upper air; here, probably blended with *wrack* (Onions). 164. *with a thought:* on the instant. 167. *presented:* represented. Ariel apparently played Ceres in the masque.

So full of valour that they smote the air
For breathing in their faces; beat the ground
For kissing of their feet; yet always bending
Towards their project. Then I beat my tabor;
At which, like unback'd colts, they prick'd their ears,
Advanced their eyelids, lifted up their noses
As they smelt music. So I charm'd their ears
That calf-like they my lowing follow'd through
Tooth'd briers, sharp furzes, pricking goss, and thorns, 180
Which enter'd their frail shins. At last I left them
I' the filthy-mantled pool beyond your cell,
There dancing up to the chins, that the foul lake
O'erstunk their feet.

Pros. This was well done, my bird.
Thy shape invisible retain thou still.
The trumpery in my house, go bring it hither,
For stale to catch these thieves.

Ari. I go, I go. [*Exit.*

Pros. A devil, a born devil, on whose nature
Nurture can never stick; on whom my pains,
Humanely taken, all, all lost, quite lost; 190
And as with age his body uglier grows,
So his mind cankers. I will plague them all,
Even to roaring.

Re-enter ARIEL, *loaden with glistering apparel, &c.*

Come, hang them on this line.

PROSPERO *and* ARIEL *remain, invisible. Enter* CALIBAN, STEPHANO, *and* TRINCULO, *all wet.*

Cal. Pray you, tread softly, that the blind mole may not
Hear a foot fall. We now are near his cell.

Ste. Monster, your fairy—which you say is a harmless fairy—has done little better than played the Jack with us.

176. *unback'd:* unridden. 180. *goss:* gorse. 187. *stale:* bait or decoy. 189. *Nurture:* education, training. 193. *line:* a lime tree or linden (cf. V, i, 10) or, possibly, a rope. 198. *Jack:* knave.

Trin. Monster, I do smell all horse-piss, at which my nose is in great indignation. 200

Ste. So is mine. Do you hear, monster? If I should take a displeasure against you, look you—

Trin. Thou wert but a lost monster.

Cal. Good my lord, give me thy favour still.
Be patient, for the prize I'll bring thee to
Shall hoodwink this mischance; therefore, speak softly.
All's hush'd as midnight yet.

Trin. Ay, but to lose our bottles in the pool—

Ste. There is not only disgrace and dishonour in that, monster, but an infinite loss. 210

Trin. That's more to me than my wetting. Yet this is your harmless fairy, monster.

Ste. I will fetch off my bottle, though I be o'er ears for my labour.

Cal. Prithee, my king, be quiet. See'st thou here,
This is the mouth o' the cell. No noise, and enter.
Do that good mischief which may make this island
Thine own for ever, and I, thy Caliban, 218
For aye thy foot-licker.

Ste. Give me thy hand. I do begin to have bloody thoughts.

Trin. [*Spying the clothes*] O King Stephano! O peer! O worthy Stephano! Look what a wardrobe here is for thee!

Cal. Let it alone, thou fool; it is but trash.

Trin. O, ho, monster! We know what belongs to a frippery. O King Stephano!

Ste. Put off that gown, Trinculo; by this hand, I'll have that gown. [*Snatching it.*

Trin. Thy Grace shall have it.

Cal. The dropsy drown this fool! What do you mean 230
To dote thus on such luggage? Let 't alone

206. *hoodwink:* cover up; literally, "blindfold." 221–2. *O . . . Stephano.* Stephano is apparently thinking of an old song quoted in *Othello*, II, iii, 92 ff.:

> King Stephan was a worthy peer;
> His breeches cost him but a crown . . .

And do the murder first. If he awake,
From toe to crown he'll fill our skins with pinches,
Make us strange stuff.

Ste. Be you quiet, monster. Mistress Line, is not this my jerkin? Now is the jerkin under the line. Now, jerkin, you are like to lose your hair and prove a bald jerkin.

Trin. Do, do. We steal by line and level, an't like your Grace. 240

Ste. I thank thee for that jest; [*Tossing him a jerkin.*] here's a garment for't. Wit shall not go unrewarded while I am king of this country. "Steal by line and level" is an excellent pass of pate; [*Throwing him another.*] there's another garment for't.

Trin. Monster, come, put some lime upon your fingers, and away with the rest.

Cal. I will have none on't. We shall lose our time
And all be turn'd to barnacles, or to apes
With foreheads villainous low. 250

Ste. Monster, lay to your fingers. Help to bear this away where my hogshead of wine is, or I'll turn you out of my kingdom. [*Loading Caliban.*] Go to, carry this.

Trin. And this.

Ste. Ay, and this.

A noise of hunters heard. Enter divers Spirits, in shape of dogs and hounds, and hunt them about, PROSPERO *and* ARIEL *setting them on.*

Pros. Hey, Mountain, hey!

Ari. Silver! There it goes, Silver!

238. *bald jerkin:* close-fitting jacket made of leather. 239. *by line and level:* by means of instruments for determining horizontal and vertical position; hence, methodically. 244. *pass of pate:* sally of wit. 246. *lime:* birdlime. 249. *barnacles:* geese supposed to grow on trees or to be hatched from seashells growing on trees. "There are in the north parts of Scotland . . . certain trees, whereon do grow certain shell-fishes, . . . which falling into the water do become fowls, whom we call barnacles, in the north of England brant geese, and in Lancashire tree geese." (John Gerard, *Herbal*, 1597.) Barnacle geese are mentioned in the twelfth-century *Bestiarius*.

Pros. Fury, Fury! There, Tyrant, there! Hark! Hark!
[*Caliban, Stephano, and Trinculo are driven out screaming.*
Go charge my goblins that they grind their joints
With dry convulsions, shorten up their sinews 260
With aged cramps, and more pinch-spotted make them
Than pard or cat o' mountain.
Ari. Hark, they roar!
Pros. Let them be hunted soundly. At this hour
Lie at my mercy all mine enemies.
Shortly shall all my labours end, and thou
Shalt have the air at freedom. For a little
Follow, and do me service. [*Exeunt.*

ACT V

SCENE I. *Before* PROSPERO'S *cell.*

Enter PROSPERO *in his magic robes, and* ARIEL.

Pros. Now does my project gather to a head.
My charms crack not, my spirits obey, and time
Goes upright with his carriage. How's the day?
Ari. On the sixth hour, at which time, my lord,
You said our work should cease.
Pros. I did say so,
When first I raised the tempest. Say, my spirit,
How fares the king and 's followers?
Ari. Confined together
In the same fashion as you gave in charge,
Just as you left them; all prisoners, sir,
In the line-grove which weather-fends your cell; 10
They cannot budge till your release. The king,
His brother, and yours, abide all three distracted,

260. *convulsions:* cramps. 261. *aged:* caused by age. 262. *pard:* leopard. *cat o' mountain:* wildcat.

[V. i] 2. *crack:* break. 3. *carriage:* burden, load. 10. *line-grove:* lime- or linden-grove. *weather-fends:* protects from the weather. 11. *till your release:* till you release them. 12. *distracted:* distraught, mad.

And the remainder mourning over them,
Brimful of sorrow and dismay; but chiefly
Him that you term'd, sir, "the good old lord, Gonzalo";
His tears run down his beard, like winter's drops
From eaves of reeds. Your charm so strongly works 'em
That if you now beheld them, your affections
Would become tender.

Pros. Dost thou think so, spirit?

Ari. Mine would, sir, were I human.

Pros. And mine shall. 20
Hast thou, which art but air, a touch, a feeling
Of their afflictions, and shall not myself,
One of their kind, that relish all as sharply,
Passion as they, be kindlier moved than thou art?
Though with their high wrongs I am struck to the quick,
Yet with my nobler reason 'gainst my fury
Do I take part. The rarer action is
In virtue than in vengeance. They being penitent,
The sole drift of my purpose doth extend
Not a frown further. Go release them, Ariel. 30
My charms I'll break, their senses I'll restore,
And they shall be themselves.

Ari. I'll fetch them, sir. [*Exit.*

Pros. [*Drawing a magic circle*] Ye elves of hills, brooks, standing lakes, and groves;
And ye that on the sands with printless foot
Do chase the ebbing Neptune and do fly him
When he comes back; you demi-puppets that
By moonshine do the green sour ringlets make,
Whereof the ewe not bites; and you whose pastime
Is to make midnight mushrooms, that rejoice

17. *eaves of reeds:* thatch. 23. *all:* quite. 24. *Passion:* suffer. 33–50. *Ye . . . art.* These lines are based in part upon a passage in Ovid's *Metamorphoses*, as translated by Arthur Golding, and in part upon English folklore. 36. *demi-puppets:* diminutive creatures. 37. *ringlets:* fairy rings, circles of luxuriant grass formed by certain mushroom fungi, but popularly believed to be the fairies' dancing places.

To hear the solemn curfew, by whose aid 40
(Weak masters though ye be) I have bedimm'd
The noontide sun, call'd forth the mutinous winds,
And 'twixt the green sea and the azured vault
Set roaring war. To the dread rattling thunder
Have I given fire, and rifted Jove's stout oak
With his own bolt. The strong-based promontory
Have I made shake, and by the spurs pluck'd up
The pine and cedar. Graves at my command
Have waked their sleepers, oped, and let 'em forth
By my so potent art. But this rough magic 50
I here abjure, and, when I have required
Some heavenly music (which even now I do)
To work mine end upon their senses that
This airy charm is for, I'll break my staff,
Bury it certain fathoms in the earth,
And deeper than did ever plummet sound
I'll drown my book. [*Solemn music.*

Re-enter ARIEL *before; then* ALONSO, *with a frantic gesture, attended by* GONZALO; SEBASTIAN *and* ANTONIO *in like manner, attended by* ADRIAN *and* FRANCISCO. *They all enter the circle which* PROSPERO *had made, and there stand charmed; which* PROSPERO *observing, speaks:*

A solemn air and the best comforter
To an unsettled fancy cure thy brains,
Now useless, boil'd within thy skull! There stand, 60
For you are spell-stopp'd.
Holy Gonzalo, honourable man,
Mine eyes, even sociable to the show of thine,
Fall fellowly drops. The charm dissolves apace,
And as the morning steals upon the night,
Melting the darkness, so their rising senses

44–5. *To . . . fire:* the dread rattling thunderbolt I have discharged. 52. *music.* The soothing effects of music seem to have been frequently resorted to by physicians (Cf. *King Lear*, IV, vii, 25). 59. *fancy:* mind. 61. *spell-stopp'd:* spellbound. 63. *sociable:* sympathetic. *show:* appearance. 64. *Fall:* let fall.

Begin to chase the ignorant fumes that mantle
Their clearer reason. O good Gonzalo,
My true preserver, and a loyal sir
To him thou follow'st! I will pay thy graces 70
Home both in word and deed. Most cruelly
Didst thou, Alonso, use me and my daughter.
Thy brother was a furtherer in the act.
Thou art pinch'd for't now, Sebastian. Flesh and blood,
You, brother mine, that entertain'd ambition,
Expell'd remorse and nature; who, with Sebastian,
Whose inward pinches therefore are most strong,
Would here have kill'd your king. I do forgive thee,
Unnatural though thou art. Their understanding
Begins to swell, and the approaching tide 80
Will shortly fill the reasonable shores
That now lie foul and muddy. Not one of them
That yet looks on me, or would know me. Ariel,
Fetch me the hat and rapier in my cell;

[*Ariel enters the cell and brings out a courtly costume.*

I will discase me, and myself present
As I was sometime Milan. Quickly, spirit;
Thou shalt ere long be free.

Ariel *sings and helps to attire him.*

Where the bee sucks, there suck I;
In a cowslip's bell I lie;
There I couch when owls do cry. 90
On the bat's back I do fly
After summer merrily.
Merrily, merrily, shall I live now
Under the blossom that hangs on the bough.

Pros. Why, that's my dainty Ariel! I shall miss thee;
But yet thou shalt have freedom. So, so, so.
To the king's ship, invisible as thou art.

67. *ignorant:* causing ignorance or insensibility. 71. *Home:* thoroughly. 76. *remorse:* pity, compassion. *nature:* natural feeling. 85. *discase:* undress, change clothes. 86. *Milan:* Duke of Milan. S. D. *Ariel sings.* Compare Caliban's song of freedom (II, ii, 182 ff.).

There shalt thou find the mariners asleep
Under the hatches; the master and the boatswain
Being awake, enforce them to this place, 100
And presently, I prithee.

Ari. I drink the air before me, and return
Or ere your pulse twice beat. [*Exit.*

Gon. All torment, trouble, wonder, and amazement
Inhabits here. Some heavenly power guide us
Out of this fearful country!

Pros. Behold, sir king,
The wronged Duke of Milan, Prospero.
For more assurance that a living prince
Does now speak to thee, I embrace thy body;
And to thee and thy company I bid 110
A hearty welcome.

Alon. Whe'er thou beëst he or no,
Or some enchanted trifle to abuse me,
As late I have been, I not know. Thy pulse
Beats as of flesh and blood; and, since I saw thee,
The affliction of my mind amends, with which,
I fear, a madness held me. This must crave,
An if this be at all, a most strange story.
Thy dukedom I resign and do entreat
Thou pardon me my wrongs. But how should Prospero
Be living and be here?

Pros. [*To Gonzalo*] First, noble friend, 120
Let me embrace thine age, whose honour cannot
Be measured or confined.

Gon. Whether this be
Or be not, I'll not swear.

Pros. You do yet taste
Some subtilties o' the isle, that will not let you
Believe things certain. Welcome, my friends all!
[*Aside to Sebastian and Antonio.*] But you, my brace of lords,
were I so minded,

101. *presently:* immediately. 112. *trifle:* phantom, trick of magic. *abuse:* impose upon, deceive. 124. *subtilties:* illusions. 126. *brace:* pair.

I here could pluck his Highness' frown upon you
And justify you traitors. At this time
I will tell no tales.

Seb. [*Aside to Antonio*] The Devil speaks in him.

Pros. No.
[*To Antonio.*] For you, most wicked sir, whom to call brother
Would even infect my mouth, I do forgive 131
Thy rankest fault—all of them—and require
My dukedom of thee, which perforce I know
Thou must restore.

Alon. If thou be'st Prospero,
Give us particulars of thy preservation;
How thou hast met us here, who three hours since
Were wrack'd upon this shore; where I have lost—
How sharp the point of this remembrance is!—
My dear son Ferdinand.

Pros. I am woe for't, sir.

Alon. Irreparable is the loss, and Patience 140
Says it is past her cure.

Pros. I rather think
You have not sought her help, of whose soft grace
For the like loss I have her sovereign aid
And rest myself content.

Alon. You the like loss?

Pros. As great to me as late; and, supportable
To make the dear loss, have I means much weaker
Than you may call to comfort you, for I
Have lost my daughter.

Alon. A daughter?
O heavens, that they were living both in Naples,
The king and queen there! That they were, I wish 150
Myself were mudded in that oozy bed
Where my son lies. When did you lose your daughter?

Pros. In this last tempest. I perceive, these lords
At this encounter do so much admire

128. *justify:* prove. 139. *woe:* sorry. 145. *as late:* as it is recent.
154. *encounter:* meeting. *admire:* wonder.

That they devour their reason and scarce think
Their eyes do offices of truth. Their words
Are natural breath. But, howsoe'er you have
Been justled from your senses, know for certain
That I am Prospero and that very duke
Which was thrust forth of Milan, who most strangely 160
Upon this shore, where you were wrack'd, was landed,
To be the lord on't. No more yet of this;
For 'tis a chronicle of day by day,
Not a relation for a breakfast nor
Befitting this first meeting. Welcome, sir.
This cell's my court. Here have I few attendants
And subjects none abroad. Pray you, look in.
My dukedom since you have given me again,
I will requite you with as good a thing;
At least bring forth a wonder, to content ye 170
As much as me my dukedom.

Here PROSPERO *discovers* FERDINAND *and* MIRANDA *playing at chess.*

Mir. Sweet lord, you play me false.
Fer. No, my dear'st love,
I would not for the world.
Mir. Yes, for a score of kingdoms you should wrangle,
And I would call it fair play.
Alon. If this prove
A vision of the island, one dear son
Shall I twice lose.
Seb. A most high miracle!
Fer. Though the seas threaten, they are merciful;
I have cursed them without cause. [*Kneels.*
Alon. Now all the blessings

155. *devour:* make inoperative. 156. *do . . . truth:* perform their functions truthfully. S. D. *discovers:* reveals (by drawing the curtain of the inner stage of the Elizabethan theatre). 174. *score of kingdoms:* (a) account or tally of kingdoms, (b) twenty kingdoms. *wrangle:* (a) contend, play, (b) argue. 175. *fair play:* (a) honest play, (b) worthy of you.

Of a glad father compass thee about! 180
Arise, and say how thou camest here.
Mir. O, wonder!
How many goodly creatures are there here!
How beauteous mankind is! O brave new world,
That has such people in 't!
Pros. 'Tis new to thee.
Alon. What is this maid with whom thou wast at play?
Your eld'st acquaintance cannot be three hours.
Is she the goddess that hath sever'd us,
And brought us thus together?
Fer. Sir, she is mortal;
But by immortal Providence she's mine.
I chose her when I could not ask my father 190
For his advice, nor thought I had one. She
Is daughter to this famous Duke of Milan,
Of whom so often I have heard renown,
But never saw before; of whom I have
Received a second life; and second father
This lady makes him to me.
Alon. I am hers.
But, O, how oddly will it sound that I
Must ask my child forgiveness!
Pros. There, sir, stop.
Let us not burden our remembrances with
A heaviness that's gone.
Gon. I have inly wept 200
Or should have spoke ere this. Look down, you gods,
And on this couple drop a blessed crown;
For it is you that have chalk'd forth the way
Which brought us hither.
Alon. I say, Amen, Gonzalo!
Gon. Was Milan thrust from Milan, that his issue
Should become kings of Naples? O, rejoice

186. *eld'st:* oldest, longest. 193. *renown:* report. 200. *heaviness:* sadness. 203. *chalk'd forth:* marked out. 205. *Was . . . Milan:* was the Duke of Milan exiled from Milan.

Beyond a common joy, and set it down
With gold on lasting pillars. In one voyage
Did Claribel her husband find at Tunis;
And Ferdinand, her brother, found a wife 210
Where he himself was lost; Prospero his dukedom
In a poor isle; and all of us ourselves
When no man was his own.

Alon. [*To Ferdinand and Miranda*] Give me your hands.
Let grief and sorrow still embrace his heart
That doth not wish you joy!

Gon. Be it so! Amen!

Re-enter ARIEL, *with the* Master *and* Boatswain *amazedly following.*

O, look, sir, look, sir! Here is more of us.
I prophesied, if a gallows were on land,
This fellow could not drown. Now, Blasphemy,
That swear'st Grace o'erboard, not an oath on shore?
Hast thou no mouth by land? What is the news? 220

Boats. The best news is, that we have safely found
Our king and company; the next, our ship—
Which, but three glasses since, we gave out split—
Is tight and yare and bravely rigg'd as when
We first put out to sea.

Ari. [*To Prospero*] Sir, all this service
Have I done since I went.

Pros. [*To Ariel*] My tricksy spirit!

Alon. These are not natural events; they strengthen
From strange to stranger. Say, how came you hither?

Boats. If I did think, sir, I were well awake,
I'ld strive to tell you. We were dead of sleep, 230
And—how we know not—all clapp'd under hatches,
Where but even now with strange and several noises
Of roaring, shrieking, howling, jingling chains,

213. *his own:* master of his senses. 214. *still:* always. 221. *safely found:* found safe. 223. *glasses:* hours. *gave out:* declared. 224. *yare:* ready.

And moe diversity of sounds, all horrible,
We were awaked; straightway, at liberty;
Where we, in all her trim, freshly beheld
Our royal, good, and gallant ship, our master
Capering to eye her. On a trice, so please you,
Even in a dream, were we divided from them
And were brought moping hither.

Ari. [*To Prospero*] Was 't well done? 240

Pros. [*To Ariel*] Bravely, my diligence. Thou shalt be free.

Alon. This is as strange a maze as e'er men trod,
And there is in this business more than nature
Was ever conduct of. Some oracle
Must rectify our knowledge.

Pros. Sir, my liege,
Do not infest your mind with beating on
The strangeness of this business. At pick'd leisure,
Which shall be shortly, single I'll resolve you
(Which to you shall seem probable) of every
These happen'd accidents. Till when, be cheerful 250
And think of each thing well. [*To Ariel.*] Come hither, spirit.
Set Caliban and his companions free;
Untie the spell. [*Exit Ariel.*] How fares my gracious sir?
There are yet missing of your company
Some few odd lads that you remember not.

Re-enter Ariel, *driving in* Caliban, Stephano *and* Trinculo, *in their stolen apparel.*

Ste. Every man shift for all the rest, and let no man take care for himself; for all is but fortune. Coragio, bully-monster, coragio!

234. *moe:* more. 236. *freshly beheld:* beheld her fresh and fair. 238. *Capering . . . her:* dancing with joy to see her. 240. *moping:* in a state of bewilderment. 244. *conduct of:* responsible for; literally, "leader of." 246. *infest:* harass, distrust. 248. *single:* alone, in private. *resolve:* inform. 249. *every:* all severally. 250. *accidents:* events. 258. *Coragio:* courage. *bully:* a familiar term of address.

Trin. If these be true spies which I wear in my head, here's
a goodly sight. 260

Cal. O Setebos, these be brave spirits indeed!
How fine my master is! I am afraid
He will chastise me.

Seb. Ha, ha!
What things are these, my lord Antonio?
Will money buy 'em?

Ant. Very like; one of them
Is a plain fish, and, no doubt, marketable.

Pros. Mark but the badges of these men, my lords,
Then say if they be true. This mis-shapen knave—
His mother was a witch, and one so strong
That could control the moon, make flows and ebbs, 270
And deal in her command without her power.
These three have robb'd me, and this demi-devil—
For he's a bastard one—had plotted with them
To take my life. Two of these fellows you
Must know and own; this thing of darkness I
Acknowledge mine.

Cal. I shall be pinch'd to death.

Alon. Is not this Stephano, my drunken butler?

Seb. He is drunk now. Where had he wine?

Alon. And Trinculo is reeling ripe. Where should they
Find this grand liquor that hath gilded 'em? 280
How camest thou in this pickle?

Trin. I have been in such a pickle since I saw you last that
I fear me will never out of my bones. I shall not fear fly-blowing.

Seb. Why, how now, Stephano?

Ste. O, touch me not; I am not Stephano, but a cramp.

Pros. You'ld be king o' the isle, sirrah?

261. *brave:* splendid. 267. *badges:* (a) outward marks, (b) silver devices bearing their master's arms usually worn by household servants. 268. *true:* (a) honest, (b) yours. 271. *deal . . . power:* wield the moon's power either beyond the moon's rightful sphere of influence (?) or without her authority (?). The meaning is not clear. 280. *gilded:* flushed.

Ste. I should have been a sore one then.
Alon. This is a strange thing as e'er I look'd on.
[*Pointing to Caliban.*
Pros. He is as disproportion'd in his manners 290
As in his shape. [*To Caliban.*] Go, sirrah, to my cell;
Take with you your companions. As you look
To have my pardon, trim it handsomely.
Cal. Ay, that I will; and I'll be wise hereafter
And seek for grace. What a thrice-double ass
Was I to take this drunkard for a god
And worship this dull fool!
Pros. [*To Caliban*] Go to; away!
Alon. [*To Trinculo and Stephano*] Hence, and bestow your luggage where you found it.
Seb. Or stole it, rather.
[*Exeunt Caliban, Stephano, and Trinculo.*
Pros. Sir, I invite your Highness and your train 300
To my poor cell, where you shall take your rest
For this one night; which, part of it, I'll waste
With such discourse as, I not doubt, shall make it
Go quick away—the story of my life
And the particular accidents gone by
Since I came to this isle. And in the morn
I'll bring you to your ship and so to Naples
Where I have hope to see the nuptial
Of these our dear-beloved solemnized;
And thence retire me to my Milan, where 310
Every third thought shall be my grave.
Alon. I long
To hear the story of your life, which must
Take the ear strangely.
Pros. I'll deliver all,
And promise you calm seas, auspicious gales,
And sail so expeditious that shall catch
Your royal fleet far off. [*To Ariel.*] My Ariel, chick,

298. *bestow:* stow away. 302. *waste:* spend, use. 305. *accidents:* events. 313. *Take:* strike, charm (?). 315. *catch:* overtake.

That is thy charge; then to the elements
Be free, and fare thou well! [*To his guests.*] Please you, draw
near. [*Exeunt.*

EPILOGUE

Spoken by PROSPERO.

Now my charms are all o'erthrown,
And what strength I have's mine own,
Which is most faint. Now, 'tis true,
I must be here confined by you,
Or sent to Naples. Let me not,
Since I have my dukedom got
And pardon'd the deceiver, dwell
In this bare island by your spell;
But release me from my bands
With the help of your good hands. 10
Gentle breath of yours my sails
Must fill, or else my project fails,
Which was to please. Now I want
Spirits to enforce, art to enchant,
And my ending is despair,
Unless I be relieved by prayer,
Which pierces so that it assaults
Mercy itself and frees all faults.
As you from crimes would pardon'd be,
Let your indulgence set me free. 20

[Epilogue.] 10. *hands:* i.e., applause. A noise would break a spell. 13. *want:* lack. 16. *prayer:* an allusion to the despair that was supposed to overtake necromancers in their last moments. 18. *Mercy:* i.e., the Almighty.